Jesus Saves
Be with Him in Paradise

Everyone is destined to die, but life does not end with death. The Bible says that after death there will be a judgment where each person will give an account of his life to God (Hebrews 9:27). When God created Adam and Eve in His own image in the garden of Eden, He gave them an abundant life, and the freedom to choose between good and evil. They chose to disobey God and go their own way. As a consequence, death was introduced into the human race, not only physical death, but also spiritual death. For this reason, all human beings are separated from God.

Unfortunately, man continues to disobey God: *for all have sinned and fall short of the glory of God (Romans 3:23)*. This is humanity's problem: because of sin everyone is separated from God (Isaiah 59:2).

People have tried to overcome this separation in many ways: by doing good, through religion or philosophy, or by attempting to live morally and justly. However, none of these things is enough to cross the barrier of separation between God and humanity, because God is holy and human beings are sinful.

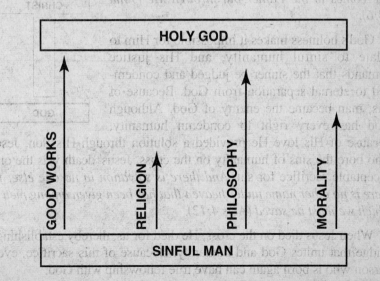

This spiritual separation has become the natural and normal condition of mankind, and because of this they are condemned: *He who believes in Him is not judged; he who does not believe has been judged already, because he has not believed in the name of the only begotten Son of God (John 3:18).* There is only one solution to the problem: *Unless one is born again he cannot see the kingdom of God (John 3:3);* that is, it is necessary to be born again in the spiritual sense. God Himself has provided the means that makes it possible for anyone to be born again, and this is the plan that He has for us because He loves us.

God's love and plan

Jesus Christ said:

For God so loved the world that He gave His only begotten Son, that whoever believes in Him shall not perish, but have eternal life (John 3:16).

I came that they may have life, and have it abundantly (John 10:10).

He who believes in the Son has eternal life; but he who does not obey the Son will not see life, but the wrath of God abides on him (John 3:36).

I am the way, and the truth, and the life; no one comes to the Father but through Me (John 14:6).

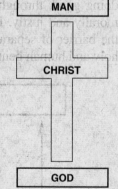

God's holiness makes it impossible for Him to relate to sinful humanity, and His justice demands that the sinner be judged and condemned to eternal separation from God. Because of this, man became the enemy of God. Although God has every right to condemn humanity, because of His love He provided a solution through His Son, Jesus, who bore the sins of humanity on the cross. Jesus' death was the only acceptable sacrifice for sin: *And there is salvation in no one else; for there is no other name under heaven that has been given among men by which we must be saved (Acts 4:12).*

When Jesus died on the cross, He died for us, thereby establishing a bridge that unites God and humanity. Because of this sacrifice, every person who is born again can have true fellowship with God.

Jesus Christ is alive today

After Jesus Christ died on the cross at Calvary, where He received the punishment that we deserved, the Bible says that He was buried in a tomb. But He did not remain there: He resurrected! For all those who believe in Jesus Christ, the resurrection is a guarantee that they will also be resurrected to eternal life in the presence of God. This is very good news! *Christ died for our sins...was buried, and...He was raised on the third day according to the Scriptures (1 Corinthians 15:3,4).*

How to receive God's love and plan

In His mercy, God has determined that salvation is free. To receive it, you need to do only four things:

1. Acknowledge the problem (separation from God because of sin).
2. Admit to being a sinner, and that you need salvation.
3. Recognize that Jesus Christ died on the cross for your sins.
4. Commit yourself to Jesus Christ so that He can save and guide you.
5. Receive Jesus Christ as your personal Savior and Lord, now.

The Bible says:

that if you confess with your mouth Jesus as Lord, and believe in your heart that God raised Him from the dead, you will be saved (Romans 10:9).

For whoever will call on the name of the Lord will be saved (Romans 10:13).

A prayer to receive Jesus Christ

Lord Jesus, I know that I have sinned against You and that I do not live according to Your plan; therefore, I ask You to forgive me. I believe that You died for me, and in doing so, You paid the debt for my sins. I repent of my sin and now I want to live the kind of life that You want me to live. I ask you to come into my life and be my personal Savior. Help me to follow You and to obey You as Lord. Allow me to discover Your good and perfect will for my life.

My personal decision

On (date) _____, I, _____
accepted Jesus Chist as my personal Savior and Lord.

You have received eternal life!

When you prayed to receive Jesus Christ as the Savior and Lord of your life, He heard you, and several things took place: your sins were forgiven (Colossians 2:13), you became a child of God (John 1:12), and you received eternal life (John 3:16).

You may feel certain emotions because of this decision, but do not let yourself be carried away by them because your feelings can change from day to day. Put your confidence in your heavenly Father, *casting all your anxiety on Him, because He cares for you (1 Peter 5:7).*

Talk and fellowship with God daily through prayer and by reading His word, the Bible. Try to have fellowship with other Christians so that you can receive support and spiritual guidance from them.

The promises of God are fulfilled

He who has the Son has the life; he who does not have the Son of God does not have the life. These things I have written to you who believe in the name of the Son of God, so that you may know that you have eternal life (1 John 5:12,13). This is the beginning of the abundant life that Jesus Christ came to offer, because God desires to restore what was lost in the Garden of Eden. Now, you *will* be with Him in Paradise!

Preface

Scriptural Promise

The New American Standard Bible has been produced with the conviction that the words of Scripture as originally penned in the Hebrew, Aramaic, and Greek were inspired by God. Since they are the eternal Word of God, the Holy Scriptures speak with fresh power to each generation, to give wisdom that leads to salvation, that men may serve Christ to the glory of God.

The Fourfold Aim
of
The Lockman Foundation

1. These publications shall be true to the original Hebrew, Aramaic, and Greek.
2. They shall be grammatically correct.
3. They shall be understandable.
4. They shall give the Lord Jesus Christ His proper place, the place which the Word gives Him; therefore, no work will ever be personalized.

In the history of English Bible translations, the King James Version is the most prestigious. This time-honored version of 1611, itself a revision of the Bishops' Bible of 1568, became the basis for the English Revised Version appearing in 1881 (New Testament) and 1885 (Old Testament). The American counterpart of this last work was published in 1901 as the American Standard Version. The ASV, a product of both British and American scholarship, has been highly regarded for its scholarship and accuracy. Recognizing the values of the American Standard Version, The Lockman Foundation felt an urgency to preserve these and other lasting values of the ASV by incorporating recent discoveries of Hebrew and Greek textual sources and by rendering it into more current English. Therefore, in 1959 a new translation project was launched, based on the time-honored principles of translation of the ASV and KJV. The result is the New American Standard Bible.

Translation work for the NASB was begun in 1959. In the preparation of this work numerous other translations have been consulted along with the linguistic tools and literature of biblical scholarship. Decisions about English renderings were made by consensus of a team composed of educators and pastors. Subsequently, review and evaluation by other Hebrew and Greek scholars outside the Editorial Board were sought and carefully considered.

The Editorial Board has continued to function since publication of the complete Bible in 1971. This edition of the NASB represents revisions and refinements recommended over the last several years as well as thorough research based on modern English usage.

Principles of Translation

Modern English Usage: The attempt has been made to render the grammar and terminology in contemporary English. When it was felt that the word-for-word literalness was unacceptable to the modern reader, a change was made in the direction of a more current English idiom. In the instances where this has been done, the more literal rendering has been indicated in the notes. There are a few exceptions to this procedure. In particular, frequently "And" is not translated at the beginning of sentences because of differences in style between ancient and modern writing. Punctuation is a relatively modern invention, and ancient writers often linked most of their sentences with "and" or other connectives. Also, the Hebrew idiom "answered and said" is sometimes reduced to "answered" or "said" as demanded by the context. For current English the idiom "it came about that" has not been translated in the New Testament except when a major transition is needed.

Greek Text: Consideration was given to the latest available manuscripts with a view to determining the best Greek text. In most instances the 26th edition of Eberhard Nestle's *Novum Testamentum Graece* was followed.

Greek Tenses: A careful distinction has been made in the treatment of the Greek aorist tense (usually translated as the English past, "He did") and the Greek imperfect tense (normally rendered either as English past progressive, "He was doing"; or, if inceptive, as "He began to do" or "He started to do"; or else if customary past, as "He used to do"). "Began" is italicized if it renders an imperfect tense, in order to distinguish it from the Greek verb for "begin." In some contexts the difference between the Greek imperfect and the English past is conveyed better by the choice of vocabulary or by other words in the context, and in such cases the Greek imperfect may be rendered as a simple past tense (e.g. "had an illness for many years" would be preferable to "was having an illness for many years" and would be understood in the same way).

On the other hand, not all aorists have been rendered as English pasts ("He did"), for some of them are clearly to be rendered as English perfects ("He has done"), or even as past perfects ("He had done"), judging from the context in which they occur. Such aorists have been rendered as perfects or past perfects in this translation.

As for the distinction between aorist and present imperatives, the translators have usually rendered these imperatives in the customary manner, rather than attempting any such fine distinction as "Begin to do!" (for the aorist imperative), or, "Continually do!" (for the present imperative).

As for sequence of tenses, the translators took care to follow English rules rather than Greek in translating Greek presents, imperfects, and aorists. Thus, where English says, "We knew that he was doing," Greek puts it, "We knew that he does"; similarly, "We knew that he had done" is the Greek, "We knew that he did." Likewise, the English, "When he had come, they met him," is represented in Greek by, "When he came, they met him." In all cases a consistent transfer has been made from the Greek tense in the subordinate clause to the appropriate tense in English.

In the rendering of negative questions introduced by the particle *mē* (which always expects the answer "No") the wording has been altered from a mere, "Will he not do this?" to a more accurate, "He will not do this, will he?"

The Lockman Foundation

Explanation of General Format

Paragraphs are designated by bold face verse numbers or letters.

Quotation Marks are used in the text in accordance with modern English usage.

"Thy," "Thee" and "Thou" are not used in this edition and have been rendered as "Your" and "You."

Personal Pronouns are capitalized when pertaining to Deity.

Italics are used in the text to indicate words which are not found in the original Hebrew, Aramaic, or Greek but implied by it. Italics are used in the marginal notes to signify alternate readings for the text. Roman text in the marginal alternate readings is the same as italics in the Bible text.

Small Caps in the New Testament are used in the text to indicate Old Testament quotations or obvious references to Old Testament texts. Variations of Old Testament wording are found in New Testament citations depending on whether the New Testament writer translated from a Hebrew text, used existing Greek or Aramaic translations, or paraphrased the material. It should be noted that modern rules for the indication of direct quotation were not used in biblical times; thus, the ancient writer would use exact quotations or references to quotation without specific indication of such.

A star (★) is used to mark verbs that are historical presents in the Greek which have been translated with an English past tense in order to conform to modern usage. The translators recognized that in some contexts the present tense seems more unexpected and unjustified to the English reader than a past tense would have been. But Greek authors frequently used the present tense for the sake of heightened vividness, thereby transporting their readers in imagination to the actual scene at the time of occurrence. However, the translators felt that it would be wise to change these historical presents to English past tenses.

The Books of the New Testament

The Genealogy of Jesus the Messiah

1 The record of the genealogy of Jesus the Messiah, ᵃthe son of David, the son of Abraham: ᵃ*Is 9:6f; 11:1*

2 Abraham was the father of Isaac, Isaac the father of Jacob, and Jacob the father of Judah and his brothers.

3 Judah was the father of Perez and Zerah by Tamar, ᵃPerez was the father of Hezron, and Hezron the father of Ram. ᵃ*Ruth 4:18-22; 1 Chr 2:1-15*

4 Ram was the father of Amminadab, Amminadab the father of Nahshon, and Nahshon the father of Salmon.

5 Salmon was the father of Boaz by Rahab, Boaz was the father of Obed by Ruth, and Obed the father of Jesse.

6 Jesse was the father of David the king.

David ᵃwas the father of Solomon by Bathsheba who had been the wife of Uriah. ᵃ*2 Sam 11:27; 12:24*

7 Solomon ᵃwas the father of Rehoboam, Rehoboam the father of Abijah, and Abijah the father of Asa. ᵃ*1 Chr 3:10ff*

8 Asa was the father of Jehoshaphat, Jehoshaphat the father of Joram, and Joram the father of Uzziah.

9 Uzziah was the father of Jotham, Jotham the father of Ahaz, and Ahaz the father of Hezekiah.

10 Hezekiah was the father of Manasseh, Manasseh the father of Amon, and Amon the ᵃfather of Josiah. ᵃ*1 Chr 3:14*

11 Josiah became the father of Jeconiah and his brothers, at the time of the ᵃdeportation to Babylon. ᵃ*2 Kin 24:14f; Jer 27:20*

12 After the ᵃdeportation to Babylon: Jeconiah became the father of Shealtiel, and Shealtiel the father of Zerubbabel. ᵃ*2 Kin 24:14f; Jer 27:20*

13 Zerubbabel was the father of Abihud, Abihud the father of Eliakim, and Eliakim the father of Azor.

14 Azor was the father of Zadok, Zadok the father of Achim, and Achim the father of Eliud.

15 Eliud was the father of Eleazar, Eleazar the father of Matthan, and Matthan the father of Jacob.

16 Jacob was the father of Joseph the husband of Mary, by whom Jesus was born, ᵃwho is called the Messiah. ᵃ*Matt 27:17, 22; Luke 2:11*

17 So all the generations from Abraham to David are fourteen generations; from David to the ᵃdeportation to Babylon, fourteen generations; and from the ᵃdeportation to Babylon to the Messiah, fourteen generations. ᵃ*2 Kin 24:14f; Jer 27:20*

Conception and Birth of Jesus

18 Now the birth of Jesus Christ was as follows: when His ᵃmother Mary had been betrothed to Joseph, before they came together she was found to be with child by the Holy Spirit. ᵃ*Matt 12:46; Luke 1:27*

19 And Joseph her husband, being a righteous man and not wanting to disgrace her, planned ᵃto send her away secretly. ᵃ*Deut 22:20-24; 24:1-4*

20 But when he had considered this, behold, an angel of the Lord appeared to him in a dream, saying, "ᵃJoseph, son of David, do not be afraid to take Mary as your wife; for the Child who has been conceived in her is of the Holy Spirit. ᵃ*Luke 2:4*

21 "She will bear a Son; and you shall call His name Jesus, for He ᵃwill save His people from their sins." ᵃ*Luke 2:11; John 1:29*

22 Now all this took place to fulfill what was ᵃspoken by the Lord through the prophet: ᵃ*Luke 24:44; Rom 1:2-4*

23 "ᵃBEHOLD, THE VIRGIN SHALL BE WITH ᵇCHILD AND SHALL BEAR A SON, AND THEY SHALL CALL HIS NAME IMMANUEL," which translated means, "GOD WITH US." ᵃ*Is 7:14* ᵇ*Is 9:6, 7*

24 And Joseph awoke from his sleep and did as the angel of the Lord commanded him, and took *Mary* as his wife,

25 but kept her a virgin until she gave birth to a Son; and ᵃhe called His name Jesus. ᵃ*Matt 1:21; Luke 2:21*

The Visit of the Magi

2 Now after Jesus was ᵃborn in Bethlehem of Judea in the days of Herod the king, magi from the east arrived in Jerusalem, saying, ᵃ*Mic 5:2; Luke 2:4-7*

2 "Where is He who has been born ᵃKing of the Jews? For we saw His star in the east and have come to worship Him." ᵃ*Jer 23:5; 30:9*

3 When Herod the king heard *this,* he was troubled, and all Jerusalem with him.

4 Gathering together all the chief priests and scribes of the people, he inquired of them where the Messiah was to be born.

5 They said to him, "ᵃIn Bethlehem of Judea; for this is what has been written by the prophet: ᵃ*John 7:42*

6 'ᵃAND YOU, BETHLEHEM, LAND OF JUDAH,
ARE BY NO MEANS LEAST AMONG THE LEADERS OF JUDAH;
FOR OUT OF YOU SHALL COME FORTH A RULER WHO WILL SHEPHERD MY PEOPLE ISRAEL.' " ᵃ*Mic 5:2; John 7:42*

7 Then Herod secretly called the magi and determined from them the exact time ᵃthe star appeared. ᵃ*Num 24:17*

8 And he sent them to Bethlehem and said, "Go and search carefully for the Child; and when you have found *Him*, report to me, so that I too may come and worship Him."

9 After hearing the king, they went their way; and the star, which they had seen in the east, went on before them until it came and stood over *the place* where the Child was.

10 When they saw the star, they rejoiced exceedingly with great joy.

11 After coming into the house they saw the Child with Mary His mother; and they fell to the ground and ªworshiped Him. Then, opening their treasures, they presented to Him gifts of gold, frankincense, and myrrh. ªMatt 14:33

12 And having been warned *by God* ªin a dream not to return to Herod, the magi left for their own country by another way. ªJob 33:15, 16; Matt 1:20

The Flight to Egypt

13 Now when they had gone, behold, an angel of the Lord *ªappeared to Joseph in a dream and said, "Get up! Take the Child and His mother and flee to Egypt, and remain there until I tell you; for Herod is going to search for the Child to destroy Him." ªMatt 2:12, 19

14 So Joseph got up and took the Child and His mother while it was still night, and left for Egypt.

15 He remained there until the death of Herod. *This was* to fulfill what had been spoken by the Lord through the prophet: "ªOUT OF EGYPT I CALLED MY SON." ªHos 11:1; Num 24:8

Herod Slaughters Babies

16 Then when Herod saw that he had been tricked by ªthe magi, he became very enraged, and sent and slew all the male children who were in Bethlehem and all its vicinity, from two years old and under, according to the time which he had determined from the magi. ªMatt 2:1

17 Then what had been spoken through Jeremiah the prophet was fulfilled:

18 "ªA VOICE WAS HEARD IN RAMAH,
WEEPING AND GREAT MOURNING,
RACHEL WEEPING FOR HER CHILDREN;
AND SHE REFUSED TO BE COMFORTED,
BECAUSE THEY WERE NO MORE." ªJer 31:15

19 But when Herod died, behold, an angel of the Lord *ªappeared in a dream to Joseph in Egypt, and said, ªMatt 1:20; 2:12, 13, 22

20 "Get up, take the Child and His mother, and go into the land of Israel; for those who sought the Child's life are dead."

21 So Joseph got up, took the Child and His mother, and came into the land of Israel.

22 But when he heard that Archelaus was reigning over Judea in place of his father Herod, he was afraid to go there. Then after

being ªwarned *by God* in a dream, he left for the regions of Galilee, ªMatt 2:12, 13, 19

23 and came and lived in a city called ªNazareth. *This was* to fulfill what was spoken through the prophets: "He shall be called a Nazarene." ªLuke 1:26; 2:39

The Preaching of John the Baptist

3 Now ªin those days John the Baptist *came, preaching in the wilderness of Judea, saying, ªJohn 1:6-8, 19-28

2 "ªRepent, for the kingdom of heaven is at hand." ªMatt 4:17

3 For this is the ªone referred to by Isaiah the prophet when he said,

"ᵇTHE VOICE OF ONE CRYING IN THE WILDER-
NESS,
'MAKE READY THE WAY OF THE LORD,
MAKE HIS PATHS STRAIGHT!' " ªLuke 1:17, 76
ᵇIs 40:3

4 Now John himself had ªa garment of camel's hair and a leather belt around his waist; and his food was locusts and wild honey. ª2 Kin 1:8; Zech 13:4

5 Then Jerusalem ªwas going out to him, and all Judea and all the district around the Jordan; ªMark 1:5

6 and they were being ªbaptized by him in the Jordan River, as they confessed their sins. ªMatt 3:11, 13-16; Mark 1:5

7 But when he saw many of the ªPharisees and ᵇSadducees coming for baptism, he said to them, "You brood of vipers, who warned you to flee from the wrath to come? ªMatt 16:1ff ᵇMatt 22:23

8 "ªTherefore bear fruit in keeping with repentance; ªLuke 3:8; Eph 5:8, 9

9 and do not suppose that you can say to yourselves, 'ªWe have Abraham for our father'; for I say to you that from these stones God is able to raise up children to Abraham. ªLuke 3:8; 16:24

10 "The ªaxe is already laid at the root of the trees; therefore every tree that does not bear good fruit is cut down and thrown into the fire. ªLuke 3:9

11 "As for me, ªI baptize you with water for repentance, but He who is coming after me is mightier than I, and I am not fit to remove His sandals; He will baptize you with the Holy Spirit and fire. ªMark 1:4, 8; Luke 3:16

12 "His ªwinnowing fork is in His hand, and He will thoroughly clear His threshing floor; and He will gather His wheat into the barn, but He will burn up the chaff with unquenchable fire." ªIs 30:24; 41:16

The Baptism of Jesus

13 ªThen Jesus *arrived from Galilee at the Jordan *coming* to John, to be baptized by him. ªJohn 1:31-34

14 But John tried to prevent Him, saying, "I have need to be baptized by You, and do You come to me?"

15 But Jesus answering said to him, "Permit *it* at this time; for in this way it is fitting for us ªto fulfill all righteousness." Then he *permitted Him. ªPs 40:7, 8; John 4:34

16 After being baptized, Jesus came up immediately from the water; and behold, the heavens were opened, and ªhe saw the Spirit of God descending as a dove *and* lighting on Him, ªMark 1:10; Luke 3:22

17 and behold, a voice out of the heavens said, "ªThis is My beloved Son, in whom I am well-pleased." ªPs 2:7; Is 42:1

The Temptation of Jesus

4 ªThen Jesus was led up by the Spirit into the wilderness to be tempted by the devil. ªMark 1:12, 13; Luke 4:1-13

2 And after He had ªfasted forty days and forty nights, He then became hungry. ªEx 34:28; 1 Kin 19:8

3 And ªthe tempter came and said to Him, "If You are the ᵇSon of God, command that these stones become bread." ª1 Thess 3:5 ᵇMatt 14:33

4 But He answered and said, "It is written, 'ªMAN SHALL NOT LIVE ON BREAD ALONE, BUT ON EVERY WORD THAT PROCEEDS OUT OF THE MOUTH OF GOD.' " ªDeut 8:3

5 Then the devil *took Him into ªthe holy city and had Him stand on the pinnacle of the temple, ªNeh 11:1, 18; Dan 9:24

6 and *said to Him, "If You are the Son of God, throw Yourself down; for it is written, 'ªHE WILL COMMAND HIS ANGELS CONCERNING YOU';
and
'ON *their* HANDS THEY WILL BEAR YOU UP, SO THAT YOU WILL NOT STRIKE YOUR FOOT AGAINST A STONE.' " ªPs 91:11, 12

7 Jesus said to him, "On the other hand, it is written, 'ªYOU SHALL NOT PUT THE LORD YOUR GOD TO THE TEST.' " ªDeut 6:16

8 ªAgain, the devil *took Him to a very high mountain and *showed Him all the kingdoms of the world and their glory; ªMatt 16:26; 1 John 2:15-17

9 and he said to Him, "ªAll these things I will give You, if You fall down and worship me." ª1 Cor 10:20f

10 Then Jesus *said to him, "Go, Satan! For it is written, 'ªYOU SHALL WORSHIP THE LORD YOUR GOD, AND SERVE HIM ONLY,' " ªDeut 6:13; 10:20

11 Then the devil *left Him; and behold, ªangels came and *began* to minister to Him. ªMatt 26:53; Luke 22:43

Jesus Begins His Ministry

12 Now when Jesus heard that ªJohn had been taken into custody, He withdrew into Galilee; ªMatt 14:3; Mark 1:14

13 and leaving Nazareth, He came and ªsettled in Capernaum, which is by the sea, in the region of Zebulun and Naphtali. ªMatt 11:23; Mark 1:21

14 *This was* to fulfill what was spoken through Isaiah the prophet:

15 "ªTHE LAND OF ZEBULUN AND THE LAND OF NAPHTALI,
BY THE WAY OF THE SEA, BEYOND THE JORDAN, GALILEE OF THE GENTILES—
ªIs 9:1

16 ªTHE PEOPLE WHO WERE SITTING IN DARKNESS SAW A GREAT LIGHT,
AND THOSE WHO WERE SITTING IN THE LAND AND SHADOW OF DEATH,
UPON THEM A LIGHT DAWNED." ªIs 9:2; 60:1-3

17 ªFrom that time Jesus began to preach and say, "Repent, for the kingdom of heaven is at hand." ªMark 1:14, 15

The First Disciples

18 ªNow as Jesus was walking by the Sea of Galilee, He saw two brothers, Simon who was called Peter, and Andrew his brother, casting a net into the sea; for they were fishermen. ªLuke 5:2-11; John 1:40-42

19 And He *said to them, "Follow Me, and I will make you fishers of men."

20 Immediately they left their nets and followed Him.

21 Going on from there He saw two other brothers, ªJames the *son* of Zebedee, and John his brother, in the boat with Zebedee their father, mending their nets; and He called them. ªMatt 10:2; 20:20

22 Immediately they left the boat and their father, and followed Him.

Ministry in Galilee

23 Jesus was going throughout all Galilee, ªteaching in their synagogues and proclaiming the gospel of the kingdom, and healing every kind of disease and every kind of sickness among the people. ªMatt 9:35; 13:54

24 The news about Him spread ªthroughout all Syria; and they brought to Him all who were ill, those suffering with various diseases and pains, demoniacs, epileptics, paralytics; and He healed them. ªMark 7:26; Luke 2:2

25 Large crowds ªfollowed Him from Galilee and *the* Decapolis and Jerusalem and Judea and *from* beyond the Jordan. ªMark 3:7, 8; Luke 6:17

The Sermon on the Mount; The Beatitudes

5 ªWhen Jesus saw the crowds, He went up on the mountain; and after He sat down,

His disciples came to Him. ᵃMatt ch 5-7; Luke 6:20-49

2 ᵃHe opened His mouth and *began* to teach them, saying, ᵃMatt 13:35; Acts 8:35

3 "ᵃBlessed are the poor in spirit, for theirs is the kingdom of heaven. ᵃMatt 5:3-12; Luke 6:20-23

4 "Blessed are ᵃthose who mourn, for they shall be comforted. ᵃIs 61:2; John 16:20

5 "Blessed are ᵃthe gentle, for they shall inherit the earth. ᵃPs 37:11

6 "Blessed are ᵃthose who hunger and thirst for righteousness, for they shall be satisfied. ᵃIs 55:1, 2; John 4:14

7 "Blessed are ᵃthe merciful, for they shall receive mercy. ᵃProv 11:17; Matt 6:14, 15

8 "Blessed are ᵃthe pure in heart, for they shall see God. ᵃPs 24:4

9 "Blessed are the peacemakers, for ᵃthey shall be called sons of God. ᵃMatt 5:45; Luke 6:35

10 "Blessed are those who have been ᵃpersecuted for the sake of righteousness, for theirs is the kingdom of heaven. ᵃ1 Pet 3:14

11 "Blessed are you when *people* ᵃinsult you and persecute you, and falsely say all kinds of evil against you because of Me. ᵃ1 Pet 4:14

12 "Rejoice and be glad, for your reward in heaven is great; for ᵃin the same way they persecuted the prophets who were before you. ᵃ2 Chr 36:16; Matt 23:37

Disciples and the World

13 "You are the salt of the earth; but ᵃif the salt has become tasteless, how can it be made salty *again?* It is no longer good for anything, except to be thrown out and trampled under foot by men. ᵃMark 9:50; Luke 14:34f

14 "You are ᵃthe light of the world. A city set on a hill cannot be hidden; ᵃProv 4:18; John 8:12

15 ᵃnor does *anyone* light a lamp and put it under a basket, but on the lampstand, and it gives light to all who are in the house. ᵃMark 4:21; Luke 8:16

16 "Let your light shine before men in such a way that they may ᵃsee your good works, and glorify your Father who is in heaven. ᵃ1 Pet 2:12

17 "Do not think that I came to abolish the ᵃLaw or the Prophets; I did not come to abolish but to fulfill. ᵃMatt 7:12

18 "For truly I say to you, ᵃuntil heaven and earth pass away, not the smallest letter or stroke shall pass from the Law until all is accomplished. ᵃMatt 24:35; Luke 16:17

19 "Whoever then annuls one of the least of these commandments, and teaches others *to do* the same, shall be called least ᵃin the kingdom of heaven; but whoever keeps and teaches *them,* he shall be called great in the kingdom of heaven. ᵃMatt 11:11

20 "For I say to you that unless your ᵃrighteousness surpasses *that* of the scribes and Pharisees, you will not enter the kingdom of heaven. ᵃLuke 18:11, 12

Personal Relationships

21 "You have heard that the ancients were told, 'ᵃYOU SHALL NOT COMMIT MURDER' and 'Whoever commits murder shall be liable to the court.' ᵃEx 20:13; Deut 5:17

22 "But I say to you that everyone who is angry with his brother shall be guilty before ᵃthe court; and whoever says to his brother, 'You good-for-nothing,' shall be guilty before the supreme court; and whoever says, 'You fool,' shall be guilty *enough to go* into the fiery hell. ᵃDeut 16:18; 2 Chr 19:5f

23 "Therefore if you are ᵃpresenting your offering at the altar, and there remember that your brother has something against you, ᵃMatt 5:24

24 leave your offering there before the altar and go; first be ᵃreconciled to your brother, and then come and present your offering. ᵃRom 12:17, 18

25 "ᵃMake friends quickly with your opponent at law while you are with him on the way, so that your opponent may not hand you over to the judge, and the judge to the officer, and you be thrown into prison. ᵃProv 25:8f; Luke 12:58

26 "Truly I say to you, ᵃyou will not come out of there until you have paid up the last cent. ᵃLuke 12:59

27 "You have heard that it was said, 'ᵃYOU SHALL NOT COMMIT ADULTERY'; ᵃEx 20:14; Deut 5:18

28 but I say to you that everyone who looks at a woman ᵃwith lust for her has already committed adultery with her in his heart. ᵃ2 Sam 11:2-5; Job 31:1

29 "ᵃIf your right eye makes you stumble, tear it out and throw it from you; for it is better for you to lose one of the parts of your body, than for your whole body to be thrown into hell. ᵃMatt 18:9; Mark 9:47

30 "ᵃIf your right hand makes you stumble, cut it off and throw it from you; for it is better for you to lose one of the parts of your body, than for your whole body to go into hell. ᵃMatt 18:8; Mark 9:43

31 "It was said, 'ᵃWHOEVER SENDS HIS WIFE AWAY, LET HIM GIVE HER A CERTIFICATE OF DIVORCE'; ᵃDeut 24:1, 3; Jer 3:1

32 ᵃbut I say to you that everyone who divorces his wife, except for *the* reason of unchastity, makes her commit adultery; and whoever marries a divorced woman commits adultery. ᵃMatt 19:9; Mark 10:11f

33 "Again, you have heard that the ancients were told, 'ᵃYOU SHALL NOT MAKE FALSE VOWS, BUT SHALL FULFILL YOUR VOWS TO THE LORD.' ᵃLev 19:12; Num 30:2

34 "But I say to you, ᵃmake no oath at all,

19 "aEvery tree that does not bear good fruit is cut down and thrown into the fire. aMatt 3:10; Luke 3:9

20 "So then, you will know them aby their fruits. aMatt 7:16; 12:33

21 "aNot everyone who says to Me, 'Lord, Lord,' will enter the kingdom of heaven, but he who does the will of My Father who is in heaven will enter. aLuke 6:46

22 "aMany will say to Me on that day, 'Lord, Lord, did we not prophesy in Your name, and in Your name cast out demons, and in Your name perform many miracles?' aMatt 25:11f; Luke 13:25ff

23 "And then I will declare to them, 'I never knew you; aDEPART FROM ME, YOU WHO PRACTICE LAWLESSNESS.' aPs 6:8; Matt 25:41

The Two Foundations

24 "Therefore aeveryone who hears these words of Mine and acts on them, may be compared to a wise man who built his house on the rock. aMatt 16:18; James 1:22-25

25 "And the rain fell, and the floods came, and the winds blew and slammed against that house; and yet it did not fall, for it had been founded on the rock.

26 "Everyone who hears these words of Mine and does not act on them, will be like a foolish man who built his house on the sand.

27 "The rain fell, and the floods came, and the winds blew and slammed against that house; and it fell—and great was its fall."

28 When Jesus had finished these words, athe crowds were amazed at His teaching; aMatt 13:54; 22:33

29 for He was teaching them as one having authority, and not as their scribes.

Jesus Cleanses a Leper; The Centurion's Faith

8 When Jesus came down from the mountain, large crowds followed Him.

2 And aa leper came to Him and bowed down before Him, and said, "Lord, if You are willing, You can make me clean." aMark 1:40-44; Luke 5:12-14

3 Jesus stretched out His hand and touched him, saying, "I am willing; be cleansed." And immediately his aleprosy was cleansed. aMatt 11:5; Luke 4:27

4 And Jesus *said to him, "See that you tell no one; but ago, show yourself to the priest and present the offering that Moses commanded, as a testimony to them." aMark 1:44; Luke 5:14

5 And awhen Jesus entered Capernaum, a centurion came to Him, imploring Him, aLuke 7:1-10

6 and saying, "Lord, my servant is lying apar-alyzed at home, fearfully tormented." aMatt 4:24

7 Jesus *said to him, "I will come and heal him."

8 But the centurion said, "Lord, I am not worthy for You to come under my roof, but just say the word, and my servant will be healed.

9 "For I also am a man under aauthority, with soldiers under me; and I say to this one, 'Go!' and he goes, and to another, 'Come!' and he comes, and to my slave, 'Do this!' and he does it." aMark 1:27; Luke 9:1

10 Now when Jesus heard this, He marveled and said to those who were following, "Truly I say to you, I have not found such great faith with anyone in Israel.

11 "I say to you that many awill come from east and west, and recline at the table with Abraham, Isaac and Jacob in the kingdom of heaven; aIs 49:12; 59:19

12 but athe sons of the kingdom will be cast out into bthe outer darkness; in that place there will be weeping and gnashing of teeth." aMatt 13:38 bMatt 22:13

13 And Jesus said to the centurion, "Go; it shall be done for you aas you have believed." And the servant was healed that very moment. aMatt 9:22, 29

Peter's Mother-in-law and Many Others Healed

14 aWhen Jesus came into Peter's home, He saw his mother-in-law lying sick in bed with a fever. aMark 1:29-34; Luke 4:38-41

15 He touched her hand, and the fever left her; and she got up and waited on Him.

16 When evening came, they brought to Him many awho were demon-possessed; and He cast out the spirits with a word, and bhealed all who were ill. aMatt 4:24 bMatt 4:23

17 This was to fulfill what was spoken through Isaiah the prophet: "aHE HIMSELF TOOK OUR INFIRMITIES AND CARRIED AWAY OUR DISEASES." aIs 53:4

Discipleship Tested

18 Now when Jesus saw a crowd around Him, aHe gave orders to depart to the other side of the sea. aMark 4:35; Luke 8:22

19 aThen a scribe came and said to Him, "Teacher, I will follow You wherever You go." aLuke 9:57-60

20 Jesus *said to him, "The foxes have holes and the birds of the air have nests, but athe Son of Man has nowhere to lay His head." aDan 7:13; Matt 9:6

21 Another of the disciples said to Him, "Lord, permit me first to go and bury my father."

22 But Jesus *said to him, "aFollow Me, and allow the dead to bury their own dead." aMatt 9:9; Mark 2:14

23 ᵃWhen He got into the boat, His disciples followed Him. ᵃ*Mark 4:36-41; Luke 8:22-25*

24 And behold, there arose a great storm on the sea, so that the boat was being covered with the waves; but Jesus Himself was asleep.

25 And they came to *Him* and woke Him, saying, "ᵃSave *us,* Lord; we are perishing!" ᵃ*Matt 8:2; 9:18*

26 He *said to them, "Why are you afraid, ᵃyou men of little faith?" Then He got up and rebuked the winds and the sea, and it became perfectly calm. ᵃ*Matt 6:30; 14:31*

27 The men were amazed, and said, "What kind of a man is this, that even the winds and the sea obey Him?"

Jesus Casts Out Demons

28 ᵃWhen He came to the other side into the country of the Gadarenes, two men who were demon-possessed met Him as they were coming out of the tombs. *They were* so extremely violent that no one could pass by that way. ᵃ*Mark 5:1-17; Luke 8:26-37*

29 And they cried out, saying, "ᵃWhat business do we have with each other, Son of God? Have You come here to torment us before the time?" ᵃ*Judg 11:12; 2 Sam 16:10*

30 Now there was a herd of many swine feeding at a distance from them.

31 The demons *began* to entreat Him, saying, "If You *are going to* cast us out, send us into the herd of swine."

32 And He said to them, "Go!" And they came out and went into the swine, and the whole herd rushed down the steep bank into the sea and perished in the waters.

33 The herdsmen ran away, and went to the city and reported everything, including what had happened to the ᵃdemoniacs. ᵃ*Matt 4:24*

34 And behold, the whole city came out to meet Jesus; and when they saw Him, ᵃthey implored Him to leave their region. ᵃ*Amos 7:12; Acts 16:39*

A Paralytic Healed

9 Getting into a boat, Jesus crossed over *the sea* and came to ᵃHis own city. ᵃ*Matt 4:13; Mark 5:21*

2 ᵃAnd they brought to Him a paralytic lying on a bed. Seeing their faith, Jesus said to the paralytic, "Take courage, son; your sins are forgiven." ᵃ*Mark 2:3-12; Luke 5:18-26*

3 And some of the scribes said to themselves, "This *fellow* ᵃblasphemes." ᵃ*Mark 3:28, 29*

4 And Jesus ᵃknowing their thoughts said, "Why are you thinking evil in your hearts? ᵃ*Matt 12:25; Luke 6:8*

5 "Which is easier, to say, 'ᵃYour sins are forgiven,' or to say, 'Get up, and walk'? ᵃ*Matt 9:2, 6; Mark 2:5, 9*

6 "But so that you may know that ᵃthe Son of Man has authority on earth to forgive sins"—then He *said to the paralytic, "Get up, pick up your bed and go home." ᵃ*Matt 8:20; John 5:27*

7 And he got up and went home.

8 But when the crowds saw *this,* they were awestruck, and ᵃglorified God, who had given such authority to men. ᵃ*Matt 5:16; 15:31*

Matthew Called

9 ᵃAs Jesus went on from there, He saw a man called Matthew, sitting in the tax collector's booth; and He *said to him, "Follow Me!" And he got up and followed Him. ᵃ*Mark 2:14-22; Luke 5:27-38*

10 Then it happened that as Jesus was reclining *at the table* in the house, behold, many tax collectors and sinners came and were dining with Jesus and His disciples.

11 When the Pharisees saw *this,* they said to His disciples, "ᵃWhy is your Teacher eating with the tax collectors and sinners?" ᵃ*Matt 11:19; Mark 2:16*

12 But when Jesus heard *this,* He said, "*It is* not ᵃthose who are healthy who need a physician, but those who are sick. ᵃ*Mark 2:17; Luke 5:31*

13 "But go and learn what this means: 'ᵃI DESIRE COMPASSION, AND NOT SACRIFICE,' for I did not come to call the righteous, but sinners." ᵃ*Hos 6:6*

The Question about Fasting

14 Then the disciples of John *came to Him, asking, "Why do we and ᵃthe Pharisees fast, but Your disciples do not fast?" ᵃ*Luke 18:12*

15 And Jesus said to them, "The attendants of the bridegroom cannot mourn as long as the bridegroom is with them, can they? But the days will come when the bridegroom is taken away from them, and then they will fast.

16 "But no one puts a patch of unshrunk cloth on an old garment; for the patch pulls away from the garment, and a worse tear results.

17 "Nor do *people* put new wine into old wineskins; otherwise the wineskins burst, and the wine pours out and the wineskins are ruined; but they put new wine into fresh wineskins, and both are preserved."

Miracles of Healing

18 ᵃWhile He was saying these things to them, a *synagogue* official came and bowed down before Him, and said, "My daughter has just died; but come and lay Your hand on her, and she will live." ᵃ*Mark 5:22-43; Luke 8:41-56*

19 Jesus got up and *began* to follow him, and *so did* His disciples.

20 And a woman who had been suffering from a hemorrhage for twelve years, came up behind Him and touched ᵃthe fringe of His cloak; ᵃ*Num 15:38; Deut 22:12*

21 for she was saying to herself, "If I only

ᵃtouch His garment, I will get well." ᵃ*Matt 14:36; Mark 3:10*

22 But Jesus turning and seeing her said, "Daughter, take courage; ᵃyour faith has made you well." At once the woman was made well. ᵃ*Matt 9:29; 15:28*

23 When Jesus came into the official's house, and saw ᵃthe flute-players and the crowd in noisy disorder, ᵃ2 *Chr 35:25; Jer 9:17*

24 He said, "Leave; for the girl ᵃhas not died, but is asleep." And they *began* laughing at Him. ᵃ*John 11:13; Acts 20:10*

25 But ᵃwhen the crowd had been sent out, He entered and ᵇtook her by the hand, and the girl got up. ᵃ*Acts 9:40* ᵇ*Mark 9:27*

26 ᵃThis news spread throughout all that land. ᵃ*Matt 4:24; 9:31*

27 As Jesus went on from there, two blind men followed Him, crying out, "Have mercy on us, ᵃSon of David!" ᵃ*Matt 1:1; 12:23*

28 When He entered the house, the blind men came up to Him, and Jesus *said to them, "Do you believe that I am able to do this?" They *said to Him, "Yes, Lord."

29 Then He touched their eyes, saying, "It shall be done to you ᵃaccording to your faith." ᵃ*Matt 8:13; 9:22*

30 And their eyes were opened. And Jesus ᵃsternly warned them: "See that no one knows *about this!*" ᵃ*Matt 8:4*

31 But they went out and ᵃspread the news about Him throughout all that land. ᵃ*Matt 4:24; 9:26*

32 As they were going out, ᵃa mute, demon-possessed man was brought to Him. ᵃ*Matt 12:22, 24*

33 After the demon was cast out, the mute man spoke; and the crowds were amazed, *and were* saying, "ᵃNothing like this has ever been seen in Israel." ᵃ*Mark 2:12*

34 But the Pharisees were saying, "He ᵃcasts out the demons by the ruler of the demons." ᵃ*Matt 12:24; Mark 3:22*

35 Jesus was going through all the cities and villages, ᵃteaching in their synagogues and proclaiming the gospel of the kingdom, and healing every kind of disease and every kind of sickness. ᵃ*Matt 4:23; Mark 1:14*

36 Seeing the people, He felt compassion for them, ᵃbecause they were distressed and dispirited like sheep without a shepherd. ᵃ*Num 27:17; Ezek 34:5*

37 Then He *said to His disciples, "ᵃThe harvest is plentiful, but the workers are few. ᵃ*Luke 10:2*

38 "Therefore beseech the Lord of the harvest to send out workers into His harvest."

The Twelve Disciples; Instructions for Service

10 Jesus ᵃsummoned His twelve disciples and gave them authority over unclean spirits, to cast them out, and to heal every kind of disease and every kind of sickness. ᵃ*Mark 3:13-15; 6:7*

2 ᵃNow the names of the twelve apostles are these: The first, Simon, who is called Peter, and Andrew his brother; and James the son of Zebedee, and John his brother; ᵃ*Mark 3:16-19; Luke 6:14-16*

3 ᵃPhilip and Bartholomew; ᵇThomas and Matthew the tax collector; James the son of Alphaeus, and Thaddaeus; ᵃ*John 1:43ff* ᵇ*John 11:16*

4 Simon the Zealot, and ᵃJudas Iscariot, the one who betrayed Him. ᵃ*Matt 26:14; Luke 22:3*

5 These twelve Jesus sent out after instructing them: "Do not go in *the* way of *the* Gentiles, and do not enter *any* city of the ᵃSamaritans; ᵃ2 *Kin 17:24ff; Luke 9:52*

6 but rather go to ᵃthe lost sheep of the house of Israel. ᵃ*Matt 15:24*

7 "And as you go, preach, saying, 'ᵃThe kingdom of heaven is at hand.' ᵃ*Matt 3:2*

8 "Heal *the* sick, raise *the* dead, cleanse *the* lepers, cast out demons. Freely you received, freely give.

9 "ᵃDo not acquire gold, or silver, or copper for your money belts, ᵃ*Luke 22:35*

10 or a bag for *your* journey, or even two coats, or sandals, or a staff; for ᵃthe worker is worthy of his support. ᵃ*1 Cor 9:14; 1 Tim 5:18*

11 "And whatever city or village you enter, inquire who is worthy in it, and stay at his house until you leave *that city.*

12 "As you enter the house, ᵃgive it your greeting. ᵃ*1 Sam 25:6; Ps 122:7, 8*

13 "If the house is worthy, give it your *blessing of* peace. But if it is not worthy, take back your *blessing of* peace.

14 "Whoever does not receive you, nor heed your words, as you go out of that house or that city, ᵃshake the dust off your feet. ᵃ*Acts 13:51*

15 "Truly I say to you, ᵃit will be more tolerable for *the* land of Sodom and Gomorrah in the day of judgment than for that city. ᵃ*Matt 11:22, 24*

A Hard Road before Them

16 "ᵃBehold, I send you out as sheep in the midst of wolves; so be shrewd as serpents and innocent as doves. ᵃ*Luke 10:3*

17 "But beware of men, for they will hand you over to *the* ᵃcourts and scourge you in their synagogues; ᵃ*Matt 5:22*

18 and you will even be brought before governors and kings for My sake, as a testimony to them and to the Gentiles.

19 "ᵃBut when they hand you over, do not worry about how or what you are to say; for it will be given you in that hour what you are to say. ᵃ*Mark 13:11-13; Luke 21:12-17*

20 "For ᵃit is not you who speak, but *it is* the Spirit of your Father who speaks in you. ᵃ*Luke 12:12; Acts 4:8*

21 "ᵃBrother will betray brother to death, and a father *his* child; and children will rise up against parents and cause them to be put to death. ᵃ*Matt 10:35, 36; Mark 13:12*

22 "ᵃYou will be hated by all because of My name, but it is the one who has endured to the end who will be saved. ᵃ*Matt 24:9; Luke 21:17*

23 "But whenever they persecute you in one city, flee to the next; for truly I say to you, you will not finish *going through* the cities of Israel ᵃuntil the Son of Man comes. ᵃ*Matt 16:27f*

The Meaning of Discipleship

24 "ᵃA disciple is not above his teacher, nor a slave above his master. ᵃ*Luke 6:40; John 13:16*

25 "It is enough for the disciple that he become like his teacher, and the slave like his master. If they have called the head of the house ᵃBeelzebul, how much more *will they malign* the members of his household! ᵃ*2 Kin 1:2; Matt 12:24, 27*

26 "Therefore do not fear them, ᵃfor there is nothing concealed that will not be revealed, or hidden that will not be known. ᵃ*Mark 4:22; Luke 8:17*

27 "ᵃWhat I tell you in the darkness, speak in the light; and what you hear *whispered* in *your* ear, proclaim upon the housetops. ᵃ*Luke 12:3*

28 "Do not fear those who kill the body but are unable to kill the soul; but rather ᵃfear Him who is able to destroy both soul and body in hell. ᵃ*Heb 10:31*

29 "ᵃAre not two sparrows sold for a cent? And *yet* not one of them will fall to the ground apart from your Father. ᵃ*Luke 12:6*

30 "But ᵃthe very hairs of your head are all numbered. ᵃ*1 Sam 14:45; 2 Sam 14:11*

31 "So do not fear; ᵃyou are more valuable than many sparrows. ᵃ*Matt 12:12*

32 "Therefore ᵃeveryone who confesses Me before men, I will also confess him before My Father who is in heaven. ᵃ*Luke 12:8; Rev 3:5*

33 "But ᵃwhoever denies Me before men, I will also deny him before My Father who is in heaven. ᵃ*Mark 8:38; Luke 9:26*

34 "ᵃDo not think that I came to bring peace on the earth; I did not come to bring peace, but a sword. ᵃ*Luke 12:51-53*

35 "For I came to ᵃSET A MAN AGAINST HIS FATHER, AND A DAUGHTER AGAINST HER MOTHER, AND A DAUGHTER-IN-LAW AGAINST HER MOTHER-IN-LAW; ᵃ*Mic 7:6; Matt 10:21*

36 and ᵃA MAN'S ENEMIES WILL BE THE MEMBERS OF HIS HOUSEHOLD. ᵃ*Mic 7:6; Matt 10:21*

37 "ᵃHe who loves father or mother more than Me is not worthy of Me; and he who loves son or daughter more than Me is not worthy of Me. ᵃ*Deut 33:9; Luke 14:26*

38 "And ᵃhe who does not take his cross and follow after Me is not worthy of Me. ᵃ*Matt 16:24; Mark 8:34*

39 "ᵃHe who has found his life will lose it, and he who has lost his life for My sake will find it. ᵃ*Matt 16:25; Mark 8:35*

The Reward of Service

40 "He who receives you receives Me, and ᵃhe who receives Me receives Him who sent Me. ᵃ*Mark 9:37; Luke 9:48*

41 "ᵃHe who receives a prophet in *the* name of a prophet shall receive a prophet's reward; and he who receives a righteous man in the name of a righteous man shall receive a righteous man's reward. ᵃ*Matt 25:44, 45*

42 "And ᵃwhoever in the name of a disciple gives to one of these little ones even a cup of cold water to drink, truly I say to you, he shall not lose his reward." ᵃ*Matt 25:40; Mark 9:41*

John's Questions

11 ᵃWhen Jesus had finished giving instructions to His twelve disciples, He departed from there to teach and preach in their cities. ᵃ*Matt 7:28*

2 ᵃNow when John, while imprisoned, heard of the works of Christ, he sent *word* by his disciples ᵃ*Matt 4:12*

3 and said to Him, "Are You ᵃthe Expected One, or shall we look for someone else?" ᵃ*Ps 118:26; Matt 11:10*

4 Jesus answered and said to them, "Go and report to John what you hear and see:

5 ᵃ*the* BLIND RECEIVE SIGHT and *the* lame walk, *the* lepers are cleansed and *the* deaf hear, *the* dead are raised up, and *the* POOR HAVE THE GOSPEL PREACHED TO THEM. ᵃ*Is 35:5f; Matt 8:3*

6 "And blessed is he who ᵃdoes not take offense at Me." ᵃ*Matt 5:29; 13:57*

Jesus' Tribute to John

7 As these men were going *away,* Jesus began to speak to the crowds about John, "What did you go out into ᵃthe wilderness to see? A reed shaken by the wind? ᵃ*Matt 3:1*

8 "But what did you go out to see? A man dressed in soft *clothing?* Those who wear soft *clothing* are in kings' palaces!

9 "But what did you go out to see? ᵃA prophet? Yes, I tell you, and one who is more than a prophet. ᵃ*Matt 14:5; 21:26*

10 "This is the one about whom it is written,
　'ᵃBEHOLD, I SEND MY MESSENGER AHEAD OF
　　YOU,

WHO WILL PREPARE YOUR WAY BEFORE YOU.'
    Mal 3:1; Mark 1:2

11 "Truly I say to you, among those born of women there has not arisen *anyone* greater than John the Baptist! Yet the one who is least in the kingdom of heaven is greater than he.

12 ªFrom the days of John the Baptist until now the kingdom of heaven suffers violence, and violent men take it by force. ªLuke 16:16

13 "For all the prophets and the Law prophesied until John.

14 "And if you are willing to accept *it,* John himself is ªElijah who was to come. *ªMal 4:5; Matt 17:10-13*

15 "ªHe who has ears to hear, let him hear. ªMatt 13:9, 43; Mark 4:9, 23

16 "But to what shall I compare this generation? It is like children sitting in the market places, who call out to the other *children,*

17 and say, 'We played the flute for you, and you did not dance; we sang a dirge, and you did not mourn.'

18 "For John came neither eating nor ªdrinking, and they say, 'ᵇHe has a demon!' *ªLuke 1:15* ᵇMatt 9:34; John 7:20

19 "The Son of Man came eating and drinking, and they say, 'Behold, a gluttonous man and a drunkard, ªa friend of tax collectors and sinners!' Yet wisdom is vindicated by her deeds." ªMatt 9:11; Luke 5:29-32

The Unrepenting Cities

20 Then He began to denounce the cities in which most of His ªmiracles were done, because they did not repent. ªLuke 10:13-15

21 "ªWoe to you, Chorazin! Woe to you, Bethsaida! For if the miracles had occurred in Tyre and Sidon which occurred in you, they would have repented long ago in sackcloth and ashes. ªLuke 10:13-15

22 "Nevertheless I say to you, it will be more tolerable for Tyre and Sidon in ªthe day of judgment than for you. ªMatt 10:15; 12:36

23 "And you, ªCapernaum, will not be exalted to heaven, will you? You will ᵇdescend to Hades; for if the miracles had occurred in Sodom which occurred in you, it would have remained to this day. ªMatt 4:13 ᵇIs 14:13, 15

24 "Nevertheless I say to you that ªit will be more tolerable for the land of Sodom in *the* day of judgment, than for you." *ªMatt 10:15; 11:22*

Come to Me

25 ªAt that time Jesus said, "I praise You, Father, Lord of heaven and earth, that You have hidden these things from *the* wise and intelligent and have revealed them to infants. ªLuke 10:21, 22

26 "Yes, ªFather, for this way was well-pleasing in Your sight. ªLuke 22:42; 23:34

27 "ªAll things have been handed over to Me by My Father; and no one knows the Son except the Father; nor does anyone know the Father except the Son, and anyone to whom the Son wills to reveal *Him.* ªMatt 28:18; John 3:35

28 "ªCome to Me, all who are weary and heavy-laden, and I will give you rest. ªJer 31:25; John 7:37

29 "Take My yoke upon you and ªlearn from Me, for I am gentle and humble in heart, and ᵇYOU WILL FIND REST FOR YOUR SOULS. ªJohn 13:15 ᵇJer 6:16

30 "For ªMy yoke is easy and My burden is light." ª1 John 5:3

Sabbath Questions

12 ªAt that time Jesus went through the grainfields on the Sabbath, and His disciples became hungry and began to pick the heads *of grain* and eat. ªMark 2:23-28; Luke 6:1-5

2 But when the Pharisees saw *this,* they said to Him, "Look, Your disciples do what ªis not lawful to do on a Sabbath." *ªMatt 12:10; Luke 13:14*

3 But He said to them, "Have you not read what David did when he became hungry, he and his companions,

4 how he entered the house of God, and ªthey ate the consecrated bread, which was not lawful for him to eat nor for those with him, but for the priests alone? ª1 Sam 21:6

5 "Or have you not read in the Law, that on the Sabbath the priests in the temple break the Sabbath and are innocent?

6 "But I say to you that something ªgreater than the temple is here. ª2 Chr 6:18; Is 66:1, 2

7 "But if you had known what this means, 'ªI DESIRE COMPASSION, AND NOT A SACRIFICE,' you would not have condemned the innocent. ªHos 6:6; Matt 9:13

Lord of the Sabbath

8 "For ªthe Son of Man is Lord of the Sabbath." ªMatt 8:20; 12:32, 40

9 ªDeparting from there, He went into their synagogue. ªMark 3:1-6; Luke 6:6-11

10 And a man *was there* whose hand was withered. And they questioned Jesus, asking, "ªIs it lawful to heal on the Sabbath?"—so that they might accuse Him. ªMatt 12:2; Luke 13:14

11 And He said to them, "ªWhat man is there among you who has a sheep, and if it falls into a pit on the Sabbath, will he not take hold of it and lift it out? ªLuke 14:5

12 "ªHow much more valuable then is a man than a sheep! So then, it is lawful to do good on the Sabbath." ªMatt 10:31; Luke 14:1-6

13 Then He *said to the man, "Stretch out your hand!" ªHe stretched it out, and it was restored to normal, like the other. ªMatt 8:3; Acts 28:8

14 But the Pharisees went out and ªconspired against Him, *as to* how they might destroy Him. ªMatt 26:4; Mark 14:1

15 But Jesus, aware of *this*, withdrew from there. Many followed Him, and ªHe healed them all, ªMatt 4:23

16 and ªwarned them not to tell who He was. ªMatt 8:4; 9:30

17 This *was* to fulfill what was spoken through Isaiah the prophet:

18 "ªBEHOLD, MY SERVANT WHOM I HAVE
    CHOSEN;
    ᵇMY BELOVED IN WHOM MY SOUL IS WELL-
    PLEASED;
    I WILL PUT MY SPIRIT UPON HIM,
    ªAND HE SHALL PROCLAIM JUSTICE TO THE
    GENTILES. ªIs 42:1 ᵇMatt 3:17

19 "ªHE WILL NOT QUARREL, NOR CRY OUT;
    NOR WILL ANYONE HEAR HIS VOICE IN THE
    STREETS. ªIs 42:2

20 "ªA BATTERED REED HE WILL NOT BREAK OFF,
    AND A SMOLDERING WICK HE WILL NOT PUT
    OUT,
    UNTIL HE LEADS JUSTICE TO VICTORY. ªIs 42:3

21 "ªAND IN HIS NAME THE GENTILES WILL HOPE."
    ªRom 15:12

The Pharisees Rebuked

22 ªThen a demon-possessed man *who was* blind and mute was brought to Jesus, and He healed him, so that the mute man spoke and saw. ªMatt 9:32, 34

23 All the crowds were amazed, and were saying, "This man cannot be the ªSon of David, can he?" ªMatt 9:27

24 But when the Pharisees heard *this*, they said, "This man ªcasts out demons only by Beelzebul the ruler of the demons." ªMatt 9:34

25 ªAnd knowing their thoughts Jesus said to them, "Any kingdom divided against itself is laid waste; and any city or house divided against itself will not stand. ªMark 3:23-27; Luke 11:17-22

26 "If ªSatan casts out Satan, he is divided against himself; how then will his kingdom stand? ªMatt 4:10; 13:19

27 "If I ªby Beelzebul cast out demons, ᵇby whom do your sons cast *them* out? For this reason they will be your judges. ªMatt 9:34 ᵇActs 19:13

28 "But ªif I cast out demons by the Spirit of God, then the kingdom of God has come upon you. ª1 John 3:8

29 "Or how can anyone enter the strong man's house and carry off his property, unless he first binds the strong *man*? And then he will plunder his house.

The Unpardonable Sin

30 "ªHe who is not with Me is against Me; and

he who does not gather with Me scatters. ªMark 9:40; Luke 9:50

31 "ªTherefore I say to you, any sin and blasphemy shall be forgiven people, but blasphemy against the Spirit shall not be forgiven. ªLuke 12:10

32 "ªWhoever speaks a word against the Son of Man, it shall be forgiven him; but whoever speaks against the Holy Spirit, it shall not be forgiven him, either in ᵇthis age or in the *age* to come. ªLuke 12:10 ᵇMatt 13:22, 39

Words Reveal Character

33 "Either make the tree good and its fruit good, or make the tree bad and its fruit bad; for ªthe tree is known by its fruit. ªMatt 7:16-18; Luke 6:43, 44

34 "ªYou brood of vipers, how can you, being evil, speak what is good? For the mouth speaks out of that which fills the heart. ªMatt 3:7; 23:33

35 "ªThe good man brings out of *his* good treasure what is good; and the evil man brings out of *his* evil treasure what is evil. ªProv 10:20, 21; 25:11, 12

36 "But I tell you that every careless word that people speak, they shall give an accounting for it in ªthe day of judgment. ªMatt 10:15

37 "For by your words you will be justified, and by your words you will be condemned."

The Desire for Signs

38 Then some of the scribes and Pharisees said to Him, "Teacher, ªwe want to see a sign from You." ªMatt 16:1; Mark 8:11, 12

39 But He answered and said to them, "ªAn evil and adulterous generation craves for a sign; and *yet* no sign will be given to it but the sign of Jonah the prophet; ªMatt 16:4

40 for just as ªJONAH WAS THREE DAYS AND THREE NIGHTS IN THE BELLY OF THE SEA MONSTER, so will the Son of Man be ᵇthree days and three nights in the heart of the earth. ªJon 1:17 ᵇMatt 16:21

41 "The men of Nineveh will stand up with this generation at the judgment, and will condemn it because ªthey repented at the preaching of Jonah; and behold, something greater than Jonah is here. ªJon 3:5

42 "ªThe Queen of *the* South will rise up with this generation at the judgment and will condemn it, because she came from the ends of the earth to hear the wisdom of Solomon; and behold, something greater than Solomon is here. ª1 Kin 10:1; 2 Chr 9:1

43 "ªNow when the unclean spirit goes out of a man, it passes through waterless places seeking rest, and does not find *it*. ªLuke 11:24-26

44 "Then it says, 'I will return to my house from which I came'; and when it comes, it finds *it* unoccupied, swept, and put in order.

45 "Then it goes and takes along with it seven other spirits more wicked than itself, and they

go in and live there; and ªthe last state of that man becomes worse than the first. That is the way it will also be with this evil generation."
ªMark 5:9; Luke 11:26

Changed Relationships

46 ªWhile He was still speaking to the crowds, behold, His mother and brothers were standing outside, seeking to speak to Him. ªMark 3:31-35; Luke 8:19-21

47 Someone said to Him, "Behold, Your mother and Your brothers are standing outside seeking to speak to You."

48 But Jesus answered the one who was telling Him and said, "Who is My mother and who are My brothers?"

49 And stretching out His hand toward His disciples, He said, "Behold My mother and My brothers!

50 "For whoever does the will of My Father who is in heaven, he is My brother and sister and mother."

Jesus Teaches in Parables

13 That day Jesus went out of the house and was sitting ªby the sea. ªMark 2:13

2 And large crowds gathered to Him, so ªHe got into a boat and sat down, and the whole crowd was standing on the beach. ªLuke 5:3

3 And He spoke many things to them in ªparables, saying, "Behold, the sower went out to sow; ªMatt 13:10ff; Mark 4:2ff

4 and as he sowed, some *seeds* fell beside the road, and the birds came and ate them up.

5 "Others fell on the rocky places, where they did not have much soil; and immediately they sprang up, because they had no depth of soil.

6 "But when the sun had risen, they were scorched; and because they had no root, they withered away.

7 "Others fell among the thorns, and the thorns came up and choked them out.

8 "And others fell on the good soil and *yielded a crop, some a ªhundredfold, some sixty, and some thirty. ªGen 26:12; Matt 13:23

9 ªHe who has ears, let him hear."
ªMatt 11:15; Rev 2:7, 11, 17, 29

An Explanation

10 And the disciples came and said to Him, "Why do You speak to them in parables?"

11 Jesus answered them, "ªTo you it has been granted to know the mysteries of the kingdom of heaven, but to them it has not been granted. ªMatt 19:11; 20:23

12 "ªFor whoever has, to him *more* shall be given, and he will have an abundance; but whoever does not have, even what he has shall be taken away from him. ªMatt 25:29; Mark 4:25

13 "Therefore I speak to them in parables; because while ªseeing they do not see, and while hearing they do not hear, nor do they understand. ªDeut 29:4; Is 42:19, 20

14 "In their case the prophecy of Isaiah is being fulfilled, which says,
'ªYOU WILL KEEP ON HEARING, BUT WILL NOT UNDERSTAND;
YOU WILL KEEP ON SEEING, BUT WILL NOT PERCEIVE; ªIs 6:9; Mark 4:12

15 ªFOR THE HEART OF THIS PEOPLE HAS BECOME DULL,
WITH THEIR EARS THEY SCARCELY HEAR,
AND THEY HAVE CLOSED THEIR EYES,
OTHERWISE THEY WOULD SEE WITH THEIR EYES,
HEAR WITH THEIR EARS,
AND UNDERSTAND WITH THEIR HEART AND RETURN,
AND I WOULD HEAL THEM.' ªIs 6:10; Ps 119:70

16 "ªBut blessed are your eyes, because they see; and your ears, because they hear.
ªMatt 16:17; John 20:29

17 "For truly I say to you that ªmany prophets and righteous men desired to see what you see, and did not see *it*, and to hear what you hear, and did not hear *it*. ªJohn 8:56; Heb 11:13

The Sower Explained

18 "ªHear then the parable of the sower.
ªMark 4:13-20; Luke 8:11-15

19 "When anyone hears ªthe word of the kingdom and does not understand it, the evil *one* comes and snatches away what has been sown in his heart. This is the one on whom seed was sown beside the road. ªMatt 4:23

20 "The one on whom seed was sown on the rocky places, this is the man who hears the word and immediately receives it with joy;

21 yet he has no *firm* root in himself, but is *only* temporary, and when affliction or persecution arises because of the word, immediately he ªfalls away. ªMatt 11:6

22 "And the one on whom seed was sown among the thorns, this is the man who hears the word, and the worry of the world and the ªdeceitfulness of wealth choke the word, and it becomes unfruitful. ªMatt 19:23; 1 Tim 6:9, 10, 17

23 "And the one on whom seed was sown on the good soil, this is the man who hears the word and understands it; who indeed bears fruit and brings forth, some ªa hundredfold, some sixty, and some thirty." ªMatt 13:8

Tares among Wheat

24 Jesus presented another parable to them, saying, "ªThe kingdom of heaven may be compared to a man who sowed good seed in his field. ªMatt 13:31, 33, 45, 47; 18:23

25 "But while his men were sleeping, his enemy came and sowed tares among the wheat, and went away.

26 "But when the wheat sprouted and bore grain, then the tares became evident also.

27 "The slaves of the landowner came and said to him, 'Sir, did you not sow good seed in your field? How then does it have tares?'

28 "And he said to them, 'An enemy has done this!' The slaves *said to him, 'Do you want us, then, to go and gather them up?'

29 "But he *said, 'No; for while you are gathering up the tares, you may uproot the wheat with them.

30 'Allow both to grow together until the harvest; and in the time of the harvest I will say to the reapers, "First gather up the tares and bind them in bundles to burn them up; but ªgather the wheat into my barn." ' " ªMatt 3:12

The Mustard Seed

31 He presented another parable to them, saying, "ªThe kingdom of heaven is like a mustard seed, which a man took and sowed in his field; ªMatt 13:24

32 and this is smaller than all *other* seeds, but when it is full grown, it is larger than the garden plants and becomes a tree, so that ªTHE BIRDS OF THE AIR come and NEST IN ITS BRANCHES." ªEzek 17:23; Ps 104:12

The Leaven

33 He spoke another parable to them, "ªThe kingdom of heaven is like leaven, which a woman took and hid in three pecks of flour until it was all leavened." ªMatt 13:24

34 All these things Jesus spoke to the crowds in parables, and He did not speak to them ªwithout a parable. ªMark 4:34; John 10:6

35 *This was* to fulfill what was spoken through the prophet:

"ªI WILL OPEN MY MOUTH IN PARABLES;
I WILL UTTER THINGS HIDDEN SINCE THE FOUNDATION OF THE WORLD." ªPs 78:2

The Tares Explained

36 Then He left the crowds and went into ªthe house. And His disciples came to Him and said, "ᵇExplain to us the parable of the tares of the field." ªMatt 13:1 ᵇMatt 15:15

37 And He said, "The one who sows the good seed is ªthe Son of Man, ªMatt 8:20

38 and the field is the world; and *as for* the good seed, these are ªthe sons of the kingdom; and the tares are ᵇthe sons of the evil *one;* ªMatt 8:12 ᵇJohn 8:44

39 and the enemy who sowed them is the devil, and the harvest is ªthe end of the age; and the reapers are angels. ªMatt 12:32; 13:22, 40, 49

40 "So just as the tares are gathered up and burned with fire, so shall it be at ªthe end of the age. ªMatt 12:32; 13:22, 39, 49

41 "ªThe Son of Man will send forth His angels, and they will gather out of His kingdom all stumbling blocks, and those who commit lawlessness, ªMatt 8:20

42 and ªwill throw them into the furnace of fire; in that place ᵇthere will be weeping and gnashing of teeth. ªMatt 13:50 ᵇMatt 8:12

43 "Then THE RIGHTEOUS WILL SHINE FORTH AS THE SUN in the kingdom of their Father. He who has ears, let him hear. ªDan 12:3

Hidden Treasure

44 "The kingdom of heaven is like a treasure hidden in the field, which a man found and hid *again;* and from joy over it he goes and ªsells all that he has and buys that field. ªMatt 13:46

A Costly Pearl

45 "Again, ªthe kingdom of heaven is like a merchant seeking fine pearls, ªMatt 13:24

46 and upon finding one pearl of great value, he went and sold all that he had and bought it.

A Dragnet

47 "Again, ªthe kingdom of heaven is like a dragnet cast into the sea, and gathering *fish* of every kind; ªMatt 13:44

48 and when it was filled, they drew it up on the beach; and they sat down and gathered the good *fish* into containers, but the bad they threw away.

49 "So it will be at ªthe end of the age; the angels will come forth and take out the wicked from among the righteous, ªMatt 13:39, 40

50 and ªwill throw them into the furnace of fire; in that place there will be weeping and gnashing of teeth. ªMatt 13:42

51 "Have you understood all these things?" They *said to Him, "Yes."

52 And Jesus said to them, "Therefore every scribe who has become a disciple of the kingdom of heaven is like a head of a household, who brings out of his treasure things new and old."

Jesus Revisits Nazareth

53 ªWhen Jesus had finished these parables, He departed from there. ªMatt 7:28

54 ªHe came to His hometown and ᵇ*began* teaching them in their synagogue, so that they were astonished, and said, "Where *did* this man *get* this wisdom and *these* miraculous powers? ªMark 6:1-6 ᵇMatt 4:23

55 "Is not this the carpenter's son? Is not ªHis mother called Mary, and His ªbrothers, James and Joseph and Simon and Judas? ªMatt 12:46

56 "And ªHis sisters, are they not all with us? Where then *did* this man *get* all these things?" ªMark 6:3

57 And they took ªoffense at Him. But Jesus said to them, "ᵇA prophet is not without honor

except in his hometown and in his *own* household." ᵃ*Matt 11:6* ᵇ*Mark 6:4*

58 And He did not do many miracles there because of their unbelief.

John the Baptist Beheaded

14 ᵃAt that time Herod the tetrarch heard the news about Jesus, ᵃ*Mark 6:14-29; Luke 9:7-9*

2 and said to his servants, "ᵃThis is John the Baptist; he has risen from the dead, and that is why miraculous powers are at work in him." ᵃ*Matt 16:14; Mark 6:14*

3 For when ᵃHerod had John arrested, he bound him and put him in prison because of Herodias, the wife of his brother Philip. ᵃ*Mark 8:15; Luke 3:1, 19*

4 For John had been saying to him, "It is not lawful for you to have her." ᵃ*Lev 18:16; 20:21*

5 Although Herod wanted to put him to death, he feared the crowd, because they regarded John as ᵃa prophet. ᵃ*Matt 11:9*

6 But when Herod's birthday came, the daughter of Herodias danced before *them* and pleased ᵃHerod, ᵃ*Mark 8:15; Luke 3:1, 19*

7 so *much* that he promised with an oath to give her whatever she asked.

8 Having been prompted by her mother, she *said, "Give me here on a platter the head of John the Baptist."

9 Although he was grieved, the king commanded *it* to be given because of his oaths, and because of his dinner guests.

10 He sent and had John beheaded in the prison.

11 And his head was brought on a platter and given to the girl, and she brought it to her mother.

12 His disciples came and took away the body and buried it; and they went and reported to Jesus.

Five Thousand Fed

13 ᵃNow when Jesus heard *about John,* He withdrew from there in a boat to a secluded place by Himself; and when the people heard *of this,* they followed Him on foot from the cities. ᵃ*Matt 15:32-38*

14 When He went ashore, He saw a large crowd, and felt compassion for them and ᵃhealed their sick. ᵃ*Matt 4:23*

15 When it was evening, the disciples came to Him and said, "This place is desolate and the hour is already late; so send the crowds away, that they may go into the villages and buy food for themselves."

16 But Jesus said to them, "They do not need to go away; you give them *something* to eat!"

17 They *said to Him, "We have here only ᵃfive loaves and two fish." ᵃ*Matt 16:9*

18 And He said, "Bring them here to Me."

19 Ordering the people to sit down on the grass, He took the five loaves and the two fish, and looking up toward heaven, He ᵃblessed *the food,* and breaking the loaves He gave them to the disciples, and the disciples *gave them* to the crowds, ᵃ*1 Sam 9:13; Matt 15:36*

20 and they all ate and were satisfied. They picked up what was left over of the broken pieces, twelve full ᵃbaskets. ᵃ*Matt 16:9; Mark 6:43*

21 There were about five thousand men who ate, besides women and children.

Jesus Walks on the Water

22 ᵃImmediately He made the disciples get into the boat and go ahead of Him to the other side, while He sent the crowds away. ᵃ*Mark 6:45-51; John 6:15-21*

23 After He had sent the crowds away, ᵃHe went up on the mountain by Himself to pray; and when it was evening, He was there alone. ᵃ*Mark 6:46; Luke 6:12*

24 But the boat was already a long distance from the land, battered by the waves; for the wind was ᵃcontrary. ᵃ*Acts 27:4*

25 And in the fourth watch of the night He came to them, walking on the sea.

26 When the disciples saw Him walking on the sea, they were terrified, and said, "It is ᵃa ghost!" And they cried out in fear. ᵃ*Luke 24:37*

27 But immediately Jesus spoke to them, saying, "ᵃTake courage; it is I; ᵇdo not be afraid." ᵃ*Matt 9:2* ᵇ*Matt 17:7*

28 Peter said to Him, "Lord, if it is You, command me to come to You on the water."

29 And He said, "Come!" And Peter got out of the boat, and walked on the water and came toward Jesus.

30 But seeing the wind, he became frightened, and beginning to sink, he cried out, "Lord, save me!"

31 Immediately Jesus stretched out His hand and took hold of him, and *said to him, "ᵃYou of little faith, why did you doubt?" ᵃ*Matt 6:30; 8:26*

32 When they got into the boat, the wind stopped.

33 And those who were in the boat worshiped Him, saying, "You are certainly ᵃGod's Son!" ᵃ*Matt 4:3*

34 ᵃWhen they had crossed over, they came to land at Gennesaret. ᵃ*John 6:24, 25*

35 And when the men of that place recognized Him, they sent *word* into all that surrounding district and brought to Him all who were sick;

36 and they implored Him that they might just touch the fringe of His cloak; and as many as ᵃtouched *it* were cured. ᵃ*Matt 9:21; Mark 3:10*

Tradition and Commandment

15 [a]Then some Pharisees and scribes *came to Jesus from Jerusalem and said, [a]Mark 7:1-23

2 "Why do Your disciples break the tradition of the elders? For they [a]do not wash their hands when they eat bread." [a]Luke 11:38

3 And He answered and said to them, "Why do you yourselves transgress the commandment of God for the sake of your tradition?

4 "For God said, '[a]HONOR YOUR FATHER AND MOTHER,' and, '[b]HE WHO SPEAKS EVIL OF FATHER OR MOTHER IS TO BE PUT TO DEATH.' [a]Ex 20:12 [b]Ex 21:17

5 "But you say, 'Whoever says to *his* father or mother, "Whatever I have that would help you has been given *to God*,"

6 he is not to honor his father or his mother.' And *by this* you invalidated the word of God for the sake of your tradition.

7 "You hypocrites, rightly did Isaiah prophesy of you:

8 '[a]THIS PEOPLE HONORS ME WITH THEIR LIPS,
BUT THEIR HEART IS FAR AWAY FROM ME.
　[a]Is 29:13

9 'BUT IN VAIN DO THEY WORSHIP ME,
TEACHING AS [a]DOCTRINES THE PRECEPTS OF
MEN.' " [a]Col 2:22

10 After Jesus called the crowd to Him, He said to them, "Hear and understand.

11 "[a]*It is* not what enters into the mouth *that* defiles the man, but what proceeds out of the mouth, this defiles the man." [a]Matt 15:18; Acts 10:14, 15

12 Then the disciples *came and *said to Him, "Do You know that the Pharisees were offended when they heard this statement?"

13 But He answered and said, "[a]Every plant which My heavenly Father did not plant shall be uprooted. [a]Is 60:21; 61:3

14 "Let them alone; [a]they are blind guides of the blind. And [b]if a blind man guides a blind man, both will fall into a pit." [a]Matt 23:16, 24 [b]Luke 6:39

The Heart of Man

15 Peter said to Him, "[a]Explain the parable to us." [a]Matt 13:36

16 Jesus said, "Are you still lacking in understanding also?

17 "Do you not understand that everything that goes into the mouth passes into the stomach, and is eliminated?

18 "But [a]the things that proceed out of the mouth come from the heart, and those defile the man. [a]Matt 12:34; Mark 7:20

19 "[a]For out of the heart come evil thoughts, murders, adulteries, fornications, thefts, false witness, slanders. [a]Gal 5:19ff

20 "These are the things which defile the man; but to eat with unwashed hands does not defile the man."

The Syrophoenician Woman

21 Jesus went away from there, and withdrew into the district of [a]Tyre and Sidon. [a]Matt 11:21

22 And a Canaanite woman from that region came out and *began* to cry out, saying, "Have mercy on me, Lord, Son of David; my daughter is cruelly [a]demon-possessed." [a]Matt 4:24

23 But He did not answer her a word. And His disciples came and implored Him, saying, "Send her away, because she keeps shouting at us."

24 But He answered and said, "I was sent only to [a]the lost sheep of the house of Israel." [a]Matt 10:6

25 But she came and [a]began to bow down before Him, saying, "Lord, help me!" [a]Matt 8:2

26 And He answered and said, "It is not good to take the children's bread and throw it to the dogs."

27 But she said, "Yes, Lord; but even the dogs feed on the crumbs which fall from their masters' table."

28 Then Jesus said to her, "O woman, [a]your faith is great; it shall be done for you as you wish." And her daughter was healed at once. [a]Matt 9:22

Healing Crowds

29 [a]Departing from there, Jesus went along by the Sea of Galilee, and having gone up on the mountain, He was sitting there. [a]Matt 15:29-31; Mark 7:31-37

30 And large crowds came to Him, bringing with them *those who were* lame, crippled, blind, mute, and many others, and they laid them down at His feet; and [a]He healed them. [a]Matt 4:23

31 So the crowd marveled as they saw the mute speaking, the crippled restored, and the lame walking, and the blind seeing; and they [a]glorified the God of Israel. [a]Matt 9:8

Four Thousand Fed

32 [a]And Jesus called His disciples to Him, and said, "I feel compassion for the people, because they have remained with Me now three days and have nothing to eat; and I do not want to send them away hungry, for they might faint on the way." [a]Matt 14:13-21

33 The disciples *said to Him, "Where would we get so many loaves in *this* desolate place to satisfy such a large crowd?"

34 And Jesus *said to them, "How many loaves do you have?" And they said, "Seven, and a few small fish."

35 And He directed the people to sit down on the ground;

36 and He took the seven loaves and the fish; and [a]giving thanks, He broke them and started

giving them to the disciples, and the disciples *gave them* to the people. ªMatt 14:19; 26:27

37 And they all ate and were satisfied, and they picked up what was left over of the broken pieces, seven large ªbaskets full. ªMatt 16:10; Mark 8:8, 20

38 And those who ate were four thousand men, besides women and children.

39 And sending away the crowds, Jesus got into the boat and came to the region of ªMagadan. ªMark 8:10

Pharisees Test Jesus

16 ªThe Pharisees and Sadducees came up, and testing Jesus, they asked Him to show them a sign from heaven. ªMark 8:11-21

2 But He replied to them, "When it is evening, you say, '*It will be* fair weather, for the sky is red.' ªLuke 12:54f

3 "And in the morning, '*There will be* a storm today, for the sky is red and threatening.' ªDo you know how to discern the appearance of the sky, but cannot *discern* the signs of the times? ªLuke 12:56

4 "ªAn evil and adulterous generation seeks after a sign; and a sign will not be given it, except the sign of Jonah." And He left them and went away. ªMatt 12:39; Luke 11:29

5 And the disciples came to the other side *of the sea*, but they had forgotten to bring *any* bread.

6 And Jesus said to them, "Watch out and ªbeware of the leaven of the Pharisees and Sadducees." ªMark 8:15; Luke 12:1

7 They began to discuss *this* among themselves, saying, "*He said that* because we did not bring *any* bread."

8 But Jesus, aware of this, said, "ªYou men of little faith, why do you discuss among yourselves that you have no bread? ªMatt 6:30; 8:26

9 "Do you not yet understand or remember ªthe five loaves of the five thousand, and how many baskets *full* you picked up? ªMatt 14:17-21

10 "Or ªthe seven loaves of the four thousand, and how many large baskets *full* you picked up? ªMatt 15:34-38

11 "How is it that you do not understand that I did not speak to you concerning bread? But beware of the leaven of the ªPharisees and Sadducees." ªMatt 3:7; 16:6, 12

12 Then they understood that He did not say to beware of the leaven of bread, but of the teaching of the ªPharisees and Sadducees. ªMatt 3:7; 5:20

Peter's Confession of Christ

13 ªNow when Jesus came into the district of Caesarea Philippi, He was asking His disciples, "Who do people say that the Son of Man is?" ªMark 8:27-29; Luke 9:18-20

14 And they said, "Some *say* ªJohn the Baptist; and others, ᵇElijah; but still others, Jeremiah, or one of the prophets." ªMatt 14:2 ᵇMatt 17:10

15 He *said to them, "But who do you say that I am?"

16 Simon Peter answered, "You are the Christ, ªthe Son of ᵇthe living God." ªMatt 4:3 ᵇPs 42:2

17 And Jesus said to him, "Blessed are you, Simon Barjona, because ªflesh and blood did not reveal *this* to you, but My Father who is in heaven. ª1 Cor 15:50; Gal 1:16

18 "I also say to you that you are ªPeter, and upon this rock I will build My church; and the gates of ᵇHades will not overpower it. ªMatt 4:18 ᵇMatt 11:23

19 "I will give you the keys of the kingdom of heaven; and ªwhatever you bind on earth shall have been bound in heaven, and whatever you loose on earth shall have been loosed in heaven." ªMatt 18:18; John 20:23

20 ªThen He warned the disciples that they should tell no one that He was the Christ. ªMatt 8:4; Mark 8:30

Jesus Foretells His Death

21 ªFrom that time Jesus began to show His disciples that He must go to Jerusalem, and suffer many things from the elders and chief priests and scribes, and be killed, and be raised up on the third day. ªMark 8:31-9:1; Luke 9:22-27

22 Peter took Him aside and began to rebuke Him, saying, "God forbid *it*, Lord! This shall never happen to You."

23 But He turned and said to Peter, "Get behind Me, ªSatan! You are a stumbling block to Me; for you are not setting your mind on God's interests, but man's." ªMatt 4:10

Discipleship Is Costly

24 Then Jesus said to His disciples, "If anyone wishes to come after Me, he must deny himself, and ªtake up his cross and follow Me. ªMatt 10:38; Luke 14:27

25 "For ªwhoever wishes to save his life will lose it; but whoever loses his life for My sake will find it. ªMatt 10:39

26 "For what will it profit a man if he gains the whole world and forfeits his soul? Or what will a man give in exchange for his soul?

27 "For the Son of Man ªis going to come in the glory of His Father with His angels, and WILL THEN REPAY EVERY MAN ACCORDING TO HIS DEEDS. ªMark 8:38; 1 Thess 4:16

28 "Truly I say to you, there are some of those who are standing here who will not taste death until they see the Son of Man ªcoming in His kingdom." ªMatt 10:23; 24:3, 27, 37, 39

The Transfiguration

17 [a]Six days later Jesus *took with Him [b]Peter and James and John his brother, and *led them up on a high mountain by themselves. [a]Mark 9:2-8 [b]Matt 26:37

2 And He was transfigured before them; and His face shone like the sun, and His garments became as white as light.

3 And behold, Moses and Elijah appeared to them, talking with Him.

4 Peter said to Jesus, "Lord, it is good for us to be here; if You wish, [a]I will make three tabernacles here, one for You, and one for Moses, and one for Elijah." [a]Mark 9:5; Luke 9:33

5 While he was still speaking, a bright cloud overshadowed them, and behold, [a]a voice out of the cloud said, "This is My beloved Son, with whom I am well-pleased; listen to Him!" [a]Mark 1:11; Luke 3:22

6 When the disciples heard *this,* they fell face down to the ground and were terrified.

7 And Jesus came to *them* and touched them and said, "Get up, and [a]do not be afraid." [a]Matt 14:27

8 And lifting up their eyes, they saw no one except Jesus Himself alone.

9 [a]As they were coming down from the mountain, Jesus commanded them, saying, "Tell the vision to no one until the Son of Man has [b]risen from the dead." [a]Mark 9:9-13 [b]Matt 16:21

10 And His disciples asked Him, "Why then do the scribes say that [a]Elijah must come first?" [a]Mal 4:5; Matt 11:14

11 And He answered and said, "Elijah is coming and will restore all things;

12 but I say to you that Elijah already came, and they did not recognize him, but did to him whatever they wished. So also [a]the Son of Man is going to suffer at their hands." [a]Matt 8:20; 17:9, 22

13 Then the disciples understood that He had spoken to them about John the Baptist.

The Demoniac

14 [a]When they came to the crowd, a man came up to Jesus, falling on his knees before Him and saying, [a]Mark 9:14-28; Luke 9:37-42

15 "Lord, have mercy on my son, for he is a [a]lunatic and is very ill; for he often falls into the fire and often into the water. [a]Matt 4:24

16 "I brought him to Your disciples, and they could not cure him."

17 And Jesus answered and said, "You unbelieving and perverted generation, how long shall I be with you? How long shall I put up with you? Bring him here to Me."

18 And Jesus rebuked him, and the demon came out of him, and the boy was cured at once.

19 Then the disciples came to Jesus privately and said, "Why could we not drive it out?"

20 And He *said to them, "Because of the littleness of your faith; for truly I say to you, [a]if you have faith the size of a mustard seed, you will say to this mountain, 'Move from here to there,' and it will move; and nothing will be impossible to you. [a]Matt 21:21f; Mark 11:23f

21 ["[a]But this kind does not go out except by prayer and fasting."] [a]Mark 9:29

22 [a]And while they were gathering together in Galilee, Jesus said to them, "The Son of Man is going to be delivered into the hands of men; [a]Mark 9:30-32; Luke 9:44, 45

23 and [a]they will kill Him, and He will be raised on the third day." And they were deeply grieved. [a]Matt 16:21; 17:9

The Tribute Money

24 When they came to Capernaum, those who collected [a]the two-drachma *tax* came to Peter and said, "Does your teacher not pay [a]the two-drachma *tax?*" [a]Ex 30:13; 38:26

25 He *said, "Yes." And when he came into the house, Jesus spoke to him first, saying, "What do you think, Simon? From whom do the kings of the earth collect [a]customs or [b]poll-tax, from their sons or from strangers?" [a]Rom 13:7 [b]Matt 22:17, 19

26 When Peter said, "From strangers," Jesus said to him, "Then the sons are exempt.

27 "However, so that we do not [a]offend them, go to the sea and throw in a hook, and take the first fish that comes up; and when you open its mouth, you will find a shekel. Take that and give it to them for you and Me." [a]Matt 5:29, 30; 18:6, 8, 9

Rank in the Kingdom

18 [a]At that time the disciples came to Jesus and said, "Who then is greatest in the kingdom of heaven?" [a]Mark 9:33-37; Luke 9:46-48

2 And He called a child to Himself and set him before them,

3 and said, "Truly I say to you, unless you are converted and [a]become like children, you will not enter the kingdom of heaven. [a]Matt 19:14; Mark 10:15

4 "Whoever then humbles himself as this child, he is the greatest in the kingdom of heaven.

5 "And whoever receives one such child in My name receives Me;

6 but [a]whoever causes one of these little ones who believe in Me to stumble, it would be better for him to have a heavy millstone hung around his neck, and to be drowned in the depth of the sea. [a]Mark 9:42; Luke 17:2

Stumbling Blocks

7 "Woe to the world because of *its* stumbling

blocks! For [a]it is inevitable that stumbling blocks come; but woe to that man through whom the stumbling block comes! [a]*Luke 17:1; 1 Cor 11:19*

8 "[a]If your hand or your foot causes you to stumble, cut it off and throw it from you; it is better for you to enter life crippled or lame, than to have two hands or two feet and be cast into the eternal fire. [a]*Matt 5:30; Mark 9:43*

9 "[a]If your eye causes you to stumble, pluck it out and throw it from you. It is better for you to enter life with one eye, than to have two eyes and be cast into the fiery hell. [a]*Matt 5:29; Mark 9:47*

10 "See that you do not despise one of these little ones, for I say to you that [a]their angels in heaven continually see the face of My Father who is in heaven. [a]*Luke 1:19; Acts 12:15*

11 ["[a]For the Son of Man has come to save that which was lost.] [a]*Luke 19:10*

Ninety-nine Plus One

12 "What do you think? [a]If any man has a hundred sheep, and one of them has gone astray, does he not leave the ninety-nine on the mountains and go and search for the one that is straying? [a]*Luke 15:4-7*

13 "If it turns out that he finds it, truly I say to you, he rejoices over it more than over the ninety-nine which have not gone astray.

14 "So it is not *the* will of your Father who is in heaven that one of these little ones perish.

Discipline and Prayer

15 "[a]If your brother sins, go and show him his fault in private; if he listens to you, you have won your brother. [a]*Lev 19:17; Luke 17:3*

16 "But if he does not listen *to you,* take one or two more with you, so that [a]BY THE MOUTH OF TWO OR THREE WITNESSES EVERY FACT MAY BE CONFIRMED. [a]*Deut 19:15; John 8:17*

17 "If he refuses to listen to them, tell it to the church; and if he refuses to listen even to the church, [a]let him be to you as a Gentile and a tax collector. [a]*2 Thess 3:6, 14f*

18 "Truly I say to you, [a]whatever you bind on earth shall have been bound in heaven; and whatever you loose on earth shall have been loosed in heaven. [a]*Matt 16:19; John 20:23*

19 "Again I say to you, that if two of you agree on earth about anything that they may ask, [a]it shall be done for them by My Father who is in heaven. [a]*Matt 7:7*

20 "For where two or three have gathered together in My name, [a]I am there in their midst." [a]*Matt 28:20*

Forgiveness

21 Then Peter came and said to Him, "Lord, [a]how often shall my brother sin against me and I forgive him? Up to [b]seven times?" [a]*Matt 18:15* [b]*Luke 17:4*

22 Jesus *said to him, "I do not say to you, up to seven times, but up to [a]seventy times seven. [a]*Gen 4:24*

23 "For this reason [a]the kingdom of heaven may be compared to a king who wished to [b]settle accounts with his slaves. [a]*Matt 13:24* [b]*Matt 25:19*

24 "When he had begun to settle *them,* one who owed him ten thousand talents was brought to him.

25 "But since he [a]did not have *the means* to repay, his lord commanded him [b]to be sold, along with his wife and children and all that he had, and repayment to be made. [a]*Luke 7:42* [b]*Ex 21:2*

26 "So the slave fell *to the ground* and [a]prostrated himself before him, saying, 'Have patience with me and I will repay you everything.' [a]*Matt 8:2*

27 "And the lord of that slave felt compassion and released him and [a]forgave him the debt. [a]*Luke 7:42*

28 "But that slave went out and found one of his fellow slaves who owed him a hundred denarii; and he seized him and *began* to choke *him,* saying, 'Pay back what you owe.'

29 "So his fellow slave fell *to the ground* and *began* to plead with him, saying, 'Have patience with me and I will repay you.'

30 "But he was unwilling and went and threw him in prison until he should pay back what was owed.

31 "So when his fellow slaves saw what had happened, they were deeply grieved and came and reported to their lord all that had happened.

32 "Then summoning him, his lord *said to him, 'You wicked slave, I forgave you all that debt because you pleaded with me.

33 "[a]Should you not also have had mercy on your fellow slave, in the same way that I had mercy on you?' [a]*Matt 6:12; Eph 4:32*

34 "And his lord, moved with anger, handed him over to the torturers until he should repay all that was owed him.

35 "[a]My heavenly Father will also do the same to you, if each of you does not forgive his brother from your heart." [a]*Matt 6:14*

Concerning Divorce

19 When Jesus had finished these words, He departed from Galilee and [a]came into the region of Judea beyond the Jordan; [a]*Mark 10:1-12*

2 and large crowds followed Him, and [a]He healed them there. [a]*Matt 4:23*

3 *Some* Pharisees came to Jesus, testing Him and asking, "[a]Is it lawful *for a man* to divorce his wife for any reason at all?" [a]*Matt 5:31*

4 And He answered and said, "Have you not read ^athat He who created *them* from the beginning MADE THEM MALE AND FEMALE, ^a*Gen 1:27; 5:2*

5 and said, '^aFOR THIS REASON A MAN SHALL LEAVE HIS FATHER AND MOTHER AND BE JOINED TO HIS WIFE, AND THE TWO SHALL BECOME ONE FLESH'? ^a*Gen 2:24; Eph 5:31*

6 "So they are no longer two, but one flesh. What therefore God has joined together, let no man separate."

7 They *said to Him, "^aWhy then did Moses command to GIVE HER A CERTIFICATE OF DIVORCE AND SEND *her* AWAY?" ^a*Deut 24:1-4; Matt 5:31*

8 He *said to them, "Because of your hardness of heart Moses permitted you to divorce your wives; but from the beginning it has not been this way.

9 "And I say to you, ^awhoever divorces his wife, except for immorality, and marries another woman commits adultery." ^a*Matt 5:32*

10 The disciples *said to Him, "If the relationship of the man with his wife is like this, it is better not to marry."

11 But He said to them, "^aNot all men *can* accept this statement, but *only* those to whom it has been given. ^a*1 Cor 7:7ff*

12 "For there are eunuchs who were born that way from their mother's womb; and there are eunuchs who were made eunuchs by men; and there are *also* eunuchs who made themselves eunuchs for the sake of the kingdom of heaven. He who is able to accept *this,* let him accept *it.*"

Jesus Blesses Little Children

13 ^aThen *some* children were brought to Him so that He might lay His hands on them and pray; and the disciples rebuked them. ^a*Mark 10:13-16; Luke 18:15-17*

14 But Jesus said, "^aLet the children alone, and do not hinder them from coming to Me; for the kingdom of heaven belongs to such as these." ^a*Matt 18:3; Mark 10:15*

15 After laying His hands on them, He departed from there.

The Rich Young Ruler

16 ^aAnd someone came to Him and said, "Teacher, what good thing shall I do that I may obtain eternal life?" ^a*Luke 10:25-28*

17 And He said to him, "Why are you asking Me about what is good? There is *only* One who is good; but ^aif you wish to enter into life, keep the commandments." ^a*Lev 18:5; Neh 9:29*

18 *Then* he *said to Him, "Which ones?" And Jesus said, "^aYOU SHALL NOT COMMIT MURDER; YOU SHALL NOT COMMIT ADULTERY; YOU SHALL NOT STEAL; YOU SHALL NOT BEAR FALSE WITNESS; ^a*Ex 20:13-16; Deut 5:17-20*

19 ^aHONOR YOUR FATHER AND MOTHER; and ^bYOU

SHALL LOVE YOUR NEIGHBOR AS YOURSELF." ^a*Ex 20:12* ^b*Lev 19:18*

20 The young man *said to Him, "All these things I have kept; what am I still lacking?"

21 Jesus said to him, "If you wish to be complete, go *and* ^asell your possessions and give to *the* poor, and you will have treasure in heaven; and come, follow Me." ^a*Luke 12:33; 16:9*

22 But when the young man heard this statement, he went away grieving; for he was one who owned much property.

23 And Jesus said to His disciples, "Truly I say to you, ^ait is hard for a rich man to enter the kingdom of heaven. ^a*Matt 13:22; Mark 10:23f*

24 "Again I say to you, ^ait is easier for a camel to go through the eye of a needle, than for a rich man to enter the kingdom of God." ^a*Mark 10:25; Luke 18:25*

25 When the disciples heard *this,* they were very astonished and said, "Then who can be saved?"

26 And looking at *them* Jesus said to them, "^aWith people this is impossible, but with God all things are possible." ^a*Gen 18:14; Job 42:2*

The Disciples' Reward

27 Then Peter said to Him, "Behold, we have left everything and followed You; what then will there be for us?"

28 And Jesus said to them, "Truly I say to you, that you who have followed Me, in the regeneration when the Son of Man will sit on His glorious throne, ^ayou also shall sit upon twelve thrones, judging the twelve tribes of Israel. ^a*Luke 22:30; Rev 3:21*

29 "And ^aeveryone who has left houses or brothers or sisters or father or mother or children or farms for My name's sake, will receive many times as much, and will inherit eternal life. ^a*Matt 6:33; Mark 10:29f*

30 "^aBut many *who are* first will be last; and *the* last, first. ^a*Matt 20:16; Mark 10:31*

Laborers in the Vineyard

20 "For the kingdom of heaven is like a landowner who went out early in the morning to hire laborers for his ^avineyard. ^a*Matt 21:28, 33*

2 "When he had agreed with the laborers for a denarius for the day, he sent them into his vineyard.

3 "And he went out about the third hour and saw others standing idle in the market place;

4 and to those he said, 'You also go into the vineyard, and whatever is right I will give you.' And *so* they went.

5 "Again he went out about the sixth and the ninth hour, and did the same thing.

6 "And about the eleventh *hour* he went out and found others standing *around;* and he

*said to them, 'Why have you been standing here idle all day long?'

7 "They *said to him, 'Because no one hired us.' He *said to them, 'You go into the vineyard too.'

8 "When ᵃevening came, the owner of the vineyard *said to his foreman, 'Call the laborers and pay them their wages, beginning with the last *group* to the first.' ᵃ*Lev 19:13; Deut 24:15*

9 "When those *hired* about the eleventh hour came, each one received a denarius.

10 "When those *hired* first came, they thought that they would receive more; but each of them also received a denarius.

11 "When they received it, they grumbled at the landowner,

12 saying, 'These last men have worked *only* one hour, and you have made them equal to us who have borne the burden and the ᵃscorching heat of the day.' ᵃ*Jon 4:8; Luke 12:55*

13 "But he answered and said to one of them, 'ᵃFriend, I am doing you no wrong; did you not agree with me for a denarius? ᵃ*Matt 22:12; 26:50*

14 'Take what is yours and go, but I wish to give to this last man the same as to you.

15 'Is it not lawful for me to do what I wish with what is my own? Or is your ᵃeye envious because I am generous?' ᵃ*Deut 15:9; Matt 6:23*

16 "So ᵃthe last shall be first, and the first last." ᵃ*Matt 19:30; Mark 10:31*

Death, Resurrection Foretold

17 ᵃAs Jesus was about to go up to Jerusalem, He took the twelve *disciples* aside by themselves, and on the way He said to them, ᵃ*Mark 10:32-34; Luke 18:31-33*

18 "Behold, we are going up to Jerusalem; and the Son of Man ᵃwill be delivered to the chief priests and scribes, and they will condemn Him to death, ᵃ*Matt 16:21*

19 and will hand Him over to the Gentiles to mock and scourge and crucify *Him*, and on ᵃthe third day He will be raised up." ᵃ*Matt 16:21; 17:23*

Preferment Asked

20 ᵃThen the mother of the sons of Zebedee came to Jesus with her sons, bowing down and making a request of Him. ᵃ*Mark 10:35-45*

21 And He said to her, "What do you wish?" She *said to Him, "Command that in Your kingdom these two sons of mine ᵃmay sit one on Your right and one on Your left." ᵃ*Matt 19:28*

22 But Jesus answered, "You do not know what you are asking. Are you able ᵃto drink the cup that I am about to drink?" They *said to Him, "We are able." ᵃ*Is 51:17, 22; Jer 49:12*

23 He *said to them, "ᵃMy cup you shall drink; but to sit on My right and on *My* left, this is not Mine to give, but it is for those for whom it has been ᵇprepared by My Father." ᵃ*Acts 12:2* ᵇ*Matt 25:34*

24 And hearing *this,* the ten became indignant with the two brothers.

25 ᵃBut Jesus called them to Himself and said, "You know that the rulers of the Gentiles lord it over them, and *their* great men exercise authority over them. ᵃ*Matt 20:25-28; Luke 22:25-27*

26 "It is not this way among you, ᵃbut whoever wishes to become great among you shall be your servant, ᵃ*Matt 23:11; Mark 9:35*

27 and whoever wishes to be first among you shall be your slave;

28 just as the Son of Man ᵃdid not come to be served, but to serve, and to give His life a ransom for many." ᵃ*Matt 26:28; John 13:13ff*

Sight for the Blind

29 ᵃAs they were leaving Jericho, a large crowd followed Him. ᵃ*Matt 9:27-31*

30 And two blind men sitting by the road, hearing that Jesus was passing by, cried out, "Lord, ᵃhave mercy on us, Son of David!" ᵃ*Matt 9:27*

31 The crowd sternly told them to be quiet, but they cried out all the more, "Lord, ᵃSon of David, have mercy on us!" ᵃ*Matt 9:27*

32 And Jesus stopped and called them, and said, "What do you want Me to do for you?"

33 They *said to Him, "Lord, *we want* our eyes to be opened."

34 Moved with compassion, Jesus touched their eyes; and immediately they regained their sight and followed Him.

The Triumphal Entry

21 ᵃWhen they had approached Jerusalem and had come to Bethphage, at the Mount of Olives, then Jesus sent two disciples, ᵃ*Mark 11:1-10; Luke 19:29-38*

2 saying to them, "Go into the village opposite you, and immediately you will find a donkey tied *there* and a colt with her; untie them and bring them to Me.

3 "If anyone says anything to you, you shall say, 'The Lord has need of them,' and immediately he will send them."

4 ᵃThis took place to fulfill what was spoken through the prophet: ᵃ*Mark 11:7-10; Luke 19:35-38*

5 "ᵃSAY TO THE DAUGHTER OF ZION,
'BEHOLD YOUR KING IS COMING TO YOU,
GENTLE, AND MOUNTED ON A DONKEY,
EVEN ON A COLT, THE FOAL OF A BEAST OF
BURDEN.' " ᵃ*Is 62:11; Zech 9:9*

6 The disciples went and did just as Jesus had instructed them,

7 and brought the donkey and the colt, and laid their coats on them; and He sat on the coats.

8 Most of the crowd ᵃspread their coats in the road, and others were cutting branches from the trees and spreading them in the road. ᵃ*2 Kin 9:13*

9 The crowds going ahead of Him, and those who followed, were shouting,

"Hosanna to the Son of David;
ᵃBLESSED IS HE WHO COMES IN THE NAME OF THE LORD;
Hosanna ᵇin the highest!" ᵃ*Ps 118:26*
ᵇ*Luke 2:14*

10 When He had entered Jerusalem, all the city was stirred, saying, "Who is this?"
11 And the crowds were saying, "This is ᵃthe prophet Jesus, from Nazareth in Galilee."
ᵃ*Matt 21:26; Mark 6:15*

Cleansing the Temple

12 ᵃAnd Jesus entered the temple and drove out all those who were buying and selling in the temple, and overturned the tables of the money changers and the seats of those who were selling doves. ᵃ*Mark 11:15-18; Luke 19:45-47;*
13 And He *said to them, "It is written, 'ᵃMY HOUSE SHALL BE CALLED A HOUSE OF PRAYER'; but you are making it a ᵇROBBERS' DEN." ᵃ*Is 56:7* ᵇ*Jer 7:11*
14 And *the* blind and *the* lame came to Him in the temple, and ᵃHe healed them. ᵃ*Matt 4:23*
15 But when the chief priests and the scribes saw the wonderful things that He had done, and the children who were shouting in the temple, "Hosanna to the ᵃSon of David," they became indignant ᵃ*Matt 9:27*
16 and said to Him, "Do you hear what these *children* are saying?" And Jesus *said to them, "Yes; have you never read, 'ᵃOUT OF THE MOUTH OF INFANTS AND NURSING BABIES YOU HAVE PREPARED PRAISE FOR YOURSELF'?" ᵃ*Ps 8:2; Matt 11:25*
17 And He left them and went out of the city to ᵃBethany, and spent the night there. ᵃ*Matt 26:6; Mark 11:1, 11, 12*

The Barren Fig Tree

18 ᵃNow in the morning, when He was returning to the city, He became hungry. ᵃ*Mark 11:12-14, 20-24*
19 Seeing a lone ᵃfig tree by the road, He came to it and found nothing on it except leaves only; and He *said to it, "No longer shall there ever be *any* fruit from you." And at once the fig tree withered. ᵃ*Luke 13:6-9*
20 Seeing *this,* the disciples were amazed and asked, "How did the fig tree wither *all* at once?"
21 And Jesus answered and said to them, "Truly I say to you, ᵃif you have faith and do not doubt, you will not only do what was done to the fig tree, but even if you say to this mountain, 'Be taken up and cast into the sea,' it will happen. ᵃ*Matt 17:20; Mark 11:23*
22 "And ᵃall things you ask in prayer, believing, you will receive." ᵃ*Matt 7:7*

Authority Challenged

23 ᵃWhen He entered the temple, the chief priests and the elders of the people came to Him while He was teaching, and said, "By what authority are You doing these things, and who gave You this authority?" ᵃ*Mark 11:27-33; Luke 20:1-8*
24 Jesus said to them, "I will also ask you one thing, which if you tell Me, I will also tell you by what authority I do these things.
25 "The baptism of John was from what *source,* from heaven or from men?" And they *began* reasoning among themselves, saying, "If we say, 'From heaven,' He will say to us, 'Then why did you not believe him?'
26 "But if we say, 'From men,' we fear the people; for they all regard John as ᵃa prophet." ᵃ*Matt 11:9; Mark 6:20*
27 And answering Jesus, they said, "We do not know." He also said to them, "Neither will I tell you by what authority I do these things.

Parable of Two Sons

28 "But what do you think? A man had two sons, and he came to the first and said, 'Son, go work today in the ᵃvineyard.' ᵃ*Matt 20:1; 21:33*
29 "And he answered, 'I will not'; but afterward he regretted it and went.
30 "The man came to the second and said the same thing; and he answered, 'I *will,* sir'; but he did not go.
31 "Which of the two did the will of his father?" They *said, "The first." Jesus *said to them, "Truly I say to you that ᵃthe tax collectors and prostitutes will get into the kingdom of God before you. ᵃ*Luke 7:29, 37-50*
32 "For John came to you in the way of righteousness and you did not believe him; but ᵃthe tax collectors and prostitutes did believe him; and you, seeing *this,* did not even feel remorse afterward so as to believe him. ᵃ*Luke 3:12; 7:29f*

Parable of the Landowner

33 "Listen to another parable. ᵃThere was a landowner who PLANTED A VINEYARD AND PUT A WALL AROUND IT AND DUG A WINE PRESS IN IT, AND BUILT A TOWER, and rented it out to vine-growers and went on a journey. ᵃ*Mark 12:1-12; Luke 20:9-19*
34 "When the harvest time approached, he ᵃsent his slaves to the vine-growers to receive his produce. ᵃ*Matt 22:3*
35 "The vine-growers took his slaves and beat one, and killed another, and stoned a third.
36 "Again he ᵃsent another group of slaves larger than the first; and they did the same thing to them. ᵃ*Matt 22:4*
37 "But afterward he sent his son to them, saying, 'They will respect my son.'
38 "But when the vine-growers saw the son, they said among themselves, 'This is the heir; come, let us kill him and seize his inheritance.'

39 "They took him, and threw him out of the vineyard and killed him.

40 "Therefore when the owner of the vineyard comes, what will he do to those vine-growers?"

41 They *said to Him, "He will bring those wretches to a wretched end, and ᵃwill rent out the vineyard to other vine-growers who will pay him the proceeds at the *proper* seasons."
ᵃMatt 8:11f; Acts 13:46

42 Jesus *said to them, "Did you never read in the Scriptures,

ᵃTHE STONE WHICH THE BUILDERS REJECTED,
THIS BECAME THE CHIEF CORNER *stone;*
THIS CAME ABOUT FROM THE LORD,
AND IT IS MARVELOUS IN OUR EYES'?
ᵃPs 118:22f; Acts 4:11

43 "Therefore I say to you, the kingdom of God will be taken away from you and given to a people, producing the fruit of it.

44 "And ᵃhe who falls on this stone will be broken to pieces; but on whomever it falls, it will scatter him like dust." ᵃIs 8:14, 15

45 When the chief priests and the Pharisees heard His parables, they understood that He was speaking about them.

46 When they sought to seize Him, they ᵃfeared the people, because they considered Him to be a ᵇprophet. ᵃMatt 21:26 ᵇMatt 21:11

Parable of the Marriage Feast

22 Jesus spoke to them again in parables, saying,

2 "ᵃThe kingdom of heaven may be compared to a king who gave a wedding feast for his son. ᵃMatt 13:24; 22:2-14

3 "And he ᵃsent out his slaves to call those who had been invited to the wedding feast, and they were unwilling to come. ᵃMatt 21:34

4 "Again he ᵃsent out other slaves saying, 'Tell those who have been invited, "Behold, I have prepared my dinner; my oxen and my fattened livestock are *all* butchered and everything is ready; come to the wedding feast."' ᵃMatt 21:36

5 "But they paid no attention and went their way, one to his own farm, another to his business,

6 and the rest seized his slaves and mistreated them and killed them.

7 "But the king was enraged, and he sent his armies and destroyed those murderers and set their city on fire.

8 "Then he *said to his slaves, 'The wedding is ready, but those who were invited were not worthy.

9 'Go therefore to ᵃthe main highways, and as many as you find *there,* invite to the wedding feast.' ᵃEzek 21:21; Obad 14

10 "Those slaves went out into the streets and gathered together all they found, both evil and good; and the wedding hall was filled with dinner guests.

11 "But when the king came in to look over the dinner guests, he saw ᵃa man there who was not dressed in wedding clothes, ᵃ2 Kin 10:22; Zech 3:3, 4

12 and he *said to him, 'Friend, how did you come in here without wedding clothes?' And the man was speechless. ᵃMatt 20:13; 26:50

13 "Then the king said to the servants, 'Bind him hand and foot, and throw him into ᵃthe outer darkness; in that place there will be weeping and gnashing of teeth.' ᵃMatt 8:12; 25:30

14 "For many are ᵃcalled, but few *are* chosen." ᵃMatt 24:22; 2 Pet 1:10

Tribute to Caesar

15 ᵃThen the Pharisees went and plotted together how they might trap Him in what He said. ᵃMark 12:13-17; Luke 20:20-26

16 And they *sent their disciples to Him, along with the ᵃHerodians, saying, "Teacher, we know that You are truthful and teach the way of God in truth, and defer to no one; for You are not partial to any. ᵃMark 3:6; 8:15

17 "Tell us then, what do You think? Is it lawful to give a ᵃpoll-tax to ᵇCaesar, or not?" ᵃMatt 17:25 ᵇLuke 3:1

18 But Jesus perceived their malice, and said, "Why are you testing Me, you hypocrites?

19 "Show Me the ᵃcoin *used* for the poll-tax." And they brought Him a denarius. ᵃMatt 17:25

20 And He *said to them, "Whose likeness and inscription is this?"

21 They *said to Him, "Caesar's." Then He *said to them, "ᵃThen render to Caesar the things that are Caesar's; and to God the things that are God's." ᵃMark 12:17; Luke 20:25

22 And hearing *this,* they were amazed, and ᵃleaving Him, they went away. ᵃMark 12:12

Jesus Answers the Sadducees

23 ᵃOn that day *some* Sadducees (who say there is no resurrection) came to Jesus and questioned Him, ᵃMark 12:18-27; Luke 20:27-40

24 asking, "Teacher, Moses said, 'ᵃIF A MAN DIES HAVING NO CHILDREN, HIS BROTHER AS NEXT OF KIN SHALL MARRY HIS WIFE, AND RAISE UP CHILDREN FOR HIS BROTHER.' ᵃDeut 25:5

25 "Now there were seven brothers with us; and the first married and died, and having no children left his wife to his brother;

26 so also the second, and the third, down to the seventh.

27 "Last of all, the woman died.

28 "In the resurrection, therefore, whose wife of the seven will she be? For they all had *married* her."

29 But Jesus answered and said to them, "You are mistaken, [a]not understanding the Scriptures nor the power of God. [a]John 20:9

30 "For in the resurrection they neither [a]marry nor are given in marriage, but are like angels in heaven. [a]Matt 24:38; Luke 17:27

31 "But regarding the resurrection of the dead, have you not read what was spoken to you by God:

32 '[a]I AM THE GOD OF ABRAHAM, AND THE GOD OF ISAAC, AND THE GOD OF JACOB'? He is not the God of the dead but of the living." [a]Ex 3:6

33 When the crowds heard this, [a]they were astonished at His teaching. [a]Matt 7:28

34 [a]But when the Pharisees heard that Jesus had silenced the Sadducees, they gathered themselves together. [a]Luke 10:25-37

35 One of them, [a]a lawyer, asked Him a question, testing Him, [a]Luke 7:30; 10:25

36 "Teacher, which is the great commandment in the Law?"

37 And He said to him, " '[a]YOU SHALL LOVE THE LORD YOUR GOD WITH ALL YOUR HEART, AND WITH ALL YOUR SOUL, AND WITH ALL YOUR MIND.' [a]Deut 6:5

38 "This is the great and foremost commandment.

39 "The second is like it, '[a]YOU SHALL LOVE YOUR NEIGHBOR AS YOURSELF.' [a]Lev 19:18; Matt 19:19

40 " '[a]On these two commandments depend the whole Law and the Prophets." [a]Matt 7:12

41 [a]Now while the Pharisees were gathered together, Jesus asked them a question: [a]Mark 12:35-37; Luke 20:41-44

42 "What do you think about the Christ, whose son is He?" They *said to Him, "[a]The son of David." [a]Matt 9:27

43 He *said to them, "Then how does David [a]in the Spirit call Him 'Lord,' saying, [a]2 Sam 23:2; Rev 1:10

44 '[a]THE LORD SAID TO MY LORD,
"SIT AT MY RIGHT HAND,
UNTIL I PUT YOUR ENEMIES BENEATH YOUR FEET" '? [a]Ps 110:1; Matt 26:64

45 "If David then calls Him 'Lord,' how is He his son?"

46 [a]No one was able to answer Him a word, nor did anyone dare from that day on to ask Him another question. [a]Mark 12:34; Luke 14:6

Pharisaism Exposed

23 [a]Then Jesus spoke to the crowds and to His disciples, [a]Mark 12:38, 39; Luke 20:45, 46

2 saying: "[a]The scribes and the Pharisees have seated themselves in the chair of Moses; [a]Deut 33:3f; Ezra 7:6, 25

3 therefore all that they tell you, do and observe, but do not do according to their deeds; for they say things and do not do them.

4 "[a]They tie up heavy burdens and lay them on men's shoulders, but they themselves are unwilling to move them with so much as a finger. [a]Luke 11:46; Acts 15:10

5 "But they do all their deeds [a]to be noticed by men; for they [b]broaden their phylacteries and lengthen the tassels of their garments. [a]Matt 6:1, 5, 16 [b]Ex 13:9

6 "They [a]love the place of honor at banquets and the chief seats in the synagogues, [a]Luke 11:43; 14:7

7 and respectful greetings in the market places, and being called [a]Rabbi by men. [a]Matt 23:8; 26:25, 49

8 "But do not be called [a]Rabbi; for One is your Teacher, and you are all brothers. [a]Matt 23:7; 26:25, 49

9 "Do not call anyone on earth your father; for [a]One is your Father, He who is in heaven. [a]Matt 6:9; 7:11

10 "Do not be called leaders; for One is your Leader, that is, Christ.

11 "[a]But the greatest among you shall be your servant. [a]Matt 20:26

12 "[a]Whoever exalts himself shall be humbled; and whoever humbles himself shall be exalted. [a]Luke 14:11; 18:14

Eight Woes

13 "But woe to you, scribes and Pharisees, hypocrites, [a]because you shut off the kingdom of heaven from people; for you do not enter in yourselves, nor do you allow those who are entering to go in. [a]Luke 11:52

14 ["Woe to you, scribes and Pharisees, hypocrites, because [a]you devour widows' houses, and for a pretense you make long prayers; therefore you will receive greater condemnation.] [a]Mark 12:40; Luke 20:47

15 "Woe to you, scribes and Pharisees, hypocrites, because you travel around on sea and land to make one [a]proselyte; and when he becomes one, you make him twice as much a son of hell as yourselves. [a]Acts 2:10; 6:5

16 "Woe to you, [a]blind guides, who say, 'Whoever swears by the temple, that is nothing; but whoever swears by the gold of the temple is obligated.' [a]Matt 15:14; 23:24

17 "You fools and blind men! [a]Which is more important, the gold or the temple that sanctified the gold? [a]Ex 30:29

18 "And, 'Whoever swears by the altar, that is nothing, but whoever swears by the offering on it, he is obligated.'

19 "You blind men, [a]which is more important, the offering, or the altar that sanctifies the offering? [a]Ex 29:37

20 "Therefore, whoever swears by the altar, swears both by the altar and by everything on it.

21 "And whoever swears by the temple, swears *both* by the temple and by Him who ᵃdwells within it. ª*1 Kin 8:13; Ps 26:8*

22 "And whoever swears by heaven, ᵃswears *both* by the throne of God and by Him who sits upon it. ª*Is 66:1; Matt 5:34*

23 "ᵃWoe to you, scribes and Pharisees, hypocrites! For you tithe mint and dill and cummin, and have neglected the weightier provisions of the law: justice and mercy and faithfulness; but these are the things you should have done without neglecting the others. ª*Matt 23:13; Luke 11:42*

24 "You ᵃblind guides, who strain out a gnat and swallow a camel! ª*Matt 23:16*

25 "Woe to you, scribes and Pharisees, hypocrites! For ᵃyou clean the outside of the cup and of the dish, but inside they are full of robbery and self-indulgence. ª*Mark 7:4; Luke 11:39f*

26 "You blind Pharisee, first ᵃclean the inside of the cup and of the dish, so that the outside of it may become clean also. ª*Mark 7:4; Luke 11:39f*

27 "ᵃWoe to you, scribes and Pharisees, hypocrites! For you are like whitewashed tombs which on the outside appear beautiful, but inside they are full of dead men's bones and all uncleanness. ª*Luke 11:44; Acts 23:3*

28 "So you, too, outwardly appear righteous to men, but inwardly you are full of hypocrisy and lawlessness.

29 "ᵃWoe to you, scribes and Pharisees, hypocrites! For you build the tombs of the prophets and adorn the monuments of the righteous, ª*Luke 11:47f*

30 and say, 'If we had been *living* in the days of our fathers, we would not have been partners with them in *shedding* the blood of the prophets.'

31 "So you testify against yourselves, that you ᵃare sons of those who murdered the prophets. ª*Matt 23:34, 37; Acts 7:51f*

32 "Fill up, then, the measure *of the guilt* of your fathers.

33 "You serpents, ᵃyou brood of vipers, how will you escape the sentence of hell? ª*Matt 3:7; Luke 3:7*

34 "ᵃTherefore, behold, I am sending you prophets and wise men and scribes; some of them you will kill and crucify, and some of them you will scourge in your synagogues, and persecute from city to city, ª*Matt 23:34-36; Luke 11:49-51*

35 so that upon you may fall *the guilt of* all the righteous blood shed on earth, from the blood of righteous Abel to the blood of Zechariah, the ᵃson of Berechiah, whom ᵇyou murdered between the temple and the altar. ª*Zech 1:1* ᵇ*2 Chr 24:21*

36 "Truly I say to you, all these things will come upon ᵃthis generation. ª*Matt 10:23; 24:34*

Lament over Jerusalem

37 "ᵃJerusalem, Jerusalem, who kills the prophets and stones those who are sent to her! How often I wanted to gather your children together, the way a hen gathers her chicks under her wings, and you were unwilling. ª*Luke 13:34, 35*

38 "Behold, ᵃyour house is being left to you desolate! ª*1 Kin 9:7f; Jer 22:5*

39 "For I say to you, from now on you will not see Me until you say, 'ᵃBLESSED IS HE WHO COMES IN THE NAME OF THE LORD!' " ª*Ps 118:26; Matt 21:9*

Signs of Christ's Return

24 ᵃJesus came out from the temple and was going away when His disciples came up to point out the temple buildings to Him. ª*Mark 13; Luke 21:5-36*

2 And He said to them, "Do you not see all these things? Truly I say to you, ᵃnot one stone here will be left upon another, which will not be torn down." ª*Luke 19:44*

3 As He was sitting on ᵃthe Mount of Olives, the disciples came to Him privately, saying, "Tell us, when will these things happen, and what *will be* the sign of Your coming, and of the end of the age?" ª*Matt 21:1*

4 And Jesus answered and said to them, "ᵃSee to it that no one misleads you. ª*Jer 29:8*

5 "For ᵃmany will come in My name, saying, 'I am the Christ,' and will mislead many. ª*Matt 24:11, 24; Acts 5:36f*

6 "You will be hearing of ᵃwars and rumors of wars. See that you are not frightened, for *those things* must take place, but *that* is not yet the end. ª*Rev 6:4*

7 "For ᵃnation will rise against nation, and kingdom against kingdom, and in various places there will be famines and earthquakes. ª*2 Chr 15:6; Is 19:2*

8 "ᵃBut all these things are *merely* the beginning of birth pangs. ª*Matt 24:8-20; Luke 21:12-24*

9 "ᵃThen they will deliver you to tribulation, and will kill you, and ᵇyou will be hated by all nations because of My name. ª*Matt 10:17* ᵇ*Matt 10:22*

10 "At that time many will ᵃfall away and will betray one another and hate one another. ª*Matt 11:6*

11 "Many ᵃfalse prophets will arise and will mislead many. ª*Matt 7:15; 24:24*

12 "Because lawlessness is increased, most people's love will grow cold.

13 "ᵃBut the one who endures to the end, he will be saved. ª*Matt 10:22*

14 "This ᵃgospel of the kingdom shall be preached in the whole ᵇworld as a testimony to all the nations, and then the end will come. ª*Matt 4:23* ᵇ*Luke 4:5*

Perilous Times

15 "Therefore when you see the ᵃABOMINATION OF DESOLATION which was spoken of through Daniel the prophet, standing in the holy place (let the reader understand), ᵃ*Dan 9:27; 11:31*

16 then those who are in Judea must flee to the mountains.

17 "Whoever is on ᵃthe housetop must not go down to get the things out that are in his house. ᵃ*1 Sam 9:25; 2 Sam 11:2*

18 "Whoever is in the field must not turn back to get his cloak.

19 "But ᵃwoe to those who are pregnant and to those who are nursing babies in those days! ᵃ*Luke 23:29*

20 "But pray that your flight will not be in the winter, or on a Sabbath.

21 "For then there will be a ᵃgreat tribulation, such as has not occurred since the beginning of the world until now, nor ever will. ᵃ*Dan 12:1; Joel 2:2*

22 "Unless those days had been cut short, no life would have been saved; but for ᵃthe sake of the elect those days will be cut short. ᵃ*Matt 22:14; 24:24, 31*

23 "ᵃThen if anyone says to you, 'Behold, here is the Christ,' or 'There *He is*,' do not believe *him*. ᵃ*Luke 17:23f*

24 "For false Christs and false prophets will arise and will show great ᵃsigns and wonders, so as to mislead, if possible, even ᵇthe elect. ᵃ*John 4:48* ᵇ*Matt 22:14*

25 "Behold, I have told you in advance.

26 "So if they say to you, 'Behold, He is in the wilderness,' do not go out, *or*, 'Behold, He is in the inner rooms,' do not believe *them*.

27 "ᵃFor just as the lightning comes from the east and flashes even to the west, so will the coming of the Son of Man be. ᵃ*Luke 17:24*

28 "ᵃWherever the corpse is, there the vultures will gather. ᵃ*Job 39:30; Ezek 39:17*

The Glorious Return

29 "But immediately after the tribulation of those days ᵃTHE SUN WILL BE DARKENED, AND THE MOON WILL NOT GIVE ITS LIGHT, AND THE STARS WILL FALL from the sky, and the powers of the heavens will be shaken. ᵃ*Is 13:10; 24:23*

30 "And then ᵃthe sign of the Son of Man will appear in the sky, and then all the tribes of the earth will mourn, and they will see ᵇthe SON OF MAN COMING ON THE CLOUDS OF THE SKY with power and great glory. ᵃ*Matt 24:3* ᵇ*Dan 7:13*

31 "And He will send forth His angels with ᵃA GREAT TRUMPET and THEY WILL GATHER TOGETHER His elect from the four winds, from one end of the sky to the other. ᵃ*Ex 19:16; Deut 30:4*

Parable of the Fig Tree

32 "Now learn the parable from the fig tree: when its branch has already become tender and puts forth its leaves, you know that summer is near;

33 so, you too, when you see all these things, recognize that He is near, *right* ᵃat the door. ᵃ*James 5:9; Rev 3:20*

34 "Truly I say to you, ᵃthis generation will not pass away until all these things take place. ᵃ*Matt 10:23; 16:28*

35 "ᵃHeaven and earth will pass away, but My words will not pass away. ᵃ*Matt 5:18; Mark 13:31*

36 "But ᵃof that day and hour no one knows, not even the angels of heaven, nor the Son, but the Father alone. ᵃ*Mark 13:32; Acts 1:7*

37 "For the coming of the Son of Man will be ᵃjust like the days of Noah. ᵃ*Gen 6:5; 7:6-23*

38 "For as in those days before the flood they were eating and drinking, ᵃmarrying and giving in marriage, until the day that ᵇNoah entered the ark, ᵃ*Matt 22:30* ᵇ*Gen 7:7*

39 and they did not understand until the flood came and took them all away; so will the ᵃcoming of the Son of Man be. ᵃ*Matt 16:27; 24:3, 30, 37*

40 "Then there will be two men in the field; one will be taken and one will be left.

41 "ᵃTwo women *will be* grinding at the mill; one will be taken and one will be left. ᵃ*Luke 17:35*

Be Ready for His Coming

42 "Therefore ᵃbe on the alert, for you do not know which day your Lord is coming. ᵃ*Matt 24:43, 44; 25:10, 13*

43 "But be sure of this, that ᵃif the head of the house had known ᵇat what time of the night the thief was coming, he would have been on the alert and would not have allowed his house to be broken into. ᵃ*Luke 12:39f* ᵇ*Mark 13:35*

44 "For this reason ᵃyou also must be ready; for the Son of Man is coming at an hour when you do not think *He will*. ᵃ*Matt 24:42, 43; 25:10, 13*

45 "ᵃWho then is the faithful and sensible slave whom his master put in charge of his household to give them their food at the proper time? ᵃ*Luke 12:42-46*

46 "Blessed is that slave whom his master finds so doing when he comes.

47 "Truly I say to you that ᵃhe will put him in charge of all his possessions. ᵃ*Matt 25:21, 23*

48 "But if that evil slave says in his heart, 'My master is not coming for a long time,'

49 and begins to beat his fellow slaves and eat and drink with drunkards;

50 the master of that slave will come on a day when he does not expect *him* and at an hour which he does not know,

51 and will cut him in pieces and assign him a place with the hypocrites; in that place there will be ᵃweeping and gnashing of teeth. ᵃ*Matt 8:12*

Parable of Ten Virgins

25 "Then ᵃthe kingdom of heaven will be comparable to ten virgins, who took their ᵇlamps and went out to meet the bridegroom. ᵃ*Matt 13:24* ᵇ*Acts 20:8; Rev 4:5*

2 "Five of them were foolish, and five were ᵃprudent. ᵃ*Matt 7:24; 10:16*

3 "For when the foolish took their lamps, they took no oil with them,

4 but the ᵃprudent took oil in flasks along with their lamps. ᵃ*Matt 7:24; 10:16*

5 "Now while the bridegroom was delaying, they all got drowsy and *began* to sleep.

6 "But at midnight there was a shout, 'Behold, the bridegroom! Come out to meet *him.*'

7 "Then all those virgins rose and trimmed their lamps.

8 "The foolish said to the prudent, 'Give us some of your oil, for our lamps are going out.'

9 "But the ᵃprudent answered, 'No, there will not be enough for us and you *too;* go instead to the dealers and buy *some* for yourselves.' ᵃ*Matt 7:24; 10:16*

10 "And while they were going away to make the purchase, the bridegroom came, and those who were ᵃready went in with him to ᵇthe wedding feast; and the door was shut. ᵃ*Matt 24:42ff* ᵇ*Luke 12:35f*

11 "Later the other virgins also came, saying, 'ᵃLord, lord, open up for us.' ᵃ*Matt 7:21ff; Luke 13:25*

12 "But he answered, 'Truly I say to you, I do not know you.'

13 "ᵃBe on the alert then, for you do not know the day nor the hour. ᵃ*Matt 24:42ff*

Parable of the Talents

14 "ᵃFor *it is* just like a man *about* to go on a journey, who called his own slaves and entrusted his possessions to them. ᵃ*Matt 25:14-30; Luke 19:12-27*

15 "To one he gave five talents, to another, two, and to another, one, each according to his own ability; and he ᵃwent on his journey. ᵃ*Matt 21:33*

16 "Immediately the one who had received the five ᵃtalents went and traded with them, and gained five more talents. ᵃ*Matt 18:24; Luke 19:13*

17 "In the same manner the one who had *received* the two *talents* gained two more.

18 "But he who received the one *talent* went away, and dug *a hole* in the ground and hid his master's money.

19 "Now after a long time the master of those slaves *came and *ᵃsettled accounts with them. ᵃ*Matt 18:23*

20 "The one who had received the five ᵃtalents came up and brought five more talents, saying, 'Master, you entrusted five talents to me. See, I have gained five more talents.' ᵃ*Matt 18:24; Luke 19:13*

21 "His master said to him, 'Well done, good and faithful slave. You were faithful with a few things, I will ᵃput you in charge of many things; enter into the joy of your master.' ᵃ*Luke 12:44; 22:29*

22 "Also the one who *had received* the two ᵃtalents came up and said, 'Master, you entrusted two talents to me. See, I have gained two more talents.' ᵃ*Matt 18:24; Luke 19:13*

23 "His master said to him, 'Well done, good and ᵃfaithful slave. You were faithful with a few things, I will put you in charge of many things; enter into the joy of your master.' ᵃ*Matt 24:45, 47; 25:21*

24 "And the one also who had received the one ᵃtalent came up and said, 'Master, I knew you to be a hard man, reaping where you did not sow and gathering where you scattered no *seed.* ᵃ*Matt 18:24; Luke 19:13*

25 "And I was afraid, and went away and hid your talent in the ground. See, you have what is yours.'

26 "But his master answered and said to him, 'You wicked, lazy slave, you knew that I reap where I did not sow and gather where I scattered no *seed.*

27 'Then you ought to have put my money in the bank, and on my arrival I would have received my *money* back with interest.

28 'Therefore take away the talent from him, and give it to the one who has the ten talents.'

29 "ᵃFor to everyone who has, *more* shall be given, and he will have an abundance; but from the one who does not have, even what he does have shall be taken away. ᵃ*Matt 13:12; Mark 4:25*

30 "Throw out the worthless slave into ᵃthe outer darkness; in that place there will be weeping and gnashing of teeth. ᵃ*Matt 8:12; 22:13*

The Judgment

31 "But when ᵃthe Son of Man comes in His glory, and all the angels with Him, then He will sit on His glorious throne. ᵃ*Matt 16:27f; 1 Thess 4:16*

32 "All the nations will be gathered before Him; and He will separate them from one another, ᵃas the shepherd separates the sheep from the goats; ᵃ*Ezek 34:17, 20*

33 and He will put the sheep on His right, and the goats ᵃon the left. ᵃ*Eccl 10:2*

34 "Then the King will say to those on His right, 'Come, you who are blessed of My Father, ᵃinherit the kingdom prepared for you from the foundation of the world. ᵃ*Matt 5:3; 19:29*

35 'For ᵃI was hungry, and you gave Me *something* to eat; I was thirsty, and you gave

Me *something* to drink; I was a stranger, and you invited Me in; [a]Is 58:7; Ezek 18:7, 16

36 [a]naked, and you clothed Me; I was sick, and you visited Me; I was in prison, and you came to Me.' [a]Is 58:7; Ezek 18:7, 16

37 "Then the righteous will answer Him, 'Lord, when did we see You hungry, and feed You, or thirsty, and give You *something* to drink?

38 'And when did we see You a stranger, and invite You in, or naked, and clothe You?

39 'When did we see You sick, or in prison, and come to You?'

40 "The King will answer and say to them, 'Truly I say to you, [a]to the extent that you did it to one of these brothers of Mine, *even* the least of them, you did it to Me.' [a]Prov 19:17; Matt 10:42

41 "Then He will also say to those on His left, '[a]Depart from Me, accursed ones, into the eternal fire which has been prepared for the devil and his angels; [a]Matt 7:23

42 for I was hungry, and you gave Me *nothing* to eat; I was thirsty, and you gave Me nothing to drink;

43 I was a stranger, and you did not invite Me in; naked, and you did not clothe Me; sick, and in prison, and you did not visit Me.'

44 "Then they themselves also will answer, 'Lord, when did we see You hungry, or thirsty, or a stranger, or naked, or sick, or in prison, and did not take care of You?'

45 "Then He will answer them, 'Truly I say to you, to the extent that you did not do it to one of the least of these, you did not do it to Me.'

46 "These will go away into eternal punishment, but the righteous into [a]eternal life." [a]Matt 19:29; John 3:15f, 36

The Plot to Kill Jesus

26 [a]When Jesus had finished all these words, He said to His disciples, [a]Matt 7:28

2 "[a]You know that after two days the Passover is coming, and the Son of Man is *to be* handed over for crucifixion." [a]Mark 14:1, 2; Luke 22:1, 2

3 Then the chief priests and the elders of the people were gathered together in [a]the court of the high priest, named Caiaphas; [a]Matt 26:58, 69; 27:27

4 and they [a]plotted together to seize Jesus by stealth and kill Him. [a]Matt 12:14

5 But they were saying, "Not during the festival, [a]otherwise a riot might occur among the people." [a]Matt 27:24

The Precious Ointment

6 [a]Now when Jesus was in Bethany, at the home of Simon the leper, [a]Luke 7:37-39; John 12:1-8

7 [a]a woman came to Him with an alabaster

vial of very costly perfume, and she poured it on His head as He reclined *at the table.* [a]Luke 7:37f

8 But the disciples were indignant when they saw *this,* and said, "Why this waste?

9 "For this *perfume* might have been sold for a high price and *the money* given to the poor."

10 But Jesus, aware of this, said to them, "Why do you bother the woman? For she has done a good deed to Me.

11 "For you always have [a]the poor with you; but you do not always have Me. [a]Deut 15:11; Mark 14:7

12 "For when she poured this perfume on My body, she did it [a]to prepare Me for burial. [a]John 19:40

13 "Truly I say to you, [a]wherever this gospel is preached in the whole world, what this woman has done will also be spoken of in memory of her." [a]Mark 14:9

Judas's Bargain

14 [a]Then one of the twelve, named Judas Iscariot, went to the chief priests [a]Mark 14:10, 11; Luke 22:3-6

15 and said, "What are you willing to give me to betray Him to you?" And [a]they weighed out thirty pieces of silver to him. [a]Ex 21:32; Zech 11:12

16 From then on he *began* looking for a good opportunity to betray Jesus.

17 [a]Now on the first *day* of Unleavened Bread the disciples came to Jesus and asked, "Where do You want us to prepare for You to eat the Passover?" [a]Mark 14:12-16; Luke 22:7-13

18 And He said, "Go into the city to [a]a certain man, and say to him, 'The Teacher says, "My time is near; I *am to* keep the Passover at your house with My disciples." ' " [a]Mark 14:13; Luke 22:10

19 The disciples did as Jesus had directed them; and they prepared the Passover.

The Last Passover

20 [a]Now when evening came, Jesus was reclining *at the table* with the twelve disciples. [a]Mark 14:17-21

21 As they were eating, He said, "[a]Truly I say to you that one of you will betray Me." [a]Luke 22:21-23; John 13:21f

22 Being deeply grieved, they each one began to say to Him, "Surely not I, Lord?"

23 And He answered, "[a]He who dipped his hand with Me in the bowl is the one who will betray Me. [a]Ps 41:9; John 13:18, 26

24 "The Son of Man *is to* go, [a]just as it is written of Him; but woe to that man by whom the Son of Man is betrayed! It would have been good for that man if he had not been born." [a]Matt 26:31, 54, 56; Mark 9:12

25 And [a]Judas, who was betraying Him, said,

"Surely it is not I, Rabbi?" Jesus *said to him, "You have said *it* yourself." ªMatt 26:14

The Lord's Supper Instituted

26 ªWhile they were eating, Jesus took *some* bread, and after a blessing, He broke *it* and gave *it* to the disciples, and said, "Take, eat; this is My body." ªJ Cor 10:16

27 And when He had taken a cup and given thanks, He gave *it* to them, saying, "Drink from it, all of you;

28 for ªthis is My blood of the covenant, which is poured out for many for forgiveness of sins. ªEx 24:8; Heb 9:20

29 "But I say to you, I will not drink of this fruit of the vine from now on until that day when I drink it new with you in My Father's kingdom."

30 ªAfter singing a hymn, they went out to the Mount of Olives. ªMark 14:26-31; Luke 22:31-34

31 Then Jesus *said to them, "You will all fall away because of Me this night, for it is written, ªI WILL STRIKE DOWN THE SHEPHERD, AND THE SHEEP OF THE FLOCK SHALL BE SCATTERED.' ªZech 13:7

32 "But after I have been raised, ªI will go ahead of you to Galilee." ªMatt 28:7, 10, 16; Mark 16:7

33 But Peter said to Him, "*Even* though all may fall away because of You, I will never fall away."

34 Jesus said to him, "ªTruly I say to you that this *very* night, before a rooster crows, you will deny Me three times." ªMatt 26:75; John 13:38

35 Peter *said to Him, "ªEven if I have to die with You, I will not deny You." All the disciples said the same thing too. ªJohn 13:37

The Garden of Gethsemane

36 ªThen Jesus *came with them to a place called Gethsemane, and *said to His disciples, "Sit here while I go over there and pray." ªMark 14:32-42; Luke 22:40-46

37 And He took with Him ªPeter and the two sons of Zebedee, and began to be grieved and distressed. ªMatt 4:21; 17:1; Mark 5:37

38 Then He *said to them, "ªMy soul is deeply grieved, to the point of death; remain here and keep watch with Me." ªJohn 12:27

39 And He went a little beyond *them,* and fell on His face and prayed, saying, "My Father, if it is possible, let ªthis cup pass from Me; ᵇyet not as I will, but as You will." ªMatt 20:22 ᵇMatt 26:42

40 And He *came to the disciples and *found them sleeping, and *said to Peter, "So, you *men* could not ªkeep watch with Me for one hour? ªMatt 26:38

41 "Keep watching and praying that you may not enter into temptation; ªthe spirit is willing, but the flesh is weak." ªMark 14:38

42 He went away again a second time and prayed, saying, "My Father, if this cannot pass away unless I drink it, ªYour will be done." ªMatt 26:39; Mark 14:36

43 Again He came and found them sleeping, for their eyes were heavy.

44 And He left them again, and went away and prayed a third time, saying the same thing once more.

45 Then He *came to the disciples and *said to them, "Are you still sleeping and resting? Behold, ªthe hour is at hand and the Son of Man is being betrayed into the hands of sinners. ªMark 14:41; John 12:27

46 "Get up, let us be going; behold, the one who betrays Me is at hand!"

Jesus' Betrayal and Arrest

47 ªWhile He was still speaking, behold, Judas, one of the twelve, came up accompanied by a large crowd with swords and clubs, *who came* from the chief priests and elders of the people. ªMark 14:43-50; Luke 22:47-53

48 Now he who was betraying Him gave them a sign, saying, "Whomever I kiss, He is the one; seize Him."

49 Immediately Judas went to Jesus and said, "Hail, ªRabbi!" and kissed Him. ªMatt 23:7; 26:25

50 And Jesus said to him, "ªFriend, *do* what you have come for." Then they came and laid hands on Jesus and seized Him. ªMatt 20:13; 22:12

51 And behold, ªone of those who were with Jesus reached and drew out his sword, and struck the ªslave of the high priest and cut off his ear. ªMark 14:47; Luke 22:50

52 Then Jesus *said to him, "Put your sword back into its place; for ªall those who take up the sword shall perish by the sword. ªGen 9:6; Rev 13:10

53 "Or do you think that I cannot appeal to My Father, and He will at once put at My disposal more than twelve ªlegions of ᵇangels? ªMark 5:9, 15 ᵇMatt 4:11

54 "How then will ªthe Scriptures be fulfilled, *which say* that it must happen this way?" ªMatt 26:24

55 At that time Jesus said to the crowds, "Have you come out with swords and clubs to arrest Me as *you would* against a robber? ªEvery day I used to sit in the temple teaching and you did not seize Me. ªMark 12:35; 14:49

56 "But all this has taken place to fulfill ªthe Scriptures of the prophets." Then all the disciples left Him and fled. ªMatt 26:24

Jesus before Caiaphas

57 ªThose who had seized Jesus led Him away to Caiaphas, the high priest, where the scribes and the elders were gathered together. ªMark 14:53-65; John 18:12f, 19-24

58 But ªPeter was following Him at a distance as far as the ᵇcourtyard of the high priest, and entered in, and sat down with the officers to see the outcome. ªJohn 18:15 ᵇMatt 26:3

59 Now the chief priests and the whole ªCouncil kept trying to obtain false testimony against Jesus, so that they might put Him to death. ªMatt 5:22

60 They did not find *any,* even though many false witnesses came forward. But later on ªtwo came forward. ªDeut 19:15

61 and said, "This man stated, 'ªI am able to destroy the temple of God and to rebuild it in three days.' " ªMatt 27:40; Mark 14:58

62 The high priest stood up and said to Him, "Do You not answer? What is it that these men are testifying against You?"

63 But Jesus kept silent. ªAnd the high priest said to Him, "I adjure You by the living God, that You tell us whether You are the Christ, the Son of God." ªMatt 26:63-66; Luke 22:67-71

64 Jesus *said to him, "You have said it *yourself;* nevertheless I tell you, hereafter you will see THE SON OF MAN SITTING AT THE RIGHT HAND OF POWER, and ªCOMING ON THE CLOUDS OF HEAVEN." ªDan 7:13; Matt 16:27f

65 Then the high priest ªtore his robes and said, "He has blasphemed! What further need do we have of witnesses? Behold, you have now heard the blasphemy; ªNum 14:6; Mark 14:63

66 what do you think?" They answered, "ªHe deserves death!" ªLev 24:16; John 19:7

67 ªThen they spat in His face and beat Him with their fists; and others slapped Him, ªIs 50:6; Matt 26:67, 68

68 and said, "ªProphesy to us, You Christ; who is the one who hit You?" ªMark 14:65; Luke 22:64

Peter's Denials

69 ªNow Peter was sitting outside in the courtyard, and a servant-girl came to him and said, "You too were with Jesus the Galilean." ªMark 14:66-72; Luke 22:55-62

70 But he denied *it* before them all, saying, "I do not know what you are talking about."

71 When he had gone out to the gateway, another *servant-girl* saw him and *said to those who were there, "This man was with Jesus of Nazareth."

72 And again he denied *it* with an oath, "I do not know the man."

73 A little later the bystanders came up and said to Peter, "Surely you too are *one* of them; ªfor even the way you talk gives you away." ªMark 14:70; Luke 22:59

74 Then he began to curse and swear, "I do not know the man!" And immediately a rooster crowed.

75 And Peter remembered the word which Jesus had said, "ªBefore a rooster crows, you will deny Me three times." And he went out and wept bitterly. ªMatt 26:34

Judas's Remorse

27 ªNow when morning came, all the chief priests and the elders of the people conferred together against Jesus to put Him to death; ªMark 15:1; Luke 22:66

2 and they bound Him, and led Him away and delivered Him to ªPilate the governor. ªLuke 3:1; 13:1

3 Then when ªJudas, who had betrayed Him, saw that He had been condemned, he felt remorse and returned ᵇthe thirty pieces of silver to the chief priests and elders, ªMatt 26:14 ᵇMatt 26:15

4 saying, "I have sinned by betraying innocent blood." But they said, "What is that to us? ªSee *to that* yourself!" ªMatt 27:24

5 And he threw the pieces of silver into the temple sanctuary and departed; and ªhe went away and hanged himself. ªMatt 26:24; Acts 1:18

6 The chief priests took the pieces of silver and said, "It is not lawful to put them into the temple treasury, since it is the price of blood."

7 And they conferred together and with the money bought the Potter's Field as a burial place for strangers.

8 ªFor this reason that field has been called the Field of Blood to this day. ªActs 1:19

9 Then that which was spoken through Jeremiah the prophet was fulfilled: "ªAND THEY TOOK THE THIRTY PIECES OF SILVER, THE PRICE OF THE ONE WHOSE PRICE HAD BEEN SET by the sons of Israel; ªZech 11:12

10 ªAND THEY GAVE THEM FOR THE POTTER'S FIELD, AS THE LORD DIRECTED ME." ªZech 11:13

Jesus before Pilate

11 ªNow Jesus stood before the governor, and the governor questioned Him, saying, "Are You the King of the Jews?" And Jesus said to him, "*It is as* you say." ªMark 15:2-5; Luke 23:2, 3

12 And while He was being accused by the chief priests and elders, ªHe did not answer. ªMatt 26:63; John 19:9

13 Then Pilate *said to Him, "Do You not hear how many things they testify against You?"

14 And ªHe did not answer him with regard to even a *single* charge, so the governor was quite amazed. ªMatt 27:12; Mark 15:5

15 ªNow at *the* feast the governor was accustomed to release for the people *any* one prisoner whom they wanted. ªJohn 18:39-19:16

16 At that time they were holding a notorious prisoner, called Barabbas.

17 So when the people gathered together, Pilate said to them, "Whom do you want me to

release for you? Barabbas, or Jesus ªwho is called Christ?" ªMatt 1:16; 27:22

18 For he knew that because of envy they had handed Him over.

19 ªWhile he was sitting on the judgment seat, his wife sent him *a message,* saying, "Have nothing to do with that righteous Man; for last night I suffered greatly in a dream because of Him." ªJohn 19:13; Acts 12:21

20 But the chief priests and the elders persuaded the crowds to ªask for Barabbas and to put Jesus to death. ªActs 3:14

21 But the governor said to them, "Which of the two do you want me to release for you?" And they said, "Barabbas."

22 Pilate *said to them, "Then what shall I do with Jesus ªwho is called Christ?" They all *said, "Crucify Him!" ªMatt 1:16

23 And he said, "Why, what evil has He done?" But they kept shouting all the more, saying, "Crucify Him!"

24 When Pilate saw that he was accomplishing nothing, but rather that a riot was starting, he took water and ªwashed his hands in front of the crowd, saying, "I am innocent of this Man's blood; see *to that* yourselves." ªDeut 21:6-8

25 And all the people said, "ªHis blood shall be on us and on our children!" ªJosh 2:19; Acts 5:28

26 Then he released Barabbas for them; but after having Jesus ªscourged, he handed Him over to be crucified. ªMark 15:15; Luke 23:16

Jesus Is Mocked

27 ªThen the soldiers of the governor took Jesus into the Praetorium and gathered the whole *Roman* cohort around Him. ªMark 15:16-20

28 They stripped Him and ªput a scarlet robe on Him. ªMark 15:17; John 19:2

29 ªAnd after twisting together a crown of thorns, they put it on His head, and a reed in His right hand; and they knelt down before Him and mocked Him, saying, "Hail, King of the Jews!" ªMark 15:17; John 19:2

30 ªThey spat on Him, and took the reed and *began* to beat Him on the head. ªMatt 26:67; Mark 10:34

31 ªAfter they had mocked Him, they took the *scarlet* robe off Him and put His *own* garments back on Him, and led Him away to crucify Him. ªMark 15:20

32 ªAs they were coming out, they found a man of Cyrene named Simon, whom they pressed into service to bear His cross. ªJohn 19:17

The Crucifixion

33 ªAnd when they came to a place called Golgotha, which means Place of a Skull, ªMark 15:22-32; Luke 23:33-43

34 ªthey gave Him wine to drink mixed with gall; and after tasting *it,* He was unwilling to drink. ªPs 69:21

35 And when they had crucified Him, ªthey divided up His garments among themselves by casting lots. ªPs 22:18

36 And sitting down, they *began* to ªkeep watch over Him there. ªMatt 27:54

37 And above His head they put up the charge against Him which read, "ªTHIS IS JESUS THE KING OF THE JEWS." ªMark 15:26; Luke 23:38

38 At that time two robbers *were crucified with Him, one on the right and one on the left.

39 And those passing by were hurling abuse at Him, ªwagging their heads ªJob 16:4; Ps 22:7

40 and saying, "ªYou who *are going to* destroy the temple and rebuild it in three days, save Yourself! ᵇIf You are the Son of God, come down from the cross." ªMatt 26:61 ᵇMatt 27:42

41 In the same way the chief priests also, along with the scribes and elders, were mocking *Him* and saying,

42 "ªHe saved others; He cannot save Himself. He is the King of Israel; let Him now come down from the cross, and we will believe in Him. ªMark 15:31; Luke 23:35

43 "ªHE TRUSTS IN GOD; LET GOD RESCUE *Him* now, IF HE DELIGHTS IN HIM; for He said, 'I am the Son of God.' " ªPs 22:8

44 ªThe robbers who had been crucified with Him were also insulting Him with the same words. ªLuke 23:39-43

45 ªNow from the sixth hour darkness fell upon all the land until the ninth hour. ªMark 15:33-41; Luke 23:44-49

46 About the ninth hour Jesus cried out with a loud voice, saying, "ªELI, ELI, LAMA SABACHTHANI?" that is, "MY GOD, MY GOD, WHY HAVE YOU FORSAKEN ME?" ªPs 22:1

47 And some of those who were standing there, when they heard it, *began* saying, "This man is calling for Elijah."

48 ªImmediately one of them ran, and taking a sponge, he filled it with sour wine and put it on a reed, and gave Him a drink. ªPs 69:21; Mark 15:36

49 But the rest *of them* said, "Let us see whether Elijah will come to save Him."

50 And Jesus ªcried out again with a loud voice, and yielded up His spirit. ªMark 15:37; Luke 23:46

51 ªAnd behold, ᵇthe veil of the temple was torn in two from top to bottom; and the earth

shook and the rocks were split. [a]*Luke 23:47-49* [b]*Ex 26:31ff*

52 The tombs were opened, and many bodies of the saints who had [a]fallen asleep were raised;. [a]*Acts 7:60*

53 and coming out of the tombs after His resurrection they entered [a]the holy city and appeared to many. [a]*Matt 4:5*

54 [a]Now the centurion, and those who were with him keeping guard over Jesus, when they saw the earthquake and the things that were happening, became very frightened and said, "Truly this was the Son of God!" [a]*Mark 15:39; Luke 23:47*

55 [a]Many women were there looking on from a distance, who had followed Jesus from Galilee while ministering to Him. [a]*Mark 15:40f; Luke 23:49*

56 Among them was [a]Mary Magdalene, and Mary the mother of James and Joseph, and the mother of the sons of Zebedee. [a]*Matt 28:1; Mark 15:40, 47*

Jesus Is Buried

57 [a]When it was evening, there came a rich man from Arimathea, named Joseph, who himself had also become a disciple of Jesus. [a]*Mark 15:42-47; Luke 23:50-56*

58 This man went to Pilate and asked for the body of Jesus. Then Pilate ordered it to be given *to him.*

59 And Joseph took the body and wrapped it in a clean linen cloth,

60 and laid it in his own new tomb, which he had hewn out in the rock; and he rolled [a]a large stone against the entrance of the tomb and went away. [a]*Matt 27:66; 28:2*

61 And [a]Mary Magdalene was there, and the other Mary, sitting opposite the grave. [a]*Matt 27:56; 28:1*

62 Now on the next day, the day after [a]the preparation, the chief priests and the Pharisees gathered together with Pilate, [a]*Mark 15:42; Luke 23:54*

63 and said, "Sir, we remember that when He was still alive that deceiver said, '[a]After three days I *am to* rise again.' [a]*Matt 16:21; 17:23*

64 "Therefore, give orders for the grave to be made secure until the third day, otherwise His disciples may come and steal Him away and say to the people, 'He has risen from the dead,' and the last deception will be worse than the first."

65 Pilate said to them, "You have a [a]guard; go, make it *as* secure as you know how." [a]*Matt 27:66; 28:11*

66 And they went and made the grave secure, and along with the guard they set a [a]seal on the stone. [a]*Dan 6:17*

Jesus Is Risen!

28 [a]Now after the Sabbath, as it began to dawn toward the first *day* of the week, Mary Magdalene and the other Mary came to look at the grave. [a]*John 20:1-8*

2 And behold, a severe earthquake had occurred, for [a]an angel of the Lord descended from heaven and came and rolled away [b]the stone and sat upon it. [a]*Luke 24:4* [b]*Matt 27:66*

3 And [a]his appearance was like lightning, and his clothing as white as snow. [a]*Dan 7:9; 10:6; Mark 9:3*

4 The guards shook for fear of him and became like dead men.

5 The angel said to the women, "[a]Do not be afraid; for I know that you are looking for Jesus who has been crucified. [a]*Matt 14:27; 28:10*

6 "He is not here, for He has risen, [a]just as He said. Come, see the place where He was lying. [a]*Matt 12:40; 16:21*

7 "Go quickly and tell His disciples that He has risen from the dead; and behold, He is going ahead of you [a]into Galilee, there you will see Him; behold, I have told you." [a]*Matt 26:32; 28:10, 16*

8 And they left the tomb quickly with fear and great joy and ran to report it to His disciples.

9 And behold, Jesus met them and greeted them. And they came up and took hold of His feet and worshiped Him.

10 Then Jesus *said to them, "Do not be afraid; go and take word to [a]My brethren to leave for Galilee, and there they will see Me." [a]*John 20:17; Rom 8:29*

11 Now while they were on their way, some of [a]the guard came into the city and reported to the chief priests all that had happened. [a]*Matt 27:65, 66*

12 And when they had assembled with the elders and consulted together, they gave a large sum of money to the soldiers,

13 and said, "You are to say, 'His disciples came by night and stole Him away while we were asleep.'

14 "And if this should come to [a]the governor's ears, we will win him over and keep you out of trouble." [a]*Matt 27:2*

15 And they took the money and did as they had been instructed; and this story was widely [a]spread among the Jews, *and is* to this day. [a]*Matt 9:31; Mark 1:45*

The Great Commission

16 But the eleven disciples proceeded [a]to Galilee, to the mountain which Jesus had designated. [a]*Matt 26:32; 28:7, 10*

17 When they saw Him, they worshiped *Him;* but [a]some were doubtful. [a]*Mark 16:11*

18 And Jesus came up and spoke to them, say-

ing, "ªAll authority has been given to Me in heaven and on earth. ªDan 7:13f; Matt 11:27

19 "Go therefore and make disciples of all the nations, baptizing them in the name of the Father and the Son and the Holy Spirit,

20 teaching them to observe all that I commanded you; and lo, ªI am with you always, even to the end of the age." ªMatt 18:20; Acts 18:10

The Gospel According to
MARK

Preaching of John the Baptist

1 The beginning of the gospel of Jesus Christ, ªthe Son of God. ªMatt 4:3

2 ªAs it is written in Isaiah the prophet:
"BEHOLD, I SEND MY MESSENGER AHEAD OF YOU,
WHO WILL PREPARE YOUR WAY; ªMatt 3:1-11; Luke 3:2-16

3 ªTHE VOICE OF ONE CRYING IN THE WILDERNESS,
'MAKE READY THE WAY OF THE LORD,
MAKE HIS PATHS STRAIGHT.' " ªIs 40:3; Matt 3:3

4 John the Baptist appeared in the wilderness ªpreaching a baptism of repentance for the ᵇforgiveness of sins. ªActs 13:24 ᵇLuke 1:77

5 And all the country of Judea was going out to him, and all the people of Jerusalem; and they were being baptized by him in the Jordan River, confessing their sins.

6 John was clothed with camel's hair and wore ªa leather belt around his waist, and his diet was locusts and wild honey. ª2 Kin 1:8

7 And he was preaching, and saying, "After me One is coming who is mightier than I, and I am not fit to stoop down and untie the thong of His sandals.

8 "I baptized you with water; but He will baptize you with the Holy Spirit."

The Baptism of Jesus

9 ªIn those days Jesus came from Nazareth in Galilee and was baptized by John in the Jordan. ªMatt 3:13-17; Luke 3:21, 22

10 Immediately coming up out of the water, He saw the heavens opening, and the Spirit like a dove descending upon Him;

11 and a voice came out of the heavens: "ªYou are My beloved Son, in You I am wellpleased." ªPs 2:7; Is 42:1

12 ªImmediately the Spirit *impelled Him to go out into the wilderness. ªMatt 4:1-11; Luke 4:1-13

13 And He was in the wilderness forty days being tempted by ªSatan; and He was with the wild beasts, and the angels were ministering to Him. ªMatt 4:10

Jesus Preaches in Galilee

14 ªNow after John had been taken into custody, Jesus came into Galilee, ᵇpreaching the gospel of God, ªMatt 4:12 ᵇMatt 4:23

15 and saying, "ªThe time is fulfilled, and the kingdom of God is at hand; repent and believe in the gospel." ªGal 4:4; Eph 1:10

16 ªAs He was going along by the Sea of Galilee, He saw Simon and Andrew, the brother of Simon, casting a net in the sea; for they were fishermen. ªLuke 5:2-11; John 1:40-42

17 And Jesus said to them, "Follow Me, and I will make you become fishers of men."

18 Immediately they left their nets and followed Him.

19 Going on a little farther, He saw James the son of Zebedee, and John his brother, who were also in the boat mending the nets.

20 Immediately He called them; and they left their father Zebedee in the boat with the hired servants, and went away to follow Him.

21 ªThey *went into Capernaum; and immediately on the Sabbath He entered the synagogue and began to teach. ªLuke 4:31-37

22 ªThey were amazed at His teaching; for He was teaching them as one having authority, and not as the scribes. ªMatt 7:28

23 Just then there was a man in their synagogue with an unclean spirit; and he cried out,

24 saying, "ªWhat business do we have with each other, Jesus of Nazareth? Have You come to destroy us? I know who You are—ᵇthe Holy One of God!" ªMatt 8:29 ᵇLuke 4:34

25 And Jesus rebuked him, saying, "Be quiet, and come out of him!"

26 Throwing him into convulsions, the unclean spirit cried out with a loud voice and came out of him.

27 They were all ªamazed, so that they debated among themselves, saying, "What is this? A new teaching with authority! He commands even the unclean spirits, and they obey Him." ªMark 10:24, 32; 16:5, 6

28 Immediately the news about Him spread everywhere into all the surrounding district of Galilee.

Crowds Healed

29 ªAnd immediately after they came out of the synagogue, they came into the house of Simon and Andrew, with James and John. ªMatt 8:14, 15; Luke 4:38, 39

30 Now Simon's mother-in-law was lying sick with a fever; and immediately they *spoke to Jesus about her.

31 And He came to her and raised her up, taking her by the hand, and the fever left her,

and she waited on them.

32 [a]When evening came, after the sun had set, they *began* bringing to Him all who were ill and those who were demon-possessed.
[a]*Matt 8:16, 17; Luke 4:40, 41*

33 And the whole [a]city had gathered at the door. [a]*Mark 1:21*

34 And He [a]healed many who were ill with various diseases, and cast out many demons; and He was not permitting the demons to speak, because they knew who He was. [a]*Matt 4:23*

35 [a]In the early morning, while it was still dark, Jesus got up, left *the house,* and went away to a secluded place, and was praying there. [a]*Luke 4:42, 43*

36 Simon and his companions searched for Him;

37 they found Him, and *said to Him, "Everyone is looking for You."

38 He *said to them, "Let us go somewhere else to the towns nearby, so that I may preach there also; for that is what I came for."

39 [a]And He went into their synagogues throughout all Galilee, preaching and casting out the demons. [a]*Matt 4:23; 9:35*

40 [a]And a leper *came to Jesus, beseeching Him and falling on his knees before Him, and saying, "If You are willing, You can make me clean." [a]*Matt 8:2-4; Luke 5:12-14*

41 Moved with compassion, Jesus stretched out His hand and touched him, and *said to him, "I am willing; be cleansed."

42 Immediately the leprosy left him and he was cleansed.

43 And He sternly warned him and immediately sent him away,

44 and He *said to him, "[a]See that you say nothing to anyone; but [a]go, show yourself to the priest and [b]offer for your cleansing what Moses commanded, as a testimony to them."
[a]*Matt 8:4* [b]*Lev 14:1-32*

45 But he went out and began to [a]proclaim it freely and to [a]spread the news around, to such an extent that Jesus could no longer publicly enter a city, but stayed out in unpopulated areas; and they were coming to Him from everywhere. [a]*Matt 28:15; Luke 5:15*

The Paralytic Healed

2 When He had come back to Capernaum several days afterward, it was heard that He was at home.

2 And [a]many were gathered together, so that there was no longer room, not even near the door; and He was speaking the word to them. [a]*Mark 1:45; 2:13*

3 [a]And they *came, bringing to Him a paralytic, carried by four men. [a]*Matt 9:2-8; Luke 5:18-26*

4 Being unable to get to Him because of the crowd, they [a]removed the roof above Him; and when they had dug an opening, they let down the pallet on which the [b]paralytic was lying.
[a]*Luke 5:19* [b]*Matt 4:24*

5 And Jesus seeing their faith *said to the paralytic, "Son, [a]your sins are forgiven." [a]*Matt 9:2*

6 But some of the scribes were sitting there and reasoning in their hearts,

7 "Why does this man speak that way? He is blaspheming; [a]who can forgive sins but God alone?" [a]*Is 43:25*

8 Immediately Jesus, aware in His spirit that they were reasoning that way within themselves, *said to them, "Why are you reasoning about these things in your hearts?

9 "Which is easier, to say to the [a]paralytic, 'Your sins are forgiven'; or to say, 'Get up, and pick up your pallet and walk'? [a]*Matt 4:24*

10 "But so that you may know that the Son of Man has authority on earth to forgive sins"—He *said to the paralytic,

11 "I say to you, get up, pick up your pallet and go home."

12 And he got up and immediately picked up the pallet and went out in the sight of everyone, so that they were all amazed and [a]were glorifying God, saying, "[b]We have never seen anything like this." [a]*Matt 9:8* [b]*Mark 9:33*

13 And He went out again by the seashore; and [a]all the people were coming to Him, and He was teaching them. [a]*Mark 1:45*

Levi (Matthew) Called

14 [a]As He passed by, He saw Levi the *son* of Alphaeus sitting in the tax booth, and He *said to him, "Follow Me!" And he got up and followed Him. [a]*Matt 9:9-13; Luke 5:27-32*

15 And it *happened that He was reclining *at the table* in his house, and many tax collectors and sinners were dining with Jesus and His disciples; for there were many of them, and they were following Him.

16 When [a]the scribes of the Pharisees saw that He was eating with the sinners and tax collectors, they said to His disciples, "Why is He eating and drinking with tax collectors and sinners?" [a]*Luke 5:30; Acts 23:9*

17 And hearing *this,* Jesus *said to them, "[a]It *is* not those who are healthy who need a physician, but those who are sick; I did not come to call the righteous, but sinners." [a]*Matt 9:12, 13; Luke 5:31, 32*

18 [a]John's disciples and the Pharisees were fasting; and they *came and *said to Him, "Why do John's disciples and the disciples of the Pharisees fast, but Your disciples do not fast?" [a]*Matt 9:14-17; Luke 5:33-38*

19 And Jesus said to them, "While the bride-

groom is with them, the attendants of the bridegroom cannot fast, can they? So long as they have the bridegroom with them, they cannot fast.

20 "But the ªdays will come when the bridegroom is taken away from them, and then they will fast in that day. ªMatt 9:15; Luke 17:22

21 "No one sews a patch of unshrunk cloth on an old garment; otherwise the patch pulls away from it, the new from the old, and a worse tear results.

22 "No one puts new wine into old wineskins; otherwise the wine will burst the skins, and the wine is lost and the skins *as well;* but *one puts* new wine into fresh wineskins."

Question of the Sabbath

23 ªAnd it happened that He was passing through the grainfields on the Sabbath, and His disciples began to make their way along while picking the heads *of grain.* ªMatt 12:1-8; Luke 6:1-5

24 The Pharisees were saying to Him, "Look, ªwhy are they doing what is not lawful on the Sabbath?" ªMatt 12:2

25 And He *said to them, "Have you never read what David did when he was in need and he and his companions became hungry;

26 how he entered the house of God in the time of ªAbiathar *the* high priest, and ate the consecrated bread, which is not lawful for *anyone* to eat except the priests, and he also gave it to those who were with him?" ª1 Sam 21:1; 2 Sam 8:17

27 Jesus said to them, "ªThe Sabbath was made for man, and not man for the Sabbath. ªEx 23:12; Deut 5:14

28 "So the Son of Man is Lord even of the Sabbath."

Jesus Heals on the Sabbath

3 ªHe entered again into a synagogue; and a man was there whose hand was withered. ªMatt 12:9-14; Luke 6:6-11

2 They were watching Him *to see* if He would heal him on the Sabbath, ªso that they might accuse Him. ªMatt 12:10; Luke 6:7

3 He *said to the man with the withered hand, "Get up and come forward!"

4 And He *said to them, "Is it lawful to do good or to do harm on the Sabbath, to save a life or to kill?" But they kept silent.

5 After ªlooking around at them with anger, grieved at their hardness of heart, He *said to the man, "Stretch out your hand." And he stretched it out, and his hand was restored. ªLuke 6:10

6 The Pharisees went out and immediately *began* conspiring with the ªHerodians against Him, *as to* how they might destroy Him. ªMatt 22:16; Mark 12:13

7 ªJesus withdrew to the sea with His disciples; and a great multitude from Galilee followed; and *also* from Judea, ªMatt 12:15, 16; Luke 6:17-19

8 and from Jerusalem, and from ªIdumea, and beyond the Jordan, and the vicinity of Tyre and Sidon, a great number of people heard of all that He was doing and came to Him. ªJosh 15:1, 21; Ezek 35:15

9 ªAnd He told His disciples that a boat should stand ready for Him because of the crowd, so that they would not crowd Him; ªMark 4:1; Luke 5:1-3

10 for He had ªhealed many, with the result that all those who had afflictions pressed around Him in order to ᵇtouch Him. ªMatt 4:23 ᵇMatt 9:21

11 Whenever the unclean spirits saw Him, they would fall down before Him and shout, "You are ªthe Son of God!" ªMatt 4:3

12 And He ªearnestly warned them not to tell who He was. ªMatt 8:4

The Twelve Are Chosen

13 And He *went up on ªthe mountain and *summoned those whom He Himself wanted, and they came to Him. ªMatt 5:1; Luke 6:12

14 And He appointed twelve, so that they would be with Him and that He *could* send them out to preach,

15 and to have authority to cast out the demons.

16 And He appointed the twelve: ªSimon (to whom He gave the name Peter), ªActs 1:13

17 and James, the *son* of Zebedee, and John the brother of James (to them He gave the name Boanerges, which means, "Sons of Thunder");

18 and Andrew, and Philip, and Bartholomew, and Matthew, and Thomas, and James the son of Alphaeus, and Thaddaeus, and Simon the Zealot;

19 and Judas Iscariot, who betrayed Him.

20 And He *came ªhome, and the crowd *gathered again, to such an extent that they could not even eat a meal. ªMark 2:1; 7:17

21 When His own people heard *of this,* they went out to take custody of Him; for they were saying, "ªHe has lost His senses." ªJohn 10:20; Acts 26:24

22 The scribes who came down from Jerusalem were saying, "He is possessed by ªBeelzebul," and "ᵇHe casts out the demons by the ruler of the demons." ªMatt 10:25 ᵇMatt 9:34

23 ªAnd He called them to Himself and began speaking to them in parables, "How can Satan cast out Satan? ªMatt 12:25-29; Luke 11:17-22

24 "If a kingdom is divided against itself, that kingdom cannot stand.

25 "If a house is divided against itself, that house will not be able to stand.

26 "If ªSatan has risen up against himself and is divided, he cannot stand, but he is finished! ªMatt 4:10

27 "ªBut no one can enter the strong man's house and plunder his property unless he first binds the strong man, and then he will plunder his house. ªIs 49:24, 25

28 "ªTruly I say to you, all sins shall be forgiven the sons of men, and whatever blasphemies they utter; ªMatt 12:31, 32; Mark 3:28-30

29 but ªwhoever blasphemes against the Holy Spirit never has forgiveness, but is guilty of an eternal sin"— ªLuke 12:10

30 because they were saying, "He has an unclean spirit."

31 ªThen His mother and His brothers *arrived, and standing outside they sent *word* to Him and called Him. ªMatt 12:46-50; Luke 8:19-21

32 A crowd was sitting around Him, and they *said to Him, "Behold, Your mother and Your brothers are outside looking for You."

33 Answering them, He *said, "Who are My mother and My brothers?"

34 Looking about at those who were sitting around Him, He *said, "ªBehold My mother and My brothers! ªMatt 12:49

35 "For whoever ªdoes the will of God, he is My brother and sister and mother." ªEph 6:6; Heb 10:36

Parable of the Sower and Soils

4 ªHe began to teach again by the sea. And such a very large crowd gathered to Him that He got into a boat in the sea and sat down; and the whole crowd was by the sea on the land. ªMatt 13:1-15; Luke 8:4-10

2 And He was teaching them many things in ªparables, and was saying to them in His teaching, ªMatt 13:3ff; Mark 3:23

3 "Listen *to this!* Behold, the sower went out to sow;

4 as he was sowing, some *seed* fell beside the road, and the birds came and ate it up.

5 "Other *seed* fell on the rocky *ground* where it did not have much soil; and immediately it sprang up because it had no depth of soil.

6 "And after the sun had risen, it was scorched; and because it had no root, it withered away.

7 "Other *seed* fell among the thorns, and the thorns came up and choked it, and it yielded no crop.

8 "Other *seeds* fell into the good soil, and as they grew up and increased, they yielded a crop and produced thirty, sixty, and a hundredfold."

9 And He was saying, "ªHe who has ears to hear, let him hear." ªMatt 11:15; Mark 4:23

10 As soon as He was alone, His followers, along with the twelve, *began* asking Him *about* the parables.

11 And He was saying to them, "To you has been given the mystery of the kingdom of God, but ªthose who are outside get everything in parables, ª1 Cor 5:12f; Col 4:5

12 so that ªWHILE SEEING, THEY MAY SEE AND NOT PERCEIVE, AND WHILE HEARING, THEY MAY HEAR AND NOT UNDERSTAND, OTHERWISE THEY MIGHT RETURN AND BE FORGIVEN." ªIs 6:9f; 43:8

Explanation

13 ªAnd He *said to them, "Do you not understand this parable? How will you understand all the parables? ªMatt 13:18-23; Luke 8:11-15

14 "The sower sows the word.

15 "These are the ones who are beside the road where the word is sown; and when they hear, immediately ªSatan comes and takes away the word which has been sown in them. ªMatt 4:10f; 1 Pet 5:8

16 "In a similar way these are the ones on whom seed was sown on the rocky *places,* who, when they hear the word, immediately receive it with joy;

17 and they have no *firm* root in themselves, but are *only* temporary; then, when affliction or persecution arises because of the word, immediately they fall away.

18 "And others are the ones on whom seed was sown among the thorns; these are the ones who have heard the word,

19 but the worries of ªthe world, and the ªdeceitfulness of riches, and the desires for other things enter in and choke the word, and it becomes unfruitful. ªMatt 13:22 ªProv 23:4

20 "And those are the ones on whom seed was sown on the good soil; and they hear the word and accept it and ªbear fruit, thirty, sixty, and a hundredfold." ªJohn 15:2ff; Rom 7:4

21 And He was saying to them, "ªA lamp is not brought to be put under a basket, is it, or under a bed? Is it not *brought* to be put on the lampstand? ªMatt 5:15; Luke 8:16

22 "ªFor nothing is hidden, except to be revealed; nor has *anything* been secret, but that it would come to light. ªMatt 10:26; Luke 8:17

23 "ªIf anyone has ears to hear, let him hear." ªMatt 11:15; 13:9

24 And He was saying to them, "Take care what you listen to. ªBy your standard of measure it will be measured to you; and more will be given you besides. ªMatt 7:2; Luke 6:38

25 "ªFor whoever has, to him *more* shall be given; and whoever does not have, even what he has shall be taken away from him." ªMatt 13:12; 25:29

Parable of the Seed

26 And He was saying, "The kingdom of God is like a man who casts seed upon the soil;

27 and he goes to bed at night and gets up by day, and the seed sprouts and grows—how, he himself does not know.

28 "The soil produces crops by itself; first the blade, then the head, then the mature grain in the head.

29 "But when the crop permits, he immediately ªputs in the sickle, because the harvest has come." ªJoel 3:13

Parable of the Mustard Seed

30 ªAnd He said, "How shall we picture the kingdom of God, or by what parable shall we present it? ªMatt 13:31, 32; Luke 13:18, 19

31 "It is like a mustard seed, which, when sown upon the soil, though it is smaller than all the seeds that are upon the soil,

32 yet when it is sown, it grows up and becomes larger than all the garden plants and forms large branches; so that ªTHE BIRDS OF THE AIR can NEST UNDER ITS SHADE." ªEzek 17:23; Ps 104:12

33 With many such parables He was speaking the word to them, so far as they were able to hear it;

34 and He did not speak to them ªwithout a parable; but He was explaining everything privately to His own disciples. ªMatt 13:34; John 10:6

Jesus Stills the Sea

35 ªOn that day, when evening came, He *said to them, "Let us go over to the other side." ªMatt 8:18, 23-27; Luke 8:22, 25

36 Leaving the crowd, they *took Him along with them ªin the boat, just as He was; and other boats were with Him. ªMark 3:9; 4:1

37 And there *arose a fierce gale of wind, and the waves were breaking over the boat so much that the boat was already filling up.

38 Jesus Himself was in the stern, asleep on the cushion; and they *woke Him and *said to Him, "Teacher, do You not care that we are perishing?"

39 And He got up and ªrebuked the wind and said to the sea, "Hush, be still." And the wind died down and it became perfectly calm. ªPs 65:7; 89:9

40 And He said to them, "Why are you afraid? ªDo you still have no faith?" ªMatt 14:31; Luke 8:25

41 They became very much afraid and said to one another, "Who then is this, that even the wind and the sea obey Him?"

The Gerasene Demoniac

5 ªThey came to the other side of the sea, into the country of the Gerasenes. ªMatt 8:28-34; Luke 8:26-37

2 When He got out of ªthe boat, immediately a man from the tombs with an unclean spirit met Him, ªMark 3:9; 4:1, 36

3 and he had his dwelling among the tombs. And no one was able to bind him anymore, even with a chain;

4 because he had often been bound with shackles and chains, and the chains had been torn apart by him and the shackles broken in pieces, and no one was strong enough to subdue him.

5 Constantly, night and day, he was screaming among the tombs and in the mountains, and gashing himself with stones.

6 Seeing Jesus from a distance, he ran up and bowed down before Him;

7 and shouting with a loud voice, he *said, "ªWhat business do we have with each other, Jesus, Son of ᵇthe Most High God? I implore You by God, do not torment me!" ªMatt 8:29 ᵇLuke 8:28

8 For He had been saying to him, "Come out of the man, you unclean spirit!"

9 And He was asking him, "What is your name?" And he *said to Him, "My name is ªLegion; for we are many." ªMatt 26:53; Mark 5:15

10 And he began to implore Him earnestly not to send them out of the country.

11 Now there was a large herd of swine feeding nearby on the mountain.

12 The demons implored Him, saying, "Send us into the swine so that we may enter them."

13 Jesus gave them permission. And coming out, the unclean spirits entered the swine; and the herd rushed down the steep bank into the sea, about two thousand of them; and they were drowned in the sea.

14 Their herdsmen ran away and reported it in the city and in the country. And the people came to see what it was that had happened.

15 They *came to Jesus and *observed the man who had been demon-possessed sitting down, clothed and ªin his right mind, the very man who had had the ᵇ"legion"; and they became frightened. ªLuke 8:35 ᵇMark 5:9

16 Those who had seen it described to them how it had happened to the ªdemon-possessed man, and all about the swine. ªMatt 4:24; Mark 5:15

17 And they began to ªimplore Him to leave their region. ªMatt 8:34; Acts 16:39

18 ªAs He was getting into the boat, the man who had been demon-possessed was imploring Him that he might accompany Him. ªLuke 8:38, 39

19 And He did not let him, but He *said to him, "ªGo home to your people and report to them what great things the Lord has done for you, and how He had mercy on you." ªLuke 8:39

20 And he went away and began to ªproclaim in ᵇDecapolis what great things Jesus had done for him; and everyone was amazed. ªPs 66:16 ᵇMatt 4:25

Miracles and Healing

21 When Jesus had crossed over again in ªthe boat to the other side, a large crowd gathered around Him; and so He stayed ᵇby the sea-shore. ªMark 4:36 ᵇMark 4:1

22 ªOne of the synagogue officials named Jairus *came up, and on seeing Him, *fell at His feet ªMatt 9:18-26; Luke 8:41-56

23 and *implored Him earnestly, saying, "My little daughter is at the point of death; please come and ªlay Your hands on her, so that she will get well and live." ªMark 6:5; 7:32

24 And He went off with him; and a large crowd was following Him and pressing in on Him.

25 A woman who had had a hemorrhage for twelve years,

26 and had endured much at the hands of many physicians, and had spent all that she had and was not helped at all, but rather had grown worse—

27 after hearing about Jesus, she came up in the crowd behind Him and touched His cloak.

28 For she thought, "If I just touch His garments, I will get well."

29 Immediately the flow of her blood was dried up; and she felt in her body that she was healed of her ªaffliction. ªMark 3:10; 5:34

30 Immediately Jesus, perceiving in Himself that ªthe power proceeding from Him had gone forth, turned around in the crowd and said, "Who touched My garments?" ªLuke 5:17

31 And His disciples said to Him, "You see the crowd pressing in on You, and You say, 'Who touched Me?' "

32 And He looked around to see the woman who had done this.

33 But the woman fearing and trembling, aware of what had happened to her, came and fell down before Him and told Him the whole truth.

34 And He said to her, "Daughter, ªyour faith has made you well; ᵇgo in peace and be healed of your affliction." ªMatt 9:22 ᵇLuke 7:50; 8:48

35 While He was still speaking, they *came from the house of the ªsynagogue official, saying, "Your daughter has died; why trouble the Teacher anymore?" ªMark 5:22

36 But Jesus, overhearing what was being spoken, *said to the synagogue official, "ªDo not be afraid any longer, only believe." ªLuke 8:50

37 And He allowed no one to accompany Him, except ªPeter and James and John the brother of James. ªMatt 17:1; 26:37

38 They *came to the house of the ªsynagogue official; and He *saw a commotion, and peo-ple loudly weeping and wailing. ªMark 5:22

39 And entering in, He *said to them, "Why make a commotion and weep? The child has not died, but is asleep."

40 They began laughing at Him. But putting them all out, He *took along the child's father and mother and His own companions, and *entered the room where the child was.

41 Taking the child by the hand, He *said to her, "Talitha kum!" (which translated means, "Little girl, ªI say to you, get up!"). ªLuke 7:14; Acts 9:40

42 Immediately the girl got up and began to walk, for she was twelve years old. And imme-diately they were completely astounded.

43 And He ªgave them strict orders that no one should know about this, and He said that some-thing should be given her to eat. ªMatt 8:4

Teaching at Nazareth

6 ªJesus went out from there and *came into ᵇHis hometown; and His disciples *fol-lowed Him. ªMatt 13:54-58 ᵇLuke 4:16, 23

2 When the Sabbath came, He began ªto teach in the synagogue; and the many listeners were astonished, saying, "Where did this man get these things, and what is this wisdom given to Him, and such miracles as these performed by His hands? ªMatt 4:23; Mark 10:1

3 "Is not this ªthe carpenter, the son of Mary, and brother of James and Joses and Judas and Simon? Are not His sisters here with us?" And they took ᵇoffense at Him. ªMatt 13:55 ᵇMatt 11:6

4 Jesus said to them, "ªA prophet is not with-out honor except in his hometown and among his own relatives and in his own household." ªMatt 13:57; John 4:44

5 And He could do no miracle there except that He ªlaid His hands on a few sick people and healed them. ªMark 5:23

6 And He wondered at their unbelief.

ªAnd He was going around the villages teaching. ªMatt 9:35; Mark 1:39

The Twelve Sent Out

7 ªAnd He *summoned the twelve and began to send them out ᵇin pairs, and gave them authority over the unclean spirits; ªLuke 10:4-11 ᵇLuke 10:1

8 ªand He instructed them that they should take nothing for their journey, except a mere staff—no bread, no bag, no money in their belt— ªMatt 10:10

9 but to wear sandals; and He added, "Do not put on two tunics."

10 And He said to them, "Wherever you enter a house, stay there until you leave town.

11 "Any place that does not receive you or lis-ten to you, as you go out from there, ªshake the

dust off the soles of your feet for a testimony against them." ªMatt 10:14; Acts 13:51

12 ªThey went out and preached that *men* should repent. ªMatt 11:1; Luke 9:6

13 And they were casting out many demons and ªwere anointing with oil many sick people and healing them. ªJames 5:14

John's Fate Recalled

14 ªAnd King Herod heard *of it,* for His name had become well known; and *people* were saying, "John the Baptist has risen from the dead, and that is why these miraculous powers are at work in Him." ªMatt 14:1-12; Luke 9:7-9

15 But others were saying, "He is ªElijah." And others were saying, "*He is* a prophet, like one of the prophets *of old.*" ªMatt 16:14; Mark 8:28

16 But when Herod heard *of it,* he kept saying, "John, whom I beheaded, has risen!"

17 For Herod himself had sent and had John arrested and bound in prison on account of ªHerodias, the wife of his brother Philip, because he had married her. ªMatt 14:3; Luke 3:19

18 For John had been saying to Herod, "ªIt is not lawful for you to have your brother's wife." ªMatt 14:4

19 ªHerodias had a grudge against him and wanted to put him to death and could not *do so;* ªMatt 14:3

20 for ªHerod was afraid of John, knowing that he was a righteous and holy man, and he kept him safe. And when he heard him, he was very perplexed; but he used to enjoy listening to him. ªMatt 21:26

21 A strategic day came when Herod on his birthday ªgave a banquet for his lords and military commanders and the leading men of Galilee; ªEsth 1:3; 2:18

22 and when the daughter of ªHerodias herself came in and danced, she pleased Herod and his dinner guests; and the king said to the girl, "Ask me for whatever you want and I will give it to you." ªMatt 14:3

23 And he swore to her, "Whatever you ask of me, I will give it to you; up to ªhalf of my kingdom." ªEsth 5:3, 6; 7:2

24 And she went out and said to her mother, "What shall I ask for?" And she said, "The head of John the Baptist."

25 Immediately she came in a hurry to the king and asked, saying, "I want you to give me at once the head of John the Baptist on a platter."

26 And although the king was very sorry, *yet* because of his oaths and because of his dinner guests, he was unwilling to refuse her.

27 Immediately the king sent an executioner and commanded *him* to bring *back* his head. And he went and had him beheaded in the prison,

28 and brought his head on a platter, and gave it to the girl; and the girl gave it to her mother.

29 When his disciples heard *about this,* they came and took away his body and laid it in a tomb.

30 The ªapostles *gathered together with Jesus; and they reported to Him all that they had done and taught. ªMatt 10:2; Mark 3:14

31 And He *said to them, "Come away by yourselves to a secluded place and rest a while." (For there were many *people* coming and going, and ªthey did not even have time to eat.) ªMark 3:20

32 ªThey went away in the boat to a secluded place by themselves. ªMark 8:2-9

Five Thousand Fed

33 *The people* saw them going, and many recognized *them* and ran there together on foot from all the cities, and got there ahead of them.

34 When Jesus went ashore, He ªsaw a large crowd, and He felt compassion for them because ªthey were like sheep without a shepherd; and He began to teach them many things. ªMatt 9:36 ªNum 27:17

35 When it was already quite late, His disciples came to Him and said, "This place is desolate and it is already quite late;

36 send them away so that they may go into the surrounding countryside and villages and buy themselves something to eat."

37 But He answered them, "You give them *something* to eat!" ªAnd they *said to Him, "Shall we go and spend two hundred denarii on bread and give them *something* to eat?" ªJohn 6:7

38 And He *said to them, "How many loaves do you have? Go look!" And when they found out, they *said, "Five, and two fish."

39 And He commanded them all to sit down by groups on the green grass.

40 They sat down in groups of hundreds and of fifties.

41 And He took the five loaves and the two fish, and looking up toward heaven, He ªblessed *the food* and broke the loaves and He kept giving *them* to the disciples to set before them; and He divided up the two fish among them all. ªMatt 14:19

42 They all ate and were satisfied,

43 and they picked up twelve full ªbaskets of the broken pieces, and also of the fish. ªMatt 14:20

44 There were ªfive thousand men who ate the loaves. ªMatt 14:21

Jesus Walks on the Water

45 ªImmediately Jesus made His disciples get into the boat and go ahead of *Him* to the other side to Bethsaida, while He Himself was sending the crowd away. ªMatt 14:22-32; John 6:15-21

46 After ᵃbidding them farewell, He left for the mountain to pray. ᵃ*Acts 18:18, 21; 2 Cor 2:13*

47 When it was evening, the boat was in the middle of the sea, and He was alone on the land.

48 Seeing them straining at the oars, for the wind was against them; at about the ᵃfourth watch of the night He *came to them, walking on the sea; and He intended to pass by them. ᵃ*Matt 24:43; Mark 13:35*

49 But when they saw Him walking on the sea, they supposed that it was a ghost, and cried out;

50 for they all saw Him and were terrified. But immediately He spoke with them and *said to them, "ᵃTake courage; it is I, ᵇdo not be afraid." ᵃ*Matt 9:2* ᵇ*Matt 14:27*

51 Then He got into ᵃthe boat with them, and the wind stopped; and they were utterly astonished, ᵃ*Mark 6:32*

52 for ᵃthey had not gained any insight from the *incident of* the loaves, but their heart ᵇwas hardened. ᵃ*Mark 8:17ff* ᵇ*Rom 11:7*

Healing at Gennesaret

53 ᵃWhen they had crossed over they came to land at Gennesaret, and moored to the shore. ᵃ*John 6:24, 25*

54 When they got out of the boat, immediately *the people* recognized Him,

55 and ran about that whole country and began to carry here and there on their pallets those who were sick, to the place they heard He was.

56 Wherever He entered villages, or cities, or countryside, they were laying the sick in the market places, and imploring Him that they might just ᵃtouch ᵇthe fringe of His cloak; and as many as touched it were being cured. ᵃ*Mark 3:10* ᵇ*Matt 9:20*

Followers of Tradition

7 ᵃThe Pharisees and some of the scribes gathered around Him when they had come from Jerusalem, ᵃ*Matt 15:1-20*

2 and had seen that some of His disciples were eating their bread with ᵃimpure hands, that is, unwashed. ᵃ*Matt 15:2; Mark 7:5*

3 (For the Pharisees and all the Jews do not eat unless they carefully wash their hands, *thus* observing the ᵃtraditions of the elders; ᵃ*Mark 7:5, 8, 9, 13; Gal 1:14*

4 and *when they come* from the market place, they do not eat unless they cleanse themselves; and there are many other things which they have received in order to observe, such as the washing of ᵃcups and pitchers and copper pots.) ᵃ*Matt 23:25*

5 The Pharisees and the scribes *asked Him, "Why do Your disciples not walk according to the ᵃtradition of the elders, but eat their bread with impure hands?" ᵃ*Mark 7:3, 8, 9, 13; Gal 1:14*

6 And He said to them, "Rightly did Isaiah prophesy of you hypocrites, as it is written:

'ᵃTHIS PEOPLE HONORS ME WITH THEIR LIPS,
  BUT THEIR HEART IS FAR AWAY FROM ME.
      ᵃ*Is 29:13*

7 'BUT IN VAIN DO THEY WORSHIP ME,
  TEACHING AS DOCTRINES THE PRECEPTS OF
      MEN.' ᵃ*Is 29:13*

8 "Neglecting the commandment of God, you hold to the ᵃtradition of men." ᵃ*Mark 7:3, 5, 9, 13; Gal 1:14*

9 He was also saying to them, "You are experts at setting aside the commandment of God in order to keep your tradition.

10 "For Moses said, 'ᵃHONOR YOUR FATHER AND YOUR MOTHER'; and, 'ᵇHE WHO SPEAKS EVIL OF FATHER OR MOTHER, IS TO BE PUT TO DEATH'; ᵃ*Ex 20:12* ᵇ*Ex 21:17*

11 but you say, 'If a man says to *his* father or *his* mother, whatever I have that would help you is ᵃCorban (that is to say, given *to God),*' ᵃ*Lev 1:2; Matt 27:6*

12 you no longer permit him to do anything for *his* father or *his* mother;

13 *thus* invalidating the word of God by your ᵃtradition which you have handed down; and you do many things such as that." ᵃ*Mark 7:3, 5, 8, 9; Gal 1:14*

The Heart of Man

14 After He called the crowd to Him again, He *began* saying to them, "Listen to Me, all of you, and understand:

15 there is nothing outside the man which can defile him if it goes into him; but the things which proceed out of the man are what defile the man.

16 ["If anyone has ears to hear, let him hear."]

17 When he had left the crowd *and* entered ᵃthe house, His disciples questioned Him about the parable. ᵃ*Mark 2:1; 3:20*

18 And He *said to them, "Are you so lacking in understanding also? Do you not understand that whatever goes into the man from outside cannot defile him,

19 because it does not go into his heart, but into his stomach, and is eliminated?" (*Thus He* declared all foods ᵃclean.) ᵃ*Luke 11:41; Acts 10:15*

20 And He was saying, "ᵃThat which proceeds out of the man, that is what defiles the man. ᵃ*Matt 15:18; Mark 7:23*

21 "For from within, out of the heart of men, proceed the evil thoughts, fornications, thefts, murders, adulteries,

22 deeds of coveting *and* wickedness, *as well as* deceit, sensuality, ᵃenvy, slander, pride *and* foolishness. ᵃ*Matt 6:23; 20:15*

23 "All these evil things proceed from within and defile the man."

The Syrophoenician Woman

24 ªJesus got up and went away from there to the region of Tyre. And when He had entered a house, He wanted no one to know *of it;* yet He could not escape notice. ªMatt 15:21-28

25 But after hearing of Him, a woman whose little daughter had an unclean spirit immediately came and fell at His feet.

26 Now the woman was a Gentile, of the Syrophoenician race. And she kept asking Him to cast the demon out of her daughter.

27 And He was saying to her, "Let the children be satisfied first, for it is not good to take the children's bread and throw it to the dogs."

28 But she answered and *said to Him, "Yes, Lord, *but* even the dogs under the table feed on the children's crumbs."

29 And He said to her, "Because of this answer go; the demon has gone out of your daughter."

30 And going back to her home, she found the child lying on the bed, the demon having left.

31 ªAgain He went out from the region of Tyre, and came through Sidon to the Sea of Galilee, within the region of Decapolis. ªMatt 15:29-31

32 They *brought to Him one who was deaf and spoke with difficulty, and they *implored Him to ªlay His hand on him. ªMark 5:23

33 ªJesus took him aside from the crowd, by himself, and put His fingers into his ears, and after ªspitting, He touched his tongue *with the saliva;* ªMark 8:23

34 and looking up to heaven with a deep ªsigh, He *said to him, "Ephphatha!" that is, "Be opened!" ªMark 8:12

35 And his ears were opened, and the impediment of his tongue was removed, and he *began speaking plainly.

36 And He gave them orders not to tell anyone; but the more He ordered them, the more widely they ªcontinued to proclaim it. ªMark 1:45

37 They were utterly astonished, saying, "He has done all things well; He makes even the deaf to hear and the mute to speak."

Four Thousand Fed

8 In those days, when there was again a large crowd and they had nothing to eat, ªJesus called His disciples and *said to them, ªMark 6:34-44

2 "ªI feel compassion for the people because they have remained with Me now three days and have nothing to eat. ªMatt 9:36; Mark 6:34

3 "If I send them away hungry to their homes, they will faint on the way; and some of them have come from a great distance."

4 And His disciples answered Him, "Where will anyone be able *to find enough* bread here in *this* desolate place to satisfy these people?"

5 And He was asking them, "How many loaves do you have?" And they said, "Seven."

6 And He *directed the people to sit down on the ground; and taking the seven loaves, He gave thanks and broke them, and started giving them to His disciples to serve to them, and they served them to the people.

7 They also had a few small fish; and ªafter He had blessed them, He ordered these to be served as well. ªMatt 14:19

8 And they ate and were satisfied; and they picked up seven large ªbaskets full of what was left over of the broken pieces. ªMatt 15:37; Mark 8:20

9 About four thousand were *there;* and He sent them away.

10 And immediately He entered the boat with His disciples and came to the district of ªDalmanutha. ªMatt 15:39

11 ªThe Pharisees came out and began to argue with Him, ᵇseeking from Him a sign from heaven, to test Him. ªMatt 16:1-12 ᵇMatt 12:38

12 Sighing deeply in His spirit, He *said, "Why does this generation seek for a sign? Truly I say to you, ªno sign will be given to this generation." ªMatt 12:39

13 Leaving them, He again embarked and went away to the other side.

14 And they had forgotten to take bread, and did not have more than one loaf in the boat with them.

15 And He was giving orders to them, saying, "ªWatch out! Beware of the leaven of the Pharisees and the leaven of Herod." ªMatt 16:6; Luke 12:1

16 They *began* to discuss with one another *the fact* that they had no bread.

17 And Jesus, aware of this, *said to them, "Why do you discuss *the fact* that you have no bread? ªDo you not yet see or understand? Do you have a hardened heart? ªMark 6:52

18 "ªHAVING EYES, DO YOU NOT SEE? AND HAVING EARS, DO YOU NOT HEAR? And do you not remember, ªJer 5:21; Ezek 12:2

19 when I broke ªthe five loaves for the five thousand, how many ᵇbaskets full of broken pieces you picked up?" They *said to Him, "Twelve." ªMark 6:41-44 ᵇMatt 14:20

20 "When *I broke* ªthe seven for the four thousand, how many large baskets full of broken pieces did you pick up?" And they *said to Him, "Seven." ªMark 8:6-9

21 And He was saying to them, "ªDo you not yet understand?" ªMark 6:52

22 And they *came to Bethsaida. And they *brought a blind man to Jesus and *implored Him to ªtouch him. ªMark 3:10

23 Taking the blind man by the hand, He [a]brought him out of the village; and after [a]spitting on his eyes and [b]laying His hands on him, He asked him, "Do you see anything?" [a]Mark 7:33 [b]Mark 5:23

24 And he looked up and said, "I see men, for I see *them* like trees, walking around."

25 Then again He laid His hands on his eyes; and he looked intently and was restored, and *began* to see everything clearly.

26 And He sent him to his home, saying, "Do not even enter [a]the village." [a]Mark 8:23

Peter's Confession of Christ

27 [a]Jesus went out, along with His disciples, to the villages of Caesarea Philippi; and on the way He questioned His disciples, saying to them, "Who do people say that I am?" [a]Matt 16:13-16; Luke 9:18-20

28 [a]They told Him, saying, "John the Baptist; and others *say* Elijah; but others, one of the prophets." [a]Mark 6:14; Luke 9:7, 8

29 And He *continued* by questioning them, "But who do you say that I am?" [a]Peter *answered and *said to Him, "You are the Christ." [a]John 6:68, 69

30 And [a]He warned them to tell no one about Him. [a]Matt 8:4; 16:20

31 [a]And He began to teach them that the Son of Man must suffer many things and be rejected by the elders and the chief priests and the scribes, and be killed, and after three days rise again. [a]Matt 16:21-28; Luke 9:22-27

32 And He was stating the matter [a]plainly. And Peter took Him aside and began to rebuke Him. [a]John 10:24; 11:14

33 But turning around and seeing His disciples, He rebuked Peter and *said, "Get behind Me, [a]Satan; for you are not setting your mind on God's interests, but man's." [a]Matt 4:10

34 And He summoned the crowd with His disciples, and said to them, "If anyone wishes to come after Me, he must deny himself, and [a]take up his cross and follow Me. [a]Matt 10:38; Luke 14:27

35 "For [a]whoever wishes to save his life will lose it, but whoever loses his life for My sake and the gospel's will save it. [a]Matt 10:39; Luke 17:33

36 "For what does it profit a man to gain the whole world, and forfeit his soul?

37 "For what will a man give in exchange for his soul?

38 "For [a]whoever is ashamed of Me and My words in this adulterous and sinful generation, the Son of Man will also be ashamed of him when He comes in the glory of His Father with the holy angels." [a]Matt 10:33; Luke 9:26

The Transfiguration

9 And Jesus was saying to them, "[a]Truly I say to you, there are some of those who are standing here who will not taste death until they see the kingdom of God after it has come with power." [a]Matt 16:28; Mark 13:26

2 [a]Six days later, Jesus *took with Him Peter and James and John, and *brought them up on a high mountain by themselves. And He was transfigured before them; [a]Matt 17:1-8; Luke 9:28-36

3 and [a]His garments became radiant and exceedingly white, as no launderer on earth can whiten them. [a]Matt 28:3

4 Elijah appeared to them along with Moses; and they were talking with Jesus.

5 Peter *said to Jesus, "Rabbi, it is good for us to be here; [a]let us make three tabernacles, one for You, and one for Moses, and one for Elijah." [a]Matt 17:4; Luke 9:33

6 For he did not know what to answer; for they became terrified.

7 Then a cloud formed, overshadowing them, and a voice came out of the cloud, "[a]This is My beloved Son, listen to Him!" [a]Matt 3:17; Mark 1:11

8 All at once they looked around and saw no one with them anymore, except Jesus alone.

9 [a]As they were coming down from the mountain, He gave them orders not to relate to anyone what they had seen, until the Son of Man rose from the dead. [a]Matt 17:9-13

10 They seized upon that statement, discussing with one another what rising from the dead meant.

11 They asked Him, saying, "*Why is it* that the scribes say that [a]Elijah must come first?" [a]Mal 4:5; Matt 11:14

12 And He said to them, "Elijah does first come and restore all things. And *yet* how is it written of the Son of Man that [a]He will suffer many things and be treated with contempt? [a]Matt 16:21; 26:24

13 "But I say to you that Elijah has indeed come, and they did to him whatever they wished, just as it is written of him."

All Things Possible

14 [a]When they came *back* to the disciples, they saw a large crowd around them, and *some* scribes arguing with them. [a]Matt 17:14-19; Luke 9:37-42

15 Immediately, when the entire crowd saw Him, they were [a]amazed and *began* running up to greet Him. [a]Mark 14:33; 16:5, 6

16 And He asked them, "What are you discussing with them?"

17 And one of the crowd answered Him, "Teacher, I brought You my son, possessed with a spirit which makes him mute;

18 and whenever it seizes him, it slams him *to the ground* and he foams *at the mouth,* and grinds his teeth and stiffens out. I told Your

disciples to cast it out, and they could not *do it.*"

19 And He *answered them and *said, "O unbelieving generation, how long shall I be with you? How long shall I put up with you? Bring him to Me!"

20 They brought the boy to Him. When he saw Him, immediately the spirit threw him into a convulsion, and falling to the ground, he *began* rolling around and foaming *at the mouth.*

21 And He asked his father, "How long has this been happening to him?" And he said, "From childhood.

22 "It has often thrown him both into the fire and into the water to destroy him. But if You can do anything, take pity on us and help us!"

23 And Jesus said to him, " 'If You can?' ᵃAll things are possible to him who believes."
ᵃMatt 17:20; John 11:40

24 Immediately the boy's father cried out and said, "I do believe; help my unbelief."

25 When Jesus saw that ᵃa crowd was rapidly gathering, He rebuked the unclean spirit, saying to it, "You deaf and mute spirit, I command you, come out of him and do not enter him again." ᵃMark 9:15

26 After crying out and throwing him into terrible convulsions, it came out; and *the boy* became so much like a corpse that most *of them* said, "He is dead!"

27 But Jesus took him by the hand and raised him; and he got up.

28 When He came ᵃinto *the* house, His disciples *began* questioning Him privately, "Why could we not drive it out?" ᵃMark 2:1; 7:17

29 And He said to them, "This kind cannot come out by anything but prayer."

Death and Resurrection Foretold

30 ᵃFrom there they went out and *began* to go through Galilee, and He did not want anyone to know *about it.* ᵃMatt 17:22, 23; Luke 9:43-45

31 For He was teaching His disciples and telling them, "ᵃThe Son of Man is to be delivered into the hands of men, and they will kill Him; and when He has been killed, He will rise three days later." ᵃMatt 16:21; Mark 8:31

32 But ᵃthey did not understand *this* statement, and they were afraid to ask Him. ᵃLuke 2:50; 9:45

33 ᵃThey came to Capernaum; and when He was in the house, He *began* to question them, "What were you discussing on the way?"
ᵃMatt 18:1-5; Luke 9:46-48

34 But they kept silent, for on the way ᵃthey had discussed with one another which *of them was* the greatest. ᵃMatt 18:4; Mark 9:50

35 Sitting down, He called the twelve and *said to them, "ᵃIf anyone wants to be first, he

shall be last of all and servant of all."
ᵃMatt 20:26; 23:11

36 Taking a child, He set him before them, and taking him in His arms, He said to them,

37 "ᵃWhoever receives one child like this in My name receives Me; and whoever receives Me does not receive Me, but Him who sent Me." ᵃMatt 10:40; Luke 10:16

Dire Warnings

38 ᵃJohn said to Him, "Teacher, we saw someone casting out demons in Your name, and we tried to prevent him because he was not following us." ᵃLuke 9:49, 50

39 But Jesus said, "Do not hinder him, for there is no one who will perform a miracle in My name, and be able soon afterward to speak evil of Me.

40 "ᵃFor he who is not against us is for us.
ᵃMatt 12:30; Luke 11:23

41 "For ᵃwhoever gives you a cup of water to drink because of your name as *followers* of Christ, truly I say to you, he will not lose his reward. ᵃMatt 10:42

42 "ᵃWhoever causes one of these little ones who believe to stumble, it would be better for him if, with a heavy millstone hung around his neck, he had been cast into the sea. ᵃMatt 18:6; Luke 17:2

43 "ᵃIf your hand causes you to stumble, cut it off; it is better for you to enter life crippled, than, having your two hands, to go into hell, into the ᵇunquenchable fire, ᵃMatt 5:30 ᵇMatt 3:12

44 [where THEIR WORM DOES NOT DIE, AND THE FIRE IS NOT QUENCHED.]

45 "If your foot causes you to stumble, cut it off; it is better for you to enter life lame, than, having your two feet, to be cast into ᵃhell,
ᵃMatt 5:22

46 [where THEIR WORM DOES NOT DIE, AND THE FIRE IS NOT QUENCHED.]

47 "ᵃIf your eye causes you to stumble, throw it out; it is better for you to enter the kingdom of God with one eye, than, having two eyes, to be cast into hell, ᵃMatt 5:29; 18:9

48 ᵃwhere THEIR WORM DOES NOT DIE, AND ᵇTHE FIRE IS NOT QUENCHED. ᵃIs 66:24 ᵇMatt 3:12

49 "For everyone will be salted with fire.

50 "Salt is good; but ᵃif the salt becomes unsalty, with what will you make it salty *again?* Have salt in yourselves, and be at peace with one another." ᵃMatt 5:13; Luke 14:34f

Jesus' Teaching about Divorce

10 ᵃGetting up, He *went from there to the region of Judea and beyond the Jordan; crowds *gathered around Him again, and, according to His custom, He once more *began* to teach them. ᵃMatt 19:1-9

2 *Some* Pharisees came up to Jesus, testing Him, and *began* to question Him whether it was lawful for a man to divorce a wife.

3 And He answered and said to them, "What did Moses command you?"

4 They said, "ᵃMoses permitted *a man* TO WRITE A CERTIFICATE OF DIVORCE AND SEND *her* AWAY." ᵃ*Deut 24:1, 3; Matt 5:31*

5 But Jesus said to them, "ᵃBecause of your hardness of heart he wrote you this commandment. ᵃ*Matt 19:8*

6 "But ᵃfrom the beginning of creation, *God* ᵇMADE THEM MALE AND FEMALE. ᵃ*Mark 13:19* ᵇ*Gen 1:27*

7 "ᵃFOR THIS REASON A MAN SHALL LEAVE HIS FATHER AND MOTHER, ᵃ*Gen 2:24*

8 ᵃAND THE TWO SHALL BECOME ONE FLESH; SO they are no longer two, but one flesh. ᵃ*Gen 2:24*

9 "What therefore God has joined together, let no man separate."

10 In the house the disciples *began* questioning Him about this again.

11 And He *said to them, "ᵃWhoever divorces his wife and marries another woman commits adultery against her; ᵃ*Matt 5:32*

12 and ᵃif she herself divorces her husband and marries another man, she is committing adultery." ᵃ*1 Cor 7:11, 13*

Jesus Blesses Little Children

13 ᵃAnd they were bringing children to Him so that He might touch them; but the disciples rebuked them. ᵃ*Matt 19:13-15; Luke 18:15-17*

14 But when Jesus saw this, He was indignant and said to them, "Permit the children to come to Me; do not hinder them; ᵃfor the kingdom of God belongs to such as these. ᵃ*Matt 5:3*

15 "Truly I say to you, ᵃwhoever does not receive the kingdom of God like a child will not enter it *at all*." ᵃ*Matt 18:3; 19:14*

16 And He ᵃtook them in His arms and *began* blessing them, laying His hands on them. ᵃ*Mark 9:36*

The Rich Young Ruler

17 ᵃAs He was setting out on a journey, a man ran up to Him and knelt before Him, and asked Him, "Good Teacher, what shall I do to ᵇinherit eternal life?" ᵃ*Matt 19:16-30* ᵇ*Matt 25:34*

18 And Jesus said to him, "Why do you call Me good? No one is good except God alone.

19 "You know the commandments, 'ᵃDO NOT MURDER, DO NOT COMMIT ADULTERY, DO not STEAL, DO NOT BEAR FALSE WITNESS, DO not defraud, HONOR YOUR FATHER AND MOTHER.' " ᵃ*Ex 20:12-16; Deut 5:16-20*

20 And he said to Him, "Teacher, I have kept ᵃall these things from my youth up." ᵃ*Matt 19:20*

21 Looking at him, Jesus felt a love for him and said to him, "One thing you lack: go and sell all you possess and give to the poor, and you will have ᵃtreasure in heaven; and come, follow Me." ᵃ*Matt 6:20*

22 But at these words he was saddened, and he went away grieving, for he was one who owned much property.

23 And Jesus, looking around, *said to His disciples, "ᵃHow hard it will be for those who are wealthy to enter the kingdom of God!" ᵃ*Matt 19:23*

24 The disciples ᵃwere amazed at His words. But Jesus *answered again and *said to them, "Children, how hard it is to enter the kingdom of God! ᵃ*Mark 1:27*

25 "ᵃIt is easier for a camel to go through the eye of a needle than for a rich man to enter the kingdom of God." ᵃ*Matt 19:24*

26 They were even more astonished and said to Him, "Then who can be saved?"

27 Looking at them, Jesus *said, "ᵃWith people it is impossible, but not with God; for all things are possible with God." ᵃ*Matt 19:26*

28 ᵃPeter began to say to Him, "Behold, we have left everything and followed You." ᵃ*Matt 4:20-22*

29 Jesus said, "Truly I say to you, ᵃthere is no one who has left house or brothers or sisters or mother or father or children or farms, for My sake and for the gospel's sake, ᵃ*Matt 6:33; 19:29*

30 but that he will receive a hundred times as much now in the present age, houses and brothers and sisters and mothers and children and farms, along with persecutions; and in ᵃthe age to come, eternal life. ᵃ*Matt 12:32*

31 "But ᵃmany *who are* first will be last, and the last, first." ᵃ*Matt 19:30; 20:16*

Jesus' Sufferings Foretold

32 ᵃThey were on the road going up to Jerusalem, and Jesus was walking on ahead of them; and they were amazed, and those who followed were fearful. And again He took the twelve aside and began to tell them what was going to happen to Him, ᵃ*Matt 20:17-19; Luke 18:31-33*

33 *saying,* "Behold, we are going up to Jerusalem, and ᵃthe Son of Man will be delivered to the chief priests and the scribes; and they will condemn Him to death and will hand Him over to the Gentiles. ᵃ*Mark 8:31; 9:12*

34 "They will mock Him and ᵃspit on Him, and scourge Him and kill *Him,* and three days later He will rise again." ᵃ*Matt 16:21; 26:67*

35 ᵃJames and John, the two sons of Zebedee, *came up to Jesus, saying, "Teacher, we want You to do for us whatever we ask of You." ᵃ*Matt 20:20-28*

36 And He said to them, "What do you want Me to do for you?"

37 They said to Him, "Grant that we ᵃmay sit,

one on Your right and one on *Your* left, in Your glory." [a]*Matt 19:28*

38 But Jesus said to them, "You do not know what you are asking. Are you able [a]to drink the cup that I drink, or to be baptized with the baptism with which I am baptized?" [a]*Matt 20:22*

39 They said to Him, "We are able." And Jesus said to them, "The cup that I drink [a]you shall drink; and you shall be baptized with the baptism with which I am baptized. [a]*Acts 12:2; Rev 1:9*

40 "But to sit on My right or on *My* left, this is not Mine to give; [a]but it is for those for whom it has been prepared." [a]*Matt 13:11*

41 [a]Hearing *this,* the ten began to feel indignant with James and John. [a]*Mark 10:42-45; Luke 22:25-27*

42 Calling them to Himself, Jesus *said to them, "You know that those who are recognized as rulers of the Gentiles lord it over them; and their great men exercise authority over them.

43 "But it is not this way among you, [a]but whoever wishes to become great among you shall be your servant; [a]*Matt 20:26; 23:11*

44 and whoever wishes to be first among you shall be slave of all.

45 "For even the Son of Man [a]did not come to be served, but to serve, and to give His life a ransom for many." [a]*Matt 20:28*

Bartimaeus Receives His Sight

46 [a]Then they *came to Jericho. And as He was leaving Jericho with His disciples and a large crowd, a blind beggar *named* Bartimaeus, the son of Timaeus, was sitting by the road. [a]*Matt 20:29-34; Luke 18:35-43*

47 When he heard that it was Jesus the Nazarene, he began to cry out and say, "Jesus, [a]Son of David, have mercy on me!" [a]*Matt 9:27*

48 Many were sternly telling him to be quiet, but he kept crying out all the more, "[a]Son of David, have mercy on me!" [a]*Matt 9:27*

49 And Jesus stopped and said, "Call him *here.*" So they *called the blind man, saying to him, "[a]Take courage, stand up! He is calling for you." [a]*Matt 9:2*

50 Throwing aside his cloak, he jumped up and came to Jesus.

51 And answering him, Jesus said, "What do you want Me to do for you?" And the blind man said to Him, "[a]Rabboni, *I want* to regain my sight!" [a]*Matt 23:7; John 20:16*

52 And Jesus said to him, "Go; [a]your faith has made you well." Immediately he regained his sight and *began* following Him on the road. [a]*Matt 9:22*

The Triumphal Entry

11 [a]As they *approached Jerusalem, at Bethphage and Bethany, near the Mount

of Olives, He *sent two of His disciples, [a]*Matt 21:1-9; Luke 19:29-38*

2 and *said to them, "Go into the village opposite you, and immediately as you enter it, you will find a colt tied *there,* on which no one yet has ever sat; untie it and bring it *here.*

3 "If anyone says to you, 'Why are you doing this?' you say, 'The Lord has need of it'; and immediately he will send it back here."

4 They went away and found a colt tied at the door, outside in the street; and they *untied it.

5 Some of the bystanders were saying to them, "What are you doing, untying the colt?"

6 They spoke to them just as Jesus had told *them,* and they gave them permission.

7 [a]They *brought the colt to Jesus and put their coats on it; and He sat on it. [a]*Matt 21:4-9; Luke 19:35-38*

8 And many spread their coats in the road, and others *spread* leafy branches which they had cut from the fields.

9 Those who went in front and those who followed were shouting:
"Hosanna!
[a]BLESSED IS HE WHO COMES IN THE NAME OF
THE LORD; [a]*Ps 118:26; Matt 21:9*

10 Blessed *is* the coming kingdom of our father David;
Hosanna [a]in the highest!" [a]*Matt 21:9*

11 [a]Jesus entered Jerusalem *and came* into the temple; and after looking around at everything, [b]He left for Bethany with the twelve, since it was already late. [a]*Matt 21:12* [b]*Matt 21:17*

12 [a]On the next day, when they had left Bethany, He became hungry. [a]*Matt 21:18-22*

13 Seeing at a distance a fig tree in leaf, He went *to see* if perhaps He would find anything on it; and when He came to it, He found nothing but leaves, for it was not the season for figs.

14 He said to it, "May no one ever eat fruit from you again!" And His disciples were listening.

Jesus Drives Money Changers from the Temple

15 [a]Then they *came to Jerusalem. And He entered the temple and began to drive out those who were buying and selling in the temple, and overturned the tables of the money changers and the seats of those who were selling doves; [a]*John 2:13-16*

16 and He would not permit anyone to carry merchandise through the temple.

17 And He *began* to teach and say to them, "Is it not written, '[a]MY HOUSE SHALL BE CALLED A HOUSE OF PRAYER FOR ALL THE NATIONS'? [b]But you have made it a ROBBERS' DEN." [a]*Is 56:7* [b]*Jer 7:11*

18 The chief priests and the scribes heard *this,* and [a]*began* seeking how to destroy Him; for

they were afraid of Him, for the whole crowd was astonished at His teaching. [a]Matt 21:46; Mark 12:12

19 [a]When evening came, they would go out of the city. [a]Matt 21:17; Mark 11:11

20 [a]As they were passing by in the morning, they saw the fig tree withered from the roots up. [a]Matt 21:19-22

21 Being reminded, Peter *said to Him, "[a]Rabbi, look, the fig tree which You cursed has withered." [a]Matt 23:7

22 And Jesus *answered saying to them, "[a]Have faith in God. [a]Matt 17:20; 21:21f

23 "[a]Truly I say to you, whoever says to this mountain, 'Be taken up and cast into the sea,' and does not doubt in his heart, but believes that what he says is going to happen, it will be granted him. [a]Matt 17:20; 1 Cor 13:2

24 "Therefore I say to you, [a]all things for which you pray and ask, believe that you have received them, and they will be granted you. [a]Matt 7:7f

25 "Whenever you stand praying, [a]forgive, if you have anything against anyone, so that your Father who is in heaven will also forgive you your transgressions. [a]Matt 6:14

26 ["[a]But if you do not forgive, neither will your Father who is in heaven forgive your transgressions."] [a]Matt 6:15; 18:35

Jesus' Authority Questioned

27 They *came again to Jerusalem. [a]And as He was walking in the temple, the chief priests and the scribes and the elders *came to Him, [a]Matt 21:23-27; Luke 20:1-8

28 and began saying to Him, "By what authority are You doing these things, or who gave You this authority to do these things?"

29 And Jesus said to them, "I will ask you one question, and you answer Me, and then I will tell you by what authority I do these things.

30 "Was the baptism of John from heaven, or from men? Answer Me."

31 They began reasoning among themselves, saying, "If we say, 'From heaven,' He will say, 'Then why did you not believe him?'

32 "But shall we say, 'From men'?"—they were afraid of the people, for everyone considered John to have been a real prophet.

33 Answering Jesus, they *said, "We do not know." And Jesus *said to them, "Nor will I tell you by what authority I do these things."

Parable of the Vine-growers

12 And He began to speak to them in parables: "[a]A man PLANTED A VINEYARD AND PUT A WALL AROUND IT, AND DUG A VAT UNDER THE WINE PRESS AND BUILT A TOWER, and rented it out to vine-growers and went on a journey. [a]Matt 21:33-46; Luke 20:9-19

2 "At the harvest time he sent a slave to the vine-growers, in order to receive some of the produce of the vineyard from the vine-growers.

3 "They took him, and beat him and sent him away empty-handed.

4 "Again he sent them another slave, and they wounded him in the head, and treated him shamefully.

5 "And he sent another, and that one they killed; and so with many others, beating some and killing others.

6 "He had one more to send, a beloved son; he sent him last of all to them, saying, 'They will respect my son.'

7 "But those vine-growers said to one another, 'This is the heir; come, let us kill him, and the inheritance will be ours!'

8 "They took him, and killed him and threw him out of the vineyard.

9 "What will the owner of the vineyard do? He will come and destroy the vine-growers, and will give the vineyard to others.

10 "Have you not even read this Scripture:
'[a]THE STONE WHICH THE BUILDERS REJECTED,
THIS BECAME THE CHIEF CORNER stone;
[a]Ps 118:22

11 [a]THIS CAME ABOUT FROM THE LORD,
AND IT IS MARVELOUS IN OUR EYES'?"
[a]Ps 118:23

12 And they were seeking to seize Him, and yet they feared the people, for they understood that He spoke the parable against them. And so [a]they left Him and went away. [a]Matt 22:22

Jesus Answers the Pharisees, Sadducees and Scribes

13 [a]Then they *sent some of the Pharisees and Herodians to Him in order to [b]trap Him in a statement. [a]Matt 22:15-22 [b]Luke 11:54

14 They *came and *said to Him, "Teacher, we know that You are truthful and defer to no one; for You are not partial to any, but teach the way of God in truth. Is it lawful to pay a poll-tax to Caesar, or not?

15 "Shall we pay or shall we not pay?" But He, knowing their hypocrisy, said to them, "Why are you testing Me? Bring Me a denarius to look at."

16 They brought one. And He *said to them, "Whose likeness and inscription is this?" And they said to Him, "Caesar's."

17 And Jesus said to them, "[a]Render to Caesar the things that are Caesar's, and to God the things that are God's." And they were amazed at Him. [a]Matt 22:21

18 [a]Some Sadducees (who say that there is no resurrection) *came to Jesus, and began questioning Him, saying, "[a]Matt 22:23-33; Luke 20:27-38;

19 "Teacher, Moses wrote for us that [a]IF A MAN'S BROTHER DIES and leaves behind a wife

AND LEAVES NO CHILD, HIS BROTHER SHOULD MARRY THE WIFE AND RAISE UP CHILDREN TO HIS BROTHER. ªDeut 25:5

20 "There were seven brothers; and the first took a wife, and died leaving no children.

21 "The second one married her, and died leaving behind no children; and the third likewise;

22 and so all seven left no children. Last of all the woman died also.

23 "In the resurrection, when they rise again, which one's wife will she be? For all seven had married her."

24 Jesus said to them, "Is this not the reason you are mistaken, that you do not understand the Scriptures or the power of God?

25 "For when they rise from the dead, they neither marry nor are given in marriage, but are like angels in heaven.

26 "But regarding the fact that the dead rise again, have you not read in the book of Moses, ªin the passage about the burning bush, how God spoke to him, saying, ᵇI AM THE GOD OF ABRAHAM, AND THE GOD OF ISAAC, and the God of Jacob'? ªLuke 20:37 ᵇEx 3:6

27 "ªHe is not the God of the dead, but of the living; you are greatly mistaken." ªMatt 22:32; Luke 20:38

28 ªOne of the scribes came and heard them arguing, and recognizing that He had answered them well, asked Him, "What commandment is the foremost of all?" ªLuke 10:25-28; 20:39f

29 Jesus answered, "The foremost is, 'ªHEAR, O ISRAEL! THE LORD OUR GOD IS ONE LORD; ªDeut 6:4

30 ªAND YOU SHALL LOVE THE LORD YOUR GOD WITH ALL YOUR HEART, AND WITH ALL YOUR SOUL, AND WITH ALL YOUR MIND, AND WITH ALL YOUR STRENGTH.' ªDeut 6:5

31 "The second is this, 'ªYOU SHALL LOVE YOUR NEIGHBOR AS YOURSELF.' There is no other commandment greater than these." ªLev 19:18

32 The scribe said to Him, "Right, Teacher; You have truly stated that ªHE IS ONE, AND THERE IS NO ONE ELSE BESIDES HIM; ªDeut 4:35

33 ªAND TO LOVE HIM WITH ALL THE HEART AND WITH ALL THE UNDERSTANDING AND WITH ALL THE STRENGTH, AND TO LOVE ONE'S NEIGHBOR AS HIMSELF, ᵇis much more than all burnt offerings and sacrifices." ªDeut 6:5 ᵇ1 Sam 15:22

34 When Jesus saw that he had answered intelligently, He said to him, "You are not far from the kingdom of God." ªAfter that, no one would venture to ask Him any more questions. ªMatt 22:46

35 ªAnd Jesus began to say, as He taught in the temple, "How is it that the scribes say that the Christ is the son of David? ªMatt 22:41-46; Luke 20:41-44

36 "David himself said in the Holy Spirit,

'ªTHE LORD SAID TO MY LORD,
"SIT AT MY RIGHT HAND,
UNTIL I PUT YOUR ENEMIES BENEATH YOUR FEET."' ªPs 110:1

37 "David himself calls Him 'Lord'; so in what sense is He his son?" And ªthe large crowd enjoyed listening to Him. ªJohn 12:9

38 ªIn His teaching He was saying: "Beware of the scribes who like to walk around in long robes, and like respectful greetings in the market places, ªMatt 23:1-7; Luke 20:45-47

39 and chief seats in the synagogues and places of honor at banquets,

40 ªwho devour widows' houses, and for appearance's sake offer long prayers; these will receive greater condemnation." ªLuke 20:47

The Widow's Mite

41 ªAnd He sat down opposite the treasury, and began observing how the people were putting money into the treasury; and many rich people were putting in large sums. ªLuke 21:1-4

42 A poor widow came and put in two small copper coins, which amount to a cent.

43 Calling His disciples to Him, He said to them, "Truly I say to you, this poor widow put in more than all the contributors to the treasury;

44 for they all put in out of their surplus, but she, out of her poverty, put in all she owned, all she had ªto live on." ªLuke 8:43; 15:12, 30

Things to Come

13 ªAs He was going out of the temple, one of His disciples ✱said to Him, "Teacher, behold what wonderful stones and what wonderful buildings!" ªMatt 24; Luke 21:5-36

2 And Jesus said to him, "Do you see these great buildings? ªNot one stone will be left upon another which will not be torn down." ªLuke 19:44

3 As He was sitting on ªthe Mount of Olives opposite the temple, Peter and James and John and Andrew were questioning Him privately, ªMatt 21:1

4 "Tell us, when will these things be, and what will be the sign when all these things are going to be fulfilled?"

5 And Jesus began to say to them, "See to it that no one misleads you.

6 "Many will come in My name, saying, 'ªI am He!' and will mislead many. ªJohn 8:24

7 "When you hear of wars and rumors of wars, do not be frightened; those things must take place; but that is not yet the end.

8 "For nation will rise up against nation, and kingdom against kingdom; there will be earthquakes in various places; there will also be famines. These things are merely the beginning of birth pangs.

9 "But be on your guard; for they will ^adeliver you to *the* courts, and you will be flogged ^ain *the* synagogues, and you will stand before governors and kings for My sake, as a testimony to them. ^a*Matt 10:17*

10 "^aThe gospel must first be preached to all the nations. ^a*Matt 24:14*

11 "^aWhen they arrest you and hand you over, do not worry beforehand about what you are to say, but say whatever is given you in that hour; for it is not you who speak, but *it is* the Holy Spirit. ^a*Matt 10:19-22; Luke 21:12-17*

12 "Brother will betray brother to death, and a father *his* child; and children will rise up against parents and have them put to death.

13 "^aYou will be hated by all because of My name, but the one who endures to the end, he will be saved. ^a*Matt 10:22; John 15:21*

14 "But ^awhen you see the ^bABOMINATION OF DESOLATION standing where it should not be (let the reader understand), then those who are in Judea must flee to the mountains. ^a*Matt 24:15f* ^b*Dan 9:27*

15 "^aThe one who is on the housetop must not go down, or go in to get anything out of his house; ^a*Luke 17:31*

16 and the one who is in the field must not turn back to get his coat.

17 "But woe to those who are pregnant and to those who are nursing babies in those days!

18 "But pray that it may not happen in the winter.

19 "For those days will be a *time of* tribulation such as has not occurred ^asince the beginning of the creation which God created until now, and never will. ^a*Dan 12:1; Mark 10:6*

20 "Unless the Lord had shortened *those* days, no life would have been saved; but for the sake of the elect, whom He chose, He shortened the days.

21 "And then if anyone says to you, 'Behold, here is the Christ'; or, 'Behold, *He is* there'; do not believe *him;*

22 for false Christs and false prophets will arise, and will show ^asigns and wonders, in order to lead astray, if possible, the elect. ^a*Matt 24:24; John 4:48*

23 "But take heed; behold, I have told you everything in advance.

The Return of Christ

24 "But in those days, after that tribulation, ^aTHE SUN WILL BE DARKENED AND THE MOON WILL NOT GIVE ITS LIGHT, ^a*Is 13:10; Ezek 32:7*

25 ^aAND THE STARS WILL BE FALLING from heaven, and the powers that are in the heavens will be shaken. ^a*Is 34:4; Rev 6:13*

26 "Then they will see ^aTHE SON OF MAN COMING IN CLOUDS with great power and glory. ^a*Dan 7:13; Rev 1:7*

27 "And then He will send forth the angels, and ^awill gather together His elect from the four winds, from the farthest end of the earth to the farthest end of heaven. ^a*Deut 30:4*

28 "Now learn the parable from the fig tree: when its branch has already become tender and puts forth its leaves, you know that summer is near.

29 "Even so, you too, when you see these things happening, recognize that He is near, *right* at the door.

30 "Truly I say to you, this generation will not pass away until all these things take place.

31 "Heaven and earth will pass away, but My words will not pass away.

32 "^aBut of that day or hour no one knows, not even the angels in heaven, nor the Son, but the Father *alone.* ^a*Matt 24:36; Acts 1:7*

33 "Take heed, ^akeep on the alert; for you do not know when the *appointed* time will come. ^a*Eph 6:18; Col 4:2*

34 "^a*It is* like a man away on a journey, *who* upon leaving his house and putting his slaves in charge, *assigning* to each one his task, also commanded the doorkeeper to stay on the alert. ^a*Luke 12:36-38*

35 "Therefore, be on the alert—for you do not know when the master of the house is coming, whether in the evening, at midnight, or ^awhen the rooster crows, or in the morning— ^a*Mark 14:30*

36 in case he should come suddenly and find you ^aasleep. ^a*Rom 13:11*

37 "What I say to you I say to all, '^aBe on the alert!' " ^a*Matt 24:42; Mark 13:35*

Death Plot and Anointing

14 ^aNow the Passover and Unleavened Bread were two days away; and the chief priests and the scribes were seeking how to seize Him by stealth and kill *Him;* ^a*Matt 26:2-5; Luke 22:1, 2*

2 for they were saying, "Not during the festival, otherwise there might be a riot of the people."

3 ^aWhile He was in Bethany at the home of Simon the leper, and reclining *at the table,* there came a woman with an alabaster vial of very costly perfume of pure nard; *and* she broke the vial and poured it over His head. ^a*Luke 7:37-39; John 12:1-8*

4 But some were indignantly *remarking* to one another, "Why has this perfume been wasted?

5 "For this perfume might have been sold for over three hundred denarii, and *the money* given to the poor." And they were scolding her.

6 But Jesus said, "Let her alone; why do you bother her? She has done a good deed to Me.

7 "For you always have ᵃthe poor with you, and whenever you wish you can do good to them; but you do not always have Me.
ᵃDeut 15:11; Matt 26:11

8 "She has done what she could; ᵃshe has anointed My body beforehand for the burial.
ᵃJohn 19:40

9 "Truly I say to you, ᵃwherever the gospel is preached in the whole world, what this woman has done will also be spoken of in memory of her." ᵃMatt 26:13

10 ᵃThen Judas Iscariot, who was one of the twelve, went off to the chief priests in order to betray Him to them. ᵃMatt 26:14-16; Luke 22:3-6

11 They were glad when they heard this, and promised to give him money. And he began seeking how to betray Him at an opportune time.

The Last Passover

12 ᵃOn the first day of Unleavened Bread, when the Passover lamb was being sacrificed, His disciples *said to Him, "Where do You want us to go and prepare for You to eat the Passover?" ᵃMatt 26:17-19; Luke 22:7-13

13 And He *sent two of His disciples and *said to them, "Go into the city, and a man will meet you carrying a pitcher of water; follow him;

14 and wherever he enters, say to the owner of the house, 'The Teacher says, "Where is My ᵃguest room in which I may eat the Passover with My disciples?" ' ᵃLuke 22:11

15 "And he himself will show you a large upper room furnished and ready; prepare for us there."

16 The disciples went out and came to the city, and found it just as He had told them; and they prepared the Passover.

17 ᵃWhen it was evening He *came with the twelve. ᵃJohn 13:18ff

18 As they were reclining at the table and eating, Jesus said, "Truly I say to you that one of you will betray Me—one who is eating with Me."

19 They began to be grieved and to say to Him one by one, "Surely not I?"

20 And He said to them, "It is one of the twelve, one who dips with Me in the bowl.

21 "For the Son of Man is to go just as it is written of Him; but woe to that man by whom the Son of Man is betrayed! It would have been good for that man if he had not been born."

The Lord's Supper

22 ᵃWhile they were eating, He took some bread, and after a blessing He broke it, and gave it to them, and said, "Take it; this is My body." ᵃMark 10:16

23 And when He had taken a cup and given thanks, He gave it to them, and they all drank from it.

24 And He said to them, "This is My ᵃblood of the covenant, which is poured out for many.
ᵃEx 24:8

25 "Truly I say to you, I will never again drink of the fruit of the vine until that day when I drink it new in the kingdom of God."

26 ᵃAfter singing a hymn, they went out to the Mount of Olives. ᵃMatt 26:30

27 ᵃAnd Jesus *said to them, "You will all fall away, because it is written, ᵇI WILL STRIKE DOWN THE SHEPHERD, AND THE SHEEP SHALL BE SCATTERED.' ᵃMatt 26:31-35 ᵇZech 13:7

28 "But after I have been raised, ᵃI will go ahead of you to Galilee." ᵃMatt 28:16

29 But Peter said to Him, "Even though all may fall away, yet I will not."

30 And Jesus *said to him, "Truly I say to you, that ᵃthis very night, before ᵇa rooster crows twice, you yourself will deny Me three times." ᵃMatt 26:34 ᵇMark 14:68, 72

31 But Peter kept saying insistently, "Even if I have to die with You, I will not deny You!" And they all were saying the same thing also.

Jesus in Gethsemane

32 ᵃThey *came to a place named Gethsemane; and He *said to His disciples, "Sit here until I have prayed." ᵃMatt 26:36-46; Luke 22:40-46

33 And He *took with Him Peter and James and John, and began to be very ᵃdistressed and troubled. ᵃMark 9:15; 16:5, 6

34 And He *said to them, "ᵃMy soul is deeply grieved to the point of death; remain here and keep watch." ᵃMatt 26:38; John 12:27

35 And He went a little beyond them, and fell to the ground and began to pray that if it were possible, ᵃthe hour might pass Him by.
ᵃMatt 26:45; Mark 14:41

36 And He was saying, "ᵃAbba! Father! All things are possible for You; remove this cup from Me; ᵇyet not what I will, but what You will." ᵃRom 8:15 ᵇMatt 26:39

37 And He *came and *found them sleeping, and *said to Peter, "Simon, are you asleep? Could you not keep watch for one hour?

38 "ᵃKeep watching and praying that you may not come into temptation; the spirit is willing, but the flesh is weak." ᵃMatt 26:41

39 Again He went away and prayed, saying the same words.

40 And again He came and found them sleeping, for their eyes were very heavy; and they did not know what to answer Him.

41 And He *came the third time, and *said to them, "Are you still sleeping and resting? It is enough; ᵃthe hour has come; behold, the Son of

Man is being betrayed into the hands of sinners. ªMark 14:35

42 "Get up, let us be going; behold, the one who betrays Me is at hand!"

Betrayal and Arrest

43 ªImmediately while He was still speaking, Judas, one of the twelve, *came up accompanied by a crowd with swords and clubs, *who were* from the chief priests and the scribes and the elders. ªMatt 26:47-56; Luke 22:47-53

44 Now he who was betraying Him had given them a signal, saying, "Whomever I kiss, He is the one; seize Him and lead Him away under guard."

45 After coming, Judas immediately went to Him, saying, "ªRabbi!" and kissed Him. ªMatt 23:7

46 They laid hands on Him and seized Him.

47 But one of those who stood by drew his sword, and struck the slave of the high priest and cut off his ear.

48 And Jesus said to them, "Have you come out with swords and clubs to arrest Me, as *you would* against a robber?

49 "Every day I was with you ªin the temple teaching, and you did not seize Me; but *this has taken place* to fulfill the Scriptures." ªMark 12:35; Luke 19:47

50 And they all left Him and fled.

51 A young man was following Him, wearing *nothing but* a linen sheet over *his* naked *body;* and they *seized him.

52 But he pulled free of the linen sheet and escaped naked.

Jesus before His Accusers

53 ªThey led Jesus away to the high priest; and all the chief priests and the elders and the scribes *gathered together. ªMatt 26:57-68; John 18:12f, 19-24

54 Peter had followed Him at a distance, right into the courtyard of the high priest; and he was sitting with the officers and ªwarming himself at the fire. ªMark 14:67; John 18:18

55 Now the chief priests and the whole ªCouncil kept trying to obtain testimony against Jesus to put Him to death, and they were not finding any. ªMatt 5:22

56 For many were giving false testimony against Him, but their testimony was not consistent.

57 Some stood up and *began* to give false testimony against Him, saying,

58 "We heard Him say, 'ªI will destroy this temple made with hands, and in three days I will build another made without hands.' " ªMatt 26:61; Mark 15:29

59 Not even in this respect was their testimony consistent.

60 The high priest stood up *and came* forward

and questioned Jesus, saying, "Do You not answer? What is it that these men are testifying against You?"

61 But He kept silent and did not answer. ªAgain the high priest was questioning Him, and saying to Him, "Are You the Christ, the Son of the Blessed *One?*" ªMatt 26:63ff; Luke 22:67-71

62 And Jesus said, "I am; and you shall see ªTHE SON OF MAN SITTING AT THE RIGHT HAND OF POWER, and ᵇCOMING WITH THE CLOUDS OF HEAVEN." ªPs 110:1 ᵇDan 7:13

63 ªTearing his clothes, the high priest *said, "What further need do we have of witnesses? ªNum 14:6; Matt 26:65

64 "You have heard the ªblasphemy; how does it seem to you?" And they all condemned Him to be deserving of death. ªLev 24:16

65 Some began to ªspit at Him, and to blindfold Him, and to beat Him with their fists, and to say to Him, "ᵇProphesy!" And the officers received Him with slaps *in the face.* ªMatt 26:67 ᵇLuke 22:64

Peter's Denials

66 ªAs Peter was below in the courtyard, one of the servant-girls of the high priest *came, ªMatt 26:69-75; Luke 22:56-62

67 and seeing Peter ªwarming himself, she looked at him and *said, "You also were with Jesus the ᵇNazarene." ªMark 14:54 ᵇMark 1:24

68 But he denied *it*, saying, "I neither know nor understand what you are talking about." And he went out onto the porch, and a rooster crowed.

69 The servant-girl saw him, and began once more to say to the bystanders, "This is *one* of them!"

70 But again he denied it. And after a little while the bystanders were again saying to Peter, "Surely you are *one* of them, ªfor you are a Galilean too." ªMatt 26:73; Luke 22:59

71 But he began to curse and swear, "I do not know this man you are talking about!"

72 Immediately a rooster crowed a second time. And Peter remembered how Jesus had made the remark to him, "Before ªa rooster crows twice, you will deny Me three times." And he began to weep. ªMark 14:30, 68

Jesus before Pilate

15 ªEarly in the morning the chief priests with the elders and scribes and the whole Council, immediately held a consultation; and binding Jesus, they led Him away and delivered Him to Pilate. ªMatt 27:1

2 ªPilate questioned Him, "Are You the King of the Jews?" And He *answered him, "*It is as* you say." ªMatt 27:11-14; Luke 23:2, 3

3 The chief priests *began* to accuse Him harshly.

4 Then Pilate questioned Him again, saying, "Do You not answer? See how many charges they bring against You!"

5 But Jesus ªmade no further answer; so Pilate was amazed. ªMatt 27:12

6 ªNow at the feast he used to release for them any one prisoner whom they requested. ªMatt 27:15-26; Luke 23:18-25

7 The man named Barabbas had been imprisoned with the insurrectionists who had committed murder in the insurrection.

8 The crowd went up and began asking him to do as he had been accustomed to do for them.

9 Pilate answered them, saying, "Do you want me to release for you the King of the Jews?"

10 For he was aware that the chief priests had handed Him over because of envy.

11 But the chief priests stirred up the crowd ªto ask him to release Barabbas for them instead. ªActs 3:14

12 Answering again, Pilate said to them, "Then what shall I do with Him whom you call the King of the Jews?"

13 They shouted back, "Crucify Him!"

14 But Pilate said to them, "Why, what evil has He done?" But they shouted all the more, "Crucify Him!"

15 Wishing to satisfy the crowd, Pilate released Barabbas for them, and after having Jesus ªscourged, he handed Him over to be crucified. ªMatt 27:26

Jesus Is Mocked

16 ªThe soldiers took Him away into the palace (that is, the Praetorium), and they *called together the whole Roman cohort. ªMatt 27:27-31

17 They *dressed Him up in purple, and after twisting a crown of thorns, they put it on Him;

18 and they began to acclaim Him, "Hail, King of the Jews!"

19 They kept beating His head with a reed, and spitting on Him, and kneeling and bowing before Him.

20 After they had mocked Him, they took the purple robe off Him and put His own garments on Him. And they *led Him out to crucify Him.

21 ªThey *pressed into service a passer-by coming from the country, Simon of Cyrene (the father of Alexander and Rufus), to bear His cross. ªMatt 27:32; Luke 23:26

The Crucifixion

22 ªThen they *brought Him to the place Golgotha, which is translated, Place of a Skull. ªMatt 27:33-44; Luke 23:33-43

23 They tried to give Him ªwine mixed with myrrh; but He did not take it. ªMatt 27:34

24 And they *crucified Him, and *ªdivided up His garments among themselves, casting lots for them to decide what each man should take. ªPs 22:18; John 19:24

25 It was the ªthird hour when they crucified Him. ªMark 15:33

26 The inscription of the charge against Him read, "ªTHE KING OF THE JEWS." ªMatt 27:37

27 They *crucified two robbers with Him, one on His right and one on His left.

28 [And the Scripture was fulfilled which says, "And He was numbered with transgressors."]

29 Those passing by were hurling abuse at Him, ªwagging their heads, and saying, "Ha! You who are going to ᵇdestroy the temple and rebuild it in three days, ªPs 22:7 ᵇMark 14:58

30 save Yourself, and come down from the cross!"

31 In the same way the chief priests also, along with the scribes, were mocking Him among themselves and saying, "ªHe saved others; He cannot save Himself. ªMatt 27:42; Luke 23:35

32 "Let this Christ, the King of Israel, now come down from the cross, so that we may see and believe!" ªThose who were crucified with Him were also insulting Him. ªMatt 27:44; Mark 15:27

33 ªWhen the sixth hour came, darkness fell over the whole land until the ninth hour. ªMatt 27:45-56; Luke 23:44-49

34 At the ninth hour Jesus cried out with a loud voice, "ªELOI, ELOI, LAMA SABACHTHANI?" which is translated, "MY GOD, MY GOD, WHY HAVE YOU FORSAKEN ME?" ªPs 22:1; Matt 27:46

35 When some of the bystanders heard it, they began saying, "Behold, He is calling for Elijah."

36 Someone ran and filled a sponge with sour wine, put it on a reed, and gave Him a drink, saying, "Let us see whether Elijah will come to take Him down."

37 ªAnd Jesus uttered a loud cry, and breathed His last. ªMatt 27:50; Luke 23:46

38 ªAnd the veil of the temple was torn in two from top to bottom. ªEx 26:31-33; Matt 27:51

39 ªWhen the centurion, who was standing right in front of Him, saw the way He breathed His last, he said, "Truly this man was the Son of God!" ªMatt 27:54; Mark 15:45

40 ªThere were also some women looking on from a distance, among whom were Mary Magdalene, and Mary the mother of James the Less and Joses, and Salome. ªLuke 23:49; John 19:25

41 When He was in Galilee, they used to follow Him and ªminister to Him; and there were

many other women who came up with Him to Jerusalem. [a]*Matt 27:55f*

Jesus Is Buried

42 [a]When evening had already come, because it was the preparation day, that is, the day before the Sabbath, [a]*Matt 27:57-61; Luke 23:50-56*
43 Joseph of Arimathea came, a [a]prominent member of the Council, who himself was waiting for the kingdom of God; and he [b]gathered up courage and went in before Pilate, and asked for the body of Jesus. [a]*Matt 27:57* [b]*John 19:38*
44 Pilate wondered if He was dead by this time, and summoning the centurion, he questioned him as to whether He was already dead.
45 And ascertaining this from [a]the centurion, he granted the body to Joseph. [a]*Mark 15:39*
46 Joseph bought a linen cloth, took Him down, wrapped Him in the linen cloth and laid Him in a tomb which had been hewn out in the rock; and he rolled a stone against the entrance of the tomb.
47 [a]Mary Magdalene and Mary the *mother* of Joses were looking on *to see* where He was laid. [a]*Matt 27:56; Mark 15:40*

The Resurrection

16 [a]When the Sabbath was over, Mary Magdalene, and Mary the *mother* of James, and Salome, bought spices, so that they might come and anoint Him. [a]*John 20:1-8*
2 Very early on the first day of the week, they *came to the tomb when the sun had risen.
3 They were saying to one another, "Who will roll away [a]the stone for us from the entrance of the tomb?" [a]*Matt 27:60; Mark 15:46*
4 Looking up, they *saw that the stone had been rolled away, although it was extremely large.
5 [a]Entering the tomb, they saw a young man sitting at the right, wearing a white robe; and they were amazed. [a]*John 20:11, 12*
6 And he *said to them, "Do not be amazed; you are looking for Jesus the Nazarene, who has been crucified. [a]He has risen; He is not here; behold, *here is* the place where they laid Him. [a]*Matt 28:6; Luke 24:6*
7 "But go, tell His disciples and Peter, '[a]He is going ahead of you to Galilee; there you will see Him, just as He told you.' " [a]*Matt 26:32; Mark 14:28*
8 They went out and fled from the tomb, for trembling and astonishment had gripped them;

and they said nothing to anyone, for they were afraid.

9 [Now after He had risen early on the first day of the week, He first appeared to [a]Mary Magdalene, from whom He had cast out seven demons. [a]*Matt 27:56; John 20:14*
10 [a]She went and reported to those who had been with Him, while they were mourning and weeping. [a]*John 20:18*
11 When they heard that He was alive and had been seen by her, [a]they refused to believe it. [a]*Matt 28:17; Luke 8:2*
12 After that, He appeared in a different form [a]to two of them while they were walking along on their way to the country. [a]*Luke 24:13-35*
13 They went away and reported it to the others, but they [a]did not believe them either. [a]*Matt 28:17; Mark 16:11, 14*

The Disciples Commissioned

14 Afterward He appeared [a]to the eleven themselves as they were reclining *at the table;* and He reproached them for their unbelief and hardness of heart, because they had not believed those who had seen Him after He had risen. [a]*Luke 24:36; John 20:19, 26*
15 And He said to them, "[a]Go into all the world and preach the gospel to all creation. [a]*Matt 28:19; Acts 1:8*
16 "[a]He who has believed and has been baptized shall be saved; but he who has disbelieved shall be condemned. [a]*John 3:18, 36; Acts 16:31*
17 "These signs will accompany those who have believed: [a]in My name they will cast out demons, they will speak with new tongues; [a]*Mark 9:38; Luke 10:17*
18 they will pick up serpents, and if they drink any deadly *poison,* it will not hurt them; they will [a]lay hands on the sick, and they will recover." [a]*Mark 5:23*
19 So then, when the Lord Jesus had spoken to them, He [a]was received up into heaven and sat down at the right hand of God. [a]*Luke 9:51; 24:51*
20 And they went out and preached everywhere, while the Lord worked with them, and confirmed the word by the signs that followed.]

[*And they promptly reported all these instructions to Peter and his companions. And after that, Jesus Himself sent out through them from east to west the sacred and imperishable proclamation of eternal salvation.*]

LUKE

Introduction

1 Inasmuch as many have undertaken to compile an account of the things ªaccomplished among us, ªRom 4:21; 14:5

2 just as they were handed down to us by those who ªfrom the beginning were ᵇeyewitnesses and servants of the word, ªJohn 15:27 ᵇ2 Pet 1:16

3 it seemed fitting for me as well, having investigated everything carefully from the beginning, to write *it* out for you in consecutive order, ªmost excellent Theophilus; ªActs 23:26; 24:3

4 so that you may know the exact truth about the things you have been ªtaught. ªActs 18:25; Rom 2:18

Birth of John the Baptist Foretold

5 In the days of Herod, king of Judea, there was a priest named Zacharias, of the ªdivision of Abijah; and he had a wife from the daughters of Aaron, and her name was Elizabeth. ª1 Chr 24:10

6 They were both righteous in the sight of God, walking ªblamelessly in all the commandments and requirements of the Lord. ªPhil 2:15; 3:6

7 But they had no child, because Elizabeth was barren, and they were both advanced in years.

8 Now it happened *that* while ªhe was performing his priestly service before God in the *appointed* order of his division, ª1 Chr 24:19; 2 Chr 8:14

9 according to the custom of the priestly office, he was chosen by lot ªto enter the temple of the Lord and burn incense. ªEx 30:7f

10 And the whole multitude of the people were in prayer ªoutside at the hour of the incense offering. ªLev 16:17

11 And ªan angel of the Lord appeared to him, standing to the right of the altar of incense. ªLuke 2:9; Acts 5:19

12 Zacharias was troubled when he saw *the angel*, and ªfear gripped him. ªLuke 2:9

13 But the angel said to him, "Do not be afraid, Zacharias, for your petition has been heard, and your wife Elizabeth will bear you a son, and ªyou will give him the name John. ªLuke 1:60, 63

14 "You will have joy and gladness, and many will rejoice at his birth.

15 "For he will be great in the sight of the Lord; and he will ªdrink no wine or liquor, and he will be filled with the Holy Spirit while yet in his mother's womb. ªNum 6:3; Judg 13:4

16 "And he will ªturn many of the sons of Israel back to the Lord their God. ªMatt 3:2, 6; Luke 3:3

17 "It is he who will go *as a forerunner* before Him in the spirit and power of Elijah, ªTO TURN THE HEARTS OF THE FATHERS BACK TO THE CHILDREN, and the disobedient to the attitude of the righteous, so as to make ready a people prepared for the Lord." ªMal 4:6

18 Zacharias said to the angel, "How will I know this *for certain*? For ªI am an old man and my wife is advanced in years." ªGen 17:17

19 The angel answered and said to him, "I am ªGabriel, who stands in the presence of God, and I have been sent to speak to you and to bring you this good news. ªDan 8:16; 9:21

20 "And behold, you shall be silent and unable to speak until the day when these things take place, because you did not believe my words, which will be fulfilled in their proper time."

21 The people were waiting for Zacharias, and were wondering at his delay in the temple.

22 But when he came out, he was unable to speak to them; and they realized that he had seen a vision in the temple; and he ªkept making signs to them, and remained mute. ªLuke 1:62

23 When the days of his priestly service were ended, he went back home.

24 After these days Elizabeth his wife became pregnant, and she kept herself in seclusion for five months, saying,

25 "This is the way the Lord has dealt with me in the days when He looked *with favor* upon *me,* to ªtake away my disgrace among men." ªGen 30:23; Is 4:1

Jesus' Birth Foretold

26 Now in the sixth month the angel Gabriel was sent from God to a city in Galilee called ªNazareth, ªMatt 2:23

27 to a virgin engaged to a man whose name was Joseph, ªof the descendants of David; and the virgin's name was Mary. ªMatt 1:16, 20; Luke 2:4

28 And coming in, he said to her, "Greetings, favored one! The Lord *is* with you."

29 But she ªwas very perplexed at *this* statement, and kept pondering what kind of salutation this was. ªLuke 1:12

30 The angel said to her, "ªDo not be afraid, Mary; for you have found favor with God. ªMatt 14:27; Luke 1:13

31 "And behold, you will conceive in your womb and bear a son, and you ªshall name Him Jesus. ªIs 7:14; Matt 1:21, 25

32 "He will be great and will be called the Son of [a]the Most High; and the Lord God will give Him [b]the throne of His father David; [a]*Mark 5:7* [b]*2 Sam 7:12, 13, 16*

33 And He will reign over the house of Jacob forever, [a]and His kingdom will have no end." [a]*2 Sam 7:13, 16; Ps 89:36, 37*

34 Mary said to the angel, "How can this be, since I am a virgin?"

35 The angel answered and said to her, "[a]The Holy Spirit will come upon you, and the power of the Most High will overshadow you; and for that reason the holy Child shall be called [b]the Son of God. [a]*Matt 1:18* [b]*Matt 4:3*

36 "And behold, even your relative Elizabeth has also conceived a son in her old age; and she who was called barren is now in her sixth month.

37 "For [a]nothing will be impossible with God." [a]*Gen 18:14; Jer 32:17*

38 And Mary said, "Behold, the bondslave of the Lord; may it be done to me according to your word." And the angel departed from her.

Mary Visits Elizabeth

39 Now at this time Mary arose and went in a hurry to [a]the hill country, to a city of Judah, [a]*Josh 20:7; 21:11*

40 and entered the house of Zacharias and greeted Elizabeth.

41 When Elizabeth heard Mary's greeting, the baby leaped in her womb; and Elizabeth was [a]filled with the Holy Spirit. [a]*Luke 1:67; Acts 2:4*

42 And she cried out with a loud voice and said, "Blessed *are* you among women, and blessed *is* the fruit of your womb!

43 "And how has it *happened* to me, that the mother of [a]my Lord would come to me? [a]*Luke 2:11*

44 "For behold, when the sound of your greeting reached my ears, the baby leaped in my womb for joy.

45 "And [a]blessed *is* she who believed that there would be a fulfillment of what had been spoken to her by the Lord." [a]*Luke 1:20, 48*

The Magnificat

46 And Mary said:
"[a]My soul [b]exalts the Lord, [a]*1 Sam 2:1-10* [b]*Ps 34:2f*

47 And [a]my spirit has rejoiced in God my Savior. [a]*Ps 35:9; Hab 3:18*

48 "For [a]He has had regard for the humble state of His bondslave;
For behold, from this time on all generations will count me blessed. [a]*Ps 138:6*

49 "For the Mighty One has done great things for me;
And holy is His name.

50 "[a]AND HIS MERCY IS UPON GENERATION AFTER GENERATION

TOWARD THOSE WHO FEAR HIM. [a]*Ps 103:17*

51 "[a]He has done mighty deeds with His arm;
He has scattered *those who were* proud in the thoughts of their heart. [a]*Ps 98:1; 118:15*

52 "He has brought down rulers from *their* thrones,
And has [a]exalted those who were humble. [a]*Job 5:11*

53 "[a]HE HAS FILLED THE HUNGRY WITH GOOD THINGS;
And sent away the rich empty-handed. [a]*Ps 107:9*

54 "He has given help to Israel His servant,
In remembrance of His mercy,

55 As He spoke to our fathers,
[a]To Abraham and his descendants forever." [a]*Gen 17:7*

56 And Mary stayed with her about three months, and *then* returned to her home.

John Is Born

57 Now the time had come for Elizabeth to give birth, and she gave birth to a son.

58 Her neighbors and her relatives heard that the Lord had [a]displayed His great mercy toward her; and they were rejoicing with her. [a]*Gen 19:19*

59 And it happened that on [a]the eighth day they came to circumcise the child, and they were going to call him Zacharias, after his father. [a]*Gen 17:12; Lev 12:3*

60 But his mother answered and said, "No indeed; but [a]he shall be called John." [a]*Luke 1:13, 63*

61 And they said to her, "There is no one among your relatives who is called by that name."

62 And they [a]made signs to his father, as to what he wanted him called. [a]*Luke 1:22*

63 And he asked for a tablet and wrote as follows, "[a]His name is John." And they were all astonished. [a]*Luke 1:13, 60*

64 [a]And at once his mouth was opened and his tongue *loosed,* and he *began* to speak in praise of God. [a]*Luke 1:20*

65 Fear came on all those living around them; and all these matters were being talked about in all [a]the hill country of Judea. [a]*Luke 1:39*

66 All who heard them kept them in mind, saying, "What then will this child *turn out to be?*" For [a]the hand of the Lord was certainly with him. [a]*Acts 11:21*

Zacharias's Prophecy

67 And his father Zacharias [a]was filled with the Holy Spirit, and prophesied, saying: [a]*Luke 1:41; Acts 2:4, 8*

68 "Blessed *be* the Lord God of Israel,
For He has visited us and accomplished [a]redemption for His people, [a]*Luke 2:38; Heb 9:12*

69 And has raised up a ᵃhorn of salvation for
   us
   In the house of David His servant—
      ᵃ*1 Sam 2:1, 10; Ps 18:2*
70 ᵃAs He spoke by the mouth of His holy
   prophets from of old— ᵃ*Rom 1:2*
71 Salvation ᵃFROM OUR ENEMIES,
   And from THE HAND OF ALL WHO HATE US;
      ᵃ*Ps 106:10*
72 To show mercy toward our fathers,
   ᵃAnd to remember His holy covenant,
      ᵃ*Ps 105:8f, 42; 106:45*
73 ᵃThe oath which He swore to Abraham
   our father, ᵃ*Gen 22:16ff; Heb 6:13*
74 To grant us that we, being rescued from
   the hand of our enemies,
   Might serve Him without fear,
75 ᵃIn holiness and righteousness before Him
   all our days. ᵃ*Eph 4:24*
76 "And you, child, will be called the prophet
   of the Most High;
   For you will go on ᵃBEFORE THE LORD TO
   PREPARE HIS WAYS; ᵃ*Mal 3:1; Matt 11:10*
77 To give to His people *the* knowledge of
   salvation
   By ᵃthe forgiveness of their sins, ᵃ*Jer 31:34;
      Mark 1:4*
78 Because of the tender mercy of our God,
   With which ᵃthe Sunrise from on high
   will visit us, ᵃ*Mal 4:2; Eph 5:14*
79 ᵃTO SHINE UPON THOSE WHO SIT IN DARKNESS
   AND THE SHADOW OF DEATH,
   To guide our feet into the way of peace."
      ᵃ*Is 9:2*
80 ᵃAnd the child continued to grow and to
become strong in spirit, and he lived in the
deserts until the day of his public appearance
to Israel. ᵃ*Luke 2:40*

Jesus' Birth in Bethlehem

2 Now in those days a decree went out from
ᵃCaesar Augustus, that a census be taken of
all the inhabited earth. ᵃ*Matt 22:17; Luke 3:1*
2 This was the first census taken while
Quirinius was governor of ᵃSyria. ᵃ*Matt 4:24*
3 And everyone was on his way to register
for the census, each to his own city.
4 Joseph also went up from Galilee, from
the city of Nazareth, to Judea, to the city of
David which is called Bethlehem, because ᵃhe
was of the house and family of David,
ᵃ*Luke 1:27*
5 in order to register along with Mary, who
was engaged to him, and was with child.
6 While they were there, the days were completed for her to give birth.
7 And she ᵃgave birth to her firstborn son;
and she wrapped Him in cloths, and laid Him
in a manger, because there was no room for
them in the inn. ᵃ*Matt 1:25*

8 In the same region there were *some* shepherds staying out in the fields and keeping
watch over their flock by night.
9 And ᵃan angel of the Lord suddenly stood
before them, and the glory of the Lord shone
around them; and they were terribly frightened.
ᵃ*Luke 1:11; Acts 5:19*
10 But the angel said to them, "ᵃDo not be
afraid; for behold, I bring you good news of
great joy which will be for all the people;
ᵃ*Matt 14:27*
11 for today in the city of David there has
been born for you a ᵃSavior, who is Christ the
Lord. ᵃ*Matt 1:21; John 4:42*
12 "ᵃThis *will be* a sign for you: you will find
a baby wrapped in cloths and lying in a manger." ᵃ*1 Sam 2:34; 2 Kin 19:29*
13 And suddenly there appeared with the
angel a multitude of the heavenly host praising
God and saying,
14 "ᵃGlory to God in the highest,
   And on earth peace among men with
      whom He is pleased." ᵃ*Matt 21:9;
         Luke 19:38*
15 When the angels had gone away from them
into heaven, the shepherds *began* saying to one
another, "Let us go straight to Bethlehem then,
and see this thing that has happened which the
Lord has made known to us."
16 So they came in a hurry and found their
way to Mary and Joseph, and the baby as He
lay in the manger.
17 When they had seen this, they made known
the statement which had been told them about
this Child.
18 And all who heard it wondered at the
things which were told them by the shepherds.
19 But Mary ᵃtreasured all these things, pondering them in her heart. ᵃ*Luke 2:51*
20 The shepherds went back, ᵃglorifying and
praising God for all that they had heard and
seen, just as had been told them. ᵃ*Matt 9:8*

Jesus Presented at the Temple

21 And when ᵃeight days had passed, before
His circumcision, His name was *then* called
Jesus, the name given by the angel before He
was conceived in the womb. ᵃ*Gen 17:12; Lev 12:3*
22 ᵃAnd when the days for their purification
according to the law of Moses were completed,
they brought Him up to Jerusalem to present
Him to the Lord ᵃ*Lev 12:6-8*
23 (as it is written in the Law of the Lord,
"ᵃEVERY *firstborn* MALE THAT OPENS THE WOMB
SHALL BE CALLED HOLY TO THE LORD"), ᵃ*Ex 13:2,
12; Num 3:13*
24 and to offer a sacrifice according to what
was said in the Law of the Lord, "ᵃA PAIR OF
TURTLEDOVES OR TWO YOUNG PIGEONS." ᵃ*Lev 5:11;
12:8*

25 And there was a man in Jerusalem whose name was Simeon; and this man was righteous and devout, [a]looking for the consolation of Israel; and the Holy Spirit was upon him. [a]Mark 15:43; Luke 2:38

26 And it had been revealed to him by the Holy Spirit that he would not [a]see death before he had seen the Lord's Christ. [a]Ps 89:48; John 8:51

27 And he came in the Spirit into the temple; and when the parents brought in the child Jesus, [a]to carry out for Him the custom of the Law, [a]Luke 2:22

28 then he took Him into his arms, and blessed God, and said,

29 "Now Lord, You are releasing Your
    bond-servant to depart in peace,
    [a]According to Your word; [a]Luke 2:26

30 For my eyes have [a]seen Your salvation,
    [a]Ps 119:166, 174; Is 52:10

31 Which You have prepared in the presence
    of all peoples,

32 [a]A LIGHT OF REVELATION TO THE GENTILES,
    And the glory of Your people Israel."
    [a]Is 9:2; 42:6

33 And His father and [a]mother were amazed at the things which were being said about Him. [a]Matt 12:46

34 And Simeon blessed them and said to Mary His mother, "Behold, this *Child* is appointed for [a]the fall and rise of many in Israel, and for a sign to be opposed— [a]Matt 21:44; 1 Cor 1:23

35 and a sword will pierce even your own soul—to the end that thoughts from many hearts may be revealed."

36 And there was a prophetess, Anna the daughter of Phanuel, of [a]the tribe of Asher. She was advanced in years [b]and had lived with *her* husband seven years after her marriage, [a]Josh 19:24 [b]1 Tim 5:9

37 and then as a widow to the age of eighty-four. She never left the temple, serving night and day with [a]fastings and prayers. [a]Luke 5:33; Acts 13:3

38 At that very moment she came up and *began* giving thanks to God, and continued to speak of Him to all those who were [a]looking for the redemption of Jerusalem. [a]Luke 1:68; 2:25

Return to Nazareth

39 When they had performed everything according to the Law of the Lord, they returned to Galilee, to [a]their own city of Nazareth. [a]Matt 2:23; Luke 1:26

40 [a]The Child continued to grow and become strong, increasing in wisdom; and the grace of God was upon Him. [a]Luke 1:80; 2:52

Visit to Jerusalem

41 Now His parents went to Jerusalem every year at [a]the Feast of the Passover. [a]Ex 12:11; 23:15

42 And when He became twelve, they went up *there* according to the custom of the Feast;

43 and as they were returning, after spending the [a]full number of days, the boy Jesus stayed behind in Jerusalem. But His parents were unaware of it; [a]Ex 12:15

44 but supposed Him to be in the caravan, and went a day's journey; and they *began* looking for Him among their relatives and acquaintances.

45 When they did not find Him, they returned to Jerusalem looking for Him.

46 Then, after three days they found Him in the temple, sitting in the midst of the teachers, both listening to them and asking them questions.

47 And all who heard Him [a]were amazed at His understanding and His answers. [a]Matt 7:28; 13:54

48 When they saw Him, they were astonished; and His mother said to Him, "Son, why have You treated us this way? Behold, [a]Your father and I have been anxiously looking for You." [a]Luke 2:49; 3:23

49 And He said to them, "Why is it that you were looking for Me? Did you not know that [a]I had to be in My Father's *house?*" [a]John 4:34; 5:36

50 But [a]they did not understand the statement which He had made to them. [a]Mark 9:32; Luke 9:45

51 And He went down with them and came to [a]Nazareth, and He continued in subjection to them; and His mother [b]treasured all *these* things in her heart. [a]Luke 2:39 [b]Luke 2:19

52 And Jesus kept increasing in wisdom and stature, and in [a]favor with God and men. [a]Luke 2:40

John the Baptist Preaches

3 Now in the fifteenth year of the reign of Tiberius Caesar, when [a]Pontius Pilate was governor of Judea, and [b]Herod was tetrarch of Galilee, and his brother Philip was tetrarch of the region of Ituraea and Trachonitis, and Lysanias was tetrarch of Abilene, [a]Matt 27:2 [b]Matt 14:1

2 in the high priesthood of Annas and Caiaphas, [a]the word of God came to John, the son of Zacharias, in the wilderness. [a]Matt 3:1-10; Mark 1:3-5

3 And he came into all [a]the district around the Jordan, preaching a baptism of repentance for the forgiveness of sins; [a]Matt 3:5

4 as it is written in the book of the words of Isaiah the prophet,
    "[a]THE VOICE OF ONE CRYING IN THE WILDER-
    NESS,

'MAKE READY THE WAY OF THE LORD,
MAKE HIS PATHS STRAIGHT. ªIs 40:3

5 'ªEVERY RAVINE WILL BE FILLED,
AND EVERY MOUNTAIN AND HILL WILL BE
BROUGHT LOW;
THE CROOKED WILL BECOME STRAIGHT,
AND THE ROUGH ROADS SMOOTH; ªIs 40:4

6 ªAND ALL FLESH WILL ᵇSEE THE SALVATION OF
GOD.' " ªIs 40:5 ᵇLuke 2:30

7 So he *began* saying to the crowds who were going out to be baptized by him, "ªYou brood of vipers, who warned you to flee from the wrath to come? ªMatt 12:34; 23:33

8 "Therefore bear fruits in keeping with repentance, and do not begin to say to yourselves, 'ªWe have Abraham for our father,' for I say to you that from these stones God is able to raise up children to Abraham. ªJohn 8:33

9 "Indeed the axe is already laid at the root of the trees; so ªevery tree that does not bear good fruit is cut down and thrown into the fire." ªMatt 7:19; Luke 13:6-9

10 And the crowds were questioning him, saying, "ªThen what shall we do?" ªLuke 3:12, 14; Acts 2:37, 38

11 And he would answer and say to them, "The man who has two tunics is to ªshare with him who has none; and he who has food is to do likewise." ªIs 58:7; 1 Tim 6:17, 18

12 And *some* ªtax collectors also came to be baptized, and they said to him, "Teacher, what shall we do?" ªLuke 7:29

13 And he said to them, "Collect no more than what you have been ordered to."

14 *Some* soldiers were questioning him, saying, "And *what about* us, what shall we do?" And he said to them, "Do not take money from anyone by force, or ªaccuse *anyone* falsely, and be content with your wages." ªEx 20:16; 23:1

15 Now while the people were in a state of expectation and all were wondering in their hearts about John, ªas to whether he was the Christ, ªJohn 1:19f

16 ªJohn answered and said to them all, "As for me, I baptize you with water; but One is coming who is mightier than I, and I am not fit to untie the thong of His sandals; He will baptize you with the Holy Spirit and fire. ªMatt 3:11, 12; Mark 1:7, 8

17 "His winnowing fork is in His hand to thoroughly clear His threshing floor, and to gather the wheat into His barn; but He will burn up the chaff with ªunquenchable fire." ªMark 9:43, 48

18 So with many other exhortations he preached the gospel to the people.

19 But when ªHerod the tetrarch was reprimanded by him because of ªHerodias, his brother's wife, and because of all the wicked things which Herod had done, ªMatt 14:3; Mark 6:17

20 Herod also added this to them all: ªhe locked John up in prison. ªJohn 3:24

Jesus Is Baptized

21 ªNow when all the people were baptized, Jesus was also baptized, and while He was praying, heaven was opened, ªMatt 3:13-17; Mark 1:9-11

22 and the Holy Spirit descended upon Him in bodily form like a dove, and a voice came out of heaven, "ªYou are My beloved Son, in You I am well-pleased." ªPs 2:7; Is 42:1

Genealogy of Jesus

23 ªWhen He began His ministry, Jesus Himself was about thirty years of age, being, as was supposed, the son of Joseph, the son of Eli, ªMatt 4:17; Acts 1:1

24 the son of Matthat, the son of Levi, the son of Melchi, the son of Jannai, the son of Joseph,

25 the son of Mattathias, the son of Amos, the son of Nahum, the son of Hesli, the son of Naggai,

26 the son of Maath, the son of Mattathias, the son of Semein, the son of Josech, the son of Joda,

27 the son of Joanan, the son of Rhesa, ªthe son of Zerubbabel, the son of Shealtiel, the son of Neri, ªMatt 1:12

28 the son of Melchi, the son of Addi, the son of Cosam, the son of Elmadam, the son of Er,

29 the son of Joshua, the son of Eliezer, the son of Jorim, the son of Matthat, the son of Levi,

30 the son of Simeon, the son of Judah, the son of Joseph, the son of Jonam, the son of Eliakim,

31 the son of Melea, the son of Menna, the son of Mattatha, the son of Nathan, the son of David,

32 ªthe son of Jesse, the son of Obed, the son of Boaz, the son of Salmon, the son of Nahshon, ªMatt 1:1-6

33 the son of Amminadab, the son of Admin, the son of Ram, the son of Hezron, the son of Perez, the son of Judah,

34 the son of Jacob, the son of Isaac, ªthe son of Abraham, the son of Terah, the son of Nahor, ªGen 11:26-30; 1 Chr 1:24-27

35 the son of Serug, the son of Reu, the son of Peleg, the son of Heber, the son of Shelah,

36 the son of Cainan, the son of Arphaxad, the son of Shem, ªthe son of Noah, the son of Lamech, ªGen 5:3-32; 1 Chr 1:1-4

37 the son of Methuselah, the son of Enoch, the son of Jared, the son of Mahalaleel, the son of Cainan,

38 the son of Enosh, the son of Seth, the son of Adam, the son of God.

The Temptation of Jesus

4 [a]Jesus, full of the Holy Spirit, returned from the Jordan and was led around by the Spirit in the wilderness [a]Matt 4:1-11; Mark 1:12, 13

2 for [a]forty days, being tempted by the devil. And He was nothing during those days, and when they had ended, He became hungry. [a]Ex 34:28; 1 Kin 19:8

3 And the devil said to Him, "If You are the Son of God, tell this stone to become bread."

4 And Jesus answered him, "It is written, '[a]MAN SHALL NOT LIVE ON BREAD ALONE.' " [a]Deut 8:3

5 [a]And he led Him up and showed Him all the kingdoms of the world in a moment of time. [a]Matt 4:8-10

6 And the devil said to Him, "I will give You all this domain and its glory; [a]for it has been handed over to me, and I give it to whomever I wish. [a]1 John 5:19

7 "Therefore if You worship before me, it shall all be Yours."

8 Jesus answered him, "It is written, '[a]YOU SHALL WORSHIP THE LORD YOUR GOD AND SERVE HIM ONLY.' " [a]Deut 6:13; 10:20

9 [a]And he led Him to Jerusalem and had Him stand on the pinnacle of the temple, and said to Him, "If You are the Son of God, throw Yourself down from here; [a]Matt 4:5-7

10 for it is written,

'[a]HE WILL COMMAND HIS ANGELS CONCERNING
    YOU TO GUARD YOU,' [a]Ps 91:11

11 and,

'[a]ON their HANDS THEY WILL BEAR YOU UP,
    SO THAT YOU WILL NOT STRIKE YOUR FOOT
    AGAINST A STONE.' " [a]Ps 91:12

12 And Jesus answered and said to him, "It is said, '[a]YOU SHALL NOT PUT THE LORD YOUR GOD TO THE TEST.' " [a]Deut 6:16

13 When the devil had finished every temptation, he left Him until an opportune time.

Jesus' Public Ministry

14 And [a]Jesus returned to Galilee in the power of the Spirit, and [b]news about Him spread through all the surrounding district. [a]Matt 4:12 [b]Matt 9:26

15 And He began [a]teaching in their synagogues and was praised by all. [a]Matt 4:23

16 And He came to Nazareth, where He had been brought up; and as was His custom, [a]He entered the synagogue on the Sabbath, and stood up to read. [a]Matt 13:54; Mark 6:1f

17 And the book of the prophet Isaiah was handed to Him. And He opened the book and found the place where it was written,

18 "[a]THE SPIRIT OF THE LORD IS UPON ME,
    BECAUSE HE ANOINTED ME TO PREACH THE
    GOSPEL TO THE POOR.

HE HAS SENT ME TO PROCLAIM RELEASE TO
    THE CAPTIVES,
AND RECOVERY OF SIGHT TO THE BLIND,
TO SET FREE THOSE WHO ARE OPPRESSED,
    [a]Is 61:1; Matt 11:5

19 [a]TO PROCLAIM THE FAVORABLE YEAR OF THE
    LORD." [a]Is 61:2; Lev 25:10

20 And He [a]closed the book, gave it back to the attendant and sat down; and the eyes of all in the synagogue were fixed on Him. [a]Luke 4:17

21 And He began to say to them, "Today this Scripture has been fulfilled in your hearing."

22 And all were speaking well of Him, and wondering at the gracious words which were falling from His lips; and they were saying, "[a]Is this not Joseph's son?" [a]Matt 13:55; Mark 6:3

23 And He said to them, "No doubt you will quote this proverb to Me, 'Physician, heal yourself! Whatever we heard was done [a]at Capernaum, do here in your hometown as well.' " [a]Matt 4:13; Mark 1:21ff

24 And He said, "Truly I say to you, [a]no prophet is welcome in his hometown." [a]Matt 13:57; Mark 6:4

25 "But I say to you in truth, there were many widows in Israel [a]in the days of Elijah, when the sky was shut up for three years and six months, when a great famine came over all the land; [a]1 Kin 17:1; 18:1

26 and yet Elijah was sent to none of them, but [a]only to Zarephath, in the land of Sidon, to a woman who was a widow. [a]1 Kin 17:9

27 "And there were many lepers in Israel in the time of Elisha the prophet; and none of them was cleansed, but [a]only Naaman the Syrian." [a]2 Kin 5:1-14

28 And all the people in the synagogue were filled with rage as they heard these things;

29 and they got up and [a]drove Him out of the city, and led Him to the brow of the hill on which their city had been built, in order to throw Him down the cliff. [a]Num 15:35; Acts 7:58

30 But [a]passing through their midst, He went His way. [a]John 10:39

31 And [a]He came down to Capernaum, a city of Galilee, and He was teaching them on the Sabbath; [a]Mark 1:21-28

32 and [a]they were amazed at His teaching, for [a]His message was with authority. [a]Luke 4:36; John 7:46

33 In the synagogue there was a man possessed by the spirit of an unclean demon, and he cried out with a loud voice,

34 "Let us alone! [a]What business do we have with each other, Jesus of [b]Nazareth? Have You come to destroy us? I know who You are—[b]the Holy One of God!" [a]Matt 8:29 [b]Mark 1:24

35 But Jesus [a]rebuked him, saying, "Be quiet and come out of him!" And when the demon

had thrown him down in the midst *of the people,* he came out of him without doing him any harm. ᵃ*Matt 8:26; Mark 4:39*

36 And amazement came upon them all, and they *began* talking with one another saying, "What is this message? For ᵃwith authority and power He commands the unclean spirits and they come out." ᵃ*Luke 4:32*

37 And ᵃthe report about Him was spreading into every locality in the surrounding district. ᵃ*Luke 4:14*

Many Are Healed

38 ᵃThen He got up and *left* the synagogue, and entered Simon's home. Now Simon's mother-in-law was suffering from a high fever, and they asked Him to help her. ᵃ*Matt 8:14, 15; Mark 1:29-31*

39 And standing over her, He ᵃrebuked the fever, and it left her; and she immediately got up and waited on them. ᵃ*Luke 4:35, 41*

40 ᵃWhile the sun was setting, all those who had any *who were* sick with various diseases brought them to Him; and laying His hands on each one of them, He was healing them. ᵃ*Matt 8:16, 17; Mark 1:32-34*

41 Demons also were coming out of many, shouting, "You are the Son of God!" But rebuking them, He would ᵃnot allow them to speak, because they knew Him to be the Christ. ᵃ*Matt 8:16; Mark 1:34*

42 ᵃWhen day came, Jesus left and went to a secluded place; and the crowds were searching for Him, and came to Him and tried to keep Him from going away from them. ᵃ*Mark 1:35-38*

43 But He said to them, "I must preach the kingdom of God to the other cities also, ᵃfor I was sent for this purpose." ᵃ*Mark 1:38*

44 So He kept on preaching in the synagogues ᵃof Judea. ᵃ*Matt 4:23*

The First Disciples

5 ᵃNow it happened that while the crowd was pressing around Him and listening to the word of God, He was standing by the lake of Gennesaret; ᵃ*Matt 4:18-22; Mark 1:16-20*

2 and He saw two boats lying at the edge of the lake; but the fishermen had gotten out of them and were washing their nets.

3 And ᵃHe got into one of the boats, which was Simon's, and asked him to put out a little way from the land. And He sat down and *began* teaching the people from the boat. ᵃ*Matt 13:2; Mark 3:9, 10*

4 When He had finished speaking, He said to Simon, "Put out into the deep water and ᵃlet down your nets for a catch." ᵃ*John 21:6*

5 Simon answered and said, "ᵃMaster, we worked hard all night and caught nothing, but I will do as You say *and* let down the nets." ᵃ*Luke 8:24; 9:33, 49*

6 When they had done this, ᵃthey enclosed a great quantity of fish, and their nets *began* to break; ᵃ*John 21:6*

7 so they signaled to their partners in the other boat for them to come and help them. And they came and filled both of the boats, so that they began to sink.

8 But when Simon Peter saw *that,* he fell down at Jesus' feet, saying, "Go away from me Lord, for I am a sinful man, O Lord!"

9 For amazement had seized him and all his companions because of the catch of fish which they had taken;

10 and so also *were* James and John, sons of Zebedee, who were partners with Simon. And Jesus said to Simon, "ᵃDo not fear, from now on you will be catching men." ᵃ*Matt 14:27*

11 When they had brought their boats to land, ᵃthey left everything and followed Him. ᵃ*Matt 4:20, 22; 19:29*

The Leper and the Paralytic

12 ᵃWhile He was in one of the cities, behold, *there was* a man covered with leprosy; and when he saw Jesus, he fell on his face and implored Him, saying, "Lord, if You are willing, You can make me clean." ᵃ*Matt 8:2-4; Mark 1:40-44*

13 And He stretched out His hand and touched him, saying, "I am willing; be cleansed." And immediately the leprosy left him.

14 And He ordered him to tell no one, "But go and ᵃshow yourself to the priest and make an offering for your cleansing, just as Moses commanded, as a testimony to them." ᵃ*Lev 13:49; 14:2ff*

15 But ᵃthe news about Him was spreading even farther, and large crowds were gathering to hear *Him* and to be healed of their sicknesses. ᵃ*Matt 9:26*

16 But Jesus Himself would *often* slip away to the wilderness and ᵃpray. ᵃ*Matt 14:23; Mark 1:35*

17 One day He was teaching; and there were *some* Pharisees and teachers of the law sitting *there,* who had ᵃcome from every village of Galilee and Judea and *from* Jerusalem; and ᵇthe power of the Lord was *present* for Him to perform healing. ᵃ*Mark 1:45* ᵇ*Mark 5:30*

18 And *some* men *were* carrying on a bed a man who was paralyzed; and they were trying to bring him in and to set him down in front of Him. ᵃ*Matt 9:2-8; Mark 2:3-12*

19 But not finding any *way* to bring him in because of the crowd, they went up on ᵃthe roof and let him down ᵇthrough the tiles with his stretcher, into the middle *of the crowd,* in front of Jesus. ᵃ*Matt 24:17* ᵇ*Mark 2:4*

20 Seeing their faith, He said, "Friend, ᵃyour sins are forgiven you." ᵃ*Matt 9:2*

21 The scribes and the Pharisees began to reason, saying, "ᵃWho is this *man* who speaks blasphemies? ᵇWho can forgive sins, but God alone?" ᵃLuke 7:49 ᵇIs 43:25

22 But Jesus, aware of their reasonings, answered and said to them, "Why are you reasoning in your hearts?

23 "Which is easier, to say, 'Your sins have been forgiven you,' or to say, 'Get up and walk'?

24 "But, so that you may know that the Son of Man has authority on earth to forgive sins,"—He said to the ᵃparalytic—"I say to you, get up, and pick up your stretcher and go home." ᵃMatt 4:24

25 Immediately he got up before them, and picked up what he had been lying on, and went home ᵃglorifying God. ᵃMatt 9:8

26 They were all struck with astonishment and *began* ᵃglorifying God; and they were filled with fear, saying, "We have seen remarkable things today." ᵃMatt 9:8

Call of Levi (Matthew)

27 ᵃAfter that He went out and noticed a tax collector named Levi sitting in the tax booth, and He said to him, "Follow Me." ᵃMatt 9:9-17; Mark 2:14-22

28 And he ᵃleft everything behind, and got up and *began* to follow Him. ᵃLuke 5:11

29 And ᵃLevi gave a big reception for Him in his house; and there was a great crowd of ᵇtax collectors and other *people* who were reclining *at the table* with them. ᵃMatt 9:9 ᵇLuke 15:1

30 ᵃThe Pharisees and their scribes *began* grumbling at His disciples, saying, "Why do you eat and drink with the tax collectors and sinners?" ᵃMark 2:16; Luke 15:2

31 And Jesus answered and said to them, "ᵃ*It is* not those who are well who need a physician, but those who are sick. ᵃMatt 9:12, 13; Mark 2:17

32 "I have not come to call the righteous but sinners to repentance."

33 And they said to Him, "ᵃThe disciples of John often fast and offer prayers, the *disciples* of the Pharisees also do the same, but Yours eat and drink." ᵃMatt 9:14; Mark 2:18

34 And Jesus said to them, "You cannot make the attendants of the bridegroom fast while the bridegroom is with them, can you?

35 "ᵃBut *the* days will come; and when the bridegroom is taken away from them, then they will fast in those days." ᵃMatt 9:15; Mark 2:20

36 And He was also telling them a parable: "No one tears a piece of cloth from a new garment and puts it on an old garment; otherwise he will both tear the new, and the piece from the new will not match the old.

37 "And no one puts new wine into old wineskins; otherwise the new wine will burst the skins and it will be spilled out, and the skins will be ruined.

38 "But new wine must be put into fresh wineskins.

39 "And no one, after drinking old *wine* wishes for new; for he says, 'The old is good *enough.*' "

Jesus Is Lord of the Sabbath

6 ᵃNow it happened that He was passing through *some* grainfields on a Sabbath; and His disciples were picking the heads of grain, rubbing them in their hands, and eating *the* grain. ᵃMatt 12:1-8; Mark 2:23-28

2 But some of the Pharisees said, "Why do you do what ᵃis not lawful on the Sabbath?" ᵃMatt 12:2

3 And Jesus answering them said, "Have you not even read ᵃwhat David did when he was hungry, he and those who were with him, ᵃ1 Sam 21:6

4 how he entered the house of God, and took and ate the consecrated bread which ᵃis not lawful for any to eat except the priests alone, and gave it to his companions?" ᵃLev 24:9

5 And He was saying to them, "The Son of Man is Lord of the Sabbath."

6 ᵃOn another Sabbath He entered the synagogue and was teaching; and there was a man there whose right hand was withered. ᵃMatt 12:9-14; Mark 3:1-6;

7 The scribes and the Pharisees ᵃwere watching Him closely *to see* if He healed on the Sabbath, so that they might find *reason* to accuse Him. ᵃMark 3:2

8 But He ᵃknew what they were thinking, and He said to the man with the withered hand, "Get up and come forward!" And he got up and came forward. ᵃMatt 9:4

9 And Jesus said to them, "I ask you, is it lawful to do good or to do harm on the Sabbath, to save a life or to destroy it?"

10 After ᵃlooking around at them all, He said to him, "Stretch out your hand!" And he did *so;* and his hand was restored. ᵃMark 3:5

11 But they themselves were filled with rage, and discussed together what they might do to Jesus.

Choosing the Twelve

12 It was at this time that He went off to the mountain to ᵃpray, and He spent the whole night in prayer to God. ᵃMatt 14:23; Luke 5:16

13 And when day came, ᵃHe called His disciples to Him and chose twelve of them, whom He also named as apostles: ᵃMatt 10:2-4; Mark 3:16-19

14 Simon, whom He also named Peter, and Andrew his brother; and James and John; and Philip and Bartholomew;

15 and [a]Matthew and Thomas; James *the son* of Alphaeus, and Simon who was called the Zealot; [a]*Matt 9:9*

16 Judas *the son* of James, and Judas Iscariot, who became a traitor.

17 Jesus came down with them and stood on a level place; and *there was* [a]a large crowd of His disciples, and a great throng of people from all Judea and Jerusalem and the coastal region of Tyre and Sidon, [a]*Matt 4:25; Mark 3:7, 8*

18 who had come to hear Him and to be healed of their diseases; and those who were troubled with unclean spirits were being cured.

19 And all the people were trying to [a]touch Him, for [b]power was coming from Him and healing *them* all. [a]*Matt 9:21* [b]*Luke 5:17*

The Beatitudes

20 And turning His gaze toward His disciples, He *began* to say, "[a]Blessed *are* you *who are* poor, for yours is the kingdom of God. [a]*Matt 5:3-12; Luke 6:20-23*

21 "Blessed *are* you who hunger now, for you shall be satisfied. Blessed *are* you who weep now, for you shall laugh.

22 "Blessed are you when men hate you, and [a]ostracize you, and insult you, and scorn your name as evil, for the sake of the Son of Man. [a]*John 9:22; 16:2*

23 "Be glad in that day and leap *for joy*, for behold, your reward is great in heaven. For [a]in the same way their fathers used to treat the prophets. [a]*2 Chr 36:16; Acts 7:52*

24 "But woe to [a]you who are rich, for you are receiving your comfort in full. [a]*Luke 16:25; James 5:1*

25 "Woe to you who are well-fed now, for you shall be hungry. Woe *to you* who laugh now, for you shall mourn and weep.

26 "Woe *to you* when all men speak well of you, for their fathers used to treat the [a]false prophets in the same way. [a]*Matt 7:15*

27 "But I say to you who hear, [a]love your enemies, do good to those who hate you, [a]*Matt 5:44; Luke 6:35*

28 bless those who curse you, [a]pray for those who mistreat you. [a]*Matt 5:44; Luke 6:35*

29 "[a]Whoever hits you on the cheek, offer him the other also; and whoever takes away your coat, do not withhold your shirt from him either. [a]*Matt 5:39-42*

30 "Give to everyone who asks of you, and whoever takes away what is yours, do not demand it back.

31 "[a]Treat others the same way you want them to treat you. [a]*Matt 7:12*

32 "If you love those who love you, what credit is *that* to you? For even sinners love those who love them. [a]*Matt 5:46*

33 "If you do good to those who do good to you, what credit is *that* to you? For even sinners do the same.

34 "[a]If you lend to those from whom you expect to receive, what credit is *that* to you? Even sinners lend to sinners in order to receive back the same *amount*. [a]*Matt 5:42*

35 "But love your enemies, and do good, and lend, expecting nothing in return; and your reward will be great, and you will be [a]sons of [b]the Most High; for He Himself is kind to ungrateful and evil *men*. [a]*Matt 5:9* [b]*Luke 1:32*

36 "Be merciful, just as your Father is merciful.

37 "[a]Do not judge, and you will not be judged; and do not condemn, and you will not be condemned; pardon, and you will be pardoned. [a]*Matt 7:1-5*

38 "Give, and it will be given to you. They will pour [a]into your lap a good measure—pressed down, shaken together, *and* running over. For by your standard of measure it will be measured to you in return." [a]*Mark 4:24*

39 And He also spoke a parable to them: "[a]A blind man cannot guide a blind man, can he? Will they not both fall into a pit? [a]*Matt 15:14*

40 "[a]A pupil is not above his teacher; but everyone, after he has been fully trained, will be like his teacher. [a]*Matt 10:24; John 13:16*

41 "Why do you look at the speck that is in your brother's eye, but do not notice the log that is in your own eye?

42 "Or how can you say to your brother, 'Brother, let me take out the speck that is in your eye,' when you yourself do not see the log that is in your own eye? You hypocrite, first take the log out of your own eye, and then you will see clearly to take out the speck that is in your brother's eye.

43 "[a]For there is no good tree which produces bad fruit, nor, on the other hand, a bad tree which produces good fruit. [a]*Matt 7:16, 18, 20*

44 "[a]For each tree is known by its own fruit. For men do not gather figs from thorns, nor do they pick grapes from a briar bush. [a]*Matt 7:16; 12:33*

45 "[a]The good man out of the good treasure of his heart brings forth what is good; and the evil *man* out of the evil *treasure* brings forth what is evil; [b]for his mouth speaks from that which fills his heart. [a]*Matt 12:35* [b]*Matt 12:34*

Builders and Foundations

46 "[a]Why do you call Me, 'Lord, Lord,' and do not do what I say? [a]*Mal 1:6; Matt 7:21*

47 "[a]Everyone who comes to Me and hears My words and acts on them, I will show you whom he is like: [a]*James 1:22ff*

48 he is like a man building a house, who dug deep and laid a foundation on the rock; and

when a flood occurred, the torrent burst against that house and could not shake it, because it had been well built.

49 "But the one who has heard and has not acted *accordingly,* is like a man who built a house on the ground without any foundation; and the torrent burst against it and immediately it collapsed, and the ruin of that house was great."

Jesus Heals a Centurion's Servant

7 When He had completed all His discourse in the hearing of the people, [a]He went to Capernaum. [a]*Matt 8:5-13*

2 And a centurion's slave, who was highly regarded by him, was sick and about to die.

3 When he heard about Jesus, [a]he sent some Jewish elders asking Him to come and save the life of his slave. [a]*Matt 8:5*

4 When they came to Jesus, they earnestly implored Him, saying, "He is worthy for You to grant this to him;

5 for he loves our nation and it was he who built us our synagogue."

6 Now Jesus *started* on His way with them; and when He was not far from the house, the centurion sent friends, saying to Him, "Lord, do not trouble Yourself further, for I am not worthy for You to come under my roof;

7 for this reason I did not even consider myself worthy to come to You, but *just* say the word, and my servant will be healed.

8 "For I also am a man placed under authority, with soldiers under me; and I say to this one, 'Go!' and he goes, and to another, 'Come!' and he comes, and to my slave, 'Do this!' and he does it."

9 Now when Jesus heard this, He marveled at him, and turned and said to the crowd that was following Him, "I say to you, [a]not even in Israel have I found such great faith." [a]*Matt 8:10; Luke 7:50*

10 When those who had been sent returned to the house, they found the slave in good health.

11 Soon afterwards He went to a city called Nain; and His disciples were going along with Him, accompanied by a large crowd.

12 Now as He approached the gate of the city, a dead man was being carried out, the only son of his mother, and she was a widow; and a sizeable crowd from the city was with her.

13 When [a]the Lord saw her, He felt compassion for her, and said to her, "Do not weep." [a]*Luke 7:19; 10:1*

14 And He came up and touched the coffin; and the bearers came to a halt. And He said, "Young man, I say to you, arise!"

15 The dead man sat up and began to speak. And *Jesus* gave him back to his mother.

16 [a]Fear gripped them all, and they *began* glo-rifying God, saying, "A great prophet has arisen among us!" and, "God has visited His people!" [a]*Luke 5:26*

17 [a]This report concerning Him went out all over Judea and in all the surrounding district. [a]*Matt 9:26*

A Deputation from John

18 [a]The disciples of John reported to him about all these things. [a]*Matt 11:2-19*

19 Summoning two of his disciples, John sent them to [a]the Lord, saying, "Are You the Expected One, or do we look for someone else?" [a]*Luke 7:13; 10:1*

20 When the men came to Him, they said, "John the Baptist has sent us to You, to ask, 'Are You the Expected One, or do we look for someone else?' "

21 At that very time He [a]cured many *people* of diseases and [b]afflictions and evil spirits; and He gave sight to many *who were* blind. [a]*Matt 4:23* [b]*Mark 3:10*

22 And He answered and said to them, "Go and report to John what you have seen and heard: *the* [a]BLIND RECEIVE SIGHT, *the* lame walk, *the* lepers are cleansed, and *the* deaf hear, *the* dead are raised up, *the* [b]POOR HAVE THE GOSPEL PREACHED TO THEM. [a]*Is 35:5* [b]*Is 61:1*

23 "Blessed is he who does not take offense at Me."

24 When the messengers of John had left, He began to speak to the crowds about John, "What did you go out into the wilderness to see? A reed shaken by the wind?

25 "But what did you go out to see? A man dressed in soft clothing? Those who are splen-didly clothed and live in luxury are *found* in royal palaces!

26 "But what did you go out to see? A prophet? Yes, I say to you, and one who is more than a prophet.

27 "This is the one about whom it is written,

'[a]BEHOLD, I SEND MY MESSENGER AHEAD OF YOU,

WHO WILL PREPARE YOUR WAY BEFORE YOU.'
[a]*Mal 3:1; Matt 11:10*

28 "I say to you, among those born of women there is no one greater than John; yet he who is least in the kingdom of God is greater than he."

29 When all the people and the tax collectors heard *this,* they acknowledged God's justice, [a]having been baptized with the baptism of John. [a]*Matt 21:32; Luke 3:12*

30 But the Pharisees and the [a]lawyers rejected God's purpose for themselves, not having been baptized by John. [a]*Matt 22:35*

31 "To what then shall I compare the men of this generation, and what are they like?

32 "They are like children who sit in the mar-ket place and call to one another, and they say,

'We played the flute for you, and you did not dance; we sang a dirge, and you did not weep.'
33 "For John the Baptist has come [a]eating no bread and drinking no wine, and you say, 'He has a demon!' [a]*Luke 1:15*
34 "The Son of Man has come eating and drinking, and you say, 'Behold, a gluttonous man and a drunkard, a friend of tax collectors and sinners!'
35 "Yet wisdom [a]is vindicated by all her children." [a]*Luke 7:29*
36 Now one of the Pharisees was requesting Him to dine with him, and he entered the Pharisee's house and reclined *at the table.*
37 [a]And there was a woman in the city who was a sinner; and when she learned that He was reclining *at the table* in the Pharisee's house, she brought an alabaster vial of perfume, [a]*Matt 26:6-13; Mark 14:3-9*
38 and standing behind *Him* at His feet, weeping, she began to wet His feet with her tears, and kept wiping them with the hair of her head, and kissing His feet and anointing them with the perfume.
39 Now when the Pharisee who had invited Him saw this, he said to himself, "If this man were [a]a prophet He would know who and what sort of person this woman is who is touching Him, that she is a sinner." [a]*Luke 7:16; John 4:19*

Parable of Two Debtors

40 And Jesus answered him, "Simon, I have something to say to you." And he replied, "Say it, Teacher."
41 "A moneylender had two debtors: one owed five hundred [a]denarii, and the other fifty. [a]*Matt 18:28; Mark 6:37*
42 "When they [a]were unable to repay, he graciously forgave them both. So which of them will love him more?" [a]*Matt 18:25*
43 Simon answered and said, "I suppose the one whom he forgave more." And He said to him, "You have judged correctly."
44 Turning toward the woman, He said to Simon, "Do you see this woman? I entered your house; you [a]gave Me no water for My feet, but she has wet My feet with her tears and wiped them with her hair. [a]*Gen 18:4; 19:2*
45 "You [a]gave Me no kiss; but she, since the time I came in, has not ceased to kiss My feet. [a]*2 Sam 15:5*
46 "[a]You did not anoint My head with oil, but she anointed My feet with perfume. [a]*2 Sam 12:20; Ps 23:5*
47 "For this reason I say to you, her sins, which are many, have been forgiven, for she loved much; but he who is forgiven little, loves little."
48 Then He said to her, "[a]Your sins have been forgiven." [a]*Matt 9:2; Mark 2:5, 9*

49 Those who were reclining *at the table* with Him began to say to themselves, "[a]Who is this *man* who even forgives sins?" [a]*Luke 5:21*
50 And He said to the woman, "Your faith has saved you; [a]go in peace." [a]*Mark 5:34; Luke 8:48*

Ministering Women

8 Soon afterwards, He *began* going around from one city and village to another, [a]proclaiming and preaching the kingdom of God. The twelve were with Him, [a]*Matt 4:23*
2 and *also* [a]some women who had been healed of evil spirits and sicknesses: Mary who was called Magdalene, from whom seven demons had gone out, [a]*Matt 27:55; Mark 15:40, 41*
3 and Joanna the wife of Chuza, [a]Herod's steward, and Susanna, and many others who were contributing to their support out of their private means. [a]*Matt 14:1*

Parable of the Sower

4 [a]When a large crowd was coming together, and those from the various cities were journeying to Him, He spoke by way of a parable: [a]*Matt 13:2-9; Mark 4:1-9*
5 "The sower went out to sow his seed; and as he sowed, some fell beside the road, and it was trampled under foot and the birds of the air ate it up.
6 "Other *seed* fell on rocky *soil,* and as soon as it grew up, it withered away, because it had no moisture.
7 "Other *seed* fell among the thorns; and the thorns grew up with it and choked it out.
8 "Other *seed* fell into the good soil, and grew up, and produced a crop a hundred times as great." As He said these things, He would call out, "[a]He who has ears to hear, let him hear." [a]*Matt 11:15; Mark 7:16*
9 [a]His disciples *began* questioning Him as to what this parable meant. [a]*Matt 13:10-23; Mark 4:10-20*
10 And He said, "To you it has been granted to know the mysteries of the kingdom of God, but to the rest *it is* in parables, so that [a]SEEING THEY MAY NOT SEE, AND HEARING THEY MAY NOT UNDERSTAND. [a]*Is 6:9; Matt 13:14*
11 "Now the parable is this: [a]the seed is the word of God. [a]*1 Pet 1:23*
12 "Those beside the road are those who have heard; then the devil comes and takes away the word from their heart, so that they will not believe and be saved.
13 "Those on the rocky *soil are* those who, when they hear, receive the word with joy; and these have no *firm* root; they believe for a while, and in time of temptation fall away.
14 "The *seed* which fell among the thorns, these are the ones who have heard, and as they go on their way they are choked with worries

and riches and pleasures of *this* life, and bring no fruit to maturity.

15 "But the *seed* in the good soil, these are the ones who have heard the word in an honest and good heart, and hold it fast, and bear fruit with perseverance.

Parable of the Lamp

16 "Now ᵃno one after lighting a lamp covers it over with a container, or puts it under a bed; but he puts it on a lampstand, so that those who come in may see the light. ᵃ*Matt 5:15; Mark 4:21*

17 "ᵃFor nothing is hidden that will not become evident, nor *anything* secret that will not be known and come to light. ᵃ*Matt 10:26; Mark 4:22*

18 "So take care how you listen; ᵃfor whoever has, to him *more* shall be given; and whoever does not have, even what he thinks he has shall be taken away from him." ᵃ*Matt 13:12; 25:29*

19 ᵃAnd His mother and brothers came to Him, and they were unable to get to Him because of the crowd. ᵃ*Matt 12:46-50; Mark 3:31-35*

20 And it was reported to Him, "Your mother and Your brothers are standing outside, wishing to see You."

21 But He answered and said to them, "My mother and My brothers are these ᵃwho hear the word of God and do it." ᵃ*Luke 11:28*

Jesus Stills the Sea

22 ᵃNow on one of *those* days Jesus and His disciples got into a boat, and He said to them, "Let us go over to the other side of the lake." So they launched out. ᵃ*Matt 8:23-27; Mark 4:36-41*

23 But as they were sailing along He fell asleep; and a fierce gale of wind descended on ᵃthe lake, and they *began* to be swamped and to be in danger. ᵃ*Luke 5:1f; 8:22*

24 They came to Jesus and woke Him up, saying, "ᵃMaster, Master, we are perishing!" And He got up and ᵇrebuked the wind and the surging waves, and they stopped, and it became calm. ᵃ*Luke 5:5* ᵇ*Luke 4:39*

25 And He said to them, "Where is your faith?" They were fearful and amazed, saying to one another, "Who then is this, that He commands even the winds and the water, and they obey Him?"

The Demoniac Cured

26 ᵃThen they sailed to the country of the Gerasenes, which is opposite Galilee. ᵃ*Matt 8:28-34; Mark 5:1-17*

27 And when He came out onto the land, He was met by a man from the city who was possessed with demons; and who had not put on any clothing for a long time, and was not living in a house, but in the tombs.

28 Seeing Jesus, he cried out and fell before Him, and said in a loud voice, "ᵃWhat business do we have with each other, Jesus, Son of ᵇthe Most High God? I beg You, do not torment me." ᵃ*Matt 8:29* ᵇ*Mark 5:7*

29 For He had commanded the unclean spirit to come out of the man. For it had seized him many times; and he was bound with chains and shackles and kept under guard, and *yet* he would break his bonds and be driven by the demon into the desert.

30 And Jesus asked him, "What is your name?" And he said, "ᵃLegion"; for many demons had entered him. ᵃ*Matt 26:53*

31 They were imploring Him not to command them to go away into ᵃthe abyss. ᵃ*Rom 10:7; Rev 9:1f, 11*

32 Now there was a herd of many swine feeding there on the mountain; and *the demons* implored Him to permit them to enter the swine. And He gave them permission.

33 And the demons came out of the man and entered the swine; and the herd rushed down the steep bank into ᵃthe lake and was drowned. ᵃ*Luke 5:1f; 8:22*

34 When the herdsmen saw what had happened, they ran away and reported it in the city and *out* in the country.

35 *The people* went out to see what had happened; and they came to Jesus, and found the man from whom the demons had gone out, sitting down ᵃat the feet of Jesus, clothed and in his right mind; and they became frightened. ᵃ*Luke 10:39*

36 Those who had seen it reported to them how the man who was ᵃdemon-possessed had been made well. ᵃ*Matt 4:24*

37 And all the people of the country of the Gerasenes and the surrounding district asked Him to leave them, for they were gripped with great fear; and He got into a boat and returned.

38 ᵃBut the man from whom the demons had gone out was begging Him that he might accompany Him; but He sent him away, saying, ᵃ*Mark 5:18-20*

39 "Return to your house and describe what great things God has done for you." So he went away, proclaiming throughout the whole city what great things Jesus had done for him.

Miracles of Healing

40 ᵃAnd as Jesus returned, the people welcomed Him, for they had all been waiting for Him. ᵃ*Matt 9:1; Mark 5:21*

41 ᵃAnd there came a man named Jairus, and he was an official of the synagogue; and he fell at Jesus' feet, and *began* to implore Him to come to his house; ᵃ*Matt 9:18-26; Mark 5:22-43*

42 for he had an only daughter, about twelve years old, and she was dying. But as He went, the crowds were pressing against Him.

43 And a woman who had a hemorrhage for

twelve years, and could not be healed by any-one,

44 came up behind Him and touched the fringe of His cloak, and immediately her hemorrhage stopped.

45 And Jesus said, "Who is the one who touched Me?" And while they were all denying it, Peter said, "ªMaster, the people are crowding and pressing in on You." ªLuke 5:5

46 But Jesus said, "Someone did touch Me, for I was aware that ªpower had gone out of Me." ªLuke 5:17

47 When the woman saw that she had not escaped notice, she came trembling and fell down before Him, and declared in the presence of all the people the reason why she had touched Him, and how she had been immediately healed.

48 And He said to her, "Daughter, your faith has made you well; ªgo in peace." ªMark 5:34; Luke 7:50

49 While He was still speaking, someone *came from the house of ªthe synagogue official, saying, "Your daughter has died; do not trouble the Teacher anymore." ªLuke 8:41

50 But when Jesus heard this, He answered him, "ªDo not be afraid any longer; only believe, and she will be made well." ªMark 5:36

51 When He came to the house, He did not allow anyone to enter with Him, except Peter and John and James, and the girl's father and mother.

52 Now they were all weeping and ªlamenting for her; but He said, "Stop weeping, for she has not died, but ᵇis asleep." ªLuke 23:27 ᵇJohn 11:13

53 And they began laughing at Him, knowing that she had died.

54 He, however, took her by the hand and called, saying, "Child, arise!"

55 And her spirit returned, and she got up immediately; and He gave orders for something to be given her to eat.

56 Her parents were amazed; but He ªinstructed them to tell no one what had happened. ªMatt 8:4

Ministry of the Twelve

9 ªAnd He called the twelve together, and gave them power and authority over all the demons and to heal diseases. ªMatt 10:5; Mark 6:7

2 And He sent them out to ªproclaim the kingdom of God and to perform healing. ªMatt 10:7

3 And He said to them, "ªTake nothing for your journey, neither a staff, nor a bag, nor bread, nor money; and do not even have two tunics apiece." ªLuke 10:4-12; 22:35

4 "Whatever house you enter, stay there until you leave that city.

5 "And as for those who do not receive you, as you go out from that city, ªshake the dust off your feet as a testimony against them." ªLuke 10:11; Acts 13:51

6 Departing, they began going throughout the villages, ªpreaching the gospel and healing everywhere. ªMark 6:12; Luke 8:1

7 ªNow Herod the tetrarch heard of all that was happening; and he was greatly perplexed, because it was said by some that John had risen from the dead, ªMark 6:14f

8 and by some that ªElijah had appeared, and by others that one of the prophets of old had risen again. ªMatt 16:14

9 Herod said, "I myself had John beheaded; but who is this man about whom I hear such things?" And ªhe kept trying to see Him. ªLuke 23:8

10 When the apostles returned, they gave an account to Him of all that they had done. ªTaking them with Him, He withdrew by Himself to a city called Bethsaida. ªMatt 14:13-21; Mark 6:32-44

11 But the crowds were aware of this and followed Him; and welcoming them, He began speaking to them about the kingdom of God and curing those who had need of healing.

Five Thousand Fed

12 Now the day was ending, and the twelve came and said to Him, "Send the crowd away, that they may go into the surrounding villages and countryside and find lodging and get something to eat; for here we are in a desolate place."

13 But He said to them, "You give them something to eat!" And they said, "We have no more than five loaves and two fish, unless perhaps we go and buy food for all these people."

14 (For there were about five thousand men.) And He said to His disciples, "Have them sit down to eat ªin groups of about fifty each." ªMark 6:39

15 They did so, and had them all sit down.

16 Then He took the five loaves and the two fish, and looking up to heaven, He blessed them, and broke them, and kept giving them to the disciples to set before the people.

17 And they all ate and were satisfied; and the broken pieces which they had left over were picked up, twelve ªbaskets full. ªMatt 14:20

18 ªAnd it happened that while He was praying alone, the disciples were with Him, and He questioned them, saying, "Who do the people say that I am?" ªMatt 16:13-16; Mark 8:27-29

19 They answered and said, "John the Baptist, and others say Elijah; but others, that one of the prophets of old has risen again."

20 And He said to them, "But who do you say that I am?" And Peter answered and said, "ªThe Christ of God." ªJohn 6:68f

21 But He ªwarned them and instructed *them* not to tell this to anyone, ªMatt 8:4; 16:20

22 ªsaying, "The Son of Man must suffer many things and be rejected by the elders and chief priests and scribes, and be killed and be raised up on the third day." ªMatt 16:21-28; Mark 8:31-9:1

23 And He was saying to *them* all, "ªIf anyone wishes to come after Me, he must deny himself, and take up his cross daily and follow Me. ªMatt 10:38; Luke 14:27

24 "For ªwhoever wishes to save his life will lose it, but whoever loses his life for My sake, he is the one who will save it. ªMatt 10:39; Luke 17:33

25 "For what is a man profited if he gains the whole world, and ªloses or forfeits himself? ªHeb 10:34

26 "ªFor whoever is ashamed of Me and My words, the Son of Man will be ashamed of him when He comes in His glory, and *the glory* of the Father and of the holy angels. ªMatt 10:33; Luke 12:9

27 "But I say to you truthfully, ªthere are some of those standing here who will not taste death until they see the kingdom of God." ªMatt 16:28

The Transfiguration

28 ªSome eight days after these sayings, He took along Peter and John and James, and went up on the mountain to pray. ªMatt 17:1-8; Mark 9:2-8

29 And while He was ªpraying, the appearance of His face became different, and His clothing *became* white *and* gleaming. ªLuke 3:21; 5:16

30 And behold, two men were talking with Him; and they were Moses and Elijah,

31 who, appearing in glory, were speaking of His ªdeparture which He was about to accomplish at Jerusalem. ª2 Pet 1:15

32 Now Peter and his companions ªhad been overcome with sleep; but when they were fully awake, they saw His glory and the two men standing with Him. ªMatt 26:43; Mark 14:40

33 And as these were leaving Him, Peter said to Jesus, "Master, it is good for us to be here; ªlet us make three tabernacles: one for You, and one for Moses, and one for Elijah"—not realizing what he was saying. ªMatt 17:4; Mark 9:5

34 While he was saying this, a cloud formed and *began* to overshadow them; and they were afraid as they entered the cloud.

35 Then a voice came out of the cloud, saying, "ªThis is My Son, *My* Chosen One; listen to Him!" ªIs 42:1; Matt 3:17

36 And when the voice had spoken, Jesus was found alone. And ªthey kept silent, and reported to no one in those days any of the things which they had seen. ªMatt 17:9; Mark 9:9f

37 ªOn the next day, when they came down from the mountain, a large crowd met Him. ªMatt 17:14-18; Mark 9:14-27

38 And a man from the crowd shouted, saying, "Teacher, I beg You to look at my son, for he is my only *boy,*

39 and a spirit seizes him, and he suddenly screams, and it throws him into a convulsion with foaming *at the mouth;* and only with difficulty does it leave him, mauling him *as it leaves.*

40 "I begged Your disciples to cast it out, and they could not."

41 And Jesus answered and said, "You unbelieving and perverted generation, how long shall I be with you and put up with you? Bring your son here."

42 While he was still approaching, the demon slammed him *to the ground* and threw him into a convulsion. But Jesus rebuked the unclean spirit, and healed the boy and gave him back to his father.

43 And they were all amazed at the greatness of God.

ªBut while everyone was marveling at all that He was doing, He said to His disciples, ªMatt 17:22f; Mark 9:30-32

44 "Let these words sink into your ears; ªfor the Son of Man is going to be delivered into the hands of men." ªLuke 9:22

45 But ªthey did not understand this statement, and it was concealed from them so that they would not perceive it; and they were afraid to ask Him about this statement. ªMark 9:32

The Test of Greatness

46 ªAn argument started among them as to which of them might be the greatest. ªLuke 22:24

47 But Jesus, ªknowing what they were thinking in their heart, took a child and stood him by His side, ªMark 9:4

48 and said to them, "ªWhoever receives this child in My name receives Me, and whoever receives Me receives Him who sent Me; for the one who is least among all of you, this is the one who is great." ªMatt 10:40; Luke 10:16

49 ªJohn answered and said, "Master, we saw someone casting out demons in Your name; and we tried to prevent him because he does not follow along with us." ªMark 9:38-40

50 But Jesus said to him, "Do not hinder *him;* ªfor he who is not against you is for you." ªMatt 12:30; Luke 11:23

51 When the days were approaching for His ascension, He was determined ªto go to Jerusalem; ªLuke 13:22; 17:11

52 and He sent messengers on ahead of Him, and they went and entered a village of the

aSamaritans to make arrangements for Him. aMatt 10:5; Luke 10:33

53 But they did not receive Him, abecause He was traveling toward Jerusalem. aJohn 4:9

54 When His disciples James and John saw *this,* they said, "Lord, do You want us to acommand fire to come down from heaven and consume them?" a2 Kin 1:9-16

55 But He turned and rebuked them, [and said, "You do not know what kind of spirit you are of;

56 for the Son of Man did not come to destroy men's lives, but to save them."] And they went on to another village.

Exacting Discipleship

57 As they were going along the road, asomeone said to Him, "I will follow You wherever You go." aMatt 8:19-22

58 And Jesus said to him, "The foxes have holes and the birds of the air *have* nests, but athe Son of Man has nowhere to lay His head." aMatt 8:20

59 And He said to another, "aFollow Me." But he said, "Lord, permit me first to go and bury my father." aMatt 8:22

60 But He said to him, "Allow the dead to bury their own dead; but as for you, go and aproclaim everywhere the kingdom of God." aMatt 4:23

61 Another also said, "I will follow You, Lord; but afirst permit me to say good-bye to those at home." a1 Kin 19:20

62 But Jesus said to him, "aNo one, after putting his hand to the plow and looking back, is fit for the kingdom of God." aPhil 3:13

The Seventy Sent Out

10 Now after this the Lord appointed seventy aothers, and sent them bin pairs ahead of Him to every city and place where He Himself was going to come. aLuke 9:1f, 52 bMark 6:7

2 And He was saying to them, "aThe harvest is plentiful, but the laborers are few; therefore beseech the Lord of the harvest to send out laborers into His harvest. aMatt 9:37, 38; John 4:35

3 "Go; abehold, I send you out as lambs in the midst of wolves. aMatt 10:16

4 "aCarry no money belt, no bag, no shoes; and greet no one on the way. aMatt 10:9-14; Mark 6:8-11

5 "Whatever house you enter, first say, 'Peace *be* to this house.'

6 "If a man of peace is there, your peace will rest on him; but if not, it will return to you.

7 "Stay in that house, eating and drinking what they give you; for athe laborer is worthy of his wages. Do not keep moving from house to house. aMatt 10:10; 1 Cor 9:14

8 "Whatever city you enter and they receive you, aeat what is set before you; a1 Cor 10:27

9 and heal those in it who are sick, and say to them, 'aThe kingdom of God has come near to you.' aMatt 3:2; 10:7

10 "But whatever city you enter and they do not receive you, go out into its streets and say,

11 'aEven the dust of your city which clings to our feet we wipe off *in protest* against you; yet be sure of this, that the kingdom of God has come near.' aMatt 10:14; Mark 6:11

12 "I say to you, ait will be more tolerable in that day for Sodom than for that city. aGen 19:24-28; Matt 10:15

13 "aWoe to you, Chorazin! Woe to you, Bethsaida! For if the miracles had been performed in Tyre and Sidon which occurred in you, they would have repented long ago, sitting in sackcloth and ashes. aMatt 11:21-23

14 "But it will be more tolerable for aTyre and Sidon in the judgment than for you. aMatt 11:21

15 "And you, aCapernaum, will not be exalted to heaven, will you? You will be brought down to Hades! aIs 14:13-15; Matt 4:13

16 "aThe one who listens to you listens to Me, and the one who rejects you rejects Me; and he who rejects Me rejects the One who sent Me." aMatt 10:40; Mark 9:37

The Happy Results

17 The seventy returned with joy, saying, "Lord, even athe demons are subject to us in Your name." aLuke 9:1

18 And He said to them, "I was watching aSatan fall from heaven like lightning. aMatt 4:10

19 "Behold, I have given you authority to atread on serpents and scorpions, and over all the power of the enemy, and nothing will injure you. aPs 91:13

20 "Nevertheless do not rejoice in this, that the spirits are subject to you, but rejoice that ayour names are recorded in heaven." aEx 32:32; Ps 69:28

21 aAt that very time He rejoiced greatly in the Holy Spirit, and said, "I praise You, O Father, Lord of heaven and earth, that You have hidden these things from *the* wise and intelligent and have revealed them to infants. Yes, Father, for this way was well-pleasing in Your sight. aMatt 11:25-27

22 "aAll things have been handed over to Me by My Father, and bno one knows who the Son is except the Father, and who the Father is except the Son, and anyone to whom the Son wills to reveal *Him.*" aJohn 3:35 bJohn 10:15

23 aTurning to the disciples, He said privately, "Blessed *are* the eyes which see the things you see, aMatt 13:16, 17

24 for I say to you, that many prophets and kings wished to see the things which you see, and did not see *them*, and to hear the things which you hear, and did not hear *them*."

25 ªAnd a lawyer stood up and put Him to the test, saying, "Teacher, what shall I do to inherit eternal life?" ªMatt 19:16-19

26 And He said to him, "What is written in the Law? How does it read to you?"

27 And he answered, "ªYOU SHALL LOVE THE LORD YOUR GOD WITH ALL YOUR HEART, AND WITH ALL YOUR SOUL, AND WITH ALL YOUR STRENGTH, AND WITH ALL YOUR MIND; AND YOUR NEIGHBOR AS YOURSELF." ªDeut 6:5; Lev 19:18

28 And He said to him, "You have answered correctly; ªDO THIS AND YOU WILL LIVE." ªLev 18:5; Ezek 20:11

29 But wishing ªto justify himself, he said to Jesus, "And who is my neighbor?" ªLuke 16:15

The Good Samaritan

30 Jesus replied and said, "A man was ªgoing down from Jerusalem to Jericho, and fell among robbers, and they stripped him and beat him, and went away leaving him half dead. ªLuke 18:31; 19:28

31 "And by chance a priest was going down on that road, and when he saw him, he passed by on the other side.

32 "Likewise a Levite also, when he came to the place and saw him, passed by on the other side.

33 "But a ªSamaritan, who was on a journey, came upon him; and when he saw him, he felt compassion, ªMatt 10:5; Luke 9:52

34 and came to him and bandaged up his wounds, pouring oil and wine on *them;* and he put him on his own beast, and brought him to an inn and took care of him.

35 "On the next day he took out two denarii and gave them to the innkeeper and said, 'Take care of him; and whatever more you spend, when I return I will repay you.'

36 "Which of these three do you think proved to be a neighbor to the man who fell into the robbers' *hands?*"

37 And he said, "The one who showed mercy toward him." Then Jesus said to him, "Go and do the same."

Martha and Mary

38 Now as they were traveling along, He entered a village; and a woman named ªMartha welcomed Him into her home. ªLuke 10:40f; John 11:1, 5, 19ff, 30, 39

39 She had a sister called ªMary, who was seated at the Lord's feet, listening to His word. ªLuke 10:42; John 11:1f, 19f, 28, 31f, 45

40 But ªMartha was distracted with all her preparations; and she came up *to Him* and said, "Lord, do You not care that my sister has left

me to do all the serving alone? Then tell her to help me." ªLuke 10:38, 41; John 11:1, 5, 19ff, 30, 39

41 But the Lord answered and said to her, "Martha, Martha, you are ªworried and bothered about so many things; ªMatt 6:25

42 ªbut *only* one thing is necessary, for Mary has chosen the good part, which shall not be taken away from her." ªPs 27:4; John 6:27

Instruction about Prayer

11 It happened that while Jesus was praying in a certain place, after He had finished, one of His disciples said to Him, "Lord, teach us to pray just as John also taught his disciples."

2 And He said to them, "ªWhen you pray, say:

'Father, hallowed be Your name.
Your kingdom come. ªMatt 6:9-13

3 'Give us ªeach day our daily bread. ªActs 17:11

4 'And forgive us our sins,
For we ourselves also forgive everyone
who ªis indebted to us.
And lead us not into temptation.' " ªLuke 13:4

5 Then He said to them, "Suppose one of you has a friend, and goes to him at midnight and says to him, 'Friend, lend me three loaves;

6 for a friend of mine has come to me from a journey, and I have nothing to set before him';

7 and from inside he answers and says, 'Do not bother me; the door has already been shut and my children and I are in bed; I cannot get up and give you *anything.*'

8 "I tell you, even though he will not get up and give him *anything* because he is his friend, yet ªbecause of his persistence he will get up and give him as much as he needs. ªLuke 18:1-5

9 "So I say to you, ªask, and it will be given to you; seek, and you will find; knock, and it will be opened to you. ªMatt 7:7-11

10 "For everyone who asks, receives; and he who seeks, finds; and to him who knocks, it will be opened.

11 "Now suppose one of you fathers is asked by his son for a fish; he will not give him a snake instead of a fish, will he?

12 "Or *if* he is asked for an egg, he will not give him a scorpion, will he?

13 "ªIf you then, being evil, know how to give good gifts to your children, how much more will *your* heavenly Father give the Holy Spirit to those who ask Him?" ªMatt 7:11; Luke 18:7f

Pharisees' Blasphemy

14 ªAnd He was casting out a demon, and it was mute; when the demon had gone out, the mute man spoke; and the crowds were amazed. ªMatt 9:32-34

15 But some of them said, "He casts out

demons ᵃby ᵇBeelzebul, the ruler of the demons." ᵃMatt 9:34 ᵇMatt 10:25

16 Others, to test *Him,* ᵃwere demanding of Him a sign from heaven. ᵃMatt 12:38; 16:1

17 ᵃBut He knew their thoughts and said to them, "Any kingdom divided against itself is laid waste; and a house *divided* against itself falls. ᵃMatt 12:25-29; Mark 3:23-27

18 "If ᵃSatan also is divided against himself, how will his kingdom stand? For you say that I cast out demons by Beelzebul. ᵃMatt 4:10

19 "And if I by ᵃBeelzebul cast out demons, by whom do your sons cast them out? So they will be your judges. ᵃMatt 10:25

20 "But if I cast out demons by the ᵃfinger of God, then ᵇthe kingdom of God has come upon you. ᵃEx 8:19 ᵇMatt 3:2

21 "When a strong *man,* fully armed, guards his own house, his possessions are undisturbed.

22 "But when someone stronger than he attacks him and overpowers him, he takes away from him all his armor on which he had relied and distributes his plunder.

23 "ᵃHe who is not with Me is against Me; and he who does not gather with Me, scatters. ᵃMatt 12:30; Mark 9:40

24 "ᵃWhen the unclean spirit goes out of a man, it passes through waterless places seeking rest, and not finding any, it says, 'I will return to my house from which I came.' ᵃMatt 12:43-45

25 "And when it comes, it finds it swept and put in order.

26 "Then it goes and takes *along* seven other spirits more evil than itself, and they go in and live there; and the last state of that man becomes worse than the first."

27 While Jesus was saying these things, one of the women in the crowd raised her voice and said to Him, "ᵃBlessed is the womb that bore You and the breasts at which You nursed." ᵃLuke 23:29

28 But He said, "On the contrary, blessed are ᵃthose who hear the word of God and observe it." ᵃLuke 8:21

The Sign of Jonah

29 As the crowds were increasing, He began to say, "ᵃThis generation is a wicked generation; it seeks for a sign, and *yet* no sign will be given to it but the sign of Jonah. ᵃMatt 16:4; Mark 8:12

30 "For just as ᵃJonah became a sign to the Ninevites, so will the Son of Man be to this generation. ᵃJon 3:4

31 "The ᵃQueen of the South will rise up with the men of this generation at the judgment and condemn them, because she came from the ends of the earth to hear the wisdom of Solo-

mon; and behold, something greater than Solomon is here. ᵃ1 Kin 10:1-10; 2 Chr 9:1-12

32 "The men of Nineveh will stand up with this generation at the judgment and condemn it, because ᵃthey repented at the preaching of Jonah; and behold, something greater than Jonah is here. ᵃJon 3:5

33 "ᵃNo one, after lighting a lamp, puts it away in a cellar nor under a basket, but on the lampstand, so that those who enter may see the light. ᵃMatt 5:15; Mark 4:21

34 "ᵃThe eye is the lamp of your body; when your eye is clear, your whole body also is full of light; but when it is bad, your body also is full of darkness. ᵃMatt 6:22, 23

35 "Then watch out that the light in you is not darkness.

36 "If therefore your whole body is full of light, with no dark part in it, it will be wholly illumined, as when the lamp illumines you with its rays."

Woes upon the Pharisees

37 Now when He had spoken, a Pharisee *asked Him to have lunch with him; and He went in, and reclined *at the table.*

38 When the Pharisee saw it, he was surprised that He had not first ᵃceremonially washed before the meal. ᵃMatt 15:2; Mark 7:3f

39 But the Lord said to him, "Now ᵃyou Pharisees clean the outside of the cup and of the platter; but inside of you, you are full of robbery and wickedness. ᵃMatt 23:25f

40 "ᵃYou foolish ones, did not He who made the outside make the inside also? ᵃLuke 12:20; 1 Cor 15:36

41 "But ᵃgive that which is within as charity, and then all things are ᵇclean for you. ᵃLuke 12:33 ᵇTitus 1:15

42 "ᵃBut woe to you Pharisees! For you ᵇpay tithe of mint and rue and every *kind of* garden herb, and *yet* disregard justice and the love of God; but these are the things you should have done without neglecting the others. ᵃMatt 23:23 ᵇLev 27:30

43 "Woe to you Pharisees! For you ᵃlove the chief seats in the synagogues and the respectful greetings in the market places. ᵃMatt 23:6f; Mark 12:38f

44 "ᵃWoe to you! For you are like concealed tombs, and the people who walk over *them* are unaware *of it.*" ᵃMatt 23:27

45 One of the ᵃlawyers *said to Him in reply, "Teacher, when You say this, You insult us too." ᵃMatt 22:35; Luke 11:46, 52

46 But He said, "Woe to you lawyers as well! For ᵃyou weigh men down with burdens hard to bear, while you yourselves will not even touch the burdens with one of your fingers. ᵃMatt 23:4

47 "ªWoe to you! For you build the tombs of the prophets, and *it was* your fathers *who* killed them. ªMatt 23:29ff

48 "So you are witnesses and approve the deeds of your fathers; because it was they who killed them, and you build *their* tombs.

49 "For this reason also ªthe wisdom of God said, 'I will send to them prophets and apostles, and *some* of them they will kill and *some* they will persecute, ª1 Cor 1:24, 30; Col 2:3

50 so that the blood of all the prophets, shed ªsince the foundation of the world, may be charged against this generation, ªMatt 25:34

51 from the blood of Abel to ªthe blood of Zechariah, who was killed between the altar and the house *of God;* yes, I tell you, it shall be charged against this generation.' ª2 Chr 24:20, 21

52 "Woe to you lawyers! For you have taken away the key of knowledge; ªyou yourselves did not enter, and you hindered those who were entering." ªMatt 23:13

53 When He left there, the scribes and the Pharisees began to be very hostile and to question Him closely on many subjects,

54 plotting against Him ªto catch *Him* in something He might say. ªMark 12:13

God Knows and Cares

12 Under these circumstances, after so many thousands of people had gathered together that they were stepping on one another, He began saying to His disciples first *of all,* "ªBeware of the leaven of the Pharisees, which is hypocrisy. ªMatt 16:6, 11f; Mark 8:15

2 "ªBut there is nothing covered up that will not be revealed, and hidden that will not be known. ªMatt 10:26; Mark 4:22

3 "Accordingly, whatever you have said in the dark will be heard in the light, and what you have whispered in the inner rooms will be proclaimed upon ªthe housetops. ªMatt 10:27; 24:17

4 "I say to you, ªMy friends, do not be afraid of those who kill the body and after that have no more that they can do. ªJohn 15:13-15

5 "But I will warn you whom to fear: ªfear the One who, after He has killed, has authority to cast into hell; yes, I tell you, fear Him! ªHeb 10:31

6 "Are not ªfive sparrows sold for two cents? *Yet* not one of them is forgotten before God. ªMatt 10:29

7 "ªIndeed, the very hairs of your head are all numbered. Do not fear; you are more valuable than many sparrows. ªMatt 10:30

8 "And I say to you, everyone who ªconfesses Me before men, the Son of Man will confess him also before the angels of God; ªMatt 10:32; Luke 15:10

9 but ªhe who denies Me before men will be

denied before the angels of God. ªMatt 10:33; Luke 9:26

10 "ªAnd everyone who speaks a word against the Son of Man, it will be forgiven him; but he who blasphemes against the Holy Spirit, it will not be forgiven him. ªMatt 12:31, 32; Mark 3:28-30

11 "When they bring you before the synagogues and the rulers and the authorities, do not ªworry about how or what you are to speak in your defense, or what you are to say; ªMatt 6:25; 10:19

12 for ªthe Holy Spirit will teach you in that very hour what you ought to say." ªMatt 10:20; Luke 21:15

Covetousness Denounced

13 Someone in the crowd said to Him, "Teacher, tell my brother to divide the *family* inheritance with me."

14 But He said to him, "ªMan, who appointed Me a judge or arbitrator over you?" ªMic 6:8; Rom 2:1, 3

15 Then He said to them, "ªBeware, and be on your guard against every form of greed; for not *even* when one has an abundance does his life consist of his possessions." ª1 Tim 6:6-10

16 And He told them a parable, saying, "The land of a rich man was very productive.

17 "And he began reasoning to himself, saying, 'What shall I do, since I have no place to store my crops?'

18 "Then he said, 'This is what I will do: I will tear down my barns and build larger ones, and there I will store all my grain and my goods.

19 'And I will say to my soul, "Soul, ªyou have many goods laid up for many years *to come;* take your ease, eat, drink *and* be merry." ' ªEccl 11:9

20 "But God said to him, 'You fool! This *very* night ªyour soul is required of you; and ᵇ*now* who will own what you have prepared?' ªJob 27:8 ᵇPs 39:6

21 "So is the man who ªstores up treasure for himself, and is not rich toward God." ªLuke 12:33

22 And He said to His disciples, "ªFor this reason I say to you, do not worry about *your* life, *as to* what you will eat; nor for your body, *as to* what you will put on. ªMatt 6:25-33

23 "For life is more than food, and the body more than clothing.

24 "Consider the ªravens, for they neither sow nor reap; they have no storeroom nor barn, and *yet* God feeds them; how much more valuable you are than the birds! ªJob 38:41

25 "And which of you by worrying can add a *single* ªhour to his life's span? ªPs 39:5

26 "If then you cannot do even a very little thing, why do you worry about other matters?

27 "Consider the lilies, how they grow: they neither toil nor spin; but I tell you, not even

ªSolomon in all his glory clothed himself like
one of these. ª*1 Kin 10:4-7; 2 Chr 9:3-6*
28 "But if God so clothes the grass in the field,
which is *alive* today and tomorrow is thrown
into the furnace, how much more *will He
clothe* you? ªYou men of little faith! ª*Matt 6:30*
29 "And do not seek what you will eat and
what you will drink, and do not ªkeep worrying. ª*Matt 6:31*
30 "For all these things the nations of the
world eagerly seek; but your Father knows that
you need these things.
31 "But seek His kingdom, and ªthese things
will be added to you. ª*Matt 6:33*
32 "Do not be afraid, ªlittle flock, for ᵇyour
Father has chosen gladly to give you the kingdom. ª*John 21:15-17* ᵇ*Eph 1:5, 9*
33 "ªSell your possessions and give to charity;
make yourselves money belts which do not
wear out, an unfailing treasure in heaven,
where no thief comes near nor moth destroys.
ª*Matt 19:21; Luke 11:41*
34 "For ªwhere your treasure is, there your
heart will be also. ª*Matt 6:21*

Be in Readiness

35 "Be dressed in ªreadiness, and *keep* your
lamps lit. ª*Eph 6:14; 1 Pet 1:13*
36 "Be like men who are waiting for their
master when he returns from the wedding
feast, so that they may immediately open *the
door* to him when he comes and knocks.
37 "Blessed are those slaves whom the master
will find ªon the alert when he comes; truly I
say to you, that ᵇhe will gird himself *to serve,*
and have them recline *at the table,* and will
come up and wait on them. ª*Matt 24:42* ᵇ*Luke 17:8*
38 "ªWhether he comes in the second watch,
or even in the third, and finds *them* so, blessed
are those *slaves.* ª*Matt 24:43*
39 "ªBut be sure of this, that if the head of the
house had known at what hour the thief was
coming, he would not have allowed his house
to be broken into. ª*Matt 24:43, 44*
40 "ªYou too, be ready; for the Son of Man is
coming at an hour that you do not expect."
ª*Mark 13:33; Luke 21:36*
41 Peter said, "Lord, are You addressing this
parable to us, or ªto everyone *else* as well?"
ª*Luke 12:47, 48*
42 And the Lord said, "ªWho then is the faithful and sensible steward, whom his master will
put in charge of his servants, to give them their
rations at the proper time? ª*Matt 24:45-51*
43 "Blessed is that ªslave whom his master
finds so doing when he comes. ª*Luke 12:42*
44 "Truly I say to you that he will put him in
charge of all his possessions.
45 "But if that slave says in his heart, 'My
master will be a long time in coming,' and

begins to beat the slaves, *both* men and
women, and to eat and drink and get drunk;
46 the master of that slave will come on a day
when he does not expect *him* and at an hour he
does not know, and will cut him in pieces, and
assign him a place with the unbelievers.
47 "And that slave who knew his master's will
and did not get ready or act in accord with his
will, will ªreceive many lashes, ª*Deut 25:2;
James 4:17*
48 but the one who did not ªknow *it,* and committed deeds worthy of a flogging, will receive
but few. From everyone who has been given
much, much will be required; and to whom
they entrusted much, of him they will ask all
the more. ª*Lev 5:17; Num 15:29f*

Christ Divides Men

49 "I have come to cast fire upon the earth;
and how I wish it were already kindled!
50 "But I have a ªbaptism to undergo, and how
distressed I am until it is accomplished!
ª*Mark 10:38*
51 "ªDo you suppose that I came to grant
peace on earth? I tell you, no, but rather division; ª*Matt 10:34-36*
52 for from now on five *members* in one
household will be divided, three against two
and two against three.
53 "They will be divided, ªfather against son
and son against father, mother against daughter
and daughter against mother, mother-in-law
against daughter-in-law and daughter-in-law
against mother-in-law." ª*Mic 7:6; Matt 10:21*
54 And He was also saying to the crowds,
"ªWhen you see a cloud rising in the west,
immediately you say, 'A shower is coming,'
and so it turns out. ª*Matt 16:2f*
55 "And when *you see* a south wind blowing,
you say, 'It will be a ªhot day,' and it turns out
that way. ª*Matt 20:12*
56 "You hypocrites! ªYou know how to analyze the appearance of the earth and the sky,
but why do you not analyze this present time?
ª*Matt 16:3*
57 "And ªwhy do you not even on your own
initiative judge what is right? ª*Luke 21:30*
58 "For ªwhile you are going with your opponent to appear before the magistrate, on *your*
way *there* make an effort to settle with him, so
that he may not drag you before the judge, and
the judge turn you over to the officer, and the
officer throw you into prison. ª*Matt 5:25, 26*
59 "I say to you, you will not get out of there
until you have paid the very last ªcent."
ª*Mark 12:42*

Call to Repent

13 Now on the same occasion there were
some present who reported to Him

about the Galileans whose blood ᵃPilate had mixed with their sacrifices. ᵃMatt 27

2 And Jesus said to them, "ᵃDo you suppose that these Galileans were *greater* sinners than all *other* Galileans because they suffered this *fate?* ᵃJohn 9:2f

3 "I tell you, no, but unless you repent, you will all likewise perish.

4 "Or do you suppose that those eighteen on whom the tower in ᵃSiloam fell and killed them were *worse* culprits than all the men who live in Jerusalem? ᵃNeh 3:15; Is 8:6

5 "I tell you, no, but unless you repent, you will all likewise perish."

6 And He *began* telling this parable: "A man had ᵃa fig tree which had been planted in his vineyard; and he came looking for fruit on it and did not find any. ᵃMatt 21:19

7 "And he said to the vineyard-keeper, 'Behold, for three years I have come looking for fruit on this fig tree without finding any. ᵃCut it down! Why does it even use up the ground?' ᵃMatt 3:10; 7:19

8 "And he answered and said to him, 'Let it alone, sir, for this year too, until I dig around it and put in fertilizer;

9 and if it bears fruit next year, *fine;* but if not, cut it down.'"

Healing on the Sabbath

10 And He was ᵃteaching in one of the synagogues on the Sabbath. ᵃMatt 4:23

11 And there was a woman who for eighteen years had had ᵃa sickness caused by a spirit; and she was bent double, and could not straighten up at all. ᵃLuke 13:16

12 When Jesus saw her, He called her over and said to her, "Woman, you are freed from your sickness."

13 And He ᵃlaid His hands on her; and immediately she was made erect again and *began* glorifying God. ᵃMark 5:23

14 But the synagogue official, indignant because Jesus had healed on the Sabbath, *began* saying to the crowd in response, "ᵃThere are six days in which work should be done; so come during them and get healed, and not on the Sabbath day." ᵃEx 20:9; Deut 5:13

15 But the Lord answered him and said, "You hypocrites, ᵃdoes not each of you on the Sabbath untie his ox or his donkey from the stall and lead him away to water *him?* ᵃLuke 14:5

16 "And this woman, ᵃa daughter of Abraham as she is, whom Satan has bound for eighteen long years, should she not have been released from this bond on the Sabbath day?" ᵃLuke 19:9

17 As He said this, all His opponents were being humiliated; and ᵃthe entire crowd was rejoicing over all the glorious things being done by Him. ᵃLuke 18:43

Parables of Mustard Seed and Leaven

18 So ᵃHe was saying, "What is the kingdom of God like, and to what shall I compare it? ᵃMatt 13:31, 32; Mark 4:30-32

19 "It is like a mustard seed, which a man took and threw into his own garden; and it grew and became a tree, and ᵃTHE BIRDS OF THE AIR NESTED IN ITS BRANCHES." ᵃEzek 17:23

20 And again He said, "ᵃTo what shall I compare the kingdom of God? ᵃMatt 13:24; Luke 13:18

21 "ᵃIt is like leaven, which a woman took and hid in three pecks of flour until it was all leavened." ᵃMatt 13:33

Teaching in the Villages

22 And He was passing through from one city and village to another, teaching, and ᵃproceeding on His way to Jerusalem. ᵃLuke 9:51

23 And someone said to Him, "Lord, are there *just* a few who are being saved?" And He said to them,

24 "ᵃStrive to enter through the narrow door; for many, I tell you, will seek to enter and will not be able. ᵃMatt 7:13

25 "Once the head of the house gets up and ᵃshuts the door, and you begin to stand outside and knock on the door, saying, 'Lord, open up to us!' then He will answer and say to you, 'ᵇI do not know where you are from.' ᵃMatt 25:10 ᵇMatt 7:23

26 "Then you will ᵃbegin to say, 'We ate and drank in Your presence, and You taught in our streets'; ᵃLuke 3:8

27 and He will say, 'I tell you, I do not know where you are from; ᵃDEPART FROM ME, ALL YOU EVILDOERS.' ᵃPs 6:8; Matt 25:41

28 "ᵃIn that place there will be weeping and gnashing of teeth when you see Abraham and Isaac and Jacob and all the prophets in the kingdom of God, but yourselves being thrown out. ᵃMatt 8:12; 22:13

29 "And they ᵃwill come from east and west and from north and south, and will recline *at the table* in the kingdom of God. ᵃMatt 8:11

30 "And behold, ᵃ*some* are last who will be first and *some* are first who will be last." ᵃMatt 19:30; 20:16

31 Just at that time some Pharisees approached, saying to Him, "Go away, leave here, for ᵃHerod wants to kill You." ᵃMatt 14:1; Luke 3:1

32 And He said to them, "Go and tell that fox, 'Behold, I cast out demons and perform cures today and tomorrow, and the third *day* I ᵃreach My goal.' ᵃHeb 2:10; 5:9

33 "Nevertheless I must journey on today and tomorrow and the next *day;* for it cannot be that a ᵃprophet would perish outside of Jerusalem. ᵃMatt 21:11

34 "ᵃO Jerusalem, Jerusalem, *the city* that kills

the prophets and stones those sent to her! How often I wanted to gather your children together, just as a hen *gathers* her brood under her wings, and you would not *have it!* ᵃ*Luke 19:41*

35 "Behold, your house is left to you *desolate;* and I say to you, you will not see Me until *the time* comes when you say, 'ᵃBLESSED IS HE WHO COMES IN THE NAME OF THE LORD!' " ᵃ*Ps 118:26; Matt 21:9*

Jesus Heals on the Sabbath

14 It happened that when He went into the house of one of the leaders of the Pharisees on *the* Sabbath to eat bread, ᵃthey were watching Him closely. ᵃ*Mark 3:2*

2 And there in front of Him was a man suffering from dropsy.

3 And Jesus answered and spoke to the lawyers and Pharisees, saying, "ᵃIs it lawful to heal on the Sabbath, or not?" ᵃ*Matt 12:2; Luke 13:14*

4 But they kept silent. And He took hold of him and healed him, and sent him away.

5 And He said to them, "ᵃWhich one of you will have a son or an ox fall into a well, and will not immediately pull him out on a Sabbath day?" ᵃ*Matt 12:11; Luke 13:15*

6 ᵃAnd they could make no reply to this. ᵃ*Matt 22:46; Luke 20:40*

Parable of the Guests

7 And He *began* speaking a parable to the invited guests when He noticed how ᵃthey had been picking out the places of honor *at the table,* saying to them, ᵃ*Matt 23:6*

8 "When you are invited by someone to a wedding feast, ᵃdo not take the place of honor, for someone more distinguished than you may have been invited by him, ᵃ*Prov 25:6, 7*

9 and he who invited you both will come and say to you, 'Give *your* place to this man,' and then ᵃin disgrace you proceed to occupy the last place. ᵃ*Luke 3:8*

10 "But when you are invited, go and recline at the last place, so that when the one who has invited you comes, he may say to you, 'Friend, ᵃmove up higher'; then you will have honor in the sight of all who are at the table with you. ᵃ*Prov 25:6, 7*

11 "ᵃFor everyone who exalts himself will be humbled, and he who humbles himself will be exalted." ᵃ*2 Sam 22:28; Prov 29:23*

12 And He also went on to say to the one who had invited Him, "When you give a luncheon or a dinner, do not invite your friends or your brothers or your relatives or rich neighbors, otherwise they may also invite you in return and *that* will be your repayment.

13 "But when you give a reception, invite *the* poor, *the* crippled, *the* lame, *the* blind,

14 and you will be blessed, since they do not have *the means* to repay you; for you will be

repaid at ᵃthe resurrection of the righteous." ᵃ*John 5:29; Acts 24:15*

15 When one of those who were reclining *at the table* with Him heard this, he said to Him, "ᵃBlessed is everyone who will eat bread in the kingdom of God!" ᵃ*Rev 19:9*

Parable of the Dinner

16 But He said to him, "ᵃA man was giving a big dinner, and he invited many; ᵃ*Matt 22:2-14; Luke 14:16-24*

17 and at the dinner hour he sent his slave to say to those who had been invited, 'Come; for everything is ready now.'

18 "But they all alike began to make excuses. The first one said to him, 'I have bought a piece of land and I need to go out and look at it; please consider me excused.'

19 "Another one said, 'I have bought five yoke of oxen, and I am going to try them out; please consider me excused.'

20 "Another one said, 'ᵃI have married a wife, and for that reason I cannot come.' ᵃ*Deut 24:5; 1 Cor 7:33*

21 "And the slave came *back* and reported this to his master. Then the head of the household became angry and said to his slave, 'Go out at once into the streets and lanes of the city and bring in here the poor and crippled and blind and lame.'

22 "And the slave said, 'Master, what you commanded has been done, and still there is room.'

23 "And the master said to the slave, 'Go out into the highways and along the hedges, and compel *them* to come in, so that my house may be filled.

24 'For I tell you, none of those men who were invited shall taste of my dinner.' "

Discipleship Tested

25 Now large crowds were going along with Him; and He turned and said to them,

26 "ᵃIf anyone comes to Me, and does not hate his own father and mother and wife and children and brothers and sisters, yes, and even his own life, he cannot be My disciple. ᵃ*Matt 10:37*

27 "Whoever does not ᵃcarry his own cross and come after Me cannot be My disciple. ᵃ*Matt 10:38; 16:24*

28 "For which one of you, when he wants to build a tower, does not first sit down and calculate the cost to see if he has enough to complete it?

29 "Otherwise, when he has laid a foundation and is not able to finish, all who observe it begin to ridicule him,

30 saying, 'This man began to build and was not able to finish.'

31 "Or what king, when he sets out to meet another king in battle, will not first sit down

and [a]consider whether he is strong enough with ten thousand *men* to encounter the one coming against him with twenty thousand? [a]*Prov 20:18*

32 "Or else, while the other is still far away, he sends a delegation and asks for terms of peace.

33 "So then, none of you can be My disciple who [a]does not give up all his own possessions. [a]*Phil 3:7; Heb 11:26*

34 "Therefore, salt is good; but [a]if even salt has become tasteless, with what will it be seasoned? [a]*Matt 5:13; Mark 9:50*

35 "It is useless either for the soil or for the manure pile; it is thrown out. [a]He who has ears to hear, let him hear." [a]*Matt 11:15*

The Lost Sheep

15 Now all the [a]tax collectors and the sinners were coming near Him to listen to Him. [a]*Luke 5:29*

2 Both the Pharisees and the scribes *began* to grumble, saying, "This man receives sinners and [a]eats with them." [a]*Matt 9:11*

3 So He told them this parable, saying,

4 "[a]What man among you, if he has a hundred sheep and has lost one of them, does not leave the ninety-nine in the open pasture and go after the one which is lost until he finds it? [a]*Matt 18:12-14; Luke 15:4-7*

5 "When he has found it, he lays it on his shoulders, rejoicing.

6 "And when he comes home, he calls together his friends and his neighbors, saying to them, 'Rejoice with me, for I have found my sheep which was lost!'

7 "I tell you that in the same way, there will be *more* joy in heaven over one sinner who repents than over ninety-nine righteous persons who need no repentance.

The Lost Coin

8 "Or what woman, if she has ten silver coins and loses one coin, does not light a lamp and sweep the house and search carefully until she finds it?

9 "When she has found it, she calls together her friends and neighbors, saying, 'Rejoice with me, for I have found the coin which I had lost!'

10 "In the same way, I tell you, there is joy [a]in the presence of the angels of God over one sinner who repents." [a]*Matt 10:32; Luke 15:7*

The Prodigal Son

11 And He said, "A man had two sons.

12 "The younger of them said to his father, 'Father, give me [a]the share of the estate that falls to me.' So he divided his [b]wealth between them. [a]*Deut 21:17* [b]*Luke 15:30*

13 "And not many days later, the younger son gathered everything together and went on a journey into a distant country, and there he squandered his estate with loose living.

14 "Now when he had spent everything, a severe famine occurred in that country, and he began to be impoverished.

15 "So he went and hired himself out to one of the citizens of that country, and he sent him into his fields to feed swine.

16 "And he would have gladly filled his stomach with the pods that the swine were eating, and no one was giving *anything* to him.

17 "But when he came to his senses, he said, 'How many of my father's hired men have more than enough bread, but I am dying here with hunger!

18 'I will get up and go to my father, and will say to him, "Father, I have sinned against heaven, and in your sight;

19 I am no longer worthy to be called your son; make me as one of your hired men."'

20 "So he got up and came to his father. But while he was still a long way off, his father saw him and felt compassion *for him,* and ran and [a]embraced him and kissed him. [a]*Gen 45:14; 46:29*

21 "And the son said to him, 'Father, I have sinned against heaven and in your sight; I am no longer worthy to be called your son.'

22 "But the father said to his slaves, 'Quickly bring out [a]the best robe and put it on him, and [b]put a ring on his hand and sandals on his feet; [a]*Zech 3:4* [b]*Gen 41:42*

23 and bring the fattened calf, kill it, and let us eat and celebrate;

24 for this son of mine was [a]dead and has come to life again; he was lost and has been found.' And they began to celebrate. [a]*Matt 8:22; Luke 9:60*

25 "Now his older son was in the field, and when he came and approached the house, he heard music and dancing.

26 "And he summoned one of the servants and *began* inquiring what these things could be.

27 "And he said to him, 'Your brother has come, and your father has killed the fattened calf because he has received him back safe and sound.'

28 "But he became angry and was not willing to go in; and his father came out and *began* pleading with him.

29 "But he answered and said to his father, 'Look! For so many years I have been serving you and I have never neglected a command of yours; and *yet* you have never given me a young goat, so that I might celebrate with my friends;

30 but when this son of yours came, who has devoured your [a]wealth with prostitutes, you

killed the fattened calf for him.' ᵃ*Prov 29:3;*
Luke 15:12

31 "And he said to him, 'Son, you have
always been with me, and all that is mine is
yours.

32 'But we had to celebrate and rejoice, for
this brother of yours was ᵃdead and *has begun*
to live, and *was* lost and has been found.' "
ᵃ*Luke 15:24*

The Unrighteous Steward

16 Now He was also saying to the disciples, "There was a rich man who had a
manager, and this *manager* was reported to
him as ᵃsquandering his possessions. ᵃ*Luke 15:13*

2 "And he called him and said to him, 'What
is this I hear about you? Give an accounting of
your management, for you can no longer be
manager.'

3 "The manager said to himself, 'What shall
I do, since my master is taking the management away from me? I am not strong enough
to dig; I am ashamed to beg.

4 'I know what I shall do, so that when I am
removed from the management people will
welcome me into their homes.'

5 "And he summoned each one of his master's debtors, and he *began* saying to the first,
'How much do you owe my master?'

6 "And he said, 'A hundred measures of oil.'
And he said to him, 'Take your bill, and sit
down quickly and write fifty.'

7 "Then he said to another, 'And how much
do you owe?' And he said, 'A hundred measures of wheat.' He *said to him, 'Take your
bill, and write eighty.'

8 "And his master praised the unrighteous
manager because he had acted shrewdly; for
the sons of this age are more shrewd in relation
to their own kind than the ᵃsons of light.
ᵃ*John 12:36; Eph 5:8*

9 "And I say to you, make friends for yourselves by means of the ᵃwealth of unrighteousness, so that when it fails, they will receive you
into the eternal dwellings.   ᵃ*Matt 6:24; Luke*
16:11, 13

10 "ᵃHe who is faithful in a very little thing is
faithful also in much; and he who is unrighteous in a very little thing is unrighteous also in
much. ᵃ*Matt 25:21, 23*

11 "Therefore if you have not been faithful in
the *use of* unrighteous ᵃwealth, who will entrust
the true *riches* to you? ᵃ*Luke 16:9*

12 "And if you have not been faithful in *the*
use of that which is another's, who will give
you that which is your own?

13 "ᵃNo servant can serve two masters; for
either he will hate the one and love the other,
or else he will be devoted to one and despise

the other. You cannot serve God and wealth."
ᵃ*Matt 6:24*

14 Now the Pharisees, who were ᵃlovers of
money, were listening to all these things and
were scoffing at Him. ᵃ*2 Tim 3:2*

15 And He said to them, "You are those who
justify yourselves in the sight of men, but ᵃGod
knows your hearts; for that which is highly
esteemed among men is detestable in the sight
of God. ᵃ*1 Sam 16:7; Prov 21:2*

16 "ᵃThe Law and the Prophets *were pro-*
claimed until John; since that time ᵇthe gospel
of the kingdom of God has been preached, and
everyone is forcing his way into it.
ᵃ*Matt 11:12f* ᵇ*Matt 4:23*

17 "ᵃBut it is easier for heaven and earth to
pass away than for one stroke of a letter of the
Law to fail. ᵃ*Matt 5:18*

18 "ᵃEveryone who divorces his wife and
marries another commits adultery, and he who
marries one who is divorced from a husband
commits adultery. ᵃ*Matt 5:32; 1 Cor 7:10, 11*

The Rich Man and Lazarus

19 "Now there was a rich man, and he habitu-
ally dressed in purple and fine linen, joyously
living in splendor every day.

20 "And a poor man named Lazarus ᵃwas laid
at his gate, covered with sores, ᵃ*Acts 3:2*

21 and longing to be fed with the *crumbs*
which were falling from the rich man's table;
besides, even the dogs were coming and lick-
ing his sores.

22 "Now the poor man died and was carried
away by the angels to ᵃAbraham's bosom; and
the rich man also died and was buried.
ᵃ*John 1:18; 13:23*

23 "In ᵃHades he lifted up his eyes, being in
torment, and *saw Abraham far away and Lazarus in his bosom. ᵃ*Matt 11:23*

24 "And he cried out and said, 'ᵃFather Abraham, have mercy on me, and send Lazarus so
that he may dip the tip of his finger in water
and cool off my tongue, for I am in agony in
ᵇthis flame.' ᵃ*Luke 3:8* ᵇ*Matt 25:41*

25 "But Abraham said, 'Child, remember that
ᵃduring your life you received your good
things, and likewise Lazarus bad things; but
now he is being comforted here, and you are in
agony. ᵃ*Luke 6:24*

26 'And besides all this, between us and you
there is a great chasm fixed, so that those who
wish to come over from here to you will not be
able, and *that* none may cross over from there
to us.'

27 "And he said, 'Then I beg you, father, that
you send him to my father's house—

28 for I have five brothers—in order that he
may ᵃwarn them, so that they will not also
come to this place of torment.' ᵃ*Acts 2:40; 8:25*

29 "But Abraham *said, 'They have ᵃMoses and the Prophets; let them hear them.'
ᵃLuke 4:17; John 5:45-47

30 "But he said, 'No, ᵃfather Abraham, but if someone goes to them from the dead, they will repent!'   ᵃLuke 3:8; 16:24

31 "But he said to him, 'If they do not listen to Moses and the Prophets, they will not be persuaded even if someone rises from the dead.' "

Instructions

17 He said to His disciples, "ᵃIt is inevitable that stumbling blocks come, but woe to him through whom they come!   ᵃMatt 18:7; 1 Cor 11:19

2 "ᵃIt would be better for him if a millstone were hung around his neck and he were thrown into the sea, than that he would cause one of these little ones to stumble.   ᵃMatt 18:6; Mark 9:42

3 "Be on your guard! ᵃIf your brother sins, rebuke him; and if he repents, forgive him.
ᵃMatt 18:15

4 "And if he sins against you ᵃseven times a day, and returns to you seven times, saying, 'I repent,' forgive him."   ᵃMatt 18:21f

5 The apostles said to the Lord, "Increase our faith!"

6 And the Lord said, "If you had faith like ᵃa mustard seed, you would say to this mulberry tree, 'Be uprooted and be planted in the sea'; and it would obey you.   ᵃMatt 13:31; 17:20

7 "Which of you, having a slave plowing or tending sheep, will say to him when he has come in from the field, 'Come immediately and sit down to eat'?

8 "But will he not say to him, 'ᵃPrepare something for me to eat, and *properly* clothe yourself and serve me while I eat and drink; and afterward you may eat and drink'?
ᵃLuke 12:37

9 "He does not thank the slave because he did the things which were commanded, does he?

10 "So you too, when you do all the things which are commanded you, say, 'We are unworthy slaves; we have done *only* that which we ought to have done.' "

Ten Lepers Cleansed

11 While He was on the way to Jerusalem, ᵃHe was passing between Samaria and Galilee.
ᵃLuke 9:52ff; John 4:3f

12 As He entered a village, ten leprous men who ᵃstood at a distance met Him;   ᵃLev 13:45f

13 and they raised their voices, saying, "Jesus, ᵃMaster, have mercy on us!"   ᵃLuke 5:5

14 When He saw them, He said to them, "ᵃGo and show yourselves to the priests." And as they were going, they were cleansed.   ᵃLev 14:1-32; Matt 8:4

15 Now one of them, when he saw that he had been healed, turned back, ᵃglorifying God with a loud voice,   ᵃMatt 9:8

16 and he fell on his face at His feet, giving thanks to Him. And he was a ᵃSamaritan.
ᵃMatt 10:5

17 Then Jesus answered and said, "Were there not ten cleansed? But the nine—where are they?

18 "Was no one found who returned to ᵃgive glory to God, except this foreigner?"   ᵃMatt 9:8

19 And He said to him, "Stand up and go; ᵃyour faith has made you well."   ᵃMatt 9:22; Luke 18:42

20 Now having been questioned by the Pharisees ᵃas to when the kingdom of God was coming, He answered them and said, "The kingdom of God is not coming with signs to be observed;   ᵃLuke 19:11; Acts 1:6

21 nor will ᵃthey say, 'Look, here *it is!*' or, 'There *it is!*' For behold, the kingdom of God is in your midst."   ᵃLuke 17:23

Second Coming Foretold

22 And He said to the disciples, "ᵃThe days will come when you will long to see one of the days of the Son of Man, and you will not see it.
ᵃMatt 9:15; Mark 2:20

23 "ᵃThey will say to you, 'Look there! Look here!' Do not go away, and do not run after *them*.   ᵃMatt 24:23; Mark 13:21

24 "ᵃFor just like the lightning, when it flashes out of one part of the sky, shines to the other part of the sky, so will the Son of Man be in His day.   ᵃMatt 24:27

25 "ᵃBut first He must suffer many things and be rejected by this generation.   ᵃMatt 16:21; Luke 9:22

26 "ᵃAnd just as it happened in the days of Noah, so it will be also in the days of the Son of Man: ᵃMatt 24:37-39

27 they were eating, they were drinking, they were marrying, they were being given in marriage, until the day that Noah entered the ark, and the flood came and destroyed them all.

28 "It was the same as happened in ᵃthe days of Lot: they were eating, they were drinking, they were buying, they were selling, they were planting, they were building;   ᵃGen 19

29 but on the day that Lot went out from Sodom it rained fire and brimstone from heaven and destroyed them all.

30 "It will be just the same on the day that the Son of Man ᵃis revealed.   ᵃMatt 16:27; 1 Cor 1:7

31 "On that day, the one who is ᵃon the housetop and whose goods are in the house must not go down to take them out; and likewise the one who is in the field must not turn back.
ᵃMatt 24:17, 18; Mark 13:15f

32 "ᵃRemember Lot's wife.   ᵃGen 19:26

33 "ᵃWhoever seeks to keep his life will lose

it, and whoever loses *his life* will preserve it.
[a]*Matt 10:39*

34 "I tell you, on that night there will be two in one bed; one will be taken and the other will be left.

35 "[a]There will be two women grinding at the same place; one will be taken and the other will be left. [a]*Matt 24:41*

36 ["[a]Two men will be in the field; one will be taken and the other will be left."] [a]*Matt 24:40*

37 And answering they *said to Him, "Where, Lord?" And He said to them, "[a]Where the body *is*, there also the vultures will be gathered." [a]*Matt 24:28*

Parables on Prayer

18 Now He was telling them a parable to show that at all times they [a]ought to pray and not to [b]lose heart, [a]*Luke 11:5-10* [b]*2 Cor 4:1*

2 saying, "In a certain city there was a judge who did not fear God and did not [a]respect man. [a]*Luke 18:4; 20:13*

3 "There was a widow in that city, and she kept coming to him, saying, 'Give me legal protection from my opponent.'

4 "For a while he was unwilling; but afterward he said to himself, 'Even though I do not fear God nor [a]respect man, [a]*Luke 18:2; 20:13*

5 yet [a]because this widow bothers me, I will give her legal protection, otherwise by continually coming she will wear me out.' " [a]*Luke 11:8*

6 And [a]the Lord said, "Hear what the unrighteous judge *said; [a]*Luke 7:13*

7 now, will not God bring about justice for His [a]elect who cry to Him day and night, and will He [b]delay long over them? [a]*Matt 24:22* [b]*2 Pet 3:9*

8 "I tell you that He will bring about justice for them quickly. However, when the Son of Man comes, [a]will He find faith on the earth?" [a]*Luke 17:26ff*

The Pharisee and the Publican

9 And He also told this parable to some people who [a]trusted in themselves that they were righteous, and [b]viewed others with contempt: [a]*Luke 16:15* [b]*Rom 14:3, 10*

10 "Two men [a]went up into the temple to pray, one a Pharisee and the other a tax collector. [a]*1 Kin 10:5; 2 Kin 20:5, 8*

11 "The Pharisee [a]stood and was praying this to himself: 'God, I thank You that I am not like other people: swindlers, unjust, adulterers, or even like this tax collector. [a]*Matt 6:5; Mark 11:25*

12 'I fast twice a week; I [a]pay tithes of all that I get.' [a]*Luke 11:42*

13 "But the tax collector, standing some distance away, [a]was even unwilling to lift up his eyes to heaven, but [b]was beating his breast,

saying, 'God, be merciful to me, the sinner!' [a]*Ezra 9:6* [b]*Luke 23:48*

14 "I tell you, this man went to his house justified rather than the other; [a]for everyone who exalts himself will be humbled, but he who humbles himself will be exalted." [a]*Matt 23:12; Luke 14:11*

15 [a]And they were bringing even their babies to Him so that He would touch them, but when the disciples saw it, they *began* rebuking them. [a]*Matt 19:13-15; Mark 10:13-16*

16 But Jesus called for them, saying, "Permit the children to come to Me, and do not hinder them, for the kingdom of God belongs to such as these.

17 "Truly I say to you, [a]whoever does not receive the kingdom of God like a child will not enter it *at all.*" [a]*Matt 18:3; 19:14*

The Rich Young Ruler

18 [a]A ruler questioned Him, saying, "Good Teacher, what shall I do to inherit eternal life?" [a]*Luke 10:25-28*

19 And Jesus said to him, "Why do you call Me good? No one is good except God alone.

20 "You know the commandments, '[a]DO NOT COMMIT ADULTERY, DO NOT MURDER, DO NOT STEAL, DO NOT BEAR FALSE WITNESS, HONOR YOUR FATHER AND MOTHER.' " [a]*Ex 20:12-16; Deut 5:16-20*

21 And he said, "All these things I have kept from *my* youth."

22 When Jesus heard *this*, He said to him, "One thing you still lack; [a]sell all that you possess and distribute it to the poor, and you shall have treasure in heaven; and come, follow Me." [a]*Matt 19:21; Luke 12:33*

23 But when he had heard these things, he became very sad, for he was extremely rich.

24 And Jesus looked at him and said, "[a]How hard it is for those who are wealthy to enter the kingdom of God! [a]*Matt 19:23; Mark 10:23f*

25 "For [a]it is easier for a camel to go through the eye of a needle than for a rich man to enter the kingdom of God." [a]*Matt 19:24; Mark 10:25*

26 They who heard it said, "Then who can be saved?"

27 But He said, "[a]The things that are impossible with people are possible with God." [a]*Matt 19:26*

28 Peter said, "Behold, [a]we have left our own *homes* and followed You." [a]*Luke 5:11*

29 And He said to them, "Truly I say to you, [a]there is no one who has left house or wife or brothers or parents or children, for the sake of the kingdom of God, [a]*Matt 6:33; 19:29*

30 who will not receive many times as much at this time and in [a]the age to come, eternal life." [a]*Matt 12:32*

31 [a]Then He took the twelve aside and said to them, "Behold, we are going up to Jerusalem,

and all things which are written through the prophets about the Son of Man will be accomplished. ᵃ*Matt 20:17-19; Mark 10:32-34*

32 "ᵃFor He will be handed over to the Gentiles, and will be mocked and mistreated and spit upon, ᵃ*Matt 16:21*

33 and after they have scourged Him, they will kill Him; and the third day He will rise again."

34 But ᵃthe disciples understood none of these things, and *the meaning of* this statement was hidden from them, and they did not comprehend the things that were said. ᵃ*Mark 9:32; Luke 9:45*

Bartimaeus Receives Sight

35 ᵃAs Jesus was approaching Jericho, a blind man was sitting by the road begging. ᵃ*Matt 20:29-34; Mark 10:46-52*

36 Now hearing a crowd going by, he *began* to inquire what this was.

37 They told him that Jesus of Nazareth was passing by.

38 And he called out, saying, "Jesus, ᵃSon of David, have mercy on me!" ᵃ*Matt 9:27; Luke 18:39*

39 Those who led the way were sternly telling him to be quiet; but he kept crying out all the more, "ᵃSon of David, have mercy on me!" ᵃ*Luke 18:38*

40 And Jesus stopped and commanded that he be brought to Him; and when he came near, He questioned him,

41 "What do you want Me to do for you?" And he said, "Lord, *I want* to regain my sight!"

42 And Jesus said to him, "Receive your sight; ᵃyour faith has made you well." ᵃ*Matt 9:22*

43 Immediately he regained his sight and *began* following Him, ᵃglorifying God; and when all the people saw it, they gave praise to God. ᵃ*Matt 9:8*

Zaccheus Converted

19 He ᵃentered Jericho and was passing through. ᵃ*Luke 18:35*

2 And there was a man called by the name of Zaccheus; he was a chief tax collector and he was rich.

3 Zaccheus was trying to see who Jesus was, and was unable because of the crowd, for he was small in stature.

4 So he ran on ahead and climbed up into a ᵃsycamore tree in order to see Him, for He was about to pass through that way. ᵃ*1 Kin 10:27; 1 Chr 27:28*

5 When Jesus came to the place, He looked up and said to him, "Zaccheus, hurry and come down, for today I must stay at your house."

6 And he hurried and came down and received Him gladly.

7 When they saw it, they all *began* to grumble, saying, "He has gone to be the guest of a man who is a sinner."

8 Zaccheus stopped and said to the Lord, "Behold, Lord, half of my possessions I will give to the poor, and if I have defrauded anyone of anything, I will give back ᵃfour times as much." ᵃ*Ex 22:1; Lev 6:5*

9 And Jesus said to him, "Today salvation has come to this house, because he, too, is ᵃa son of Abraham. ᵃ*Luke 3:8; 13:16*

10 "For ᵃthe Son of Man has come to seek and to save that which was lost." ᵃ*Matt 18:11*

Parable of Money Usage

11 While they were listening to these things, Jesus went on to tell a parable, because ᵃHe was near Jerusalem, and they supposed that ᵇthe kingdom of God was going to appear immediately. ᵃ*Luke 9:51* ᵇ*Luke 17:20*

12 So He said, "ᵃA nobleman went to a distant country to receive a kingdom for himself, and *then* return. ᵃ*Matt 25:14-30; Luke 19:12-27*

13 "And he called ten of his slaves, and gave them ten minas and said to them, 'Do business *with this* until I come *back.*'

14 "But his citizens hated him and sent a delegation after him, saying, 'We do not want this man to reign over us.'

15 "When he returned, after receiving the kingdom, he ordered that these slaves, to whom he had given the money, be called to him so that he might know what business they had done.

16 "The first appeared, saying, 'Master, your mina has made ten minas more.'

17 "And he said to him, 'Well done, good slave, because you have been ᵃfaithful in a very little thing, you are to be in authority over ten cities.' ᵃ*Luke 16:10*

18 "The second came, saying, 'Your mina, master, has made five minas.'

19 "And he said to him also, 'And you are to be over five cities.'

20 "Another came, saying, 'Master, here is your mina, which I kept put away in a handkerchief;

21 for I was afraid of you, because you are an exacting man; you take up what you did not lay down and reap what you did not sow.'

22 "He *said to him, 'By your own words I will judge you, you worthless slave. Did you know that I am an exacting man, taking up what I did not lay down and reaping what I did not sow?

23 'Then why did you not put my money in the bank, and having come, I would have collected it with interest?'

24 "Then he said to the bystanders, 'Take the mina away from him and give it to the one who has the ten minas.'

25 "And they said to him, 'Master, he has ten minas *already*.'
26 "ªI tell you that to everyone who has, more shall be given, but from the one who does not have, even what he does have shall be taken away. ªMatt 13:12; Mark 4:25
27 "But ªthese enemies of mine, who did not want me to reign over them, bring them here and slay them in my presence." ªLuke 19:14

Triumphal Entry

28 After He had said these things, He ªwas going on ahead, ᵇgoing up to Jerusalem. ªMark 10:32 ᵇLuke 9:51
29 ªWhen He approached Bethphage and Bethany, near the mount that is called Olivet, He sent two of the disciples, ªMatt 21:1-9; Mark 11:1-10
30 saying, "Go into the village ahead of *you;* there, as you enter, you will find a colt tied on which no one yet has ever sat; untie it and bring it *here.*
31 "If anyone asks you, 'Why are you untying it?' you shall say, 'The Lord has need of it.' "
32 So those who were sent went away and found it just as He had told them.
33 As they were untying the colt, its owners said to them, "Why are you untying the colt?"
34 They said, "The Lord has need of it."
35 They brought it to Jesus, ªand they threw their coats on the colt and put Jesus *on it.* ªMatt 21:4-9; Mark 11:7-10
36 As He was going, they were spreading their coats on the road.
37 As soon as He was approaching, near the descent of the Mount of Olives, the whole crowd of the disciples began to ªpraise God joyfully with a loud voice for all the miracles which they had seen, ªLuke 18:43
38 shouting:
   "ªBLESSED IS THE KING WHO COMES IN THE
      NAME OF THE LORD;
   Peace in heaven and glory in the high-
      est!" ªPs 118:26
39 ªSome of the Pharisees in the crowd said to Him, "Teacher, rebuke Your disciples." ªMatt 21:15f
40 But Jesus answered, "I tell you, if these become silent, ªthe stones will cry out!" ªHab 2:11
41 When He approached *Jerusalem,* He saw the city and ªwept over it, ªLuke 13:34, 35
42 saying, "If you had known in this day, even you, the things which make for peace! But now they have been hidden from your eyes.
43 "For the days will come upon you when your enemies will ªthrow up a barricade against you, and surround you and hem you in on every side, ªEccl 9:14; Is 29:3

44 and they will level you to the ground and your children within you, and ªthey will not leave in you one stone upon another, because you did not recognize the time of your visitation." ªMatt 24:2; Mark 13:2

Traders Driven from the Temple

45 ªJesus entered the temple and began to drive out those who were selling, ªJohn 2:13-16
46 saying to them, "It is written, 'ªAND MY HOUSE SHALL BE A HOUSE OF PRAYER,' but you have made it a ROBBERS' DEN." ªIs 56:7; Jer 7:11
47 And ªHe was teaching daily in the temple; but the chief priests and the scribes and the leading men among the people were trying to destroy Him, ªMatt 26:55; Luke 21:37
48 and they could not find anything that they might do, for all the people were hanging on to every word He said.

Jesus' Authority Questioned

20 ªOn one of the days while He was teaching the people in the temple and preaching the gospel, the chief priests and the scribes with the elders confronted *Him,* ªMatt 21:23-27; Mark 11:27-33
2 and they spoke, saying to Him, "Tell us by what authority You are doing these things, or who is the one who gave You this authority?"
3 Jesus answered and said to them, "I will also ask you a question, and you tell Me:
4 "Was the baptism of John from heaven or from men?"
5 They reasoned among themselves, saying, "If we say, 'From heaven,' He will say, 'Why did you not believe him?'
6 "But if we say, 'From men,' all the people will stone us to death, for they are convinced that John was a ªprophet." ªMatt 11:9; Luke 7:29, 30
7 So they answered that they did not know where *it came* from.
8 And Jesus said to them, "Nor will I tell you by what authority I do these things."

Parable of the Vine-growers

9 ªAnd He began to tell the people this parable: "A man planted a vineyard and rented it out to vine-growers, and went on a journey for a long time. ªMatt 21:33-46; Mark 12:1-12
10 "At the *harvest* time he sent a slave to the vine-growers, so that they would give him *some* of the produce of the vineyard; but the vine-growers beat him and sent him away empty-handed.
11 "And he proceeded to send another slave; and they beat him also and treated him shamefully and sent him away empty-handed.
12 "And he proceeded to send a third; and this one also they wounded and cast out.

13 "The owner of the vineyard said, 'What shall I do? I will send my beloved son; perhaps they will [a]respect him.' [a]Luke 18:2

14 "But when the vine-growers saw him, they reasoned with one another, saying, 'This is the heir; let us kill him so that the inheritance will be ours.'

15 "So they threw him out of the vineyard and killed him. What, then, will the owner of the vineyard do to them?

16 "He will come and [a]destroy these vine-growers and will give the vineyard to others." When they heard it, they said, "May it never be!" [a]Matt 21:41; Mark 12:9

17 But Jesus looked at them and said, "What then is this that is written:

'[a]THE STONE WHICH THE BUILDERS REJECTED,
THIS BECAME [b]THE CHIEF CORNER *stone*'?
[a]Ps 118:22 [b]Eph 2:20

18 "[a]Everyone who falls on that stone will be broken to pieces; but on whomever it falls, it will scatter him like dust." [a]Matt 21:44

Tribute to Caesar

19 The scribes and the chief priests [a]tried to lay hands on Him that very hour, and they feared the people; for they understood that He spoke this parable against them. [a]Luke 19:47

20 [a]So they watched Him, and sent spies who pretended to be righteous, in order that they might catch Him in some statement, so that they *could* deliver Him to the rule and the authority of the governor. [a]Mark 3:2

21 They questioned Him, saying, "Teacher, we know that You speak and teach correctly, and You are not partial to any, but teach the way of God in truth.

22 "Is it lawful for us [a]to pay taxes to Caesar, or not?" [a]Matt 17:25; Luke 23:2

23 But He detected their trickery and said to them,

24 "Show Me a denarius. Whose likeness and inscription does it have?" They said, "Caesar's."

25 And He said to them, "Then [a]render to Caesar the things that are Caesar's, and to God the things that are God's." [a]Matt 22:21; Mark 12:17

26 And they were unable to [a]catch Him in a saying in the presence of the people; and being amazed at His answer, they became silent. [a]Luke 11:54

Is There a Resurrection?

27 [a]Now there came to Him some of the Sadducees (who say that there is no resurrection), [a]Matt 22:23-33; Mark 12:18-27

28 and they questioned Him, saying, "Teacher, Moses wrote for us that [a]IF A MAN'S BROTHER DIES, having a wife, AND HE IS CHILDLESS, HIS BROTHER SHOULD MARRY THE WIFE AND RAISE UP CHILDREN TO HIS BROTHER. [a]Deut 25:5

29 "Now there were seven brothers; and the first took a wife and died childless;

30 and the second

31 and the third married her; and in the same way all seven died, leaving no children.

32 "Finally the woman died also.

33 "In the resurrection therefore, which one's wife will she be? For all seven had married her."

34 Jesus said to them, "The sons of [a]this age marry and are given in marriage, [a]Matt 12:32; Luke 16:8

35 but those who are considered worthy to attain to [a]that age and the resurrection from the dead, neither marry nor are given in marriage; [a]Matt 12:32; Luke 16:8

36 for they cannot even die anymore, because they are like angels, and are [a]sons of God, being sons of the resurrection. [a]Rom 8:16f; 1 John 3:1, 2

37 "But that the dead are raised, even Moses showed, in [a]the *passage about the burning* bush, where he calls the Lord [b]THE GOD OF ABRAHAM, AND THE GOD OF ISAAC, AND THE GOD OF JACOB. [a]Mark 12:26 [b]Ex 3:6

38 "Now He is not the God of the dead but of the living; for [b]all live to Him." [a]Matt 22:32 [b]Rom 14:8

39 Some of the scribes answered and said, "Teacher, You have spoken well."

40 For [a]they did not have courage to question Him any longer about anything. [a]Matt 22:46; Luke 14:6

41 [a]Then He said to them, "How *is it that* they say the Christ is David's son? [a]Matt 22:41-46; Mark 12:35-37

42 "For David himself says in the book of Psalms,

'[a]THE LORD SAID TO MY LORD,
"SIT AT MY RIGHT HAND, [a]Ps 110:1

43 [a]UNTIL I MAKE YOUR ENEMIES A FOOTSTOOL
　　FOR YOUR FEET." ' [a]Ps 110:1

44 "Therefore David calls Him 'Lord,' and how is He his son?"

45 [a]And while all the people were listening, He said to the disciples, [a]Matt 23:1-7; Mark 12:38-40

46 "Beware of the scribes, [a]who like to walk around in long robes, and love respectful greetings in the market places, and chief seats in the synagogues and places of honor at banquets, [a]Luke 11:43; 14:7

47 who devour widows' houses, and for appearance's sake offer long prayers. These will receive greater condemnation."

The Widow's Gift

21 [a]And He looked up and saw the rich putting their gifts into the treasury. [a]Mark 12:41-44

2 And He saw a poor widow putting in ªtwo small copper coins. ªMark 12:42

3 And He said, "Truly I say to you, this poor widow put in more than all *of them;*

4 for they all out of their surplus put into the offering; but she out of her poverty put in all that she had ªto live on." ªMark 12:44

5 ªAnd while some were talking about the temple, that it was adorned with beautiful stones and votive gifts, He said, ªMatt 24; Mark 13

6 "*As for* these things which you are looking at, the days will come in which ªthere will not be left one stone upon another which will not be torn down." ªLuke 19:44

7 They questioned Him, saying, "Teacher, when therefore will these things happen? And what *will be* the sign when these things are about to take place?"

8 And He said, "See to it that you are not misled; for many will come in My name, saying, 'ªI am *He*,' and, 'The time is near.' ᵇDo not go after them. ªJohn 8:24 ᵇLuke 17:23

9 "When you hear of wars and disturbances, do not be terrified; for these things must take place first, but the end *does* not *follow* immediately."

Things to Come

10 Then He continued by saying to them, "Nation will rise against nation and kingdom against kingdom,

11 and there will be great earthquakes, and in various places plagues and famines; and there will be terrors and great signs from heaven.

12 "But before all these things, ªthey will lay their hands on you and will persecute you, delivering you to the synagogues and prisons, bringing you before kings and governors for My name's sake. ªMatt 10:19-22; Mark 13:11-13

13 "ªIt will lead to an opportunity for your testimony. ªPhil 1:12

14 "ªSo make up your minds not to prepare beforehand to defend yourselves; ªLuke 12:11

15 for ªI will give you utterance and wisdom which none of your opponents will be able to resist or refute. ªLuke 12:12

16 "But you will be betrayed even by parents and brothers and relatives and friends, and they will put *some* of you to death,

17 and you will be hated by all because of My name.

18 "Yet ªnot a hair of your head will perish. ªMatt 10:30; Luke 12:7

19 "ªBy your endurance you will gain your lives. ªMatt 10:22; 24:13

20 "But when you see Jerusalem ªsurrounded by armies, then recognize that her desolation is near. ªLuke 19:43

21 "Then those who are in Judea must flee to the mountains, and those who are in the midst

of the city must leave, and ªthose who are in the country must not enter the city; ªLuke 17:31

22 because these are ªdays of vengeance, so that all things which are written will be fulfilled. ªIs 63:4; Dan 9:24-27

23 "Woe to those who are pregnant and to those who are nursing babies in those days; for ªthere will be great distress upon the land and wrath to this people; ªDan 8:19; 1 Cor 7:26

24 and they will fall by the edge of the sword, and will be led captive into all the nations; and Jerusalem will be ªtrampled under foot by the Gentiles until ᵇthe times of the Gentiles are fulfilled. ªRev 11:2 ᵇRom 11:25

The Return of Christ

25 "There will be signs in sun and moon and stars, and on the earth dismay among nations, in perplexity at the roaring of the sea and the waves,

26 men fainting from fear and the expectation of the things which are coming upon the world; for the powers of the heavens will be shaken.

27 "Then they will see ªTHE SON OF MAN COMING IN A CLOUD with power and great glory. ªDan 7:13; Rev 1:7

28 "But when these things begin to take place, straighten up and lift up your heads, because ªyour redemption is drawing near." ªLuke 18:7

29 Then He told them a parable: "Behold the fig tree and all the trees;

30 as soon as they put forth *leaves,* you see it and ªknow for yourselves that summer is now near. ªLuke 12:57

31 "So you also, when you see these things happening, recognize that ªthe kingdom of God is near. ªMatt 3:2

32 "Truly I say to you, this generation will not pass away until all things take place.

33 "ªHeaven and earth will pass away, but My words will not pass away. ªMatt 5:18; Luke 16:17

34 "ªBe on guard, so that your hearts will not be weighted down with dissipation and drunkenness and the worries of life, and that day will not come on you suddenly like a trap; ªMatt 24:42-44; Mark 4:19

35 for it will come upon all those who dwell on the face of all the earth.

36 "But ªkeep on the alert at all times, praying that you may have strength to escape all these things that are about to take place, and to stand before the Son of Man." ªMark 13:33; Luke 12:40

37 Now during the day He was ªteaching in the temple, but at evening He would go out and spend the night on ᵇthe mount that is called Olivet. ªMatt 26:55 ᵇMatt 21:1

38 And all the people would get up early in the morning *to come* to Him in the temple to listen to Him.

Preparing the Passover

22 [a]Now the Feast of Unleavened Bread, which is called the Passover, was approaching. [a]Ex 12:1-27

2 The chief priests and the scribes [a]were seeking how they might put Him to death; for they were afraid of the people. [a]Matt 12:14

3 [a]And Satan entered into Judas who was called Iscariot, belonging to the number of the twelve. [a]Matt 26:14-16; Mark 14:10, 11

4 And he went away and discussed with the chief priests and [a]officers how he might betray Him to them. [a]1 Chr 9:11; Neh 11:11

5 They were glad and agreed to give him money.

6 So he consented, and *began* seeking a good opportunity to betray Him to them apart from the crowd.

7 [a]Then came the *first* day of Unleavened Bread on which the Passover *lamb* had to be sacrificed. [a]Matt 26:17-19; Mark 14:12-16

8 And Jesus sent [a]Peter and John, saying, "Go and prepare the Passover for us, so that we may eat it." [a]Acts 3:1, 11; 4:13, 19

9 They said to Him, "Where do You want us to prepare it?"

10 And He said to them, "When you have entered the city, a man will meet you carrying a pitcher of water; follow him into the house that he enters.

11 "And you shall say to the owner of the house, 'The Teacher says to you, "Where is the guest room in which I may eat the Passover with My disciples?" '

12 "And he will show you a large, furnished upper room; prepare it there."

13 And they left and found *everything* just as He had told them; and they prepared the Passover.

The Lord's Supper

14 [a]When the hour had come, He reclined *at the table*, and the apostles with Him. [a]Matt 26:20; Mark 14:17

15 And He said to them, "I have earnestly desired to eat this Passover with you before I suffer;

16 for I say to you, I shall never again eat it [a]until it is fulfilled in the kingdom of God." [a]Luke 14:15; 22:18, 30

17 [a]And when He had taken a cup *and* given thanks, He said, "Take this and share it among yourselves; [a]1 Cor 10:16

18 for [a]I say to you, I will not drink of the fruit of the vine from now on until the kingdom of God comes." [a]Matt 26:29; Mark 14:25

19 And when He had taken *some* bread *and* [a]given thanks, He broke it and gave it to them, saying, "This is My body which is given for you; do this in remembrance of Me." [a]Matt 14:19

20 And in the same way *He took* the cup after they had eaten, saying, "This cup which is [a]poured out for you is the [b]new covenant in My blood. [a]Matt 26:28 [b]Ex 24:8

21 "[a]But behold, the hand of the one betraying Me is with Mine on the table. [a]Ps 41:9; John 13:18, 21, 22, 26

22 "For indeed, the Son of Man is going [a]as it has been determined; but woe to that man by whom He is betrayed!" [a]Acts 2:23; 4:28

23 And they began to discuss among themselves which one of them it might be who was going to do this thing.

Who Is Greatest

24 And there arose also [a]a dispute among them *as to* which one of them was regarded to be greatest. [a]Mark 9:34; Luke 9:46

25 [a]And He said to them, "The kings of the Gentiles lord it over them; and those who have authority over them are called 'Benefactors.' [a]Matt 20:25-28; Mark 10:42-45

26 "But *it is* not this way with you, [a]but the one who is the greatest among you must become like the youngest, and the leader like the servant. [a]Matt 23:11; Mark 9:35

27 "For who is greater, the one who reclines *at the table* or the one who serves? Is it not the one who reclines *at the table?* But [a]I am among you as the one who serves. [a]Matt 20:28; John 13:12-15

28 "You are those who have stood by Me in My [a]trials; [a]Heb 2:18; 4:15

29 and just as My Father has granted Me a [a]kingdom, I grant you [a]Matt 5:3; 2 Tim 2:12

30 that you may eat and drink at My table in My kingdom, and [a]you will sit on thrones judging the twelve tribes of Israel. [a]Matt 19:28

31 "Simon, Simon, behold, [a]Satan has demanded *permission* to [b]sift you like wheat; [a]Job 1:6-12 [b]Amos 9:9

32 but I [a]have prayed for you, that your faith may not fail; and you, when once you have turned again, strengthen your brothers." [a]John 17:9, 15

33 [a]But he said to Him, "Lord, with You I am ready to go both to prison and to death!" [a]Matt 26:33-35; Mark 14:29-31

34 And He said, "I say to you, Peter, the rooster will not crow today until you have denied three times that you know Me."

35 And He said to them, "[a]When I sent you out without money belt and bag and sandals, you did not lack anything, did you?" They said, "*No,* nothing." [a]Matt 10:9f; Mark 6:8

36 And He said to them, "But now, whoever has a money belt is to take it along, likewise

also a bag, and whoever has no sword is to sell his coat and buy one.

37 "For I tell you that this which is written must be fulfilled in Me, ^a'AND HE WAS NUMBERED WITH TRANSGRESSORS'; for ^bthat which refers to Me has *its* fulfillment." ^a*Is 53:12* ^b*John 17:4*

38 They said, "Lord, look, here are two ^aswords." And He said to them, "It is enough." ^a*Luke 22:36, 49*

The Garden of Gethsemane

39 And He came out and proceeded ^aas was His custom to the Mount of Olives; and the disciples also followed Him. ^a*Luke 21:37*

40 ^aWhen He arrived at the place, He said to them, "Pray that you may not enter into temptation." ^a*Matt 26:36-46; Mark 14:32-42*

41 And He withdrew from them about a stone's throw, and He ^aknelt down and *began* to pray, ^a*Matt 26:39; Mark 14:35*

42 saying, "Father, if You are willing, remove this cup from Me; ^ayet not My will, but Yours be done." ^a*Matt 26:39*

43 Now an ^aangel from heaven appeared to Him, strengthening Him. ^a*Matt 4:11*

44 And ^abeing in agony He was praying very fervently; and His sweat became like drops of blood, falling down upon the ground. ^a*Heb 5:7*

45 When He rose from prayer, He came to the disciples and found them sleeping from sorrow,

46 and said to them, "Why are you sleeping? Get up and ^apray that you may not enter into temptation." ^a*Luke 22:40*

Jesus Betrayed by Judas

47 ^aWhile He was still speaking, behold, a crowd *came,* and the one called Judas, one of the twelve, was preceding them; and he approached Jesus to kiss Him. ^a*Matt 26:47-56; Mark 14:43-50*

48 But Jesus said to him, "Judas, are you betraying the Son of Man with a kiss?"

49 When those who were around Him saw what was going to happen, they said, "Lord, shall we strike with the ^asword?" ^a*Luke 22:38*

50 And one of them struck the slave of the high priest and cut off his right ear.

51 But Jesus answered and said, "Stop! No more of this." And He touched his ear and healed him.

52 Then Jesus said to the chief priests and ^aofficers of the temple and elders who had come against Him, "Have you come out with swords and clubs as you would against a robber? ^a*Luke 22:4*

53 "While I was with you daily in the temple, you did not lay hands on Me; but this hour and the power of darkness are yours."

Jesus' Arrest

54 Having arrested Him, they led Him *away* and brought Him to the house of the high priest; but ^aPeter was following at a distance. ^a*Matt 26:58; Mark 14:54*

55 ^aAfter they had kindled a fire in the middle of the courtyard and had sat down together, Peter was sitting among them. ^a*Matt 26:69-75*

56 And a servant-girl, seeing him as he sat in the firelight and looking intently at him, said, "This man was with Him too."

57 But he denied *it,* saying, "Woman, I do not know Him."

58 A little later, ^aanother saw him and said, "You are *one* of them too!" But Peter said, "Man, I am not!" ^a*John 18:26*

59 After about an hour had passed, another man *began* to insist, saying, "Certainly this man also was with Him, ^afor he is a Galilean too." ^a*Matt 26:73; Mark 14:70*

60 But Peter said, "Man, I do not know what you are talking about." Immediately, while he was still speaking, a rooster crowed.

61 The Lord turned and looked at Peter. And Peter remembered the word of the Lord, how He had told him, "^aBefore a rooster crows today, you will deny Me three times." ^a*Luke 22:34*

62 And he went out and wept bitterly.

63 ^aNow the men who were holding Jesus in custody were mocking Him and beating Him, ^a*Matt 26:67f; Mark 14:65*

64 and they blindfolded Him and were asking Him, saying, "^aProphesy, who is the one who hit You?" ^a*Matt 26:68; Mark 14:65*

65 And they were saying many other things against Him, ^ablaspheming. ^a*Matt 27:39*

Jesus before the Sanhedrin

66 ^aWhen it was day, the Council of elders of the people assembled, both chief priests and scribes, and they led Him away to their council chamber, saying, ^a*Matt 27:1f; Mark 15:1*

67 "If You are the Christ, tell us." But He said to them, "If I tell you, you will not believe; ^a*Matt 26:63-66; Mark 14:61-63*

68 and if I ask a question, you will not answer.

69 "^aBut from now on ^bTHE SON OF MAN WILL BE SEATED AT THE RIGHT HAND of the power OF GOD." ^a*Matt 26:64* ^b*Ps 110:1*

70 And they all said, "Are You the Son of God, then?" And He said to them, "^aYes, I am." ^a*Matt 26:64; 27:11*

71 Then they said, "What further need do we have of testimony? For we have heard it ourselves from His own mouth."

Jesus before Pilate

23 Then the whole body of them got up and ^abrought Him before Pilate. ^a*Matt 27:2; Mark 15:1*

2 [a]And they began to accuse Him, saying, "We found this man misleading our nation and forbidding to pay taxes to Caesar, and saying that He Himself is Christ, a King." [a]Matt 27:11-14; Mark 15:2-5

3 So Pilate asked Him, saying, "Are You the King of the Jews?" And He answered him and said, "[a]It is as you say." [a]Luke 22:70

4 Then Pilate said to the chief priests and the crowds, "[a]I find no guilt in this man." [a]Matt 27:23; Mark 15:14

5 But they kept on insisting, saying, "He stirs up the people, teaching all over Judea, [a]starting from Galilee even as far as this place." [a]Matt 4:12

6 When Pilate heard it, he asked whether the man was a Galilean.

7 And when he learned that He belonged to Herod's jurisdiction, he sent Him to [a]Herod, who himself also was in Jerusalem at that time. [a]Matt 14:1; Mark 6:14

Jesus before Herod

8 Now Herod was very glad when he saw Jesus; for [a]he had wanted to see Him for a long time, because he had been hearing about Him and was hoping to see some sign performed by Him. [a]Luke 9:9

9 And he questioned Him at some length; but [a]He answered him nothing. [a]Matt 27:12, 14; Mark 15:5

10 And the chief priests and the scribes were standing there, accusing Him vehemently.

11 And Herod with his soldiers, after treating Him with contempt and mocking Him, [a]dressed Him in a gorgeous robe and sent Him back to Pilate. [a]Matt 27:28

12 Now [a]Herod and Pilate became friends with one another that very day; for before they had been enemies with each other. [a]Acts 4:27

Pilate Seeks Jesus' Release

13 Pilate summoned the chief priests and the [a]rulers and the people, [a]Luke 23:35; John 7:26, 48

14 and said to them, "You brought this man to me as one who [a]incites the people to rebellion, and behold, having examined Him before you, I [b]have found no guilt in this man regarding the charges which you make against Him. [a]Luke 23:2 [b]Luke 23:4

15 "No, nor has [a]Herod, for he sent Him back to us; and behold, nothing deserving death has been done by Him. [a]Luke 9:9

16 "Therefore I will [a]punish Him and release Him." [a]Matt 27:26; Mark 15:15

17 [Now he was obliged to release to them at the feast one prisoner.]

18 But they cried out all together, saying, "[a]Away with this man, and release for us Barabbas!" [a]John 18:39-19:16

19 (He was one who had been thrown into

prison for an insurrection made in the city, and for murder.)

20 Pilate, wanting to release Jesus, addressed them again,

21 but they kept on calling out, saying, "Crucify, crucify Him!"

22 And he said to them the third time, "Why, what evil has this man done? I have found in Him no guilt demanding death; therefore I will [a]punish Him and release Him." [a]Luke 23:16

23 But they were insistent, with loud voices asking that He be crucified. And their voices began to prevail.

24 And Pilate pronounced sentence that their demand be granted.

25 And he released the man they were asking for who had been thrown into prison for insurrection and murder, but he delivered Jesus to their will.

Simon Bears the Cross

26 [a]When they led Him away, they seized a man, Simon of Cyrene, coming in from the country, and placed on him the cross to carry behind Jesus. [a]John 19:17

27 And following Him was a large crowd of the people, and of women who were [a]mourning and lamenting Him. [a]Luke 8:52

28 But Jesus turning to them said, "Daughters of Jerusalem, stop weeping for Me, but weep for yourselves and for your children.

29 "For behold, the days are coming when they will say, '[a]Blessed are the barren, and the wombs that never bore, and the breasts that never nursed.' [a]Matt 24:19; Luke 11:27

30 "Then they will begin to [a]SAY TO THE MOUNTAINS, 'FALL ON US,' AND TO THE HILLS, 'COVER US.' [a]Hos 10:8; Is 2:19, 20

31 "For if they do these things when the tree is green, what will happen when it is dry?"

32 [a]Two others also, who were criminals, were being led away to be put to death with Him. [a]Matt 27:38; Mark 15:27

The Crucifixion

33 [a]When they came to the place called The Skull, there they crucified Him and the criminals, one on the right and the other on the left. [a]Matt 27:33-44; Mark 15:22-32

34 But Jesus was saying, "Father, forgive them; for they do not know what they are doing." [a]And they cast lots, dividing up His garments among themselves. [a]Ps 22:18; John 19:24

35 And the people stood by, looking on. And even the rulers were sneering at Him, saying, "He saved others; [a]let Him save Himself if this is the Christ of God, His Chosen One." [a]Matt 27:43

36 The soldiers also mocked Him, coming up to Him, [a]offering Him sour wine, [a]Matt 27:48

37 and saying, "ªIf You are the King of the Jews, save Yourself!" ªMatt 27:43

38 Now there was also an inscription above Him, "ªTHIS IS THE KING OF THE JEWS." ªMatt 27:37; Mark 15:26

39 ªOne of the criminals who were hanged *there* was hurling abuse at Him, saying, "Are You not the Christ? Save Yourself and us!" ªMatt 27:44; Mark 15:32

40 But the other answered, and rebuking him said, "Do you not even fear God, since you are under the same sentence of condemnation?

41 "And we indeed *are suffering* justly, for we are receiving what we deserve for our deeds; but this man has done nothing wrong."

42 And he was saying, "Jesus, remember me when You come in Your kingdom!"

43 And He said to him, "Truly I say to you, today you shall be with Me in ªParadise." ª2 Cor 12:4; Rev 2:7

44 ªIt was now about the sixth hour, and darkness fell over the whole land until the ninth hour, ªMatt 27:45-56; Mark 15:33-41

45 because the sun was obscured; and ªthe veil of the temple was torn in two. ªEx 26:31-33; Matt 27:51

46 And Jesus, crying out with a loud voice, said, "Father, ªINTO YOUR HANDS I COMMIT MY SPIRIT." Having said this, He breathed His last. ªPs 31:5

47 ªNow when the centurion saw what had happened, he *began* praising God, saying, "Certainly this man was innocent." ªMatt 27:54; Mark 15:39

48 And all the crowds who came together for this spectacle, when they observed what had happened, *began* to return, ªbeating their breasts. ªLuke 8:52; 18:13

49 ªAnd all His acquaintances and the women who accompanied Him from Galilee were standing at a distance, seeing these things. ªMatt 27:55f; Mark 15:40f

Jesus Is Buried

50 ªAnd a man named Joseph, who was a member of the Council, a good and righteous man ªMatt 27:57-61; Mark 15:42-47

51 (he had not consented to their plan and action), *a man* from Arimathea, a city of the Jews, who was ªwaiting for the kingdom of God; ªMark 15:43; Luke 2:25

52 this man went to Pilate and asked for the body of Jesus.

53 And he took it down and wrapped it in a linen cloth, and laid Him in a tomb cut into the rock, where no one had ever lain.

54 It was ªthe preparation day, and the Sabbath was about to begin. ªMatt 27:62; Mark 15:42

55 Now ªthe women who had come with Him out of Galilee followed, and saw the tomb and how His body was laid. ªLuke 23:49

56 Then they returned and ªprepared spices and perfumes.

And on the Sabbath they rested according to the commandment. ªMark 16:1; Luke 24:1

The Resurrection

24 ªBut on the first day of the week, at early dawn, they came to the tomb bringing the spices which they had prepared. ªJohn 20:1-8

2 And they found the stone rolled away from the tomb,

3 but when they entered, they did not find the body of ªthe Lord Jesus. ªLuke 7:13; Acts 1:21

4 While they were perplexed about this, behold, ªtwo men suddenly stood near them in dazzling clothing; ªJohn 20:12

5 and as *the women* were terrified and bowed their faces to the ground, *the men* said to them, "Why do you seek the living One among the dead?

6 "He is not here, but He ªhas risen. Remember how He spoke to you ᵇwhile He was still in Galilee, ªMark 16:6 ᵇMatt 17:22f

7 saying that ªthe Son of Man must be delivered into the hands of sinful men, and be crucified, and the third day rise again." ªMatt 16:21; Luke 24:46

8 And ªthey remembered His words, ªJohn 2:22

9 and returned from the tomb and reported all these things to the eleven and to all the rest.

10 Now they were ªMary Magdalene and Joanna and Mary the *mother* of James; also the other women with them were telling these things to the apostles. ªMatt 27:56

11 But these words appeared to them as nonsense, and they would not believe them.

12 But Peter got up and ªran to the tomb; stooping and looking in, he *saw the linen wrappings only; and he went away ᵇto his home, marveling at what had happened. ªJohn 20:3-6 ᵇJohn 20:10

The Road to Emmaus

13 And behold, two of them were going that very day to a village named Emmaus, which was about seven miles from Jerusalem.

14 And they were talking with each other about all these things which had taken place.

15 While they were talking and discussing, Jesus Himself approached and *began* traveling with them.

16 But ªtheir eyes were prevented from recognizing Him. ªLuke 24:31; John 20:14

17 And He said to them, "What are these words that you are exchanging with one

another as you are walking?" And they stood still, looking sad.

18 One *of them*, named Cleopas, answered and said to Him, "Are You the only one visiting Jerusalem and unaware of the things which have happened here in these days?"

19 And He said to them, "What things?" And they said to Him, "The things about Jesus the Nazarene, who was a [a]prophet mighty in deed and word in the sight of God and all the people, [a]*Matt 21:11*

20 and how the chief priests and our [a]rulers delivered Him to the sentence of death, and crucified Him. [a]*Luke 23:13*

21 "But we were hoping that it was He who was going to [a]redeem Israel. Indeed, besides all this, it is the third day since these things happened. [a]*Luke 1:68*

22 "But also some women among us amazed us. [a]When they were at the tomb early in the morning, [a]*Luke 24:1ff*

23 and did not find His body, they came, saying that they had also seen a vision of angels who said that He was alive.

24 "Some of those who were with us went to the tomb and found it just exactly as the women also had said; but Him they did not see."

25 And He said to them, "O foolish men and slow of heart to believe in all that [a]the prophets have spoken! [a]*Matt 26:24*

26 "[a]Was it not necessary for the Christ to suffer these things and to enter into His glory?" [a]*Luke 24:7, 44ff; Heb 2:10*

27 Then beginning with [a]Moses and with all the prophets, He explained to them the things concerning Himself in all the Scriptures. [a]*Gen 3:15*

28 And they approached the village where they were going, and [a]He acted as though He were going farther. [a]*Mark 6:48*

29 But they urged Him, saying, "Stay with us, for it is *getting* toward evening, and the day is now nearly over." So He went in to stay with them.

30 When He had reclined *at the table* with them, He took the bread and [a]blessed *it*, and breaking *it*, He *began* giving *it* to them. [a]*Matt 14:19*

31 Then their [a]eyes were opened and they recognized Him; and He vanished from their sight. [a]*Luke 24:16*

32 They said to one another, "Were not our hearts burning within us while He was speaking to us on the road, while He [a]was explaining the Scriptures to us?" [a]*Luke 24:45*

33 And they got up that very hour and returned to Jerusalem, and found gathered together the eleven and [a]those who were with them, [a]*Acts 1:14*

34 saying, "[a]The Lord has really risen and [b]has appeared to Simon." [a]*Luke 24:6* [b]*1 Cor 15:5*

35 They *began* to relate their experiences on the road and how [a]He was recognized by them in the breaking of the bread. [a]*Luke 24:30f*

Other Appearances

36 While they were telling these things, He Himself stood in their midst and *said to them, "Peace be to you."

37 But they were startled and frightened and thought that they were seeing [a]a spirit. [a]*Matt 14:26; Mark 6:49*

38 And He said to them, "Why are you troubled, and why do doubts arise in your hearts?

39 "See My hands and My feet, that it is I Myself; [a]touch Me and see, for a spirit does not have flesh and bones as you see that I have." [a]*John 20:27; 1 John 1:1*

40 And when He had said this, He showed them His hands and His feet.

41 While they still [a]could not believe *it* because of their joy and amazement, He said to them, "Have you anything here to eat?" [a]*Luke 24:11*

42 They gave Him a piece of a broiled fish;

43 and He took it and [a]ate *it* before them. [a]*Acts 10:41*

44 Now He said to them, "These are My words which I spoke to you while I was still with you, that all things which are written about Me in the [a]Law of Moses and the Prophets and the Psalms must be fulfilled." [a]*Luke 24:27*

45 Then He [a]opened their minds to understand the Scriptures, [a]*Luke 24:32; Acts 16:14*

46 and He said to them, "[a]Thus it is written, that the Christ would suffer and [b]rise again from the dead the third day, [a]*Luke 24:26, 44* [b]*Luke 24:7*

47 and that repentance for forgiveness of sins would be proclaimed in His name to [a]all the nations, beginning from Jerusalem. [a]*Matt 28:19*

48 "You are [a]witnesses of these things. [a]*Acts 1:8, 22; 2:32*

49 "And behold, [a]I am sending forth the promise of My Father upon you; but [b]you are to stay in the city until you are clothed with power from on high." [a]*John 14:26* [b]*Acts 1:4*

The Ascension

50 And He led them out as far as [a]Bethany, and He lifted up His hands and blessed them. [a]*Matt 21:17; Acts 1:12*

51 While He was blessing them, He parted from them and was carried up into heaven.

52 And they, after worshiping Him, returned to Jerusalem with great joy,

53 and were continually in the temple praising God.

The Gospel According to
JOHN

The Deity of Jesus Christ

1 In the beginning was the Word, and the Word was ᵃwith God, and the Word was God. ᵃ*John 17:5*

2 He was in the beginning with God.

3 ᵃAll things came into being through Him, and apart from Him nothing came into being that has come into being. ᵃ*John 1:10; 1 Cor 8:6*

4 ᵃIn Him was life, and the life was ᵇthe Light of men. ᵃ*John 5:26* ᵇ*John 8:12*

5 ᵃThe Light shines in the darkness, and the darkness did not comprehend it. ᵃ*John 3:19*

The Witness John

6 There came a man sent from God, whose name was ᵃJohn. ᵃ*Matt 3:1*

7 He came as a witness, to testify about the Light, ᵃso that all might believe through him. ᵃ*John 1:12; Acts 19:4*

8 ᵃHe was not the Light, but *he came* to testify about the Light. ᵃ*John 1:20*

9 There was ᵃthe true Light which, coming into the world, enlightens every man. ᵃ*1 John 2:8*

10 He was in the world, and ᵃthe world was made through Him, and the world did not know Him. ᵃ*1 Cor 8:6; Col 1:16*

11 He came to His own, and those who were His own did not receive Him.

12 But as many as received Him, to them He gave the right to become ᵃchildren of God, *even* to those who believe in His name, ᵃ*John 11:52; Gal 3:26*

13 ᵃwho were born, not of blood nor of the will of the flesh nor of the will of man, but of God. ᵃ*John 3:5f; James 1:18*

The Word Made Flesh

14 And the Word ᵃbecame flesh, and dwelt among us, and ᵇwe saw His glory, glory as of the only begotten from the Father, full of grace and truth. ᵃ*Phil 2:7f* ᵇ*Luke 9:32*

15 John *testified about Him and cried out, saying, "This was He of whom I said, 'ᵃHe who comes after me has a higher rank than I, for He existed before me.' " ᵃ*Matt 3:11; John 1:27, 30*

16 For of His ᵃfullness we have all received, and grace upon grace. ᵃ*Eph 1:23; 3:19*

17 For ᵃthe Law was given through Moses; grace and truth were realized through Jesus Christ. ᵃ*John 7:19*

18 No one has seen God at any time; ᵃthe only begotten God who is ᵇin the bosom of the Father, He has explained *Him*. ᵃ*John 3:16, 18* ᵇ*Luke 16:22*

The Testimony of John

19 This is ᵃthe testimony of John, when the Jews sent to him priests and Levites from Jerusalem to ask him, "Who are you?" ᵃ*John 1:7*

20 And he confessed and did not deny, but confessed, "ᵃI am not the Christ." ᵃ*Luke 3:15f; John 3:28*

21 They asked him, "What then? Are you Elijah?" And he *said, "I am not." "Are you ᵃthe Prophet?" And he answered, "No." ᵃ*Deut 18:15, 18; Matt 21:11*

22 Then they said to him, "Who are you, so that we may give an answer to those who sent us? What do you say about yourself?"

23 He said, "I am ᵃA VOICE OF ONE CRYING IN THE WILDERNESS, 'MAKE STRAIGHT THE WAY OF THE LORD,' as Isaiah the prophet said." ᵃ*Is 40:3; Matt 3:3*

24 Now they had been sent from the Pharisees.

25 They asked him, and said to him, "Why then are you baptizing, if you are not the Christ, nor Elijah, nor ᵃthe Prophet?" ᵃ*Deut 18:15, 18; Matt 21:11*

26 John answered them saying, "ᵃI baptize in water, *but* among you stands One whom you do not know. ᵃ*Matt 3:11; Mark 1:8*

27 *It is* He who comes after me, the ᵃthong of whose sandal I am not worthy to untie." ᵃ*Matt 3:11; Mark 1:7*

28 These things took place in Bethany ᵃbeyond the Jordan, where John was baptizing. ᵃ*John 3:26; 10:40*

29 The next day he *saw Jesus coming to him and *said, "Behold, ᵃthe Lamb of God who takes away the sin of the world! ᵃ*Is 53:7; John 1:36*

30 "This is He on behalf of whom I said, 'ᵃAfter me comes a Man who has a higher rank than I, for He existed before me.' ᵃ*Matt 3:11; John 1:27*

31 "I did not recognize Him, but so that He might be manifested to Israel, I came baptizing in water."

32 John testified saying, "ᵃI have seen the Spirit descending as a dove out of heaven, and He remained upon Him. ᵃ*Matt 3:16; Mark 1:10*

33 "I did not recognize Him, but He who sent me to baptize in water said to me, 'He upon whom you see the Spirit descending and remaining upon Him, ᵃthis is the One who baptizes in the Holy Spirit.' ᵃ*Matt 3:11; Mark 1:8*

34 "I myself have seen, and have testified that this is ᵃthe Son of God." ᵃ*Matt 4:3; John 1:49*

Jesus' Public Ministry, First Converts

35 Again [a]the next day John was standing with two of his disciples. [a]*John 1:29*

36 and he looked at Jesus as He walked, and *said, "Behold, [a]the Lamb of God!" [a]*John 1:29*

37 The two disciples heard him speak, and they followed Jesus.

38 And Jesus turned and saw them following, and *said to them, "What do you seek?" They said to Him, "[a]Rabbi (which translated means Teacher), where are You staying?" [a]*Matt 23:7f; John 1:49*

39 He *said to them, "Come, and you will see." So they came and saw where He was staying; and they stayed with Him that day, for it was about the tenth hour.

40 [a]One of the two who heard John *speak* and followed Him, was Andrew, Simon Peter's brother. [a]*Matt 4:18-22; Mark 1:16-20*

41 He *found first his own brother Simon and *said to him, "We have found the [a]Messiah" (which translated means Christ). [a]*Dan 9:25; John 4:25*

42 He brought him to Jesus. Jesus looked at him and said, "You are Simon the son of [a]John; you shall be called Cephas" (which is translated Peter). [a]*Matt 16:17; John 21:15-17*

43 The next day He purposed to go into [a]Galilee, and He *found Philip. And Jesus *said to him, "Follow Me." [a]*Matt 4:12; John 1:28*

44 Now Philip was from [a]Bethsaida, of the city of Andrew and Peter. [a]*Matt 11:21*

45 Philip *found Nathanael and *said to him, "We have found Him of whom [a]Moses in the Law and *also* [a]the Prophets wrote—Jesus of Nazareth, the son of Joseph." [a]*Luke 24:27*

46 Nathanael said to him, "[a]Can any good thing come out of Nazareth?" Philip *said to him, "Come and see." [a]*John 7:41, 52*

47 Jesus saw Nathanael coming to Him, and *said of him, "Behold, an [a]Israelite indeed, in whom there is no deceit!" [a]*Rom 9:4*

48 Nathanael *said to Him, "How do You know me?" Jesus answered and said to him, "Before [a]Philip called you, when you were under the fig tree, I saw you." [a]*Matt 10:3; John 1:44-48*

49 Nathanael answered Him, "Rabbi, You are the Son of God; You are the [a]King of Israel." [a]*Matt 2:2; 27:42*

50 Jesus answered and said to him, "Because I said to you that I saw you under the fig tree, do you believe? You will see greater things than these."

51 And He *said to him, "Truly, truly, I say to you, you will see [a]the heavens opened and the angels of God ascending and descending on the Son of Man." [a]*Ezek 1:1; Matt 3:16*

Miracle at Cana

2 On the third day there was a wedding in [a]Cana of Galilee, and the mother of Jesus was there; [a]*John 2:11; 4:46*

2 and both Jesus and His [a]disciples were invited to the wedding. [a]*John 1:40-49; 2:12, 17, 22*

3 When the wine ran out, the mother of Jesus *said to Him, "They have no wine."

4 And Jesus *said to her, "Woman, what does that have to do with us? [a]My hour has not yet come." [a]*John 7:6, 8, 30; 8:20*

5 His [a]mother *said to the servants, "Whatever He says to you, do it." [a]*Matt 12:46*

6 Now there were six stone waterpots set there [a]for the Jewish custom of purification, containing twenty or thirty gallons each. [a]*Mark 7:3f; John 3:25*

7 Jesus *said to them, "Fill the waterpots with water." So they filled them up to the brim.

8 And He *said to them, "Draw *some* out now and take it to the headwaiter." So they took it *to him.*

9 When the headwaiter tasted the water [a]which had become wine, and did not know where it came from (but the servants who had drawn the water knew), the headwaiter *called the bridegroom, [a]*John 4:46*

10 and *said to him, "Every man serves the good wine first, and when *the people* [a]have drunk freely, *then he serves* the poorer *wine; but* you have kept the good wine until now." [a]*Matt 24:49; Luke 12:45*

11 This beginning of *His* signs Jesus did in Cana of Galilee, and manifested His [a]glory, and His disciples believed in Him. [a]*John 1:14*

12 After this He went down to [a]Capernaum, He and His [b]mother and *His* brothers and His disciples; and they stayed there a few days. [a]*Matt 4:13* [b]*Matt 12:46*

First Passover—Cleansing the Temple

13 [a]The Passover of the Jews was near, and Jesus went up to Jerusalem. [a]*Deut 16:1-6; John 5:1*

14 [a]And He found in the temple those who were selling oxen and sheep and doves, and the money changers seated *at their tables.* [a]*Mal 3:1ff*

15 And He made a scourge of cords, and drove *them* all out of the temple, with the sheep and the oxen; and He poured out the coins of the money changers and overturned their tables;

16 and to those who were selling [a]the doves He said, "Take these things away; stop making [b]My Father's house a place of business." [a]*Matt 21:12* [b]*Luke 2:49*

17 His [a]disciples remembered that it was written, "[b]ZEAL FOR YOUR HOUSE WILL CONSUME ME." [a]*John 2:2* [b]*Ps 69:9*

18 The Jews then said to Him, "[a]What sign do

You show us as your authority for doing these things?" ªMatt 12:38

19 Jesus answered them, "ªDestroy this temple, and in three days I will raise it up." ªMatt 26:61; 27:40

20 The Jews then said, "It took ªforty-six years to build this temple, and will You raise it up in three days?" ªEzra 5:16

21 But He was speaking of ªthe temple of His body. ª1 Cor 6:19

22 So when He was raised from the dead, His disciples remembered that He said this; and they believed ªthe Scripture and the word which Jesus had spoken. ªPs 16:10; Luke 24:26f

23 Now when He was in Jerusalem at ªthe Passover, during the feast, many believed in His name, observing His signs which He was doing. ªJohn 2:13

24 But Jesus, on His part, was not entrusting Himself to them, for ªHe knew all men, ªActs 1:24; 15:8

25 and because He did not need anyone to testify concerning man, ªfor He Himself knew what was in man. ªMatt 9:4; John 1:42, 47

The New Birth

3 Now there was a man of the Pharisees, named ªNicodemus, a ruler of the Jews; ªJohn 7:50; 19:39

2 this man came to Jesus by night and said to Him, "ªRabbi, we know that You have come from God as a teacher; for no one can do these signs that You do unless ªGod is with him." ªMatt 23:7 ªJohn 9:33

3 Jesus answered and said to him, "Truly, truly, I say to you, unless one ªis born again he cannot see the kingdom of God." ª2 Cor 5:17; 1 Pet 1:23

4 Nicodemus *said to Him, "How can a man be born when he is old? He cannot enter a second time into his mother's womb and be born, can he?"

5 Jesus answered, "Truly, truly, I say to you, unless one is born of ªwater and the Spirit he cannot enter into the kingdom of God. ªEzek 36:25-27; Eph 5:26

6 "ªThat which is born of the flesh is flesh, and that which is born of the Spirit is spirit. ªJohn 1:13; 1 Cor 15:50

7 "Do not be amazed that I said to you, 'You must be born again.'

8 "ªThe wind blows where it wishes and you hear the sound of it, but do not know where it comes from and where it is going; so is everyone who is born of the Spirit." ªPs 135:7; Eccl 11:5

9 Nicodemus said to Him, "How can these things be?"

10 Jesus answered and said to him, "Are you ªthe teacher of Israel and do not understand these things? ªLuke 2:46; 5:17

11 "Truly, truly, I say to you, ªwe speak of what we know and testify of what we have seen, and you do not accept our testimony. ªJohn 1:18; 7:16f

12 "If I told you earthly things and you do not believe, how will you believe if I tell you heavenly things?

13 "ªNo one has ascended into heaven, but He who descended from heaven: the Son of Man. ªProv 30:4; Acts 2:34

14 "As ªMoses lifted up the serpent in the wilderness, even so must the Son of Man ªbe lifted up; ªNum 21:9 ªJohn 12:34

15 so that whoever believes will ªin Him have eternal life. ªJohn 20:31; 1 John 5:11-13

16 "For God so ªloved the world, that He gave His only begotten Son, that whoever believes in Him shall not perish, but have eternal life. ªRom 5:8; Eph 2:4

17 "For God did not send the Son into the world ªto judge the world, but that the world might be saved through Him. ªLuke 19:10; John 8:15

18 "He who believes in Him is not judged; he who does not believe has been judged already, because he has not believed in the name of ªthe only begotten Son of God. ªJohn 1:18; 1 John 4:9

19 "This is the judgment, that ªthe Light has come into the world, and men loved the darkness rather than the Light, for their deeds were evil. ªJohn 1:4; 8:12

20 "ªFor everyone who does evil hates the Light, and does not come to the Light for fear that his deeds will be exposed. ªJohn 3:20, 21; Eph 5:11, 13

21 "But he who ªpractices the truth comes to the Light, so that his deeds may be manifested as having been wrought in God." ª1 John 1:6

John's Last Testimony

22 After these things Jesus and His disciples came into the land of Judea, and there He was spending time with them and ªbaptizing. ªJohn 4:1, 2

23 John also was baptizing in Aenon near Salim, because there was much water there; and people were coming and were being baptized—

24 for ªJohn had not yet been thrown into prison. ªMatt 4:12; 14:3

25 Therefore there arose a discussion on the part of John's disciples with a Jew about ªpurification. ªJohn 2:6

26 And they came to John and said to him, "ªRabbi, He who was with you beyond the Jordan, to whom you have testified, behold, He is

baptizing and all are coming to Him."
[a]*Matt 23:7; John 3:2*

27 John answered and said, "[a]A man can receive nothing unless it has been given him from heaven. [a]*1 Cor 4:7; Heb 5:4*

28 "You yourselves are my witnesses that I said, '[a]I am not the Christ,' but, 'I have been sent ahead of Him.' [a]*John 1:20, 23*

29 "He who has the bride is [a]the bridegroom; but the friend of the bridegroom, who stands and hears him, rejoices greatly because of the bridegroom's voice. So this joy of mine has been made full. [a]*Matt 9:15; 25:1*

30 "He must increase, but I must decrease.

31 "[a]He who comes from above is above all, he who is of the earth is from the earth and speaks of the earth. [a]He who comes from heaven is above all. [a]*Matt 28:18; John 3:13*

32 "What He has seen and heard, of that He [a]testifies; and [a]no one receives His testimony. [a]*John 3:11*

33 "He who has received His testimony [a]has set his seal to *this,* that God is true. [a]*John 6:27; Rom 4:11*

34 "For He whom God has sent speaks the words of God; [a]for He gives the Spirit without measure. [a]*Matt 12:18; Luke 4:18*

35 "[a]The Father loves the Son and has given all things into His hand. [a]*Matt 28:18; John 5:20*

36 "He who [a]believes in the Son has eternal life; but he who does not obey the Son will not see life, but the wrath of God abides on him." [a]*John 3:16*

Jesus Goes to Galilee

4 Therefore when [a]the Lord knew that the Pharisees had heard that Jesus was making and baptizing more disciples than John [a]*Luke 7:13*

2 (although [a]Jesus Himself was not baptizing, but His disciples were), [a]*John 3:22, 26; 1 Cor 1:17*

3 He left [a]Judea and went away [b]again into Galilee. [a]*John 3:22* [b]*John 2:11f*

4 And He had to pass through [a]Samaria. [a]*Luke 9:52*

5 So He *came to a city of Samaria called Sychar, near [a]the parcel of ground that Jacob gave to his son Joseph; [a]*Gen 33:19; Josh 24:32*

6 and Jacob's well was there. So Jesus, being wearied from His journey, was sitting thus by the well. It was about the sixth hour.

The Woman of Samaria

7 There *came a woman of Samaria to draw water. Jesus *said to her, "Give Me a drink."

8 For His [a]disciples had gone away into the city to buy food. [a]*John 2:2*

9 Therefore the Samaritan woman *said to Him, "How is it that You, being a Jew, ask me for a drink since I am a Samaritan woman?"

(For [a]Jews have no dealings with Samaritans.) [a]*Ezra 4:3-6, 11ff; Matt 10:5*

10 Jesus answered and said to her, "If you knew the gift of God, and who it is who says to you, 'Give Me a drink,' you would have asked Him, and He would have given you [a]living water." [a]*Jer 2:13; John 4:14*

11 She *said to Him, "Sir, You have nothing to draw with and the well is deep; where then do You get that [a]living water? [a]*Jer 2:13; John 4:14*

12 "You are not greater than our father Jacob, are You, who [a]gave us the well, and drank of it himself and his sons and his cattle?" [a]*John 4:6*

13 Jesus answered and said to her, "Everyone who drinks of this water will thirst again;

14 but whoever drinks of the water that I will give him shall never thirst; but the water that I will give him will become in him a well of water springing up to [a]eternal life." [a]*Matt 25:46; John 6:27*

15 The woman *said to Him, "Sir, [a]give me this water, so I will not be thirsty nor come all the way here to draw." [a]*John 6:35*

16 He *said to her, "Go, call your husband and come here."

17 The woman answered and said, "I have no husband." Jesus *said to her, "You have correctly said, 'I have no husband';

18 for you have had five husbands, and the one whom you now have is not your husband; this you have said truly."

19 The woman *said to Him, "Sir, I perceive that You are [a]a prophet. [a]*Matt 21:11; Luke 7:16, 39*

20 "Our fathers worshiped in [a]this mountain, and you *people* say that in Jerusalem is the place where men ought to worship." [a]*Deut 11:29; Josh 8:33*

21 Jesus *said to her, "Woman, believe Me, an hour is coming when [a]neither in this mountain nor in Jerusalem will you worship the Father. [a]*Mal 1:11; 1 Tim 2:8*

22 "You worship what you do not know; we worship what we know, for [a]salvation is from the Jews. [a]*Is 2:3; Rom 3:1f*

23 "But [a]an hour is coming, and now is, when the true worshipers will worship the Father in spirit and truth; for such people the Father seeks to be His worshipers. [a]*John 4:21; 5:25, 28*

24 "God is spirit, and those who worship Him must worship [a]in spirit and truth." [a]*Phil 3:3*

25 The woman *said to Him, "I know that [a]Messiah is coming ([b]He who is called Christ); when that One comes, He will declare all things to us." [a]*Dan 9:25* [b]*Matt 1:16*

26 Jesus *said to her, "I who speak to you am *He*." [a]*John 8:24, 28, 58; 9:37*

27 At this point His [a]disciples came, and they were amazed that He had been speaking with a woman, yet no one said, "What do You seek?" or, "Why do You speak with her?" [a]*John 4:8*

28 So the woman left her waterpot, and went into the city and *said to the men,

29 "Come, see a man who told me all the things that I *have* done; ªthis is not the Christ, is it?" ªMatt 12:23; John 7:26, 31

30 They went out of the city, and were coming to Him.

31 Meanwhile the disciples were urging Him, saying, "ªRabbi, eat." ªMatt 23:7; 26:25, 49

32 But He said to them, "I have food to eat that you do not know about."

33 So the ªdisciples were saying to one another, "No one brought Him *anything* to eat, did he?" ªLuke 6:13-16; John 1:40-49

34 Jesus *said to them, "My food is to do the will of Him who sent Me and to ªaccomplish His work. ªJohn 5:36; 17:4

35 "Do you not say, 'There are yet four months, and *then* comes the harvest'? Behold, I say to you, lift up your eyes and look on the fields, that they are white ªfor harvest. ªMatt 9:37, 38; Luke 10:2

36 "Already he who reaps is receiving wages and is gathering fruit for ªlife eternal; so that he who sows and he who reaps may rejoice together. ªMatt 19:29; John 3:36

37 "For in this *case* the saying is true, 'ªOne sows and another reaps.' ªJob 31:8; Mic 6:15

38 "I sent you to reap that for which you have not labored; others have labored and you have entered into their labor."

The Samaritans

39 From ªthat city many of the Samaritans believed in Him because of the word of the woman who testified, "ᵇHe told me all the things that I *have* done." ªJohn 4:5, 30 ᵇJohn 4:29

40 So when the Samaritans came to Jesus, they were asking Him to stay with them; and He stayed there two days.

41 Many more believed because of His word;

42 and they were saying to the woman, "It is no longer because of what you said that we believe, for we have heard for ourselves and know that this One is indeed ªthe Savior of the world." ªMatt 1:21; Luke 2:11

43 After ªthe two days He went forth from there into Galilee. ªJohn 4:40

44 For Jesus Himself testified that ªa prophet has no honor in his own country. ªMatt 13:57; Mark 6:4

45 So when He came to Galilee, the Galileans received Him, ªhaving seen all the things that He did in Jerusalem at the feast; for they themselves also went to the feast. ªJohn 2:23

Healing a Nobleman's Son

46 Therefore He came again to ªCana of Galilee where He had made the water wine. And there was a royal official whose son was sick at Capernaum. ªJohn 2:1

47 When he heard that Jesus had come ªout of Judea into Galilee, he went to Him and was imploring *Him* to come down and heal his son; for he was at the point of death. ªJohn 4:3, 54

48 So Jesus said to him, "Unless you *people* see ªsigns and wonders, you *simply* will not believe." ªDan 4:2f; 6:27

49 The royal official *said to Him, "Sir, come down before my child dies."

50 Jesus *said to him, "ªGo; your son lives." The man believed the word that Jesus spoke to him and started off. ªMatt 8:13

51 As he was now going down, *his* slaves met him, saying that his son was living.

52 So he inquired of them the hour when he began to get better. Then they said to him, "Yesterday at the seventh hour the fever left him."

53 So the father knew that *it was* at that hour in which Jesus said to him, "Your son lives"; and he himself believed and ªhis whole household. ªActs 11:14

54 This is again a second sign that Jesus performed when He had ªcome out of Judea into Galilee. ªJohn 4:45f

The Healing at Bethesda

5 After these things there was ªa feast of the Jews, and Jesus went up to Jerusalem. ªDeut 16:1; John 2:13

2 Now there is in Jerusalem by ªthe sheep *gate* a pool, which is called in Hebrew Bethesda, having five porticoes. ªNeh 3:1, 32; 12:39

3 In these lay a multitude of those who were sick, blind, lame, and withered, [waiting for the moving of the waters;

4 for an angel of the Lord went down at certain seasons into the pool and stirred up the water; whoever then first, after the stirring up of the water, stepped in was made well from whatever disease with which he was afflicted.]

5 A man was there who had been ill for thirty-eight years.

6 When Jesus saw him lying *there,* and knew that he had already been a long time *in that condition,* He *said to him, "Do you wish to get well?"

7 The sick man answered Him, "Sir, I have no man to put me into the pool when ªthe water is stirred up, but while I am coming, another steps down before me." ªJohn 5:4

8 Jesus *said to him, "ªGet up, pick up your pallet and walk." ªMatt 9:6; Mark 2:11

9 Immediately the man became well, and picked up his pallet and *began* to walk.

ªNow it was the Sabbath on that day. ªJohn 9:14

10 So the Jews were saying to the man who was cured, "It is the Sabbath, and ªit is not per-

missible for you to carry your pallet."
[a]Neh 13:19; Jer 17:21f

11 But he answered them, "He who made me well was the one who said to me, 'Pick up your pallet and walk.' "

12 They asked him, "Who is the man who said to you, 'Pick up *your pallet* and walk'?"

13 But the man who was healed did not know who it was, for Jesus had slipped away while there was a crowd in *that* place.

14 Afterward Jesus *found him in the temple and said to him, "Behold, you have become well; do not [a]sin anymore, [b]so that nothing worse happens to you." [a]Mark 2:5 [b]Ezra 9:14

15 The man went away, and told [a]the Jews that it was Jesus who had made him well. [a]John 1:19; 5:16, 18

16 For this reason [a]the Jews were persecuting Jesus, because He was doing these things on the Sabbath. [a]John 1:19; 5:10, 15, 18

17 But He answered them, "My Father is working until now, and I Myself am working."

Jesus' Equality with God

18 For this reason therefore the Jews were seeking all the more to kill Him, because He not only was breaking the Sabbath, but also was calling God His own Father, [a]making Himself equal with God. [a]John 10:33; 19:7

19 Therefore Jesus answered and was saying to them, "Truly, truly, I say to you, [a]the Son can do nothing of Himself, unless *it is* something He sees the Father doing; for whatever the Father does, these things the Son also does in like manner. [a]Matt 26:39; John 5:30

20 "[a]For the Father loves the Son, and shows Him all things that He Himself is doing; and *the Father* will show Him [b]greater works than these, so that you will marvel. [a]John 3:35 [b]John 14:12

21 "For just as the Father raises the dead and [a]gives them life, even so [b]the Son also gives life to whom He wishes. [a]Rom 4:17 [b]John 11:25

22 "For not even the Father judges anyone, but [a]He has given all judgment to the Son, [a]John 5:27; 9:39

23 so that all will honor the Son even as they honor the Father. [a]He who does not honor the Son does not honor the Father who sent Him. [a]Luke 10:16; 1 John 2:23

24 "Truly, truly, I say to you, he who hears My word, and [a]believes Him who sent Me, has eternal life, and [b]does not come into judgment, but has passed out of death into life. [a]John 12:44 [b]John 3:18

Two Resurrections

25 "Truly, truly, I say to you, an hour is coming and now is, when [a]the dead will hear the voice of the Son of God, and those who [b]hear will live. [a]Luke 15:24 [b]John 6:60

26 "For just as the Father has life in Himself, even so He [a]gave to the Son also to have life in Himself; [a]John 1:4; 6:57

27 and He gave Him authority to [a]execute judgment, because He is *the* Son of Man. [a]John 9:39; Acts 10:42

28 "Do not marvel at this; for an hour is coming, in which [a]all who are in the tombs will hear His voice, [a]John 11:24; 1 Cor 15:52

29 and will come forth; [a]those who did the good *deeds* to a resurrection of life, those who committed the evil *deeds* to a resurrection of judgment. [a]Dan 12:2; Matt 25:46

30 "I can do nothing on My own initiative. As I hear, I judge; and [a]My judgment is just, because I do not seek My own will, but [b]the will of Him who sent Me. [a]John 8:16 [b]John 4:34

31 "[a]If I *alone* testify about Myself, My testimony is not true. [a]John 8:14

32 "There is [a]another who testifies of Me, and I know that the testimony which He gives about Me is true. [a]John 5:37

Witness of John

33 "You have sent to John, and he [a]has testified to the truth. [a]John 1:7, 15, 19, 32; 3:26-30

34 "But [a]the testimony which I receive is not from man, but I say these things so that you may be saved. [a]John 5:32; 1 John 5:9

35 "He was the lamp that was burning and was shining and you [a]were willing to rejoice for a while in his light. [a]Mark 1:5

Witness of Works

36 "But the testimony which I have is greater than *the testimony of* John; for [a]the works which the Father has given Me [b]to accomplish—the very works that I do—testify about Me, that the Father has sent Me. [a]John 10:25, 38 [b]John 4:34

Witness of the Father

37 "And the Father who sent Me, [a]He has testified of Me. You have neither heard His voice at any time nor seen His form. [a]Matt 3:17; Mark 1:11

38 "You do not have [a]His word abiding in you, for you do not believe Him whom He sent. [a]1 John 2:14

Witness of the Scripture

39 "[a]You search the Scriptures because you think that in them you have eternal life; it is these that testify about Me; [a]John 7:52; Rom 2:17ff

40 and you are unwilling to come to Me so that you may have life.

41 "[a]I do not receive glory from men; [a]John 5:44; 7:18

42 but I know you, that you do not have the love of God in yourselves.

43 "I have come in My Father's name, and

you do not receive Me; [a]if another comes in his own name, you will receive him. [a]Matt 24:5

44 "How can you believe, when you receive glory from one another and you do not seek [a]the glory that is from [b]the *one and* only God? [a]Rom 2:29 [b]John 17:3

45 "Do not think that I will accuse you before the Father; the one who accuses you is [a]Moses, in whom you have set your hope. [a]John 9:28; Rom 2:17ff

46 "For if you believed Moses, you would believe Me, for [a]he wrote about Me. [a]Luke 24:27

47 "But [a]if you do not believe his writings, how will you believe My words?"   [a]Luke 16:29, 31

Five Thousand Fed

6 After these things [a]Jesus went away to the other side of the Sea of Galilee (or Tiberias). [a]Matt 14:13-21; Mark 6:32-44

2 A large crowd followed Him, because they saw the [a]signs which He was performing on those who were sick. [a]John 2:11, 23; 3:2

3 Then [a]Jesus went up on the mountain, and there He sat down with His disciples. [a]Matt 5:1; Mark 3:13

4 Now [a]the Passover, the feast of the Jews, was near. [a]Deut 16:1; John 2:13

5 Therefore Jesus, lifting up His eyes and seeing that a large crowd was coming to Him, *said to [a]Philip, "Where are we to buy bread, so that these may eat?" [a]John 1:43

6 This He was saying to [a]test him, for He Himself knew what He was intending to do. [a]2 Cor 13:5; Rev 2:2

7 Philip answered Him, "[a]Two hundred denarii worth of bread is not sufficient for them, for everyone to receive a little." [a]Mark 6:37

8 One of His disciples, [a]Andrew, Simon Peter's brother, *said to Him, [a]John 1:40

9 "There is a lad here who has five barley loaves and two [a]fish, but what are these for so many people?" [a]John 6:11; 21:9, 10, 13

10 Jesus said, "Have the people sit down." Now there was [a]much grass in the place. So the men sat down, in number about [b]five thousand. [a]Mark 6:39 [b]Matt 14:21

11 Jesus then took the loaves, and [a]having given thanks, He distributed to those who were seated; likewise also of the fish as much as they wanted. [a]Matt 15:36; John 6:23

12 When they were filled, He *said to His [a]disciples, "Gather up the leftover fragments so that nothing will be lost." [a]John 2:2

13 So they gathered them up, and filled twelve [a]baskets with fragments from the five barley loaves which were left over by those who had eaten. [a]Matt 14:20

14 Therefore when the people saw the sign which He had performed, they said, "This is truly the [a]Prophet who is to come into the world." [a]Matt 11:3; 21:11

Jesus Walks on the Water

15 So Jesus, perceiving that they were intending to come and take Him by force to make Him king, [a]withdrew again to the mountain by Himself alone. [a]Matt 14:22-33; Mark 6:45-51

16 Now when evening came, His [a]disciples went down to the sea, [a]John 2:2

17 and after getting into a boat, they *started to cross the sea [a]to Capernaum. It had already become dark, and Jesus had not yet come to them. [a]Mark 6:45; John 6:24, 59

18 The sea *began* to be stirred up because a strong wind was blowing.

19 Then, when they had rowed about three or four miles, they *saw Jesus walking on the sea and drawing near to the boat; and they were frightened.

20 But He *said to them, "It is I; [a]do not be afraid." [a]Matt 14:27

21 So they were willing to receive Him into the boat, and immediately the boat was at the land to which they were going.

22 The next day [a]the crowd that stood on the other side of the sea saw that there was no other small boat there, except one, and that Jesus had not entered with His disciples into the boat, but *that* His disciples had gone away alone. [a]John 6:2

23 There came other small boats from Tiberias near to the place where they ate the bread after the Lord [a]had given thanks. [a]John 6:11

24 So when the crowd saw that Jesus was not there, nor His disciples, they themselves got into the small boats, and [a]came to Capernaum seeking Jesus. [a]Matt 14:34; Mark 6:53

25 When they found Him on the other side of the sea, they said to Him, "[a]Rabbi, when did You get here?" [a]Matt 23:7

Words to the People

26 Jesus answered them and said, "Truly, truly, I say to you, you seek Me, not because you saw [a]signs, but because you ate of the loaves and were filled. [a]John 6:2, 14, 30

27 "Do not [a]work for the food which perishes, but for the food which endures to eternal life, which the Son of Man will give to you, for on Him the Father, God, [b]has set His seal." [a]Is 55:2 [b]John 3:33

28 Therefore they said to Him, "What shall we do, so that we may work the works of God?"

29 Jesus answered and said to them, "This is [a]the work of God, that you believe in Him whom He has sent." [a]1 Thess 1:3; James 2:22

30 So they said to Him, "ᵃWhat then do You do for a sign, so that we may see, and believe You? What work do You perform? ᵃMatt 12:38

31 "Our fathers ate the manna in the wilderness; as it is written, 'ᵃHE GAVE THEM BREAD OUT OF HEAVEN TO EAT.' " ᵃPs 78:24; Ex 16:4, 15

32 Jesus then said to them, "Truly, truly, I say to you, it is not Moses who has given you the bread out of heaven, but it is My Father who gives you the true bread out of heaven.

33 "For the bread of God is that which ᵃcomes down out of heaven, and gives life to the world." ᵃJohn 6:41, 50

34 Then they said to Him, "Lord, always ᵃgive us this bread." ᵃJohn 4:15

35 Jesus said to them, "ᵃI am the bread of life; he who comes to Me will not hunger, and he who believes in Me ᵇwill never thirst. ᵃJohn 6:48, 51 ᵇJohn 4:14

36 "But ᵃI said to you that you have seen Me, and yet do not believe. ᵃJohn 6:26

37 "ᵃAll that the Father gives Me will come to Me, and the one who comes to Me I will certainly not cast out. ᵃJohn 6:39; 17:2, 24

38 "For ᵃI have come down from heaven, ᵇnot to do My own will, but the will of Him who sent Me. ᵃJohn 3:13 ᵇMatt 26:39

39 "This is the will of Him who sent Me, that of all that He has given Me I ᵃlose nothing, but raise it up on the last day. ᵃJohn 17:12; 18:9

40 "For this is the will of My Father, that everyone who beholds the Son and ᵃbelieves in Him will have eternal life, and I Myself will ᵇraise him up on the last day." ᵃJohn 3:16 ᵇMatt 10:15

Words to the Jews

41 Therefore the Jews were grumbling about Him, because He said, "I am the bread that ᵃcame down out of heaven." ᵃJohn 6:33, 51, 58

42 They were saying, "ᵃIs not this Jesus, the son of Joseph, whose father and mother ᵇwe know? How does He now say, 'I have come down out of heaven'?" ᵃLuke 4:22 ᵇJohn 7:27f

43 Jesus answered and said to them, "Do not grumble among yourselves.

44 "No one can come to Me unless the Father who sent Me ᵃdraws him; and I will raise him up on the last day. ᵃJer 31:3; Hos 11:4

45 "It is written in the prophets, 'ᵃAND THEY SHALL ALL BE TAUGHT OF GOD.' Everyone who has heard and learned from the Father, comes to Me. ᵃIs 54:13; Jer 31:34

46 "ᵃNot that anyone has seen the Father, except the One who is from God; He has seen the Father. ᵃJohn 1:18

47 "Truly, truly, I say to you, he who believes ᵃhas eternal life. ᵃJohn 3:36; 5:24

48 "ᵃI am the bread of life. ᵃJohn 6:35, 51

49 "ᵃYour fathers ate the manna in the wilderness, and they died. ᵃJohn 6:31, 58

50 "This is the bread which comes down out of heaven, so that one may eat of it and ᵃnot die. ᵃJohn 3:36; 5:24

51 "I am the living bread that came down out of heaven; if anyone eats of this bread, he will live forever; and the bread also which I will give ᵃfor the life of the world is My flesh." ᵃJohn 1:29; 3:14f

52 Then the Jews ᵃbegan to argue with one another, saying, "How can this man give us His flesh to eat?" ᵃJohn 9:16; 10:19

53 So Jesus said to them, "Truly, truly, I say to you, unless you eat the flesh of ᵃthe Son of Man and drink His blood, you have no life in yourselves. ᵃMatt 8:20; John 6:27, 62

54 "He who eats My flesh and drinks My blood has eternal life, and I will ᵃraise him up on the last day. ᵃJohn 6:39

55 "For My flesh is true food, and My blood is true drink.

56 "He who eats My flesh and drinks My blood ᵃabides in Me, and I in him. ᵃJohn 15:4f; 17:23

57 "As the ᵃliving Father sent Me, and I live because of the Father, so he who eats Me, he also will live because of Me. ᵃMatt 16:16; John 5:26

58 "This is the bread which came down out of heaven; not as the fathers ate and died; he who eats this bread ᵃwill live forever." ᵃJohn 3:36; 5:24

Words to the Disciples

59 These things He said ᵃin the synagogue as He taught in Capernaum. ᵃMatt 4:23

60 Therefore many of His ᵃdisciples, when they heard this said, "This is a difficult statement; who can listen to it?" ᵃJohn 2:2; 6:66

61 But Jesus, conscious that His disciples grumbled at this, said to them, "Does this ᵃcause you to stumble? ᵃMatt 11:6

62 "What then if you see the Son of Man ᵃascending to where He was before? ᵃJohn 3:13

63 "ᵃIt is the Spirit who gives life; the flesh profits nothing; the words that I have spoken to you are spirit and are life. ᵃ2 Cor 3:6

64 "But there are some of you who do not believe." For Jesus ᵃknew from the beginning who they were who did not believe, and ᵇwho it was that would betray Him. ᵃJohn 2:25 ᵇMatt 10:4

65 And He was saying, "For this reason I have said to you, that no one can come to Me unless ᵃit has been granted him from the Father." ᵃMatt 13:11; John 3:27

Peter's Confession of Faith

66 As a result of this many of His ᵃdisciples withdrew and were not walking with Him anymore. ᵃJohn 2:2; 7:3

67 So Jesus said to ªthe twelve, "You do not want to go away also, do you?" ªMatt 10:2; John 2:2

68 Simon Peter answered Him, "Lord, to whom shall we go? You have ªwords of eternal life. ªJohn 6:63; 12:49f

69 "We have believed and have come to know that You are ªthe Holy One of God." ªMark 1:24; 8:29

70 Jesus answered them, "ªDid I Myself not choose you, the twelve, and yet one of you is a devil?" ªJohn 15:16, 19

71 Now He meant Judas ªthe son of Simon Iscariot, for he, one of the twelve, was going to betray Him. ªJohn 12:4; 13:2, 26

Jesus Teaches at the Feast

7 After these things Jesus ªwas walking in Galilee, for He was unwilling to walk in Judea because the Jews ᵇwere seeking to kill Him. ªJohn 4:3 ᵇJohn 5:18

2 Now the feast of the Jews, ªthe Feast of Booths, was near. ªLev 23:34; Deut 16:13, 16

3 Therefore His ªbrothers said to Him, "Leave here and go into Judea, so that Your disciples also may see Your works which You are doing. ªMatt 12:46; Mark 3:21

4 "For no one does anything in secret when he himself seeks to be known publicly. If You do these things, show Yourself to the world."

5 For not even His ªbrothers were believing in Him. ªMatt 12:46; Mark 3:21

6 So Jesus ⁺said to them, "ªMy time is not yet here, but your time is always opportune. ªMatt 26:18; John 2:4

7 "ªThe world cannot hate you, but it hates Me because I testify of it, that ᵇits deeds are evil. ªJohn 15:18f ᵇJohn 3:19f

8 "Go up to the feast yourselves; I do not go up to this feast because ªMy time has not yet fully come." ªJohn 7:6

9 Having said these things to them, He stayed in Galilee.

10 But when His ªbrothers had gone up to the feast, then He Himself also went up, not publicly, but as if, in secret.   ªMatt 12:46; Mark 3:21

11 So the Jews ªwere seeking Him at the feast and were saying, "Where is He?" ªJohn 11:56

12 There was much grumbling among the crowds concerning Him; ªsome were saying, "He is a good man"; others were saying, "No, on the contrary, He leads the people astray." ªJohn 7:40-43

13 Yet no one was speaking openly of Him for ªfear of the Jews. ªJohn 9:22; 12:42

14 But when it was now the midst of the feast Jesus went up into the temple, and began to ªteach. ªMatt 26:55; John 7:28

15 ªThe Jews then were astonished, saying, "How has this man become learned, having never been educated?" ªJohn 1:19; 7:11, 13, 35

16 So Jesus answered them and said, "ªMy teaching is not Mine, but His who sent Me. ªJohn 3:11

17 "ªIf anyone is willing to do His will, he will know of the teaching, whether it is of God or whether I speak from Myself. ªPs 25:9, 14; Prov 3:32

18 "He who speaks from himself ªseeks his own glory; but He who is seeking the glory of the One who sent Him, He is true, and there is no unrighteousness in Him. ªJohn 5:41; 8:50, 54

19 "ªDid not Moses give you the Law, and yet none of you carries out the Law? Why do you ᵇseek to kill Me?" ªJohn 1:17 ᵇMark 11:18

20 The crowd answered, "ªYou have a demon! Who seeks to kill You?" ªMatt 11:18; John 8:48f, 52

21 Jesus answered them, "I did ªone deed, and you all marvel. ªJohn 5:2-9, 16; 7:23

22 "For this reason ªMoses has given you circumcision (not because it is from Moses, but from ᵇthe fathers), and on the Sabbath you circumcise a man. ªLev 12:3 ᵇGen 17:10ff

23 "ªIf a man receives circumcision on the Sabbath so that the Law of Moses will not be broken, are you angry with Me because I made an entire man well on the Sabbath? ªMatt 12:2; John 5:9, 10

24 "Do not ªjudge according to appearance, but judge with righteous judgment." ªLev 19:15; Is 11:3

25 So some of the people of Jerusalem were saying, "Is this not the man whom they are seeking to kill?

26 "Look, He is speaking publicly, and they are saying nothing to Him. ªThe rulers do not really know that this is the Christ, do they? ªLuke 23:13; John 3:1

27 "However, ªwe know where this man is from; but whenever the Christ may come, no one knows where He is from." ªJohn 6:42; 7:41f

28 Then Jesus cried out in the temple, teaching and saying, "You both know Me and know where I am from; and ªI have not come of Myself, but He who sent Me is true, whom you do not know. ªJohn 8:42

29 "I know Him, because ªI am from Him, and ᵇHe sent Me." ªJohn 6:46 ᵇJohn 3:17

30 So they ªwere seeking to seize Him; and no man laid his hand on Him, because His hour had not yet come. ªMatt 21:46; John 7:32, 44

31 But ªmany of the crowd believed in Him; and they were saying, "When the Christ comes, He will not perform more ᵇsigns than those which this man has, will He?" ªJohn 2:23 ᵇJohn 2:11

32 The Pharisees heard the crowd muttering these things about Him, and the chief priests

and the Pharisees sent [a]officers to seize Him.
[a]*Matt 26:58; John 7:45f*

33 Therefore Jesus said, "[a]For a little while longer I am with you, then I go to Him who sent Me. [a]*John 12:35; 13:33*

34 "[a]You will seek Me, and will not find Me; and where I am, you cannot come." [a]*John 7:36; 8:21*

35 The Jews then said to one another, "Where does this man intend to go that we will not find Him? He is not intending to go to [a]the Dispersion among the Greeks, and teach the Greeks, is He? [a]*Ps 147:2; Is 11:12*

36 "What is this statement that He said, '[a]You will seek Me, and will not find Me; and where I am, you cannot come'?" [a]*John 7:34; 8:21*

37 Now on [a]the last day, the great *day* of the feast, Jesus stood and cried out, saying, "If anyone is thirsty, let him come to Me and drink. [a]*Lev 23:36; Num 29:35*

38 "He who believes in Me, [a]as the Scripture said, 'From his innermost being will flow rivers of living water.' " [a]*Is 44:3; 55:1*

39 But this He spoke [a]of the Spirit, whom those who believed in Him were to receive; for the Spirit was not yet *given*, because Jesus was not yet glorified. [a]*Joel 2:28; John 1:33*

Division of People over Jesus

40 *Some* of the people therefore, when they heard these words, were saying, "This certainly is [a]the Prophet." [a]*Matt 21:11; John 1:21*

41 Others were saying, "This is the Christ." Still others were saying, "[a]Surely the Christ is not going to come from Galilee, is He? [a]*John 1:46; 7:52*

42 "Has not the Scripture said that the Christ comes from [a]the descendants of David, and from Bethlehem, the village where David was?" [a]*Ps 89:4; Mic 5:2*

43 So [a]a division occurred in the crowd because of Him. [a]*John 9:16; 10:19*

44 [a]Some of them wanted to seize Him, but no one laid hands on Him. [a]*John 7:30*

45 The [a]officers then came to the chief priests and Pharisees, and they said to them, "Why did you not bring Him?" [a]*John 7:32*

46 The officers answered, "[a]Never has a man spoken the way this man speaks." [a]*Matt 7:28*

47 The Pharisees then answered them, "[a]You have not also been led astray, have you? [a]*John 7:12*

48 "No one of [a]the rulers or Pharisees has believed in Him, has he? [a]*Luke 23:13; John 7:26*

49 "But this crowd which does not know the Law is accursed."

50 [a]Nicodemus (he who came to Him before, being one of them) *said to them, [a]*John 3:1; 19:39*

51 "[a]Our Law does not judge a man unless it

first hears from him and knows what he is doing, does it?" [a]*Ex 23:1; Deut 17:6*

52 They answered him, "[a]You are not also from Galilee, are you? Search, and see that no prophet arises out of Galilee." [a]*John 1:46; 7:41*

53 [Everyone went to his home.

The Adulterous Woman

8 But Jesus went to [a]the Mount of Olives.
   [a]*Matt 21:1*

2 Early in the morning He came again into the temple, and all the people were coming to Him; and [a]He sat down and *began* to teach them. [a]*Matt 26:55; John 8:20*

3 The scribes and the Pharisees *brought a woman caught in adultery, and having set her in the center *of the court*,

4 they *said to Him, "Teacher, this woman has been caught in adultery, in the very act.

5 "Now in the Law [a]Moses commanded us to stone such women; what then do You say?" [a]*Lev 20:10; Deut 22:22f*

6 They were saying this, [a]testing Him, so that they might have grounds for accusing Him. But Jesus stooped down and with His finger wrote on the ground. [a]*Matt 16:1; 19:3*

7 But when they persisted in asking Him, He straightened up, and said to them, "He who is without sin among you, let him *be the* [a]first to throw a stone at her." [a]*Deut 17:7*

8 Again He stooped down and wrote on the ground.

9 When they heard it, they *began* to go out one by one, beginning with the older ones, and He was left alone, and the woman, where she was, in the center *of the court.*

10 [a]Straightening up, Jesus said to her, "Woman, where are they? Did no one condemn you?" [a]*John 8:7*

11 She said, "No one, Lord." And Jesus said, "[a]I do not condemn you, either. Go. From now on [b]sin no more."] [a]*John 3:17* [b]*John 5:14*

Jesus Is the Light of the World

12 Then Jesus again spoke to them, saying, "[a]I am the Light of the world; he who follows Me will not walk in the darkness, but will have the Light of life." [a]*John 1:4; 9:5*

13 So the Pharisees said to Him, "[a]You are testifying about Yourself; Your testimony is not true." [a]*John 5:31*

14 Jesus answered and said to them, "Even if I testify about Myself, My testimony is true, for I know [a]where I came from and where I am going; but you do not know where I come from or where I am going. [a]*John 8:42; 13:3*

15 "You judge according to the flesh; [a]I am not judging anyone. [a]*John 3:17*

16 "But even [a]if I do judge, My judgment is true; for I am not alone *in it,* but I and the Father who sent Me. [a]*John 5:30*

17 "Even in ^ayour law it has been written that the testimony of ^btwo men is true. ^aDeut 17:6 ^bMatt 18:16

18 "I am He who testifies about Myself, and ^athe Father who sent Me testifies about Me." ^aJohn 5:37; 1 John 5:9

19 So they were saying to Him, "Where is Your Father?" Jesus answered, "You know neither Me nor My Father; ^aif you knew Me, you would know My Father also." ^aJohn 7:28; 8:55

20 These words He spoke in the treasury, as ^aHe taught in the temple; and no one seized Him, because ^bHis hour had not yet come. ^aJohn 7:14 ^bJohn 7:30

21 Then He said again to them, "I go away, and ^ayou will seek Me, and will die in your sin; where I am going, you cannot come." ^aJohn 7:34

22 So the Jews were saying, "Surely He will not kill Himself, will He, since He says, '^aWhere I am going, you cannot come'?" ^aJohn 7:35

23 And He was saying to them, "^aYou are from below, I am from above; you are of this world, ^bI am not of this world. ^aJohn 3:31 ^bJohn 17:14, 16

24 "Therefore I said to you that you will die in your sins; for unless you believe that ^aI am He, you will die in your sins." ^aMatt 24:5; Mark 13:6

25 So they were saying to Him, "Who are You?" Jesus said to them, "What have I been saying to you from the beginning?

26 "I have many things to speak and to judge concerning you, but ^aHe who sent Me is true; and the things which I heard from Him, these I speak to the world." ^aJohn 3:33; 7:28

27 They did not realize that He had been speaking to them about the Father.

28 So Jesus said, "When you ^alift up the Son of Man, then you will know that I am He, and I do nothing on My own initiative, but I speak these things as the Father taught Me. ^aJohn 3:14; 12:32

29 "And He who sent Me is with Me; ^aHe has not left Me alone, for I always do the things that are pleasing to Him." ^aJohn 8:16; 16:32

30 As He spoke these things, ^amany came to believe in Him. ^aJohn 7:31

The Truth Will Make You Free

31 So Jesus was saying to those Jews who had believed Him, "^aIf you continue in My word, then you are truly disciples of Mine; ^aJohn 15:7; 2 John 9

32 and you will know the truth, and ^athe truth will make you free." ^aJohn 8:36; Rom 8:2

33 They answered Him, "^aWe are Abraham's descendants and have never yet been enslaved to anyone; how is it that You say, 'You will become free'?" ^aMatt 3:9; Luke 3:8

34 Jesus answered them, "Truly, truly, I say to you, ^aeveryone who commits sin is the slave of sin. ^aRom 6:16; 2 Pet 2:19

35 "The slave does not remain in the house forever; ^athe son does remain forever. ^aLuke 15:31

36 "So if the Son ^amakes you free, you will be free indeed. ^aJohn 8:32

37 "I know that you are ^aAbraham's descendants; yet you seek to kill Me, because My word has no place in you. ^aMatt 3:9; John 8:39

38 "I speak the things which I have seen with My Father; therefore you also do the things which you heard from ^ayour father." ^aJohn 8:41, 44

39 They answered and said to Him, "Abraham is our father." Jesus *said to them, "^aIf you are Abraham's children, do the deeds of Abraham. ^aRom 9:7; Gal 3:7

40 "But as it is, you are seeking to kill Me, a man who has ^atold you the truth, which I heard from God; this Abraham did not do. ^aJohn 8:26

41 "You are doing the deeds of your father." They said to Him, "We were not born of fornication; ^awe have one Father: God." ^aDeut 32:6; Is 63:16

42 Jesus said to them, "If God were your Father, ^ayou would love Me, for I proceeded forth and have come from God, for I have not even come on My own initiative, but He sent Me. ^a1 John 5:1

43 "Why do you not understand what I am saying? It is because you cannot ^ahear My word. ^aJohn 5:25

44 "^aYou are of your father the devil, and ^byou want to do the desires of your father. He was a murderer from the beginning, and does not stand in the truth because there is no truth in him. Whenever he speaks a lie, he speaks from his own nature, for he is a liar and the father of lies. ^a1 John 3:8 ^bJohn 7:17

45 "But because ^aI speak the truth, you do not believe Me. ^aJohn 18:37

46 "Which one of you convicts Me of sin? If I speak truth, why do you not believe Me?

47 "^aHe who is of God hears the words of God; for this reason you do not hear them, because you are not of God." ^a1 John 4:6

48 The Jews answered and said to Him, "Do we not say rightly that You are a ^aSamaritan and have a demon?" ^aMatt 10:5; John 4:9

49 Jesus answered, "I do not ^ahave a demon; but I honor My Father, and you dishonor Me. ^aJohn 7:20

50 "But ^aI do not seek My glory; there is One who seeks and judges. ^aJohn 5:41; 8:54

51 "Truly, truly, I say to you, if anyone keeps My word he will never ^asee death." ^aMatt 16:28; Luke 2:26

52 The Jews said to Him, "Now we know that

You have a demon. Abraham died, and the prophets *also;* and You say, 'If anyone ªkeeps My word, he will never taste of death.'
ªJohn 8:55; 14:23

53 "Surely You ªare not greater than our father Abraham, who died? The prophets died too; whom do You make Yourself out *to be?"*
ªJohn 4:12

54 Jesus answered, "If I glorify Myself, My glory is nothing; ªit is My Father who glorifies Me, of whom you say, 'He is our God';
ªJohn 7:39

55 and you have not come to know Him, ªbut I know Him; and if I say that I do not know Him, I will be a liar like you, ªbut I do know Him and keep His word. ªJohn 7:29

56 "Your father Abraham ªrejoiced to see My day, and he saw *it* and was glad." ªMatt 13:17; Heb 11:13

57 ªSo the Jews said to Him, "You are not yet fifty years old, and have You seen Abraham?"
ªJohn 1:19

58 Jesus said to them, "Truly, truly, I say to you, before Abraham was born, ªI am."
ªEx 3:14; John 1:1

59 Therefore they ªpicked up stones to throw at Him, but Jesus ᵇhid Himself and went out of the temple. ªJohn 10:31 ᵇJohn 12:36

Healing the Man Born Blind

9 As He passed by, He saw a man blind from birth.

2 And His disciples asked Him, "Rabbi, who sinned, this man or his ªparents, that he would be born blind?" ªEx 20:5

3 Jesus answered, "*It was* neither *that* this man sinned, nor his parents; but *it was* so ªthat the works of God might be displayed in him.
ªJohn 11:4

4 "We must work the works of Him who sent Me ªas long as it is day; night is coming when no one can work. ªJohn 7:33; 11:9

5 "While I am in the world, I am ªthe Light of the world." ªMatt 5:14; John 1:4

6 When He had said this, He ªspat on the ground, and made clay of the spittle, and applied the clay to his eyes, ªMark 7:33; 8:23

7 and said to him, "Go, wash in ªthe pool of Siloam" (which is translated, Sent). So he went away and washed, and came *back* seeing.
ªNeh 3:15; Is 8:6

8 Therefore the neighbors, and those who previously saw him as a beggar, were saying, "Is not this the one who used to ªsit and beg?"
ªActs 3:2, 10

9 Others were saying, "This is he," *still* others were saying, "No, but he is like him." He kept saying, "I am the one."

10 So they were saying to him, "How then were your eyes opened?"

11 He answered, "The man who is called Jesus made clay, and anointed my eyes, and said to me, 'Go to ªSiloam and wash'; so I went away and washed, and I received sight."
ªJohn 9:7

12 They said to him, "Where is He?" He *said, "I do not know."

Controversy over the Man

13 They *brought to the Pharisees the man who was formerly blind.

14 ªNow it was a Sabbath on the day when Jesus made the clay and opened his eyes.
ªJohn 5:9

15 ªThen the Pharisees also were asking him again how he received his sight. And he said to them, "He applied clay to my eyes, and I washed, and I see." ªJohn 9:10

16 Therefore some of the Pharisees were saying, "This man is not from God, because He ªdoes not keep the Sabbath." But others were saying, "How can a man who is a sinner perform such signs?" And there was a division among them. ªMatt 12:2; Luke 13:14

17 So they *said to the blind man again, "What do you say about Him, since He opened your eyes?" And he said, "He is a ªprophet."
ªDeut 18:15; Matt 21:11

18 ªThe Jews then did not believe *it* of him, that he had been blind and had received sight, until they called the parents of the very one who had received his sight, ªJohn 1:19; 9:22

19 and questioned them, saying, "Is this your son, who you say was born blind? Then how does he now see?"

20 His parents answered them and said, "We know that this is our son, and that he was born blind;

21 but how he now sees, we do not know; or who opened his eyes, we do not know. Ask him; he is of age, he will speak for himself."

22 His parents said this because they ªwere afraid of the Jews; for the Jews had already agreed that if anyone confessed Him to be Christ, ᵇhe was to be put out of the synagogue.
ªJohn 7:13 ᵇLuke 6:22

23 For this reason his parents said, "ªHe is of age; ask him." ªJohn 9:21

24 So a second time they called the man who had been blind, and said to him, "ªGive glory to God; we know that this man is a sinner."
ªJosh 7:19; Ezra 10:11

25 He then answered, "Whether He is a sinner, I do not know; one thing I do know, that though I was blind, now I see."

26 So they said to him, "What did He do to you? How did He open your eyes?"

27 He answered them, "ªI told you already and you did not ᵇlisten; why do you want to hear *it*

again? You do not want to become His disciples too, do you?" [a]John 9:15 [b]John 8:43, 47

28 They reviled him and said, "You are His disciple, but [a]we are disciples of Moses. [a]John 5:45; Rom 2:17

29 "We know that God has spoken to Moses, but as for this man, [a]we do not know where He is from." [a]John 8:14

30 The man answered and said to them, "Well, here is an amazing thing, that you do not know where He is from, and *yet* He opened my eyes.

31 "We know that [a]God does not hear sinners; but if anyone is God-fearing and does His will, He hears him. [a]Job 27:8f; 35:13

32 "Since the beginning of time it has never been heard that anyone opened the eyes of a person born blind.

33 "[a]If this man were not from God, He could do nothing." [a]John 3:2; 9:16

34 They answered him, "You were born entirely in sins, and are you teaching us?" So they [a]put him out. [a]John 9:22, 35; 3 John 10

Jesus Affirms His Deity

35 Jesus heard that they had [a]put him out, and finding him, He said, "Do you believe in the Son of Man?" [a]John 9:22, 34; 3 John 10

36 He answered, "[a]Who is He, Lord, that I may believe in Him?" [a]Rom 10:14

37 Jesus said to him, "You have both seen Him, and [a]He is the one who is talking with you." [a]John 4:26

38 And he said, "Lord, I believe." And he [a]worshiped Him. [a]Matt 8:2

39 And Jesus said, "[a]For judgment I came into this world, so that [b]those who do not see may see, and that those who see may become blind." [a]John 5:22, 27 [b]Luke 4:18

40 Those of the Pharisees who were with Him heard these things and said to Him, "[a]We are not blind too, are we?" [a]Rom 2:19

41 Jesus said to them, "[a]If you were blind, you would have no sin; but since you say, 'We see,' your sin remains. [a]John 15:22, 24

Parable of the Good Shepherd

10 "Truly, truly, I say to you, he who does not enter by the door into the fold of the sheep, but climbs up some other way, he is [a]a thief and a robber. [a]John 10:8

2 "But he who enters by the door is [a]a shepherd of the sheep. [a]John 10:11f

3 "To him the doorkeeper opens, and the sheep hear [a]his voice, and he calls his own sheep by name and leads them out. [a]John 10:4f, 16, 27

4 "When he puts forth all his own, he goes ahead of them, and the sheep follow him because they know [a]his voice. [a]John 10:5, 16, 27

5 "A stranger they simply will not follow, but will flee from him, because they do not know [a]the voice of strangers." [a]John 10:4, 16, 27

6 This [a]figure of speech Jesus spoke to them, but they did not understand what those things were which He had been saying to them. [a]John 16:25, 29; 2 Pet 2:22

7 So Jesus said to them again, "Truly, truly, I say to you, I am [a]the door of the sheep. [a]John 10:1f, 9

8 "All who came before Me are [a]thieves and robbers, but the sheep did not hear them. [a]Jer 23:1f; Ezek 34:2ff

9 "[a]I am the door; if anyone enters through Me, he will be saved, and will go in and out and find pasture. [a]John 10:1f, 9

10 "The thief comes only to steal and kill and destroy; I came that they [a]may have life, and have *it* abundantly. [a]John 5:40

11 "[a]I am the good shepherd; the good shepherd lays down His life for the sheep. [a]Is 40:11; Ezek 34:11-16, 23

12 "He who is a hired hand, and not a [a]shepherd, who is not the owner of the sheep, sees the wolf coming, and leaves the sheep and flees, and the wolf snatches them and scatters *them.* [a]John 10:2

13 "*He flees* because he is a hired hand and is not concerned about the sheep.

14 "I am the good shepherd, and [a]I know My own and My own know Me, [a]John 10:27

15 even as [a]the Father knows Me and I know the Father; and I lay down My life for the sheep. [a]Matt 11:27; Luke 10:22

16 "I have [a]other sheep, which are not of this fold; I must bring them also, and they will hear My voice; and they will become one flock *with* one shepherd. [a]Is 56:8

17 "For this reason the Father loves Me, because I [a]lay down My life so that I may take it again. [a]John 10:11, 15, 18

18 "[a]No one has taken it away from Me, but I lay it down on My own initiative. I have authority to lay it down, and I have authority to take it up again. This commandment I received from My Father." [a]Matt 26:53; John 2:19

19 [a]A division occurred again among the Jews because of these words. [a]John 7:43; 9:16

20 Many of them were saying, "He [a]has a demon and [b]is insane. Why do you listen to Him?" [a]John 7:20 [b]Mark 3:21

21 Others were saying, "These are not the sayings of one demon-possessed. [a]A demon cannot open the eyes of the blind, can he?" [a]Ex 4:11; John 9:32f

Jesus Asserts His Deity

22 At that time the Feast of the Dedication took place at Jerusalem;

23 it was winter, and Jesus was walking in the

temple in the portico of ᵃSolomon. ᵃ*Acts 3:11; 5:12*

24 The Jews then gathered around Him, and were saying to Him, "How long will You keep us in suspense? If You are the Christ, tell us ᵃplainly." ᵃ*Luke 22:67; John 16:25*

25 Jesus answered them, "I told you, and you do not believe; ᵃthe works that I do in My Father's name, these testify of Me. ᵃ*John 5:36; 10:38*

26 "But you do not believe because ᵃyou are not of My sheep. ᵃ*John 8:47*

27 "My sheep ᵃhear My voice, and I know them, and they follow Me; ᵃ*John 10:4, 16*

28 and I give ᵃeternal life to them, and they will never perish; and no one will snatch them out of My hand. ᵃ*John 17:2f; 1 John 2:25*

29 "My Father, who has given *them* to Me, is greater than all; and no one is able to snatch *them* out of the Father's hand.

30 "ᵃI and the Father are one." ᵃ*John 17:21ff*

31 The Jews ᵃpicked up stones again to stone Him. ᵃ*John 8:59*

32 Jesus answered them, "I showed you many good works from the Father; for which of them are you stoning Me?"

33 The Jews answered Him, "For a good work we do not stone You, but for ᵃblasphemy; and because You, being a man, ᵇmake Yourself out *to be* God." ᵃ*Lev 24:16* ᵇ*John 5:18*

34 Jesus answered them, "Has it not been written in your Law, 'ᵃI SAID, YOU ARE GODS'? ᵃ*Ps 82:6*

35 "If he called them gods, to whom the word of God came (and the Scripture cannot be broken),

36 do you say of Him, whom the Father sanctified and ᵃsent into the world, 'You are blaspheming,' because I said, 'I am the Son of God'? ᵃ*John 3:17*

37 "ᵃIf I do not do the works of My Father, do not believe Me; ᵃ*John 10:25; 15:24*

38 but if I do them, though you do not believe Me, believe the works, so that you may know and understand that ᵃthe Father is in Me, and I in the Father." ᵃ*John 14:10f, 20; 17:21, 23*

39 Therefore ᵃthey were seeking again to seize Him, and He eluded their grasp. ᵃ*John 7:30*

40 And He went away ᵃagain beyond the Jordan to the place where John was first baptizing, and He was staying there. ᵃ*John 1:28*

41 Many came to Him and were saying, "While John performed no sign, yet ᵃevery-thing John said about this man was true." ᵃ*John 1:27, 30, 34; 3:27-30*

42 ᵃMany believed in Him there. ᵃ*John 7:31*

The Death and Resurrection of Lazarus

11 Now a certain man was sick, Lazarus of Bethany, the village of Mary and her sister ᵃMartha. ᵃ*Luke 10:38; John 11:5, 19ff*

2 It was the Mary who ᵃanointed the Lord with ointment, and wiped His feet with her hair, whose brother Lazarus was sick. ᵃ*Luke 7:38; John 12:3*

3 So the sisters sent *word* to Him, saying, "Lord, behold, ᵃhe whom You love is sick." ᵃ*John 11:5, 11, 36*

4 But when Jesus heard *this,* He said, "This sickness is not to end in death, but for ᵃthe glory of God, so that the Son of God may be glorified by it." ᵃ*John 9:3; 10:38*

5 Now Jesus loved ᵃMartha and her sister and Lazarus. ᵃ*John 11:1*

6 So when He heard that he was sick, He then stayed two days *longer* in the place where He was.

7 Then after this He *said to the disciples, "ᵃLet us go to Judea again." ᵃ*John 10:40*

8 The disciples *said to Him, "Rabbi, the Jews were just now seeking ᵃto stone You, and are You going there again?" ᵃ*John 8:59; 10:31*

9 Jesus answered, "ᵃAre there not twelve hours in the day? If anyone walks in the day, he does not stumble, because he sees the light of this world. ᵃ*Luke 13:33; John 9:4*

10 "But if anyone walks in the night, he stumbles, because the light is not in him."

11 This He said, and after that He *said to them, "Our friend Lazarus ᵃhas fallen asleep; but I go, so that I may awaken him out of sleep." ᵃ*Matt 27:52; Mark 5:39*

12 The disciples then said to Him, "Lord, if he has fallen asleep, he will recover."

13 Now ᵃJesus had spoken of his death, but they thought that He was speaking of literal sleep. ᵃ*Matt 9:24; Luke 8:52*

14 So Jesus then said to them plainly, "Lazarus is dead,

15 and I am glad for your sakes that I was not there, so that you may believe; but let us go to him."

16 Therefore Thomas, who is called ᵃDidymus, said to *his* fellow disciples, "Let us also go, so that we may die with Him." ᵃ*John 20:24; 21:2*

17 So when Jesus came, He found that he had already been in the tomb ᵃfour days. ᵃ*John 11:39*

18 Now ᵃBethany was near Jerusalem, about two miles off; ᵃ*John 11:1*

19 and many of the Jews had come to Martha and Mary, ᵃto console them concerning *their* brother. ᵃ*Job 2:11; John 11:31*

20 ᵃMartha therefore, when she heard that Jesus was coming, went to meet Him, but ᵃMary stayed at the house. ᵃ*Luke 10:38-42*

21 Martha then said to Jesus, "Lord, ᵃif You had been here, my brother would not have died. ᵃ*John 11:32, 37*

22 "Even now I know that ᵃwhatever You ask of God, God will give You." ᵃ*John 9:31; 11:41f*

23 Jesus *said to her, "Your brother will rise again."

24 Martha *said to Him, "ªI know that he will rise again in the resurrection on the last day."
ªDan 12:2; John 5:28f

25 Jesus said to her, "ªI am the resurrection and the life; he who believes in Me will live even if he dies, ªJohn 1:4; 5:26

26 and everyone who lives and believes in Me ªwill never die. Do you believe this?" ªJohn 6:47, 50, 51; 8:51

27 She *said to Him, "Yes, Lord; I have believed that You are ªthe Christ, the Son of God, *even* He who comes into the world."
ªMatt 16:16; Luke 2:11

28 When she had said this, she went away and called Mary her sister, saying secretly, "ªThe Teacher is here and is calling for you."
ªMatt 26:18; Mark 14:14

29 And when she heard it, she *got up quickly and was coming to Him.

30 Now Jesus had not yet come into the village, but ªwas still in the place where Martha met Him. ªJohn 11:20

31 ªThen the Jews who were with her in the house, and consoling her, when they saw that Mary got up quickly and went out, they followed her, supposing that she was going to the tomb to weep there. ªJohn 11:19, 33

32 Therefore, when Mary came where Jesus was, she saw Him, and fell at His feet, saying to Him, "Lord, ªif You had been here, my brother would not have died." ªJohn 11:21

33 When Jesus therefore saw her weeping, and the Jews who came with her *also* weeping, He ªwas deeply moved in spirit and was troubled, ªJohn 11:38

34 and said, "Where have you laid him?" They *said to Him, "Lord, come and see."

35 Jesus ªwept. ªLuke 19:41; John 11:33

36 So the Jews were saying, "See how He ªloved him!" ªJohn 11:3, 5

37 But some of them said, "Could not this man, who ªopened the eyes of the blind man, have kept this man also from dying?" ªJohn 9:7

38 So Jesus, again being deeply moved within, *came to the tomb. Now it was a ªcave, and a stone was lying against it. ªMatt 27:60; Mark 15:46

39 Jesus *said, "Remove the stone." Martha, the sister of the deceased, *said to Him, "Lord, by this time there will be a stench, for he has been *dead* ªfour days." ªJohn 11:17

40 Jesus *said to her, "ªDid I not say to you that if you believe, you will see the glory of God?" ªJohn 11:4, 23ff

41 So they removed the stone. Then Jesus ªraised His eyes, and said, "ᵇFather, I thank You that You have heard Me. ªJohn 17:1 ᵇMatt 11:25

42 "I knew that You always hear Me; but ªbecause of the people standing around I said it, so that they may believe that You sent Me."
ªJohn 12:30; 17:21

43 When He had said these things, He cried out with a loud voice, "Lazarus, come forth."

44 The man who had died came forth, ªbound hand and foot with wrappings, and ᵇhis face was wrapped around with a cloth. Jesus *said to them, "Unbind him, and let him go."
ªJohn 19:40 ᵇJohn 20:7

45 Therefore many of the Jews ªwho came to Mary, and saw what He had done, believed in Him. ªJohn 11:19; 12:17f

46 But some of them went to the ªPharisees and told them the things which Jesus had done.
ªJohn 7:32, 45; 11:57

Conspiracy to Kill Jesus

47 Therefore ªthe chief priests and the Pharisees ᵇconvened a council, and were saying, "What are we doing? For this man is performing many signs. ªJohn 7:32, 45 ᵇMatt 26:3

48 "If we let Him *go on* like this, all men will believe in Him, and the Romans will come and take away both our ªplace and our nation."
ªMatt 24:15

49 But one of them, Caiaphas, ªwho was high priest that year, said to them, "You know nothing at all, ªJohn 11:51; 18:13

50 nor do you take into account that ªit is expedient for you that one man die for the people, and that the whole nation not perish."
ªJohn 18:14

51 Now he did not say this on his own initiative, but ªbeing high priest that year, he prophesied that Jesus was going to die for the nation, ªJohn 18:13

52 and not for the nation only, but in order that He might also ªgather together into one the children of God who are scattered abroad.
ªJohn 10:16

53 So from that day on they ªplanned together to kill Him. ªMatt 26:4

54 Therefore Jesus ªno longer continued to walk publicly among the Jews, but went away from there to the country near the wilderness, into a city called Ephraim; and there He stayed with the disciples. ªJohn 7:1

55 Now the Passover of the Jews was near, and many went up to Jerusalem out of the country before the Passover ªto purify themselves. ªNum 9:10; 2 Chr 30:17f

56 So they ªwere seeking for Jesus, and were saying to one another as they stood in the temple, "What do you think; that He will not come to the feast at all?" ªJohn 7:11

57 Now ªthe chief priests and the Pharisees had given orders that if anyone knew where He

was, he was to report it, so that they might seize Him. ªJohn 11:47

Mary Anoints Jesus

12 ªJesus, therefore, six days before the Passover, came to Bethany where Lazarus was, whom Jesus had raised from the dead. ªMatt 26:6-13; Mark 14:3-9

2 So they made Him a supper there, and ªMartha was serving; but Lazarus was one of those reclining *at the table* with Him. ªLuke 10:38

3 ªMary then took a pound of very costly ᵇperfume of pure nard, and anointed the feet of Jesus and wiped His feet with her hair; and the house was filled with the fragrance of the perfume. ªLuke 7:37fᵇMark 14:3

4 But ªJudas Iscariot, one of His disciples, who was intending to betray Him, *said, ªJohn 6:71

5 "Why was this perfume not sold for three hundred denarii and given to poor *people?*"

6 Now he said this, not because he was concerned about the poor, but because he was a thief, and as he ªhad the money box, he used to pilfer ᵇwhat was put into it. ªJohn 13:29 ᵇLuke 8:3

7 Therefore Jesus said, "Let her alone, so that she may keep it for ªthe day of My burial. ªJohn 19:40

8 "ªFor you always have the poor with you, but you do not always have Me." ªDeut 15:11; Matt 26:11

9 The large crowd of the Jews then learned that He was there; and they came, not for Jesus' sake only, but that they might also see Lazarus, ªwhom He raised from the dead. ªJohn 11:43f; 12:1, 17f

10 But the chief priests planned to put Lazarus to death also;

11 because ªon account of him many of the Jews were going away and were believing in Jesus. ªJohn 11:45f; 12:18

Jesus Enters Jerusalem

12 On the next day ªthe large crowd who had come to the feast, when they heard that Jesus was coming to Jerusalem, ªMatt 21:4-9; Mark 11:7-10

13 took the branches of the palm trees and went out to meet Him, and *began* to shout, "ªHosanna! BLESSED IS HE WHO COMES IN THE NAME OF THE LORD, even the King of Israel." ªPs 118:26

14 Jesus, finding a young donkey, sat on it; as it is written,

15 "ªFEAR NOT, DAUGHTER OF ZION; BEHOLD, YOUR KING IS COMING, SEATED ON A DONKEY'S COLT." ªZech 9:9

16 ªThese things His disciples did not understand at the first; but when Jesus was glorified, then they remembered that these things were

written of Him, and that they had done these things to Him. ªMark 9:32; John 2:22

17 So ªthe people, who were with Him when He called Lazarus out of the tomb and raised him from the dead, continued to testify *about Him.* ªJohn 11:42

18 ªFor this reason also the people went and met Him, because they heard that He had performed this sign. ªLuke 19:37; John 12:12

19 So the Pharisees said to one another, "You see that you are not doing any good; look, the world has gone after Him."

Greeks Seek Jesus

20 Now there were some ªGreeks among those who were going up to worship at the feast; ªJohn 7:35

21 these then came to Philip, who was from ªBethsaida of Galilee, and *began to* ask him, saying, "Sir, we wish to see Jesus." ªMatt 11:21

22 Philip *came and *told ªAndrew; Andrew and Philip *came and *told Jesus. ªJohn 1:44

23 And Jesus *answered them, saying, "The hour has come for the Son of Man to ªbe glorified. ªJohn 7:39; 12:16

24 "Truly, truly, I say to you, ªunless a grain of wheat falls into the earth and dies, it remains alone; but if it dies, it bears much fruit. ªRom 14:9; 1 Cor 15:36

25 "ªHe who loves his life loses it, and he who hates his life in this world will keep it to life eternal. ªMatt 10:39; 16:25

26 "If anyone serves Me, he must follow Me; and ªwhere I am, there My servant will be also; if anyone serves Me, the Father will honor him. ªJohn 14:3; 17:24

Jesus Foretells His Death

27 "ªNow My soul has become troubled; and what shall I say, 'Father, save Me from this hour'? But for this purpose I came to this hour. ªMatt 26:38; Mark 14:34

28 "Father, glorify Your name." Then a ªvoice came out of heaven: "I have both glorified it, and will glorify it again." ªMatt 3:17; 17:5

29 So the crowd *of people* who stood by and heard it were saying that it had thundered; others were saying, "ªAn angel has spoken to Him." ªActs 23:9

30 Jesus answered and said, "ªThis voice has not come for My sake, but for your sakes. ªJohn 11:42

31 "Now judgment is upon this world; now ªthe ruler of this world will be cast out. ªJohn 14:30; 16:11

32 "And I, if I ªam lifted up from the earth, will ᵇdraw all men to Myself." ªJohn 3:14 ᵇJohn 6:44

33 But He was saying this ªto indicate the kind of death by which He was to die. ªJohn 18:32; 21:19

34 The crowd then answered Him, "We have heard out of the Law that [a]the Christ is to remain forever; and how can You say, 'The Son of Man must be lifted up'? Who is this Son of Man?" [a]Ps 110:4; Is 9:7

35 So Jesus said to them, "For a little while longer the Light is among you. Walk while you have the Light, so that darkness will not overtake you; he who [a]walks in the darkness does not know where he goes. [a]1 John 1:6; 2:11

36 "While you have the Light, believe in the Light, so that you may become [a]sons of Light."

These things Jesus spoke, and He went away and hid Himself from them. [a]Luke 16:8; John 8:12

37 But though He had performed so many signs before them, yet they were not believing in Him.

38 This was to fulfill the word of Isaiah the prophet which he spoke: "[a]LORD, WHO HAS BELIEVED OUR REPORT? AND TO WHOM HAS THE ARM OF THE LORD BEEN REVEALED?" [a]Is 53:1; Rom 10:16

39 For this reason they could not believe, for Isaiah said again,

40 "[a]HE HAS BLINDED THEIR EYES AND HE HARDENED THEIR HEART, SO THAT THEY WOULD NOT SEE WITH THEIR EYES AND PERCEIVE WITH THEIR HEART, AND BE CONVERTED AND I HEAL THEM." [a]Is 6:10; Matt 13:14f

41 These things Isaiah said because [a]he saw His glory, and he spoke of Him. [a]Is 6:1ff

42 Nevertheless many even of [a]the rulers believed in Him, but because of the Pharisees they were not confessing Him, for fear that they would be [b]put out of the synagogue; [a]Luke 23:13 [b]John 9:22

43 [a]for they loved the approval of men rather than the approval of God. [a]John 5:41, 44

44 And Jesus cried out and said, "[a]He who believes in Me, does not believe in Me but in Him who sent Me. [a]Matt 10:40; John 5:24

45 "[a]He who sees Me sees the One who sent Me. [a]John 14:9

46 "[a]I have come as Light into the world, so that everyone who believes in Me will not remain in darkness. [a]John 1:4; 3:19

47 "If anyone hears My sayings and does not keep them, I do not judge him; for [a]I did not come to judge the world, but to save the world. [a]John 3:17; 8:15f

48 "[a]He who rejects Me and does not receive My sayings, has one who judges him; [b]the word I spoke is what will judge him at the last day. [a]Luke 10:16 [b]Deut 18:18f

49 "For I did not speak on My own initiative, but the Father Himself who sent Me [a]has given Me a commandment as to what to say and what to speak. [a]John 14:31; 17:8

50 "I know that [a]His commandment is eternal life; therefore the things I speak, I speak [b]just as the Father has told Me." [a]John 6:68 [b]John 5:19; 8:28

The Lord's Supper

13 Now before the Feast of [a]the Passover, Jesus knowing that His hour had come that He would depart out of this world [b]to the Father, having loved His own who were in the world, He loved them to the end. [a]John 11:55 [b]John 13:3

2 During supper, [a]the devil having already put into the heart of Judas Iscariot, the son of Simon, to betray Him, [a]John 6:70; 13:27

3 Jesus, [a]knowing that the Father had given all things into His hands, and that [b]He had come forth from God and was going back to God, [a]John 3:35 [b]John 8:42

4 *got up from supper, and *laid aside His garments; and taking a towel, He [a]girded Himself. [a]Luke 12:37; 17:8

Jesus Washes the Disciples' Feet

5 Then He *poured water into the basin, and began to [a]wash the disciples' feet and to wipe them with the towel with which He was girded. [a]Gen 18:4; 19:2

6 So He *came to Simon Peter. He *said to Him, "Lord, do You wash my feet?"

7 Jesus answered and said to him, "What I do you do not realize now, but you will understand [a]hereafter." [a]John 13:12ff

8 Peter *said to Him, "Never shall You wash my feet!" Jesus answered him, "[a]If I do not wash you, you have no part with Me." [a]Ps 51:2, 7; Ezek 36:25

9 Simon Peter *said to Him, "Lord, then wash not only my feet, but also my hands and my head."

10 Jesus *said to him, "He who has bathed needs only to wash his feet, but is completely clean; and [a]you are clean, but not all of you." [a]John 15:3; Eph 5:26

11 For [a]He knew the one who was betraying Him; for this reason He said, "Not all of you are clean." [a]John 6:64; 13:2

12 So when He had washed their feet, and [a]taken His garments and reclined at the table again, He said to them, "Do you know what I have done to you? [a]John 13:4

13 "You call Me Teacher and [a]Lord; and you are right, for so I am. [a]John 11:2; 1 Cor 12:3

14 "If I then, [a]the Lord and the Teacher, washed your feet, you also ought to wash one another's feet. [a]John 11:2; 1 Cor 12:3

15 "For I gave you [a]an example that you also should do as I did to you. [a]1 Pet 5:3

16 "Truly, truly, I say to you, [a]a slave is not greater than his master, nor is one who is sent greater than the one who sent him. [a]Matt 10:24; Luke 6:40

17 "If you know these things, you are ᵃblessed if you do them. ᵃ*Matt 7:24ff; Luke 11:28*

18 "I do not speak of all of you. I know the ones I have chosen; but *it is* that the Scripture may be fulfilled, 'ᵃHE WHO EATS MY BREAD HAS LIFTED UP HIS HEEL AGAINST ME.' ᵃ*Ps 41:9; Matt 26:21ff*

19 "From now on ᵃI am telling you before *it* comes to pass, so that when it does occur, you may believe that ᵇI am *He.* ᵃ*John 14:29* ᵇ*John 8:24*

20 "Truly, truly, I say to you, ᵃhe who receives whomever I send receives Me; and he who receives Me receives Him who sent Me." ᵃ*Matt 10:40; Mark 9:37*

Jesus Predicts His Betrayal

21 When Jesus had said this, He ᵃbecame troubled in spirit, and testified and said, "Truly, truly, I say to you, that one of you will betray Me." ᵃ*John 11:33*

22 The disciples *began* looking at one another, ᵃat a loss *to know* of which one He was speaking. ᵃ*Matt 26:21ff; Mark 14:18ff*

23 There was reclining on Jesus' bosom one of His disciples, ᵃwhom Jesus loved. ᵃ*John 19:26; 20:2*

24 So Simon Peter *gestured to him, and *said to him, "Tell *us* who it is of whom He is speaking."

25 He, ᵃleaning back thus on Jesus' bosom, *said to Him, "Lord, who is it?" ᵃ*John 21:20*

26 Jesus then *answered, "That is the one for whom I shall dip the morsel and give it to him." So when He had dipped the morsel, He *took and *gave it to Judas, ᵃ*the son* of Simon Iscariot. ᵃ*John 6:71*

27 After the morsel, Satan then ᵃentered into him. Therefore Jesus *said to him, "What you do, do quickly." ᵃ*Luke 22:3; John 13:2*

28 Now no one of those reclining *at the table* knew for what purpose He had said this to him.

29 For some were supposing, because Judas ᵃhad the money box, that Jesus was saying to him, "Buy the things we have need of for the feast"; or else, that he should give something to the poor. ᵃ*John 12:6*

30 So after receiving the morsel he went out immediately; and ᵃit was night. ᵃ*Luke 22:53*

31 Therefore when he had gone out, Jesus *said, "Now is the Son of Man glorified, and ᵃGod is glorified in Him; ᵃ*John 14:13; 17:4*

32 if God is glorified in Him, ᵃGod will also glorify Him in Himself, and will glorify Him immediately. ᵃ*John 17:1*

33 "Little children, I am with you ᵃa little while longer. ᵇYou will seek Me; and as I said to the Jews, now I also say to you, 'Where I am going, you cannot come.' ᵃ*John 7:33* ᵇ*John 7:34*

34 "A new commandment I give to you, ᵃthat you love one another, even as I have loved

you, that you also love one another. ᵃ*Lev 19:18; Matt 5:44*

35 "ᵃBy this all men will know that you are My disciples, if you have love for one another." ᵃ*1 John 3:14; 4:20*

36 Simon Peter *said to Him, "Lord, where are You going?" Jesus answered, "ᵃWhere I go, you cannot follow Me now; but you will follow later." ᵃ*John 13:33; 14:2*

37 Peter *said to Him, "Lord, why can I not follow You right now? ᵃI will lay down my life for You." ᵃ*Matt 26:33-35; Mark 14:29-31*

38 Jesus ᵃanswered, "Will you lay down your life for Me? Truly, truly, I say to you, ᵃa rooster will not crow until you deny Me three times. ᵃ*Mark 14:30; John 18:27*

Jesus Comforts His Disciples

14 "ᵃDo not let your heart be troubled; believe in God, believe also in Me. ᵃ*John 14:27; 16:22, 24*

2 "In My Father's house are many dwelling places; if it were not so, I would have told you; for ᵃI go to prepare a place for you. ᵃ*John 13:33, 36*

3 "If I go and prepare a place for you, ᵃI will come again and receive you to Myself, that ᵇwhere I am, *there* you may be also. ᵃ*John 14:18, 28* ᵇ*John 12:26*

4 "And you know the way where I am going."

5 ᵃThomas *said to Him, "Lord, we do not know where You are going, how do we know the way?" ᵃ*John 11:16*

6 Jesus *said to him, "I am ᵃthe way, and the truth, and the life; no one comes to the Father but through Me. ᵃ*John 10:9; Rom 5:2*

Oneness with the Father

7 "ᵃIf you had known Me, you would have known My Father also; from now on you know Him, and have seen Him." ᵃ*John 8:19*

8 ᵃPhilip *said to Him, "Lord, show us the Father, and it is enough for us." ᵃ*John 1:43*

9 Jesus *said to him, "Have I been so long with you, and *yet* you have not come to know Me, Philip? ᵃHe who has seen Me has seen the Father; how *can* you say, 'Show us the Father'? ᵃ*John 1:14; 12:45*

10 "Do you not believe that ᵃI am in the Father, and the Father is in Me? ᵇThe words that I say to you I do not speak on My own initiative, but the Father abiding in Me does His works. ᵃ*John 10:38* ᵇ*John 5:19*

11 "Believe Me that ᵃI am in the Father and the Father is in Me; otherwise ᵇbelieve because of the works themselves. ᵃ*John 10:38* ᵇ*John 5:36*

12 "Truly, truly, I say to you, he who believes in Me, the works that I do, he will do also; and ᵃgreater *works* than these he will do; because I go to the Father. ᵃ*John 5:20*

13 "ªWhatever you ask in My name, that will I do, so that the Father may be glorified in the Son. ªMatt 7:7

14 "If you ask Me anything ªin My name, I will do it. ªJohn 15:16; 16:23f

15 "ªIf you love Me, you will keep My commandments. ªJohn 14:21, 23; 15:10

Role of the Spirit

16 "I will ask the Father, and He will give you another ªHelper, that He may be with you forever; ªJohn 7:39; 14:26

17 that is ªthe Spirit of truth, whom the world cannot receive, because it does not see Him or know Him, but you know Him because He abides with you and will be in you. ªJohn 15:26; 16:13

18 "I will not leave you as orphans; ªI will come to you. ªJohn 14:3, 28

19 "After a little while ªthe world will no longer see Me, but you will see Me; ᵇbecause I live, you will live also. ªJohn 16:16, 22 ᵇJohn 6:57

20 "In that day you will know that ªI am in My Father, and you in Me, and I in you. ªJohn 10:38; 14:11

21 "ªHe who has My commandments and keeps them is the one who loves Me; and he who loves Me will be loved by My Father, and I will love him and will disclose Myself to him." ªJohn 14:15, 23; 15:10

22 Judas (not Iscariot) *said to Him, "Lord, what then has happened ªthat You are going to disclose Yourself to us and not to the world?" ªActs 10:40, 41

23 Jesus answered and said to him, "If anyone loves Me, he will ªkeep My word; and My Father will love him, and We will come to him and make Our abode with him. ªJohn 8:51; 1 John 2:5

24 "He who does not love Me does not keep My words; and ªthe word which you hear is not Mine, but the Father's who sent Me. ªJohn 7:16; 14:10

25 "These things I have spoken to you while abiding with you.

26 "But the Helper, the Holy Spirit, whom the Father will send in My name, ªHe will teach you all things, and bring to your remembrance all that I said to you. ªJohn 16:13f; 1 John 2:20, 27

27 "ªPeace I leave with you; My peace I give to you; not as the world gives do I give to you. Do not let your heart be troubled, nor let it be fearful. ªJohn 16:33; 20:19

28 "You heard that I said to you, 'I go away, and I will come to you.' If you loved Me, you would have rejoiced because I go to the Father, for ªthe Father is greater than I. ªJohn 10:29; Phil 2:6

29 "Now ªI have told you before it happens, so

that when it happens, you may believe. ªJohn 13:19

30 "I will not speak much more with you, for ªthe ruler of the world is coming, and he has nothing in Me; ªJohn 12:31

31 but so that the world may know that I love the Father, I do exactly as ªthe Father commanded Me. Get up, let us go from here. ªJohn 10:18; 12:49

Jesus Is the Vine—Followers Are Branches

15 "ªI am the true vine, and My Father is the vinedresser. ªPs 80:8ff; Is 5:1ff

2 "Every branch in Me that does not bear fruit, He takes away; and every branch that bears fruit, He prunes it so that it may bear more fruit.

3 "ªYou are already clean because of the word which I have spoken to you. ªJohn 13:10; 17:17

4 "ªAbide in Me, and I in you. As the branch cannot bear fruit of itself unless it abides in the vine, so neither can you unless you abide in Me. ªJohn 6:56; 15:4-7

5 "I am the vine, you are the branches; he who abides in Me and I in him, he ªbears much fruit, for apart from Me you can do nothing. ªJohn 15:16

6 "If anyone does not abide in Me, he is ªthrown away as a branch and dries up; and they gather them, and cast them into the fire and they are burned. ªJohn 15:2

7 "If you abide in Me, and My words abide in you, ªask whatever you wish, and it will be done for you. ªMatt 7:7; John 15:16

8 "My ªFather is glorified by this, that you bear much fruit, and so ᵇprove to be My disciples. ªMatt 5:16 ᵇJohn 8:31

9 "Just as ªthe Father has loved Me, I have also loved you; abide in My love. ªJohn 3:35; 17:23, 24, 26

10 "If you keep My commandments, you will abide in My love; just as ªI have kept My Father's commandments and abide in His love. ªJohn 8:29

11 "These things I have spoken to you so that My joy may be in you, and that your ªjoy may be made full. ªJohn 3:29

Disciples' Relation to Each Other

12 "This is ªMy commandment, that you love one another, just as I have loved you. ªJohn 13:34; 15:17

13 "Greater love has no one than this, that one ªlay down his life for his friends. ªJohn 10:11

14 "You are My friends if ªyou do what I command you. ªMatt 12:50

15 "No longer do I call you slaves, for the slave does not know what his master is doing; but I have called you friends, for ªall things that

I have heard from My Father I have made known to you. ªJohn 8:26; 16:12

16 "ªYou did not choose Me but I chose you, and appointed you that you would go and bear fruit, and *that* your fruit would remain, so that whatever you ask of the Father in My name He may give to you. ªJohn 6:70; 13:18

17 "This ªI command you, that you love one another. ªJohn 15:12

Disciples' Relation to the World

18 "ªIf the world hates you, you know that it has hated Me before *it hated* you. ªJohn 7:7; 1 John 3:13

19 "If you were of the world, the world would love its own; but because you are not of the world, but I chose you out of the world, ªbecause of this the world hates you. ªMatt 10:22; 24:9

20 "Remember the word that I said to you, 'A slave is not greater than his master.' If they persecuted Me, ªthey will also persecute you; if they kept My word, they will keep yours also. ª1 Cor 4:12; 2 Cor 4:9

21 "But all these things they will do to you for My name's sake, ªbecause they do not know the One who sent Me. ªJohn 8:19, 55; 16:3

22 "ªIf I had not come and spoken to them, they would not have sin, but now they have no excuse for their sin. ªJohn 9:41; 15:24

23 "He who hates Me hates My Father also.

24 "ªIf I had not done among them the works which no one else did, they would not have sin; but now they have both seen and hated Me and My Father as well. ªJohn 9:41; 15:22

25 "But *they have done this* to fulfill the word that is written in their ªLaw, ᵇTHEY HATED ME WITHOUT A CAUSE.' ªJohn 10:34 ᵇPs 35:19

26 "When the ªHelper comes, whom I will send to you from the Father, *that is* the Spirit of truth who proceeds from the Father, He will testify about Me, ªJohn 14:16

27 and ªyou *will* testify also, because you have been with Me from the beginning. ªLuke 24:48; John 21:24

Jesus' Warning

16 "ªThese things I have spoken to you so that you may be kept from stumbling. ªJohn 15:18-27

2 "They will ªmake you outcasts from the synagogue, but an hour is coming for everyone who kills you to think that he is offering service to God. ªJohn 9:22

3 "These things they will do ªbecause they have not known the Father or Me. ªJohn 8:19, 55; 15:21

4 "But these things I have spoken to you, ªso that when their hour comes, you may remember that I told you of them. These things I did

not say to you at the beginning, because I was with you. ªJohn 13:19

The Holy Spirit Promised

5 "But now ªI am going to Him who sent Me; and none of you asks Me, 'Where are You going?' ªJohn 7:33; 16:10, 17, 28

6 "But because I have said these things to you, ªsorrow has filled your heart. ªJohn 14:1; 16:22

7 "But I tell you the truth, it is to your advantage that I go away; for if I do not go away, the ªHelper will not come to you; but if I go, ᵇI will send Him to you. ªJohn 14:16 ᵇJohn 14:26

8 "And He, when He comes, will convict the world concerning sin and righteousness and judgment;

9 concerning sin, ªbecause they do not believe in Me; ªJohn 15:22, 24

10 and concerning ªrighteousness, because I go to the Father and you no longer see Me; ªActs 3:14; 7:52

11 ªand concerning judgment, because the ruler of this world has been judged. ªJohn 12:31

12 "I have many more things to say to you, but you cannot bear *them* now.

13 "But when He, ªthe Spirit of truth, comes, He will ᵇguide you into all the truth; for He will not speak on His own initiative, but whatever He hears, He will speak; and He will disclose to you what is to come. ªJohn 14:17 ᵇJohn 14:26

14 "He will ªglorify Me, for He will take of Mine and will disclose *it* to you. ªJohn 7:39

15 "ªAll things that the Father has are Mine; therefore I said that He takes of Mine and will disclose *it* to you. ªJohn 17:10

Jesus' Death and Resurrection Foretold

16 "A little while, and ªyou will no longer see Me; and again a little while, and you will see Me." ªJohn 14:18-24; 16:16-24

17 *Some* of His disciples then said to one another, "What is this thing He is telling us, 'A little while, and you will not see Me; and again a little while, and you will see Me'; and, 'because ªI go to the Father'?" ªJohn 16:5

18 So they were saying, "What is this that He says, 'A little while'? We do not know what He is talking about."

19 ªJesus knew that they wished to question Him, and He said to them, "Are you deliberating together about this, that I said, 'A little while, and you will not see Me, and again a little while, and you will see Me'? ªMark 9:32; John 6:61

20 "Truly, truly, I say to you, that ªyou will weep and lament, but the world will rejoice; you will grieve, but ᵇyour grief will be turned into joy. ªLuke 23:27 ᵇJohn 20:20

21 "ªWhenever a woman is in labor she has

pain, because her hour has come; but when she gives birth to the child, she no longer remembers the anguish because of the joy that a child has been born into the world. ᵃ*Is 13:8; 21:3*

22 "Therefore ᵃyou too have grief now; but ᵇI will see you again, and your heart will rejoice, and no one *will* take your joy away from you. ᵃ*John 16:6* ᵇ*John 16:16*

Prayer Promises

23 "In that day ᵃyou will not question Me about anything. Truly, truly, I say to you, ᵇif you ask the Father for anything in My name, He will give it to you. ᵃ*John 16:19, 30* ᵇ*John 15:16*

24 "ᵃUntil now you have asked for nothing in My name; ask and you will receive, so that your joy may be made full. ᵃ*John 14:14*

25 "These things I have spoken to you in ᵃfigurative language; an hour is coming when I will no longer speak to you in figurative language, but will tell you plainly of the Father. ᵃ*Matt 13:34; John 10:6*

26 "In that day ᵃyou will ask in My name, and I do not say to you that I will request of the Father on your behalf; ᵃ*John 16:19, 30*

27 for ᵃthe Father Himself loves you, because you have loved Me and have believed that ᵇI came forth from the Father. ᵃ*John 14:21, 23* ᵇ*John 8:42*

28 "I came forth from the Father and have come into the world; I am leaving the world again and ᵃgoing to the Father." ᵃ*John 13:1, 3; 16:5, 10, 17*

29 His disciples ✶said, "Lo, now You are speaking plainly and are not using ᵃa figure of speech. ᵃ*Matt 13:34; John 10:6*

30 "Now we know that You know all things, and have no need for anyone to question You; by this we ᵃbelieve that You came from God." ᵃ*John 2:11; 16:27*

31 Jesus answered them, "Do you now believe?

32 "Behold, an hour is coming, and has *already* come, for ᵃyou to be scattered, each to his own *home*, and to leave Me alone; and *yet* ᵇI am not alone, because the Father is with Me. ᵃ*Zech 13:7* ᵇ*John 8:29*

33 "These things I have spoken to you, so that ᵃin Me you may have peace. In the world you have tribulation, but take courage; ᵇI have overcome the world." ᵃ*John 14:27* ᵇ*Rom 8:37*

The High Priestly Prayer

17 Jesus spoke these things; and ᵃlifting up His eyes to heaven, He said, "Father, the hour has come; ᵇglorify Your Son, that the Son may glorify You, ᵃ*John 11:41* ᵇ*John 13:31f*

2 even as ᵃYou gave Him authority over all flesh, that ᵇto all whom You have given Him, He may give eternal life. ᵃ*John 3:35* ᵇ*John 10:28*

3 "This is eternal life, that they may know You, ᵃthe only true God, and Jesus Christ whom You have sent. ᵃ*John 5:44*

4 "ᵃI glorified You on the earth, ᵇhaving accomplished the work which You have given Me to do. ᵃ*John 13:31* ᵇ*John 4:34*

5 "Now, Father, glorify Me together with Yourself, with the glory which I had ᵃwith You before the world was. ᵃ*John 1:1; 8:58*

6 "I have manifested Your name to the men whom ᵃYou gave Me out of the world; they were Yours and You gave them to Me, and they have kept Your word. ᵃ*John 6:37, 39; 17:2, 9, 24*

7 "Now they have come to know that everything You have given Me is from You;

8 for ᵃthe words which You gave Me I have given to them; and they received *them* and truly understood that ᵇI came forth from You, and they believed that ᶜYou sent Me. ᵃ*John 12:49* ᵇ*John 8:42*

9 "ᵃI ask on their behalf; ᵇI do not ask on behalf of the world, but of those whom You have given Me; for they are Yours; ᵃ*Luke 22:32* ᵇ*John 17:20f*

10 and ᵃall things that are Mine are Yours, and Yours are Mine; and I have been glorified in them. ᵃ*John 16:15*

11 "I am no longer in the world; and *yet* they themselves are in the world, and I come to You. Holy Father, keep them in Your name, *the name* ᵃwhich You have given Me, that ᵇthey may be one even as We *are.* ᵃ*Phil 2:9* ᵇ*John 17:21f*

12 "While I was with them, I was keeping them in Your name which You have given Me; and I guarded them and not one of them perished but ᵃthe son of perdition, so that the ᵇScripture would be fulfilled. ᵃ*John 6:70* ᵇ*John 13:18*

The Disciples in the World

13 "But now ᵃI come to You; and ᵇthese things I speak in the world so that they may have My joy made full in themselves. ᵃ*John 7:33* ᵇ*John 15:11*

14 "I have given them Your word; and ᵃthe world has hated them, because they are not of the world, even as I am not of the world. ᵃ*John 15:19*

15 "I do not ask You to take them out of the world, but to keep them from ᵃthe evil *one.* ᵃ*Matt 5:37*

16 "ᵃThey are not of the world, even as I am not of the world. ᵃ*John 17:14*

17 "ᵃSanctify them in the truth; Your word is truth. ᵃ*John 15:3*

18 "As You sent Me into the world, ᵃI also have sent them into the world. ᵃ*Matt 10:5; John 4:38*

19 "For their sakes I sanctify Myself, that they

themselves also may be ªsanctified in truth.
ªJohn 15:3

20 "I do not ask on behalf of these alone, but for those also who believe in Me through their word;

21 that they may all be one; ªeven as You, Father, *are* in Me and I in You, that they also may be in Us, so that the world may believe that You sent Me. ªJohn 10:38; 17:11, 23

Their Future Glory

22 "The ªglory which You have given Me I have given to them, that they may be one, just as We are one; ªJohn 1:14; 17:24

23 ªI in them and You in Me, that they may be perfected in unity, so that the world may know that You sent Me, and ᵇloved them, even as You have loved Me. ªJohn 10:38 ᵇJohn 16:27

24 "Father, I desire that they also, whom You have given Me, be with Me where I am, so that they may see My glory which You have given Me, for You loved Me before ªthe foundation of the world. ªMatt 25:34; John 17:5

25 "O ªrighteous Father, although the world has not known You, yet I have known You; and these have known that You sent Me; ªJohn 17:11; 1 John 1:9

26 and ªI have made Your name known to them, and will make it known, so that ᵇthe love with which You loved Me may be in them, and I in them." ªJohn 17:6 ᵇJohn 15:9

Judas Betrays Jesus

18 When Jesus had spoken these words, He went forth with His disciples over the ravine of the Kidron, where there was ªa garden, in which He entered with His disciples. ªMatt 26:36; Mark 14:32

2 Now Judas also, who was betraying Him, knew the place, for Jesus had ªoften met there with His disciples. ªLuke 21:37; 22:39

3 ªJudas then, having received the *Roman* cohort and officers from the chief priests and the Pharisees, *came there with lanterns and torches and weapons. ªMatt 26:47-56; Mark 14:43-50

4 So Jesus, ªknowing all the things that were coming upon Him, went forth and *said to them, "Whom do you seek?" ªJohn 6:64; 13:1, 11

5 They answered Him, "Jesus the Nazarene." He *said to them, "I am *He.*" And Judas also, who was betraying Him, was standing with them.

6 So when He said to them, "I am *He,*" they drew back and fell to the ground.

7 Therefore He again asked them, "ªWhom do you seek?" And they said, "Jesus the Nazarene." ªJohn 18:4

8 Jesus answered, "I told you that I am *He;* so if you seek Me, let these go their way,"

9 to fulfill the word which He spoke, "ªOf those whom You have given Me I lost not one." ªJohn 17:12

10 Simon Peter then, ªhaving a sword, drew it and struck the high priest's slave, and cut off his right ear; and the slave's name was Malchus. ªMatt 26:51; Mark 14:47

11 So Jesus said to Peter, "Put the sword into the sheath; ªthe cup which the Father has given Me, shall I not drink it?" ªMatt 20:22; 26:39

Jesus before the Priests

12 ªSo the *Roman* cohort and the commander and the officers of the Jews, arrested Jesus and bound Him, ªMatt 26:57ff

13 and led Him to Annas first; for he was father-in-law of ªCaiaphas, who was high priest that year. ªMatt 26:3; John 11:49, 51

14 Now Caiaphas was the one who had advised the Jews that ªit was expedient for one man to die on behalf of the people. ªJohn 11:50

15 ªSimon Peter was following Jesus, and *so was* another disciple. Now that disciple was known to the high priest, and entered with Jesus into the court of the high priest, ªMatt 26:58; Mark 14:54

16 ªbut Peter was standing at the door outside. So the other disciple, who was known to the high priest, went out and spoke to the doorkeeper, and brought Peter in. ªMatt 26:69f; Mark 14:66-68

17 Then the slave-girl who kept the door *said to Peter, "ªYou are not also *one* of this man's disciples, are you?" He *said, "I am not." ªJohn 18:25

18 Now the slaves and the officers were standing *there,* having made a charcoal fire, for it was cold and they were ªwarming themselves; and Peter was also with them, standing and warming himself. ªMark 14:54, 67

19 ªThe high priest then questioned Jesus about His disciples, and about His teaching. ªMatt 26:59-68; Mark 14:55-65

20 Jesus answered him, "I ªhave spoken openly to the world; I always taught in synagogues and in the temple, where all the Jews come together; and I spoke nothing in secret. ªJohn 7:26; 8:26

21 "Why do you question Me? Question those who have heard what I spoke to them; they know what I said."

22 When He had said this, one of the ªofficers standing nearby ᵇstruck Jesus, saying, "Is that the way You answer the high priest?" ªJohn 18:3 ᵇJohn 19:3

23 ªJesus answered him, "If I have spoken wrongly, testify of the wrong; but if rightly, why do you strike Me?" ªMatt 5:39; Acts 23:2-5

24 ªSo Annas sent Him bound to Caiaphas the high priest. ªJohn 18:13

Peter's Denial of Jesus

25 ᵃNow Simon Peter was standing and warming himself. So they said to him, "You are not also *one* of His disciples, are you?" He denied *it*, and said, "I am not." ᵃ*Matt 26:71-75; Mark 14:69-72*

26 One of the slaves of the high priest, being a relative of the one ᵃwhose ear Peter cut off, *said, "Did I not see you in ᵇthe garden with Him?" ᵃ*John 18:10* ᵇ*John 18:1*

27 Peter then denied *it* again, and immediately ᵃa rooster crowed. ᵃ*John 13:38*

Jesus before Pilate

28 ᵃThen they *led Jesus from Caiaphas into the Praetorium, and it was early; and they themselves did not enter into the Praetorium so that they would not be defiled, but might eat the Passover. ᵃ*Matt 27:2; Mark 15:1*

29 ᵃTherefore Pilate went out to them and *said, "What accusation do you bring against this Man?" ᵃ*Matt 27:11-14; Mark 15:2-5*

30 They answered and said to him, "If this Man were not an evildoer, we would not have delivered Him to you."

31 So Pilate said to them, "Take Him yourselves, and judge Him according to your law." The Jews said to him, "We are not permitted to put anyone to death,"

32 to fulfill ᵃthe word of Jesus which He spoke, signifying by what kind of death He was about to die. ᵃ*Matt 20:19; 26:2*

33 Therefore Pilate entered again into the Praetorium, and summoned Jesus and said to Him, "ᵃAre You the King of the Jews?" ᵃ*Luke 23:3; John 19:12*

34 Jesus answered, "Are you saying this on your own initiative, or did others tell you about Me?"

35 Pilate answered, "I am not a Jew, am I? Your own nation and the chief priests delivered You to me; what have You done?"

36 Jesus answered, "ᵃMy kingdom is not of this world. If My kingdom were of this world, then My servants would be fighting so that I would not be handed over to the Jews; but as it is, My kingdom is not of this realm." ᵃ*Matt 26:53; Luke 17:21*

37 Therefore Pilate said to Him, "So You are a king?" Jesus answered, "ᵃYou say *correctly* that I am a king. For this I have been born, and for this I have come into the world, to testify to the truth. Everyone who is of the truth hears My voice." ᵃ*Matt 27:11; Mark 15:2*

38 Pilate *said to Him, "What is truth?"

And when he had said this, he went out again to the Jews and *said to them, "ᵃI find no guilt in Him. ᵃ*Luke 23:4; John 19:4, 6*

39 "ᵃBut you have a custom that I release someone for you at the Passover; do you wish

then that I release for you the King of the Jews?" ᵃ*Matt 27:15-26; Mark 15:6-15*

40 So they cried out again, saying, "ᵃNot this Man, but Barabbas." Now Barabbas was a robber. ᵃ*Acts 3:14*

The Crown of Thorns

19 Pilate then took Jesus and ᵃscourged Him. ᵃ*Matt 27:26*

2 ᵃAnd the soldiers twisted together a crown of thorns and put it on His head, and put a purple robe on Him; ᵃ*Mark 15:16-19*

3 and they *began* to come up to Him and say, "Hail, King of the Jews!" and to ᵃgive Him slaps *in the face.* ᵃ*Is 50:6; John 18:22*

4 Pilate came out again and *said to them, "Behold, I am bringing Him out to you so that you may know that ᵃI find no guilt in Him." ᵃ*Luke 23:4; John 18:38*

5 Jesus then came out, ᵃwearing the crown of thorns and the purple robe. *Pilate* *said to them, "Behold, the Man!" ᵃ*John 19:2*

6 So when the chief priests and the officers saw Him, they cried out saying, "Crucify, crucify!" Pilate *said to them, "Take Him yourselves and crucify Him, for ᵃI find no guilt in Him." ᵃ*Luke 23:4; John 18:38*

7 The Jews answered him, "ᵃWe have a law, and by that law He ought to die because He made Himself out *to be* the Son of God." ᵃ*Lev 24:16; Matt 26:63-66*

8 Therefore when Pilate heard this statement, he was *even* more afraid;

9 and he entered into the Praetorium again and *said to Jesus, "Where are You from?" But ᵃJesus gave him no answer. ᵃ*Matt 26:63; 27:12, 14*

10 So Pilate *said to Him, "You do not speak to me? Do You not know that I have authority to release You, and I have authority to crucify You?"

11 Jesus answered, "ᵃYou would have no authority over Me, unless it had been given you from above; for this reason he who delivered Me to you has *the* greater sin." ᵃ*Rom 13:1*

12 As a result of this Pilate made efforts to release Him, but the Jews cried out saying, "If you release this Man, you are no friend of Caesar; everyone who makes himself out *to be* a king opposes Caesar." ᵃ*Luke 23:2; John 18:33ff*

13 Therefore when Pilate heard these words, he brought Jesus out, and ᵃsat down on the judgment seat at a place called The Pavement, but in Hebrew, Gabbatha. ᵃ*Matt 27:19*

14 Now it was ᵃthe day of preparation for the Passover; it was about the sixth hour. And he *said to the Jews, "Behold, your King!" ᵃ*Matt 27:62; John 19:31, 42*

15 So they cried out, "ᵃAway with *Him,* away with *Him,* crucify Him!" Pilate *said to them,

"Shall I crucify your King?" The chief priests answered, "We have no king but Caesar." [a]Luke 23:18

The Crucifixion

16 So he then [a]handed Him over to them to be crucified. [a]Matt 27:26; Mark 15:15

17 [a]They took Jesus, therefore, and He went out, bearing His own cross, to the place called the Place of a Skull, which is called in Hebrew, Golgotha. [a]Matt 27:33-44; Mark 15:22-32

18 There they crucified Him, and with Him [a]two other men, one on either side, and Jesus in between. [a]Luke 23:32

19 Pilate also wrote an inscription and put it on the cross. It was written, "[a]JESUS THE NAZARENE, THE KING OF THE JEWS." [a]Matt 27:37; Mark 15:26

20 Therefore many of the Jews read this inscription, for the place where Jesus was crucified was near the city; and it was written [a]in Hebrew, Latin and in Greek. [a]John 19:13

21 So the chief priests of the Jews were saying to Pilate, "Do not write, '[a]The King of the Jews'; but that He said, 'I am [a]King of the Jews.'" [a]John 19:14, 19

22 Pilate answered, "[a]What I have written I have written." [a]Gen 43:14; Esth 4:16

23 Then [a]the soldiers, when they had crucified Jesus, took His outer garments and made four parts, a part to every soldier and *also* the tunic; now the tunic was seamless, woven in one piece. [a]Matt 27:35; Mark 15:24

24 So they said to one another, "Let us not tear it, but cast lots for it, *to decide* whose it shall be"; *this was* to fulfill the Scripture: "[a]THEY [a]DIVIDED MY OUTER GARMENTS AMONG THEM, AND FOR MY CLOTHING THEY CAST LOTS." [a]Ps 22:18

25 So the soldiers did these things. [a]Matt 27:55f; Mark 15:40f

But standing by the cross of Jesus were His mother, and His mother's sister, Mary the *wife* of Clopas, and Mary Magdalene.

26 When Jesus then saw His mother, and [a]the disciple whom He loved standing nearby, He *said to His mother, "Woman, behold, your son!" [a]John 13:23

27 Then He *said to the disciple, "Behold, your mother!" From that hour the disciple took her into [a]his own *household*. [a]Luke 18:28; John 1:11

28 After this, Jesus, knowing that all things had already been accomplished, to fulfill the Scripture, *said, "[a]I am thirsty." [a]Ps 69:21

29 A jar full of sour wine was standing there; so [a]they put a sponge full of the sour wine upon *a branch of* hyssop and brought it up to His mouth. [a]Matt 27:48, 50; Mark 15:36f

30 Therefore when Jesus had received the sour wine, He said, "It is finished!" And He

bowed His head and [a]gave up His spirit. [a]Matt 27:50; Mark 15:37

Care of the Body of Jesus

31 Then the Jews, because it was the day of preparation, so that [a]the bodies would not remain on the cross on the Sabbath (for that Sabbath was a high day), asked Pilate that their legs might be broken, and *that* they might be taken away. [a]Deut 21:23; Josh 8:29

32 So the soldiers came, and broke the legs of the first man and of the other who was [a]crucified with Him; [a]John 19:18

33 but coming to Jesus, when they saw that He was already dead, they did not break His legs.

34 But one of the soldiers pierced His side with a spear, and immediately [a]blood and water came out. [a]1 John 5:6, 8

35 And he who has seen has [a]testified, and his testimony is true; and he knows that he is telling the truth, so that you also may believe. [a]John 15:27; 21:24

36 For these things came to pass to fulfill the Scripture, "[a]NOT A BONE OF HIM SHALL BE BROKEN." [a]Ex 12:46; Num 9:12

37 And again another Scripture says, "[a]THEY SHALL LOOK ON HIM WHOM THEY PIERCED." [a]Zech 12:10; Rev 1:7

38 [a]After these things Joseph of Arimathea, being a disciple of Jesus, but a secret *one* for fear of the Jews, asked Pilate that he might take away the body of Jesus; and Pilate granted permission. So he came and took away His body. [a]Matt 27:57-61; Mark 15:42-47

39 [a]Nicodemus, who had first come to Him by night, also came, bringing a mixture of myrrh and aloes, about a hundred pounds *weight*. [a]John 3:1

40 So they took the body of Jesus and [a]bound it in [b]linen wrappings with the spices, as is the burial custom of the Jews. [a]John 11:44 [b]Luke 24:12

41 Now in the place where He was crucified there was a garden, and in the garden a [a]new tomb [b]in which no one had yet been laid. [a]Matt 27:60 [b]Luke 23:53

42 Therefore because of the Jewish day of [a]preparation, since the tomb was nearby, they laid Jesus there. [a]John 19:14, 31

The Empty Tomb

20 [a]Now on the first *day* of the week Mary Magdalene *came early to the tomb, while it *was still dark, and *saw the stone *already* taken away from the tomb. [a]Matt 28:1-8; Mark 16:1-8

2 So she *ran and *came to Simon Peter and to the other [a]disciple whom Jesus loved, and *said to them, "[b]They have taken away the Lord out of the tomb, and we do not know

where they have laid Him." [a]*John 13:23*
[b]*John 20:13*

3 [a]So Peter and the other disciple went forth, and they were going to the tomb. [a]*Luke 24:12; John 20:3-10*

4 The two were running together; and the other disciple ran ahead faster than Peter and came to the tomb first;

5 and stooping and looking in, he *saw the [a]linen wrappings lying *there;* but he did not go in. [a]*John 19:40*

6 And so Simon Peter also *came, following him, and entered the tomb; and he *saw the linen wrappings lying *there,*

7 and [a]the face-cloth which had been on His head, not lying with the linen wrappings, but rolled up in a place by itself. [a]*John 11:44*

8 So the other disciple who [a]had first come to the tomb then also entered, and he saw and believed. [a]*John 20:4*

9 For as yet [a]they did not understand the Scripture, that He must rise again from the dead. [a]*Matt 22:29; John 2:22*

10 So the disciples went away again [a]to their own homes. [a]*Luke 24:12*

11 [a]But Mary was standing outside the tomb weeping; and so, as she wept, she stooped and looked into the tomb; [a]*Mark 16:5*

12 and she *saw [a]two angels in white sitting, one at the head and one at the feet, where the body of Jesus had been lying. [a]*Matt 28:2f; Mark 16:5*

13 And they *said to her, "[a]Woman, why are you weeping?" She *said to them, "Because [b]they have taken away my Lord, and I do not know where they have laid Him." [a]*John 20:15* [b]*John 20:2*

14 When she had said this, she turned around and *[a]saw Jesus standing *there,* and [b]did not know that it was Jesus. [a]*Matt 28:9* [b]*John 21:4*

15 Jesus *said to her, "[a]Woman, why are you weeping? Whom are you seeking?" Supposing Him to be the gardener, she *said to Him, "Sir, if you have carried Him away, tell me where you have laid Him, and I will take Him away." [a]*John 20:13*

16 Jesus *said to her, "Mary!" She turned and *said to Him in Hebrew, "[a]Rabboni!" (which means, Teacher). [a]*Mark 10:51*

17 Jesus *said to her, "Stop clinging to Me, for I have not yet ascended to the Father; but go to [a]My brethren and say to them, 'I [b]ascend to My Father and your Father, and My God and your God.' " [a]*Matt 28:10* [b]*John 7:33*

18 Mary Magdalene *came, [a]announcing to the disciples, "I have seen the Lord," and *that* He had said these things to her. [a]*Luke 24:10, 23*

Jesus among His Disciples

19 So when it was evening on that day, the first *day* of the week, and when the doors were shut where the disciples were, for fear of the Jews, Jesus came and stood in their midst and *said to them, "[a]Peace *be* with you." [a]*Luke 24:36; John 14:27*

20 And when He had said this, [a]He showed them both His hands and His side. The disciples then rejoiced when they saw the Lord. [a]*Luke 24:39, 40; John 19:34*

21 So Jesus said to them again, "Peace *be* with you; [a]as the Father has sent Me, I also send you." [a]*John 17:18*

22 And when He had said this, He breathed on them and *said to them, "Receive the Holy Spirit.

23 "[a]If you forgive the sins of any, *their sins* have been forgiven them; if you retain the *sins* of any, they have been retained." [a]*Matt 16:19; 18:18*

24 But [a]Thomas, one of the twelve, called [a]Didymus, was not with them when Jesus came. [a]*John 11:16*

25 So the other disciples were saying to him, "We have seen the Lord!" But he said to them, "Unless I see in [a]His hands the imprint of the nails, and put my finger into the place of the nails, and put my hand into His side, I will not believe." [a]*John 20:20*

26 After eight days His disciples were again inside, and Thomas with them. Jesus *came, the doors having been shut, and stood in their midst and said, "[a]Peace *be* with you." [a]*Luke 24:36; John 14:27*

27 Then He *said to Thomas, "[a]Reach here with your finger, and see My hands; and reach here your hand and put it into My side; and do not be unbelieving, but believing." [a]*Luke 24:40; John 20:25*

28 Thomas answered and said to Him, "My Lord and my God!"

29 Jesus *said to him, "Because you have seen Me, have you believed? [a]Blessed *are* they who did not see, and *yet* believed." [a]*1 Pet 1:8*

Why This Gospel Was Written

30 [a]Therefore many other signs Jesus also performed in the presence of the disciples, which are not written in this book; [a]*John 21:25*

31 but these have been written so that you may believe that Jesus is the Christ, the Son of God; and that [a]believing you may have life in His name. [a]*John 3:15*

Jesus Appears at the Sea of Galilee

21 After these things Jesus manifested Himself again to the disciples at the [a]Sea of Tiberias, and He manifested *Himself* in this way. [a]*John 6:1*

2 Simon Peter, and Thomas called Didymus, and Nathanael of Cana in Galilee, and [a]the

sons of Zebedee, and two others of His disciples were together. [a]*Matt 4:21; Mark 1:19*

3 Simon Peter *said to them, "I am going fishing." They *said to him, "We will also come with you." They went out and got into the boat; and [a]that night they caught nothing. [a]*Luke 5:5*

4 But when the day was now breaking, Jesus stood on the beach; yet the disciples did not [a]know that it was Jesus. [a]*Luke 24:16; John 20:14*

5 So Jesus *said to them, "Children, [a]you do not have any fish, do you?" They answered Him, "No." [a]*Luke 24:41*

6 And He said to them, "[a]Cast the net on the right-hand side of the boat and you will find *a catch.*" So they cast, and then they were not able to haul it in because of the great number of fish. [a]*Luke 5:4ff*

7 [a]Therefore that disciple whom Jesus loved *said to Peter, "It is the Lord." So when Simon Peter heard that it was the Lord, he put his outer garment on (for he was stripped *for work),* and threw himself into the sea. [a]*John 13:23; 21:20*

8 But the other disciples came in the little boat, for they were not far from the land, but about one hundred yards away, dragging the net *full* of fish.

9 So when they got out on the land, they *saw a charcoal [a]fire *already* laid and fish placed on it, and bread. [a]*John 18:18*

10 Jesus *said to them, "Bring some of the [a]fish which you have now caught." [a]*John 6:9, 11; 21:9, 13*

11 Simon Peter went up and drew the net to land, full of large fish, a hundred and fifty-three; and although there were so many, the net was not torn.

Jesus Provides

12 Jesus *said to them, "Come *and* have [a]breakfast." None of the disciples ventured to question Him, "Who are You?" knowing that it was the Lord. [a]*John 21:15*

13 Jesus *came and *took [a]the bread and *gave *it* to them, and the fish likewise. [a]*John 21:9*

14 This is now the [a]third time that Jesus was manifested to the disciples, after He was raised from the dead. [a]*John 20:19, 26*

The Love Motivation

15 So when they had finished breakfast, Jesus *said to Simon Peter, "Simon, *son* of John, do you [a]love Me more than these?" He *said to Him, "Yes, Lord; You know that I love You." He *said to him, "Tend My lambs." [a]*Matt 26:33; Mark 14:29*

16 He *said to him again a second time, "Simon, *son* of John, do you love Me?" He *said to Him, "Yes, Lord; You know that I love You." He *said to him, "[a]Shepherd My sheep." [a]*Matt 2:6; Acts 20:28*

17 He *said to him the third time, "Simon, *son* of John, do you love Me?" Peter was grieved because He said to him the third time, "Do you love Me?" And he said to Him, "Lord, [a]You know all things; You know that I love You." Jesus *said to him, "Tend My sheep. [a]*John 16:30*

Our Times Are in His Hand

18 "Truly, truly, I say to you, when you were younger, you used to gird yourself and walk wherever you wished; but when you grow old, you will stretch out your hands and someone else will gird you, and bring you where you do not wish to *go.*"

19 Now this He said, signifying by [a]what kind of death he would glorify God. And when He had spoken this, He *said to him, "Follow Me!" [a]*2 Pet 1:14*

20 Peter, turning around, *saw the [a]disciple whom Jesus loved following *them;* the one who also had [b]leaned back on His bosom at the supper and said, "Lord, who is the one who betrays You?" [a]*John 21:7* [b]*John 13:25*

21 So Peter seeing him *said to Jesus, "Lord, and what about this man?"

22 Jesus *said to him, "If I want him to remain until I come, what *is that* to you? You [a]follow Me!" [a]*Matt 8:22; 16:24*

23 Therefore this saying went out among the brethren that that disciple would not die; yet Jesus did not say to him that he would not die, but *only,* "If I want him to remain [a]until I come, what *is that* to you?" [a]*Matt 16:27f; 1 Cor 4:5*

24 This is the disciple who [a]is testifying to these things and wrote these things, and we know that his testimony is true. [a]*John 15:27*

25 And there are also [a]many other things which Jesus did, which if they *were written in detail, I suppose that even the world itself *would not contain the books that *would be written. [a]*John 20:30*

THE ACTS
of the Apostles

Introduction

1 The first account I composed, ᵃTheophilus, about all that Jesus ᵇbegan to do and teach,
ᵃLuke 1:3 ᵇLuke 3:23

2 until the day when He was taken up *to heaven,* after He ᵃhad by the Holy Spirit given orders to the apostles whom He had chosen.
ᵃMatt 28:19f; John 20:21f

3 To these ᵃHe also presented Himself alive after His suffering, by many convincing proofs, appearing to them over *a period of* forty days and speaking of the things concerning the kingdom of God. ᵃMatt 28:17; Luke 24:34, 36

4 Gathering them together, He commanded them ᵃnot to leave Jerusalem, but to wait for ᵇwhat the Father had promised, "Which," *He said,* "you heard of from Me; ᵃLuke 24:49 ᵇJohn 14:16, 26

5 for John baptized with water, but you will be baptized with the Holy Spirit ᵃnot many days from now." ᵃActs 2:1-4

6 So when they had come together, they were asking Him, saying, "Lord, ᵃis it at this time You are restoring the kingdom to Israel?"
ᵃMatt 17:11; Mark 9:12

7 He said to them, "It is not for you to know times or epochs which ᵃthe Father has fixed by His own authority; ᵃMatt 24:36; Mark 13:32

8 but you will receive power ᵃwhen the Holy Spirit has come upon you; and you shall be ᵇMy witnesses both in Jerusalem, and in all Judea and Samaria, and even to the remotest part of the earth." ᵃActs 2:1-4 ᵇLuke 24:48

The Ascension

9 And after He had said these things, ᵃHe was lifted up while they were looking on, and a cloud received Him out of their sight.
ᵃLuke 24:50, 51; Acts 1:2

10 And as they were gazing intently into the sky while He was going, behold, ᵃtwo men in white clothing stood beside them. ᵃLuke 24:4; John 20:12

11 They also said, "Men of Galilee, why do you stand looking into the sky? This Jesus, who has been taken up from you into heaven, will ᵃcome in just the same way as you have watched Him go into heaven." ᵃMatt 16:27f; Acts 3:21

The Upper Room

12 Then they ᵃreturned to Jerusalem from the mount called Olivet, which is near Jerusalem, a Sabbath day's journey away. ᵃLuke 24:52

13 When they had entered *the city,* they went up to ᵃthe upper room where they were staying; ᵇthat is, Peter and John and James and Andrew,

Philip and Thomas, Bartholomew and Matthew, James *the son* of Alphaeus, and Simon the Zealot, and Judas *the son* of James.
ᵃMark 14:15 ᵇMatt 10:2-4

14 These all with one mind ᵃwere continually devoting themselves to prayer, along with *the* women, and Mary the mother of Jesus, and with His brothers. ᵃActs 2:42; 6:4

15 At this time Peter stood up in the midst of ᵃthe brethren (a gathering of about one hundred and twenty persons was there together), and said, ᵃJohn 21:23; Acts 6:3

16 "Brethren, the Scripture had to be fulfilled, which the Holy Spirit foretold by the mouth of David concerning Judas, ᵃwho became a guide to those who arrested Jesus. ᵃMatt 26:47; Mark 14:43

17 "For he was counted among us and received his share in ᵃthis ministry." ᵃActs 1:25; 20:24

18 (Now this man ᵃacquired a field with the price of his wickedness, and falling headlong, he burst open in the middle and all his intestines gushed out. ᵃMatt 27:3-10

19 And it became known to all who were living in Jerusalem; so that in ᵃtheir own language that field was called Hakeldama, that is, Field of Blood.) ᵃMatt 27:8; Acts 21:40

20 "For it is written in the book of Psalms,

'ᵃLET HIS HOMESTEAD BE MADE DESOLATE,
AND LET NO ONE DWELL IN IT';

and,

'ᵇLET ANOTHER MAN TAKE HIS OFFICE.'
ᵃPs 69:25 ᵇPs 109:8

21 "Therefore it is necessary that of the men who have accompanied us all the time that ᵃthe Lord Jesus went in and out among us—
ᵃLuke 24:3

22 ᵃbeginning with the baptism of John until the day that He was taken up from us—one of these *must* become a witness with us of His resurrection." ᵃMatt 3:16; Mark 1:1-4, 9

23 So they put forward two men, Joseph called Barsabbas (who was also called Justus), and ᵃMatthias. ᵃActs 1:26

24 And they prayed and said, "You, Lord, ᵃwho know the hearts of all men, show which one of these two You have chosen ᵃ1 Sam 16:7; Jer 17:10

25 to occupy this ministry and ᵃapostleship from which Judas turned aside to go to his own place." ᵃRom 1:5; 1 Cor 9:2

26 And they ᵃdrew lots for them, and the lot fell to Matthias; and he was added to the eleven apostles. ᵃLev 16:8; Josh 14:2

The Day of Pentecost

2 When ᵃthe day of Pentecost had come, they were all together in one place. ᵃLev 23:15f; Acts 20:16

2 And suddenly there came from heaven a noise like a violent rushing wind, and it filled ᵃthe whole house where they were sitting. ᵃActs 4:31

3 And there appeared to them tongues as of fire distributing themselves, and they rested on each one of them.

4 And they were all ᵃfilled with the Holy Spirit and began to ᵇspeak with other tongues, as the Spirit was giving them utterance. ᵃActs 4:8, 31; ᵇ1 Cor 12:10f

5 Now there were Jews living in Jerusalem, ᵃdevout men from every nation under heaven. ᵃLuke 2:25; Acts 8:2

6 And when ᵃthis sound occurred, the crowd came together, and were bewildered because each one of them was hearing them speak in his own language. ᵃActs 2:2

7 They were amazed and astonished, saying, "Why, are not all these who are speaking ᵃGalileans? ᵃMatt 26:73; Acts 1:11

8 "And how is it that we each hear *them* in our own language to which we were born?

9 "Parthians and Medes and Elamites, and residents of Mesopotamia, Judea and Cappadocia, ᵃPontus and ᵇAsia, ᵃActs 18:2 ᵇActs 6:9

10 Phrygia and Pamphylia, Egypt and the districts of Libya around Cyrene, and visitors from Rome, both Jews and ᵃproselytes, ᵃMatt 23:15

11 Cretans and Arabs—we hear them in our *own* tongues speaking of the mighty deeds of God."

12 And ᵃthey all continued in amazement and great perplexity, saying to one another, "What does this mean?" ᵃActs 2:7

13 But others were mocking and saying, "ᵃThey are full of sweet wine." ᵃ1 Cor 14:23

Peter's Sermon

14 But Peter, taking his stand with ᵃthe eleven, raised his voice and declared to them: "Men of Judea and all you who live in Jerusalem, let this be known to you and give heed to my words. ᵃActs 1:26

15 "For these men are not drunk, as you suppose, ᵃfor it is *only* the third hour of the day; ᵃ1 Thess 5:7

16 but this is what was spoken of through the prophet Joel:

17 'ᵃAND IT SHALL BE IN THE LAST DAYS,' God says,

'THAT I WILL POUR FORTH OF MY SPIRIT ON
   ALL MANKIND;
AND YOUR SONS AND YOUR DAUGHTERS SHALL
   PROPHESY,

AND YOUR YOUNG MEN SHALL SEE VISIONS,
AND YOUR OLD MEN SHALL DREAM DREAMS;
   ᵃJoel 2:28-32

18 EVEN ON MY BONDSLAVES, BOTH MEN AND
      WOMEN,
I WILL IN THOSE DAYS POUR FORTH OF MY
   SPIRIT
And they shall prophesy.

19 'AND I WILL GRANT WONDERS IN THE SKY
      ABOVE
AND SIGNS ON THE EARTH BELOW,
BLOOD, AND FIRE, AND VAPOR OF SMOKE.

20 'THE SUN WILL BE TURNED INTO DARKNESS
AND THE MOON INTO BLOOD,
BEFORE THE GREAT AND GLORIOUS DAY OF THE
   LORD SHALL COME.

21 'AND IT SHALL BE THAT ᵃEVERYONE WHO CALLS
   ON THE NAME OF THE LORD WILL BE
   SAVED.' ᵃRom 10:13

22 "Men of Israel, listen to these words: ᵃJesus the Nazarene, a man attested to you by God with miracles and wonders and signs which God performed through Him in your midst, just as you yourselves know— ᵃActs 3:6; 4:10

23 this *Man*, delivered over by the ᵃpredetermined plan and foreknowledge of God, you nailed to a cross by the hands of godless men and put *Him* to death. ᵃLuke 22:22; Acts 3:18

24 "But ᵃGod raised Him up again, putting an end to the agony of death, since it was impossible for Him to be held in its power. ᵃMatt 28:5, 6; Mark 16:6

25 "For David says of Him,

'ᵃI SAW THE LORD ALWAYS IN MY PRESENCE;
FOR HE IS AT MY RIGHT HAND, SO THAT I WILL
   NOT BE SHAKEN. ᵃPs 16:8-11

26 'THEREFORE MY HEART WAS GLAD AND MY
      TONGUE EXULTED;
MOREOVER MY FLESH ALSO WILL LIVE IN HOPE;

27 BECAUSE YOU WILL NOT ABANDON MY SOUL
      TO ᵃHADES,
ᵇNOR ALLOW YOUR HOLY ONE TO UNDERGO
   DECAY. ᵃActs 2:31 ᵇActs 13:35

28 'YOU HAVE MADE KNOWN TO ME THE WAYS OF
      LIFE;
YOU WILL MAKE ME FULL OF GLADNESS WITH
   YOUR PRESENCE.'

29 "Brethren, I may confidently say to you regarding the patriarch David that he both died and ᵃwas buried, and his tomb is with us to this day. ᵃ1 Kin 2:10

30 "And so, because he was a prophet and knew that ᵃGOD HAD SWORN TO HIM WITH AN OATH TO SEAT *one* OF HIS DESCENDANTS ON HIS THRONE, ᵃPs 132:11; 2 Sam 7:12f

31 he looked ahead and spoke of the resurrection of the Christ, that ᵃHE WAS NEITHER ABANDONED TO HADES, NOR DID His flesh SUFFER DECAY. ᵃMatt 11:23; Acts 2:27

32 "This Jesus ªGod raised up again, to which we are all witnesses. ªActs 2:24; 3:15, 26

33 "Therefore having been exalted ªto the right hand of God, and ᵇhaving received from the Father the promise of the Holy Spirit, He has poured forth this which you both see and hear. ªActs 5:31 ᵇActs 1:4

34 "For it was not David who ascended into heaven, but he himself says:

'ªTHE LORD SAID TO MY LORD,

"SIT AT MY RIGHT HAND, ªPs 110:1; Matt 22:44f

35 UNTIL I MAKE YOUR ENEMIES A FOOTSTOOL FOR YOUR FEET." '

36 "Therefore let all the house of Israel know for certain that God has made Him both ªLord and Christ—this Jesus ᵇwhom you crucified." ªLuke 2:11 ᵇActs 2:23

The Ingathering

37 Now when they heard *this,* they were pierced to the heart, and said to Peter and the rest of the apostles, "Brethren, ªwhat shall we do?" ªLuke 3:10, 12, 14

38 Peter *said* to them, "ªRepent, and each of you be ᵇbaptized in the name of Jesus Christ for the forgiveness of your sins; and you will receive the gift of the Holy Spirit. ªMark 1:15 ᵇActs 8:12, 16

39 "For ªthe promise is for you and your children and for all who are far off, as many as the Lord our God will call to Himself." ªIs 44:3; 54:13

40 And with many other words he solemnly testified and kept on exhorting them, saying, "Be saved from this ªperverse generation!" ªDeut 32:5; Matt 17:17

41 So then, those who had received his word were baptized; and that day there were added about three thousand ªsouls. ªActs 3:23; 7:14

42 They were ªcontinually devoting themselves to the apostles' teaching and to fellowship, to ᵇthe breaking of bread and ªto prayer. ªActs 1:14 ᵇLuke 24:30

43 Everyone kept feeling a sense of awe; and many ªwonders and signs were taking place through the apostles. ªActs 2:22

44 And all those who had believed were together and ªhad all things in common; ªActs 4:32, 37; 5:2

45 and they ªbegan selling their property and possessions and were sharing them with all, as anyone might have need. ªMatt 19:21; Acts 4:34

46 ªDay by day continuing with one mind in the temple, and breaking bread from house to house, they were taking their meals together with gladness and sincerity of heart, ªActs 5:42

47 praising God and ªhaving favor with all the people. And the Lord ᵇwas adding to their number day by day those who were being saved. ªActs 5:13 ᵇActs 2:41

Healing the Lame Beggar

3 Now Peter and John were going up to the temple at the ninth *hour,* ªthe hour of prayer. ªPs 55:17; Matt 27:45

2 And a man who had been lame from his mother's womb was being carried along, whom they ªused to set down every day at the gate of the temple which is called Beautiful, in order to beg alms of those who were entering the temple. ªLuke 16:20

3 When he saw ªPeter and John about to go into the temple, he *began* asking to receive alms. ªLuke 22:8; Acts 3:1, 4, 11

4 But Peter, along with John, ªfixed his gaze on him and said, "Look at us!" ªActs 10:4

5 And he *began* to give them his attention, expecting to receive something from them.

6 But Peter said, "I do not possess silver and gold, but what I do have I give to you: ªIn the name of Jesus Christ the Nazarene—walk!" ªActs 2:22; 3:16

7 And seizing him by the right hand, he raised him up; and immediately his feet and his ankles were strengthened.

8 ªWith a leap he stood upright and *began* to walk; and he entered the temple with them, walking and leaping and praising God. ªActs 14:10

9 And ªall the people saw him walking and praising God; ªActs 4:16, 21

10 and they were taking note of him as being the one who used to ªsit at the Beautiful Gate of the temple to *beg* alms, and they were filled with wonder and amazement at what had happened to him. ªJohn 9:8; Acts 3:2

Peter's Second Sermon

11 While he was clinging to Peter and John, all the people ran together to them at the so-called ªportico of Solomon, full of amazement. ªJohn 10:23; Acts 5:12

12 But when Peter saw *this,* he replied to the people, "Men of Israel, why are you amazed at this, or why do you gaze at us, as if by our own power or piety we had made him walk?

13 "The God of Abraham, Isaac and Jacob, the God of our fathers, has glorified His ªservant Jesus, *the one* whom you delivered and disowned in the presence of Pilate, when he had decided to release Him. ªActs 3:26; 4:27, 30

14 "But you disowned the Holy and Righteous One and ªasked for a murderer to be granted to you, ªMatt 27:20; Mark 15:11

15 but put to death the Prince of life, *the one* whom ªGod raised from the dead, *a fact* to which we are ᵇwitnesses. ªActs 2:24 ᵇLuke 24:48

16 "And on the basis of faith ªin His name, *it is* the name of Jesus which has strengthened this man whom you see and know; and the faith which *comes* through Him has given him

this perfect health in the presence of you all. ᵃActs 3:6

17 "And now, brethren, I know that you acted ᵃin ignorance, just as your rulers did also. ᵃJohn 15:21; Acts 13:27

18 "But the things which ᵃGod announced beforehand by the mouth of all the prophets, ᵇthat His Christ would suffer, He has thus fulfilled. ᵃActs 2:23 ᵇActs 17:3

19 "Therefore ᵃrepent and return, so that your sins may be wiped away, in order that times of refreshing may come from the presence of the Lord; ᵃActs 2:38; 26:20

20 and that He may send Jesus, the Christ appointed for you,

21 whom heaven must receive until the period of ᵃrestoration of all things about which ᵇGod spoke by the mouth of His holy prophets from ancient time. ᵃMatt 17:11 ᵇLuke 1:70

22 "Moses said, 'ᵃTHE LORD GOD WILL RAISE UP FOR YOU A PROPHET LIKE ME FROM YOUR BRETHREN; TO HIM YOU SHALL GIVE HEED to everything He says to you. ᵃDeut 18:15, 18; Acts 7:37

23 'ᵃAnd it will be that every soul that does not heed that prophet ᵇshall be utterly destroyed from among the people.' ᵃDeut 18:19 ᵇLev 23:29

24 "And likewise, ᵃall the prophets who have spoken, from Samuel and his successors onward, also announced these days. ᵃLuke 24:27; Acts 17:3

25 "It is you who are the sons of the prophets and of the covenant which God made with your fathers, saying to Abraham, 'ᵃAND IN YOUR SEED ALL THE FAMILIES OF THE EARTH SHALL BE BLESSED.' ᵃGen 22:18

26 "For you ᵃfirst, God ᵇraised up His Servant and sent Him to bless you by turning every one of you from your wicked ways." ᵃMatt 15:24 ᵇActs 2:24

Peter and John Arrested

4 As they were speaking to the people, the priests and the captain of the temple guard and ᵃthe Sadducees came up to them, ᵃMark 12:18; Acts 5:17

2 being greatly disturbed because they were teaching the people and proclaiming ᵃin Jesus the resurrection from the dead. ᵃActs 3:15; 17:18

3 And they laid hands on them and ᵃput them in jail until the next day, for it was already evening. ᵃActs 5:18

4 But many of those who had heard the message believed; and ᵃthe number of the men came to be about five thousand. ᵃActs 2:41

5 On the next day, their ᵃrulers and elders and scribes were gathered together in Jerusalem; ᵃLuke 23:13; Acts 4:8

6 and ᵃAnnas the high priest was there, and

Caiaphas and John and Alexander, and all who were of high-priestly descent. ᵃLuke 3:2

7 When they had placed them in the center, they began to inquire, "By what power, or in what name, have you done this?"

8 Then Peter, ᵃfilled with the Holy Spirit, said to them, "Rulers and elders of the people, ᵃActs 2:4; 13:9

9 if we are on trial today for ᵃa benefit done to a sick man, as to how this man has been made well, ᵃActs 3:7f

10 let it be known to all of you and to all the people of Israel, that ᵃby the name of Jesus Christ the Nazarene, whom you crucified, whom God raised from the dead—by this name this man stands here before you in good health. ᵃActs 2:22; 3:6

11 "He is the ᵃSTONE WHICH WAS REJECTED by you, THE BUILDERS, but WHICH BECAME THE CHIEF CORNER stone. ᵃPs 118:22

12 "And there is salvation in ᵃno one else; for there is no other name under heaven that has been given among men by which we must be saved." ᵃMatt 1:21; Acts 10:43

Threat and Release

13 Now as they observed the ᵃconfidence of Peter and John and understood that they were uneducated and untrained men, they were amazed, and ᵇbegan to recognize them as having been with Jesus. ᵃActs 4:31 ᵇJohn 7:15

14 And seeing the man who had been healed standing with them, they had nothing to say in reply.

15 But when they had ordered them to leave the ᵃCouncil, they began to confer with one another, ᵃMatt 5:22

16 saying, "ᵃWhat shall we do with these men? For the fact that a ᵇnoteworthy miracle has taken place through them is apparent to all who live in Jerusalem, and we cannot deny it. ᵃJohn 11:47 ᵇActs 3:7-10

17 "But so that it will not spread any further among the people, let us warn them to speak no longer to any man ᵃin this name." ᵃJohn 15:21

18 And when they had summoned them, they ᵃcommanded them not to speak or teach at all in the name of Jesus. ᵃActs 5:28f

19 But Peter and John answered and said to them, "ᵃWhether it is right in the sight of God to give heed to you rather than to God, you be the judge; ᵃActs 5:28f

20 for ᵃwe cannot stop speaking about what we have seen and heard." ᵃI Cor 9:16

21 When they had threatened them further, they let them go (finding no basis on which to punish them) ᵃon account of the people, because they were all ᵇglorifying God for what had happened; ᵃActs 5:26 ᵇMatt 9:8

22 for the man was more than forty years old

on whom this miracle of healing had been performed.

23 When they had been released, they went to their own *companions* and reported all that the chief priests and the elders had said to them.

24 And when they heard *this,* they lifted their voices to God with one accord and said, "O Lord, it is You who ªMADE THE HEAVEN AND THE EARTH AND THE SEA, AND ALL THAT IS IN THEM, ªEx 20:11; Neh 9:6

25 who ªby the Holy Spirit, *through* the mouth of our father David Your servant, said,

'ᵇWHY DID THE GENTILES RAGE,
AND THE PEOPLES DEVISE FUTILE THINGS?
ªActs 1:16 ᵇPs 2:1

26 'ªTHE KINGS OF THE EARTH TOOK THEIR STAND,
AND THE RULERS WERE GATHERED TOGETHER
AGAINST THE LORD AND AGAINST HIS
CHRIST.' ªPs 2:2

27 "For truly in this city there were gathered together against Your holy ªservant Jesus, whom You anointed, both Herod and Pontius Pilate, along with the Gentiles and the peoples of Israel, ªActs 3:13; 4:30

28 to do whatever Your hand and ªYour purpose predestined to occur. ªActs 2:23

29 "And now, Lord, take note of their threats, and grant that Your bond-servants may ªspeak Your word with all confidence, ªPhil 1:14

30 while You extend Your hand to heal, and ªsigns and wonders take place through the name of Your holy servant Jesus." ªJohn 4:48

31 And when they had prayed, the place where they had gathered together was shaken, and they were all ªfilled with the Holy Spirit and *began* to ᵇspeak the word of God with boldness. ªActs 2:4 ᵇPhil 1:14

Sharing among Believers

32 And the congregation of those who believed were of one heart and soul; and not one *of them* claimed that anything belonging to him was his own, but ªall things were common property to them. ªActs 2:44

33 And ªwith great power the apostles were giving testimony to the resurrection of the Lord Jesus, and abundant grace was upon them all. ªActs 1:8

34 For there was not a needy person among them, for all who were owners of land or houses ªwould sell them and bring the proceeds of the sales ªMatt 19:21; Acts 2:45

35 and ªlay them at the apostles' feet, and they would be ᵇdistributed to each as any had need. ªActs 4:37 ᵇActs 2:45

36 Now Joseph, a Levite of ªCyprian birth, who was also called Barnabas by the apostles (which translated means Son of ᵇEncouragement), ªActs 13:4 ᵇActs 11:23

37 and who owned a tract of land, sold it and

brought the money and ªlaid it at the apostles' feet. ªActs 4:35; 5:2

Fate of Ananias and Sapphira

5 But a man named Ananias, with his wife Sapphira, sold a piece of property,

2 and kept back *some* of the price for himself, with his wife's full knowledge, and bringing a portion of it, he ªlaid it at the apostles' feet. ªActs 4:35, 37

3 But Peter said, "Ananias, why has ªSatan filled your heart to lie to the Holy Spirit and to keep back *some* of the price of the land? ªMatt 4:10; Luke 22:3

4 "While it remained *unsold,* did it not remain your own? And after it was sold, was it not under your control? Why is it that you have conceived this deed in your heart? You have not lied to men but ªto God." ªActs 5:3, 9

5 And as he heard these words, Ananias fell down and breathed his last; and ªgreat fear came over all who heard of it. ªActs 2:43; 5:11

6 The young men got up and ªcovered him up, and after carrying him out, they buried him. ªJohn 19:40

7 Now there elapsed an interval of about three hours, and his wife came in, not knowing what had happened.

8 And Peter responded to her, "Tell me whether you sold the land ªfor such and such a price?" And she said, "Yes, that was the price." ªActs 5:2

9 Then Peter *said* to her, "Why is it that you have agreed together to ªput the Spirit of the Lord to the test? Behold, the feet of those who have buried your husband are at the door, and they will carry you out *as well.*" ªActs 15:10

10 And immediately she ªfell at her feet and breathed her last, and the young men came in and found her dead, and they carried her out and buried her beside her husband. ªEzek 11:13; Acts 5:5

11 And ªgreat fear came over the whole church, and over all who heard of these things. ªActs 2:43; 5:5

12 At the hands of the apostles many ªsigns and wonders were taking place among the people; and they were all with one accord in ᵇSolomon's portico. ªJohn 4:48 ᵇJohn 10:23

13 But none of the rest dared to associate with them; however, ªthe people held them in high esteem. ªActs 2:47; 4:21

14 And all the more ªbelievers in the Lord, multitudes of men and women, were constantly added to *their number,* ª2 Cor 6:15

15 to such an extent that they even carried the sick out into the streets and laid them on cots and pallets, so that when Peter came by ªat least his shadow might fall on any one of them. ªActs 19:12

16 Also the people from the cities in the vicinity of Jerusalem were coming together, bringing people who were sick or afflicted with unclean spirits, and they were all being healed.

Imprisonment and Release

17 But the high priest rose up, along with all his associates (that is the sect of ªthe Sadducees), and they were filled with jealousy. ªMatt 3:7; Acts 4:1

18 They laid hands on the apostles and ªput them in a public jail. ªActs 4:3

19 But during the night ªan angel of the Lord opened the gates of the prison, and taking them out he said, ªMatt 1:20, 24; 2:13, 19

20 "Go, stand and speak to the people in the temple ªthe whole message of this Life." ªJohn 6:63, 68

21 Upon hearing *this,* they entered into the temple about daybreak and *began* to teach.

Now when ªthe high priest and his associates came, they called the Council together, even all the Senate of the sons of Israel, and sent *orders* to the prison house for them to be brought. ªActs 4:6

22 But ªthe officers who came did not find them in the prison; and they returned and reported back, ªMatt 26:58; Acts 5:26

23 saying, "We found the prison house locked quite securely and the guards standing at the doors; but when we had opened up, we found no one inside."

24 Now when ªthe captain of the temple *guard* and the chief priests heard these words, they were greatly perplexed about them as to what would come of this. ªActs 4:1; 5:26

25 But someone came and reported to them, "The men whom you put in prison are standing in the temple and teaching the people!"

26 Then the captain went along with the officers and *proceeded* to bring them *back* without violence (for ªthey were afraid of the people, that they might be stoned). ªActs 4:21; 5:13

27 When they had brought them, they stood them before ªthe Council. The high priest questioned them, ªMatt 5:22; Acts 5:21, 34, 41

28 saying, "We gave you strict orders not to continue teaching in this name, and yet, you have filled Jerusalem with your teaching and ªintend to bring this man's blood upon us." ªMatt 23:35; 27:25

29 But Peter and the apostles answered, "ªWe must obey God rather than men. ªActs 4:19

30 "ªThe God of our fathers ᵇraised up Jesus, whom you had put to death by hanging Him on a cross. ªActs 3:13 ᵇActs 2:24

31 "ªHe is the one whom God exalted to His right hand as a Prince and a ᵇSavior, to grant repentance to Israel, and forgiveness of sins. ªActs 2:33 ᵇLuke 2:11

32 "And we are ªwitnesses of these things; and *so is* the Holy Spirit, whom God has given to those who obey Him." ªLuke 24:48

Gamaliel's Counsel

33 But when they heard this, they were ªcut to the quick and intended to kill them. ªActs 2:37; 7:54

34 But a Pharisee named ªGamaliel, a teacher of the Law, respected by all the people, stood up in the Council and gave orders to put the men outside for a short time. ªActs 22:3

35 And he said to them, "Men of Israel, take care what you propose to do with these men.

36 "For some time ago Theudas rose up, ªclaiming to be somebody, and a group of about four hundred men joined up with him. But he was killed, and all who followed him were dispersed and came to nothing. ªActs 8:9; Gal 2:6

37 "After this man, Judas of Galilee rose up in the days of ªthe census and drew away *some* people after him; he too perished, and all those who followed him were scattered. ªLuke 2:2

38 "So in the present case, I say to you, stay away from these men and let them alone, for if this plan or action ªis of men, it will be overthrown; ªMark 11:30

39 but if it is of God, you will not be able to overthrow them; or else you may even be found ªfighting against God." ªProv 21:30; Acts 11:17

40 They took his advice; and after calling the apostles in, they ªflogged them and ordered them not to speak in the name of Jesus, and *then* released them. ªMatt 10:17

41 So they went on their way from the presence of the Council, ªrejoicing that they had been considered worthy to suffer shame ᵇfor *His* name. ª1 Pet 4:14, 16 ᵇJohn 15:21

42 ªAnd every day, in the temple and from house to house, they kept right on teaching and preaching Jesus *as* the Christ. ªActs 2:46

Choosing of the Seven

6 Now at this time while the ªdisciples were increasing *in number,* a complaint arose on the part of the ᵇHellenistic *Jews* against the *native* Hebrews, because their widows were being overlooked in the daily serving *of food.* ªActs 11:26 ᵇActs 9:29

2 So the twelve summoned the congregation of the disciples and said, "It is not desirable for us to neglect the word of God in order to serve tables.

3 "Therefore, brethren, select from among you seven men of good reputation, ªfull of the Spirit and of wisdom, whom we may put in charge of this task. ªActs 2:4

4 "But we will ªdevote ourselves to prayer and to the ministry of the word." ªActs 1:14

5 The statement found approval with the whole congregation; and they chose ªStephen, a man full of faith and of the Holy Spirit, and Philip, Prochorus, Nicanor, Timon, Parmenas and Nicolas, a proselyte from Antioch. ªActs 6:8ff; 11:19

6 And these they brought before the apostles; and after ªpraying, they ᵇlaid their hands on them. ªActs 1:24 ᵇNum 8:10

7 The word of God kept on spreading; and the number of the disciples continued to increase greatly in Jerusalem, and a great many of the priests were becoming obedient to ªthe faith. ªActs 13:8; 14:22

8 And Stephen, full of grace and power, was performing great ªwonders and signs among the people. ªJohn 4:48

9 But some men from what was called the Synagogue of the Freedmen, *including* both ªCyrenians and Alexandrians, and some from Cilicia and Asia, rose up and argued with Stephen. ªMatt 27:32; Acts 2:10

10 But they were unable to cope with the wisdom and the Spirit with which he was speaking.

11 Then they secretly induced men to say, "We have heard him speak blasphemous words against Moses and *against* God."

12 And they stirred up the people, the elders and the scribes, and they ªcame up to him and dragged him away and brought him before the Council. ªLuke 20:1; Acts 4:1

13 They put forward ªfalse witnesses who said, "This man incessantly speaks against this ᵇholy place and the Law; ªMatt 26:59-61 ᵇMatt 24:15

14 for we have heard him say that ªthis Nazarene, Jesus, will destroy this place and alter the customs which Moses handed down to us." ªMatt 26:61

15 And fixing their gaze on him, all who were sitting in the ªCouncil saw his face like the face of an angel. ªMatt 5:22

Stephen's Defense

7 The high priest said, "Are these things so?"
2 And he said, "Hear me, ªbrethren and fathers! The God of glory ᵇappeared to our father Abraham when he was in Mesopotamia, before he lived in Haran, ªActs 22:1 ᵇGen 11:31

3 and said to him, 'ªLEAVE YOUR COUNTRY AND YOUR RELATIVES, AND COME INTO THE LAND THAT I WILL SHOW YOU.' ªGen 12:1

4 "ªThen he left the land of the Chaldeans and settled in Haran. ᵇFrom there, after his father died, *God* had him move to this country in which you are now living. ªGen 11:31 ᵇGen 12:4, 5

5 "But He gave him no inheritance in it, not even a foot of ground, and *yet*, even when he

had no child, ªHe promised that HE WOULD GIVE IT TO HIM AS A POSSESSION, AND TO HIS DESCENDANTS AFTER HIM. ªGen 12:7; 13:15

6 "But ªGod spoke to this effect, that his DESCENDANTS WOULD BE ALIENS IN A FOREIGN LAND, AND THAT THEY WOULD BE ENSLAVED AND MISTREATED FOR FOUR HUNDRED YEARS. ªGen 15:13f

7 " 'AND WHATEVER NATION TO WHICH THEY WILL BE IN BONDAGE I MYSELF WILL JUDGE,' said God, 'AND ªAFTER THAT THEY WILL COME OUT AND SERVE ME IN THIS PLACE.' ªEx 3:12

8 "And He ªgave him the covenant of circumcision; and so ᵇ*Abraham* became the father of Isaac, and circumcised him on the eighth day; and Isaac *became the father of* Jacob, and Jacob *of* the twelve patriarchs. ªGen 17:10ff ᵇGen 21:2-4

9 "The patriarchs ªbecame jealous of Joseph and sold him into Egypt. *Yet* God was with him, ªGen 37:11, 28; 39:2, 21f

10 and rescued him from all his afflictions, and ªgranted him favor and wisdom in the sight of Pharaoh, king of Egypt, and he made him governor over Egypt and all his household. ªGen 39:21; 41:40-46

11 "Now ªa famine came over all Egypt and Canaan, and great affliction *with it*, and our fathers could find no food. ªGen 41:54f; 42:5

12 "But ªwhen Jacob heard that there was grain in Egypt, he sent our fathers *there* the first time. ªGen 42:2

13 "On the second *visit* ªJoseph made himself known to his brothers, and ᵇJoseph's family was disclosed to Pharaoh. ªGen 45:1-4 ᵇGen 45:16

14 "Then ªJoseph sent *word* and invited Jacob his father and all his relatives to come to him, seventy-five persons *in all.* ªGen 45:9, 10, 17, 18

15 "And ªJacob went down to Egypt and *there* he and our fathers died. ªGen 46:1-7; 49:33

16 "*From there* they were removed to ªShechem and laid in the tomb which Abraham had purchased for a sum of money from the sons of Hamor in Shechem. ªGen 23:16; 33:19

17 "But as the ªtime of the promise was approaching which God had assured to Abraham, ᵇthe people increased and multiplied in Egypt, ªGen 15:13 ᵇEx 1:7f

18 until ªTHERE AROSE ANOTHER KING OVER EGYPT WHO KNEW NOTHING ABOUT JOSEPH. ªEx 1:8

19 "It was he who took shrewd advantage of our race and mistreated our fathers so that they would ªexpose their infants and they would not survive. ªEx 1:22

20 "It was at this time that ªMoses was born; and he was lovely in the sight of God, and he was nurtured three months in his father's home. ªEx 2:2; Heb 11:23

21 "And after he had been set outside, ªPharaoh's daughter took him away and nurtured him as her own son. ªEx 2:5f, 10

22 "Moses was educated in all ªthe learning of the Egyptians, and he was a man of power in words and deeds. ª*1 Kin 4:30; Is 19:11*

23 "But when he was approaching the age of forty, ªit entered his mind to visit his brethren, the sons of Israel. ª*Ex 2:11f; Heb 11:24-26*

24 "And when he saw one *of them* being treated unjustly, he defended him and took vengeance for the oppressed by striking down the Egyptian.

25 "And he supposed that his brethren understood that God was granting them deliverance through him, but they did not understand.

26 "ªOn the following day he appeared to them as they were fighting together, and he tried to reconcile them in peace, saying, 'Men, you are brethren, why do you injure one another?' ª*Ex 2:13f*

27 "But the one who was injuring his neighbor pushed him away, saying, 'ªWHO MADE YOU A RULER AND JUDGE OVER US? ª*Ex 2:14; Acts 7:35*

28 'ªYOU DO NOT MEAN TO KILL ME AS YOU KILLED THE EGYPTIAN YESTERDAY, DO YOU?' ª*Ex 2:14*

29 "At this remark, ªMOSES FLED AND BECAME AN ALIEN IN THE LAND OF MIDIAN, where he became the father of two sons. ª*Ex 2:15, 22*

30 "After forty years had passed, ªAN ANGEL APPEARED TO HIM IN THE WILDERNESS OF MOUNT SINAI, IN THE FLAME OF A BURNING THORN BUSH. ª*Ex 3:1f; Is 63:9*

31 "When Moses saw it, he marveled at the sight; and as he approached to look *more* closely, there came the voice of the Lord:

32 'ªI AM THE GOD OF YOUR FATHERS, THE GOD OF ABRAHAM AND ISAAC AND JACOB.' Moses shook with fear and would not venture to look. ª*Ex 3:6; Matt 22:32*

33 'ªBUT THE LORD SAID TO HIM, 'TAKE OFF THE SANDALS FROM YOUR FEET, FOR THE PLACE ON WHICH YOU ARE STANDING IS HOLY GROUND. ª*Ex 3:5*

34 'ªI HAVE CERTAINLY SEEN THE OPPRESSION OF MY PEOPLE IN EGYPT AND HAVE HEARD THEIR GROANS, AND I HAVE COME DOWN TO RESCUE THEM; COME NOW, AND I WILL SEND YOU TO EGYPT.' ª*Ex 3:7f*

35 "This Moses whom they ªdisowned, saying, 'WHO MADE YOU A RULER AND A JUDGE?' is the one whom God sent *to be* both a ruler and a deliverer with the help of the angel who appeared to him in the thorn bush. ª*Ex 2:14; Acts 7:27*

36 "ªThis man led them out, performing ᵇwonders and signs in the land of Egypt and in the Red Sea and in the wilderness for forty years. ª*Ex 12:41* ᵇ*Ex 7:3*

37 "This is the Moses who said to the sons of Israel, 'ªGOD WILL RAISE UP FOR YOU A PROPHET LIKE ME FROM YOUR BRETHREN.' ª*Deut 18:15, 18; Acts 3:22*

38 "This is the one who was in ªthe congrega-

tion in the wilderness together with the angel who was speaking to him on Mount Sinai, and *who was* with our fathers; and he received ᵇliving oracles to pass on to you. ª*Ex 19:17* ᵇ*Deut 32:47*

39 "Our fathers were unwilling to be obedient to him, but ªrepudiated him and in their hearts turned back to Egypt, ª*Num 14:3f*

40 ªSAYING TO AARON, 'MAKE FOR US GODS WHO WILL GO BEFORE US; FOR THIS MOSES WHO LED US OUT OF THE LAND OF EGYPT—WE DO NOT KNOW WHAT HAPPENED TO HIM.' ª*Ex 32:1, 23*

41 "At that time ªthey made a calf and brought a sacrifice to the idol, and were rejoicing in ᵇthe works of their hands. ª*Ex 32:4, 6* ᵇ*Rev 9:20*

42 "But God turned away and delivered them up to serve the host of heaven; as it is written in the book of the prophets, 'ªIT WAS NOT TO ME THAT YOU OFFERED VICTIMS AND SACRIFICES FORTY YEARS IN THE WILDERNESS, WAS IT, O HOUSE OF ISRAEL? ª*Amos 5:25*

43 'ªYOU ALSO TOOK ALONG THE TABERNACLE OF MOLOCH AND THE STAR OF THE GOD ROMPHA, THE IMAGES WHICH YOU MADE TO WORSHIP. I ALSO WILL REMOVE YOU BEYOND BABYLON.' ª*Amos 5:26, 27*

44 "Our fathers had ªthe tabernacle of testimony in the wilderness, just as He who spoke to Moses directed *him* to make it ᵇaccording to the pattern which he had seen. ª*Ex 25:8, 9* ᵇ*Ex 25:40*

45 "And having received it in their turn, our fathers ªbrought it in with Joshua upon dispossessing the nations whom God drove out before our fathers, until the time of David. ª*Deut 32:49; Josh 3:14ff*

46 "ªDavid found favor in God's sight, and asked that he might find a dwelling place for the God of Jacob. ª*2 Sam 7:8ff; Ps 132:1-5*

47 "But it was ªSolomon who built a house for Him. ª*1 Kin 6:1-38; 8:20*

48 "However, ªthe Most High does not dwell in *houses* made by *human* hands; as the prophet says: ª*Luke 1:32*

49 'ªHEAVEN IS MY THRONE,
    AND EARTH IS THE FOOTSTOOL OF MY FEET;
    WHAT KIND OF HOUSE WILL YOU BUILD FOR
      ME?' says the Lord,
   'OR WHAT PLACE IS THERE FOR MY REPOSE?
      ª*Is 66:1; Matt 5:34f*

50 'ªWAS IT NOT MY HAND WHICH MADE ALL
    THESE THINGS?' ª*Is 66:2*

51 "You men who are ªstiff-necked and uncircumcised in heart and ears are always resisting the Holy Spirit; you are doing just as your fathers did. ª*Ex 32:9; 33:3, 5*

52 "Which one of the prophets did your fathers not persecute? They killed those who had previously announced the coming of ᵇthe Righteous One, whose betrayers and murderers you have now become; ª*2 Chr 36:15f* ᵇ*Acts 3:14*

53 you who received the law as ^aordained by angels, and *yet* did not keep it." ^a*Deut 33:2; Acts 7:38*

Stephen Put to Death

54 Now when they heard this, they were ^acut to the quick, and they *began* gnashing their teeth at him. ^a*Acts 5:33*

55 But being ^afull of the Holy Spirit, he gazed intently into heaven and saw the glory of God, and Jesus standing at the right hand of God; ^a*Acts 2:4*

56 and he said, "Behold, I see the ^aheavens opened up and the Son of Man standing at the right hand of God." ^a*John 1:51*

57 But they cried out with a loud voice, and covered their ears and rushed at him with one impulse.

58 When they had ^adriven him out of the city, they *began* stoning *him;* and the witnesses ^blaid aside their robes at the feet of a young man named Saul. ^a*Lev 24:14, 16* ^b*Acts 22:20*

59 They went on stoning Stephen as he ^acalled on *the Lord* and said, "Lord Jesus, receive my spirit!" ^a*Acts 9:14, 21; 22:16*

60 Then ^afalling on his knees, he cried out with a loud voice, "Lord, do not hold this sin against them!" Having said this, he fell asleep. ^a*Luke 22:41*

Saul Persecutes the Church

8 ^aSaul was in hearty agreement with putting him to death.

And on that day a great persecution began against the church in Jerusalem, and they were all scattered throughout the regions of Judea and Samaria, except the apostles. ^a*Acts 7:58; 22:20*

2 *Some* devout men buried Stephen, and made loud lamentation over him.

3 But ^aSaul *began* ravaging the church, entering house after house, and dragging off men and women, he would put them in prison. ^a*Acts 9:1, 13, 21; 22:4, 19*

Philip in Samaria

4 Therefore, those ^awho had been scattered went about preaching the word. ^a*Acts 8:1*

5 ^aPhilip went down to the city of Samaria and *began* proclaiming Christ to them. ^a*Acts 6:5; 8:26, 30*

6 The crowds with one accord were giving attention to what was said by Philip, as they heard and saw the signs which he was performing.

7 For *in the case of* many who had unclean spirits, they were coming out *of them* shouting with a loud voice; and many who had been ^aparalyzed and lame were healed. ^a*Matt 4:24*

8 So there was ^amuch rejoicing in that city. ^a*John 4:40-42; Acts 8:39*

9 Now there was a man named Simon, who formerly was practicing ^amagic in the city and astonishing the people of Samaria, claiming to be someone great; ^a*Acts 8:11; 13:6*

10 and they all, from smallest to greatest, were giving attention to him, saying, "^aThis man is what is called the Great Power of God." ^a*Acts 14:11; 28:6*

11 And they were giving him attention because he had for a long time astonished them with his ^amagic arts. ^a*Acts 8:9; 13:6*

12 But when they believed Philip ^apreaching the good news about the kingdom of God and the name of Jesus Christ, they were being baptized, men and women alike. ^a*Acts 1:3; 8:4*

13 Even Simon himself believed; and after being baptized, he continued on with Philip, and as he observed ^asigns and ^bgreat miracles taking place, he was constantly amazed. ^a*Acts 8:6* ^b*Acts 19:11*

14 Now when ^athe apostles in Jerusalem heard that Samaria had received the word of God, they sent them ^bPeter and John, ^a*Acts 8:1* ^b*Luke 22:8*

15 who came down and prayed for them ^athat they might receive the Holy Spirit. ^a*Acts 2:38; 19:2*

16 For He had ^anot yet fallen upon any of them; they had simply been baptized in the name of the Lord Jesus. ^a*Matt 28:19; Acts 19:2*

17 Then they ^a*began* laying their hands on them, and they were ^breceiving the Holy Spirit. ^a*Acts 6:6* ^b*Acts 2:4*

18 Now when Simon saw that the Spirit was bestowed through the laying on of the apostles' hands, he offered them money,

19 saying, "Give this authority to me as well, so that everyone on whom I lay my hands may receive the Holy Spirit."

20 But Peter said to him, "May your silver perish with you, because you thought you could ^aobtain the gift of God with money! ^a*2 Kin 5:16; Is 55:1*

21 "You have ^ano part or portion in this matter, for your heart is not right before God. ^a*Deut 10:9; 12:12*

22 "Therefore repent of this wickedness of yours, and pray the Lord that, ^aif possible, the intention of your heart may be forgiven you. ^a*Is 55:7*

23 "For I see that you are in the gall of bitterness and in ^athe bondage of iniquity." ^a*Is 58:6*

24 But Simon answered and said, "^aPray to the Lord for me yourselves, so that nothing of what you have said may come upon me." ^a*Gen 20:7; Ex 8:8*

An Ethiopian Receives Christ

25 So, when they had solemnly testified and spoken ^athe word of the Lord, they started back to Jerusalem, and were preaching the gospel to many villages of the Samaritans. ᵃ*Acts 13:12*

26 But ᵃan angel of the Lord spoke to Philip saying, "Get up and go south to the road that descends from Jerusalem to Gaza." (This is a desert *road.*) ᵃ*Acts 5:19; 8:29*

27 So he got up and went; and ᵃthere was an Ethiopian eunuch, a court official of Candace, queen of the Ethiopians, who was in charge of all her treasure; and he ᵇhad come to Jerusalem to worship, ᵃ*Ps 68:31;* ᵇ*1 Kin 8:41f*

28 and he was returning and sitting in his chariot, and was reading the prophet Isaiah.

29 Then ᵃthe Spirit said to Philip, "Go up and join this chariot." ᵃ*Acts 8:39; 10:19*

30 Philip ran up and heard him reading Isaiah the prophet, and said, "Do you understand what you are reading?"

31 And he said, "Well, how could I, unless someone guides me?" And he invited Philip to come up and sit with him.

32 Now the passage of Scripture which he was reading was this:

"ᵃHE WAS LED AS A SHEEP TO SLAUGHTER;
AND AS A LAMB BEFORE ITS SHEARER IS SILENT,
SO HE DOES NOT OPEN HIS MOUTH. ᵃ*Is 53:7*

33 "IN HUMILIATION HIS JUDGMENT WAS TAKEN AWAY;
WHO WILL RELATE HIS GENERATION?
FOR HIS LIFE IS REMOVED FROM THE EARTH."

34 The eunuch answered Philip and said, "Please *tell me,* of whom does the prophet say this? Of himself or of someone else?"

35 Then Philip opened his mouth, and ᵃbeginning from this Scripture he preached Jesus to him. ᵃ*Luke 24:27; Acts 17:2*

36 As they went along the road they came to some water; and the eunuch *said, "Look! Water! ᵃWhat prevents me from being baptized?" ᵃ*Acts 10:47*

37 [And Philip said, "If you believe with all your heart, you may." And he answered and said, "I believe that Jesus Christ is the Son of God."]

38 And he ordered the chariot to stop; and they both went down into the water, Philip as well as the eunuch, and he baptized him.

39 When they came up out of the water, ᵃthe Spirit of the Lord snatched Philip away; and the eunuch no longer saw him, but went on his way rejoicing. ᵃ*1 Kin 18:12; 2 Kin 2:16*

40 But Philip found himself at ᵃAzotus, and as he passed through he ᵇkept preaching the gospel to all the cities until he came to Caesarea. ᵃ*Josh 11:22* ᵇ*Acts 8:25*

The Conversion of Saul

9 ᵃNow Saul, still breathing threats and murder against the disciples of the Lord, went to the high priest, ᵃ*Acts 9:1-22; 22:3-16*

2 and asked for ᵃletters from him to the synagogues at Damascus, so that if he found any belonging to the Way, both men and women, he might bring them bound to Jerusalem. ᵃ*Acts 9:14, 21; 22:5*

3 As he was traveling, it happened that he was approaching Damascus, and ᵃsuddenly a light from heaven flashed around him; ᵃ*1 Cor 15:8*

4 and ᵃhe fell to the ground and heard a voice saying to him, "Saul, Saul, why are you persecuting Me?" ᵃ*Acts 22:7; 26:14*

5 And he said, "Who are You, Lord?" And He *said,* "I am Jesus whom you are persecuting,

6 but get up and enter the city, and ᵃit will be told you what you must do." ᵃ*Acts 9:16*

7 The men who traveled with him stood speechless, ᵃhearing the voice but seeing no one. ᵃ*John 12:29f; Acts 22:9*

8 Saul got up from the ground, and ᵃthough his eyes were open, he could see nothing; and leading him by the hand, they brought him into Damascus. ᵃ*Acts 9:18; 22:11*

9 And he was three days without sight, and neither ate nor drank.

10 Now there was a disciple at Damascus named ᵃAnanias; and the Lord said to him in ᵇa vision, "Ananias." And he said, "Here I am, Lord." ᵃ*Acts 22:12* ᵇ*Acts 10:3, 17, 19*

11 And the Lord *said* to him, "Get up and go to the street called Straight, and inquire at the house of Judas for a man from ᵃTarsus named Saul, for he is praying, ᵃ*Acts 9:30; 11:25*

12 and he has seen in a vision a man named Ananias come in and ᵃlay his hands on him, so that he might regain his sight." ᵃ*Mark 5:23; Acts 6:6*

13 But Ananias answered, "Lord, I have heard from many about this man, ᵃhow much harm he did to Your saints at Jerusalem; ᵃ*Acts 8:3*

14 and here he ᵃhas authority from the chief priests to bind all who ᵇcall on Your name." ᵃ*Acts 9:2, 21* ᵇ*Acts 7:59*

15 But the Lord said to him, "Go, for ᵃhe is a chosen instrument of Mine, to bear My name before the Gentiles and kings and the sons of Israel; ᵃ*Acts 13:2; Rom 1:1*

16 for ᵃI will show him how much he must suffer for My name's sake." ᵃ*Acts 20:23; 21:4, 11, 13*

17 So Ananias departed and entered the house, and after ᵃlaying his hands on him said, "Brother Saul, the Lord Jesus, who appeared to you on the road by which you were coming, has sent me so that you may regain your sight and be ᵇfilled with the Holy Spirit." ᵃ*Mark 5:23* ᵇ*Acts 2:4*

18 And immediately there fell from his eyes

something like scales, and he regained his sight, and he got up and was baptized.
19 and he took food and was strengthened.

Saul Begins to Preach Christ

Now for several days he was with the disciples who were at Damascus,
20 and immediately he *began* to proclaim Jesus ªin the synagogues, saying, "He is ᵇthe Son of God." ªActs 13:5, 14 ᵇActs 13:33
21 All those hearing him continued to be amazed, and were saying, "Is this not he who in Jerusalem ªdestroyed those who called on this name, and *who* had come here for the purpose of bringing them bound before the chief priests?" ªActs 8:3; 9:13
22 But Saul kept increasing in strength and confounding the Jews who lived at Damascus by proving that this *Jesus* is the Christ.
23 When ªmany days had elapsed, the Jews plotted together to do away with him,   ªGal 1:17, 18
24 but their plot became known to Saul. ªThey were also watching the gates day and night so that they might put him to death; ª2 Cor 11:32f
25 but his disciples took him by night and let him down through *an opening in* the wall, lowering him in a large basket.
26 ªWhen he came to Jerusalem, he was trying to associate with the disciples; but they were all afraid of him, not believing that he was a disciple. ªActs 22:17-20; 26:20
27 But ªBarnabas took hold of him and brought him to the apostles and described to them how he had seen the Lord on the road, and that He had talked to him, and how at Damascus he had spoken out boldly in the name of Jesus. ªActs 4:36
28 And he was with them, moving about freely in Jerusalem, ªspeaking out boldly in the name of the Lord. ªActs 4:13, 29; 9:29
29 And he was talking and arguing with the ªHellenistic *Jews;* but they were attempting to put him to death. ªActs 6:1
30 But when the brethren learned *of it,* they brought him down to ªCaesarea and ᵇsent him away to Tarsus. ªActs 8:40 ᵇGal 1:21
31 So ªthe church throughout all Judea and Galilee and Samaria enjoyed peace, being built up; and going on in the fear of the Lord and in the comfort of the Holy Spirit, it continued to increase. ªActs 5:11; 8:1

Peter's Ministry

32 Now as Peter was traveling through all *those regions,* he came down also to ªthe saints who lived at Lydda. ªActs 9:13
33 There he found a man named Aeneas, who had been bedridden eight years, for he was paralyzed.
34 Peter said to him, "Aeneas, Jesus Christ

heals you; get up and make your bed." Immediately he got up.
35 And all who lived at Lydda and Sharon saw him, and they ªturned to the Lord. ªActs 2:47; 9:42
36 Now in ªJoppa there was a disciple named Tabitha (which translated *in Greek* is called Dorcas); this woman was abounding with deeds of kindness and charity which she continually did. ªJosh 19:46; 2 Chr 2:16
37 And it happened at that time that she fell sick and died; and when they had washed her body, they laid it in an ªupper room. ªActs 1:13; 9:39
38 Since Lydda was near Joppa, ªthe disciples, having heard that Peter was there, sent two men to him, imploring him, "Do not delay in coming to us." ªActs 11:26
39 So Peter arose and went with them. When he arrived, they brought him into the ªupper room; and all the widows stood beside him, weeping and showing all the tunics and garments that Dorcas used to make while she was with them. ªActs 1:13; 9:37
40 But Peter sent them all out and knelt down and prayed, and turning to the body, he said, "ªTabitha, arise." And she opened her eyes, and when she saw Peter, she sat up. ªMark 5:41
41 And he gave her his hand and raised her up; and calling ªthe saints and widows, he presented her alive. ªActs 9:13, 32
42 It became known all over Joppa, and ªmany believed in the Lord. ªActs 9:35
43 And Peter stayed many days in Joppa with ªa tanner *named* Simon. ªActs 10:6

Cornelius's Vision

10 Now *there was* a man at ªCaesarea named Cornelius, a centurion of what was called the Italian cohort, ªActs 8:40; 10:24
2 a devout man and ªone who feared God with all his household, and ᵇgave many alms to the *Jewish* people and prayed to God continually. ªActs 10:22, 35 ᵇLuke 7:4f
3 About ªthe ninth hour of the day he clearly saw ᵇin a vision an angel of God who had *just* come in and said to him, "Cornelius!" ªActs 3:1 ᵇActs 9:10
4 And fixing his gaze on him and being much alarmed, he said, "What is it, Lord?" And he said to him, "Your prayers and alms have ascended ªas a memorial before God. ªHeb 6:10
5 "Now dispatch *some* men to ªJoppa and send for a man *named* Simon, who is also called Peter; ªActs 9:36
6 he is staying with a tanner *named* ªSimon, whose house is by the sea." ªActs 9:43
7 When the angel who was speaking to him had left, he summoned two of his servants and

a devout soldier of those who were his personal attendants,

8 and after he had explained everything to them, he sent them to ªJoppa. ªActs 9:36

9 On the next day, as they were on their way and approaching the city, ªPeter went up on the housetop about the sixth hour to pray. ªActs 10:9-32; 11:5-14

10 But he became hungry and was desiring to eat; but while they were making preparations, he ªfell into a trance; ªActs 11:5; 22:17

11 and he *saw ªthe sky opened up, and an object like a great sheet coming down, lowered by four corners to the ground, ªJohn 1:51

12 and there were in it all *kinds of* four-footed animals and crawling creatures of the earth and birds of the air.

13 A voice came to him, "Get up, Peter, kill and eat!"

14 But Peter said, "By no means, Lord, for ªI have never eaten anything unholy and unclean." ªLev 11:20-25; Deut 14:4-20

15 Again a voice *came* to him a second time, "ªWhat God has cleansed, no *longer* consider unholy." ªMatt 15:11; Mark 7:19

16 This happened three times, and immediately the object was taken up into the sky.

17 Now while Peter was greatly perplexed in mind as to what the vision which he had seen might be, behold, ªthe men who had been sent by Cornelius, having asked directions for Simon's house, appeared at the gate; ªActs 10:8

18 and calling out, they were asking whether Simon, who was also called Peter, was staying there.

19 While Peter was reflecting on the vision, ªthe Spirit said to him, "Behold, three men are looking for you. ªActs 8:29

20 "But get up, go downstairs and ªaccompany them without misgivings, for I have sent them Myself." ªActs 15:7-9

21 Peter went down to the men and said, "Behold, I am the one you are looking for; what is the reason for which you have come?"

22 They said, "Cornelius, a centurion, a righteous and ªGod-fearing man well spoken of by the entire nation of the Jews, was *divinely* directed by a holy angel to send for you *to come* to his house and hear ᵇa message from you." ªActs 10:2 ᵇActs 11:14

23 So he invited them in and gave them lodging.

Peter at Caesarea

And on the next day he got up and went away with them, and some of the brethren from Joppa accompanied him.

24 On the following day he entered ªCaesarea. Now Cornelius was waiting for them and had called together his relatives and close friends. ªActs 8:40; 10:1

25 When Peter entered, Cornelius met him, and fell at his feet and ªworshiped *him*. ªMatt 8:2

26 But Peter raised him up, saying, "ªStand up; I too am *just* a man." ªActs 14:15; Rev 19:10

27 As he talked with him, he entered and *found ªmany people assembled. ªActs 10:24

28 And he said to them, "You yourselves know how unlawful it is for a man who is a Jew to associate with a foreigner or to visit him; and *yet* ªGod has shown me that I should not call any man unholy or unclean. ªActs 10:14f, 35; 15:9

29 "That is why I came without even raising any objection when I was sent for. So I ask for what reason you have sent for me."

30 Cornelius said, "Four days ago to this hour, I was praying in my house during the ninth hour; and behold, ªa man stood before me in shining garments, ªActs 10:3-6, 30-32

31 and he *said, 'Cornelius, your prayer has been heard and your alms have been remembered before God.

32 'Therefore send to ªJoppa and invite Simon, who is also called Peter, to come to you; he is staying at the house of Simon *the* tanner by the sea.' ªJohn 4:9; 18:28

33 "So I sent for you immediately, and you have been kind enough to come. Now then, we are all here present before God to hear all that you have been commanded by the Lord."

Gentiles Hear Good News

34 ªOpening his mouth, Peter said:

"I most certainly understand *now* that ᵇGod is not one to show partiality, ªMatt 5:2 ᵇDeut 10:17

35 but in every nation the man who ªfears Him and does what is right is welcome to Him. ªActs 10:2

36 "The word which He sent to the sons of Israel, preaching ªpeace through Jesus Christ (He is ᵇLord of all)— ªEph 2:17 ᵇRom 10:12

37 you yourselves know the thing which took place throughout all Judea, starting from Galilee, after the baptism which John proclaimed.

38 "*You know of* Jesus of Nazareth, how God anointed Him with the Holy Spirit and with power, ªand *how* He went about doing good and healing all who were oppressed by the devil, for God was with Him. ªMatt 4:23

39 "We are witnesses of all the things He did both in the land of the Jews and in Jerusalem. They also ªput Him to death by hanging Him on a cross. ªActs 5:30

40 "ªGod raised Him up on the third day and granted that He become visible, ªActs 2:24

41 ªnot to all the people, but to witnesses who were chosen beforehand by God, *that is,* to us

who ate and drank with Him after He arose
from the dead. ^a*John 14:19, 22; 15:27*

42 "And He ordered us to preach to the people, and solemnly to testify that this is the One
who has been appointed by God as ^aJudge of
the living and the dead. ^a*John 5:22, 27; Acts 17:31*

43 "Of Him all the prophets bear witness that
through ^aHis name everyone who believes in
Him receives forgiveness of sins." ^a*Luke 24:47;
Acts 2:38*

44 While Peter was still speaking these words,
^athe Holy Spirit fell upon all those who were
listening to the message. ^a*Acts 11:15; 15:8*

45 ^aAll the circumcised believers who came
with Peter were amazed, because the gift of the
Holy Spirit had been ^bpoured out on the
Gentiles also. ^a*Acts 10:23* ^b*Acts 2:33, 38*

46 For they were hearing them ^aspeaking with
tongues and exalting God. Then Peter
answered, ^a*Acts 2:4; 19:6*

47 "^aSurely no one can refuse the water for
these to be baptized who ^bhave received the
Holy Spirit just as we *did*, can he?" ^a*Acts 8:36*
^b*Acts 2:4*

48 And he ordered them to be baptized ^ain the
name of Jesus Christ. Then they asked him to
stay on for a few days. ^a*Acts 2:38; 8:16*

Peter Reports at Jerusalem

11 Now the apostles and ^athe brethren who
were throughout Judea heard that the
Gentiles also had received the word of God.
^a*Acts 1:15*

2 And when Peter came up to Jerusalem,
^athose who were circumcised took issue with
him, ^a*Acts 10:45*

3 saying, "^aYou went to uncircumcised men
and ate with them." ^a*Matt 9:11; Acts 10:28*

4 But Peter began *speaking* and *proceeded* to
explain to them ^ain orderly sequence, saying,
^a*Luke 1:3*

5 "^aI was in the city of Joppa praying; and in
a trance I saw a vision, an object coming down
like a great sheet lowered by four corners from
the sky; and it came right down to me,
^a*Acts 10:9-32; 11:5-14*

6 and when I had fixed my gaze on it and
was observing it I saw the four-footed animals
of the earth and the wild beasts and the crawling creatures and the birds of the air.

7 "I also heard a voice saying to me, 'Get up,
Peter; kill and eat.'

8 "But I said, 'By no means, Lord, for nothing unholy or unclean has ever entered my
mouth.'

9 "But a voice from heaven answered a second time, '^aWhat God has cleansed, no longer
consider unholy.' ^a*Acts 10:15*

10 "This happened three times, and everything
was drawn back up into the sky.

11 "And behold, at that moment three men
appeared at the house in which we were *staying,* having been sent to me from ^aCaesarea.
^a*Acts 8:40*

12 "The Spirit told me to go with them ^awith-
out misgivings. These six brethren also went
with me and we entered the man's house.
^a*Acts 15:9; Rom 3:22*

13 "And he reported to us how he had seen the
angel standing in his house, and saying, 'Send
to Joppa and have Simon, who is also called
Peter, brought here;

14 and he will speak ^awords to you by which
you will be saved, you and ^ball your household.' ^a*Acts 10:22* ^b*John 4:53*

15 "And as I began to speak, ^athe Holy Spirit
fell upon them just ^bas *He did* upon us at the
beginning. ^a*Acts 10:44* ^b*Acts 2:4*

16 "And I remembered the word of the Lord,
how He used to say, '^aJohn baptized with
water, but you will be baptized with the Holy
Spirit.' ^a*Acts 1:5*

17 "Therefore if ^aGod gave to them the same
gift as *He gave* to us also after believing in the
Lord Jesus Christ, who was I that I could stand
in God's way?" ^a*Acts 10:45, 47*

18 When they heard this, they quieted down
and glorified God, saying, "Well then, God has
granted to the Gentiles also the ^arepentance
that leads to life." ^a*2 Cor 7:10*

The Church at Antioch

19 ^aSo then those who were scattered because
of the persecution that occurred in connection
with Stephen made their way to Phoenicia and
Cyprus and Antioch, speaking the word to no
one except to Jews alone. ^a*Acts 8:1, 4*

20 But there were some of them, men of
Cyprus and Cyrene, who came to Antioch and
began speaking to the Greeks also, ^apreaching
the Lord Jesus. ^a*Acts 5:42*

21 And ^athe hand of the Lord was with them,
and a large number who believed turned to the
Lord. ^a*Luke 1:66*

22 The news about them reached the ears of
the church at Jerusalem, and they sent ^aBarna-
bas off to Antioch. ^a*Acts 4:36*

23 Then when he arrived and witnessed ^athe
grace of God, he rejoiced and *began* to encourage them all with resolute heart to remain *true*
to the Lord; ^a*Acts 13:43; 14:26*

24 for he was a good man, and ^afull of the
Holy Spirit and of faith. And considerable
numbers were brought to the Lord. ^a*Acts 2:4*

25 And he left for ^aTarsus to look for Saul;
^a*Acts 9:11*

26 and when he had found him, he brought
him to Antioch. And for an entire year they
met with the church and taught considerable

numbers; and the disciples were first called ªChristians in Antioch. ªActs 26:28; 1 Pet 4:16

27 Now at this time ªsome prophets came down from Jerusalem to Antioch. ªLuke 11:49; Acts 2:17

28 One of them named ªAgabus stood up and *began* to indicate by the Spirit that there would certainly be a great famine all over the world. And this took place in the *reign* of Claudius. ªActs 21:10

29 And in the proportion that any of the disciples had means, each of them determined to send *a contribution* for the relief of ªthe brethren living in Judea. ªActs 11:1

30 ªAnd this they did, sending it in charge of Barnabas and Saul to the elders. ªActs 12:25

Peter's Arrest and Deliverance

12 Now about that time Herod the king laid hands on some who belonged to the church in order to mistreat them.

2 And he ªhad James the brother of John put to death with a sword. ªMatt 4:21; 20:23

3 When he saw that it ªpleased the Jews, he proceeded to arrest Peter also. Now it was during the days of Unleavened Bread. ªActs 24:27; 25:9

4 When he had seized him, he put him in prison, delivering him to four squads of soldiers to guard him, intending after ªthe Passover to bring him out before the people. ªEx 12:1-27; Mark 14:1

5 So Peter was kept in the prison, but prayer for him was being made fervently by the church to God.

6 On the very night when Herod was about to bring him forward, Peter was sleeping between two soldiers, ªbound with two chains, and guards in front of the door were watching over the prison. ªActs 21:33

7 And behold, ªan angel of the Lord suddenly ᵇappeared and a light shone in the cell; and he struck Peter's side and woke him up, saying, "Get up quickly." And his chains fell off his hands. ªActs 5:19 ᵇLuke 2:9

8 And the angel said to him, "Gird yourself and put on your sandals." And he did so. And he *said to him, "Wrap your cloak around you and follow me."

9 And he went out and continued to follow, and he did not know that what was being done by the angel was real, but thought he was seeing ªa vision. ªActs 9:10

10 When they had passed the first and second guard, they came to the iron gate that leads into the city, which ªopened for them by itself; and they went out and went along one street, and immediately the angel departed from him. ªActs 5:19; 16:26

11 When Peter came to himself, he said,

"Now I know for sure that ªthe Lord has sent forth His angel and rescued me from the hand of Herod and from all that the Jewish people were expecting." ªDan 3:28; 6:22

12 And when he realized *this,* he went to the house of Mary, the mother of ªJohn who was also called Mark, where many were gathered together and were praying. ªActs 12:25; 13:5, 13

13 When he knocked at the door of the gate, ªa servant-girl named Rhoda came to answer. ªJohn 18:16f

14 When she recognized Peter's voice, ªbecause of her joy she did not open the gate, but ran in and announced that Peter was standing in front of the gate. ªLuke 24:41

15 They said to her, "You are out of your mind!" But she kept insisting that it was so. They kept saying, "It is ªhis angel." ªMatt 18:10

16 But Peter continued knocking; and when they had opened *the door,* they saw him and were amazed.

17 But motioning to them with his hand to be silent, he described to them how the Lord had led him out of the prison. And he said, "Report these things to ªJames and the brethren." Then he left and went to another place. ªMark 6:3

18 Now when day came, there was no small disturbance among the soldiers *as to* what could have become of Peter.

19 When Herod had searched for him and had not found him, he examined the guards and ordered that they ªbe led away *to execution.* Then he went down from Judea to Caesarea and was spending time there. ªActs 16:27; 27:42

Death of Herod

20 Now he was very angry with the people of Tyre and Sidon; and with one accord they came to him, and having won over Blastus the king's chamberlain, they were asking for peace, because ªtheir country was fed by the king's country. ª1 Kin 5:11; Ezra 3:7

21 On an appointed day Herod, having put on his royal apparel, took his seat on the rostrum and *began* delivering an address to them.

22 The people kept crying out, "The voice of a god and not of a man!"

23 And immediately ªan angel of the Lord struck him because he did not give God the glory, and he was eaten by worms and died. ª2 Sam 24:16; 2 Kin 19:35

24 But ªthe word of the Lord continued to grow and to be multiplied. ªActs 6:7; 19:20

25 And Barnabas and Saul returned from Jerusalem ªwhen they had fulfilled their mission, taking along with *them* ᵇJohn, who was also called Mark. ªActs 11:30 ᵇActs 12:12

First Missionary Journey

13 Now there were at Antioch, in the church that was *there,* prophets and

[a]teachers: Barnabas, and Simeon who was called Niger, and Lucius of Cyrene, and Manaen who had been brought up with Herod the tetrarch, and Saul. [a]Rom 12:6f; 1 Cor 12:28f

2 While they were ministering to the Lord and fasting, the Holy Spirit said, "Set apart for Me Barnabas and Saul for [a]the work to which I have called them." [a]Acts 9:15

3 Then, when they had fasted and prayed and [a]laid their hands on them, they sent them away. [a]Acts 6:6

4 So, being sent out by the Holy Spirit, they went down to Seleucia and from there they sailed to [a]Cyprus. [a]Acts 4:36

5 When they reached Salamis, they *began* to proclaim the word of God in the synagogues of the Jews; and they also had [a]John as their helper. [a]Acts 12:12

6 When they had gone through the whole island as far as Paphos, they found a [a]magician, a Jewish [b]false prophet whose name was Bar-Jesus, [a]Acts 8:9 [b]Matt 7:15

7 who was with the [a]proconsul, Sergius Paulus, a man of intelligence. This man summoned Barnabas and Saul and sought to hear the word of God. [a]Acts 13:8, 12; 18:12

8 But Elymas the magician (for so his name is translated) was opposing them, seeking to turn the proconsul away from [a]the faith. [a]Acts 6:7

9 But Saul, who was also *known as* Paul, [a]filled with the Holy Spirit, fixed his gaze on him, [a]Acts 2:4; 4:8

10 and said, "You who are full of all deceit and fraud, you [a]son of the devil, you enemy of all righteousness, will you not cease to make crooked the straight ways of the Lord? [a]Matt 13:38; John 8:44

11 "Now, behold, [a]the hand of the Lord is upon you, and you will be blind and not see the sun for a time." And immediately a mist and a darkness fell upon him, and he went about seeking those who would lead him by the hand. [a]Ex 9:3; 1 Sam 5:6f

12 Then the proconsul believed when he saw what had happened, being amazed at [a]the teaching of the Lord. [a]Acts 8:25; 13:49

13 Now Paul and his companions put out to sea from Paphos and came to Perga in Pamphylia; but [a]John left them and returned to Jerusalem. [a]Acts 12:12

14 But going on from Perga, they arrived at Pisidian [a]Antioch, and on the Sabbath day they went into the synagogue and sat down. [a]Acts 14:19, 21; 2 Tim 3:11

15 After [a]the reading of the Law and [b]the Prophets the synagogue officials sent to them, saying, "Brethren, if you have any word of exhortation for the people, say it." [a]Acts 15:21 [b]Acts 13:27

16 Paul stood up, and motioning with his hand said,
"Men of Israel, and [a]you who fear God, listen: [a]Acts 10:2; 13:26

17 "The God of this people Israel chose our fathers and [a]made the people great during their stay in the land of Egypt, and with an uplifted arm [b]He led them out from it. [a]Ex 1:7 [b]Ex 12:51

18 "For [a]a period of about forty years He put up with them in the wilderness. [a]Num 14:34; Acts 7:36

19 "When He had destroyed [a]seven nations in the land of Canaan, He [b]distributed their land as an inheritance—*all of which took* about four hundred and fifty years. [a]Deut 7:1 [b]Josh 14:1

20 "After these things He [a]gave *them* judges until Samuel the prophet. [a]Judg 2:16

21 "Then they [a]asked for a king, and God gave them [b]Saul the son of Kish, a man of the tribe of Benjamin, for forty years. [a]1 Sam 8:5 [b]1 Sam 9:1f

22 "After He had removed him, He raised up David to be their king, concerning whom He also testified and said, '[a]I HAVE FOUND DAVID the son of Jesse, A MAN AFTER MY HEART, who will do all My will.' [a]1 Sam 13:14; Ps 89:20

23 "From the descendants of this man, according to promise, God has brought to Israel [a]a Savior, Jesus, [a]Luke 2:11; John 4:42

24 after [a]John had proclaimed before His coming a baptism of repentance to all the people of Israel. [a]Mark 1:1-4; Acts 1:22

25 "And while John was completing his course, [a]he kept saying, 'What do you suppose that I am? I am not *He.* But behold, one is coming after me the sandals of whose feet I am not worthy to untie.' [a]Matt 3:11; Mark 1:7

26 "Brethren, sons of Abraham's family, and those among you who fear God, to us the message of [a]this salvation has been sent. [a]John 6:68; Acts 4:12

27 "For those who live in Jerusalem, and their rulers, [a]recognizing neither Him nor the utterances of the prophets which are read every Sabbath, fulfilled *these* by condemning *Him.* [a]Acts 3:17

28 "And though they found no ground for *putting Him to* death, they [a]asked Pilate that He be executed. [a]Matt 27:22, 23; Mark 15:13, 14

29 "When they had [a]carried out all that was written concerning Him, [b]they took Him down from the cross and laid Him in a tomb. [a]Acts 26:22 [b]Luke 23:53

30 "But God [a]raised Him from the dead; [a]Acts 2:24; 13:33, 34, 37

31 and for many days [a]He appeared to those who came up with Him from Galilee to Jerusalem, the very ones who are now [b]His witnesses to the people. [a]Acts 1:3 [b]Luke 24:48

32 "And we preach to you the good news of ^athe promise made to the fathers, ^a*Rom 4:13*

33 that God has fulfilled this *promise* to our children in that He raised up Jesus, as it is also written in the second Psalm, '^aYOU ARE MY SON; TODAY I HAVE BEGOTTEN YOU.' ^a*Ps 2:7*

34 "*As for the fact* that He raised Him up from the dead, no longer to return to decay, He has spoken in this way: '^aI WILL GIVE YOU THE HOLY *and* SURE *blessings* OF DAVID.' ^a*Is 55:3*

35 "Therefore He also says in another *Psalm,* '^aYOU WILL NOT ALLOW YOUR HOLY ONE TO UNDERGO DECAY.' ^a*Ps 16:10; Acts 2:27*

36 "For David, after he had served ^athe purpose of God in his own generation, fell asleep, and was laid among his fathers and underwent decay; ^a*Acts 13:22; 20:27*

37 but He whom God ^araised did not undergo decay. ^a*Acts 2:24; 13:30, 33, 34*

38 "Therefore let it be known to you, brethren, that ^athrough Him forgiveness of sins is proclaimed to you, ^a*Luke 24:47; Acts 2:38*

39 and through Him ^aeveryone who believes is freed from all things, from which you could not be freed through the Law of Moses. ^a*Acts 10:43; Rom 3:28*

40 "Therefore take heed, so that the thing spoken of ^ain the Prophets may not come upon *you:* ^a*Luke 24:44; John 6:45*

41 '^aBEHOLD, YOU SCOFFERS, AND MARVEL, AND PERISH;

FOR I AM ACCOMPLISHING A WORK IN YOUR DAYS,

A WORK WHICH YOU WILL NEVER BELIEVE, THOUGH SOMEONE SHOULD DESCRIBE IT TO YOU.' " ^a*Hab 1:5*

42 As Paul and Barnabas were going out, the people kept begging that these things might be spoken to them the next ^aSabbath. ^a*Acts 13:14*

43 Now when *the meeting of* the synagogue had broken up, many of the Jews and of the ^aGod-fearing proselytes followed Paul and Barnabas, who, speaking to them, were urging them to continue in ^bthe grace of God. ^a*Acts 17:4, 17* ^b*Acts 11:23*

Paul Turns to the Gentiles

44 The next ^aSabbath nearly the whole city assembled to hear the word of the Lord. ^a*Acts 13:14*

45 But when ^athe Jews saw the crowds, they were filled with jealousy and *began* contradicting the things spoken by Paul, and were blaspheming. ^a*Acts 13:50; 14:2, 4, 5, 19*

46 Paul and Barnabas spoke out boldly and said, "It was necessary that the word of God be spoken to you ^afirst; since you repudiate it and judge yourselves unworthy of eternal life, behold, ^bwe are turning to the Gentiles. ^a*Acts 3:26* ^b*Acts 18:6; 22:21*

47 "For so the Lord has commanded us,

'^aI HAVE PLACED YOU AS A LIGHT FOR THE GENTILES,

THAT YOU MAY BRING SALVATION TO THE END OF THE EARTH.' " ^a*Is 42:6; 49:6*

48 When the Gentiles heard this, they *began* rejoicing and glorifying the word of the Lord; and as many as ^ahad been appointed to eternal life believed. ^a*Rom 8:28ff; Eph 1:4f, 11*

49 And ^athe word of the Lord was being spread through the whole region. ^a*Acts 13:12*

50 But the Jews incited the ^adevout women of prominence and the leading men of the city, and instigated a persecution against Paul and Barnabas, and drove them out of their district. ^a*Acts 16:14; 17:4*

51 But ^athey shook off the dust of their feet *in protest* against them and went to Iconium. ^a*Matt 10:14; Mark 6:11*

52 And the disciples were continually ^afilled with joy and with the Holy Spirit. ^a*Acts 2:4*

Acceptance and Opposition

14 In Iconium ^athey entered the synagogue of the Jews together, and spoke in such a manner ^bthat a large number of people believed, both of Jews and of Greeks. ^a*Acts 13:5* ^b*Acts 2:47*

2 But the Jews who ^adisbelieved stirred up the minds of the Gentiles and embittered them against the brethren. ^a*John 3:36*

3 Therefore they spent a long time *there* ^aspeaking boldly *with reliance* upon the Lord, who was testifying to the word of His grace, granting that signs and wonders be done by their hands. ^a*Acts 4:29f; 20:32*

4 ^aBut the people of the city were divided; and some sided with ^bthe Jews, and some with the apostles. ^a*Acts 17:4* ^b*Acts 13:45, 50*

5 And when an attempt was made by both the Gentiles and the Jews with their rulers, to mistreat and to ^astone them, ^a*Acts 14:19*

6 they became aware of it and fled to the cities of Lycaonia, Lystra and ^aDerbe, and the surrounding region; ^a*Acts 14:20; 16:1*

7 and there they continued to ^apreach the gospel. ^a*Acts 14:15, 21; 16:10*

8 At Lystra ^aa man was sitting who had no strength in his feet, lame from his mother's womb, who had never walked. ^a*Acts 3:2*

9 This man was listening to Paul as he spoke, who, when he had fixed his gaze on him and had seen that he had ^afaith to be made well, ^a*Matt 9:28*

10 said with a loud voice, "Stand upright on your feet." ^aAnd he leaped up and *began* to walk. ^a*Acts 3:8*

11 When the crowds saw what Paul had done, they raised their voice, saying in the Lycaonian

language, "ªThe gods have become like men and have come down to us." ªActs 28:6

12 And they *began* calling Barnabas, Zeus, and Paul, Hermes, because he was the chief speaker.

13 The priest of Zeus, whose *temple* was just outside the city, brought oxen and garlands to the gates, and ªwanted to offer sacrifice with the crowds. ªDan 2:46

14 But when the apostles Barnabas and Paul heard of it, they ªtore their robes and rushed out into the crowd, crying out ªNum 14:6; Matt 26:65

15 and saying, "Men, why are you doing these things? We are also men of the same nature as you, and we preach the gospel to you that you should turn from these vain things to a living God, ªWHO MADE THE HEAVEN AND THE EARTH AND THE SEA AND ALL THAT IS IN THEM. ªEx 20:11; Ps 146:6

16 "In the generations gone by He ªpermitted all the nations to go their own ways; ªActs 17:30

17 and yet ªHe did not leave Himself without witness, in that He did good and gave you rains from heaven and fruitful seasons, satisfying your hearts with food and gladness."
ªActs 17:26f; Rom 1:19f

18 *Even* saying these things, with difficulty they restrained the crowds from offering sacrifice to them.

19 But Jews came from Antioch and Iconium, and having won over the crowds, they ªstoned Paul and dragged him out of the city, supposing him to be dead. ªActs 14:5; 2 Cor 11:25

20 But while ªthe disciples stood around him, he got up and entered the city. The next day he went away with Barnabas to Derbe. ªActs 11:26; 14:22, 28

21 After they had preached the gospel to that city and had ªmade many disciples, they returned to Lystra and to Iconium and to Antioch, ªActs 2:47

22 strengthening the souls of the disciples, encouraging them to continue in ªthe faith, and *saying*, "ᵇThrough many tribulations we must enter the kingdom of God." ªActs 6:7 ᵇJohn 16:33

23 When ªthey had appointed elders for them in every church, having ᵇprayed with fasting, they commended them to the Lord in whom they had believed. ªTitus 1:5 ᵇActs 13:3

24 They passed through ªPisidia and came into ᵇPamphylia. ªActs 13:14 ᵇActs 13:13

25 When they had spoken the word in ªPerga, they went down to Attalia. ªActs 13:13

26 From there they sailed to Antioch, from which they had been ªcommended to the grace of God for the work that they had accomplished. ªActs 11:23; 15:40

27 When they had arrived and gathered the church together, they *began* to report all things that God had done with them and how He had opened a ªdoor of faith to the Gentiles.
ª1 Cor 16:9; 2 Cor 2:12

28 And they spent a long time with ªthe disciples. ªActs 11:26; 14:22

The Council at Jerusalem

15 ªSome men came down from Judea and *began* teaching the brethren, "Unless you are circumcised according to the custom of Moses, you cannot be saved." ªActs 15:24

2 And when Paul and Barnabas had great dissension and ªdebate with them, *the brethren* determined that Paul and Barnabas and some others of them should go up to Jerusalem to the apostles and elders concerning this issue.
ªActs 15:7

3 Therefore, being ªsent on their way by the church, they were passing through both Phoenicia and Samaria, describing in detail the conversion of the Gentiles, and were bringing great joy to all the brethren. ªActs 20:38; 21:5

4 When they arrived at Jerusalem, they were received by the church and the apostles and the elders, and they ªreported all that God had done with them. ªActs 14:27; 15:12

5 But some of ªthe sect of the Pharisees who had believed stood up, saying, "It is necessary to ᵇcircumcise them and to direct them to observe the Law of Moses." ªActs 26:5 ᵇ1 Cor 7:18

6 ªThe apostles and the elders came together to look into this matter. ªActs 11:30; 15:4, 22, 23

7 After there had been much debate, Peter stood up and said to them, "Brethren, you know that in the early days God made a choice among you, that by my mouth the Gentiles would hear the word of ªthe gospel and believe. ªActs 20:24

8 "And God, ªwho knows the heart, testified to them ᵇgiving them the Holy Spirit, just as He also did to us; ªActs 1:24 ᵇActs 2:4

9 and ªHe made no distinction between us and them, cleansing their hearts by faith.
ªActs 10:28, 34; 11:12

10 "Now therefore why do you ªput God to the test by placing upon the neck of the disciples a yoke which neither our fathers nor we have been able to bear? ªActs 5:9

11 "But we believe that we are saved through ªthe grace of the Lord Jesus, in the same way as they also are." ªRom 3:24; 5:15

12 All the people kept silent, and they were listening to Barnabas and Paul as they were ªrelating what signs and wonders God had done through them among the Gentiles.
ªActs 14:27; 15:3, 4

James's Judgment

13 After they had stopped speaking, ªJames answered, saying, "Brethren, listen to me.
ªActs 12:17

14 "ªSimeon has related how God first con-

cerned Himself about taking from among the Gentiles a people for His name. ªActs 15:7; 2 Pet 1:1

15 "With this the words of ªthe Prophets agree, just as it is written, ªActs 13:40

16 'ªAFTER THESE THINGS I will return,
AND I WILL REBUILD THE TABERNACLE OF
DAVID WHICH HAS FALLEN,
AND I WILL REBUILD ITS RUINS,
AND I WILL RESTORE IT, ªAmos 9:11

17 ªSO THAT THE REST OF MANKIND MAY SEEK
THE LORD,
AND ALL THE GENTILES WHO ARE CALLED BY
MY NAME,' ªAmos 9:12

18 SAYS THE LORD, WHO ªMAKES THESE THINGS
KNOWN FROM LONG AGO. ªIs 45:21

19 "Therefore it is ªmy judgment that we do not trouble those who are turning to God from among the Gentiles, ªActs 15:28; 21:25

20 but that we write to them that they abstain from things contaminated by idols and from ªfornication and from ᵇwhat is strangled and from blood. ªLev 18:6-23 ᵇLev 17:14

21 "For ªMoses from ancient generations has in every city those who preach him, since he is read in the synagogues every Sabbath." ªActs 13:15; 2 Cor 3:14f

22 Then it seemed good to the apostles and the elders, with the whole church, to choose men from among them to send to Antioch with Paul and Barnabas—Judas called Barsabbas, and ªSilas, leading men among the brethren, ªActs 15:27, 32, 40; 16:19, 25, 29

23 and they sent this letter by them,
"ªThe apostles and the brethren who are elders, to the brethren in Antioch and Syria and Cilicia who are from the Gentiles, greetings. ªActs 15:2

24 "Since we have heard that some of our number to whom we gave no instruction have ªdisturbed you with *their* words, unsettling your souls, ªGal 1:7; 5:10

25 ªit seemed good to us, having become of one mind, to select men to send to you with our beloved Barnabas and Paul, ªActs 15:28

26 men who have ªrisked their lives for the name of our Lord Jesus Christ. ªActs 9:23ff; 14:19

27 "Therefore we have sent ªJudas and Silas, who themselves will also report the same things by word *of mouth.* ªActs 15:22, 32

28 "For it seemed good to ªthe Holy Spirit and to us to lay upon you no greater burden than these essentials: ªActs 5:32; 15:8

29 that you abstain from ªthings sacrificed to idols and from ªblood and from things strangled and from fornication; if you keep yourselves free from such things, you will do well. Farewell." ªActs 15:20

30 So when they were sent away, ªthey went down to Antioch; and having gathered the congregation together, they delivered the letter. ªActs 15:22f

31 When they had read it, they rejoiced because of its encouragement.

32 Judas and Silas, also being ªprophets themselves, encouraged and strengthened the brethren with a lengthy message. ªActs 13:1

33 After they had spent time *there,* they were sent away from the brethren ªin peace to those who had sent them out. ªMark 5:34; Acts 16:36

34 [But it seemed good to Silas to remain there.]

35 But Paul and Barnabas stayed in Antioch, teaching and ªpreaching with many others also, the word of the Lord. ªActs 8:4

Second Missionary Journey

36 After some days Paul said to Barnabas, "Let us return and visit the brethren in ªevery city in which we proclaimed the word of the Lord, *and see* how they are." ªActs 13:4, 13, 14, 51; 14:6, 24f

37 Barnabas wanted to take ªJohn, called Mark, along with them also. ªActs 12:12

38 But Paul kept insisting that they should not take him along who had ªdeserted them in Pamphylia and had not gone with them to the work. ªActs 13:13

39 And there occurred such a sharp disagreement that they separated from one another, and Barnabas took Mark with him and sailed away to ªCyprus. ªActs 4:36

40 But Paul chose ªSilas and left, being committed by the brethren to the grace of the Lord. ªActs 15:22

41 And he was traveling through ªSyria and Cilicia, strengthening the churches. ªMatt 4:24; Acts 15:23

The Macedonian Vision

16 Paul came also to Derbe and to Lystra. And a disciple was there, named ªTimothy, the son of a ᵇJewish woman who was a believer, but his father was a Greek, ªActs 17:14f ᵇ2 Tim 1:5

2 and he was well spoken of by ªthe brethren who were in Lystra and Iconium. ªActs 16:40

3 Paul wanted this man to go with him; and he ªtook him and circumcised him because of the Jews who were in those parts, for they all knew that his father was a Greek. ªGal 2:3

4 Now while they were passing through the cities, they were delivering ªthe decrees which had been decided upon by the apostles and elders who were in Jerusalem, for them to observe. ªActs 15:28f

5 So ªthe churches were being strengthened in the faith, and were ᵇincreasing in number daily. ªActs 9:31 ᵇActs 2:47

6 They passed through the Phrygian and aGalatian region, having been forbidden by the Holy Spirit to speak the word in Asia; aActs 18:23; 1 Cor 16:1

7 and after they came to Mysia, they were trying to go into Bithynia, and the aSpirit of Jesus did not permit them; aLuke 24:49; Acts 8:29

8 and passing by Mysia, they came down to aTroas. aActs 16:11; 20:5f

9 A vision appeared to Paul in the night: a man of aMacedonia was standing and appealing to him, and saying, "Come over to Macedonia and help us." aActs 16:10, 12; 18:5

10 When he had seen the vision, immediately awe sought to go into Macedonia, concluding that God had called us to preach the gospel to them. aActs 16:10-17; 20:5-15

11 So putting out to sea from aTroas, we ran a straight course to Samothrace, and on the day following to Neapolis; aActs 16:8; 20:5f

12 and from there to aPhilippi, which is a leading city of the district of Macedonia, a *Roman* colony; and we were staying in this city for some days. aActs 20:6; Phil 1:1

13 And on athe Sabbath day we went outside the gate to a riverside, where we were supposing that there would be a place of prayer; and we sat down and began speaking to the women who had assembled. aActs 13:14

First Convert in Europe

14 A woman named Lydia, from the city of Thyatira, a seller of purple fabrics, aa worshiper of God, was listening; and the Lord bopened her heart to respond to the things spoken by Paul. aActs 18:7 bLuke 24:45

15 And when she and aher household had been baptized, she urged us, saying, "If you have judged me to be faithful to the Lord, come into my house and stay." And she prevailed upon us. aActs 11:14

16 It happened that as we were going to the place of prayer, a slave-girl having aa spirit of divination met us, who was bringing her masters much profit by fortune-telling. aLev 19:31; 20:6, 27

17 Following after Paul and us, she kept crying out, saying, "These men are bond-servants of athe Most High God, who are proclaiming to you the way of salvation." aMark 5:7

18 She continued doing this for many days. But Paul was greatly annoyed, and turned and said to the spirit, "I command you ain the name of Jesus Christ to come out of her!" And it came out at that very moment. aLuke 10:17

19 But when her masters saw that their hope of aprofit was gone, they seized Paul and Silas and bdragged them into the market place before the authorities, aActs 16:16 bActs 17:6f

20 and when they had brought them to the chief magistrates, they said, "These men are throwing our city into confusion, being Jews,

21 and aare proclaiming customs which it is not lawful for us to accept or to observe, being Romans." aEsth 3:8

Paul and Silas Imprisoned

22 The crowd rose up together against them, and the chief magistrates tore their robes off them and proceeded to order *them* to be abeaten with rods. a2 Cor 11:25; 1 Thess 2:2

23 When they had struck them with many blows, they threw them into prison, commanding athe jailer to guard them securely; aActs 16:27, 36

24 and he, having received such a command, threw them into the inner prison and fastened their feet in athe stocks. aJob 13:27; 33:11

25 But about midnight Paul and Silas were praying and asinging hymns of praise to God, and the prisoners were listening to them; aEph 5:19

26 and suddenly there came a great earthquake, so that the foundations of the prison house were shaken; and immediately aall the doors were opened and everyone's bchains were unfastened. aActs 12:10 bActs 12:7

27 When athe jailer awoke and saw the prison doors opened, he drew his sword and was about bto kill himself, supposing that the prisoners had escaped. aActs 16:23, 36 bActs 12:19

28 But Paul cried out with a loud voice, saying, "Do not harm yourself, for we are all here!"

29 And he called for lights and rushed in, and trembling with fear he fell down before aPaul and Silas, aActs 16:19

30 and after he brought them out, he said, "Sirs, awhat must I do to be saved?" aActs 2:37; 22:10

The Jailer Converted

31 They said, "Believe in the Lord Jesus, and you will be saved, you and ayour household." aActs 11:14; 16:15

32 And they spoke the word of the Lord to him together with all who were in his house.

33 And he took them athat *very* hour of the night and washed their wounds, and immediately he was baptized, he and all his *household*. aActs 16:25

34 And he brought them into his house and set food before them, and rejoiced greatly, having believed in God with ahis whole household. aActs 11:14; 16:15

35 Now when day came, the chief magistrates sent their policemen, saying, "Release those men."

36 And athe jailer reported these words to Paul, *saying*, "The chief magistrates have sent to release you. Therefore come out now and go *bin peace.*" ᵃActs 16:27 ᵇActs 15:33

37 But Paul said to them, "They have beaten us in public without trial, ᵃmen who are Romans, and have thrown us into prison; and now are they sending us away secretly? No indeed! But let them come themselves and bring us out." ᵃActs 22:25-29

38 The policemen reported these words to the chief magistrates. They were afraid when they heard that they were Romans, ᵃActs 22:29

39 and they came and appealed to them, and when they had brought them out, they kept begging them ᵃto leave the city. ᵃMatt 8:34

40 They went out of the prison and entered *the house of* ᵃLydia, and when they saw the brethren, they encouraged them and departed. ᵃActs 16:14

Paul at Thessalonica

17 Now when they had traveled through Amphipolis and Apollonia, they came to ᵃThessalonica, where there was a synagogue of the Jews. ᵃActs 17:11, 13; 20:4

2 And according to Paul's custom, he went to them, and for three ᵃSabbaths reasoned with them from the Scriptures, ᵃActs 13:14

3 explaining and giving evidence that the Christ ᵃhad to suffer and ᵇrise again from the dead, and *saying,* "This Jesus whom I am proclaiming to you is the Christ." ᵃActs 3:18 ᵇJohn 20:9

4 And some of them were persuaded and joined Paul and Silas, along with a large number of the ᵃGod-fearing Greeks and a number of the ᵇleading women. ᵃActs 13:43 ᵇActs 13:50

5 But ᵃthe Jews, becoming jealous and taking along some wicked men from the market place, formed a mob and set the city in an uproar; and attacking the house of Jason, they were seeking to bring them out to the people. ᵃActs 17:13; 1 Thess 2:14ff

6 When they did not find them, they *began* dragging Jason and some brethren before the city authorities, shouting, "These men who have upset ᵃthe world have come here also; ᵃMatt 24:14; Acts 17:31

7 and Jason ᵃhas welcomed them, and they all act contrary to the decrees of Caesar, saying that there is another king, Jesus." ᵃLuke 10:38; James 2:25

8 They stirred up the crowd and the city authorities who heard these things.

9 And when they had received a pledge from ᵃJason and the others, they released them. ᵃActs 17:5

Paul at Berea

10 The brethren immediately sent Paul and Silas away by night to ᵃBerea, and when they arrived, they went into the synagogue of the Jews. ᵃActs 17:13; 20:4

11 Now these were more noble-minded than those in ᵃThessalonica, for they received the word with great eagerness, examining the Scriptures daily *to see* whether these things were so. ᵃActs 17:1

12 Therefore many of them believed, along with a number of prominent Greek ᵃwomen and men. ᵃActs 13:50

13 But when the Jews of Thessalonica found out that the word of God had been proclaimed by Paul in ᵃBerea also, they came there as well, agitating and stirring up the crowds. ᵃActs 17:10; 20:4

14 Then immediately the brethren sent Paul out to go as far as the sea; and ᵃSilas and ᵇTimothy remained there. ᵃActs 15:22 ᵇActs 16:1

15 Now those who escorted Paul brought him as far as ᵃAthens; and receiving a command for Silas and Timothy to come to him as soon as possible, they left. ᵃActs 17:16, 21f; 18:1

Paul at Athens

16 Now while Paul was waiting for them at ᵃAthens, his spirit was being provoked within him as he was observing the city full of idols. ᵃActs 17:15, 21f; 18:1

17 So he was reasoning ᵃin the synagogue with the Jews and ᵇthe God-fearing *Gentiles,* and in the market place every day with those who happened to be present. ᵃActs 9:20 ᵇActs 17:4

18 And also some of the Epicurean and Stoic philosophers were conversing with him. Some were saying, "What would this idle babbler wish to say?" Others, "He seems to be a proclaimer of strange deities,"—because he was preaching ᵃJesus and the resurrection. ᵃActs 4:2; 17:31f

19 And they ᵃtook him and brought him to the Areopagus, saying, "May we know what this new teaching is which you are proclaiming? ᵃActs 23:19

20 "For you are bringing some strange things to our ears; so we want to know what these things mean."

21 (Now all the Athenians and the strangers ᵃvisiting there used to spend their time in nothing other than telling or hearing something new.) ᵃActs 2:10

Sermon on Mars Hill

22 So Paul stood in the midst of the Areopagus and said, "Men of Athens, I observe that you are very ᵃreligious in all respects. ᵃActs 25:19

23 "For while I was passing through and examining the ᵃobjects of your worship, I also found an altar with this inscription, 'TO AN UNKNOWN GOD.' Therefore what you wor-

ship in ignorance, this I proclaim to you. [a]2 Thess 2:4

24 "[a]The God who made the world and all things in it, since He is [b]Lord of heaven and earth, does not dwell in temples made with hands; [a]Is 42:5 [b]Deut 10:14

25 nor is He served by human hands, [a]as though He needed anything, since He Himself gives to all *people* life and breath and all things; [a]Job 22:2; Ps 50:10-12

26 and He made from one *man* every nation of mankind to live on all the face of the earth, having [a]determined *their* appointed times and the boundaries of their habitation, [a]Deut 32:8; Job 12:23

27 that they would seek God, if perhaps they might grope for Him and find Him, [a]though He is not far from each one of us; [a]Deut 4:7; Jer 23:23f

28 for [a]in Him we live and move and exist, as even some of your own poets have said, 'For we also are His children.' [a]Job 12:10; Dan 5:23

29 "Being then the children of God, we [a]ought not to think that the Divine Nature is like gold or silver or stone, an image formed by the art and thought of man. [a]Is 40:18ff; Rom 1:23

30 "Therefore having [a]overlooked the times of ignorance, God is now declaring to men that all *people* everywhere should repent, [a]Acts 14:16; Rom 3:25

31 because He has fixed a day in which [a]He will judge the world in righteousness through a Man whom He has appointed, having furnished proof to all men by raising Him from the dead." [a]Ps 9:8; 96:13

32 Now when they heard of [a]the resurrection of the dead, some *began* to sneer, but others said, "We shall hear you again concerning this." [a]Acts 17:18, 31

33 So Paul went out of their midst.

34 But some men joined him and believed, among whom also were Dionysius the [a]Areopagite and a woman named Damaris and others with them. [a]Acts 17:19, 22

Paul at Corinth

18 After these things he left Athens and went to [a]Corinth. [a]Acts 18:8; 19:1

2 And he found a Jew named [a]Aquila, a native of Pontus, having recently come from Italy with his wife [a]Priscilla, because Claudius had commanded all the Jews to leave Rome. He came to them, [a]Acts 18:18, 26; Rom 16:3

3 and because he was of the same trade, he stayed with them and [a]they were working, for by trade they were tent-makers. [a]Acts 20:34; 1 Cor 4:12

4 And he was reasoning in the synagogue every [a]Sabbath and trying to persuade Jews and Greeks. [a]Acts 13:14

5 But when Silas and Timothy came down from Macedonia, Paul *began* devoting himself completely to the word, solemnly [a]testifying to the Jews that [b]Jesus was the Christ. [a]Acts 20:21 [b]Acts 17:3

6 But when they resisted and blasphemed, he shook out his garments and said to them, "Your [a]blood *be* on your own heads! I am clean. From now on I will go [b]to the Gentiles." [a]2 Sam 1:16 [b]Acts 13:46

7 Then he left there and went to the house of a man named Titius Justus, [a]a worshiper of God, whose house was next to the synagogue. [a]Acts 13:43; 16:14

8 [a]Crispus, the leader of the synagogue, believed in the Lord [b]with all his household, and many of the Corinthians when they heard were believing and being baptized. [a]1 Cor 1:14 [b]Acts 11:14

9 And the Lord said to Paul in the night by [a]a vision, "Do not be afraid *any longer,* but go on speaking and do not be silent; [a]Acts 9:10

10 for I am with you, and no man will attack you in order to harm you, for I have many people in this city."

11 And he settled *there* a year and six months, teaching the word of God among them.

12 But while Gallio was proconsul of Achaia, [a]the Jews with one accord rose up against Paul and brought him before [b]the judgment seat, [a]1 Thess 2:14ff [b]Matt 27:19

13 saying, "This man persuades men to worship God contrary to [a]the law." [a]John 19:7; Acts 18:15

14 But when Paul was about to [a]open his mouth, Gallio said to the Jews, "If it were a matter of wrong or of vicious crime, O Jews, it would be reasonable for me to put up with you; [a]Matt 5:2

15 but if there are [a]questions about words and names and your own law, look after it yourselves; I am unwilling to be a judge of these matters." [a]Acts 23:29; 25:19

16 And he drove them away from [a]the judgment seat. [a]Matt 27:19

17 And they all took hold of [a]Sosthenes, the leader of the synagogue, and *began* beating him in front of the judgment seat. But Gallio was not concerned about any of these things. [a]1 Cor 1:1

18 Paul, having remained many days longer, took leave of the brethren and put out to sea for Syria, and with him were Priscilla and Aquila. In Cenchrea he [a]had his hair cut, for he was keeping a vow. [a]Num 6:2, 5, 9, 18; Acts 21:24

19 They came to [a]Ephesus, and he left them there. Now he himself entered the synagogue and reasoned with the Jews. [a]Acts 18:21, 24; 19:1, 17, 26, 28, 34f

20 When they asked him to stay for a longer time, he did not consent,

21 but taking leave of them and saying, "I will return to you again ᵃif God wills," he set sail from Ephesus. ᵃRom 1:10; 15:32

22 When he had landed at ᵃCaesarea, he went up and greeted the church, and went down to ᵇAntioch. ᵃActs 8:40 ᵇActs 11:19

Third Missionary Journey

23 And having spent some time *there,* he left and passed successively through the ᵃGalatian region and Phrygia, strengthening all the disciples. ᵃActs 16:6

24 Now a Jew named ᵃApollos, an Alexandrian by birth, an eloquent man, came to Ephesus; and he was mighty in the Scriptures. ᵃActs 19:1; 1 Cor 1:12

25 This man had been instructed in ᵃthe way of the Lord; and being fervent in spirit, he was speaking and teaching accurately the things concerning Jesus, being acquainted only with ᵇthe baptism of John; ᵃActs 9:2 ᵇLuke 7:29

26 and he began to speak out boldly in the synagogue. But when ᵃPriscilla and Aquila heard him, they took him aside and explained to him the way of God more accurately. ᵃActs 18:2, 18

27 And when he wanted to go across to Achaia, the brethren encouraged him and wrote to ᵃthe disciples to welcome him; and when he had arrived, he greatly helped those who had believed through grace, ᵃActs 11:26

28 for he powerfully refuted the Jews in public, demonstrating ᵃby the Scriptures that ᵇJesus was the Christ. ᵃActs 8:35 ᵇActs 18:5

Paul at Ephesus

19 It happened that while ᵃApollos was at Corinth, Paul passed through the ᵇupper country and came to Ephesus, and found some disciples. ᵃ1 Cor 1:12 ᵇActs 18:23

2 He said to them, "ᵃDid you receive the Holy Spirit when you believed?" And they *said* to him, "No, we have not even heard whether there is a Holy Spirit." ᵃActs 8:15f; 11:16f

3 And he said, "Into what then were you baptized?" And they said, "ᵃInto John's baptism." ᵃLuke 7:29; Acts 18:25

4 Paul said, "ᵃJohn baptized with the baptism of repentance, telling the people to believe in Him who was coming after him, that is, in Jesus." ᵃMatt 3:11; Mark 1:4, 7, 8

5 When they heard this, they were ᵃbaptized in the name of the Lord Jesus. ᵃActs 8:12, 16; 10:48

6 And when Paul had ᵃlaid his hands upon them, the Holy Spirit came on them, and they *began* ᵇspeaking with tongues and prophesying. ᵃActs 8:17 ᵇActs 2:4; 10:46

7 There were in all about twelve men.

8 And he entered ᵃthe synagogue and continued speaking out boldly for three months, reasoning and persuading *them* ᵇabout the kingdom of God. ᵃActs 9:20 ᵇActs 1:3

9 But when ᵃsome were becoming hardened and disobedient, speaking evil of ᵇthe Way before the people, he withdrew from them and took away the disciples, reasoning daily in the school of Tyrannus. ᵃActs 14:4 ᵇActs 9:2

10 This took place for two years, so that all who lived in ᵃAsia heard the word of the Lord, both Jews and Greeks. ᵃActs 16:6; 19:22, 26, 27

Miracles at Ephesus

11 God was performing ᵃextraordinary miracles by the hands of Paul, ᵃActs 8:13

12 ᵃso that handkerchiefs or aprons were even carried from his body to the sick, and the diseases left them and the evil spirits went out. ᵃActs 5:15

13 But also some of the Jewish ᵃexorcists, who went from place to place, attempted to name over those who had the evil spirits the name of the Lord Jesus, saying, "I adjure you by Jesus whom Paul preaches." ᵃMatt 12:27; Luke 11:19

14 Seven sons of one Sceva, a Jewish chief priest, were doing this.

15 And the evil spirit answered and said to them, "I recognize Jesus, and I know about Paul, but who are you?"

16 And the man, in whom was the evil spirit, leaped on them and subdued all of them and overpowered them, so that they fled out of that house naked and wounded.

17 This became known to all, both Jews and Greeks, who lived in ᵃEphesus; and fear fell upon them all and the name of the Lord Jesus was being magnified. ᵃActs 18:19

18 Many also of those who had believed kept coming, confessing and disclosing their practices.

19 And many of those who practiced magic brought their books together and *began* burning them in the sight of everyone; and they counted up the price of them and found it fifty thousand ᵃpieces of silver. ᵃLuke 15:8

20 So the word of the Lord ᵃwas growing mightily and prevailing. ᵃActs 6:7; 12:24

21 Now after these things were finished, Paul purposed in the spirit to ᵃgo to Jerusalem after he had passed through Macedonia and Achaia, saying, "After I have been there, ᵇI must also see Rome." ᵃActs 20:16, 22 ᵇActs 23:11

22 And having sent into Macedonia two of those who ministered to him, ᵃTimothy and ᵇErastus, he himself stayed in Asia for a while. ᵃActs 16:1 ᵇRom 16:23

23 About that time there occurred no small disturbance concerning ᵃthe Way. ᵃActs 19:9

24 For a man named Demetrius, a silversmith,

who made silver shrines of Artemis, [a]was bringing no little business to the craftsmen; [a]Acts 16:16, 19f

25 these he gathered together with the workmen of similar *trades,* and said, "Men, you know that our prosperity depends upon this business.

26 "You see and hear that not only in Ephesus, but in almost all of Asia, this Paul has persuaded and turned away a considerable number of people, saying that [a]gods made with hands are no gods *at all.* [a]Deut 4:28; Ps 115:4

27 "Not only is there danger that this trade of ours fall into disrepute, but also that the temple of the great goddess Artemis be regarded as worthless and that she whom all of Asia and [a]the world worship will even be dethroned from her magnificence." [a]Matt 24:14

28 When they heard *this* and were filled with rage, they *began* crying out, saying, "Great is Artemis of the [a]Ephesians!" [a]Acts 18:19

29 The city was filled with the confusion, and they rushed with one accord into the theater, dragging along Gaius and [a]Aristarchus, Paul's traveling companions from Macedonia. [a]Acts 20:4; 27:2

30 And when Paul wanted to go into the assembly, [a]the disciples would not let him. [a]Acts 19:9

31 Also some of the Asiarchs who were friends of his sent to him and repeatedly urged him not to venture into the theater.

32 [a]So then, some were shouting one thing and some another, for the assembly was in confusion and the majority did not know for what reason they had come together. [a]Acts 21:34

33 Some of the crowd concluded *it was* Alexander, since the Jews had put him forward; and having [a]motioned with his hand, Alexander was intending to make a defense to the assembly. [a]Acts 12:17

34 But when they recognized that he was a Jew, a *single* outcry arose from them all as they shouted for about two hours, "Great is Artemis of the Ephesians!"

35 After quieting the crowd, the town clerk *said, "Men of [a]Ephesus, what man is there after all who does not know that the city of the Ephesians is guardian of the temple of the great Artemis and of the *image* which fell down from heaven? [a]Acts 18:19

36 "So, since these are undeniable facts, you ought to keep calm and to do nothing rash.

37 "For you have brought these men *here* who are neither [a]robbers of temples nor blasphemers of our goddess. [a]Rom 2:22

38 "So then, if Demetrius and the craftsmen who are with him have a complaint against any man, the courts are in session and [a]proconsuls are *available;* let them bring charges against one another. [a]Acts 13:7

39 "But if you want anything beyond this, it shall be settled in the lawful assembly.

40 "For indeed we are in danger of being accused of a riot in connection with today's events, since there is no *real* cause *for it,* and in this connection we will be unable to account for this disorderly gathering."

41 After saying this he dismissed the assembly.

Paul in Macedonia and Greece

20 After the uproar had ceased, Paul sent for [a]the disciples, and when he had exhorted them and taken his leave of them, he left to go to [b]Macedonia. [a]Acts 11:26 [b]Acts 16:9

2 When he had gone through those districts and had given them much exhortation, he came to Greece.

3 And *there* he spent three months, and when [a]a plot was formed against him by the Jews as he was about to set sail for Syria, he decided to return through Macedonia. [a]Acts 9:23f; 20:19

4 And he was accompanied by Sopater of Berea, *the son* of Pyrrhus, and by [a]Aristarchus and Secundus of the Thessalonians, and [a]Gaius of Derbe, and Timothy, and Tychicus and [b]Trophimus of Asia. [a]Acts 19:29 [b]Acts 21:29

5 But these had gone on ahead and were waiting for [b]us at [b]Troas. [a]Acts 16:10 [b]Acts 16:8

6 We sailed from [a]Philippi after [b]the days of Unleavened Bread, and came to them at Troas within five days; and there we stayed seven days. [a]Acts 16:12 [b]Acts 12:3

7 On the first day of the week, when we were gathered together to [a]break bread, Paul *began* talking to them, intending to leave the next day, and he prolonged his message until midnight. [a]Acts 2:42; 20:11

8 There were many lamps in the [a]upper room where we were gathered together. [a]Acts 1:13

9 And there was a young man named Eutychus sitting on the window sill, sinking into a deep sleep; and as Paul kept on talking, he was overcome by sleep and fell down from the third floor and was picked up dead.

10 But Paul went down and fell upon him, and after embracing him, he [a]said, "Do not be troubled, for his life is in him." [a]Matt 9:23f; Mark 5:39

11 When he had gone *back* up and had [a]broken the bread and eaten, he talked with them a long while until daybreak, and then left. [a]Acts 2:42; 20:7

12 They took away the boy alive, and were greatly comforted.

Troas to Miletus

13 But [a]we, going ahead to the ship, set sail for Assos, intending from there to take Paul on

board; for so he had arranged it, intending himself to go by land. ᵃActs 16:10; 20:5-15

14 And when he met us at Assos, we took him on board and came to Mitylene.

15 Sailing from there, we arrived the following day opposite Chios; and the next day we crossed over to Samos; and the day following we came to ᵃMiletus. ᵃActs 20:17; 2 Tim 4:20

16 For Paul had decided to sail past Ephesus so that he would not have to spend time in Asia; for he was hurrying ᵃto be in Jerusalem, if possible, ᵇon the day of Pentecost. ᵃActs 19:21 ᵇActs 2:1

Farewell to Ephesus

17 From Miletus he sent to Ephesus and called to him ᵃthe elders of the church. ᵃActs 11:30

18 And when they had come to him, he said to them,

"You yourselves know, ᵃfrom the first day that I set foot in Asia, how I was with you the whole time, ᵃActs 18:19; 19:1, 10

19 serving the Lord with all humility and with tears and with trials which came upon me through ᵃthe plots of the Jews; ᵃActs 20:3

20 how I ᵃdid not shrink from declaring to you anything that was profitable, and teaching you publicly and from house to house, ᵃActs 20:27

21 solemnly testifying to both Jews and Greeks of ᵃrepentance toward God and faith in our Lord Jesus Christ. ᵃActs 2:38; 11:18

22 "And now, behold, bound in spirit, ᵃI am on my way to Jerusalem, not knowing what will happen to me there, ᵃActs 17:16; 20:16

23 except that the Holy Spirit solemnly testifies to me in every city, saying that ᵃbonds and afflictions await me. ᵃActs 9:16; 21:33

24 "But ᵃI do not consider my life of any account as dear to myself, so that I may ᵇfinish my course and the ministry which I received from the Lord Jesus, to testify solemnly of the gospel of the grace of God. ᵃActs 21:13 ᵇActs 13:25

25 "And now, behold, I know that all of you, among whom I went about ᵃpreaching the kingdom, will no longer see my face. ᵃMatt 4:23; Acts 28:31

26 "Therefore, I testify to you this day that ᵃI am innocent of the blood of all men. ᵃActs 18:6

27 "For I did not shrink from declaring to you the whole ᵃpurpose of God. ᵃActs 13:36

28 "Be on guard for yourselves and for all the flock, among which the Holy Spirit has made you overseers, to shepherd the church of God which ᵃHe purchased with His own blood. ᵃEph 1:7, 14; 1 Pet 1:19

29 "I know that after my departure ᵃsavage wolves will come in among you, not sparing the flock; ᵃEzek 22:27; Matt 7:15

30 and from among your own selves men will arise, speaking perverse things, to draw away ᵃthe disciples after them. ᵃActs 11:26

31 "Therefore be on the alert, remembering that night and day for a period of three years I did not cease to admonish each one ᵃwith tears. ᵃActs 20:19

32 "And now I ᵃcommend you to God and to the word of His grace, which is able to build *you* up and to give *you* the inheritance among all those who are sanctified. ᵃActs 14:23

33 "ᵃI have coveted no one's silver or gold or clothes. ᵃ1 Cor 9:4-18; 2 Cor 11:7-12

34 "You yourselves know that ᵃthese hands ministered to my *own* needs and to the men who were with me. ᵃActs 18:3

35 "In everything I showed you that by working hard in this manner you must help the weak and remember the words of the Lord Jesus, that He Himself said, 'It is more blessed to give than to receive.' "

36 When he had said these things, he ᵃknelt down and prayed with them all. ᵃActs 9:40; 21:5

37 And they *began* to weep aloud and ᵃembraced Paul, and repeatedly kissed him, ᵃLuke 15:20

38 grieving especially over ᵃthe word which he had spoken, that they would not see his face again. And they were accompanying him to the ship. ᵃActs 20:25

Paul Sails from Miletus

21 When ᵃwe had parted from them and had set sail, we ran a straight course to Cos and the next day to Rhodes and from there to Patara; ᵃActs 16:10; 21:1-18

2 and having found a ship crossing over to ᵃPhoenicia, we went aboard and set sail. ᵃActs 11:19; 21:3

3 When we came in sight of ᵃCyprus, leaving it on the left, we kept sailing to Syria and landed at Tyre; for there the ship was to unload its cargo. ᵃActs 4:36; 21:16

4 After looking up the disciples, we stayed there seven days; and they kept telling Paul ᵃthrough the Spirit not to set foot in Jerusalem. ᵃActs 20:23; 21:11

5 When our days there were ended, we left and started on our journey, while they all, with wives and children, escorted us until *we were* out of the city. After ᵃkneeling down on the beach and praying, we said farewell to one another. ᵃLuke 22:41; Acts 9:40

6 Then we went on board the ship, and they returned ᵃhome again. ᵃJohn 19:27

7 When we had finished the voyage from ᵃTyre, we arrived at Ptolemais, and after greeting the brethren, we stayed with them for a day. ᵃActs 12:20; 21:3

8 On the next day we left and came to Caesarea, and entering the house of ᵃPhilip the

evangelist, who was one of the seven, we stayed with him. ᵃActs 6:5; 8:5

9 Now this man had four virgin daughters who were ᵃprophetesses. ᵃLuke 2:36; Acts 13:1

10 As we were staying there for some days, a prophet named ᵃAgabus came down from Judea. ᵃActs 11:28

11 And coming to us, he took Paul's belt and bound his own feet and hands, and said, "This ᵃis what the Holy Spirit says: 'In this way the Jews at Jerusalem will ᵇbind the man who owns this belt and deliver him into the hands of the Gentiles.' " ᵃActs 8:29 ᵇActs 21:33

12 When we had heard this, we as well as the local residents *began* begging him ᵃnot to go up to Jerusalem. ᵃActs 21:15

13 Then Paul answered, "What are you doing, weeping and breaking my heart? For I am ready not only to be bound, but even to die at Jerusalem for ᵃthe name of the Lord Jesus." ᵃActs 5:41; 9:16

14 And since he would not be persuaded, we fell silent, remarking, "ᵃThe will of the Lord be done!" ᵃLuke 22:42

Paul at Jerusalem

15 After these days we got ready and ᵃstarted on our way up to Jerusalem. ᵃActs 21:12

16 *Some* of the disciples from Caesarea also came with us, taking us to Mnason of Cyprus, a ᵃdisciple of long standing with whom we were to lodge. ᵃActs 15:7

17 After we arrived in Jerusalem, ᵃthe brethren received us gladly. ᵃActs 1:15; 21:7

18 And the following day Paul went in with us to ᵃJames, and all the elders were present. ᵃActs 12:17

19 After he had greeted them, he ᵃ*began* to relate one by one the things which God had done among the Gentiles through his ᵇministry. ᵃActs 14:27 ᵇActs 1:17

20 And when they heard it they *began* ᵃglorifying God; and they said to him, "You see, brother, how many thousands there are among the Jews of those who have believed, and they are all ᵇzealous for the Law; ᵃMatt 9:8 ᵇActs 15:1

21 and they have been told about you, that you are teaching all the Jews who are among the Gentiles to forsake Moses, telling them ᵃnot to circumcise their children nor to walk according to ᵇthe customs. ᵃ1 Cor 7:18f ᵇActs 6:14

22 "What, then, is *to be done?* They will certainly hear that you have come.

23 "Therefore do this that we tell you. We have four men who ᵃare under a vow; ᵃNum 6:13-21; Acts 18:18

24 take them and ᵃpurify yourself along with them, and pay their expenses so that they may shave their heads; and all will know that there is nothing to the things which they have been

told about you, but that you yourself also walk orderly, keeping the Law. ᵃJohn 11:55; Acts 21:26

25 "But concerning the Gentiles who have believed, we wrote, ᵃhaving decided that they should abstain from meat sacrificed to idols and from blood and from what is strangled and from fornication." ᵃActs 15:19f, 29

26 Then Paul took the men, and the next day, purifying himself along with them, ᵃwent into the temple giving notice of the completion of the days of purification, until the sacrifice was offered for each one of them. ᵃNum 6:13; Acts 24:18

Paul Seized in the Temple

27 When ᵃthe seven days were almost over, ᵇthe Jews from Asia, upon seeing him in the temple, *began* to stir up all the crowd and laid hands on him, ᵃNum 6:9, 13-20 ᵇActs 20:19

28 crying out, "Men of Israel, come to our aid! ᵃThis is the man who preaches to all men everywhere against our people and the Law and this place; and besides he has even brought Greeks into the temple and has defiled this holy place." ᵃActs 6:13

29 For they had previously seen Trophimus the ᵃEphesian in the city with him, and they supposed that Paul had brought him into the temple. ᵃActs 18:19

30 Then all the city was provoked, and the people rushed together, and taking hold of Paul they ᵃdragged him out of the temple, and immediately the doors were shut. ᵃ2 Kin 11:15; Acts 16:19

31 While they were seeking to kill him, a report came up to the commander of the ᵃRoman cohort that all Jerusalem was in confusion. ᵃActs 10:1

32 At once he ᵃtook along *some* soldiers and centurions and ran down to them; and when they saw the commander and the soldiers, they stopped beating Paul. ᵃActs 23:27

33 Then the commander came up and took hold of him, and ordered him to be ᵃbound with ᵇtwo chains; and he *began* asking who he was and what he had done. ᵃActs 20:23 ᵇActs 12:6

34 But among the crowd ᵃsome were shouting one thing *and* some another, and when he could not find out the facts because of the uproar, he ordered him to be brought into the barracks. ᵃActs 19:32

35 When he got to ᵃthe stairs, he was carried by the soldiers because of the violence of the mob; ᵃActs 21:40

36 for the multitude of the people kept following them, shouting, "ᵃAway with him!" ᵃLuke 23:18; John 19:15

37 As Paul was about to be brought into ᵃthe barracks, he said to the commander, "May I

say something to you?" And he *said, "Do you know Greek? ᵃ*Acts 21:34; 22:24*

38 "Then you are not ᵃthe Egyptian who some time ago stirred up a revolt and led the four thousand men of the Assassins out into the wilderness?" ᵃ*Acts 5:36*

39 But Paul said, "ᵃI am a Jew of Tarsus in Cilicia, a citizen of no insignificant city; and I beg you, allow me to speak to the people." ᵃ*Acts 9:11; 22:3*

40 When he had given him permission, Paul, standing on the stairs, motioned to the people with his hand; and when there was a great hush, he spoke to them in the ᵃHebrew dialect, saying, ᵃ*John 5:2; Acts 1:19*

Paul's Defense before the Jews

22 "ᵃBrethren and fathers, hear my defense which I now *offer* to you." ᵃ*Acts 7:2*

2 And when they heard that he was addressing them in the ᵃHebrew dialect, they became even more quiet; and he *said, ᵃ*Acts 21:40*

3 "ᵃI am a Jew, born in Tarsus of Cilicia, but brought up in this city, educated under ᵇGamaliel, strictly according to the law of our fathers, being zealous for God just as you all are today. ᵃ*Acts 9:1-22* ᵇ*Acts 5:34*

4 "I persecuted this ᵇWay to the death, binding and putting both men and women into prisons, ᵃ*Acts 8:3* ᵇ*Acts 9:2*

5 as also ᵃthe high priest and all ᵇthe Council of the elders can testify. From them I also received letters to the brethren, and started off for Damascus in order to bring even those who were there to Jerusalem as prisoners to be punished. ᵃ*Acts 9:1* ᵇ*Luke 22:66*

6 "ᵃBut it happened that as I was on my way, approaching Damascus about noontime, a very bright light suddenly flashed from heaven all around me, ᵃ*Acts 9:3-8; 26:12-18*

7 and I fell to the ground and heard a voice saying to me, 'Saul, Saul, why are you persecuting Me?'

8 "And I answered, 'Who are You, Lord?' And He said to me, 'I am ᵃJesus the Nazarene, whom you are persecuting.' ᵃ*Acts 26:9*

9 "And those who were with me ᵃsaw the light, to be sure, but ᵇdid not understand the voice of the One who was speaking to me. ᵃ*Acts 26:13* ᵇ*Acts 9:7*

10 "And I said, 'ᵃWhat shall I do, Lord?' And the Lord said to me, 'Get up and go on into Damascus, and there you will be told of all that has been appointed for you to do.' ᵃ*Acts 16:30*

11 "But since I ᵃcould not see because of the brightness of that light, I was led by the hand by those who were with me and came into Damascus. ᵃ*Acts 9:8*

12 "A certain ᵃAnanias, a man who was devout by the standard of the Law, *and* well

spoken of by all the Jews who lived there, ᵃ*Acts 9:10*

13 came to me, and standing near said to me, 'ᵃBrother Saul, receive your sight!' And at that very time I looked up at him. ᵃ*Acts 9:17*

14 "And he said, 'ᵃThe God of our fathers has appointed you to know His will and to ᵇsee the Righteous One and to hear an utterance from His mouth. ᵃ*Acts 3:13* ᵇ*Acts 9:17*

15 'For you will be ᵃa witness for Him to all men of what you have seen and heard. ᵃ*Acts 23:11; 26:16*

16 'Now why do you delay? Get up and be baptized, and ᵃwash away your sins, calling on His name.' ᵃ*Acts 2:38; 1 Cor 6:11*

17 "It happened when I returned to Jerusalem and was praying in the temple, that I ᵃfell into a trance, ᵃ*Acts 10:10*

18 and I saw Him saying to me, 'ᵃMake haste, and get out of Jerusalem quickly, because they will not accept your testimony about Me.' ᵃ*Acts 9:29*

19 "And I said, 'Lord, they themselves understand that in one synagogue after another ᵃI used to imprison and beat those who believed in You. ᵃ*Acts 8:3; 22:4*

20 'And ᵃwhen the blood of Your witness Stephen was being shed, I also was standing by approving, and watching out for the coats of those who were slaying him.' ᵃ*Acts 7:58f; 8:1*

21 "And He said to me, 'Go! For I will send you far away ᵃto the Gentiles.' " ᵃ*Acts 9:15*

22 They listened to him up to this statement, and *then* they raised their voices and said, "Away with such a fellow from the earth, for ᵃhe should not be allowed to live!" ᵃ*Acts 25:24*

23 And as they were crying out and ᵃthrowing off their cloaks and tossing dust into the air, ᵃ*Acts 7:58*

24 the commander ordered him to be brought into the barracks, stating that he should be ᵃexamined by scourging so that he might find out the reason why they were shouting against him that way. ᵃ*Acts 22:29*

25 But when they stretched him out with thongs, Paul said to the centurion who was standing by, "Is it lawful for you to scourge ᵃa man who is a Roman and uncondemned?" ᵃ*Acts 16:37*

26 When the centurion heard *this*, he went to the commander and told him, saying, "What are you about to do? For this man is a Roman."

27 The commander came and said to him, "Tell me, are you a Roman?" And he said, "Yes."

28 The commander answered, "I acquired this citizenship with a large sum of money." And Paul said, "But I was actually born *a citizen*."

29 Therefore those who were about to ᵃexamine him immediately let go of him; and the

commander also was afraid when he found out that he was a Roman, and because he had put him in chains. ªActs 22:24

30 But on the next day, ªwishing to know for certain why he had been accused by the Jews, he released him and ordered the chief priests and all the Council to assemble, and brought Paul down and set him before them. ªActs 23:28

Paul before the Council

23 Paul, looking intently at the Council, said, "Brethren, ªI have lived my life with a perfectly good conscience before God up to this day." ªActs 24:16; 2 Cor 1:12

2 The high priest Ananias commanded those standing beside him ªto strike him on the mouth. ªJohn 18:22

3 Then Paul said to him, "God is going to strike you, you whitewashed wall! Do you ªsit to try me according to the Law, and in violation of the Law order me to be struck?" ªLev 19:15; Deut 25:2

4 But the bystanders said, "Do you revile God's high priest?"

5 And Paul said, "I was not aware, brethren, that he was high priest; for it is written, 'ªYOU SHALL NOT SPEAK EVIL OF A RULER OF YOUR PEOPLE.'" ªEx 22:28

6 But perceiving that one group were Sadducees and the other Pharisees, Paul *began* crying out in the Council, "Brethren, I am a Pharisee, a son of Pharisees; I am on trial for ªthe hope and resurrection of the dead!" ªActs 24:15, 21; 26:8

7 As he said this, there occurred a dissension between the Pharisees and Sadducees, and the assembly was divided.

8 For ªthe Sadducees say that there is no resurrection, nor an angel, nor a spirit, but the Pharisees acknowledge them all. ªMatt 22:23; Mark 12:18

9 And there occurred a great uproar; and some of the scribes of the Pharisaic party stood up and *began* to argue heatedly, saying, "We find nothing wrong with this man; ªsuppose a spirit or an angel has spoken to him?" ªJohn 12:29; Acts 22:6ff

10 And as a great dissension was developing, the commander was afraid Paul would be torn to pieces by them and ordered the troops to go down and take him away from them by force, and bring him into ªthe barracks. ªActs 21:34; 23:16, 32

11 But on the night *immediately* following, the Lord stood at his side and said, "Take courage; for ªas you have solemnly witnessed to My cause at Jerusalem, so you must witness at Rome also." ªActs 19:21

A Conspiracy to Kill Paul

12 When it was day, ªthe Jews formed a conspiracy and bound themselves under an oath, saying that they would neither eat nor drink until they had killed Paul. ªActs 9:23; 23:30

13 There were more than forty who formed this plot.

14 They came to the chief priests and the elders and said, "We have ªbound ourselves under a solemn oath to taste nothing until we have killed Paul. ªActs 23:12, 21

15 "Now therefore, you and ªthe Council notify the commander to bring him down to you, as though you were going to determine his case by a more thorough investigation; and we for our part are ready to slay him before he comes near *the place*." ªActs 22:30; 23:1, 6, 20, 28

16 But the son of Paul's sister heard of their ambush, and he came and entered ªthe barracks and told Paul. ªActs 21:34; 23:10, 32

17 Paul called one of the centurions to him and said, "Lead this young man to the commander, for he has something to report to him."

18 So he took him and led him to the commander and *said, "Paul ªthe prisoner called me to him and asked me to lead this young man to you since he has something to tell you." ªEph 3:1

19 The commander took him by the hand and stepping aside, *began* to inquire of him privately, "What is it that you have to report to me?"

20 And he said, "The Jews have agreed to ask you to bring Paul down tomorrow to ªthe Council, as though they were going to inquire somewhat more thoroughly about him. ªActs 22:30; 23:1, 6, 15, 28

21 "So do not listen to them, for more than forty of them are ªlying in wait for him who have bound themselves under a curse not to eat or drink until they slay him; and now they are ready and waiting for the promise from you." ªActs 23:12, 14

22 So the commander let the young man go, instructing him, "Tell no one that you have notified me of these things."

Paul Moved to Caesarea

23 And he called to him two of the centurions and said, "Get two hundred soldiers ready by the third hour of the night to proceed to ªCaesarea, with seventy horsemen and two hundred spearmen." ªActs 8:40; 23:33

24 *They were* also to provide mounts to put Paul on and bring him safely to ªFelix the governor. ªActs 23:26, 33; 24:1, 3, 10

25 And he wrote a letter having this form:

26 "Claudius Lysias, to the ªmost excellent governor Felix, greetings. ªLuke 1:3; Acts 24:3

27 "When this man was arrested by the Jews

and was about to be slain by them, [a]I came up to them with the troops and rescued him, [b]having learned that he was a Roman. [a]Acts 21:32f [b]Acts 22:25-29

28 "And [a]wanting to ascertain the charge for which they were accusing him, I brought him down to their Council; [a]Acts 22:30

29 and I found him to be accused over questions about their Law, but under [a]no accusation deserving death or imprisonment. [a]Acts 23:9; 25:25

30 "When I was [a]informed that there would be a plot against the man, I sent him to you at once, also instructing his accusers to bring charges against him before you." [a]Acts 23:20f

31 So the soldiers, in accordance with their orders, took Paul and brought him by night to Antipatris.

32 But the next day, leaving [a]the horsemen to go on with him, they returned to the barracks. [a]Acts 23:23

33 When these had come to Caesarea and delivered the letter to [a]the governor, they also presented Paul to him. [a]Acts 23:24, 26; 24:1, 3, 10

34 When he had read it, he asked from what [a]province he was, and when he learned that [b]he was from Cilicia, [a]Acts 25:1 [b]Acts 21:39

35 he said, "I will give you a hearing after your [a]accusers arrive also," giving orders for him to be kept in Herod's Praetorium. [a]Acts 23:30; 24:19

Paul before Felix

24 After five days the high priest [a]Ananias came down with some elders, with an attorney *named* Tertullus, and they brought charges to the governor against Paul. [a]Acts 23:2

2 After *Paul* had been summoned, Tertullus began to accuse him, saying *to the governor,* "Since we have through you attained much peace, and since by your providence reforms are being carried out for this nation,

3 we acknowledge *this* in every way and everywhere, [a]most excellent Felix, with all thankfulness. [a]Acts 23:26; 26:25

4 "But, that I may not weary you any further, I beg you to grant us, by your kindness, a brief hearing.

5 "For we have found this man a real pest and a fellow who stirs up dissension among all the Jews throughout the world, and a ringleader of the [a]sect of the Nazarenes. [a]Acts 15:5; 24:14

6 "And he even tried to [a]desecrate the temple; and then we arrested him. [We wanted to judge him according to our own Law. [a]Acts 21:28

7 "But Lysias the commander came along,

and with much violence took him out of our hands,

8 ordering his accusers to come before you.] By examining him yourself concerning all these matters you will be able to ascertain the things of which we accuse him."

9 [a]The Jews who joined in the attack, asserting that these things were so. [a]1 Thess 2:16

10 When [a]the governor had nodded for him to speak, Paul responded:
"Knowing that for many years you have been a judge to this nation, I cheerfully make my defense, [a]Acts 23:24

11 since you can take note of the fact that no more than [a]twelve days ago I went up to Jerusalem to worship. [a]Acts 21:18, 27; 24:1

12 "[a]Neither in the temple, nor in the synagogues, nor in the city *itself* did they find me carrying on a discussion with anyone or [b]causing a riot. [a]Acts 25:8 [b]Acts 24:18

13 "[a]Nor can they prove to you *the charges* of which they now accuse me. [a]Acts 25:7

14 "But this I admit to you, that according to [a]the Way which they call a sect I do serve the God of our fathers, believing everything that is in accordance with the Law and that is written in the Prophets; [a]Acts 9:2; 24:22

15 having a hope in God, which [a]these men cherish themselves, that there shall certainly be a resurrection of both the righteous and the wicked. [a]Dan 12:2; John 5:28f

16 "In view of this, [a]I also do my best to maintain always a blameless conscience *both* before God and before men. [a]Acts 23:1

17 "Now after several years I [a]came to bring alms to my nation and to present offerings; [a]Acts 11:29f; Rom 15:25-28

18 in which they found me *occupied* in the temple, having been [a]purified, without *any* crowd or uproar. But *there were* some Jews from Asia— [a]Acts 21:26

19 who ought to have been present before you and to [a]make accusation, if they should have anything against me. [a]Acts 23:30

20 "Or else let these men themselves tell what misdeed they found when I stood before [a]the Council, [a]Matt 5:22

21 other than for this one statement which [a]I shouted out while standing among them, 'For the resurrection of the dead I am on trial before you today.' " [a]Acts 23:6; 24:15

22 But Felix, having a more exact knowledge about [a]the Way, put them off, saying, "When Lysias the commander comes down, I will decide your case." [a]Acts 24:14

23 Then he gave orders to the centurion for him to be [a]kept in custody and *yet* have *some* freedom, and not to prevent any of [b]his friends from ministering to him. [a]Acts 23:35 [b]Acts 23:16

24 But some days later Felix arrived with

Drusilla, his wife who was a Jewess, and sent for Paul and heard him *speak* about ªfaith in Christ Jesus. ªActs 20:21

25 But as he was discussing righteousness, self-control and ªthe judgment to come, Felix became frightened and said, "Go away for the present, and when I find time I will summon you." ªActs 10:42

26 At the same time too, he was hoping that ªmoney would be given him by Paul; therefore he also used to send for him quite often and converse with him. ªActs 24:17

27 But after two years had passed, Felix was succeeded by Porcius Festus, and wishing to do the Jews a favor, Felix left Paul ªimprisoned. ªActs 23:35; 25:14

Paul before Festus

25 Festus then, having arrived in ªthe province, three days later went up to Jerusalem from Caesarea. ªActs 23:34

2 And the chief priests and the leading men of the Jews ªbrought charges against Paul, and they were urging him, ªActs 24:1; 25:15

3 requesting a concession against Paul, that he might have him brought to Jerusalem (*at the same time*, ªsetting an ambush to kill him on the way). ªActs 9:24

4 Festus then answered that Paul ªwas being kept in custody at Caesarea and that he himself was about to leave shortly. ªActs 24:23

5 "Therefore," he *said, "let the influential men among you go *there with me, and if there is anything wrong about the man, let them prosecute him."

6 After he had spent not more than eight or ten days among them, he went down to Caesarea, and on the next day he took his seat on ªthe tribunal and ordered Paul to be brought. ªMatt 27:19; Acts 25:10, 17

7 After Paul arrived, the Jews who had come down from Jerusalem stood around him, bringing many and serious charges against him ªwhich they could not prove, ªActs 24:13

8 while Paul said in his own defense, "ªI have committed no offense either against the Law of the Jews or against the temple or against Caesar." ªActs 6:13; 24:12

9 But Festus, ªwishing to do the Jews a favor, answered Paul and said, "Are you willing to go up to Jerusalem and stand trial before me on these *charges?*" ªActs 12:3; 24:27

10 But Paul said, "I am standing before Caesar's ªtribunal, where I ought to be tried. I have done no wrong to *the* Jews, as you also very well know. ªMatt 27:19; Acts 25:6, 17

11 "If, then, I am a wrongdoer and have committed anything worthy of death, I do not refuse to die; but if none of those things is *true* of which these men accuse me, no one can

hand me over to them. I ªappeal to Caesar." ªActs 25:21, 25; 26:32

12 Then when Festus had conferred with his council, he answered, "You have appealed to Caesar, to Caesar you shall go."

13 Now when several days had elapsed, King Agrippa and Bernice arrived at ªCaesarea and paid their respects to Festus. ªActs 8:40; 25:1, 4, 6

14 While they were spending many days there, Festus laid Paul's case before the king, saying, "There is a man who was ªleft as a prisoner by Felix; ªActs 24:27

15 and when I was at Jerusalem, the chief priests and the elders of the Jews ªbrought charges against him, asking for a sentence of condemnation against him. ªActs 24:1; 25:2

16 "I ªanswered them that it is not the custom of the Romans to hand over any man before the accused meets his accusers face to face and has an opportunity to make his defense against the charges. ªActs 25:4f

17 "So after they had assembled here, I did not delay, but on the next day took my seat on ªthe tribunal and ordered the man to be brought before me. ªMatt 27:19; Acts 25:6, 10

18 "When the accusers stood up, they *began* bringing charges against him not of such crimes as I was expecting,

19 but they *simply* had some ªpoints of disagreement with him about their own religion and about a dead man, Jesus, whom Paul asserted to be alive. ªActs 18:15; 23:29

20 "ªBeing at a loss how to investigate such matters, I asked whether he was willing to go to Jerusalem and there stand trial on these matters. ªActs 25:9

21 "But when Paul ªappealed to be held in custody for the Emperor's decision, I ordered him to be kept in custody until I send him to Caesar." ªActs 25:11f

22 Then ªAgrippa *said* to Festus, "I also would like to hear the man myself." "Tomorrow," he *said, "you shall hear him." ªActs 9:15

Paul before Agrippa

23 So, on the next day when ªAgrippa came together with ªBernice amid great pomp, and entered the auditorium accompanied by the commanders and the prominent men of the city, at the command of Festus, Paul was brought in. ªActs 25:13; 26:30

24 Festus *said, "King Agrippa, and all you gentlemen here present with us, you see this man about whom ªall the people of the Jews appealed to me, both at Jerusalem and here, loudly declaring that ᵇhe ought not to live any longer. ªActs 25:2, 7 ᵇActs 22:22

25 "But I found that he had committed ªnothing worthy of death; and since he himself

[b]appealed to the Emperor, I decided to send him. [a]*Acts 23:29* [b]*Acts 25:11f*

26 "Yet I have nothing definite about him to write to my lord. Therefore I have brought him before you *all* and especially before you, King Agrippa, so that after the investigation has taken place, I may have something to write.

27 "For it seems absurd to me in sending a prisoner, not to indicate also the charges against him."

Paul's Defense before Agrippa

26 [a]Agrippa said to Paul, "You are permitted to speak for yourself." Then Paul stretched out his hand and *proceeded* to make his defense: [a]*Acts 9:15*

2 "In regard to all the things of which I am accused by the Jews, I consider myself fortunate, King Agrippa, that I am about to make my defense before you today;

3 especially because you are an expert in all [a]customs and questions among *the* Jews; therefore I beg you to listen to me patiently. [a]*Acts 6:14; 25:19; 26:7*

4 "So then, all Jews know [a]my manner of life from my youth up, which from the beginning was spent among my *own* nation and at Jerusalem; [a]*Gal 1:13f; Phil 3:5*

5 since they have known about me for a long time, if they are willing to testify, that I lived *as* a [a]Pharisee according to the strictest sect of our religion. [a]*Acts 23:6; Phil 3:5*

6 "And now I am standing trial [a]for the hope of [b]the promise made by God to our fathers; [a]*Acts 24:15* [b]*Acts 13:32*

7 *the promise* to which our twelve tribes hope to attain, as they earnestly serve *God* night and day. And for this [a]hope, O King, I am being accused by Jews. [a]*Acts 24:15*

8 "Why is it considered incredible among you *people* [a]if God does raise the dead? [a]*Acts 23:6*

9 "So then, [a]I thought to myself that I had to do many things hostile to the name of Jesus of Nazareth. [a]*John 16:2; 1 Tim 1:13*

10 "And this is just what I [a]did in Jerusalem; not only did I lock up many of the saints in prisons, having received authority from the chief priests, but also when they were being put to death I cast my vote against them. [a]*Acts 8:3*

11 "And [a]as I punished them often in all the synagogues, I tried to force them to blaspheme; and being furiously enraged at them, I kept pursuing them even to foreign cities. [a]*Matt 10:17; Acts 22:19*

12 "While so engaged [a]as I was journeying to Damascus with the authority and commission of the chief priests, [a]*Acts 9:3-8; 22:6-11*

13 at midday, O King, I saw on the way a light

from heaven, brighter than the sun, shining all around me and those who were journeying with me.

14 "And when we had all fallen to the ground, I heard a voice saying to me in the [a]Hebrew dialect, 'Saul, Saul, why are you persecuting Me? It is hard for you to kick against the goads.' [a]*Acts 21:40*

15 "And I said, 'Who are You, Lord?' And the Lord said, 'I am Jesus whom you are persecuting.

16 'But get up and stand on your feet; for this purpose I have appeared to you, to [a]appoint you a minister and a witness not only to the things which you have seen, but also to the things in which I will appear to you; [a]*Acts 22:14*

17 rescuing you [a]from the *Jewish* people and from the Gentiles, to whom I am sending you, [a]*1 Chr 16:35; Acts 9:15*

18 to [a]open their eyes so that they may turn from darkness to light and from the dominion of Satan to God, that they may receive forgiveness of sins and an inheritance among those who have been sanctified by faith in Me.' [a]*Is 35:5; 42:7, 16*

19 "So, King Agrippa, I did not prove disobedient to the heavenly vision,

20 but *kept* declaring both [a]to those of Damascus first, and *also* at Jerusalem and *then* throughout all the region of Judea, and *even* to the Gentiles, that they should repent and turn to God, performing deeds appropriate to repentance. [a]*Acts 9:19ff*

21 "For this reason *some* Jews [a]seized me in the temple and tried to put me to death. [a]*Acts 21:27, 30*

22 "So, having obtained help from God, I stand to this day testifying both to small and great, stating nothing but what [a]the Prophets and Moses said was going to take place; [a]*Acts 10:43; 24:14*

23 that the Christ was to suffer, *and* that [a]by reason of *His* resurrection from the dead He would be the first to proclaim light both to the *Jewish* people and to the Gentiles." [a]*1 Cor 15:20, 23; Col 1:18*

24 While *Paul* was saying this in his defense, Festus *said in a loud voice, "Paul, you are out of your mind! *Your* great [a]learning is driving you mad." [a]*John 7:15; 2 Tim 3:15*

25 But Paul *said, "I am not out of my mind, [a]most excellent Festus, but I utter words of sober truth. [a]*Acts 23:26; 24:3*

26 "For the king [a]knows about these matters, and I speak to him also with confidence, since I am persuaded that none of these things escape his notice; for this has not been done in a corner. [a]*Acts 26:3*

27 "King Agrippa, do you believe the Prophets? I know that you do."

28 Agrippa *replied* to Paul, "In a short time you will persuade me to become a ªChristian."
ªActs 11:26

29 And Paul *said*, "I would wish to God, that whether in a short or long time, not only you, but also all who hear me this day, might become such as I am, except for these ªchains."
ªActs 21:33

30 ªThe king stood up and the governor and Bernice, and those who were sitting with them,
ªActs 25:23

31 and when they had gone aside, they *began* talking to one another, saying, "ªThis man is not doing anything worthy of death or imprisonment." ªActs 23:29

32 And Agrippa said to Festus, "This man might have been ªset free if he had not appealed to Caesar." ªActs 28:18

Paul Is Sent to Rome

27 When it was decided that we would sail for ªItaly, they proceeded to deliver Paul and some other prisoners to a centurion of the Augustan cohort named Julius. ªActs 18:2; 27:6

2 And embarking in an Adramyttian ship, which was about to sail to the regions along the coast of Asia, we put out to sea accompanied by ªAristarchus, a Macedonian of Thessalonica. ªActs 19:29

3 The next day we put in at Sidon; and Julius ªtreated Paul with consideration and ᵇallowed him to go to his friends and receive care.
ªActs 27:43 ᵇActs 24:23

4 From there we put out to sea and sailed under the shelter of ªCyprus because the winds were contrary. ªActs 4:36

5 When we had sailed through the sea along the coast of ªCilicia and Pamphylia, we landed at Myra in Lycia. ªActs 21:39

6 There the centurion found an ªAlexandrian ship sailing for Italy, and he put us aboard it.
ªActs 28:11

7 When we had sailed slowly for a good many days, and with difficulty had arrived off Cnidus, since the wind did not permit us *to go* farther, we sailed under the shelter of ªCrete, off Salmone; ªActs 2:11; 27:12f, 21

8 and with difficulty ªsailing past it we came to a place called Fair Havens, near which was the city of Lasea. ªActs 27:13

9 When considerable time had passed and the voyage was now dangerous, since even ªthe fast was already over, Paul *began* to admonish them, ªLev 16:29-31; 23:27-29

10 and said to them, "Men, I perceive that the voyage will certainly be with ªdamage and great loss, not only of the cargo and the ship, but also of our lives." ªActs 27:21

11 But the centurion was more persuaded by the ªpilot and the captain of the ship than by what was being said by Paul. ªRev 18:17

12 Because the harbor was not suitable for wintering, the majority reached a decision to put out to sea from there, if somehow they could reach Phoenix, a harbor of ªCrete, facing southwest and northwest, and spend the winter *there.* ªActs 2:11; 27:13, 21

13 When a moderate south wind came up, supposing that they had attained their purpose, they weighed anchor and *began* ªsailing along Crete, close *inshore.* ªActs 27:8

Shipwreck

14 But before very long there ªrushed down from the land a violent wind, called Euraquilo;
ªMark 4:37

15 and when the ship was caught *in it* and could not face the wind, we gave way *to it* and let ourselves be driven along.

16 Running under the shelter of a small island called Clauda, we were scarcely able to get the *ship's* boat under control.

17 After they had hoisted it up, they used supporting cables in undergirding the ship; and fearing that they might ªrun aground on *the shallows* of Syrtis, they let down the sea anchor and in this way let themselves be driven along. ªActs 27:26, 29

18 The next day as we were being violently storm-tossed, they began to ªjettison the cargo;
ªJon 1:5; Acts 27:38

19 and on the third day they threw the ship's tackle overboard with their own hands.

20 Since neither sun nor stars appeared for many days, and no small storm was assailing *us,* from then on all hope of our being saved was gradually abandoned.

21 When they had gone a long time without food, then Paul stood up in their midst and said, "ªMen, you ought to have followed my advice and not to have set sail from Crete and incurred this ªdamage and loss. ªActs 27:10

22 "*Yet* now I urge you to ªkeep up your courage, for there will be no loss of life among you, but *only* of the ship. ªActs 27:25, 36

23 "For this very night an angel of the God to whom I belong and ªwhom I serve stood before me, ªRom 1:9

24 saying, 'Do not be afraid, Paul; ªyou must stand before Caesar; and behold, God has granted you all those who are sailing with you.' ªActs 23:11

25 "Therefore, ªkeep up your courage, men, for I believe God that it will turn out exactly as I have been told. ªActs 27:22, 36

26 "But we must ªrun aground on a certain ᵇisland." ªActs 27:29, 41 ᵇActs 28:1

27 But when the fourteenth night came, as we were being driven about in the Adriatic Sea, about midnight the sailors *began* to surmise that they were approaching some land.

28 They took soundings and found *it to be* twenty fathoms; and a little farther on they took another sounding and found *it to be* fifteen fathoms.

29 Fearing that we might ªrun aground somewhere on the rocks, they cast four anchors from the stern and wished for daybreak. ªActs 27:17, 26

30 But as the sailors were trying to escape from the ship and had let down ªthe *ship's* boat into the sea, on the pretense of intending to lay out anchors from the bow, ªActs 27:16

31 Paul said to the centurion and to the soldiers, "Unless these men remain in the ship, you yourselves cannot be saved."

32 Then the soldiers cut away the ropes of the *ship's* boat and let it fall away.

33 Until the day was about to dawn, Paul was encouraging them all to take some food, saying, "Today is the fourteenth day that you have been constantly watching and going without eating, having taken nothing.

34 "Therefore I encourage you to take some food, for this is for your preservation, for ªnot a hair from the head of any of you will perish." ªMatt 10:30

35 Having said this, he took bread and ªgave thanks to God in the presence of all, and he broke it and began to eat. ªMatt 14:19

36 All ªof them were encouraged and they themselves also took food. ªActs 27:22, 25

37 All of us in the ship were two hundred and seventy-six ªpersons. ªActs 2:41

38 When they had eaten enough, they *began* to lighten the ship by ªthrowing out the wheat into the sea. ªJon 1:5; Acts 27:18

39 When day came, ªthey could not recognize the land; but they did observe a bay with a beach, and they resolved to drive the ship onto it if they could. ªActs 28:1

40 And casting off ªthe anchors, they left them in the sea while at the same time they were loosening the ropes of the rudders; and hoisting the foresail to the wind, they were heading for the beach. ªActs 27:29

41 But striking a reef where two seas met, they ran the vessel aground; and the prow stuck fast and remained immovable, but the stern *began* to be broken up by the force *of the waves.*

42 The soldiers' plan was to ªkill the prisoners, so that none *of them* would swim away and escape; ªActs 12:19

43 but the centurion, ªwanting to bring Paul safely through, kept them from their intention, and commanded that those who could swim should jump overboard first and get to land, ªActs 27:3

44 and the rest *should follow,* some on planks, and others on various things from the ship. And so it happened that ªthey all were brought safely to land. ªActs 27:22, 31

Safe at Malta

28 When they had been brought safely through, ªthen we found out that ᵇthe island was called Malta. ªActs 27:39 ᵇActs 27:26

2 ªThe natives showed us extraordinary kindness; for because of the rain that had set in and because of the cold, they kindled a fire and received us all. ªActs 28:4; Rom 1:14

3 But when Paul had gathered a bundle of sticks and laid them on the fire, a viper came out because of the heat and fastened itself on his hand.

4 When the natives saw the creature hanging from his hand, they *began* saying to one another, "ªUndoubtedly this man is a murderer, and though he has been saved from the sea, justice has not allowed him to live." ªLuke 13:2, 4

5 However he shook the creature off into the fire and suffered no harm.

6 But they were expecting that he was about to swell up or suddenly fall down dead. But after they had waited a long time and had seen nothing unusual happen to him, they changed their minds and ªbegan to say that he was a god. ªActs 14:11

7 Now in the neighborhood of that place were lands belonging to the leading man of the island, named Publius, who welcomed us and entertained us courteously three days.

8 And it happened that the father of Publius was lying *in bed* afflicted with *recurrent* fever and dysentery; and Paul went in *to see* him and after he had prayed, he ªlaid his hands on him and healed him. ªMatt 9:18; Mark 5:23

9 After this had happened, the rest of the people on the island who had diseases were coming to him and getting cured.

10 They also honored us with many marks of respect; and when we were setting sail, they supplied *us* with all we needed.

Paul Arrives at Rome

11 At the end of three months we set sail on ªan Alexandrian ship which had wintered at the island, and which had the Twin Brothers for its figurehead. ªActs 27:6

12 After we put in at Syracuse, we stayed there for three days.

13 From there we sailed around and arrived at Rhegium, and a day later a south wind sprang up, and on the second day we came to Puteoli.

14 There we found *some* ªbrethren, and were invited to stay with them for seven days; and thus we came to Rome. ªJohn 21:23; Acts 1:15

15 And the ªbrethren, when they heard about

us, came from there as far as the Market of Appius and Three Inns to meet us; and when Paul saw them, he thanked God and took courage. ªActs 1:15; 10:23

16 When we entered Rome, Paul was ªallowed to stay by himself, with the soldier who was guarding him. ªActs 24:23

17 After three days Paul called together those who were the leading men of the Jews, and when they came together, he *began* saying to them, "Brethren, ªthough I had done nothing against our people or ᵇthe customs of our fathers, yet I was delivered as a prisoner from Jerusalem into the hands of the Romans. ªActs 25:8 ᵇActs 6:14

18 "And when they had examined me, they were willing to release me because there was ªno ground for putting me to death. ªActs 23:29; 25:25

19 "But when the Jews objected, I was forced to ªappeal to Caesar, not that I had any accusation against my nation. ªActs 25:11, 21, 25; 26:32

20 "For this reason, therefore, I requested to see you and to speak with you, for I am wearing this chain for ªthe sake of the hope of Israel." ªActs 24:15; 26:6ff

21 They said to him, "We have neither received letters from Judea concerning you, nor have any of ªthe brethren come here and reported or spoken anything bad about you. ªActs 3:17; 22:5

22 "But we desire to hear from you what your views are; for concerning this ªsect, it is known to us that it is spoken against everywhere." ªActs 24:14

23 When they had set a day for Paul, they came to him at his lodging in large numbers; and he was explaining to them by solemnly ªtestifying about the kingdom of God and trying to persuade them concerning Jesus, from both the Law of Moses and from the Prophets, from morning until evening. ªActs 1:3

24 ªSome were being persuaded by the things spoken, but others would not believe. ªActs 14:4

25 And when they did not agree with one another, they *began* leaving after Paul had spoken one *parting* word, "The Holy Spirit rightly spoke through Isaiah the prophet to your fathers,

26 saying,

ªGO TO THIS PEOPLE AND SAY,
"YOU WILL KEEP ON HEARING, BUT WILL NOT
  UNDERSTAND;
AND YOU WILL KEEP ON SEEING, BUT WILL NOT
  PERCEIVE; ªIs 6:9

27 ªFOR THE HEART OF THIS PEOPLE HAS BECOME
  DULL,
AND WITH THEIR EARS THEY SCARCELY HEAR,
AND THEY HAVE CLOSED THEIR EYES;
OTHERWISE THEY MIGHT SEE WITH THEIR EYES,
AND HEAR WITH THEIR EARS,
AND UNDERSTAND WITH THEIR HEART AND
  RETURN,
AND I WOULD HEAL THEM." ' · ªIs 6:10

28 "Therefore let it be known to you that ªthis salvation of God has been sent to the Gentiles; they will also listen." ªPs 98:3; Luke 2:30

29 [When he had spoken these words, the Jews departed, having a great dispute among themselves.]

30 And he stayed two full years in his own rented quarters and was welcoming all who came to him,

31 ªpreaching the kingdom of God and teaching concerning the Lord Jesus Christ with all openness, unhindered. ªMatt 4:23; Acts 20:25

The Letter of Paul to the
ROMANS

The Gospel Exalted

1 Paul, a bond-servant of Christ Jesus, called *as* an apostle, ªset apart for the gospel of God, ªActs 9:15; 13:2

2 which He promised beforehand through His ªprophets in the holy Scriptures, ªLuke 1:70; Rom 3:21

3 concerning His Son, who was born of a descendant of David ªaccording to the flesh, ªJohn 1:14; Rom 4:1

4 who was declared ªthe Son of God with power by the resurrection from the dead, according to the Spirit of holiness, Jesus Christ our Lord, ªMatt 4:3

5 through whom we have received grace and apostleship to bring about *the* ªobedience of faith among all the Gentiles for His name's sake, ªActs 6:7; Rom 16:26

6 among whom you also are the ªcalled of Jesus Christ; ªJude 1; Rev 17:14

7 to all who are beloved of God in Rome, called *as* ªsaints: Grace to you and peace from God our Father and the Lord Jesus Christ. ªActs 9:13; Rom 8:28ff

8 First, ªI thank my God through Jesus Christ for you all, because your faith is being proclaimed throughout the whole world. ª1 Cor 1:4; Eph 1:15f

9 For God, whom I ªserve in my spirit in the *preaching* of the gospel of His Son, is my witness *as to* how unceasingly I make mention of you, ªActs 24:14; 2 Tim 1:3

10 always in my prayers making request, if

perhaps now at last by [a]the will of God I may succeed in coming to you. [a]*Acts 18:21; Rom 15:32*

11 For [a]I long to see you so that I may impart some spiritual gift to you, that you may be established; [a]*Acts 19:21; Rom 15:23*

12 that is, that I may be encouraged together with you *while* among you, each of us by the other's faith, both yours and mine.

13 I do not want you to be unaware, brethren, that often I have planned to come to you (and have been prevented so far) so that I may obtain some [a]fruit among you also, even as among the rest of the Gentiles. [a]*John 4:36; 15:16*

14 [a]I am under obligation both to Greeks and to barbarians, both to the wise and to the foolish. [a]*1 Cor 9:16*

15 So, for my part, I am eager to [a]preach the gospel to you also who are in Rome. [a]*Rom 15:20*

16 For I am not [a]ashamed of the gospel, for [b]it is the power of God for salvation to everyone who believes, to the Jew first and also to the Greek. [a]*Mark 8:38* [b]*1 Cor 1:18, 24*

17 For in it *the* righteousness of God is revealed from faith to faith; as it is written, "[a]BUT THE RIGHTEOUS *man* SHALL LIVE BY FAITH." [a]*Hab 2:4; Gal 3:11*

Unbelief and Its Consequences

18 For [a]the wrath of God is revealed from heaven against all ungodliness and unrighteousness of men who suppress the truth in unrighteousness. [a]*Rom 5:9; Eph 5:6*

19 because [a]that which is known about God is evident within them; for God made it evident to them. [a]*Acts 14:17; 17:24ff*

20 For since the creation of the world His invisible attributes, His eternal power and divine nature, have been clearly seen, [a]being understood through what has been made, so that they are without excuse. [a]*Job 12:7-9; Ps 19:1-6*

21 For even though they knew God, they did not honor Him as God or give thanks, but they became [a]futile in their speculations, and their foolish heart was darkened. [a]*2 Kin 17:15; Jer 2:5*

22 [a]Professing to be wise, they became fools, [a]*Jer 10:14; 1 Cor 1:20*

23 and [a]exchanged the glory of the incorruptible God for an image in the form of corruptible man and of birds and four-footed animals and crawling creatures. [a]*Deut 4:16-18; Ps 106:20*

24 Therefore [a]God gave them over in the lusts of their hearts to impurity, so that their bodies would be dishonored among them. [a]*Rom 1:26, 28; Eph 4:19*

25 For they exchanged the truth of God for a [a]lie, and worshiped and served the creature rather than the Creator, who is blessed forever. Amen. [a]*Is 44:20; Jer 10:14*

26 For this reason God gave them over to [a]degrading passions; for their women exchanged the natural function for that which is unnatural, [a]*1 Thess 4:5*

27 and in the same way also the men abandoned the natural function of the woman and burned in their desire toward one another, [a]men with men committing indecent acts and receiving in their own persons the due penalty of their error. [a]*Lev 18:22; 20:13*

28 And just as they did not see fit to acknowledge God any longer, [a]God gave them over to a depraved mind, to do those things which are not proper, [a]*Rom 1:24*

29 being filled with all unrighteousness, wickedness, greed, evil; full of envy, murder, strife, deceit, malice; *they are* [a]gossips, [a]*2 Cor 12:20*

30 slanderers, haters of God, insolent, arrogant, boastful, inventors of evil, [a]disobedient to parents, [a]*2 Tim 3:2*

31 without understanding, untrustworthy, [a]unloving, unmerciful; [a]*2 Tim 3:3*

32 and although they know the ordinance of God, that those who practice such things are worthy of [a]death, they not only do the same, but also give hearty approval to those who practice them. [a]*Rom 6:21*

The Impartiality of God

2 Therefore you have no excuse, everyone of you who passes judgment, for in that which [a]you judge another, you condemn yourself; for you who judge practice the same things. [a]*2 Sam 12:5-7; Matt 7:1*

2 And we know that the judgment of God rightly falls upon those who practice such things.

3 But do you suppose this, [a]O man, when you pass judgment on those who practice such things and do the same *yourself,* that you will escape the judgment of God? [a]*Luke 12:14; Rom 2:1*

4 Or do you think lightly of [a]the riches of His kindness and tolerance and patience, not knowing that the kindness of God leads you to repentance? [a]*Rom 9:23; 11:33*

5 But because of your stubbornness and unrepentant heart [a]you are storing up wrath for yourself [b]in the day of wrath and revelation of the righteous judgment of God, [a]*Deut 32:34f* [b]*Ps 110:5*

6 [a]who WILL RENDER TO EACH PERSON ACCORDING TO HIS DEEDS: [a]*Ps 62:12; Prov 24:12*

7 to those who by [a]perseverance in doing good seek for glory and honor and immortality, eternal life; [a]*Luke 8:15; Heb 10:36*

8 but to those who are [a]selfishly ambitious and do not obey the truth, but obey unrighteousness, wrath and indignation. [a]*2 Cor 12:20; Gal 5:20*

9 *There will be* tribulation and distress for every soul of man who does evil, of the Jew [a]first and also of the Greek, [a]*Rom 1:16; 1 Pet 4:17*

10 but [a]glory and honor and peace to everyone who does good, to the Jew first and also to the Greek. [a]Rom 2:7; Heb 2:7

11 For [a]there is no partiality with God. [a]Deut 10:17; Acts 10:34

12 For all who have sinned [a]without the Law will also perish without the Law, and all who have sinned under the Law will be judged by the Law; [a]Acts 2:23; 1 Cor 9:21

13 for it is [a]not the hearers of the Law who are just before God, but the doers of the Law will be justified. [a]Matt 7:21, 24ff; John 13:17

14 For when Gentiles who do not have the Law do [a]instinctively the things of the Law, these, not having the Law, are a law to themselves, [a]Acts 10:35; Rom 1:19

15 in that they show [a]the work of the Law written in their hearts, their conscience bearing witness and their thoughts alternately accusing or else defending them, [a]Rom 2:14, 27

16 on the day when, according to my gospel, [a]God will judge the secrets of men through Christ Jesus. [a]Acts 10:42; 17:31

The Jew Is Condemned by the Law

17 But if you bear the name "Jew" and [a]rely upon the Law and boast in God, [a]Mic 3:11; John 5:45

18 and know His will and [a]approve the things that are essential, being instructed out of the Law, [a]Phil 1:10

19 and are confident that you yourself are a guide to the blind, a light to those who are in darkness,

20 a corrector of the foolish, a teacher of the immature, having in the Law [a]the embodiment of knowledge and of the truth, [a]Rom 3:31; 2 Tim 1:13

21 you, therefore, [a]who teach another, do you not teach yourself? You who preach that one shall not steal, do you steal? [a]Matt 23:3ff

22 You who say that one should not commit adultery, do you commit adultery? You who abhor idols, do you [a]rob temples? [a]Acts 19:37

23 You who [a]boast in the Law, through your breaking the Law, do you dishonor God? [a]Mic 3:11; John 5:45

24 For "[a]THE NAME OF GOD IS BLASPHEMED AMONG THE GENTILES BECAUSE OF YOU," just as it is written. [a]Is 52:5; Ezek 36:20ff

25 For indeed circumcision is of value if you practice the Law; but if you are a transgressor of the Law, [a]your circumcision has become uncircumcision. [a]Jer 4:4; 9:25f

26 [a]So if the uncircumcised man [b]keeps the requirements of the Law, will not his uncircumcision be regarded as circumcision? [a]1 Cor 7:19 [b]Rom 8:4

27 And he who is physically uncircumcised, if he keeps the Law, will he not [a]judge you who though having the letter of the Law and circumcision are a transgressor of the Law? [a]Matt 12:41

28 For [a]he is not a Jew who is one outwardly, nor is circumcision that which is outward in the flesh. [a]John 8:39; Rom 2:17

29 But he is a Jew who is one inwardly; and [a]circumcision is that which is of the heart, by the Spirit, not by the letter; [b]and his praise is not from men, but from God. [a]Deut 30:6 [b]John 5:44

All the World Guilty

3 Then what advantage has the Jew? Or what is the benefit of circumcision?

2 Great in every respect. First of all, that [a]they were entrusted with the oracles of God. [a]Deut 4:8; Ps 147:19

3 What then? If [a]some did not believe, their unbelief will not nullify the faithfulness of God, will it? [a]Rom 10:16; Heb 4:2

4 May it never be! Rather, let God be found true, though every man be found a liar, as it is written,

"[a]THAT YOU MAY BE JUSTIFIED IN YOUR
        WORDS,
    AND PREVAIL WHEN YOU ARE JUDGED."
            [a]Ps 51:4

5 But if our unrighteousness demonstrates the righteousness of God, what shall we say? The God who inflicts wrath is not unrighteous, is He? ([a]I am speaking in human terms.) [a]Rom 6:19; 1 Cor 9:8

6 May it never be! For otherwise, how will [a]God judge the world? [a]Rom 2:16

7 But if through my lie [a]the truth of God abounded to His glory, [b]why am I also still being judged as a sinner? [a]Rom 3:4 [b]Rom 9:19

8 And why not say (as we are slanderously reported and as some claim that we say), "[a]Let us do evil that good may come"? Their condemnation is just. [a]Rom 6:1

9 What then? Are we better than they? Not at all; for we have already charged that both Jews and Greeks are [a]all under sin; [a]Rom 3:19, 23; 11:32

10 as it is written,

"[a]THERE IS NONE RIGHTEOUS, NOT EVEN ONE;
            [a]Ps 14:1-3; 53:1-3

11 THERE IS NONE WHO UNDERSTANDS,
    THERE IS NONE WHO SEEKS FOR GOD;

12 ALL HAVE TURNED ASIDE, TOGETHER THEY
        HAVE BECOME USELESS;
    THERE IS NONE WHO DOES GOOD,
    THERE IS NOT EVEN ONE."

13 "[a]THEIR THROAT IS AN OPEN GRAVE,
    WITH THEIR TONGUES THEY KEEP DECEIVING,"
    "[b]THE POISON OF ASPS IS UNDER THEIR LIPS";
            [a]Ps 5:9 [b]Ps 140:3

14 "[a]WHOSE MOUTH IS FULL OF CURSING AND BIT-
    TERNESS"; [a]Ps 10:7

15 "ªTHEIR FEET ARE SWIFT TO SHED BLOOD,
ªIs 59:7f

16 DESTRUCTION AND MISERY ARE IN THEIR
PATHS,

17 AND THE PATH OF PEACE THEY HAVE NOT
KNOWN."

18 "ªTHERE IS NO FEAR OF GOD BEFORE THEIR
EYES." ªPs 36:1

19 Now we know that whatever the Law says, it speaks to ªthose who are under the Law, so that every mouth may be closed and ᵇall the world may become accountable to God; ªRom 2:12 ᵇRom 3:9

20 because ªby the works of the Law no flesh will be justified in His sight; for through the Law *comes* the knowledge of sin. ªPs 143:2; Acts 13:39

Justification by Faith

21 But now apart from the Law ª*the* righteousness of God has been manifested, being witnessed by the Law and the Prophets, ªRom 1:17; 9:30

22 even *the* righteousness of God through faith in Jesus Christ for all those who believe; for ªthere is no distinction; ªRom 10:12; Gal 3:28

23 for all ªhave sinned and fall short of the glory of God, ªRom 3:9

24 being justified as a gift ªby His grace through the redemption which is in Christ Jesus; ªRom 4:4f, 16; Eph 2:8

25 whom God displayed publicly as ªa propitiation in His blood through faith. *This was* to demonstrate His righteousness, because in the forbearance of God He passed over the sins previously committed; ª1 John 2:2; 4:10

26 for the demonstration, *I say,* of His righteousness at the present time, so that He would be just and the justifier of the one who has faith in Jesus.

27 Where then is ªboasting? It is excluded. By what kind of law? Of works? No, but by a law of faith. ªRom 2:17, 23; 4:2

28 For ªwe maintain that a man is justified by faith apart from works of the Law. ªActs 13:39; Rom 3:20, 21

29 Or ªis God *the God* of Jews only? Is He not *the God* of Gentiles also? Yes, of Gentiles also, ªActs 10:34f; Rom 9:24

30 since indeed God ªwho will justify the circumcised by faith and the uncircumcised through faith is one. ªRom 3:22; 4:11f, 16

31 Do we then nullify the Law through faith? May it never be! On the contrary, we ªestablish the Law. ªMatt 5:17; Rom 3:4, 6

Justification by Faith Evidenced in Old Testament

4 What then shall we say that Abraham, our forefather ªaccording to the flesh, has found? ªRom 1:3

2 For if Abraham was justified by works, he has something to boast about, but ªnot before God. ª1 Cor 1:31

3 For what does the Scripture say? "ªABRAHAM BELIEVED GOD, AND IT WAS CREDITED TO HIM AS RIGHTEOUSNESS." ªGen 15:6; Rom 4:9, 22

4 Now to the one who ªworks, his wage is not credited as a favor, but as what is due. ªRom 11:6

5 But to the one who does not work, but ªbelieves in Him who justifies the ungodly, his faith is credited as righteousness, ªJohn 6:29; Rom 3:22

6 just as David also speaks of the blessing on the man to whom God credits righteousness apart from works:

7 "ªBLESSED ARE THOSE WHOSE LAWLESS DEEDS
HAVE BEEN FORGIVEN,
AND WHOSE SINS HAVE BEEN COVERED.
ªPs 32:1

8 "ªBLESSED IS THE MAN WHOSE SIN THE LORD
WILL NOT TAKE INTO ACCOUNT." ªPs 32:2

9 Is this blessing then on the circumcised, or on the uncircumcised also? For we say, "ªFAITH WAS CREDITED TO ABRAHAM AS RIGHTEOUSNESS." ªGen 15:6

10 How then was it credited? While he was circumcised, or uncircumcised? Not while circumcised, but while uncircumcised;

11 and he ªreceived the sign of circumcision, a seal of the righteousness of the faith which he had while uncircumcised, so that he might be the father of ᵇall who believe without being circumcised, that righteousness might be credited to them, ªGen 17:10f ᵇRom 3:22

12 and the father of circumcision to those who not only are of the circumcision, but who also follow in the steps of the faith of our father Abraham which he had while uncircumcised.

13 For the promise to Abraham or to his descendants ªthat he would be heir of the world was not through the Law, but through the righteousness of faith. ªGen 17:4-6

14 For ªif those who are of the Law are heirs, faith is made void and the promise is nullified; ªGal 3:18

15 for the Law brings about wrath, but ªwhere there is no law, there also is no violation. ªRom 3:20

16 For this reason *it is* by faith, in order that *it may be* in accordance with ªgrace, so that the promise will be guaranteed to all the descendants, not only to those who are of the Law, but also to ᵇthose who are of the faith of Abraham, who is the father of us all, ªRom 3:24 ᵇGal 3:7

17 (as it is written, "ªA FATHER OF MANY NATIONS HAVE I MADE YOU") in the presence of Him whom he believed, *even* God, who gives

life to the dead and calls into being that which does not exist. ªGen 17:5

18 In hope against hope he believed, so that he might become a father of many nations according to that which had been spoken, "ªSo SHALL YOUR DESCENDANTS BE." ªGen 15:5

19 Without becoming weak in faith he contemplated his own body, now as good as dead since ªhe was about a hundred years old, and ᵇthe deadness of Sarah's womb; ªGen 17:17 ᵇGen 18:11

20 yet, with respect to the promise of God, he did not waver in unbelief but grew strong in faith, ªgiving glory to God, ªMatt 9:8

21 and ªbeing fully assured that what God had promised, He was able also to perform. ªRom 14:5

22 Therefore ªIT WAS ALSO CREDITED TO HIM AS RIGHTEOUSNESS. ªGen 15:6; Rom 4:3

23 Now ªnot for his sake only was it written that it was credited to him, ªRom 15:4; 1 Cor 9:9f

24 but for our sake also, to whom it will be credited, as those ªwho believe in Him who raised Jesus our Lord from the dead, ªRom 10:9; 1 Pet 1:21

25 He who was ªdelivered over because of our transgressions, and was raised because of our justification. ªIs 53:4, 5; Rom 8:32

Results of Justification

5 ªTherefore, having been justified by faith, we have peace with God through our Lord Jesus Christ, ªRom 3:28

2 through whom also we have ªobtained our introduction by faith into this grace in which we stand; and we exult in hope of the glory of God. ªEph 2:18; 3:12

3 And not only this, but we also ªexult in our tribulations, knowing that tribulation brings about perseverance; ªMatt 5:12; James 1:2f

4 and perseverance, ªproven character; and proven character, hope; ªPhil 2:22; James 1:12

5 and hope ªdoes not disappoint, because the love of God has been poured out within our hearts through the Holy Spirit who was given to us. ªPs 119:116; Rom 9:33

6 For while we were still helpless, at the right time ªChrist died for the ungodly. ªRom 4:25; 5:8

7 For one will hardly die for a righteous man; though perhaps for the good man someone would dare even to die.

8 But God demonstrates ªHis own love toward us, in that while we were yet sinners, Christ died for us. ªJohn 3:16; 15:13

9 Much more then, having now been justified ªby His blood, we shall be saved ᵇfrom the wrath of God through Him. ªRom 3:25 ᵇRom 1:18

10 For if while we were ªenemies we were reconciled to God through the death of His Son, much more, having been reconciled, we shall be saved by His life. ªRom 11:28; Col 1:21f

11 And not only this, but we also exult in God through our Lord Jesus Christ, through whom we have now received ªthe reconciliation. ªRom 5:10; 11:15

12 Therefore, just as through one man sin entered into the world, and ªdeath through sin, and so death spread to all men, because all sinned— ªRom 6:23; 1 Cor 15:56

13 for until the Law sin was in the world, but ªsin is not imputed when there is no law. ªRom 4:15

14 Nevertheless death reigned from Adam until Moses, even over those who had not sinned ªin the likeness of the offense of Adam, who is a ᵇtype of Him who was to come. ªHos 6:7 ᵇ1 Cor 15:45

15 But the free gift is not like the transgression. For if by the transgression of the one the many died, much more did the grace of God and the gift by ªthe grace of the one Man, Jesus Christ, abound to the many. ªActs 15:11

16 The gift is not like that which came through the one who sinned; for on the one hand ªthe judgment arose from one transgression resulting in condemnation, but on the other hand the free gift arose from many transgressions resulting in justification. ª1 Cor 11:32

17 For if by the transgression of the one, death reigned through the one, much more those who receive the abundance of grace and of the gift of righteousness will ªreign in life through the One, Jesus Christ. ª2 Tim 2:12; Rev 22:5

18 So then as through one transgression there resulted condemnation to all men, even so through one act of righteousness there resulted ªjustification of life to all men. ªRom 4:25

19 For as through the one man's disobedience the many were made sinners, even so through ªthe obedience of the One the many will be made righteous. ªPhil 2:8

20 The Law came in so that the transgression would increase; but where sin increased, ªgrace abounded all the more, ªRom 6:1; 1 Tim 1:14

21 so that, as sin reigned in death, even so ªgrace would reign through righteousness to eternal life through Jesus Christ our Lord. ªJohn 1:17; Rom 6:23

Believers Are Dead to Sin, Alive to God

6 What shall we say then? Are we to ªcontinue in sin so that grace may increase? ªRom 3:8; 6:15

2 May it never be! How shall we who ªdied to sin still live in it? ªRom 6:11; 7:4, 6

3 Or do you not know that all of us who have been baptized into ªChrist Jesus have been baptized into His death? ªActs 2:38; 8:16

4 Therefore we have been ªburied with Him

through baptism into death, so that as Christ was raised from the dead through the glory of the Father, so we too might walk in newness of life. [a]*Col 2:12*

5 For [a]if we have become united with *Him* in the likeness of His death, certainly we shall also be *in the likeness* of His resurrection, [a]*2 Cor 4:10; Phil 3:10f*

6 knowing this, that our [a]old self was crucified with *Him*, in order that our body of sin might be done away with, so that we would no longer be slaves to sin; [a]*Eph 4:22; Col 3:9*

7 for [a]he who has died is freed from sin. [a]*1 Pet 4:1*

8 Now [a]if we have died with Christ, we believe that we shall also live with Him, [a]*Rom 6:4; 2 Cor 4:10*

9 knowing that Christ, having been [a]raised from the dead, is never to die again; death no longer is master over Him. [a]*Acts 2:24; Rom 6:4*

10 For the death that He died, He died to sin once for all; but the life that He lives, He lives to God.

11 Even so consider yourselves to be [a]dead to sin, but alive to God in Christ Jesus. [a]*Rom 6:2; 7:4, 6*

12 Therefore do not let sin [a]reign in your mortal body so that you obey its lusts. [a]*Rom 6:14*

13 and do not go on presenting the members of your body to sin *as* instruments of unrighteousness; but [a]present yourselves to God as those alive from the dead, and your members *as* instruments of righteousness to God. [a]*Rom 12:1; 2 Cor 5:14f*

14 For [a]sin shall not be master over you, for [b]you are not under law but under grace. [a]*Rom 8:2, 12* [b]*Rom 7:4, 6*

15 What then? [a]Shall we sin because we are not under law but under grace? May it never be! [a]*Rom 6:1*

16 Do you not know that when you present yourselves to someone *as* [a]slaves for obedience, you are slaves of the one whom you obey, either of sin resulting in death, or of obedience resulting in righteousness? [a]*John 8:34; 2 Pet 2:19*

17 But thanks be to God that though you were slaves of sin, you became obedient from the heart to that [a]form of teaching to which you were committed, [a]*2 Tim 1:13*

18 and having been [a]freed from sin, you became slaves of righteousness. [a]*John 8:32; Rom 6:22*

19 I am speaking in human terms because of the weakness of your flesh. For just [a]as you presented your members as slaves to impurity and to lawlessness, resulting in *further* lawlessness, so now present your members as slaves to righteousness, resulting in sanctification. [a]*Rom 6:13*

20 For [a]when you were slaves of sin, you were free in regard to righteousness. [a]*Matt 6:24; Rom 6:16*

21 Therefore what [a]benefit were you then deriving from the things of which you are now ashamed? For the outcome of those things is death. [a]*Jer 12:13; Ezek 16:63*

22 But now having been [a]freed from sin and enslaved to God, you derive your benefit, resulting in sanctification, and the outcome, eternal life. [a]*John 8:32; Rom 6:18*

23 For the wages of [a]sin is death, but the free gift of God is eternal life in Christ Jesus our Lord. [a]*Rom 6:16; 8:6, 13*

Believers United to Christ

7 Or do you not know, [a]brethren (for I am speaking to those who know the law), that the law has jurisdiction over a person as long as he lives? [a]*Rom 1:13*

2 For [a]the married woman is bound by law to her husband while he is living; but if her husband dies, she is released from the law concerning the husband. [a]*1 Cor 7:39*

3 So then, if while her husband is living she is joined to another man, she shall be called an adulteress; but if her husband dies, she is free from the law, so that she is not an adulteress though she is joined to another man.

4 Therefore, my brethren, you also were [a]made to die [b]to the Law through the body of Christ, so that you might be joined to another, to Him who was raised from the dead, in order that we might bear fruit for God. [a]*Rom 7:6* [b]*Gal 2:19*

5 For while we were in the flesh, the sinful passions, which were [a]aroused by the Law, were at work [b]in the members of our body to bear fruit for death. [a]*Rom 7:7f* [b]*Rom 6:13, 21, 23*

6 But now we have been released from the Law, having [a]died to that by which we were bound, so that we serve in newness of the Spirit and not in oldness of the letter. [a]*Rom 6:2*

7 What shall we say then? Is the Law sin? May it never be! On the contrary, I would not have come to know sin except through the Law; for I would not have known about coveting if the Law had not said, "[a]YOU SHALL NOT COVET." [a]*Ex 20:17; Deut 5:21*

8 But sin, taking opportunity [a]through the commandment, produced in me coveting of every kind; for apart from the Law sin *is* dead. [a]*Rom 3:20; 7:11*

9 I was once alive apart from the Law; but when the commandment came, sin became alive and I died;

10 and this commandment, which was [a]to result in life, proved to result in death for me; [a]*Lev 18:5; Luke 10:28*

11 for sin, taking an opportunity through the

commandment, ªdeceived me and through it killed me. ªGen 3:13

12 ªSo then, the Law is holy, and the commandment is holy and righteous and good. ªRom 7:16; 1 Tim 1:8

13 Therefore did that which is good become *a cause of* death for me? ªMay it never be! Rather it was sin, in order that it might be shown to be sin by effecting my death through that which is good, so that through the commandment sin would become utterly sinful. ªLuke 20:16

The Conflict of Two Natures

14 For we know that the Law is ªspiritual, but I am of flesh, sold into bondage to sin. ª1 Cor 3:1

15 For what I am doing, I do not understand; for I am not practicing ªwhat I *would* like to *do,* but I am doing the very thing I hate. ªRom 7:19; Gal 5:17

16 But if I do the very thing I do not want *to do,* I agree with ªthe Law, *confessing* that the Law is good. ªRom 7:12; 1 Tim 1:8

17 So now, ªno longer am I the one doing it, but sin which dwells in me. ªRom 7:20

18 For I know that nothing good dwells in me, that is, in my ªflesh; for the willing is present in me, but the doing of the good *is* not. ªJohn 3:6; Rom 7:25

19 For ªthe good that I want, I do not do, but I practice the very evil that I do not want. ªRom 7:15

20 But if I am doing the very thing I do not want, ªI am no longer the one doing it, but sin which dwells in me. ªRom 7:17

21 I find then ªthe principle that evil is present in me, the one who wants to do good. ªRom 7:23, 25; 8:2

22 For I joyfully concur with the law of God in ªthe inner man, ª2 Cor 4:16; Eph 3:16

23 but I see ªa different law in the members of my body, waging war against the law of my mind and making me a prisoner of the law of sin which is in my members. ªRom 6:19; Gal 5:17

24 Wretched man that I am! Who will set me free from ªthe body of this death? ªRom 6:6; Col 2:11

25 ªThanks be to God through Jesus Christ our Lord! So then, on the one hand I myself with my mind am serving the law of God, but on the other, with my flesh the law of sin. ª1 Cor 15:57

Deliverance from Bondage

8 Therefore there is now no ªcondemnation for those who are ᵇin Christ Jesus. ªRom 8:34 ᵇRom 8:9f

2 For ªthe law of the Spirit of life in Christ Jesus has set you free from the law of sin and of death. ª1 Cor 15:45

3 For ªwhat the Law could not do, weak as it was through the flesh, God *did:* sending His own Son in the likeness of sinful flesh and *as an offering* for sin, He condemned sin in the flesh, ªActs 13:39; Heb 10:1ff

4 so that the requirement of the Law might be fulfilled in us, who ªdo not walk according to the flesh but according to the Spirit. ªGal 5:16, 25

5 For those who are according to the flesh set their minds on ªthe things of the flesh, but those who are according to the Spirit, ᵇthe things of the Spirit. ªGal 5:19-21 ᵇGal 5:22-25

6 ªFor the mind set on the flesh is death, but the mind set on the Spirit is life and peace, ªGal 6:8

7 because the mind set on the flesh is ªhostile toward God; for it does not subject itself to the law of God, for it is not even able *to do so,* ªJames 4:4

8 and those who are ªin the flesh cannot please God. ªRom 7:5

9 However, you are not in the flesh but in the Spirit, if indeed the Spirit of God ªdwells in you. But if anyone does not have the Spirit of Christ, he does not belong to Him. ᵇJohn 14:23; Rom 8:11

10 ªIf Christ is in you, though the body is dead because of sin, yet the spirit is alive because of righteousness. ªJohn 17:23; Gal 2:20

11 But if the Spirit of Him who ªraised Jesus from the dead dwells in you, He who raised Christ Jesus from the dead will also give life to your mortal bodies through His Spirit who dwells in you. ªActs 2:24; Rom 6:4

12 So then, brethren, we are under obligation, not to the flesh, to live according to the flesh—

13 for if you are living according to the flesh, you must die; but if by the Spirit you are ªputting to death the deeds of the body, you will live. ªCol 3:5

14 For all who are ªbeing led by the Spirit of God, these are sons of God. ªGal 5:18

15 For you ªhave not received a spirit of slavery leading to fear again, but you ᵇhave received a spirit of adoption as sons by which we cry out, "Abba! Father!" ªHeb 2:15 ᵇRom 8:23

16 The Spirit Himself ªtestifies with our spirit that we are children of God, ªActs 5:32

17 and if children, ªheirs also, heirs of God and fellow heirs with Christ, if indeed we suffer with *Him* so that we may also be glorified with *Him.* ªActs 20:32; Gal 3:29

18 For I consider that the sufferings of this present time ªare not worthy to be compared with the glory that is to be revealed to us. ª2 Cor 4:17; 1 Pet 4:13

19 For the anxious longing of the creation waits eagerly for ªthe revealing of the sons of God. ªRom 8:18; 1 Cor 1:7f

20 For the creation ªwas subjected to ᵇfutility,

not willingly, but because of Him who subjected it, in hope. [a]*Gen 3:17-19* [b]*Ps 39:5f*

21 that [a]the creation itself also will be set free from its slavery to corruption into the freedom of the glory of the children of God. [a]*Acts 3:21; 2 Pet 3:13*

22 For we know that the whole creation [a]groans and suffers the pains of childbirth together until now. [a]*Jer 12:4, 11*

23 And not only this, but also we ourselves, having [a]the first fruits of the Spirit, even we ourselves groan within ourselves, waiting eagerly for *our* adoption as sons, the redemption of our body. [a]*Rom 8:16; 2 Cor 1:22*

24 For in hope we have been saved, but [a]hope that is seen is not hope; for who hopes for what he *already* sees? [a]*Rom 4:18; 2 Cor 5:7*

25 But [a]if we hope for what we do not see, with perseverance we wait eagerly for it. [a]*1 Thess 1:3*

Our Victory in Christ

26 In the same way the Spirit also helps our weakness; for we do not know how to pray as we should, but [a]the Spirit Himself intercedes for *us* with groanings too deep for words; [a]*John 14:16; Rom 8:15f*

27 and [a]He who searches the hearts knows what the mind of the Spirit is, because He intercedes for the saints according to *the will of* God. [a]*Ps 139:1f; Luke 16:15*

28 And we know that God causes [a]all things to work together for good to those who love God, to those who are [b]called according to *His* purpose. [a]*Rom 8:32* [b]*Rom 8:30*

29 For those whom He [a]foreknew, He also predestined *to become* conformed to the image of His Son, so that He would be the firstborn among many brethren; [a]*Rom 11:2; 1 Cor 8:3*

30 and these whom He predestined, He also called; and these whom He called, He also [a]justified; and these whom He justified, He also [b]glorified. [a]*1 Cor 6:11* [b]*John 17:22*

31 What then shall we say to these things? [a]If God *is* for us, who *is* against us? [a]*Ps 118:6; Matt 1:23*

32 He who [a]did not spare His own Son, but delivered Him over for us all, how will He not also with Him freely give us all things? [a]*John 3:16; Rom 5:8*

33 Who will bring a charge against God's elect? [a]God is the one who justifies; [a]*Is 50:8f*

34 who is the one who condemns? Christ Jesus is He who died, yes, rather who was raised, who is at the right hand of God, who also [a]intercedes for us. [a]*Rom 8:27; Heb 7:25*

35 Who will separate us from the love of Christ? Will [a]tribulation, or distress, or [b]persecution, or famine, or [b]nakedness, or peril, or sword? [a]*2 Cor 4:8* [b]*1 Cor 4:11*

36 Just as it is written,
"[a]FOR YOUR SAKE WE ARE BEING PUT TO DEATH
    ALL DAY LONG;
WE WERE CONSIDERED AS SHEEP TO BE
    SLAUGHTERED." [a]*Ps 44:22; Acts 20:24*

37 But in all these things we overwhelmingly [a]conquer through Him who loved us. [a]*John 16:33; 1 Cor 15:57*

38 For I am convinced that neither [a]death, nor life, nor angels, nor principalities, nor [a]things present, nor things to come, nor powers, [a]*1 Cor 3:22*

39 nor height, nor depth, nor any other created thing, will be able to separate us from [a]the love of God, which is in Christ Jesus our Lord. [a]*Rom 5:8*

Solicitude for Israel

9 [a]I am telling the truth in Christ, I am not lying, my conscience testifies with me in the Holy Spirit, [a]*2 Cor 11:10; Gal 1:20*

2 that I have great sorrow and unceasing grief in my heart.

3 For [a]I could wish that I myself were accursed, *separated* from Christ for the sake of my brethren, my kinsmen [b]according to the flesh, [a]*Ex 32:32* [b]*Rom 11:14*

4 who are Israelites, to whom belongs the adoption as sons, and the glory and the covenants and the giving of the Law and the *temple* service and the promises, [a]*Ex 4:22; Rom 8:15*

5 whose are the fathers, and [a]from whom is the Christ according to the flesh, [b]who is over all, God blessed forever. Amen. [a]*Matt 1:1-16* [b]*Col 1:16-19*

6 But *it is* not as though the word of God has failed. [a]For they are not all Israel who are *descended* from Israel; [a]*Rom 2:28f; Gal 6:16*

7 nor are they all children [a]because they are Abraham's descendants, but: "[b]THROUGH ISAAC YOUR DESCENDANTS WILL BE NAMED." [a]*John 8:23* [b]*Gen 21:12*

8 That is, it is not the children of the flesh who are children of God, but the [a]children of the promise are regarded as descendants. [a]*Rom 4:13, 16; Gal 3:29*

9 For this is the word of promise: "[a]AT THIS TIME I WILL COME, AND SARAH SHALL HAVE A SON." [a]*Gen 18:10*

10 And not only this, but there was [a]Rebekah also, when she had conceived *twins* by one man, our father Isaac; [a]*Gen 25:21*

11 for though *the twins* were not yet born and had not done anything good or bad, so that [a]God's purpose according to *His* choice would stand, not because of works but because of Him who calls, [a]*Rom 4:17; 8:28*

12 it was said to her, "[a]THE OLDER WILL SERVE THE YOUNGER." [a]*Gen 25:23*

13 Just as it is written, "ᵃJACOB I LOVED, BUT ESAU I HATED." ᵃMal 1:2f

14 What shall we say then? ᵃThere is no injustice with God, is there? May it never be! ᵃ2 Chr 19:7; Rom 2:11

15 For He says to Moses, "ᵃI WILL HAVE MERCY ON WHOM I HAVE MERCY, AND I WILL HAVE COMPASSION ON WHOM I HAVE COMPASSION." ᵃEx 33:19

16 So then it *does* not *depend* on the man who wills or the man who runs, but on ᵃGod who has mercy. ᵃEph 2:8

17 For the Scripture says to Pharaoh, "ᵃFOR THIS VERY PURPOSE I RAISED YOU UP, TO DEMONSTRATE MY POWER IN YOU, AND THAT MY NAME MIGHT BE PROCLAIMED THROUGHOUT THE WHOLE EARTH." ᵃEx 9:16

18 So then He has mercy on whom He desires, and He ᵃhardens whom He desires. ᵃEx 4:21; 7:3

19 You will say to me then, "Why does He still find fault? For ᵃwho resists His will?" ᵃ2 Chr 20:6; Job 9:12

20 On the contrary, who are you, O man, who ᵃanswers back to God? ᵇThe thing molded will not say to the molder, "Why did you make me like this," will it? ᵃJob 33:13 ᵇIs 29:16

21 Or does not the potter have a right over the clay, to make from the same lump one vessel for honorable use and another for common use?

22 What if God, although willing to demonstrate His wrath and to make His power known, endured with much patience vessels of wrath ᵃprepared for destruction? ᵃProv 16:4; 1 Pet 2:8

23 And *He did so* to make known ᵃthe riches of His glory upon vessels of mercy, which He prepared beforehand for glory, ᵃRom 2:4; Eph 3:16

24 *even* us, whom He also called, ᵃnot from among Jews only, but also from among Gentiles. ᵃRom 3:29

25 As He says also in Hosea,
"ᵃI WILL CALL THOSE WHO WERE NOT MY PEOPLE, 'MY PEOPLE,'
AND HER WHO WAS NOT BELOVED,
'BELOVED.' " ᵃHos 2:23; 1 Pet 2:10

26 "ᵃAND IT SHALL BE THAT IN THE PLACE WHERE IT WAS SAID TO THEM, 'YOU ARE NOT MY PEOPLE,'
THERE THEY SHALL BE CALLED SONS OF THE LIVING GOD." ᵃHos 1:10

27 Isaiah cries out concerning Israel, "ᵃTHOUGH THE NUMBER OF THE SONS OF ISRAEL BE LIKE THE SAND OF THE SEA, IT IS THE REMNANT THAT WILL BE SAVED; ᵃIs 10:22

28 ᵃFOR THE LORD WILL EXECUTE HIS WORD ON THE EARTH, THOROUGHLY AND QUICKLY." ᵃIs 10:23

29 And just as Isaiah foretold,
"ᵃUNLESS THE LORD OF SABAOTH HAD LEFT TO US A POSTERITY,
WE WOULD HAVE BECOME LIKE SODOM, AND WOULD HAVE RESEMBLED GOMORRAH." ᵃIs 1:9

30 What shall we say then? That Gentiles, who did not pursue righteousness, attained righteousness, even ᵃthe righteousness which is by faith; ᵃRom 1:17; 3:21f

31 but Israel, ᵃpursuing a law of righteousness, did not arrive at *that* law. ᵃIs 51:1; Rom 9:30

32 Why? Because *they did* not *pursue it* by faith, but as though *it were* by works. They stumbled over ᵃthe stumbling stone, ᵃIs 8:14; 1 Pet 2:6, 8

33 just as it is written,
"ᵃBEHOLD, I LAY IN ZION ᵇA STONE OF STUMBLING AND A ROCK OF OFFENSE,
AND HE WHO BELIEVES IN HIM WILL NOT BE DISAPPOINTED." ᵃIs 28:16 ᵇIs 8:14

The Word of Faith Brings Salvation

10 Brethren, my heart's desire and my prayer to God for them is for *their* salvation.

2 For I testify about them that they have ᵃa zeal for God, but not in accordance with knowledge. ᵃActs 21:20

3 For not knowing about ᵃGod's righteousness and seeking to establish their own, they did not subject themselves to the righteousness of God. ᵃRom 1:17

4 For ᵃChrist is the end of the law for righteousness to everyone who believes. ᵃRom 7:1-4; Gal 3:24

5 For Moses writes that the man who practices the righteousness which is based on law ᵃshall live by that righteousness. ᵃLev 18:5; Neh 9:29

6 But ᵃthe righteousness based on faith speaks as follows: "ᵇDO NOT SAY IN YOUR HEART, 'WHO WILL ASCEND INTO HEAVEN?' (that is, to bring Christ down), ᵃRom 9:30 ᵇDeut 30:12

7 or 'WHO WILL DESCEND INTO THE ABYSS?' (that is, to ᵃbring Christ up from the dead)." ᵃHeb 13:20

8 But what does it say? "THE WORD IS NEAR YOU, IN YOUR MOUTH AND IN YOUR HEART"—that is, the word of faith which we are preaching,

9 that if you confess with your mouth Jesus *as* Lord, and believe in your heart that ᵃGod raised Him from the dead, you will be saved; ᵃActs 2:24

10 for with the heart a person believes, resulting in righteousness, and with the mouth he confesses, resulting in salvation.

11 For the Scripture says, "ᵃWHOEVER BELIEVES IN HIM WILL NOT BE DISAPPOINTED." ᵃIs 28:16; Rom 9:33

12 For ᵃthere is no distinction between Jew and Greek; for the same *Lord* is Lord of all, abounding in riches for all who call on Him; ᵃRom 3:22, 29

13 for "ᵃWHOEVER WILL CALL ON THE NAME OF THE LORD WILL BE SAVED." ᵃJoel 2:32; Acts 2:21

14 How then will they call on Him in whom they have not believed? How will they believe in Him ᵃwhom they have not heard? And how will they hear without ᵇa preacher? ᵃEph 2:17 ᵇActs 8:31

15 How will they preach unless they are sent? Just as it is written, "ᵃHOW BEAUTIFUL ARE THE FEET OF THOSE WHO BRING GOOD NEWS OF GOOD THINGS!" ᵃIs 52:7

16 However, they did not all heed the good news; for Isaiah says, "ᵃLORD, WHO HAS BELIEVED OUR REPORT?" ᵃIs 53:1; John 12:38

17 So faith comes from ᵃhearing, and hearing by ᵇthe word of Christ. ᵃGal 3:2, 5 ᵇCol 3:16

18 But I say, surely they have never heard, have they? Indeed they have;
"ᵃTHEIR VOICE HAS GONE OUT INTO ALL THE EARTH,
AND THEIR WORDS TO THE ENDS OF THE WORLD." ᵃPs 19:4; Rom 1:8

19 But I say, surely Israel did not know, did they? First Moses says,
"ᵃI WILL MAKE YOU JEALOUS BY THAT WHICH IS NOT A NATION,
BY A NATION WITHOUT UNDERSTANDING WILL I ANGER YOU." ᵃDeut 32:21

20 And Isaiah is very bold and says,
"ᵃI WAS FOUND BY THOSE WHO DID NOT SEEK ME,
I BECAME MANIFEST TO THOSE WHO DID NOT ASK FOR ME." ᵃIs 65:1; Rom 9:30

21 But as for Israel He says, "ᵃALL THE DAY LONG I HAVE STRETCHED OUT MY HANDS TO A DISOBEDIENT AND OBSTINATE PEOPLE." ᵃIs 65:2

Israel Is Not Cast Away

11 I say then, God has not ᵃrejected His people, has He? May it never be! For I too am an Israelite, a descendant of Abraham, of the tribe of Benjamin. ᵃ1 Sam 12:22; Jer 31:37

2 God ᵃhas not rejected His people whom He foreknew. Or do you not know what the Scripture says in the passage about Elijah, how he pleads with God against Israel? ᵃPs 94:14

3 "Lord, ᵃTHEY HAVE KILLED YOUR PROPHETS, THEY HAVE TORN DOWN YOUR ALTARS, AND I ALONE AM LEFT, AND THEY ARE SEEKING MY LIFE." ᵃ1 Kin 19:10, 14

4 But what is the divine response to him? "ᵃI HAVE KEPT for Myself SEVEN THOUSAND MEN WHO HAVE NOT BOWED THE KNEE TO BAAL." ᵃ1 Kin 19:18

5 In the same way then, there has also come to be at the present time ᵃa remnant according to God's gracious choice. ᵃ2 Kin 19:4; Rom 9:27

6 But ᵃif it is by grace, it is no longer on the basis of works, otherwise grace is no longer grace. ᵃRom 4:4

7 What then? What ᵃIsrael is seeking, it has not obtained, but those who were chosen obtained it, and the rest were ᵇhardened; ᵃRom 9:31 ᵇMark 6:52

8 just as it is written,
"ᵃGOD GAVE THEM A SPIRIT OF STUPOR,
EYES TO SEE NOT AND EARS TO HEAR NOT,
DOWN TO THIS VERY DAY." ᵃDeut 29:4; Is 29:10

9 And David says,
"ᵃLET THEIR TABLE BECOME A SNARE AND A TRAP,
AND A STUMBLING BLOCK AND A RETRIBUTION TO THEM. ᵃPs 69:22

10 "ᵃLET THEIR EYES BE DARKENED TO SEE NOT,
AND BEND THEIR BACKS FOREVER." ᵃPs 69:23

11 I say then, they did not stumble so as to fall, did they? May it never be! But by their transgression ᵃsalvation has come to the Gentiles, to make them jealous. ᵃActs 28:28

12 Now if their transgression is riches for the world and their failure is riches for the Gentiles, how much more will their ᵃfulfillment be! ᵃRom 11:25

13 But I am speaking to you who are Gentiles. Inasmuch then as ᵃI am an apostle of Gentiles, I magnify my ministry; ᵃActs 9:15

14 if somehow I might move to jealousy my fellow countrymen and ᵃsave some of them. ᵃ1 Cor 1:21; 9:22

15 For if their rejection is the ᵃreconciliation of the world, what will their acceptance be but life from the dead? ᵃRom 5:11

16 If the ᵃfirst piece of dough is holy, the lump is also; and if the root is holy, the branches are too. ᵃNum 15:18ff; Neh 10:37

17 But if some of the ᵃbranches were broken off, and ᵇyou, being a wild olive, were grafted in among them and became partaker with them of the rich root of the olive tree, ᵃJohn 15:2 ᵇEph 2:11ff

18 do not be arrogant toward the branches; but if you are arrogant, remember that ᵃit is not you who supports the root, but the root supports you. ᵃJohn 4:22

19 ᵃYou will say then, "Branches were broken off so that I might be grafted in." ᵃRom 9:19

20 Quite right, they were broken off for their unbelief, but you ᵃstand by your faith. Do not be conceited, but fear; ᵃRom 5:2; 2 Cor 1:24

21 for if God did not spare the natural branches, He will not spare you, either.

22 Behold then the kindness and severity of God; to those who fell, severity, but to you, God's kindness, ᵃif you continue in His kindness; otherwise you also will be cut off. ᵃ1 Cor 15:2; Heb 3:6, 14

23 And they also, ᵃif they do not continue in their unbelief, will be grafted in, for God is able to graft them in again. ᵃ2 Cor 3:16

24 For if you were cut off from what is by nature a wild olive tree, and were grafted con-

trary to nature into a cultivated olive tree, how much more will these who are the natural *branches* be grafted into their own olive tree? **25** For I do not want you, brethren, to be uninformed of this mystery—so that you will not be ªwise in your own estimation—that a partial hardening has happened to Israel until the fullness of the Gentiles has come in; ªRom 12:16

26 and so all Israel will be saved; just as it is written,

"ªTHE DELIVERER WILL COME FROM ZION,
    HE WILL REMOVE UNGODLINESS FROM JACOB."
        ªIs 59:20

27 "ªTHIS IS MY COVENANT WITH THEM,
    WHEN I TAKE AWAY THEIR SINS." ªIs 59:21;
        Jer 31:33, 34

28 From the standpoint of the gospel they are enemies for your sake, but from the standpoint of *God's* choice they are beloved for ªthe sake of the fathers; ªDeut 7:8; 10:15

29 for the gifts and the ªcalling of God are irrevocable. ªRom 8:28; 1 Cor 1:26

30 For just as you once were disobedient to God, but now have been shown mercy because of their disobedience,

31 so these also now have been disobedient, that because of the mercy shown to you they also may now be shown mercy.

32 For ªGod has shut up all in disobedience so that He may show mercy to all. ªRom 3:9; Gal 3:22f

33 Oh, the depth of ªthe riches both of the ᵇwisdom and knowledge of God! How unsearchable are His judgments and unfathomable His ways! ªRom 2:4 ᵇCol 2:3

34 For ªWHO HAS KNOWN THE MIND OF THE LORD, OR WHO BECAME HIS COUNSELOR? ªIs 40:13f; 1 Cor 2:16

35 Or ªWHO HAS FIRST GIVEN TO HIM THAT IT MIGHT BE PAID BACK TO HIM AGAIN? ªJob 35:7; 41:11

36 For ªfrom Him and through Him and to Him are all things. To Him *be* the glory forever. Amen. ª1 Cor 8:6; Col 1:16

Dedicated Service

12 Therefore I urge you, brethren, by the mercies of God, to ªpresent your bodies a living and holy sacrifice, acceptable to God, *which is* your spiritual service of worship. ªRom 6:13, 19; 1 Pet 2:5

2 And do not be conformed to this world, but be transformed by the ªrenewing of your mind, so that you may ᵇprove what the will of God is, that which is good and acceptable and perfect. ªEph 4:23 ᵇEph 5:10, 17

3 For through the grace given to me I say to everyone among you ªnot to think more highly of himself than he ought to think; but to think so as to have sound judgment, as God has

allotted to each a measure of faith. ªRom 11:20; 12:16

4 For ªjust as we have many members in one body and all the members do not have the same function, ª1 Cor 12:12-14; Eph 4:4, 16

5 so we, ªwho are many, are ᵇone body in Christ, and individually members one of another. ª1 Cor 10:17 ᵇ1 Cor 12:20, 27

6 Since we have gifts that ªdiffer according to the grace given to us, *each of us is to exercise them accordingly:* if prophecy, according to the proportion of his faith; ªRom 12:3; 1 Cor 7:7

7 if ªservice, in his serving; or he who ᵇteaches, in his teaching; ªActs 6:1 ᵇActs 13:1

8 or he who exhorts, in his exhortation; he who gives, with liberality; ªhe who leads, with diligence; he who shows mercy, with cheerfulness. ª1 Tim 5:17

9 *Let* ªlove *be* without hypocrisy. Abhor what is evil; cling to what is good. ª2 Cor 6:6; 1 Tim 1:5

10 *Be* ªdevoted to one another in brotherly love; give preference to one another in honor; ªJohn 13:34; 1 Thess 4:9

11 not lagging behind in diligence, ªfervent in spirit, ᵇserving the Lord; ªActs 18:25 ᵇActs 20:19

12 ªrejoicing in hope, persevering in tribulation, ᵇdevoted to prayer, ªRom 5:2 ᵇActs 1:14

13 ªcontributing to the needs of the saints, ᵇpracticing hospitality. ª2 Cor 9:1 ᵇMatt 25:35

14 ªBless those who persecute you; bless and do not curse. ªMatt 5:44; Luke 6:28

15 ªRejoice with those who rejoice, and weep with those who weep. ªJob 30:25; Heb 13:3

16 Be of the same mind toward one another; do not be haughty in mind, but associate with the lowly. ªDo not be wise in your own estimation. ªProv 3:7; Rom 11:25

17 ªNever pay back evil for evil to anyone. ᵇRespect what is right in the sight of all men. ªProv 20:22 ᵇ2 Cor 8:21

18 If possible, so far as it depends on you, ªbe at peace with all men. ªMark 9:50; Rom 14:19

19 Never take your own revenge, beloved, but leave room for the wrath *of God*, for it is written, "ªVENGEANCE IS MINE, I WILL REPAY," says the Lord. ªDeut 32:35; Ps 94:1

20 "ªBUT IF YOUR ENEMY IS HUNGRY, FEED HIM, AND IF HE IS THIRSTY, GIVE HIM A DRINK; FOR IN SO DOING YOU WILL HEAP BURNING COALS ON HIS HEAD." ª2 Kin 6:22; Prov 25:21f

21 Do not be overcome by evil, but overcome evil with good.

Be Subject to Government

13 Every person is to be in ªsubjection to the governing authorities. For there is no authority except from God, and those which exist are established by God. ªTitus 3:1; 1 Pet 2:13f

2 Therefore whoever resists authority has opposed the ordinance of God; and they who have opposed will receive condemnation upon themselves.

3 For ªrulers are not a cause of fear for good behavior, but for evil. Do you want to have no fear of authority? Do what is good and you will have praise from the same; ª*1 Pet 2:14*

4 for it is a minister of God to you for good. But if you do what is evil, be afraid; for it does not bear the sword for nothing; for it is a minister of God, an ªavenger who brings wrath on the one who practices evil. ª*1 Thess 4:6*

5 Therefore it is necessary to be in subjection, not only because of wrath, but also ªfor conscience' sake. ª*Eccl 8; 1 Pet 2:13, 19*

6 For because of this you also pay taxes, for *rulers* are servants of God, devoting themselves to this very thing.

7 ªRender to all what is due them: tax to whom tax *is due;* custom to whom custom; fear to whom fear; honor to whom honor. ª*Matt 22:21; Mark 12:17*

8 Owe nothing to anyone except to love one another; for ªhe who loves his neighbor has fulfilled *the* law. ª*Matt 7:12; 22:39f*

9 For this, "ªYOU SHALL NOT COMMIT ADULTERY, YOU SHALL NOT MURDER, YOU SHALL NOT STEAL, YOU SHALL NOT COVET," and if there is any other commandment, it is summed up in this saying, "ᵇYOU SHALL LOVE YOUR NEIGHBOR AS YOURSELF." ª*Ex 20:13ff* ᵇ*Lev 19:18*

10 Love does no wrong to a neighbor; therefore ªlove is the fulfillment of *the* law. ª*Matt 7:12; 22:39f*

11 *Do* this, knowing the time, that it is already the hour for you to ªawaken from sleep; for now salvation is nearer to us than when we believed. ª*Mark 13:37; 1 Cor 15:34*

12 The night is almost gone, and the day is near. Therefore let us lay aside ªthe deeds of darkness and put on ᵇthe armor of light. ª*Eph 5:11* ᵇ*Eph 6:11, 13*

13 Let us ªbehave properly as in the day, not in carousing and drunkenness, not in sexual promiscuity and sensuality, not in strife and jealousy. ª*1 Thess 4:12*

14 But ªput on the Lord Jesus Christ, and make no provision for the flesh in regard to *its* lusts. ª*Job 29:14; Gal 3:27*

Principles of Conscience

14 Now ªaccept the one who is weak in faith, *but* not for *the purpose of* passing judgment on his opinions. ª*Acts 28:2; Rom 11:15*

2 One person has faith that he may eat all things, but he who is ªweak eats vegetables *only.* ª*Rom 14:1; 15:1*

3 The one who eats is not to ªregard with contempt the one who does not eat, and the one who does not eat is not to judge the one

who eats, for God has accepted him. ª*Luke 18:9; Rom 14:10*

4 ªWho are you to judge the servant of another? To his own master he stands or falls; and he will stand, for the Lord is able to make him stand. ª*Rom 9:20; James 4:12*

5 ªOne person regards one day above another, another regards every day *alike*. Each person must be ᵇfully convinced in his own mind. ª*Gal 4:10* ᵇ*Rom 4:21*

6 He who observes the day, observes it for the Lord, and he who eats, does so for the Lord, for he ªgives thanks to God; and he who eats not, for the Lord he does not eat, and gives thanks to God. ª*Matt 14:19; 15:36*

7 For not one of us ªlives for himself, and not one dies for himself; ª*Rom 8:38f; 2 Cor 5:15*

8 for if we live, we live for the Lord, or if we die, we die for the Lord; therefore ªwhether we live or die, we are the Lord's. ª*Luke 20:38; Phil 1:20*

9 For to this end ªChrist died and lived again, that He might be ᵇLord both of the dead and of the living. ª*Rev 1:18* ᵇ*Phil 2:11*

10 But you, why do you judge your brother? Or you again, why do you regard your brother with contempt? For ªwe will all stand before the judgment seat of God. ª*Rom 2:16; 2 Cor 5:10*

11 For it is written,
  "ªAS I LIVE, SAYS THE LORD, EVERY KNEE
     SHALL BOW TO ME,
  AND EVERY TONGUE SHALL GIVE PRAISE TO
     GOD." ª*Is 45:23*

12 So then ªeach one of us will give an account of himself to God. ª*Matt 12:36; 16:27*

13 Therefore let us not ªjudge one another anymore, but rather determine this—ᵇnot to put an obstacle or a stumbling block in a brother's way. ª*Matt 7:1* ᵇ*1 Cor 8:13*

14 I know and am convinced in the Lord Jesus that ªnothing is unclean in itself; but to him who thinks anything to be unclean, to him it is unclean. ª*Acts 10:15; Rom 14:20*

15 For if because of food your brother is hurt, you are no longer ªwalking according to love. ᵇDo not destroy with your food him for whom Christ died. ª*Eph 5:2* ᵇ*1 Cor 8:11*

16 Therefore ªdo not let what is for you a good thing be spoken of as evil; ª*1 Cor 10:30; Titus 2:5*

17 for the kingdom of God is not eating and drinking, but righteousness and ªpeace and joy in the Holy Spirit. ª*Rom 15:13; Gal 5:22*

18 For he who in this *way* serves Christ is ªacceptable to God and approved by men. ª*2 Cor 8:21; Phil 4:8*

19 So then we ªpursue the things which make for peace and the building up of one another. ª*Ps 34:14; Rom 12:18*

20 Do not tear down the work of God for the sake of food. All things indeed are clean, but

[a]they are evil for the man who eats and gives offense. [a]*1 Cor 8:9-12*

21 [a]It is good not to eat meat or to drink wine, or *to do anything* by which your brother stumbles. [a]*1 Cor 8:13*

22 The faith which you have, have as your own conviction before God. Happy is he who [a]does not condemn himself in what he approves. [a]*1 John 3:21*

23 But [a]who doubts is condemned if he eats, because *his eating is* not from faith; and whatever is not from faith is sin. [a]*Rom 14:5*

Self-denial on Behalf of Others

15 Now we who are strong ought to bear the weaknesses of [a]those without strength and not *just* please ourselves. [a]*Rom 14:1; Gal 6:2*

2 Each of us is to [a]please his neighbor for his good, to his edification. [a]*1 Cor 9:22; 10:24, 33*

3 For even [a]Christ did not please Himself; but as it is written, "[b]THE REPROACHES OF THOSE WHO REPROACHED YOU FELL ON ME." [a]*2 Cor 8:9* [b]*Ps 69:9*

4 For [a]whatever was written in earlier times was written for our instruction, so that through perseverance and the encouragement of the Scriptures we might have hope. [a]*Rom 4:23f; 2 Tim 3:16*

5 Now may the God who gives perseverance and encouragement grant you [a]to be of the same mind with one another according to Christ Jesus, [a]*Rom 12:16*

6 so that with one accord you may with one voice glorify [a]the God and Father of our Lord Jesus Christ. [a]*Rev 1:6*

7 Therefore, [a]accept one another, just as Christ also accepted us to the glory of God. [a]*Rom 14:1*

8 For I say that Christ has become a servant to [a]the circumcision on behalf of the truth of God to confirm the promises *given* to the fathers, [a]*Matt 15:24; Acts 3:26*

9 and for the Gentiles to glorify God for His mercy; as it is written,
"[a]THEREFORE I WILL GIVE PRAISE TO YOU
    AMONG THE GENTILES,
AND I WILL SING TO YOUR NAME."
        [a]*2 Sam 22:50; Ps 18:49*

10 Again he says,
"[a]REJOICE, O GENTILES, WITH HIS PEOPLE."
        [a]*Deut 32:43*

11 And again,
"[a]PRAISE THE LORD ALL YOU GENTILES,
AND LET ALL THE PEOPLES PRAISE HIM."
        [a]*Ps 117:1*

12 Again Isaiah says,
"[a]THERE SHALL COME THE ROOT OF JESSE,
AND HE WHO ARISES TO RULE OVER THE
    GENTILES,
IN HIM SHALL THE GENTILES HOPE." [a]*Is 11:10*

13 Now may the God of hope fill you with all [a]joy and peace in believing, so that you will abound in hope by the power of the Holy Spirit. [a]*Rom 14:17*

14 And concerning you, my brethren, I myself also am convinced that you yourselves are full of goodness, filled with [a]all knowledge and able also to admonish one another. [a]*1 Cor 1:5; 8:1, 7, 10*

15 But I have written very boldly to you on some points so as to remind you again, because of [a]the grace that was given me from God, [a]*Rom 12:3*

16 to be [a]a minister of Christ Jesus to the Gentiles, ministering as a priest the gospel of God, so that *my* [b]offering of the Gentiles may become acceptable, sanctified by the Holy Spirit. [a]*Acts 9:15* [b]*Rom 12:1*

17 Therefore in Christ Jesus I have found reason for boasting in [a]things pertaining to God. [a]*Heb 2:17; 5:1*

18 For I will not presume to speak of anything except what [a]Christ has accomplished through me, resulting in the obedience of the Gentiles by word and deed, [a]*Acts 15:12; 21:19*

19 in the power of signs and wonders, [a]in the power of the Spirit; so that from Jerusalem and round about as far as Illyricum I have fully preached the gospel of Christ. [a]*Rom 15:13; 1 Cor 2:4*

20 And thus I aspired to preach the gospel, not where Christ was *already* named, [a]so that I would not build on another man's foundation; [a]*1 Cor 3:10; 2 Cor 10:15f*

21 but as it is written,
"[a]THEY WHO HAD NO NEWS OF HIM SHALL SEE,
    AND THEY WHO HAVE NOT HEARD SHALL
        UNDERSTAND." [a]*Is 52:15*

22 For this reason [a]I have often been prevented from coming to you; [a]*Rom 1:13; 1 Thess 2:18*

23 but now, with no further place for me in these regions, and since I [a]have had for many years a longing to come to you [a]*Acts 19:21; Rom 1:10f*

24 whenever I go to Spain—for I hope to see you in passing, and to be [a]helped on my way there by you, when I have first [b]enjoyed your company for a while— [a]*Acts 15:3* [b]*Rom 1:12*

25 but now, [a]I am going to Jerusalem [b]serving the saints. [a]*Acts 19:21* [b]*Acts 24:17*

26 For [a]Macedonia and Achaia have been pleased to make a contribution for the poor among the saints in Jerusalem. [a]*Acts 16:9; 1 Cor 16:5*

27 Yes, they were pleased *to do so,* and they are indebted to them. For if the Gentiles have shared in their spiritual things, they are indebted to minister to them also in material things.

28 Therefore, when I have finished this, and [a]have put my seal on this fruit of theirs, I will go on by way of you to Spain. [a]*John 3:33*

29 I know that when [a]I come to you, I will come in the fullness of the blessing of Christ. [a]*Acts 19:21; Rom 1:10f*

30 Now I urge you, brethren, by our Lord Jesus Christ and by [a]the love of the Spirit, to [b]strive together with me in your prayers to God for me, [a]*Col 1:8* [b]*1 Cor 1:11*

31 that I may be rescued from those who are disobedient in Judea, and *that* my [a]service for Jerusalem may prove acceptable to the saints; [a]*Rom 15:25f; 2 Cor 8:4*

32 so that I may come to you in joy by [a]the will of God and find *refreshing* rest in your company. [a]*Acts 18:21; Rom 1:10*

33 Now [a]the God of peace be with you all. Amen. [a]*Rom 16:20; 2 Cor 13:11*

Greetings and Love Expressed

16 I [a]commend to you our sister Phoebe, who is a servant of the church which is at Cenchrea; [a]*2 Cor 3:1*

2 that you [a]receive her in the Lord in a manner worthy of the saints, and that you help her in whatever matter she may have need of you; for she herself has also been a helper of many, and of myself as well. [a]*Phil 2:29*

3 Greet [a]Prisca and Aquila, my fellow workers in Christ Jesus, [a]*Acts 18:2*

4 who for my life risked their own necks, to whom not only do I give thanks, but also all the churches of the Gentiles;

5 also *greet* [a]the church that is in their house. Greet Epaenetus, my beloved, who is the first convert to Christ from Asia. [a]*1 Cor 16:19; Col 4:15*

6 Greet Mary, who has worked hard for you.

7 Greet Andronicus and Junias, my kinsmen and my [a]fellow prisoners, who are outstanding among the apostles, who also were in Christ before me. [a]*Col 4:10; Philem 23*

8 Greet Ampliatus, my beloved in the Lord.

9 Greet Urbanus, our fellow worker [a]in Christ, and Stachys my beloved. [a]*Rom 8:11ff; 16:3, 7, 10*

10 Greet Apelles, the approved [a]in Christ. Greet those who are of the *household* of Aristobulus. [a]*Rom 8:11ff; 16:3, 7, 9*

11 Greet Herodion, my [a]kinsman. Greet those of the *household* of Narcissus, who are in the Lord. [a]*Rom 9:3; 16:7, 21*

12 Greet Tryphaena and Tryphosa, workers in the Lord. Greet Persis the beloved, who has worked hard in the Lord.

13 Greet [a]Rufus, a choice man in the Lord, also his mother and mine. [a]*Mark 15:21*

14 Greet Asyncritus, Phlegon, Hermes, Patrobas, Hermas and the brethren with them.

15 Greet Philologus and Julia, Nereus and his sister, and Olympas, and all [a]the saints who are with them. [a]*Rom 16:2, 14*

16 [a]Greet one another with a holy kiss. All the churches of Christ greet you. [a]*1 Cor 16:20; 2 Cor 13:12*

17 Now I urge you, brethren, keep your eye on those who cause dissensions and hindrances contrary to the teaching which you learned, and [a]turn away from them. [a]*Matt 7:15; Gal 1:8f*

18 For such men are slaves, not of our Lord Christ but of their own appetites; and by their [a]smooth and flattering speech they deceive the hearts of the unsuspecting. [a]*Col 2:4; 2 Pet 2:3*

19 For the report of your obedience [a]has reached to all; therefore I am rejoicing over you, but I want you to be wise in what is good and innocent in what is evil. [a]*Rom 1:8*

20 [a]The God of peace will soon crush Satan under your feet.

The grace of our Lord Jesus be with you. [a]*Rom 15:33*

21 [a]Timothy my fellow worker greets you, and *so do* Lucius and Jason and Sosipater, my kinsmen. [a]*Acts 16:1*

22 I, Tertius, who [a]write this letter, greet you in the Lord. [a]*1 Cor 16:21; Gal 6:11*

23 [a]Gaius, host to me and to the whole church, greets you. Erastus, the city treasurer greets you, and Quartus, the brother. [a]*Acts 19:29; 20:4*

24 [The grace of our Lord Jesus Christ be with you all. Amen.]

25 [a]Now to Him who is able to establish you according to my gospel and the preaching of Jesus Christ, according to the revelation of the mystery which has been kept secret for long ages past, [a]*Eph 3:20; Jude 24*

26 but now is manifested, and by [a]the Scriptures of the prophets, according to the commandment of the eternal God, has been made known to all the nations, *leading* to [b]obedience of faith; [a]*Rom 1:2* [b]*Rom 1:5*

27 to the only wise God, through Jesus Christ, [a]be the glory forever. Amen. [a]*Rom 11:36*

The First Letter of Paul to the
CORINTHIANS

Appeal to Unity

1 Paul, called *as* an apostle of Jesus Christ by ᵃthe will of God, and Sosthenes our brother, ᵃRom 1:10; 2 Tim 1:1

2 To the church of God which is at Corinth, to those who have been sanctified in Christ Jesus, saints ᵃby calling, with all who in every place call on the name of our Lord Jesus Christ, their *Lord* and ours: ᵃRom 1:7; 8:28

3 ᵃGrace to you and peace from God our Father and the Lord Jesus Christ. ᵃRom 1:7

4 ᵃI thank my God always concerning you for the grace of God which was given you in Christ Jesus, ᵃRom 1:8

5 that in everything you were enriched in Him, in all ᵃspeech and all knowledge, ᵃRom 15:14; 2 Cor 8:7

6 even as ᵃthe testimony concerning Christ was confirmed in you, ᵃ2 Thess 1:10; 1 Tim 2:6

7 so that you are not lacking in any gift, ᵃawaiting eagerly the revelation of our Lord Jesus Christ, ᵃLuke 17:30; Rom 8:19, 23

8 ᵃwho will also confirm you to the end, blameless in the day of our Lord Jesus Christ. ᵃRom 8:19; Phil 1:62

9 ᵃGod is faithful, through whom you were called into fellowship with His Son, Jesus Christ our Lord. ᵃDeut 7:9; Is 49:7

10 Now I exhort you, brethren, by the name of our Lord Jesus Christ, that you all agree and that there be no ᵃdivisions among you, but that you be made complete in ᵇthe same mind and in the same judgment. ᵃ1 Cor 11:18 ᵇRom 12:16

11 For I have been informed concerning you, my brethren, by Chloe's *people*, that there are quarrels among you.

12 Now I mean this, that ᵃeach one of you is saying, "I am of Paul," and "I of ᵇApollos," and "I of Cephas," and "I of Christ." ᵃ1 Cor 3:4 ᵇActs 18:24

13 Has Christ been divided? Paul was not crucified for you, was he? Or were you ᵃbaptized in the name of Paul? ᵃMatt 28:19; Acts 2:38

14 I thank God that I ᵃbaptized none of you except ᵃCrispus and Gaius, ᵃActs 18:8

15 so that no one would say you were baptized in my name.

16 Now I did baptize also the ᵃhousehold of Stephanas; beyond that, I do not know whether I baptized any other. ᵃ1 Cor 16:15, 17

17 ᵃFor Christ did not send me to baptize, but to preach the gospel, ᵇnot in cleverness of speech, so that the cross of Christ would not be made void. ᵃJohn 4:2 ᵇ1 Cor 2:1, 4, 13

The Wisdom of God

18 For the word of the cross is foolishness to ᵃthose who are perishing, but to us who are being saved it is the power of God. ᵃ2 Cor 2:15; 2 Thess 2:10

19 For it is written,

"ᵃI WILL DESTROY THE WISDOM OF THE WISE,
AND THE CLEVERNESS OF THE CLEVER I WILL
SET ASIDE." ᵃIs 29:14

20 Where is the wise man? Where is the scribe? Where is the debater of ᵃthis age? Has not God made foolish the wisdom of the world? ᵃJob 12:17; Is 19:11f

21 For since in the wisdom of God ᵃthe world through its wisdom did not *come to* know God, ᵇGod was well-pleased through the foolishness of the message preached to save those who believe. ᵃ1 Cor 1:27f ᵇLuke 12:32

22 For indeed ᵃJews ask for signs and Greeks search for wisdom; ᵃMatt 12:38

23 but we preach ᵃChrist crucified, ᵇto Jews a stumbling block and to Gentiles foolishness, ᵃ1 Cor 2:2 ᵇ1 Pet 2:8

24 but to those who are the called, both Jews and Greeks, Christ ᵃthe power of God and ᵇthe wisdom of God. ᵃ1 Cor 1:18 ᵇ1 Cor 1:30

25 Because the foolishness of God is wiser than men, and ᵃthe weakness of God is stronger than men. ᵃ2 Cor 13:4

26 For consider your calling, brethren, that there were ᵃnot many wise according to the flesh, not many mighty, not many noble; ᵃMatt 11:25; 1 Cor 1:20

27 but God has chosen the foolish things of ᵃthe world to shame the wise, and God has chosen the weak things of ᵃthe world to shame the things which are strong, ᵃ1 Cor 1:20

28 and the base things of the world and the despised God has chosen, ᵃthe things that are not, so that He may nullify the things that are, ᵃRom 4:17

29 so that ᵃno man may boast before God. ᵃEph 2:9

30 But by His doing you are in Christ Jesus, who became to us ᵃwisdom from God, and ᵇrighteousness and sanctification, and redemption, ᵃ1 Cor 1:24 ᵇJer 23:5f

31 so that, just as it is written, "ᵃLET HIM WHO BOASTS, BOAST IN THE LORD." ᵃJer 9:23f; 2 Cor 10:17

Paul's Reliance upon the Spirit

2 And when I came to you, brethren, I ᵃdid not come with superiority of speech or of wisdom, proclaiming to you the testimony of God. ᵃ1 Cor 1:17; 2:4, 13

2 For I determined to know nothing among you except ᵃJesus Christ, and Him crucified. ᵃ1 Cor 1:23; Gal 6:14

3 I was with you in ªweakness and in fear and in much trembling. ª*1 Cor 4:10; 2 Cor 11:30*

4 and my message and my preaching were ªnot in persuasive words of wisdom, but in demonstration of the Spirit and of power, ª*1 Cor 1:17; 2:1, 13*

5 so that your faith would not rest on the wisdom of men, but on ªthe power of God. ª*2 Cor 4:7; 6:7*

6 Yet we do speak wisdom among those who are ªmature; a wisdom, however, not of this age nor of the rulers of this age, who are passing away; ª*Eph 4:13; Phil 3:15*

7 but we speak God's wisdom in a mystery, the hidden *wisdom* which God ªpredestined before the ages to our glory; ª*Rom 8:29f*

8 *the wisdom* ªwhich none of the rulers of ᵇthis age has understood; for if they had understood it they would not have crucified the Lord of glory; ª*1 Cor 2:6* ᵇ*1 Cor 1:20*

9 but just as it is written,
"ªTHINGS WHICH EYE HAS NOT SEEN AND EAR HAS NOT HEARD,
AND *which* HAVE NOT ENTERED THE HEART OF MAN,
ALL THAT GOD HAS PREPARED FOR THOSE WHO LOVE HIM." ª*Is 64:4; 65:17*

10 For to us God revealed *them* ªthrough the Spirit; for the Spirit searches all things, even the ᵇdepths of God. ª*John 14:26* ᵇ*Rom 11:33ff*

11 For who among men knows the *thoughts* of a man except the ªspirit of the man which is in him? Even so the *thoughts* of God no one knows except the Spirit of God. ª*Prov 20:27*

12 Now we ªhave received, not the spirit of the world, but the Spirit who is from God, so that we may know the things freely given to us by God. ª*Rom 8:15*

13 which things we also speak, ªnot in words taught by human wisdom, but in those taught by the Spirit, combining spiritual *thoughts* with spiritual *words*. ª*1 Cor 1:17; 2:1, 4*

14 But a natural man ªdoes not accept the things of the Spirit of God, for they are ᵇfoolishness to him; and he cannot understand them, because they are spiritually appraised. ª*John 14:17* ᵇ*1 Cor 1:18*

15 But he who is ªspiritual appraises all things, yet he himself is appraised by no one. ª*1 Cor 3:1; 14:37*

16 For ªWHO HAS KNOWN THE MIND OF THE LORD, THAT HE WILL INSTRUCT HIM? But we have the mind of Christ. ª*Is 40:13; Rom 11:34*

Foundations for Living

3 And I, brethren, could not speak to you as to spiritual men, but as to men of flesh, as to ªinfants in Christ. ª*1 Cor 2:6; Eph 4:14*

2 I gave you ªmilk to drink, not solid food; for you were not yet able *to receive it.* Indeed, even now you are not yet able, ª*Heb 5:12f; 1 Pet 2:2*

3 for you are still fleshly. For since there is ªjealousy and strife among you, are you not fleshly, and are you not walking like mere men? ª*Rom 13:13; 1 Cor 1:10f*

4 For when ªone says, "I am of Paul," and another, "I am of Apollos," are you not *mere* men? ª*1 Cor 1:12*

5 What then is Apollos? And what is Paul? Servants through whom you believed, even ªas the Lord gave *opportunity* to each one. ª*Rom 12:6; 1 Cor 3:10*

6 I planted, Apollos watered, but ªGod was causing the growth. ª*1 Cor 15:10*

7 So then neither the one who plants nor the one who waters is anything, but God who causes the growth.

8 Now he who plants and he who waters are one; but each will ªreceive his own reward according to his own labor. ª*1 Cor 3:14; 4:5*

9 For we are God's ªfellow workers; you are God's field, God's building. ª*Mark 16:20; 2 Cor 6:1*

10 According to ªthe grace of God which was given to me, like a wise master builder I laid a foundation, and another is building on it. But each man must be careful how he builds on it. ª*Rom 12:3; 1 Cor 15:10*

11 For no man can lay a ªfoundation other than the one which is laid, which is Jesus Christ. ª*Is 28:16; Eph 2:20*

12 Now if any man builds on the foundation with gold, silver, precious stones, wood, hay, straw,

13 ªeach man's work will become evident; for the day will show it because it is *to be* revealed with fire, and the fire itself will test the quality of each man's work. ª*1 Cor 4:5*

14 If any man's work which he has built on it remains, he will ªreceive a reward. ª*1 Cor 3:8; 4:5*

15 If any man's work is burned up, he will suffer loss; but he himself will be saved, yet ªso as through fire. ª*Job 23:10; Ps 66:10, 12*

16 Do you not know that ªyou are a temple of God and *that* the Spirit of God dwells in you? ª*Rom 8:9; 1 Cor 6:19*

17 If any man destroys the temple of God, God will destroy him, for the temple of God is holy, and that is what you are.

18 Let no man deceive himself. ªIf any man among you thinks that he is wise in this age, he must become foolish, so that he may become wise. ª*1 Cor 8:2; Gal 6:3*

19 For the wisdom of this world is foolishness before God. For it is written, "*He is* ªTHE ONE WHO CATCHES THE WISE IN THEIR CRAFTINESS"; ª*Job 5:13*

20 and again, "ªTHE LORD KNOWS THE REASONINGS of the wise, THAT THEY ARE USELESS." ª*Ps 94:11*

21 So then let no one boast in men. For [a]all things belong to you, [a]Rom 8:32

22 [a]whether Paul or Apollos or Cephas or the world or [b]life or death or things present or things to come; all things belong to you, [a]1 Cor 1:12 [b]Rom 8:38

23 and [a]you belong to Christ; and [b]Christ belongs to God. [a]2 Cor 10:7 [b]1 Cor 11:3

Servants of Christ

4 Let a man regard us in this manner, as servants of Christ and [a]stewards of the mysteries of God. [a]Titus 1:7; 1 Pet 4:10

2 In this case, moreover, it is required of stewards that one be found trustworthy.

3 But to me it is a very small thing that I may be examined by you, or by *any* human court; in fact, I do not even examine myself.

4 For I [a]am conscious of nothing against myself, yet I am not by this acquitted; but the one who examines me is the Lord. [a]Acts 23:1; 2 Cor 1:12

5 Therefore [a]do not go on passing judgment before the time, *but wait* [b]until the Lord comes who will both bring to light the things hidden in the darkness and disclose the motives of *men's* hearts; and then each man's praise will come to him from God. [a]Rom 2:1 [b]Rom 2:16

6 Now these things, brethren, I have figuratively applied to myself and Apollos for your sakes, so that in us you may learn not to exceed what is written, so that no one of you will become arrogant [a]in behalf of one against the other. [a]1 Cor 1:12; 3:4

7 For who regards you as superior? [a]What do you have that you did not receive? And if you did receive it, why do you boast as if you had not received it? [a]John 3:27; Rom 12:3, 6

8 You are [a]already filled, you have already become rich, you have become kings without us; and indeed, *I* wish that you had become kings so that we also might reign with you. [a]Rev 3:17f

9 For, I think, God has exhibited us apostles last of all, as men [a]condemned to death; because we [b]have become a spectacle to the world, both to angels and to men. [a]Rom 8:36 [b]Heb 10:33

10 We are fools for Christ's sake, but [a]you are prudent in Christ; we are weak, but you are strong; you are distinguished, but we are without honor. [a]1 Cor 3:18; 2 Cor 11:19

11 To this present hour we are both [a]hungry and thirsty, and are poorly clothed, and are roughly treated, and are homeless; [a]Rom 8:35; 2 Cor 11:23-27

12 and we toil, [a]working with our own hands; when we are [b]reviled, we bless; when we are persecuted, we endure; [a]Acts 18:3 [b]1 Pet 3:9

13 when we are slandered, we try to concili-

ate; we have [a]become as the scum of the world, the dregs of all things, *even* until now. [a]Lam 3:45

14 I do not write these things to [a]shame you, but to admonish you as my beloved children. [a]1 Cor 6:5; 15:34

15 For if you were to have countless tutors in Christ, yet *you would* not *have* many fathers, for in Christ Jesus I [a]became your father through the gospel. [a]Num 11:12; Gal 4:19

16 Therefore I exhort you, be [a]imitators of me. [a]1 Cor 11:1; Phil 3:17

17 For this reason I [a]have sent to you Timothy, who is my beloved and faithful child in the Lord, and he will remind you of my ways which are in Christ, just as I teach everywhere in every church. [a]1 Cor 16:10

18 Now some have become [a]arrogant, as though I were not coming to you. [a]1 Cor 4:6

19 But I [a]will come to you soon, [b]if the Lord wills, and I shall find out, not the words of those who are arrogant but their power. [a]Acts 20:2; 1 Cor 11:34 [b]Acts 18:21

20 For the kingdom of God does [a]not consist in words but in power. [a]1 Cor 2:4

21 What do you desire? [a]Shall I come to you with a rod, or with love and a spirit of gentleness? [a]2 Cor 1:23; 2:1, 3

Immorality Rebuked

5 It is actually reported that there is immorality among you, and immorality of such a kind as does not exist even among the Gentiles, that someone has [a]his father's wife. [a]Lev 18:8; Deut 22:30

2 You have become arrogant and have not mourned instead, so that the one who had done this deed would be [a]removed from your midst. [a]1 Cor 5:13

3 For I, on my part, though [a]absent in body but present in spirit, have already judged him who has so committed this, as though I were present. [a]Col 2:5; 1 Thess 2:17

4 In the name of our Lord Jesus, when you are assembled, and I with you in spirit, [a]with the power of our Lord Jesus, [a]John 20:23; 2 Cor 2:10

5 *I have decided* to [a]deliver such a one to Satan for the destruction of his flesh, so that his spirit may be saved in [b]the day of the Lord Jesus. [a]Luke 22:31 [b]1 Cor 1:8

6 [a]Your boasting is not good. Do you not know that [b]a little leaven leavens the whole lump *of dough?* [a]James 4:16 [b]Matt 16:6, 12

7 Clean out the old leaven so that you may be a new lump, just as you are *in fact* unleavened. For Christ our [a]Passover also has been sacrificed. [a]Mark 14:12; 1 Pet 1:19

8 Therefore let us celebrate the feast, [a]not with old leaven, nor with the leaven of malice

and wickedness, but with the unleavened bread of sincerity and truth. [a]Ex 12:19; 13:7

9 I wrote you in my letter [a]not to associate with immoral people; [a]2 Cor 6:14; Eph 5:11

10 I *did* not at all *mean* with the immoral people of this world, or with the covetous and swindlers, or with [a]idolaters, for then you would have to go out of the world. [a]1 Cor 10:27

11 But actually, I wrote to you not to associate with any so-called [a]brother if he is an immoral person, or covetous, or an idolater, or a reviler, or a drunkard, or a swindler—not even to eat with such a one. [a]Acts 1:15; 2 Thess 3:6

12 For what have I to do with judging outsiders? [a]Do you not judge those who are within *the church?* [a]1 Cor 5:3-5; 6:1-4

13 But those who are outside, God judges. [a]REMOVE THE WICKED MAN FROM AMONG YOURSELVES. [a]Deut 13:5; 17:7, 12

Lawsuits Discouraged

6 Does any one of you, when he has a case against his neighbor, dare to go to law before the unrighteous and [a]not before the saints? [a]Matt 18:17

2 Or do you not know that [a]the saints will judge the world? If the world is judged by you, are you not competent *to constitute* the smallest law courts? [a]Dan 7:18, 22, 27; Matt 19:28

3 [a]Do you not know that we will judge angels? How much more matters of this life? [a]Rom 6:16

4 So if you have law courts dealing with matters of this life, do you appoint them as judges who are of no account in the church?

5 [a]I say *this* to your shame. *Is it* so, *that* there is not among you one wise man who will be able to decide between his brethren, [a]1 Cor 4:14; 15:34

6 but brother goes to law with brother, and that before [a]unbelievers? [a]2 Cor 6:14f; 1 Tim 5:8

7 Actually, then, it is already a defeat for you, that you have lawsuits with one another. [a]Why not rather be wronged? Why not rather be defrauded? [a]Matt 5:39f

8 On the contrary, you yourselves wrong and defraud. *You do* this even to *your* [a]brethren. [a]1 Thess 4:6

9 Or do you not know that the unrighteous will not [a]inherit the kingdom of God? Do not be deceived; neither fornicators, nor idolaters, nor adulterers, nor effeminate, nor homosexuals, [a]Acts 20:32; 1 Cor 15:50

10 nor thieves, nor *the* covetous, nor drunkards, nor revilers, nor swindlers, will [a]inherit the kingdom of God. [a]Acts 20:32; 1 Cor 15:50

11 Such were some of you; but you were washed, but you were [a]sanctified, but you were [b]justified in the name of the Lord Jesus Christ

and in the Spirit of our God. [a]1 Cor 1:2, 30 [b]Rom 8:30

The Body Is the Lord's

12 [a]All things are lawful for me, but not all things are profitable. All things are lawful for me, but I will not be mastered by anything. [a]1 Cor 10:23

13 Food is for the stomach and the stomach is for food, but God will do away with both of them. Yet the body is not for immorality, but [a]for the Lord, and the Lord is for the body. [a]1 Cor 6:15, 19

14 Now God has not only raised the Lord, but [a]will also raise us up through His power. [a]John 6:39f; 1 Cor 15:23

15 Do you not know that [a]your bodies are members of Christ? Shall I then take away the members of Christ and make them members of a prostitute? May it never be! [a]Rom 12:5; 1 Cor 6:13

16 Or do you not know that the one who joins himself to a prostitute is one body *with her?* For He says, "[a]THE TWO SHALL BECOME ONE FLESH." [a]Gen 2:24; Matt 19:5

17 But the one who joins himself to the Lord is [a]one spirit *with Him.* [a]John 17:21-23; Rom 8:9-11

18 [a]Flee immorality. Every *other* sin that a man commits is outside the body, but the immoral man sins against his own body. [a]1 Cor 6:9; 2 Cor 12:21

19 Or do you not know that [a]your body is a temple of the Holy Spirit who is in you, whom you have from God, and that you are not your own? [a]John 2:21; 1 Cor 3:16

20 For [a]you have been bought with a price: therefore glorify God in your body. [a]Acts 20:28; 1 Cor 7:23

Teaching on Marriage

7 Now concerning the things about which you wrote, it is [a]good for a man not to touch a woman. [a]1 Cor 7:8, 26

2 But because of immoralities, each man is to have his own wife, and each woman is to have her own husband.

3 The husband must fulfill his duty to his wife, and likewise also the wife to her husband.

4 The wife does not have authority over her own body, but the husband *does;* and likewise also the husband does not have authority over his own body, but the wife *does.*

5 Stop depriving one another, except by agreement for a time, so that you may devote yourselves to prayer, and come together again so that [a]Satan will not tempt you because of your lack of self-control. [a]Matt 4:10

6 But this I say by way of concession, [a]not of command. [a]2 Cor 8:8

7 Yet I wish that all men were [a]even as I

myself am. However, each man has his own gift from God, one in this manner, and another in that. ᵃ*1 Cor 7:8; 9:5*

8 But I say to the unmarried and to widows that it is ᵃgood for them if they remain even as I. ᵃ*1 Cor 7:1, 26*

9 But if they do not have self-control, ᵃlet them marry; for it is better to marry than to burn *with passion.* ᵃ*1 Tim 5:14*

10 But to the married I give instructions, ᵃnot I, but the Lord, that the wife should not leave her husband ᵃ*Mal 2:16; Matt 5:32*

11 (but if she does leave, she must remain unmarried, or else be reconciled to her husband), and that the husband should not divorce his wife.

12 But to the rest ᵃI say, not the Lord, that if any brother has a wife who is an unbeliever, and she consents to live with him, he must not divorce her. ᵃ*1 Cor 7:6; 2 Cor 11:17*

13 And a woman who has an unbelieving husband, and he consents to live with her, she must not send her husband away.

14 For the unbelieving husband is sanctified through his wife, and the unbelieving wife is sanctified through her believing husband; for otherwise your children are unclean, but now they are ᵃholy. ᵃ*Ezra 9:2; Mal 2:15*

15 Yet if the unbelieving one leaves, let him leave; the brother or the sister is not under bondage in such *cases,* but God has called us ᵃto peace. ᵃ*Rom 14:19*

16 For how do you know, O wife, whether you will ᵃsave your husband? Or how do you know, O husband, whether you will save your wife? ᵃ*Rom 11:14; 1 Pet 3:1*

17 Only, ᵃas the Lord has assigned to each one, as God has called each, in this manner let him walk. And ᵇso I direct in all the churches. ᵃ*Rom 12:3* ᵇ*1 Cor 4:17*

18 Was any man called *when he was already* circumcised? He is not to become uncircumcised. Has anyone been called in uncircumcision? ᵃHe is not to be circumcised. ᵃ*Acts 15:1ff*

19 ᵃCircumcision is nothing, and uncircumcision is nothing, but *what matters is* the keeping of the commandments of God. ᵃ*Rom 2:27, 29; Gal 5:6*

20 ᵃEach man must remain in that condition in which he was called. ᵃ*1 Cor 7:24*

21 Were you called while a slave? Do not worry about it; but if you are able also to become free, rather do that.

22 For he who was called in the Lord while a slave, is ᵃthe Lord's freedman; likewise he who was called while free, is ᵇChrist's slave. ᵃ*Philem 16* ᵇ*1 Pet 2:16*

23 ᵃYou were bought with a price; do not become slaves of men. ᵃ*1 Cor 6:20*

24 Brethren, ᵃeach one is to remain with God in that *condition* in which he was called. ᵃ*1 Cor 7:20*

25 Now concerning virgins I have no command of the Lord, but I give an opinion as one who ᵃby the mercy of the Lord is trustworthy. ᵃ*2 Cor 4:1; 1 Tim 1:13, 16*

26 I think then that this is good in view of the present distress, that ᵃit is good for a man to remain as he is. ᵃ*1 Cor 7:1, 8*

27 Are you bound to a wife? Do not seek to be released. Are you released from a wife? Do not seek a wife.

28 But if you marry, you have not sinned; and if a virgin marries, she has not sinned. Yet such will have trouble in this life, and I am trying to spare you.

29 But this I say, brethren, ᵃthe time has been shortened, so that from now on those who have wives should be as though they had none; ᵃ*Rom 13:11f; 1 Cor 7:31*

30 and those who weep, as though they did not weep; and those who rejoice, as though they did not rejoice; and those who buy, as though they did not possess;

31 and those who use the world, as though they did not ᵃmake full use of it; for ᵇthe form of this world is passing away. ᵃ*1 Cor 9:18* ᵇ*1 John 2:17*

32 But I want you to be free from concern. One who is ᵃunmarried is concerned about the things of the Lord, how he may please the Lord; ᵃ*1 Tim 5:5*

33 but one who is married is concerned about the things of the world, how he may please his wife,

34 and *his interests* are divided. The woman who is unmarried, and the virgin, is concerned about the things of the Lord, that she may be holy both in body and spirit; but one who is married is concerned about the things of the world, how she may please her husband.

35 This I say for your own benefit; not to put a restraint upon you, but to promote what is appropriate and *to secure* undistracted devotion to the Lord.

36 But if any man thinks that he is acting unbecomingly toward his virgin *daughter,* if she is past her youth, and if it must be so, let him do what he wishes, he does not sin; let her marry.

37 But he who stands firm in his heart, being under no constraint, but has authority over his own will, and has decided this in his own heart, to keep his own virgin *daughter,* he will do well.

38 So then both he who gives his own virgin *daughter* in marriage does well, and he who does not give her in marriage will do better.

39 ᵃA wife is bound as long as her husband

lives; but if her husband is dead, she is free to be married to whom she wishes, only in the Lord. ᵃ*Rom 7:2*

40 But ᵃin my opinion she is happier if she remains as she is; and I think that I also have the Spirit of God. ᵃ*1 Cor 7:6, 25*

Take Care with Your Liberty

8 Now concerning ᵃthings sacrificed to idols, we know that we all have knowledge. Knowledge makes arrogant, but love ᵇedifies. ᵃ*Acts 15:20* ᵇ*Rom 14:19*

2 ᵃIf anyone supposes that he knows anything, he has not yet ᵇknown as he ought to know; ᵃ*1 Cor 3:18* ᵇ*1 Cor 13:8-12*

3 but if anyone loves God, he ᵃis known by Him. ᵃ*Ps 1:6; Jer 1:5*

4 Therefore concerning the eating of things sacrificed to idols, we know that there is no such thing as an idol in the world, and that ᵃthere is no God but one. ᵃ*Deut 4:35, 39; 6:4*

5 For even if ᵃthere are so-called gods whether in heaven or on earth, as indeed there are many gods and many lords, ᵃ*2 Thess 2:4*

6 yet for us there is *but* one God, ᵃthe Father, ᵇfrom whom are all things and we *exist* for Him; and one Lord, Jesus Christ, by whom are all things, and we *exist* through Him. ᵃ*Mal 2:10* ᵇ*Rom 11:36*

7 However not all men have this knowledge; but ᵃsome, being accustomed to the idol until now, eat *food* as if it were sacrificed to an idol; and their conscience being weak is defiled. ᵃ*Rom 14:14, 22f*

8 But ᵃfood will not commend us to God; we are neither the worse if we do not eat, nor the better if we do eat. ᵃ*Rom 14:17*

9 But ᵃtake care that this liberty of yours does not somehow become a stumbling block to the weak. ᵃ*Rom 14:13, 21; 1 Cor 10:28*

10 For if someone sees you, who have knowledge, dining in an idol's temple, will not his conscience, if he is weak, be strengthened to eat ᵃthings sacrificed to idols? ᵃ*Acts 15:20; 1 Cor 8:1, 4, 7*

11 For through your knowledge he who is weak ᵃis ruined, the brother for whose sake Christ died. ᵃ*Rom 14:15, 20*

12 ᵃAnd so, by sinning against the brethren and wounding their conscience when it is weak, you sin against Christ. ᵃ*Matt 18:6; Rom 14:20*

13 Therefore, ᵃif food causes my brother to stumble, I will never eat meat again, so that I will not cause my brother to stumble. ᵃ*Rom 14:21; 1 Cor 10:32*

Paul's Use of Liberty

9 Am I not ᵃfree? Am I not an apostle? Have I not seen Jesus our Lord? Are you not my work in the Lord? ᵃ*1 Cor 9:19; 10:29*

2 If to others I am not an apostle, at least I am to you; for you are the ᵃseal of my apostleship in the Lord. ᵃ*John 3:33; 2 Cor 3:2f*

3 My defense to those who examine me is this:

4 ᵃDo we not have a right to eat and drink? ᵃ*1 Cor 9:14; 1 Thess 2:6, 9*

5 ᵃDo we not have a right to take along a believing wife, even as the rest of the apostles and the brothers of the Lord and Cephas? ᵃ*1 Cor 7:7f*

6 Or do only ᵃBarnabas and I not have a right to refrain from working? ᵃ*Acts 4:36*

7 Who at any time serves ᵃas a soldier at his own expense? Who ᵇplants a vineyard and does not eat the fruit of it? Or who tends a flock and does not use the milk of the flock? ᵃ*2 Tim 2:3f* ᵇ*Deut 20:6*

8 I am not speaking these things ᵃaccording to human judgment, am I? Or does not the Law also say these things? ᵃ*Rom 3:5*

9 For it is written in the Law of Moses, "ᵃYOU SHALL NOT MUZZLE THE OX WHILE HE IS THRESHING." God is not concerned about oxen, is He? ᵃ*Deut 25:4; 1 Tim 5:18*

10 Or is He speaking altogether for our sake? Yes, ᵃfor our sake it was written, because the plowman ought to plow in hope, and the thresher *to thresh* in hope of sharing *the crops.* ᵃ*Rom 4:23f*

11 ᵃIf we sowed spiritual things in you, is it too much if we reap material things from you? ᵃ*Rom 15:27; 1 Cor 9:14*

12 If others share the right over you, do we not more? Nevertheless, we ᵃdid not use this right, but we endure all things ᵇso that we will cause no hindrance to the gospel of Christ. ᵃ*Acts 20:33* ᵇ*2 Cor6:3*

13 Do you not know that those who ᵃperform sacred services eat the *food* of the temple, *and* those who attend regularly to the altar have their share from the altar? ᵃ*Lev 6:16, 26; 7:6, 31ff*

14 So also ᵃthe Lord directed those who proclaim the gospel to get their living from the gospel. ᵃ*Matt 10:10; Luke 10:7*

15 But I have ᵃused none of these things. And I am not writing these things so that it will be done so in my case; for it would be better for me to die than have any man make my boast an empty one. ᵃ*Acts 18:3; 20:33*

16 For if I preach the gospel, I have nothing to boast of, for ᵃI am under compulsion; for woe is me if I do not preach the gospel. ᵃ*Acts 9:15; Rom 1:14*

17 For if I do this voluntarily, I have a ᵃreward; but if against my will, I have a stewardship entrusted to me. ᵃ*John 4:36; 1 Cor 3:8*

18 What then is my reward? That, when I preach the gospel, I may offer the gospel ᵃwith-

out charge, so as not to make full use of my right in the gospel. ªActs 18:3; 2 Cor 11:7

19 For though I am free from all *men*, I have made myself ªa slave to all, so that I may win more. ª2 Cor 4:5; Gal 5:13

20 ªTo the Jews I became as a Jew, so that I might win Jews; to those who are under the Law, as under the Law though not being myself under the Law, so that I might win those who are under the Law; ªActs 16:3; 21:23-26

21 to those who are ªwithout law, as without law, though not being without the law of God but ᵇunder the law of Christ, so that I might win those who are without law. ªRom 2:12, 14 ᵇGal 6:2

22 To the ªweak I became weak, that I might win the weak; I have become ᵇall things to all men, so that I may by all means save some. ªRom 15:1 ᵇ1 Cor 10:33

23 I do all things for the sake of the gospel, so that I may become a fellow partaker of it.

24 Do you not know that those who run in a race all run, but *only* one receives ªthe prize? Run in such a way that you may win. ªPhil 3:14; Col 2:18

25 Everyone who competes in the games exercises self-control in all things. They then *do it* to receive a perishable ªwreath, but we an imperishable. ª2 Tim 4:8; James 1:12

26 Therefore I ªrun in such a way, as not without aim; I box in such a way, as not beating the air; ªHeb 12:1

27 but I discipline ªmy body and make it my slave, so that, after I have preached to others, I myself will not be disqualified. ªRom 8:13

Avoid Israel's Mistakes

10 For I do not want you to be unaware, brethren, that our fathers were all ªunder the cloud and all passed through the sea; ªEx 13:21; Ps 105:39

2 and all were ªbaptized into Moses in the cloud and in the sea; ªRom 6:3; 1 Cor 1:13

3 and all ªate the same spiritual food; ªEx 16:4, 35; Deut 8:3

4 and all ªdrank the same spiritual drink, for they were drinking from a spiritual rock which followed them; and the rock was Christ. ªEx 17:6; Num 20:11

5 Nevertheless, with most of them God was not well-pleased; for ªthey were laid low in the wilderness. ªNum 14:29ff, 37; 26:65

6 Now these things happened as examples for us, so that we would not crave evil things as ªthey also craved. ªNum 11:4, 34; Ps 106:14

7 Do not be idolaters, as some of them were; as it is written, "ªTʜᴇ ᴘᴇᴏᴘʟᴇ sᴀᴛ ᴅᴏᴡɴ ᴛᴏ ᴇᴀᴛ ᴀɴᴅ ᴅʀɪɴᴋ, ᴀɴᴅ sᴛᴏᴏᴅ ᴜᴘ ᴛᴏ ᴘʟᴀʏ." ªEx 32:6

8 Nor let us act immorally, as some of them

did, and ªtwenty-three thousand fell in one day. ªNum 25:9

9 Nor let us try the Lord, as ªsome of them did, and were destroyed by the serpents. ªNum 21:5f

10 Nor grumble, as some of them did, and ªwere destroyed by the destroyer. ªNum 16:49

11 Now these things happened to them as an example, and ªthey were written for our instruction, upon whom ᵇthe ends of the ages have come. ªRom 4:23 ᵇRom 13:11

12 Therefore let him who ªthinks he stands take heed that he does not fall. ªRom 11:20; 2 Pet 3:17

13 No temptation has overtaken you but such as is common to man; and ªGod is faithful, who will not allow you to be ᵇtempted beyond what you are able, but with the temptation will provide the way of escape also, so that you will be able to endure it. ª1 Cor 1:9 ᵇ2 Pet 2:9

14 Therefore, my beloved, flee from ªidolatry. ª1 Cor 10:7, 19f; 1 John 5:21

15 I speak as to wise men; you judge what I say.

16 Is not the ªcup of blessing which we bless a sharing in the blood of Christ? Is not the bread which we break a sharing in the body of Christ? ªMatt 26:27f; Mark 14:23f

17 Since there is one bread, we ªwho are many are one body; for we all partake of the one bread. ªRom 12:5; 1 Cor 12:12f, 27

18 Look at the nation Israel; are not those who ªeat the sacrifices sharers in the altar? ªLev 7:6, 14f; Deut 12:17f

19 What do I mean then? That a thing sacrificed to idols is anything, or ªthat an idol is anything? ª1 Cor 8:4

20 *No,* but *I say* that the things which the Gentiles sacrifice, they ªsacrifice to demons and not to God; and I do not want you to become sharers in demons. ªDeut 32:17; Ps 106:37

21 ªYou cannot drink the cup of the Lord and the cup of demons; you cannot partake of the table of the Lord and the table of demons. ª2 Cor 6:16

22 Or do we ªprovoke the Lord to jealousy? We are not ᵇstronger than He, are we? ªDeut 32:21 ᵇEccl 6:10

23 ªAll things are lawful, but not all things are profitable. All things are lawful, but not all things ᵇedify. ª1 Cor 6:12 ᵇRom 14:19

24 Let no one ªseek his own *good,* but that of his neighbor. ªRom 15:2; 1 Cor 10:33

25 ªEat anything that is sold in the meat market without asking questions for conscience' sake; ªActs 10:15; 1 Cor 8:7

26 ªFᴏʀ ᴛʜᴇ ᴇᴀʀᴛʜ ɪs ᴛʜᴇ Lᴏʀᴅ's, ᴀɴᴅ ᴀʟʟ ɪᴛ ᴄᴏɴᴛᴀɪɴs. ªPs 24:1; 50:12

27 If ªone of the unbelievers invites you and you want to go, ᵇeat anything that is set before

you without asking questions for conscience'
sake. a1 Cor 5:10 bLuke 10:8

28 But aif anyone says to you, "This is meat
sacrificed to idols," do not eat it, for the sake of
the one who informed you, and for conscience'
sake; a1 Cor 8:7, 10-12

29 I mean not your own conscience, but the
other man's; for awhy is my freedom judged
by another's conscience? aRom 14:16; 1 Cor 9:19

30 If I partake with thankfulness, why am I
slandered concerning that for which I agive
thanks? aRom 14:6

31 Whether, then, you eat or drink or awhat-
ever you do, do all to the glory of God.
aCol 3:17; 1 Pet 4:11

32 aGive no offense either to Jews or to
Greeks or to the church of God; aActs 24:16;
1 Cor 8:13

33 just as I also aplease all men in all things,
not seeking my own profit but the profit of the
many, so that they may be saved. aRom 15:2;
1 Cor 9:22

Christian Order

11 aBe imitators of me, just as I also am of
Christ. a1 Cor 4:16; Phil 3:17

2 Now I praise you because you aremember
me in everything and hold firmly to the traditions, just as I delivered them to you.
a1 Thess 1:6; 3:6

3 But I want you to understand that Christ is
the ahead of every man, and the man is the
head of a woman, and God is the head of
Christ. aEph 5:23

4 Every man who has something on his head
while praying or aprophesying disgraces his
head. aActs 13:1; 1 Thess 5:20

5 But every woman who has her head uncov-
ered while praying or prophesying disgraces
her head, for she is one and the same as the
woman whose head is ashaved. aDeut 21:12

6 For if a woman does not cover her head, let
her also have her hair cut off; but if it is disgraceful for a woman to have her hair cut off
or her head shaved, let her cover her head.

7 For a man ought not to have his head covered, since he is the aimage and glory of God;
but the woman is the glory of man.   aGen
1:26; 5:1

8 For aman does not originate from woman,
but woman from man; aGen 2:21-23; 1 Tim 2:13

9 for indeed man was not created for the
woman's sake, but awoman for the man's sake.
aGen 2:18

10 Therefore the woman ought to have a symbol of authority on her head, because of the
angels.

11 However, in the Lord, neither is woman
independent of man, nor is man independent of
woman.

12 For as the woman originates from the man,
so also the man has his birth through the
woman; and aall things originate bfrom God.
a2 Cor 5:18 bRom 11:36

13 aJudge for yourselves: is it proper for a
woman to pray to God with her head uncov-
ered? aLuke 12:57

14 Does not even nature itself teach you that if
a man has long hair, it is a dishonor to him,

15 but if a woman has long hair, it is a glory to
her? For her hair is given to her for a covering.

16 But if one is inclined to be contentious, awe
have no other practice, nor have bthe churches
of God. a1 Cor 4:5 b1 Cor 7:17

17 But in giving this instruction, aI do not
praise you, because you come together not for
the better but for the worse. a1 Cor 11:2, 22

18 For, in the first place, when you come
together as a church, I hear that adivisions exist
among you; and in part I believe it. a1 Cor 1:10;
3:3

19 For there amust also be factions among
you, so that those who are approved may
become evident among you. aMatt 18:7; Luke 17:1

20 Therefore when you meet together, it is not
to eat the Lord's Supper,

21 for in your eating each one takes his own
supper first; and one is hungry and aanother is
drunk. aJude 12

22 What! Do you not have houses in which to
eat and drink? Or do you despise the achurch of
God and bshame those who have nothing?
What shall I say to you? Shall I praise you? In
this I will not praise you. a1 Cor 10:32 bJames 2:6

The Lord's Supper

23 For I received from the Lord that which I
also delivered to you, that athe Lord Jesus in
the night in which He was betrayed took bread;
a1 Cor 11:23-25; Matt 26:26-28

24 and when He had given thanks, He broke it
and said, "This is My body, which is for you;
do this in remembrance of Me."

25 In the same way He took the cup also after
supper, saying, "This cup is the anew covenant
in My blood; do this, as often as you drink it,
in remembrance of Me." aLuke 22:20; 2 Cor 3:6

26 For as often as you eat this bread and drink
the cup, you proclaim the Lord's death auntil
He comes. aJohn 21:22; 1 Cor 4:5

27 Therefore whoever eats the bread or drinks
the cup of the Lord in an unworthy manner,
shall be aguilty of the body and the blood of the
Lord. aHeb 10:29

28 But a man must aexamine himself, and in
so doing he is to eat of the bread and drink of
the cup. aMatt 26:22; 2 Cor 13:5

29 For he who eats and drinks, eats and drinks
judgment to himself if he does not judge the
body rightly.

30 For this reason many among you are weak and sick, and a number ᵃsleep. ᵃ*Acts 7:60*

31 But if we judged ourselves rightly, we would not be judged.

32 But when we are judged, we are ᵃdisciplined by the Lord so that we will not be condemned along with the world. ᵃ*2 Sam 7:14; Ps 94:12*

33 So then, my brethren, when you come together to eat, wait for one another.

34 If anyone is ᵃhungry, let him eat ᵇat home, so that you will not come together for judgment. The remaining matters I will arrange when I come. ᵃ*1 Cor 11:21* ᵇ*1 Cor 11:22*

The Use of Spiritual Gifts

12 Now concerning ᵃspiritual *gifts,* brethren, I do not want you to be unaware. ᵃ*1 Cor 12:4; 14:1*

2 ᵃYou know that when you were pagans, *you were* ᵇled astray to the mute idols, however you were led. ᵃ*1 Cor 6:11* ᵇ*1 Thess 1:9*

3 Therefore I make known to you that no one speaking ᵃby the Spirit of God says, "Jesus is accursed"; and no one can say, "Jesus is Lord," except ᵃby the Holy Spirit. ᵃ*Matt 22:43; 1 John 4:2f*

4 Now there are ᵃvarieties of gifts, but the same Spirit. ᵃ*Rom 12:6f; 1 Cor 12:11*

5 And there are varieties of ministries, and the same Lord.

6 There are varieties of effects, but the same ᵃGod who works all things in all *persons.* ᵃ*1 Cor 15:28; Eph 1:23; 4:6*

7 But to each one is given the manifestation of the Spirit ᵃfor the common good. ᵃ*1 Cor 12:12-30; 14:26*

8 For to one is given the word of ᵃwisdom through the Spirit, and to another the word of knowledge according to the same Spirit; ᵃ*1 Cor 2:6*

9 to another ᵃfaith by the same Spirit, and to another ᵇgifts of healing by the one Spirit, ᵃ*1 Cor 13:2* ᵇ*1 Cor 12:28, 30*

10 and to another the effecting of miracles, and to another prophecy, and to another the ᵃdistinguishing of spirits, to another *various* kinds of tongues, and to another the interpretation of tongues. ᵃ*1 Cor 14:29; 1 John 4:1*

11 But one and the same Spirit works all these things, ᵃdistributing to each one individually just as He wills. ᵃ*1 Cor 12:4*

12 For even as the body is one and *yet* has many members, and all the members of the body, though they are many, are one body, ᵃso also is Christ. ᵃ*1 Cor 12:27*

13 For ᵃby one Spirit we were all baptized into one body, whether Jews or Greeks, whether slaves or free, and we were all made to ᵇdrink of one Spirit. ᵃ*Eph 2:18* ᵇ*John 7:37-39*

14 For ᵃthe body is not one member, but many. ᵃ*1 Cor 12:20*

15 If the foot says, "Because I am not a hand, I am not *a part* of the body," it is not for this reason any the less *a part* of the body.

16 And if the ear says, "Because I am not an eye, I am not *a part* of the body," it is not for this reason any the less *a part* of the body.

17 If the whole body were an eye, where would the hearing be? If the whole were hearing, where would the sense of smell be?

18 But now God has ᵃplaced the members, each one of them, in the body, ᵇjust as He desired. ᵃ*1 Cor 12:28* ᵇ*Rom 12:6*

19 If they were all one member, where would the body be?

20 But now ᵃthere are many members, but one body. ᵃ*1 Cor 12:12, 14*

21 And the eye cannot say to the hand, "I have no need of you"; or again the head to the feet, "I have no need of you."

22 On the contrary, it is much truer that the members of the body which seem to be weaker are necessary;

23 and those *members* of the body which we deem less honorable, on these we bestow more abundant honor, and our less presentable members become much more presentable,

24 whereas our more presentable members have no need *of it.* But God has *so* composed the body, giving more abundant honor to that *member* which lacked,

25 so that there may be no division in the body, but *that* the members may have the same care for one another.

26 And if one member suffers, all the members suffer with it; if *one* member is honored, all the members rejoice with it.

27 Now you are Christ's body, and ᵃindividually members of it. ᵃ*Rom 12:5; Eph 5:30*

28 And God has ᵃappointed in the church, first ᵇapostles, second prophets, third teachers, then miracles, then gifts of healings, helps, administrations, *various* kinds of tongues. ᵃ*1 Cor 12:18* ᵇ*Eph 4:11*

29 All are not apostles, are they? All are not prophets, are they? All are not teachers, are they? All are not *workers of* miracles, are they?

30 All do not have gifts of healings, do they? All do not speak with tongues, do they? All do not ᵃinterpret, do they? ᵃ*1 Cor 12:10*

31 But ᵃearnestly desire the greater gifts.

And I show you a still more excellent way. ᵃ*1 Cor 14:1, 39*

The Excellence of Love

13 If I speak with the ᵃtongues of men and of angels, but do not have love, I have become a noisy gong or a ᵇclanging cymbal. ᵃ*1 Cor 12:10* ᵇ*Ps 150:5*

2 If I have *the gift of* prophecy, and know all ᵃmysteries and all knowledge; and if I have all

faith, so as to remove mountains, but do not have love, I am nothing. ᵃ*1 Cor 14:2; 15:51*

3 And if I ᵃgive all my possessions to feed *the poor,* and if I ᵇsurrender my body to be burned, but do not have love, it profits me nothing. ᵃ*Matt 6:2* ᵇ*Dan 3:28*

4 Love ᵃis patient, love is kind *and* is not jealous; love does not brag *and* is not arrogant, ᵃ*Prov 10:12; 17:9*

5 does not act unbecomingly; it does not seek its own, is not provoked, ᵃdoes not take into account a wrong *suffered,* ᵃ*2 Cor 5:19*

6 does not rejoice in unrighteousness, but ᵃrejoices with the truth; ᵃ*2 John 4; 3 John 3f*

7 ᵃbears all things, believes all things, hopes all things, endures all things. ᵃ*1 Cor 9:12*

8 Love never fails; but if *there are gifts of* ᵃprophecy, they will be done away; if *there are* ᵇtongues, they will cease; if *there is* knowledge, it will be done away. ᵃ*1 Cor 13:2* ᵇ*1 Cor 13:1*

9 For we ᵃknow in part and we prophesy in part; ᵃ*1 Cor 8:2; 13:12*

10 but when the perfect comes, the partial will be done away.

11 When I was a child, I used to speak like a child, think like a child, reason like a child; when I became a man, I did away with childish things.

12 For now we see in a mirror dimly, but then ᵃface to face; now I know in part, but then I will know fully just as I also have been fully known. ᵃ*Gen 32:30; Num 12:8*

13 But now faith, hope, love, abide these three; but the greatest of these is ᵃlove. ᵃ*Gal 5:6*

Prophecy a Superior Gift

14 ᵃPursue love, yet ᵇdesire earnestly spiritual *gifts,* but especially that you may prophesy. ᵃ*1 Cor 16:14* ᵇ*1 Cor 12:31*

2 For one who ᵃspeaks in a tongue does not speak to men but to God; for no one understands, but in *his* spirit he speaks ᵇmysteries. ᵃ*1 Cor 12:10, 28, 30* ᵇ*1 Cor 13:2*

3 But one who prophesies speaks to men for ᵃedification and exhortation and consolation. ᵃ*Rom 14:19; 1 Cor 14:5, 12, 17, 26*

4 One who speaks in a tongue ᵃedifies himself; but one who prophesies ᵃedifies the church. ᵃ*Rom 14:19; 1 Cor 14:5, 12, 17, 26*

5 Now I wish that you all spoke in tongues, but ᵃ*even* more that you would prophesy; and greater is one who prophesies than one who speaks in tongues, unless he interprets, so that the church may receive edifying. ᵃ*Num 11:29*

6 But now, brethren, if I come to you speaking in tongues, what will I profit you unless I speak to you either by way of ᵃrevelation or of knowledge or of prophecy or of teaching? ᵃ*1 Cor 14:26; Eph 1:17*

7 Yet *even* lifeless things, either flute or harp,

in producing a sound, if they do not produce a distinction in the tones, how will it be known what is played on the flute or on the harp?

8 For if ᵃthe bugle produces an indistinct sound, who will prepare himself for battle? ᵃ*Num 10:9; Jer 4:19*

9 So also you, unless you utter by the tongue speech that is clear, how will it be known what is spoken? For you will be ᵃspeaking into the air. ᵃ*1 Cor 9:26*

10 There are, perhaps, a great many kinds of languages in the world, and no *kind* is without meaning.

11 If then I do not know the meaning of the language, I will be to the one who speaks a ᵃbarbarian, and the one who speaks will be a barbarian to me. ᵃ*Acts 28:2*

12 So also you, since you are zealous of spiritual *gifts,* seek to abound for the ᵃedification of the church. ᵃ*Rom 14:19; 1 Cor 14:4, 5, 17, 26*

13 Therefore let one who speaks in a tongue pray that he may interpret.

14 For if I pray in a tongue, my spirit prays, but my mind is unfruitful.

15 What is *the outcome* then? I will pray with the spirit and I will pray with the mind also; I will ᵃsing with the spirit and I will sing with the mind also. ᵃ*Eph 5:19; Col 3:16*

16 Otherwise if you bless in the spirit *only,* how will the one who fills the place of the ungifted say ᵃthe "Amen" at your giving of thanks, since he does not know what you are saying? ᵃ*Deut 27:15-26; 1 Chr 16:36*

17 For you are giving thanks well enough, but the other person is not ᵃedified. ᵃ*Rom 14:19; 1 Cor 14:4, 5, 12, 26*

18 I thank God, I speak in tongues more than you all;

19 however, in the church I desire to speak five words with my mind so that I may instruct others also, rather than ten thousand words in a tongue.

Instruction for the Church

20 Brethren, ᵃdo not be children in your thinking; yet in evil ᵇbe infants, but in your thinking be mature. ᵃ*Eph 4:14* ᵇ*Matt 18:3*

21 In the Law it is written, "ᵃBY MEN OF STRANGE TONGUES AND BY THE LIPS OF STRANGERS I WILL SPEAK TO THIS PEOPLE, AND EVEN SO THEY WILL NOT LISTEN TO ME," says the Lord. ᵃ*Is 28:11f*

22 So then tongues are for a sign, not to those who believe but to unbelievers; but ᵃprophecy *is for a sign,* not to unbelievers but to those who believe. ᵃ*1 Cor 14:1*

23 Therefore if the whole church assembles together and all speak in tongues, and ungifted men or unbelievers enter, will not they say that ᵃyou are mad? ᵃ*Acts 2:13*

24 But if all prophesy, and an unbeliever or an

ungifted man enters, he is ^aconvicted by all, he is called to account by all; ^aJohn 16:8

25 the secrets of his heart are disclosed; and so he will fall on his face and worship God, ^adeclaring that God is certainly among you. ^aIs 45:14; Dan 2:47

26 What is *the outcome* then, brethren? When you assemble, each one has a psalm, has a teaching, has a revelation, has a tongue, has an interpretation. Let ^aall things be done for edification. ^aRom 14:19

27 If anyone speaks in a tongue, *it should be* by two or at the most three, and *each* in turn, and one must ^ainterpret; ^a1 Cor 12:10; 14:5, 13, 26ff

28 but if there is no interpreter, he must keep silent in the church; and let him speak to himself and to God.

29 Let two or three ^aprophets speak, and let the others ^bpass judgment. ^a1 Cor 14:32, 37 ^b1 Cor 12:10

30 But if a revelation is made to another who is seated, the first one must keep silent.

31 For you can all prophesy one by one, so that all may learn and all may be exhorted;

32 and the spirits of prophets are subject to prophets;

33 for God is not *a God* of confusion but of peace, as in ^aall the churches of the saints. ^a1 Cor 4:17; 7:17

34 The women are to keep silent in the churches; for they are not permitted to speak, but ^aare to subject themselves, just as the Law also says. ^a1 Tim 2:11f; 1 Pet 3:1

35 If they desire to learn anything, let them ask their own husbands at home; for it is improper for a woman to speak in church.

36 Was it from you that the word of God *first* went forth? Or has it come to you only?

37 ^aIf anyone thinks he is a prophet or spiritual, let him recognize that the things which I write to you are the Lord's commandment. ^a2 Cor 10:7

38 But if anyone does not recognize *this*, he is not recognized.

39 Therefore, my brethren, ^adesire earnestly to ^bprophesy, and do not forbid to speak in tongues. ^a1 Cor 12:31 ^b1 Cor 14:1

40 But ^aall things must be done properly and in an orderly manner. ^a1 Cor 14:33

The Fact of Christ's Resurrection

15 Now I make known to you, brethren, the gospel which I preached to you, which also you received, ^ain which also you stand, ^aRom 5:2; 11:20

2 by which also you are saved, ^aif you hold fast the word which I preached to you, unless you believed in vain. ^aRom 11:22

3 For I delivered to you as of first importance what I also received, that Christ died ^afor our sins according to the Scriptures, ^aGal 1:4; 1 Pet 2:24

4 and that He was buried, and that He was raised on the third day ^aaccording to the Scriptures, ^aPs 16:8ff

5 and that ^aHe appeared to Cephas, then ^bto the twelve. ^aLuke 24:34 ^bLuke 24:36

6 After that He appeared to more than five hundred brethren at one time, most of whom remain until now, but some ^ahave fallen asleep; ^aActs 7:60; 1 Cor 15:18, 20

7 then He appeared to James, then to ^aall the apostles; ^aLuke 24:33, 36f; Acts 1:3f

8 and last of all, as to one untimely born, ^aHe appeared to me also. ^aActs 9:3-8; 22:6-11

9 For I am ^athe least of the apostles, and not fit to be called an apostle, because I ^bpersecuted the church of God. ^a1 Tim 1:15 ^bActs 8:3

10 But by ^athe grace of God I am what I am, and His grace toward me did not prove vain; but I ^blabored even more than all of them, yet not I, but the grace of God with me. ^aRom 12:3 ^b2 Cor 11:23

11 Whether then *it was* I or they, so we preach and so you believed.

12 Now if Christ is preached, that He has been raised from the dead, how do some among you say that there ^ais no resurrection of the dead? ^aActs 17:32; 23:8

13 But if there is no resurrection of the dead, not even Christ has been raised;

14 and ^aif Christ has not been raised, then our preaching is vain, your faith also is vain. ^a1 Thess 4:14

15 Moreover we are even found *to be* false witnesses of God, because we testified against God that He ^araised Christ, whom He did not raise, if in fact the dead are not raised. ^aActs 2:24

16 For if the dead are not raised, not even Christ has been raised;

17 and if Christ has not been raised, your faith is worthless; ^ayou are still in your sins. ^aRom 4:25

18 Then those also who ^ahave fallen asleep in Christ have perished. ^a1 Cor 15:6; 1 Thess 4:16

19 If we have hoped in Christ in this life only, we are ^aof all men most to be pitied. ^a1 Cor 4:9; 2 Tim 3:12

The Order of Resurrection

20 But now Christ has been raised from the dead, the ^afirst fruits of those who ^bare asleep. ^a1 Cor 15:23 ^b1 Thess 4:16

21 For since ^aby a man *came* death, by a man also *came* the resurrection of the dead. ^aRom 5:12

22 For ^aas in Adam all die, so also in Christ all will be made alive. ^aRom 5:14-18

23 But each in his own order: Christ the first

fruits, after that ªthose who are Christ's at His coming. ª*1 Thess 4:16*

24 then *comes* the end, when He hands over ªthe kingdom to the God and Father, when He has abolished all rule and all authority and power. ª*Dan 2:44; 7:14, 27*

25 For He must reign ªuntil He has put all His enemies under His feet. ª*Ps 110:1; Matt 22:44*

26 The last enemy that will be ªabolished is death. ª*2 Tim 1:10; Rev 20:14*

27 For ªHE HAS PUT ALL THINGS IN SUBJECTION UNDER HIS FEET. But when He says, "All things are put in subjection," it is evident that He is excepted who put all things in subjection to Him. ª*Ps 8:6*

28 When all things are subjected to Him, then the Son Himself also will be subjected to the One who subjected all things to Him, so that ªGod may be all in all. ª*1 Cor 12:6*

29 Otherwise, what will those do who are baptized for the dead? If the dead are not raised at all, why then are they baptized for them?

30 Why are we also ªin danger every hour? ª*2 Cor 11:26*

31 I affirm, brethren, by the boasting in you which I have in Christ Jesus our Lord, ªI die daily. ª*Rom 8:36*

32 If from human motives I fought with wild beasts at Ephesus, what does it profit me? If the dead are not raised, ªLET US EAT AND DRINK, FOR TOMORROW WE DIE. ª*Is 22:13; 56:12*

33 ªDo not be deceived: "Bad company corrupts good morals." ª*1 Cor 6:9*

34 Become sober-minded as you ought, and stop sinning; for some have ªno knowledge of God. I speak *this* to your shame. ª*Matt 22:29*

35 But someone will say, "How are ªthe dead raised? And with what kind of body do they come?" ª*Ezek 37:3*

36 You fool! That which you ªsow does not come to life unless it dies; ª*John 12:24*

37 and that which you sow, you do not sow the body which is to be, but a bare grain, perhaps of wheat or of something else.

38 But God gives it a body just as He wished, and ªto each of the seeds a body of its own. ª*Gen 1:11*

39 All flesh is not the same flesh, but there is one *flesh* of men, and another flesh of beasts, and another flesh of birds, and another of fish.

40 There are also heavenly bodies and earthly bodies, but the glory of the heavenly is one, and the *glory* of the earthly is another.

41 There is one glory of the sun, and another glory of the moon, and another glory of the stars; for star differs from star in glory.

42 So also is the resurrection of the dead. It is sown ªa perishable *body,* it is raised an imperishable *body;* ª*Rom 8:21; 1 Cor 15:50*

43 it is sown in dishonor, it is raised in ªglory;

it is sown in weakness, it is raised in power; ª*Phil 3:21; Col 3:4*

44 it is sown a ªnatural body, it is raised a spiritual body. If there is a natural body, there is also a spiritual *body.* ª*1 Cor 2:14*

45 So also it is written, "The first ªMAN, Adam, BECAME A LIVING SOUL." The last Adam *became* a life-giving spirit. ª*Gen 2:7*

46 However, the spiritual is not first, but the natural; then the spiritual.

47 The first man is ªfrom the earth, earthy; the second man is from heaven. ª*John 3:31*

48 As is the earthy, so also are those who are earthy; and as is the heavenly, ªso also are those who are heavenly. ª*Phil 3:20f*

49 Just as we have ªborne the image of the earthy, we ᵇwill also bear the image of the heavenly. ª*Gen 5:3* ᵇ*Rom 8:29*

The Mystery of Resurrection

50 Now I say this, brethren, that flesh and blood cannot ªinherit the kingdom of God; nor does the perishable inherit the imperishable. ª*1 Cor 6:9*

51 Behold, I tell you a ªmystery; we will not all sleep, but we will all be ᵇchanged, ª*1 Cor 13:2* ᵇ*2 Cor 5:2, 4*

52 in a moment, in the twinkling of an eye, at the last trumpet; for the trumpet will sound, and the dead will be raised imperishable, and ªwe will be changed. ª*1 Thess 4:15, 17*

53 For this perishable must put on the imperishable, and this ªmortal must put on immortality. ª*2 Cor 5:4*

54 But when this perishable will have put on the imperishable, and this mortal will have put on immortality, then will come about the saying that is written, "ªDEATH IS SWALLOWED UP in victory. ª*Is 25:8*

55 "ªO DEATH, WHERE IS YOUR VICTORY? O DEATH, WHERE IS YOUR STING?" ª*Hos 13:14*

56 The sting of death is sin, and ªthe power of sin is the law; ª*Rom 3:20; 7:8*

57 but thanks be to God, who gives us the ªvictory through our Lord Jesus Christ. ª*Rom 8:37; 1 John 5:4*

58 Therefore, my beloved brethren, be steadfast, immovable, always abounding in ªthe work of the Lord, knowing that your toil is not *in* vain in the Lord. ª*1 Cor 16:10*

Instructions and Greetings

16 Now concerning ªthe collection for the saints, as I directed the churches of Galatia, so do you also. ª*Acts 24:17; Rom 15:25f*

2 On the first day of every week each one of you is to put aside and save, as he may prosper, so that ªno collections be made when I come. ª*2 Cor 9:4f*

3 When I arrive, ªwhomever you may

approve, I will send them with letters to carry your gift to Jerusalem; [a]2 Cor 3:1; 8:18f

4 and if it is fitting for me to go also, they will go with me.

5 But I will come to you after I go through Macedonia, for I [a]am going through Macedonia; [a]Acts 19:21

6 and perhaps I will stay with you, or even spend the winter, so that you may [a]send me on my way wherever I may go. [a]Acts 15:3; 1 Cor 16:11

7 For I do not wish to see you now [a]just in passing; for I hope to remain with you for some time, if the Lord permits. [a]2 Cor 1:15f

8 But I will remain in [a]Ephesus until Pentecost; [a]Acts 18:19

9 for a [a]wide door for effective *service* has opened to me, and there are many adversaries. [a]Acts 14:27

10 Now if [a]Timothy comes, see that he is with you without cause to be afraid, for he is doing [b]the Lord's work, as I also am. [a]1 Cor 4:17 [b]1 Cor 15:58

11 So let no one despise him. But send him on his way [a]in peace, so that he may come to me; for I expect him with the brethren. [a]Acts 15:33

12 But concerning [a]Apollos our brother, I encouraged him greatly to come to you with the brethren; and it was not at all *his* desire to come now, but he will come when he has opportunity. [a]Acts 18:24; 1 Cor 1:12

13 [a]Be on the alert, stand firm in the faith, act like men, be strong. [a]Matt 24:42

14 Let all that you do be done [a]in love. [a]1 Cor 14:1

15 Now I urge you, brethren (you know the [a]household of Stephanas, that they were the first fruits of Achaia, and that they have devoted themselves for [b]ministry to the saints), [a]1 Cor 1:16 [b]Rom 15:31

16 that [a]you also be in subjection to such men and to everyone who helps in the work and labors. [a]1 Thess 5:12; Heb 13:17

17 I rejoice over the coming of Stephanas and Fortunatus and Achaicus, because they have supplied [a]what was lacking on your part. [a]2 Cor 11:9; Phil 2:30

18 For they have refreshed my spirit and yours. Therefore [a]acknowledge such men. [a]Phil 2:29; 1 Thess 5:12

19 The churches of Asia greet you. [a]Aquila and Prisca greet you heartily in the Lord, with [b]the church that is in their house. [a]Acts 18:2 [b]Rom 16:5

20 All the brethren greet you. [a]Greet one another with a holy kiss. [a]Rom 16:16

21 The greeting is in [a]my own hand—Paul. [a]Rom 16:22; Gal 6:11

22 If anyone does not love the Lord, he is to be accursed. [a]Maranatha. [a]Phil 4:5; Rev 22:20

23 [a]The grace of the Lord Jesus be with you. [a]Rom 16:20

24 My love be with you all in Christ Jesus. Amen.

The Second Letter of Paul to the
CORINTHIANS

Introduction

1 Paul, an apostle of Christ Jesus [a]by the will of God, and Timothy *our* brother,

To [b]the church of God which is at Corinth with all the saints who are throughout Achaia: [a]1 Cor 1:1 [b]1 Cor 10:32

2 [a]Grace to you and peace from God our Father and the Lord Jesus Christ. [a]Rom 1:7

3 [a]Blessed *be* the God and Father of our Lord Jesus Christ, the Father of mercies and God of all comfort, [a]Eph 1:3; 1 Pet 1:3

4 who [a]comforts us in all our affliction so that we will be able to comfort those who are in any affliction with the comfort with which we ourselves are comforted by God. [a]Is 51:12; 66:13

5 For just [a]as the sufferings of Christ are ours in abundance, so also our comfort is abundant through Christ. [a]2 Cor 4:10; Phil 3:10

6 But if we are afflicted, it is [a]for your comfort and salvation; or if we are comforted, it is for your comfort, which is effective in the patient enduring of the same sufferings which we also suffer; [a]2 Cor 4:15; 12:15

7 and our hope for you is firmly grounded, knowing that [a]as you are sharers of our sufferings, so also you are *sharers* of our comfort. [a]Rom 8:17

8 For we do not want you to be unaware, brethren, of our [a]affliction which came *to us* in Asia, that we were burdened excessively, beyond our strength, so that we despaired even of life; [a]Acts 19:23; 1 Cor 15:32

9 indeed, we had the sentence of death within ourselves so that we would not trust in ourselves, but in God who raises the dead;

10 who delivered us from so great a *peril of* death, and will deliver *us*, He [a]on whom we have set our hope. And He will yet deliver us, [a]1 Tim 4:10

11 you also joining in helping us through your prayers, so that thanks may be given by [a]many persons on our behalf for the favor bestowed on us through *the prayers of* many. [a]2 Cor 4:15; 9:11f

Paul's Integrity

12 For our proud confidence is this: the testimony of ᵃour conscience, that in holiness and godly sincerity, not in fleshly wisdom but in the grace of God, we have conducted ourselves in the world, and especially toward you. *ᵃActs 23:1; 1 Thess 2:10*

13 For we write nothing else to you than what you read and understand, and I hope you will understand ᵃuntil the end; *ᵃ1 Cor 1:8*

14 just as you also partially did understand us, that we are your reason to be proud as you also are ours, in ᵃthe day of our Lord Jesus. *ᵃ1 Cor 1:8*

15 In this confidence I intended at first to come to you, so that you might twice receive a ᵃblessing; *ᵃRom 1:11; 15:29*

16 that is, to ᵃpass your way into Macedonia, and again from Macedonia to come to you, and by you to be helped on my journey to Judea. *ᵃActs 19:21; 1 Cor 16:5-7*

17 Therefore, I was not vacillating when I intended to do this, was I? Or what I purpose, do I purpose ᵃaccording to the flesh, so that with me there will be yes, yes and no, no *at the same time?* *ᵃ2 Cor 10:2f; 11:18*

18 But as ᵃGod is faithful, our word to you is not yes and no. *ᵃ1 Cor 1:9*

19 For ᵃthe Son of God, Christ Jesus, who was preached among you by us—by me and Silvanus and Timothy—was not yes and no, but is yes in Him. *ᵃMatt 4:3; 16:16*

20 For ᵃas many as are the promises of God, in Him they are yes; therefore also through Him is our Amen to the glory of God through us. *ᵃRom 15:8*

21 Now He who establishes us with you in Christ and ᵃanointed us is God, *ᵃ1 John 2:20, 27*

22 who also sealed us and ᵃgave *us* the Spirit in our hearts as a pledge. *ᵃRom 8:16; 2 Cor 5:5*

23 But ᵃI call God as witness to my soul, that to spare you I did not come again to Corinth. *ᵃRom 1:9; Gal 1:20*

24 Not that we ᵃlord it over your faith, but are workers with you for your joy; for in your faith you are standing firm. *ᵃ2 Cor 4:5; 11:20*

Reaffirm Your Love

2 But I determined this for my own sake, that I ᵃwould not come to you in sorrow again. *ᵃ1 Cor 4:21; 2 Cor 12:21*

2 For if I ᵃcause you sorrow, who then makes me glad but the one whom I made sorrowful? *ᵃ2 Cor 7:8*

3 This is the very thing I wrote you, so that when I came, I would not have sorrow from those who ought to make me rejoice; having ᵃconfidence in you all that my joy would be *the joy* of you all. *ᵃGal 5:10; 2 Thess 3:4*

4 For out of much affliction and anguish of heart I ᵃwrote to you with many tears; not so that you would be made sorrowful, but that you might know the love which I have especially for you. *ᵃ2 Cor 2:9; 7:8, 12*

5 But ᵃif any has caused sorrow, he has caused sorrow not to me, but in some degree—in order not to say too much—to all of you. *ᵃ1 Cor 5:1f*

6 Sufficient for such a one is ᵃthis punishment which *was inflicted* by the majority, *ᵃ1 Cor 5:4f; 2 Cor 7:11*

7 so that on the contrary you should rather ᵃforgive and comfort *him,* otherwise such a one might be overwhelmed by excessive sorrow. *ᵃGal 6:1; Eph 4:32*

8 Wherefore I urge you to reaffirm *your* love for him.

9 For to this end also I wrote, so that I might put you to the test, whether you are ᵃobedient in all things. *ᵃ2 Cor 7:15; 10:6*

10 But one whom you forgive anything, I *forgive* also; for indeed what I have forgiven, if I have forgiven anything, *I did it* for your sakes ᵃin the presence of Christ, *ᵃ1 Cor 5:4; 2 Cor 4:6*

11 so that no advantage would be taken of us by Satan, for ᵃwe are not ignorant of his schemes. *ᵃLuke 22:31; 2 Cor 4:4*

12 Now when I came to ᵃTroas for the gospel of Christ and when a ᵇdoor was opened for me in the Lord, *ᵃActs 16:8 ᵇActs 14:27*

13 I ᵃhad no rest for my spirit, not finding Titus my brother; but taking my leave of them, I went on to Macedonia. *ᵃ2 Cor 7:5*

14 ᵃBut thanks be to God, who always leads us in triumph in Christ, and manifests through us the sweet aroma of the knowledge of Him in every place. *ᵃRom 1:8; 6:17*

15 For we are a ᵃfragrance of Christ to God among ᵇthose who are being saved and among those who are perishing; *ᵃEph 5:2 ᵇ1 Cor 1:18*

16 ᵃto the one an aroma from death to death, to the other an aroma from life to life. And who is ᵇadequate for these things? *ᵃLuke 2:34 ᵇ2 Cor 3:5f*

17 For we are not like many, peddling the word of God, but ᵃas from sincerity, but as from God, we speak in Christ in the sight of God. *ᵃ1 Cor 5:8; 2 Cor 1:12*

Ministers of a New Covenant

3 Are we beginning to ᵃcommend ourselves again? Or do we need, as some, letters of commendation to you or from you? *ᵃ2 Cor 5:12; 10:12, 18*

2 ᵃYou are our letter, written in our hearts, known and read by all men; *ᵃ1 Cor 9:2*

3 being manifested that you are a letter of Christ, cared for by us, written not with ink but with the Spirit of the living God, not on tablets of stone but on ᵃtablets of human hearts. *ᵃProv 3:3; 7:3*

4 Such ªconfidence we have through Christ toward God. ªEph 3:12

5 Not that we are adequate in ourselves to consider anything as *coming* from ourselves, but ªour adequacy is from God, ª1 Cor 15:10

6 who also made us adequate *as* servants of a ªnew covenant, not of ᵇthe letter but of the Spirit; for the letter kills, but the Spirit gives life. ªJer 31:31 ᵇRom 2:29

7 But if the ªministry of death, in letters engraved on stones, came with glory, ᵇso that the sons of Israel could not look intently at the face of Moses because of the glory of his face, fading *as* it was, ªRom 7:5fᵇEx 34:29-35

8 how will the ministry of the Spirit fail to be even more with glory?

9 For if the ministry of condemnation has glory, much more does the ªministry of righteousness abound in glory. ªRom 1:17; 3:21f

10 For indeed what had glory, in this case has no glory because of the glory that surpasses *it*.

11 For if that which fades away *was* with glory, much more that which remains *is* in glory.

12 Therefore having such a hope, ªwe use great boldness in *our* speech, ªActs 4:13, 29

13 and *are* not like Moses, ªwho used to put a veil over his face so that the sons of Israel would not look intently at the end of what was fading away. ªEx 34:33-35; 2 Cor 3:7

14 But their minds were ªhardened; for until this very day at the ᵇreading of the old covenant the same veil remains unlifted, because it is removed in Christ. ªRom 11:7 ᵇActs 13:15

15 But to this day whenever Moses is read, a veil lies over their heart;

16 ªbut whenever a person turns to the Lord, the veil is taken away. ªEx 34:34; Rom 11:23

17 Now the Lord is the Spirit, and where the Spirit of the Lord is, ªthere is liberty. ªJohn 8:32; Gal 5:1, 13

18 But we all, with unveiled face, ªbeholding as in a mirror the glory of the Lord, are being ᵇtransformed into the same image from glory to glory, just as from the Lord, the Spirit. ª1 Cor 13:12 ᵇRom 8:29

Paul's Apostolic Ministry

4 Therefore, since we have this ministry, as we ªreceived mercy, we do not lose heart, ª1 Cor 7:25

2 but we have renounced the ªthings hidden because of shame, not walking in craftiness or adulterating the word of God, but by the manifestation of truth commending ourselves to every man's conscience in the sight of God. ªRom 6:21; 1 Cor 4:5

3 And even if our gospel is ªveiled, it is veiled to those who are perishing, ª1 Cor 2:6ff; 2 Cor 3:14

4 in whose case ªthe god of this world has ᵇblinded the minds of the unbelieving so that they might not see the light of the gospel of the glory of Christ, who is the image of God. ªJohn 12:31 ᵇ2 Cor 3:14

5 For we ªdo not preach ourselves but Christ Jesus as Lord, and ourselves as your bondservants for Jesus' sake. ª1 Cor 4:15f; 1 Thess 2:6f

6 For God, who said, "ªLight shall shine out of darkness," is the One who has ᵇshone in our hearts to give the Light of the knowledge of the glory of God in the face of Christ. ªGen 1:3 ᵇ2 Pet 1:19

7 But we have this treasure in ªearthen vessels, so that the surpassing greatness of ᵇthe power will be of God and not from ourselves; ªLam 4:2 ᵇJudg 7:2

8 *we are* ªafflicted in every way, but not crushed; perplexed, but not despairing; ª2 Cor 1:8; 7:5

9 persecuted, but not ªforsaken; struck down, but not destroyed; ªPs 129:2; Heb 13:5

10 ªalways carrying about in the body the dying of Jesus, so that the life of Jesus also may be manifested in our body. ªRom 6:5; 8:36

11 For we who live are constantly being delivered over to death for Jesus' sake, so that the life of Jesus also may be manifested in our mortal flesh.

12 So death works in us, but life in you.

13 But having the same spirit of faith, according to what is written, "ªI BELIEVED, THEREFORE I SPOKE," we also believe, therefore we also speak, ªPs 116:10

14 knowing that He who ªraised the Lord Jesus ᵇwill raise us also with Jesus and will present us with you. ªActs 2:24 ᵇ1 Thess 4:14

15 For all things *are* ªfor your sakes, so that the grace which is spreading to more and more people may cause the giving of thanks to abound to the glory of God. ªRom 8:28; 2 Cor 1:6

16 Therefore we do not lose heart, but though our outer man is decaying, yet our ªinner man is being renewed day by day. ªRom 7:22

17 For momentary, ªlight affliction is producing for us an eternal weight of glory far beyond all comparison, ªRom 8:18

18 while we ªlook not at the things which are seen, but at the things which are not seen; for the things which are seen are temporal, but the things which are not seen are eternal. ªRom 8:24; 2 Cor 5:7

The Temporal and Eternal

5 For we know that if the ªearthly tent which is our house is torn down, we have a building from God, a house ᵇnot made with hands, eternal in the heavens. ªJob 4:19 ᵇActs 7:48

2 For indeed in this *house* we ªgroan, longing

to be clothed with our dwelling from heaven,
[a]Rom 8:23; 2 Cor 5:4

3 inasmuch as we, having put it on, will not be found naked.

4 For indeed while we are in this tent, we groan, being burdened, because we do not want to be unclothed but to be [a]clothed, so that what is mortal will be swallowed up by life.
[a]1 Cor 15:53f

5 Now He who prepared us for this very purpose is God, who [a]gave to us the Spirit as a pledge. [a]Rom 8:23; 2 Cor 1:22

6 Therefore, being always of good courage, and knowing that [a]while we are at home in the body we are absent from the Lord— [a]Heb 11:13f

7 for [a]we walk by faith, not by sight—
[a]1 Cor 13:12; 2 Cor 4:18

8 we are of good courage, I say, and prefer rather to be absent from the body and [a]to be at home with the Lord. [a]John 12:26; Phil 1:23

9 Therefore we also have as our ambition, whether at home or absent, to be [a]pleasing to Him. [a]Rom 14:18; Col 1:10

10 For we must all appear before [a]the judgment seat of Christ, so that each one may be recompensed for his deeds in the body, according to what he has done, whether good or bad.
[a]Matt 16:27; Acts 10:42

11 Therefore, knowing the fear of the Lord, we persuade men, but we are made manifest to God; and I hope that we are [a]made manifest also in your consciences. [a]2 Cor 4:2

12 We are not again commending ourselves to you but [a]are giving you an [a]occasion to be proud of us, so that you will have [a]an answer for those who take pride in appearance and not in heart. [a]2 Cor 1:14; Phil 1:26

13 For if we are [a]beside ourselves, it is for God; if we are of sound mind, it is for you.
[a]Mark 3:21; 2 Cor 11:1, 16ff

14 For the love of Christ controls us, having concluded this, that [a]one died for all, therefore all died; [a]Rom 5:15; 6:6f

15 and He died for all, so that they who live might no longer [a]live for themselves, but for Him who died and rose again on their behalf.
[a]Rom 14:7-9

16 Therefore from now on we recognize no one [a]according to the flesh; even though we have known Christ according to the flesh, yet now we know Him in this way no longer.
[a]John 8:15; 2 Cor 11:18

17 Therefore if anyone is in Christ, he is a new creature; [a]the old things passed away; behold, new things have come. [a]Is 43:18f; Eph 4:24

18 Now all these things are from God, [a]who reconciled us to Himself through Christ and gave us the ministry of reconciliation,
[a]Rom 5:10; Col 1:20

19 namely, that [a]God was in Christ reconciling

the world to Himself, not counting their trespasses against them, and He has committed to us the word of reconciliation. [a]Col 2:9

20 Therefore, we are ambassadors for Christ, as though God were making an appeal through us; we beg you on behalf of Christ, be [a]reconciled to God. [a]Rom 5:10; Col 1:20

21 He made Him who [a]knew no sin to be sin on our behalf, so that we might become the righteousness of God in Him. [a]Heb 4:15; 7:26

Their Ministry Commended

6 And [a]working together with Him, we also urge you not to receive the grace of God in vain— [a]1 Cor 3:9

2 for He says,

> "[a]AT THE ACCEPTABLE TIME I LISTENED TO YOU,
> AND ON THE DAY OF SALVATION I HELPED
> YOU."

Behold, now is "THE ACCEPTABLE TIME," behold, now is "THE DAY OF SALVATION"— [a]Is 49:8

3 [a]giving no cause for offense in anything, so that the ministry will not be discredited,
[a]1 Cor 8:9, 13; 9:12

4 but in everything commending ourselves as servants of God, [a]in much endurance, in afflictions, in hardships, in distresses, [a]Acts 9:16; 2 Cor 4:8-11

5 in [a]beatings, in imprisonments, in tumults, in labors, in sleeplessness, in [b]hunger,
[a]Acts 16:23 [b]1 Cor 4:11

6 in purity, in knowledge, in patience, in kindness, in the [a]Holy Spirit, in genuine love,
[a]1 Cor 2:4; 1 Thess 1:5

7 in the word of truth, in [a]the power of God; by [b]the weapons of righteousness for the right hand and the left, [a]1 Cor 2:5 [b]2 Cor 10:4

8 by glory and [a]dishonor, by evil report and good report; regarded as deceivers and yet true; [a]1 Cor 4:10

9 as unknown yet well-known, as dying yet behold, [a]we live; as punished yet not put to death, [a]2 Cor 1:8, 10; 4:11

10 as [a]sorrowful yet always rejoicing, as [b]poor yet making many rich, as having nothing yet possessing all things. [a]John 16:22 [b]2 Cor 8:9

11 [a]Our mouth has spoken freely to you, O Corinthians, our heart is opened wide.
[a]Ezek 33:22; Eph 6:19

12 You are not restrained by us, but [a]you are restrained in your own affections. [a]2 Cor 7:2

13 Now in a like exchange—I speak as to [a]children—open wide to us also. [a]1 Cor 4:14

14 Do not be bound together with unbelievers; for what [a]partnership have righteousness and lawlessness, or what fellowship has light with darkness? [a]Eph 5:7, 11; 1 John 1:6

15 Or what [a]harmony has Christ with Belial, or what has a believer in common with an unbeliever? [a]1 Cor 10:21

16 Or what agreement has the temple of God with idols? For we are the temple of the living God; just as God said,

"ªI WILL DWELL IN THEM AND WALK AMONG THEM;

AND I WILL BE THEIR GOD, AND THEY SHALL BE MY PEOPLE. ªEx 29:45; Lev 26:12

17 "ªTherefore, COME OUT FROM THEIR MIDST AND BE SEPARATE," says the Lord.

"AND DO NOT TOUCH WHAT IS UNCLEAN;

And I will welcome you. ªIs 52:11

18 "ªAnd I will be a father to you,

And you shall be sons and daughters to Me,"

Says the Lord Almighty. ª2 Sam 7:14; 1 Chr 17:13

Paul Reveals His Heart

7 Therefore, having these promises, beloved, ªlet us cleanse ourselves from all defilement of flesh and spirit, perfecting holiness in the fear of God. ª1 Pet 1:15f

2 ªMake room for us in your hearts; we wronged no one, we corrupted no one, we took advantage of no one. ª2 Cor 6:12f; 12:15

3 I do not speak to condemn you, for I have said ªbefore that you are in our hearts to die together and to live together. ª2 Cor 6:11f

4 Great is my confidence in you; great is my ªboasting on your behalf. I am filled with ᵇcomfort; I am overflowing with joy in all our affliction. ª2 Cor 7:14 ᵇ2 Cor 1:4

5 For even when we came into Macedonia our flesh had no rest, but we were ªafflicted on every side: ᵇconflicts without, fears within. ª2 Cor 4:8 ᵇDeut 32:25

6 But God, who comforts the depressed, comforted us by the coming of ªTitus; ª2 Cor 2:13; 7:13f

7 and not only by his coming, but also by the comfort with which he was comforted in you, as he reported to us your longing, your mourning, your zeal for me; so that I rejoiced even more.

8 For though I ªcaused you sorrow by my letter, I do not regret it; though I did regret it—for I see that that letter caused you sorrow, though only for a while— ª2 Cor 2:2

9 I now rejoice, not that you were made sorrowful, but that you were made sorrowful to the point of repentance; for you were made sorrowful according to the will of God, so that you might not suffer loss in anything through us.

10 For the sorrow that is according to the will of God produces a ªrepentance without regret, leading to salvation, but the sorrow of the world produces death. ªActs 11:18

11 For behold what earnestness this very thing, this godly sorrow, has produced in you:

what vindication of yourselves, what indignation, what fear, what ªlonging, what zeal, what avenging of wrong! In everything you demonstrated yourselves to be innocent in the matter. ª2 Cor 7:7

12 So although ªI wrote to you, it was not for the sake of the offender nor for the sake of the one offended, but that your earnestness on our behalf might be made known to you in the sight of God. ª2 Cor 2:3, 9; 7:8

13 For this reason we have been comforted.

And besides our comfort, we rejoiced even much more for the joy of Titus, because his ªspirit has been refreshed by you all. ª1 Cor 16:18

14 For if in anything I have ªboasted to him about you, I was not put to shame; but as we spoke all things to you in truth, so also our boasting before Titus proved to be the truth. ª2 Cor 7:4; 8:24

15 His affection abounds all the more toward you, as he remembers the obedience of you all, how you received him with ªfear and trembling. ª1 Cor 2:3; Phil 2:12

16 I rejoice that in everything ªI have confidence in you. ª2 Cor 2:3

Great Generosity

8 Now, brethren, we wish to make known to you the grace of God which has been ªgiven in the churches of Macedonia, ª2 Cor 8:5

2 that in a great ordeal of affliction their abundance of joy and their deep poverty overflowed in the ªwealth of their liberality. ªRom 2:4

3 For I testify that ªaccording to their ability, and beyond their ability, they gave of their own accord, ª1 Cor 16:2; 2 Cor 8:11

4 begging us with much urging for the favor of participation in the ªsupport of the saints, ªRom 15:31; 2 Cor 8:19f

5 and this, not as we had expected, but they first gave themselves to the Lord and to us by ªthe will of God. ª1 Cor 1:1

6 So we ªurged Titus that as he had previously made a beginning, so he would also complete in you this gracious work as well. ª2 Cor 8:17; 12:18

7 But just as you ªabound ᵇin everything, in faith and utterance and knowledge and in all earnestness and in the love we inspired in you, see that you ªabound in this gracious work also. ª2 Cor 9:8 ᵇ1 Cor 1:5

8 I ªam not speaking this as a command, but as proving through the earnestness of others the sincerity of your love also. ª1 Cor 7:6

9 For you know the grace of our Lord Jesus Christ, that ªthough He was rich, yet for your sake He became poor, so that you through His poverty might become rich. ªPhil 2:6f

10 I give *my* opinion in this matter, for this is to your advantage, who were the first to begin ᵃa year ago not only to do *this,* but also to desire *to do it.* ᵃ*1 Cor 16:2f; 2 Cor 9:2*

11 But now finish doing it also, so that just as *there was* the ᵃreadiness to desire it, so *there may be* also the completion of it by your ability. ᵃ*2 Cor 8:12, 19; 9:2*

12 For if the readiness is present, it is acceptable ᵃaccording to what *a person* has, not according to what he does not have. ᵃ*Mark 12:43f; Luke 21:3, 4*

13 For *this* is not for the ease of others *and* for your affliction, but by way of equality—

14 at this present time your abundance *being a supply* for ᵃtheir need, so that their abundance also may become *a supply* for ᵃyour need, that there may be equality; ᵃ*Acts 4:34; 2 Cor 9:12*

15 as it is written, "ᵃHᴇ ᴡʜᴏ *gathered* ᴍᴜᴄʜ ᴅɪᴅ ɴᴏᴛ ʜᴀᴠᴇ ᴛᴏᴏ ᴍᴜᴄʜ, ᴀɴᴅ ʜᴇ ᴡʜᴏ *gathered* ʟɪᴛᴛʟᴇ ʜᴀᴅ ɴᴏ ʟᴀᴄᴋ." ᵃ*Ex 16:18*

16 But ᵃthanks be to God who ᵇputs the same earnestness on your behalf in the heart of Titus. ᵃ*2 Cor 2:14* ᵇ*Rev 17:17*

17 For he not only accepted our ᵃappeal, but being himself very earnest, he has gone to you of his own accord. ᵃ*2 Cor 8:6; 12:18*

18 We have sent along with him ᵃthe brother whose fame in *the things of* the gospel *has spread* through all the churches; ᵃ*1 Cor 16:3; 2 Cor 12:18*

19 and not only *this,* but he has also been ᵃappointed by the churches to travel with us in this gracious work, which is being administered by us for the glory of the Lord Himself, and *to show* our readiness, ᵃ*1 Cor 16:3f*

20 taking precaution so that no one will discredit us in our administration of this generous gift;

21 for we ᵃhave regard for what is honorable, not only in the sight of the Lord, but also in the sight of men. ᵃ*Rom 12:17*

22 We have sent with them our brother, whom we have often tested and found diligent in many things, but now even more diligent because of *his* great confidence in you.

23 As for Titus, *he is* my partner and fellow worker among you; as for our brethren, *they are* ᵃmessengers of the churches, a glory to Christ. ᵃ*Phil 2:25*

24 Therefore openly before the churches, show them the proof of your love and of our ᵃreason for boasting about you. ᵃ*2 Cor 7:4*

God Gives Most

9 For it is superfluous for me to write to you about this ᵃministry to the saints; ᵃ*2 Cor 8:4*

2 for I know your readiness, of which I boast about you to the Macedonians, *namely,* that Achaia has been prepared since ᵃlast year, and your zeal has stirred up most of them. ᵃ*2 Cor 8:10*

3 But I have sent the brethren, in order that our ᵃboasting about you may not be made empty in this case, so that, ᵇas I was saying, you may be prepared; ᵃ*2 Cor 7:4* ᵇ*1 Cor 16:2*

4 otherwise if any ᵃMacedonians come with me and find you unprepared, we—not to speak of you—will be put to shame by this confidence. ᵃ*Rom 15:26*

5 So I thought it necessary to urge the brethren that they would go on ahead to you and arrange beforehand your previously promised ᵃbountiful gift, so that the same would be ready as a bountiful gift and not affected by covetousness. ᵃ*Gen 33:11*

6 Now this *I say,* ᵃhe who sows sparingly will also reap sparingly, and he who sows bountifully will also reap bountifully. ᵃ*Prov 11:24f; 22:9*

7 Each one *must do* just as he has purposed in his heart, not ᵃgrudgingly or under compulsion, for ᵇGod loves a cheerful giver. ᵃ*Deut 15:10* ᵇ*Ex 25:2*

8 And ᵃGod is able to make all grace abound to you, so that always having all sufficiency in everything, you may have an abundance for every good deed; ᵃ*Eph 3:20*

9 as it is written,
"ᵃHᴇ ꜱᴄᴀᴛᴛᴇʀᴇᴅ ᴀʙʀᴏᴀᴅ, ʜᴇ ɢᴀᴠᴇ ᴛᴏ ᴛʜᴇ ᴘᴏᴏʀ,
Hɪꜱ ʀɪɢʜᴛᴇᴏᴜꜱɴᴇꜱꜱ ᴇɴᴅᴜʀᴇꜱ ꜰᴏʀᴇᴠᴇʀ." ᵃ*Ps 112:9*

10 Now He who supplies ᵃseed to the sower and bread for food will supply and multiply your seed for sowing and ᵇincrease the harvest of your righteousness; ᵃ*Is 55:10* ᵇ*Hos 10:12*

11 you will be ᵃenriched in everything for all liberality, which through us is producing thanksgiving to God. ᵃ*1 Cor 1:5*

12 For the ministry of this service is not only fully supplying ᵃthe needs of the saints, but is also overflowing ᵇthrough many thanksgivings to God. ᵃ*2 Cor 8:14* ᵇ*2 Cor 1:11*

13 Because of the proof given by this ᵃministry, they will glorify God for *your* obedience to your confession of the gospel of Christ and for the liberality of your contribution to them and to all, ᵃ*Rom 15:31; 2 Cor 8:4*

14 while they also, by prayer on your behalf, yearn for you because of the surpassing grace of God in you.

15 Thanks be to God for His indescribable ᵃgift! ᵃ*Rom 5:15f*

Paul Describes Himself

10 Now I, Paul, myself urge you by the ᵃmeekness and gentleness of Christ—I who am meek when face to face with you, but

bold toward you when absent! [a]*Matt 11:29; 1 Cor 4:21*

2 I ask that when I am present I *need* not be bold with the confidence with which I propose to be courageous against [a]some, who regard us as if we walked according to the flesh. [a]*1 Cor 4:18f*

3 For though we walk in the flesh, we do not war [a]according to the flesh, [a]*Rom 8:4; 2 Cor 1:17*

4 for the [a]weapons of our warfare are not of the flesh, but divinely powerful for the destruction of fortresses. [a]*2 Cor 6:7*

5 *We are* destroying speculations and every [a]lofty thing raised up against the knowledge of God, and *we are* taking every thought captive to the obedience of Christ, [a]*Is 2:11f*

6 and we are ready to punish all disobedience, whenever [a]your obedience is complete. [a]*2 Cor 2:9*

7 [a]You are looking at things as they are outwardly. If anyone is confident in himself that he is Christ's, let him consider this again within himself, that just as he is Christ's, [b]so also are we. [a]*John 7:24* [b]*1 Cor 9:1*

8 For even if I boast somewhat further about our [a]authority, which the Lord gave for building you up and not for destroying you, I will not be put to shame, [a]*2 Cor 13:10*

9 for I do not wish to seem as if I would terrify you by my letters.

10 For they say, "His letters are weighty and strong, but his personal presence is unimpressive and [a]his speech contemptible." [a]*1 Cor 1:17; 2 Cor 11:6*

11 Let such a person consider this, that what we are in word by letters when absent, such persons *we are* also in deed when present.

12 For we are not bold to class or compare ourselves with some of those who [a]commend themselves; but when they measure themselves by themselves and compare themselves with themselves, they are without understanding. [a]*2 Cor 3:1; 10:18*

13 But we will not boast beyond *our* measure, but [a]within the measure of the sphere which God apportioned to us as a measure, to reach even as far as you. [a]*Rom 12:3; 2 Cor 10:15f*

14 For we are not overextending ourselves, as if we did not reach to you, for we were the first to come even as far as you in the [a]gospel of Christ; [a]*2 Cor 2:12*

15 not boasting beyond *our* measure, *that is,* in other men's labors, but with the hope that as [a]your faith grows, we will be, within our sphere, enlarged even more by you, [a]*2 Thess 1:3*

16 so as to preach the gospel even to the regions beyond you, *and* not to boast [a]in what has been accomplished in the sphere of another. [a]*Rom 15:20*

17 But [a]HE WHO BOASTS IS TO BOAST IN THE LORD. [a]*Jer 9:24; 1 Cor 1:31*

18 For it is not he who commends himself that is approved, but he [a]whom the Lord commends. [a]*Rom 2:29; 1 Cor 4:5*

Paul Defends His Apostleship

11 I wish that you would [a]bear with me in a little foolishness; but indeed you are bearing with me. [a]*Matt 17:17; 2 Cor 11:4, 16, 19f*

2 For I am jealous for you with a godly jealousy; for I [a]betrothed you to one husband, so that to Christ I might present you *as* a pure virgin. [a]*Hos 2:19f; Eph 5:26f*

3 But I am afraid that, as the [a]serpent deceived Eve by his craftiness, your minds will be led astray from the simplicity and purity *of devotion* to Christ. [a]*Gen 3:4, 13; John 8:44*

4 For if one comes and preaches [a]another Jesus whom we have not preached, or you receive a different spirit which you have not received, or a [b]different gospel which you have not accepted, you bear *this* beautifully. [a]*1 Cor 3:11* [b]*Gal 1:6*

5 For I consider myself [a]not in the least inferior to the most eminent apostles. [a]*2 Cor 12:11; Gal 2:6*

6 But even if I am unskilled in speech, yet I am not *so* in [a]knowledge; in fact, in every way we have made *this* evident to you in all things. [a]*1 Cor 12:8; Eph 3:4*

7 Or did I commit a sin in humbling myself so that you might be exalted, because I preached the gospel of God to you [a]without charge? [a]*Acts 18:3; 1 Cor 9:18*

8 I robbed other churches by [a]taking wages *from them* to serve you; [a]*1 Cor 4:12; 9:6*

9 and when I was present with you and was in need, I was [a]not a burden to anyone; for when [b]the brethren came from Macedonia they fully supplied my need, and in everything I kept myself from [a]being a burden to you, and will continue to do so. [a]*2 Cor 12:13f, 16* [b]*Acts 18:5*

10 [a]As the truth of Christ is in me, [b]this boasting of mine will not be stopped in the regions of Achaia. [a]*Rom 9:1* [b]*1 Cor 9:15*

11 Why? [a]Because I do not love you? [b]God knows *I do!* [a]*2 Cor 12:15* [b]*2 Cor 11:31*

12 But what I am doing I will continue to do, [a]so that I may cut off opportunity from those who desire an opportunity to be regarded just as we are in the matter about which they are boasting. [a]*1 Cor 9:12*

13 For such men are false apostles, [a]deceitful workers, disguising themselves as apostles of Christ. [a]*Phil 3:2*

14 No wonder, for even [a]Satan disguises himself as an angel of light. [a]*Matt 4:10; Eph 6:12*

15 Therefore it is not surprising if his servants also disguise themselves as servants of righ-

teousness, ªwhose end will be according to their deeds. ªRom 2:6; 3:8

16 ªAgain I say, let no one think me foolish; but if *you do,* receive me even as foolish, so that I also may boast a little. ª2 Cor 11:1

17 What I am saying, I am not saying ªas the Lord would, but as in foolishness, in this confidence of boasting. ª1 Cor 7:12, 25

18 Since ªmany boast according to the flesh, I will boast also. ªPhil 3:3f

19 For you, ªbeing *so* wise, tolerate the foolish gladly. ª1 Cor 4:10

20 For you tolerate it if anyone ªenslaves you, anyone devours you, anyone takes advantage of you, anyone exalts himself, anyone hits you in the face. ªGal 2:4; 4:3, 9

21 To *my* shame I *must* say that we have been ªweak *by comparison.*

But in whatever respect anyone *else* is bold—I speak in foolishness—I am just as bold myself. ª2 Cor 10:10

22 Are they Hebrews? ªSo am I. Are they Israelites? So am I. Are they descendants of Abraham? ᵇSo am I. ªPhil 3:5 ᵇRom 11:1

23 Are they servants of Christ?—I speak as if insane—I more so; in ªfar more labors, in ᵇfar more imprisonments, beaten times without number, often in danger of death. ª1 Cor 15:10 ᵇ2 Cor 6:5

24 Five times I received from the Jews ªthirty-nine *lashes.* ªDeut 25:3

25 Three times I was ªbeaten with rods, once I was ᵇstoned, three times I was shipwrecked, a night and a day I have spent in the deep. ªActs 16:22 ᵇActs 14:19

26 *I have been* on frequent journeys, in dangers from rivers, dangers from robbers, dangers from *my* countrymen, dangers from the Gentiles, dangers in the ªcity, dangers in the wilderness, dangers on the sea, dangers among ᵇfalse brethren; ªActs 21:31 ᵇGal 2:4

27 *I have been* in labor and hardship, through many sleepless nights, in hunger and thirst, often ªwithout food, in cold and ᵇexposure. ª2 Cor 6:5 ᵇ1 Cor 4:11

28 Apart from *such* external things, there is the daily pressure on me *of* concern for ªall the churches. ª1 Cor 7:17

29 Who is ªweak without my being weak? Who is led into sin without my intense concern? ª1 Cor 8:9, 13; 9:22

30 If I have to boast, I will boast of what pertains to my ªweakness. ª1 Cor 2:3

31 The God and Father of the Lord Jesus, ªHe who is blessed forever, knows that I am not lying. ªRom 1:25

32 In Damascus the ethnarch under Aretas the king was ªguarding the city of the Damascenes in order to seize me, ªActs 9:24

33 and I was let down in a basket ªthrough a window in the wall, and *so* escaped his hands. ªActs 9:25

Paul's Vision

12 Boasting is necessary, though it is not profitable; but I will go on to visions and ªrevelations of the Lord. ª1 Cor 14:6; 2 Cor 12:7

2 I know a man in Christ who fourteen years ago—whether in the body I do not know, or out of the body I do not know, God knows—such a man was caught up to the ªthird heaven. ªDeut 10:14; Ps 148:4

3 And I know how such a man—whether in the body or apart from the body I do not know, ªGod knows— ª2 Cor 11:11

4 was ªcaught up into ᵇParadise and heard inexpressible words, which a man is not permitted to speak. ªEzek 8:3 ᵇLuke 23:43

5 On behalf of such a man I will boast; but on my own behalf I will not boast, except in regard to *my* ªweaknesses. ª1 Cor 2:3; 2 Cor 12:9f

6 For if I do wish to boast I will not be foolish, ªfor I will be speaking the truth; but I refrain *from this,* so that no one will credit me with more than he sees *in* me or hears from me. ª2 Cor 7:14

A Thorn in the Flesh

7 Because of the surpassing greatness of the revelations, for this reason, to keep me from exalting myself, there was given me a ªthorn in the flesh, a messenger of Satan to torment me—to keep me from exalting myself! ªNum 33:55; Ezek 28:24

8 Concerning this I implored the Lord ªthree times that it might leave me. ªMatt 26:44

9 And He has said to me, "My grace is sufficient for you, for ªpower is perfected in weakness." Most gladly, therefore, I will rather boast about my weaknesses, so that the power of Christ may dwell in me. ª1 Cor 2:5; Eph 3:16

10 Therefore ªI am well content with weaknesses, with insults, with distresses, with persecutions, with difficulties, for Christ's sake; for when I am weak, then I am strong. ªRom 8:35

11 I have become foolish; you yourselves compelled me. Actually I should have been commended by you, for ªin no respect was I inferior to the most eminent apostles, even though ᵇI am a nobody. ª2 Cor 11:5 ᵇ1 Cor 3:7

12 The ªsigns of a true apostle were performed among you with all perseverance, by signs and wonders and miracles. ªJohn 4:48; Rom 15:19

13 For in what respect were you treated as inferior to the rest of the churches, except that I myself did not become a burden to you? Forgive me ªthis wrong! ª2 Cor 11:7

14 Here ªfor this third time I am ready to come to you, and I will not be a burden to you; for I

[b]do not seek what is yours, but you; for children are not responsible to save up for *their* parents, but parents for *their* children. [a]*2 Cor 13:1, 2* [b]*1 Cor 10:24, 33*

15 I will most gladly spend and be expended for your souls. If [a]I love you more, am I to be loved less? [a]*2 Cor 11:11*

16 But be that as it may, I [a]did not burden you myself; nevertheless, crafty fellow that I am, I took you in by deceit. [a]*2 Cor 11:9*

17 [a]*Certainly* I have not taken advantage of you through any of those whom I have sent to you, have I? [a]*2 Cor 9:5*

18 I [a]urged Titus *to go,* and I sent [b]the brother with him. Titus did not take any advantage of you, did he? Did we not conduct ourselves in the same spirit *and walk* in the same steps? [a]*2 Cor 8:6* [b]*2 Cor 8:18*

19 All this time you have been thinking that we are defending ourselves to you. *Actually,* [a]it is in the sight of God that we have been speaking in Christ; and [b]all for your upbuilding, beloved. [a]*2 Cor 2:17* [b]*Rom 14:19*

20 For I am afraid that perhaps when I come I may find you to be not what I wish and may be found by you to be not what you wish; that perhaps *there will be* strife, jealousy, [a]angry tempers, disputes, slanders, [b]gossip, arrogance, disturbances; [a]*Gal 5:20* [b]*Rom 1:29*

21 I am afraid that when I come again my God may humiliate me before you, and I may mourn over many of those who have [a]sinned in the past and not repented of the [b]impurity, immorality and sensuality which they have practiced. [a]*2 Cor 13:2* [b]*1 Cor 6:9, 18*

Examine Yourselves

13 This is the third time I am coming to you. [a]Every fact is to be confirmed by the testimony of two or three witnesses. [a]*Deut 17:6; 19:15*

2 I have previously said when present the second time, and though now absent I say in advance to those who have sinned in the past and to all the rest *as well,* that if I come again I will not [a]spare *anyone,* [a]*2 Cor 1:23*

3 since you are seeking for proof of the Christ who speaks in me, and who is not weak toward you, but [a]mighty in you. [a]*2 Cor 9:8; 10:4*

4 For indeed He was [a]crucified because of weakness, yet He lives [b]because of the power of God. For we also are weak in Him, yet we will live with Him because of the power of God *directed* toward you. [a]*Phil 2:7f* [b]*1 Cor 6:14*

5 Test yourselves *to see* if you are in the faith; [a]examine yourselves! Or do you not recognize this about yourselves, that Jesus Christ is in you—unless indeed you fail the test? [a]*1 Cor 11:28*

6 But I trust that you will realize that we ourselves do not fail the test.

7 Now we pray to God that you do no wrong; not that we ourselves may appear approved, but that you may do what is right, even though we may appear unapproved.

8 For we can do nothing against the truth, but *only* for the truth.

9 For we rejoice when we ourselves are weak but you are strong; this we also pray for, that you be [a]made complete. [a]*1 Cor 1:10; 2 Cor 13:11*

10 For this reason I am writing these things while absent, so that when present I *need* not use [a]severity, in accordance with the [b]authority which the Lord gave me for building up and not for tearing down. [a]*Titus 1:13* [b]*2 Cor 10:8*

11 Finally, brethren, rejoice, be made complete, be comforted, [a]be like-minded, live in peace; and the God of love and peace will be with you. [a]*Rom 12:16*

12 [a]Greet one another with a holy kiss. [a]*Rom 16:16*

13 [a]All the saints greet you. [a]*Phil 4:22*

14 The grace of the Lord Jesus Christ, and the love of God, and the [a]fellowship of the Holy Spirit, be with you all. [a]*Phil 2:1*

The Letter of Paul to the
GALATIANS

Introduction

1 Paul, an apostle ([a]not *sent* from men nor through the agency of man, but through Jesus Christ and God the Father, who raised Him from the dead), [a]*Gal 1:11f*

2 and all the brethren who are with me,

To [a]the churches of Galatia: [a]*Acts 16:6; 1 Cor 16:1*

3 [a]Grace to you and peace from God our Father and the Lord Jesus Christ, [a]*Rom 1:7*

4 who gave Himself for our sins so that He might rescue us from this present evil age, according to the will of our God and Father,

5 [a]to whom *be* the glory forevermore. Amen. [a]*Rom 11:36*

Perversion of the Gospel

6 I am amazed that you are so quickly deserting Him who called you by the grace of Christ, for a [a]different gospel; [a]*2 Cor 11:4*

7 which is *really* not another; only there are some who are [a]disturbing you and want to distort the gospel of Christ. [a]*Acts 15:24; Gal 5:10*

8 But even if we, or an angel from heaven, should preach to you a gospel contrary to what we have preached to you, he is to be accursed!

9 As we have said before, so I say again now, [a]if any man is preaching to you a gospel contrary to what you received, he is to be accursed! [a]*Rom 16:17*

10 For am I now seeking the favor of men, or of God? Or am I striving to please men? If I were still trying to please men, I would not be a [a]bond-servant of Christ. [a]*Rom 1:1; Phil 1:1*

Paul Defends His Ministry

11 For [a]I would have you know, brethren, that the gospel which was preached by me is not according to man. [a]*Rom 2:16; 1 Cor 15:1*

12 For I neither received it from man, nor was I taught it, but *I received it* through a [a]revelation of Jesus Christ. [a]*1 Cor 2:10; 2 Cor 12:1*

13 For you have heard of [a]my former manner of life in Judaism, how I used to persecute the church of God beyond measure and tried to destroy it; [a]*Acts 26:4f*

14 and I was advancing in Judaism beyond many of my contemporaries among my countrymen, being more extremely zealous for my [a]ancestral traditions. [a]*Matt 15:2; Mark 7:3*

15 But when God, who had set me apart *even* from my mother's womb and [a]called me through His grace, was pleased [a]*Is 49:1, 5; Jer 1:5*

16 to reveal His Son in me so that I might [a]preach Him among the Gentiles, I did not immediately consult with flesh and blood, [a]*Acts 9:15; Gal 2:9*

17 [a]nor did I go up to Jerusalem to those who were apostles before me; but I went away to Arabia, and returned once more to Damascus. [a]*Acts 9:19-22*

18 Then [a]three years later I went up [b]to Jerusalem to become acquainted with Cephas, and stayed with him fifteen days. [a]*Acts 9:22f* [b]*Acts 9:26*

19 But I did not see any other of the apostles except [a]James, the Lord's brother. [a]*Matt 12:46; Acts 12:17*

20 (Now in what I am writing to you, I assure you [a]before God that I am not lying.) [a]*Rom 9:1; 2 Cor 1:23*

21 Then [a]I went into the regions of Syria and Cilicia. [a]*Acts 9:30*

22 I was *still* unknown by sight to [a]the churches of Judea which were in Christ; [a]*1 Thess 2:14*

23 but only, they kept hearing, "He who once persecuted us is now preaching the faith which he once [a]tried to destroy." [a]*Acts 9:21*

24 And they [a]were glorifying God because of me. [a]*Matt 9:8*

The Council at Jerusalem

2 Then after an interval of fourteen years I [a]went up again to Jerusalem with Barnabas, taking Titus along also. [a]*Acts 15:2*

2 It was because of a revelation that I went up; and I submitted to them the gospel which I preach among the Gentiles, but *I did so* in private to those who were of reputation, for fear that I might be [a]running, or had run, in vain. [a]*1 Cor 9:24ff; Phil 2:16*

3 But not even [a]Titus, who was with me, though he was a Greek, was compelled to be circumcised. [a]*2 Cor 2:13; Gal 2:1*

4 But *it was* because of the [a]false brethren secretly brought in, who had sneaked in to spy out our liberty which we have in Christ Jesus, in order to bring us into bondage. [a]*Acts 15:1, 24; Gal 1:7*

5 But we did not yield in subjection to them for even an hour, so that [a]the truth of the gospel would remain with you. [a]*Gal 1:6; 2:14*

6 But from those who were of high reputation (what they were makes no difference to me; [a]God shows no partiality)—well, those who were of reputation contributed nothing to me. [a]*Acts 10:34*

7 But on the contrary, seeing that I had been entrusted with the [a]gospel to the uncircumcised, just as Peter *had been* to the circumcised [a]*Acts 9:15; Gal 1:16*

8 (for He who effectually worked for Peter in *his* [a]apostleship to the circumcised effectually worked for me also to the Gentiles), [a]*Acts 1:25*

9 and recognizing [a]the grace that had been given to me, James and Cephas and John, who were reputed to be pillars, gave to me and Barnabas the right hand of fellowship, so that we *might go* to the Gentiles and they to the circumcised. [a]*Rom 12:3*

10 *They* only *asked* us to remember the poor—[a]the very thing I also was eager to do. [a]*Acts 24:17*

Peter (Cephas) Opposed by Paul

11 But when [a]Cephas came to Antioch, I opposed him to his face, because he stood condemned. [a]*Gal 1:18; 2:7, 9, 14*

12 For prior to the coming of certain men from James, he used to [a]eat with the Gentiles; but when they came, he *began* to withdraw and hold himself aloof, [b]fearing the party of the circumcision. [a]*Acts 11:3* [b]*Acts 11:2*

13 The rest of the Jews joined him in hypocrisy, with the result that even [a]Barnabas was carried away by their hypocrisy. [a]*Acts 4:36; Gal 2:1, 9*

14 But when I saw that they were not straightforward about [a]the truth of the gospel, I said to Cephas in the presence of all, "If you, being a Jew, live like the Gentiles and not like the Jews, how *is it that* you compel the Gentiles to live like Jews? [a]*Gal 2:5; Col 1:5*

15 "We *are* [a]Jews by nature and not sinners from among the Gentiles; [a]*Phil 3:4f*

16 nevertheless knowing that [a]a man is not justified by the works of the Law but through

faith in Christ Jesus, even we have believed in Christ Jesus, so that we may be justified by faith in Christ and not by the works of the Law; since by the works of the Law no flesh will be justified. [a]*Acts 13:39; Gal 3:11*

17 "But if, while seeking to be justified in Christ, we ourselves have also been found [a]sinners, is Christ then a minister of sin? May it never be! [a]*Gal 2:15*

18 "For if I rebuild what I have *once* destroyed, I [a]prove myself to be a transgressor. [a]*Rom 3:5*

19 "For through the Law I [a]died to the Law, so that I might live to God. [a]*Rom 6:2; 7:4*

20 "I have been [a]crucified with Christ; and it is no longer I who live, but Christ lives in me; and the *life* which I now live in the flesh I live by faith in the Son of God, who loved me and gave Himself up for me. [a]*Rom 6:6; Gal 5:24*

21 "I do not nullify the grace of God, for [a]if righteousness *comes* through the Law, then Christ died needlessly." [a]*Gal 3:21*

Faith Brings Righteousness

3 You foolish Galatians, who has bewitched you, before whose eyes Jesus Christ [a]was publicly portrayed *as* crucified? [a]*1 Cor 1:23; Gal 5:11*

2 This is the only thing I want to find out from you: did you receive the Spirit by the works of the Law, or by [a]hearing with faith? [a]*Rom 10:17*

3 Are you so foolish? Having begun by the Spirit, are you now being perfected by the flesh?

4 Did you suffer so many things in vain—[a]if indeed it was in vain? [a]*1 Cor 15:2*

5 So then, does He who provides you with the Spirit and works miracles among you, do it by the works of the Law, or by [a]hearing with faith? [a]*Rom 10:17*

6 Even so Abraham [a]BELIEVED GOD, AND IT WAS RECKONED TO HIM AS RIGHTEOUSNESS. [a]*Gen 15:6*

7 Therefore, be sure that [a]it is those who are of faith who are sons of Abraham. [a]*Rom 4:16; Gal 3:9*

8 The Scripture, foreseeing that God would justify the Gentiles by faith, preached the gospel beforehand to Abraham, *saying,* "[a]ALL THE NATIONS WILL BE BLESSED IN YOU." [a]*Gen 12:3*

9 So then [a]those who are of faith are blessed with Abraham, the believer. [a]*Gal 3:7*

10 For as many as are of the works of the Law are under a curse; for it is written, "[a]CURSED IS EVERYONE WHO DOES NOT ABIDE BY ALL THINGS WRITTEN IN THE BOOK OF THE LAW, TO PERFORM THEM." [a]*Deut 27:26*

11 Now that [a]no one is justified by the Law before God is evident; for, "[b]THE RIGHTEOUS MAN SHALL LIVE BY FAITH." [a]*Gal 2:16* [b]*Hab 2:4*

12 However, the Law is not of faith; on the contrary, "[a]HE WHO PRACTICES THEM SHALL LIVE BY THEM." [a]*Lev 18:5; Rom 10:5*

13 Christ redeemed us from the curse of the Law, having become a curse for us—for it is written, "[a]CURSED IS EVERYONE WHO HANGS ON A TREE"— [a]*Deut 21:23*

14 in order that in Christ Jesus the blessing of Abraham might come to the Gentiles, so that we [a]would receive [b]the promise of the Spirit through faith. [a]*Gal 3:2* [b]*Acts 2:33*

Intent of the Law

15 Brethren, [a]I speak in terms of human relations: even though it is *only* a man's covenant, yet when it has been ratified, no one sets it aside or adds conditions to it. [a]*Rom 3:5*

16 Now the promises were spoken to Abraham and to his seed. He does not say, "And to seeds," as *referring* to many, but *rather* to one, "[a]And to your seed," that is, Christ. [a]*Acts 3:25*

17 What I am saying is this: the Law, which came [a]four hundred and thirty years later, does not invalidate a covenant previously ratified by God, so as to nullify the promise. [a]*Gen 15:13f; Ex 12:40*

18 For [a]if the inheritance is based on law, it is no longer based on a promise; but God has granted it to Abraham by means of a promise. [a]*Rom 4:14*

19 [a]Why the Law then? It was added because of transgressions, having been ordained through angels by the agency of a mediator, until the seed would come to whom the promise had been made. [a]*Rom 5:20*

20 Now [a]a mediator is not for one *party only;* whereas God is *only* one. [a]*1 Tim 2:5; Heb 8:6*

21 Is the Law then contrary to the promises of God? [a]May it never be! For if a law had been given which was able to impart life, then righteousness would indeed have been based on law. [a]*Luke 20:16; Gal 2:17*

22 But the Scripture has [a]shut up everyone under sin, so that the promise by faith in Jesus Christ might be given to those who believe. [a]*Rom 11:32*

23 But before faith came, we were kept in custody under the law, being shut up to the faith which was later to be revealed.

24 Therefore the Law has become our tutor *to lead us* to Christ, so that [a]we may be justified by faith. [a]*Gal 2:16*

25 But now that faith has come, we are no longer under a [a]tutor. [a]*1 Cor 4:15*

26 For you are all [a]sons of God through faith in Christ Jesus. [a]*Rom 8:14; Gal 4:5*

27 For all of you who were baptized into Christ have [a]clothed yourselves with Christ. [a]*Rom 13:14*

28 ^aThere is neither Jew nor Greek, there is neither slave nor free man, there is neither male nor female; for you are all one in Christ Jesus. ^a*Rom 3:22; 1 Cor 12:13*

29 And if you belong to Christ, then you are Abraham's descendants, heirs according to ^apromise. ^a*Rom 9:8; Gal 3:18*

Sonship in Christ

4 Now I say, as long as the heir is a child, he does not differ at all from a slave although he is owner of everything,

2 but he is under guardians and managers until the date set by the father.

3 So also we, while we were children, were held ^ain bondage under the ^belemental things of the world. ^a*Gal 2:4* ^b*Col 2:8, 20*

4 But when the fullness of the time came, God sent forth His Son, ^aborn of a woman, born under the Law, ^a*Matt 1:25;Luke 2:7*

5 so that He might redeem those who were under the Law, that we might receive the adoption as ^asons. ^a*Rom 8:14; Gal 3:26*

6 Because you are sons, ^aGod has sent forth the Spirit of His Son into our hearts, crying, "Abba! Father!" ^a*Acts 16:7; 2 Cor 3:17*

7 Therefore you are no longer a slave, but a son; and ^aif a son, then an heir through God. ^a*Rom 8:17*

8 However at that time, ^awhen you did not know God, you were slaves to those which by nature are no gods. ^a*1 Cor 1:21; Eph 2:12*

9 But now that you have come to know God, or rather to be ^aknown by God, how is it that you turn back again to the weak and worthless elemental things, to which you desire to be enslaved all over again? ^a*1 Cor 8:3*

10 You ^aobserve days and months and seasons and years. ^a*Rom 14:5; Col 2:16*

11 I fear for you, that perhaps I have labored over you in vain.

12 I beg of you, ^abrethren, become as I *am*, for I also *have become* as you *are*. You have done me no wrong; ^a*Gal 6:18*

13 but you know that it was because of a bodily illness that I preached the gospel to you the first time;

14 and that which was a trial to you in my bodily condition you did not despise or loathe, but ^ayou received me as an angel of God, as Christ Jesus *Himself*. ^a*Matt 10:40; 1 Thess 2:13*

15 Where then is that sense of blessing you had? For I bear you witness that, if possible, you would have plucked out your eyes and given them to me.

16 So have I become your enemy ^aby telling you the truth? ^a*Amos 5:10*

17 They eagerly seek you, not commendably, but they wish to shut you out so that you will seek them.

18 But it is good always to be eagerly sought in a commendable manner, and ^anot only when I am present with you. ^a*Gal 4:13f*

19 My children, with whom I am again in labor until ^aChrist is formed in you— ^a*Eph 4:13*

20 but I could wish to be present with you now and to change my tone, for ^aI am perplexed about you. ^a*2 Cor 4:8*

Bond and Free

21 Tell me, you who want to be under law, do you not ^alisten to the law? ^a*Luke 16:29*

22 For it is written that Abraham had two sons, ^aone by the bondwoman and ^bone by the free woman. ^a*Gen 16:15* ^b*Gen 21:2*

23 But ^athe son by the bondwoman was born according to the flesh, and ^bthe son by the free woman through the promise. ^a*Rom 9:7* ^b*Gen 17:16ff*

24 This is allegorically speaking, for these *women* are two covenants: one *proceeding* from Mount Sinai bearing children who are to be ^aslaves; she is Hagar. ^a*Gal 4:3*

25 Now this Hagar is Mount Sinai in Arabia and corresponds to the present Jerusalem, for she is in slavery with her children.

26 But ^athe Jerusalem above is free; she is our mother. ^a*Heb 12:22; Rev 3:12;*

27 For it is written,

"^aRejoice, barren woman who does not
    bear;
Break forth and shout, you who are not
    in labor;
For more numerous are the children of
    the desolate
Than of the one who has a husband."
    ^a*Is 54:1*

28 And you brethren, like Isaac, are ^achildren of promise. ^a*Rom 9:7ff; Gal 3:29*

29 But as at that time he who was born according to the flesh ^apersecuted him *who was born* according to the Spirit, so it is now also. ^a*Gen 21:9*

30 But what does the Scripture say?

"^aCast out the bondwoman and her son,
For the son of the bondwoman shall not
    be an heir with the son of the free
    woman." ^a*Gen 21:10, 12*

31 So then, brethren, we are not children of a bondwoman, but of the free woman.

Walk by the Spirit

5 ^aIt was for freedom that Christ set us free; therefore keep standing firm and do not be subject again to a yoke of slavery. ^a*John 8:32, 36; Rom 8:15*

2 Behold I, Paul, say to you that if you receive ^acircumcision, Christ will be of no benefit to you. ^a*Acts 15:1; Gal 5:3, 6, 11*

3 And I testify again to every man who

receives circumcision, that he is under obligation to [a]keep the whole Law. [a]*Rom 2:25*

4 You have been severed from Christ, you who are seeking to be justified by law; you have [a]fallen from grace. [a]*Heb 12:15; 2 Pet 3:17*

5 For we through the Spirit, by faith, are [a]waiting for the hope of righteousness. [a]*Rom 8:23; 1 Cor 1:7*

6 For in Christ Jesus [a]neither circumcision nor uncircumcision means anything, but faith working through love. [a]*1 Cor 7:19; Gal 6:15*

7 You were [a]running well; who hindered you from obeying the truth? [a]*Gal 2:2*

8 This persuasion *did* not *come* from [a]Him who calls you. [a]*Rom 8:28; Gal 1:6*

9 [a]A little leaven leavens the whole lump *of dough.* [a]*1 Cor 5:6*

10 I have confidence in you in the Lord that you will adopt no other view; but the one who is [a]disturbing you will bear his judgment, whoever he is. [a]*Gal 1:7; 5:12*

11 But I, brethren, if I still preach circumcision, why am I still [a]persecuted? Then the stumbling block of the cross has been abolished. [a]*Gal 6:12*

12 I wish that those who are troubling you would even [a]mutilate themselves. [a]*Deut 23:1*

13 For you were called to freedom, brethren; [a]only *do* not *turn* your freedom into an opportunity for the flesh, but through love serve one another. [a]*1 Cor 8:9; 1 Pet 2:16*

14 For the whole Law is fulfilled in one word, in the *statement,* "[a]YOU SHALL LOVE YOUR NEIGHBOR AS YOURSELF." [a]*Lev 19:18; Matt 19:19*

15 But if you [a]bite and devour one another, take care that you are not consumed by one another. [a]*Gal 5:20; Phil 3:2*

16 But I say, [a]walk by the Spirit, and you will not carry out the desire of the flesh. [a]*Rom 8:4; 13:14*

17 For [a]the flesh sets its desire against the Spirit, and the Spirit against the flesh; for these are in opposition to one another, [b]so that you may not do the things that you please. [a]*Rom 8:5ff* [b]*Rom 7:15ff*

18 But if you are [a]led by the Spirit, you are not under the Law. [a]*Rom 8:14*

19 Now the deeds of the flesh are evident, which are: [a]immorality, impurity, sensuality, [a]*1 Cor 6:9, 18; 2 Cor 12:21*

20 idolatry, sorcery, enmities, [a]strife, jealousy, outbursts of anger, disputes, dissensions, factions, [a]*2 Cor 12:20*

21 envying, drunkenness, carousing, and things like these, of which I forewarn you, just as I have forewarned you, that those who practice such things will not [a]inherit the kingdom of God. [a]*1 Cor 6:9*

22 But [a]the fruit of the Spirit is love, joy, peace, patience, kindness, goodness, faithfulness, [a]*Matt 7:16ff; Eph 5:9*

23 gentleness, [a]self-control; against such things there is no law. [a]*Acts 24:25*

24 Now those who belong to Christ Jesus have [a]crucified the flesh with its passions and desires. [a]*Rom 6:6; Gal 2:20*

25 If we live by the Spirit, let us also walk [a]by the Spirit. [a]*Gal 5:16*

26 Let us not become [a]boastful, challenging one another, envying one another. [a]*Phil 2:3*

Bear One Another's Burdens

6 Brethren, even if anyone is caught in any trespass, you who are [a]spiritual, restore such a one in a spirit of gentleness; *each one* looking to yourself, so that you too will not be tempted. [a]*1 Cor 2:15*

2 [a]Bear one another's burdens, and thereby fulfill the law of Christ. [a]*Rom 15:1*

3 For [a]if anyone thinks he is something when he is nothing, he deceives himself. [a]*Acts 5:36; 1 Cor 3:18*

4 But each one must [a]examine his own work, and then he will have *reason for* boasting in regard to himself alone, and not in regard to another. [a]*1 Cor 11:28*

5 For [a]each one will bear his own load. [a]*Prov 9:12; Rom 14:12*

6 [a]The one who is taught the word is to share all good things with the one who teaches *him.* [a]*1 Cor 9:11, 14*

7 Do not be deceived, [a]God is not mocked; for whatever a man sows, this he will also reap. [a]*Job 13:9*

8 For the one who sows to his own flesh will from the flesh reap corruption, but [a]the one who sows to the Spirit will from the Spirit reap eternal life. [a]*Rom 8:11; James 3:18*

9 [a]Let us not lose heart in doing good, for in due time we will reap if we do not grow weary. [a]*1 Cor 15:58; 2 Cor 4:1*

10 So then, [a]while we have opportunity, let us do good to all people, and especially to those who are of the household of the faith. [a]*Prov 3:27*

11 See with what large letters I am writing to you [a]with my own hand. [a]*1 Cor 16:21*

12 Those who desire [a]to make a good showing in the flesh try to compel you to be circumcised, simply so that they will not be persecuted for the cross of Christ. [a]*Matt 23:27f*

13 For those who are circumcised do not even [a]keep the Law themselves, but they desire to have you circumcised so that they may boast in your flesh. [a]*Rom 2:25*

14 But may it never be that I would boast, except in the cross of our Lord Jesus Christ, through which the world has been crucified to me, and [a]I to the world. [a]*Rom 6:2, 6; Gal 2:19f*

15 For [a]neither is circumcision anything, nor

uncircumcision, but a new creation. ^a*Rom 2:26, 28; 1 Cor 7:19*

16 And those who will walk by this rule, peace and mercy *be* upon them, and upon the ^aIsrael of God. ^a*Rom 9:6; Gal 3:7, 29*

17 From now on let no one cause trouble for me, for I bear on my body the ^abrand-marks of Jesus. ^a*Is 44:5; Ezek 9:4*

18 ^aThe grace of our Lord Jesus Christ be with your spirit, brethren. Amen. ^a*Rom 16:20*

The Letter of Paul to the
EPHESIANS

The Blessings of Redemption

1 Paul, ^aan apostle of Christ Jesus by the will of God,

To the saints who are at Ephesus and ^b*who are* faithful in Christ Jesus: ^a*2 Cor 1:1* ^b*Col 1:2*

2 ^aGrace to you and peace from God our Father and the Lord Jesus Christ. ^a*Rom 1:7*

3 Blessed *be* the God and Father of our Lord Jesus Christ, who has blessed us with every spiritual blessing in ^athe heavenly *places* in Christ, ^a*Eph 1:20; 2:6*

4 just as ^aHe chose us in Him before the foundation of the world, that we would be holy and blameless before Him. In love ^a*Eph 2:10; 2 Thess 2:13f*

5 He ^apredestined us to adoption as sons through Jesus Christ to Himself, according to the kind intention of His will, ^a*Rom 8:29f*

6 ^ato the praise of the glory of His grace, which He freely bestowed on us in ^bthe Beloved. ^a*Eph 1:12, 14* ^b*Matt 3:17*

7 ^aIn Him we have redemption through His blood, the forgiveness of our trespasses, according to the riches of His grace ^a*Col 1:14*

8 which He lavished on us. In all wisdom and insight

9 He ^amade known to us the mystery of His will, according to His kind intention which He purposed in Him ^a*Rom 11:25; Eph 3:3*

10 with a view to an administration suitable to ^athe fullness of the times, *that is,* ^bthe summing up of all things in Christ, things in the heavens and things on the earth. In Him ^a*Mark 1:15* ^b*Col 1:16, 20*

11 also we have obtained an inheritance, having been predestined ^aaccording to His purpose who works all things ^bafter the counsel of His will, ^a*Rom 8:28f* ^b*Rom 9:11*

12 to the end that we who were the first to hope in Christ would be ^ato the praise of His glory. ^a*Eph 1:6, 14*

13 In Him, you also, after listening to the message of truth, the gospel of your salvation—having also believed, you were ^asealed in Him with ^bthe Holy Spirit of promise, ^a*Eph 4:30* ^b*Acts 2:33*

14 who is ^agiven as a pledge of our inheritance, with a view to the redemption of *God's*

own possession, to the praise of His glory. ^a*2 Cor 1:22*

15 For this reason I too, ^ahaving heard of the faith in the Lord Jesus which *exists* among you and your love for all the saints, ^a*Col 1:4; Philem 5*

16 ^ado not cease giving thanks for you, while making mention *of you* in my prayers; ^a*Rom 1:8f; Col 1:9*

17 that the ^aGod of our Lord Jesus Christ, the Father of glory, may give to you a spirit of wisdom and of revelation in the knowledge of Him. ^a*John 20:17; Rom 15:6*

18 *I pray that* ^athe eyes of your heart may be enlightened, so that you will know what is the hope of His calling, what are the riches of the glory of His inheritance in the saints, ^a*2 Cor 4:6*

19 and what is the surpassing greatness of His power toward us who believe. ^a*These are* in accordance with the working of the strength of His might ^a*Eph 3:7; Col 1:29*

20 which He brought about in Christ, when He ^araised Him from the dead and seated Him at His right hand in the heavenly *places,* ^a*Acts 2:24*

21 far above ^aall rule and authority and power and dominion, and every name that is named, not only in this age but also in the one to come. ^a*Matt 28:18; Col 1:16*

22 And He ^aput all things in subjection under His feet, and gave Him as head over all things to the church, ^a*Ps 8:6; 1 Cor 15:27*

23 which is His ^abody, the fullness of Him who fills all in all. ^a*1 Cor 12:27; Eph 4:12*

Made Alive in Christ

2 And you were ^adead in your trespasses and sins, ^a*Eph 2:5; Col 2:13*

2 in which you formerly walked according to the course of this world, according to ^athe prince of the power of the air, of the spirit that is now working in ^bthe sons of disobedience. ^a*John 12:31* ^b*Eph 5:6*

3 Among them we too all formerly lived in ^athe lusts of our flesh, indulging the desires of the flesh and of the mind, and were ^bby nature children of wrath, even as the rest. ^a*Gal 5:16f* ^b*Rom 2:14*

4 But God, being rich in mercy, because of ^aHis great love with which He loved us, ^a*John 3:16*

5 even when we were dead in our transgressions, made us alive together with Christ (ªby grace you have been saved), ªActs 15:11

6 and ªraised us up with Him, and seated us with Him in the heavenly *places* in Christ Jesus, ªCol 2:12

7 so that in the ages to come He might show the surpassing ªriches of His grace in kindness toward us in Christ Jesus. ªRom 2:4; Eph 1:7

8 For ªby grace you have been saved through faith; and that not of yourselves, *it is* the gift of God; ªActs 15:11; Eph 2:5

9 ªnot as a result of works, so that no one may boast. ªRom 3:28; 2 Tim 1:9

10 For we are His workmanship, ªcreated in Christ Jesus for good works, which God prepared beforehand so that we would walk in them. ªCol 3:10

11 Therefore remember that formerly you, the Gentiles in the flesh, who are called "ªUncircumcision" by the so-called "ªCircumcision," *which is* performed in the flesh by human hands— ªRom 2:28f; Col 2:11

12 *remember* that you were at that time separate from Christ, excluded from the commonwealth of Israel, and strangers to ªthe covenants of promise, having no hope and without God in the world. ªGal 3:17; Heb 8:6

13 But now in Christ Jesus you who formerly were far off have been brought near ªby the blood of Christ. ªRom 3:25; Col 1:20

14 For He Himself is ªour peace, who made both *groups into* one and broke down the barrier of the dividing wall, ªIs 9:6

15 by abolishing in His flesh the enmity, *which is* the Law of commandments *contained* in ordinances, so that in Himself He might make the two into ªone new man, *thus* establishing peace, ªGal 3:28; Col 3:10f

16 and might ªreconcile them both in one body to God through the cross, by it having put to death the enmity. ª2 Cor 5:18; Col 1:20, 22

17 AND ªHE CAME AND PREACHED PEACE TO YOU WHO WERE FAR AWAY, AND PEACE TO THOSE WHO WERE NEAR; ªIs 57:19; Rom 10:14

18 for through Him we both have our access in ªone Spirit to the Father. ª1 Cor 12:13; Eph 4:4

19 So then you are no longer strangers and aliens, but you are ªfellow citizens with the saints, and are of God's household, ªPhil 3:20; Heb 12:22f

20 having been built on the foundation of the apostles and prophets, Christ Jesus Himself being the ªcorner *stone*, ªPs 118:22; Luke 20:17

21 in whom the whole building, being fitted together, is growing into ªa holy temple in the Lord, ª1 Cor 3:16f

22 in whom you also are being ªbuilt together into a dwelling of God in the Spirit. ª1 Cor 3:9, 16; 2 Cor 6:16

Paul's Stewardship

3 For this reason I, Paul, ªthe prisoner of Christ Jesus for the sake of you Gentiles— ªActs 23:18; Eph 4:1

2 if indeed you have heard of the ªstewardship of God's grace which was given to me for you; ªEph 1:10; 3:9

3 that ªby revelation there was made known to me the mystery, as I wrote before in brief. ªGal 1:12

4 By referring to this, when you read you can understand my insight into the ªmystery of Christ, ªRom 11:25; 16:25

5 which in other generations was not made known to the sons of men, as it has now been revealed to His holy ªapostles and prophets in the Spirit; ª1 Cor 12:28; Eph 2:20

6 *to be specific,* that the Gentiles are ªfellow heirs and fellow members of the body, and fellow partakers of the promise in Christ Jesus through the gospel, ªGal 3:29

7 ªof which I was made a minister, according to the gift of God's grace which was given to me according to the working of His power. ªCol 1:23, 25

8 To me, the very least of all saints, this grace was given, to preach to the Gentiles the unfathomable ªriches of Christ, ªRom 2:4; Eph 1:7

9 and to bring to light what is the administration of the ªmystery which for ages has been hidden in God who created all things; ªRom 16:25; Col 1:26f

10 so that the manifold wisdom of God might now be ªmade known through the church to the ᵇrulers and the authorities in the heavenly *places.* ª1 Pet 1:12 ᵇEph 6:12

11 *This was* in ªaccordance with the eternal purpose which He carried out in Christ Jesus our Lord, ªEph 1:11

12 in whom we have boldness and confident ªaccess through faith in Him. ªEph 2:18

13 Therefore I ask you not to lose heart at my tribulations ªon your behalf, for they are your glory. ªEph 3:1

14 For this reason I ªbow my knees before the Father, ªPhil 2:10

15 from whom every family in heaven and on earth derives its name,

16 that He would grant you, according to the riches of His glory, to be ªstrengthened with power through His Spirit in the inner man, ªPhil 4:13; Col 1:11

17 so that ªChrist may dwell in your hearts through faith; *and* that you, being ᵇrooted and grounded in love, ªJohn 14:23 ᵇCol 2:7

18 may be able to comprehend with all the saints what is ªthe breadth and length and height and depth, ªJob 11:8f

19 and to know ªthe love of Christ which sur-

passes knowledge, that you may be filled up to all the fullness of God. ªRom 8:35, 39

20 Now to Him who is ªable to do far more abundantly beyond all that we ask or think, according to the power that works within us, ª2 Cor 9:8

21 ªto Him *be* the glory in the church and in Christ Jesus to all generations forever and ever. Amen. ªRom 11:36

Unity of the Spirit

4 Therefore I, the prisoner of the Lord, implore you to ªwalk in a manner worthy of the calling with which you have been called, ªEph 2:10; Col 1:10

2 with all ªhumility and gentleness, with patience, showing tolerance for one another in love, ªCol 3:12f

3 being diligent to preserve the unity of the Spirit in the ªbond of peace. ªCol 3:14f

4 *There is* ªone body and one Spirit, just as also you were called in one ᵇhope of your calling; ª1 Cor 12:4ff ᵇEph 1:18

5 ªone Lord, one faith, one baptism, ª1 Cor 8:6

6 one God and Father of all ªwho is over all and through all and in all. ªRom 11:36

7 But to each one of us grace was given ªaccording to the measure of Christ's gift. ªRom 12:3

8 Therefore it says,

"ªWHEN HE ASCENDED ON HIGH,
 HE LED CAPTIVE A HOST OF CAPTIVES,
 AND HE GAVE GIFTS TO MEN."   ªPs 68:18

9 (Now this *expression,* "He ªascended," what does it mean except that He also had descended into the lower parts of the earth? ªJohn 3:13

10 He who descended is Himself also He who ascended ªfar above all the heavens, so that He might ᵇfill all things.) ªHeb 7:26 ᵇEph 1:23

11 And He gave ªsome *as* apostles, and some *as* prophets, and some *as* evangelists, and some *as* pastors and teachers, ªActs 13:1; 1 Cor 12:28

12 ªfor the equipping of the saints for the work of service, to the building up of the body of Christ; ª2 Cor 13:9

13 until we all attain to the unity of the faith, and of the ªknowledge of the Son of God, to a ᵇmature man, to the measure of the stature which belongs to the fullness of Christ. ªEph 1:17 ᵇHeb 5:14

14 As a result, we are ªno longer to be children, tossed here and there by waves and carried about by every wind of doctrine, by the trickery of men, by craftiness in deceitful scheming; ª1 Cor 14:20

15 but speaking the truth in love, we are to ªgrow up in all *aspects* into Him who is the head, *even* Christ, ªEph 2:21

16 from whom ªthe whole body, being fitted and held together by what every joint supplies, according to the proper working of each individual part, causes the growth of the body for the building up of itself in love. ªRom 12:4f; Col 2:19

The Christian's Walk

17 So this I say, and affirm together with the Lord, ªthat you walk no longer just as the Gentiles also walk, in the futility of their mind, ªEph 2:2; 4:22

18 being ªdarkened in their understanding, ᵇexcluded from the life of God because of the ignorance that is in them, because of the hardness of their heart; ªRom 1:21 ᵇEph 2:12

19 and they, having become callous, ªhave given themselves over to ᵇsensuality for the practice of every kind of impurity with greediness. ªRom 1:24 ᵇCol 3:5

20 But you did not ªlearn Christ in this way, ªMatt 11:29

21 if indeed you ªhave heard Him and have ᵇbeen taught in Him, just as truth is in Jesus, ªRom 10:14 ᵇCol 2:7

22 that, in reference to your former manner of life, you ªlay aside the ᵇold self, which is being corrupted in accordance with the lusts of deceit, ªHeb 12:1 ᵇRom 6:6

23 and that you be ªrenewed in the spirit of your mind, ªRom 12:2

24 and put on the ªnew self, which in *the likeness of* God has been created in righteousness and holiness of the truth. ªCol 3:10

25 Therefore, laying aside falsehood, ªSPEAK TRUTH EACH ONE *of you* WITH HIS NEIGHBOR, for we are members of one another. ªZech 8:16; Eph 4:15

26 ªBE ANGRY, AND Y*et* DO NOT SIN; do not let the sun go down on your anger, ªPs 4:4

27 and do not ªgive the devil an opportunity. ªRom 12:19; James 4:7

28 He who steals must steal no longer; but rather he must labor, ªperforming with his own hands what is good, so that he will have *something* to share with one who has need. ª1 Thess 4:11; 2 Thess 3:8, 11f

29 Let no unwholesome word proceed from your mouth, but only such *a word* as is good for ªedification according to the need *of the moment,* so that it will give grace to those who hear. ªRom 14:19; Col 4:6

30 Do not grieve the Holy Spirit of God, by whom you were ªsealed for the day of redemption. ªJohn 3:33; Eph 1:13

31 ªLet all bitterness and wrath and anger and clamor and slander be put away from you, along with all malice. ªRom 3:14; Col 3:8, 19

32 Be kind to one another, tender-hearted, forgiving each other, [a]just as God in Christ also has forgiven you. [a]*Matt 6:14f; 2 Cor 2:10*

Be Imitators of God

5 [a]Therefore be imitators of God, as beloved children; [a]*Matt 5:48; Luke 6:36*

2 and [a]walk in love, just as Christ also loved you and [b]gave Himself up for us, an offering and a sacrifice to God as a fragrant aroma. [a]*Rom 14:15* [b]*Gal 2:20*

3 But [a]immorality or any impurity or greed must not even be named among you, as is proper among saints; [a]*Col 3:5*

4 and *there must be no* [a]filthiness and silly talk, or coarse jesting, which are not fitting, but rather [b]giving of thanks. [a]*Matt 12:34* [b]*Eph 5:20*

5 For this you know with certainty, that [a]no immoral or impure person or covetous man, who is an idolater, has an inheritance in the kingdom [b]of Christ and God. [a]*1 Cor 6:9* [b]*Col 1:13*

6 [a]Let no one deceive you with empty words, for because of these things the wrath of God comes upon the sons of disobedience. [a]*Col 2:8*

7 Therefore do not be [a]partakers with them; [a]*Eph 3:6*

8 for [a]you were formerly darkness, but now you are Light in the Lord; walk as children of Light [a]*Eph 2:2*

9 (for [a]the fruit of the Light *consists* in all goodness and righteousness and truth), [a]*Gal 5:22*

10 [a]trying to learn what is pleasing to the Lord. [a]*Rom 12:2*

11 Do not participate in the unfruitful [a]deeds of darkness, but instead even [b]expose them; [a]*Rom 13:12* [b]*1 Tim 5:20*

12 for it is disgraceful even to speak of the things which are done by them in secret.

13 But all things become visible [a]when they are exposed by the light, for everything that becomes visible is light. [a]*John 3:20f*

14 For this reason it says,
"[a]Awake, sleeper,
    And arise from the dead,
    And Christ will shine on you." [a]*Is 51:17; 60:1*

15 Therefore be careful how you [a]walk, not as unwise men but as wise, [a]*Eph 5:2*

16 [a]making the most of your time, because the days are evil. [a]*Col 4:5*

17 So then do not be foolish, but [a]understand what the will of the Lord is. [a]*Rom 12:2; Col 1:9*

18 And [a]do not get drunk with wine, for that is dissipation, but be filled with the Spirit, [a]*Prov 20:1; Rom 13:13*

19 [a]speaking to one another in psalms and hymns and spiritual songs, singing and making melody with your heart to the Lord; [a]*Col 3:16*

20 [a]always giving thanks for all things in the name of our Lord Jesus Christ to [b]God, even the Father; [a]*Rom 1:8* [b]*1 Cor 15:24*

21 [a]and be subject to one another in the [b]fear of Christ. [a]*Gal 5:13* [b]*2 Cor 5:11*

Marriage Like Christ and the Church

22 [a]Wives, *be subject* to your own husbands, as to the Lord. [a]*Eph 5:22-6:9; Col 3:18-4:1*

23 For [a]the husband is the head of the wife, as Christ also is the head of the church, He Himself *being* the Savior of the body. [a]*1 Cor 11:3*

24 But as the church is subject to Christ, so also the wives *ought to be* to their husbands in everything.

25 [a]Husbands, love your wives, just as Christ also loved the church and [b]gave Himself up for her, [a]*Eph 5:28, 33* [b]*Eph 5:2*

26 [a]so that He might sanctify her, having cleansed her by the washing of water with the word, [a]*Titus 2:14; Heb 10:10, 14, 29*

27 that He might present to Himself the church in all her glory, having no spot or wrinkle or any such thing; but that she would be [a]holy and blameless. [a]*Eph 1:4*

28 So husbands ought also to [a]love their own wives as their own bodies. He who loves his own wife loves himself; [a]*Eph 5:25, 33; 1 Pet 3:7*

29 for no one ever hated his own flesh, but nourishes and cherishes it, just as Christ also *does* the church,

30 because we are [a]members of His body. [a]*1 Cor 6:15; 12:27*

31 [a]FOR THIS REASON A MAN SHALL LEAVE HIS FATHER AND MOTHER AND SHALL BE JOINED TO HIS WIFE, AND THE TWO SHALL BECOME ONE FLESH. [a]*Gen 2:24; Matt 19:5*

32 This mystery is great; but I am speaking with reference to Christ and the church.

33 Nevertheless, each individual among you also is to love his own wife even as himself, and the wife must *see to it* that she [a]respects her husband. [a]*1 Pet 3:2, 5f*

Family Relationships

6 [a]Children, obey your parents in the Lord, for this is right. [a]*Prov 6:20; 23:22*

2 [a]HONOR YOUR FATHER AND MOTHER (which is the first commandment with a promise), [a]*Ex 20:12; Deut 5:16*

3 SO THAT IT MAY BE WELL WITH YOU, AND THAT YOU MAY LIVE LONG ON THE EARTH.

4 [a]Fathers, do not provoke your children to anger, but [b]bring them up in the discipline and instruction of the Lord. [a]*Col 3:21* [b]*Gen 18:19*

5 [a]Slaves, be obedient to those who are your masters according to the flesh, with fear and trembling, in the sincerity of your heart, as to Christ; [a]*Col 3:22; 1 Tim 6:1*

6 not by way of eyeservice, as [a]men-pleasers, but as slaves of Christ, doing the will of God from the heart. [a]*Gal 1:10*

7 With good will render service, [a]as to the Lord, and not to men, [a]Col 3:23

8 knowing that [a]whatever good thing each one does, this he will receive back from the Lord, whether slave or free. [a]Matt 16:27; 2 Cor 5:10

9 And masters, do the same things to them, and give up threatening, knowing that [a]both their Master and yours is in heaven, and there is no partiality with Him. [a]Job 31:13ff; Col 4:1

The Armor of God

10 Finally, [a]be strong in the Lord and in [b]the strength of His might. [a]1 Cor 16:13 [b]Eph 1:19

11 [a]Put on the full armor of God, so that you will be able to stand firm against the schemes of the devil. [a]Rom 13:12; Eph 6:13

12 For our struggle is not against [a]flesh and blood, but against the rulers, against the powers, against the world forces of this darkness, against the spiritual *forces* of wickedness in the heavenly *places*. [a]Matt 16:17

13 Therefore, take up the full armor of God, so that you will be able to [a]resist in the evil day, and having done everything, to stand firm. [a]James 4:7

14 Stand firm therefore, [a]HAVING GIRDED YOUR LOINS WITH TRUTH, and HAVING [b]PUT ON THE BREASTPLATE OF RIGHTEOUSNESS,

15 and having [a]shod YOUR FEET WITH THE PREPARATION OF THE GOSPEL OF PEACE; [a]Is 52:7; Rom 10:15

16 in addition to all, taking up the [a]shield of faith with which you will be able to extinguish all the flaming arrows of the evil *one*. [a]1 Thess 5:8

17 And take [a]THE HELMET OF SALVATION, and the [b]sword of the Spirit, which is the word of God. [a]Is 59:17 [b]Heb 4:12

18 With all [a]prayer and petition pray at all times in the Spirit, and with this in view, be on the alert with all perseverance and petition for all the saints, [a]Phil 4:6

19 and [a]*pray* on my behalf, that utterance may be given to me in the opening of my mouth, to make known with boldness the mystery of the gospel, [a]Col 4:3; 1 Thess 5:25

20 for which I am an [a]ambassador in chains; that in *proclaiming* it I may speak boldly, as I ought to speak. [a]2 Cor 5:20

21 [a]But that you also may know about my circumstances, how I am doing, Tychicus, the beloved brother and faithful minister in the Lord, will make everything known to you. [a]Eph 6:21, 22; Col 4:7-9

22 I have sent him to you for this very purpose, so that you may know about us, and that he may [a]comfort your hearts. [a]Col 2:2; 4:8

23 Peace be to the brethren, and [a]love with faith, from God the Father and the Lord Jesus Christ. [a]Gal 5:6; 1 Thess 5:8

24 Grace be with all those who love our Lord Jesus Christ with incorruptible *love*.

The Letter of Paul to the
PHILIPPIANS

Thanksgiving

1 Paul and Timothy, bond-servants of Christ Jesus,

To all the saints in Christ Jesus who are in Philippi, including the [a]overseers and deacons: [a]Acts 20:28; 1 Tim 3:1f

2 [a]Grace to you and peace from God our Father and the Lord Jesus Christ. [a]Rom 1:7

3 [a]I thank my God in all my remembrance of you, [a]Rom 1:8

4 always offering prayer with joy in [a]my every prayer for you all, [a]Rom 1:9

5 in view of your participation in the [a]gospel from the first day until now. [a]Phil 1:7; 2:22

6 *For I am* confident of this very thing, that He who began a good work in you will perfect it until [a]the day of Christ Jesus. [a]1 Cor 1:8; Phil 1:10

7 For it is only right for me to feel this way about you all, because I [a]have you in my heart, since both in my [b]imprisonment and in the defense and confirmation of the gospel, you all are partakers of grace with me. [a]2 Cor 7:3 [b]Acts 21:33

8 For [a]God is my witness, how I long for you all with the affection of Christ Jesus. [a]Rom 1:9

9 And this I pray, that [a]your love may abound still more and more in [b]real knowledge and all discernment, [a]1 Thess 3:12 [b]Col 1:9

10 so that you may [a]approve the things that are excellent, in order to be sincere and blameless until [b]the day of Christ; [a]Rom 2:18 [b]1 Cor 1:8

11 having been filled with the [a]fruit of righteousness which *comes* through Jesus Christ, to the glory and praise of God. [a]James 3:18

The Gospel Is Preached

12 Now I want you to know, brethren, that my circumstances [a]have turned out for the greater progress of the gospel, [a]Luke 21:13

13 so that my [a]imprisonment in *the cause of* Christ has become well known throughout the whole praetorian guard and to everyone else, [a]Phil 1:7; 2 Tim 2:9

14 and that most of the brethren, trusting in the Lord because of my imprisonment, have [a]far more courage to speak the word of God without fear. [a]Acts 4:31; Phil 1:20

15 ªSome, to be sure, are preaching Christ even from envy and strife, but some also from good will; ª2 Cor 11:13

16 the latter *do it* out of love, knowing that I am appointed for the defense of the ªgospel; ªPhil 1:5, 7, 12, 27; 2:22

17 the former proclaim Christ ªout of selfish ambition rather than from pure motives, thinking to cause me distress in my imprisonment. ªRom 2:8; Phil 2:3

18 What then? Only that in every way, whether in pretense or in truth, Christ is proclaimed; and in this I rejoice.

Yes, and I will rejoice,

19 for I know that this will turn out for my deliverance ªthrough your prayers and the provision of ᵇthe Spirit of Jesus Christ, ª2 Cor 1:11 ᵇActs 16:7

20 according to my earnest expectation and hope, that I will not be put to shame in anything, but *that* with all boldness, Christ will even now, as always, be ªexalted in my body, ᵇwhether by life or by death. ª1 Cor 6:20 ᵇRom 14:8

To Live Is Christ

21 For to me, ªto live is Christ and to die is gain. ªGal 2:20

22 But if *I am* to live *on* in the flesh, this *will mean* ªfruitful labor for me; and I do not know which to choose. ªRom 1:13

23 But I am hard-pressed from both *directions,* having the ªdesire to depart and be with Christ, for *that* is very much better; ª2 Cor 5:8; 2 Tim 4:6

24 yet to remain on in the flesh is more necessary for your sake.

25 ªConvinced of this, I know that I will remain and continue with you all for your progress and joy in the faith, ªPhil 2:24

26 so that your ªproud confidence in me may abound in Christ Jesus through my coming to you again, ª2 Cor 5:12; 7:4

27 Only conduct yourselves in a manner ªworthy of the gospel of Christ, so that whether I come and see you or remain absent, I will hear of you that you are standing firm in one spirit, with one mind striving together for the faith of the gospel; ªEph 4:1

28 in no way alarmed by *your* opponents—which is a ªsign of destruction for them, but of salvation for you, and that *too,* from God. ª2 Thess 1:5

29 For to you ªit has been granted for Christ's sake, not only to believe in Him, but also to suffer for His sake, ªMatt 5:11, 12

30 experiencing the same ªconflict which you saw in me, and now hear *to be* in me. ªCol 1:29; 2:1

Be Like Christ

2 Therefore if there is any encouragement in Christ, if there is any consolation of love, if there is any ªfellowship of the Spirit, if any affection and compassion, ª2 Cor 13:14

2 ªmake my joy complete by being of the same mind, maintaining the same love, united in spirit, intent on one purpose. ªJohn 3:29

3 Do nothing from selfishness or empty conceit, but with humility of mind ªregard one another as more important than yourselves; ªRom 12:10; Eph 5:21

4 ªdo not *merely* look out for your own personal interests, but also for the interests of others. ªRom 15:1f

5 ªHave this attitude in yourselves which was also in Christ Jesus, ªMatt 11:29; Rom 15:3

6 who, although He existed in the form of God, ªdid not regard equality with God a thing to be grasped, ªJohn 5:18; 10:33

7 but ªemptied Himself, taking the form of a bond-servant, *and* ᵇbeing made in the likeness of men. ª2 Cor 8:9 ᵇHeb 2:17

8 Being found in appearance as a man, He humbled Himself by becoming ªobedient to the point of death, even death on a cross. ªMatt 26:39; John 10:18

9 For this reason also, God ªhighly exalted Him, and bestowed on Him ᵇthe name which is above every name, ªMatt 28:18 ᵇEph 1:21

10 so that at the name of Jesus ªEVERY KNEE WILL BOW, of those who are in heaven and on earth and under the earth, ªIs 45:23; Rom 14:11

11 and that every tongue will confess that Jesus Christ is ªLord, to the glory of God the Father. ªJohn 13:13; Rom 10:9

12 So then, my beloved, just as you have always obeyed, not as in my presence only, but now much more in my absence, work out your ªsalvation with ᵇfear and trembling; ªHeb 5:9 ᵇ2 Cor 7:15

13 for it is ªGod who is at work in you, both to will and to work for *His* good pleasure. ªRom 12:3; 1 Cor 12:6

14 Do all things without ªgrumbling or disputing; ª1 Cor 10:10; 1 Pet 4:9

15 so that you will prove yourselves to be ªblameless and innocent, children of God above reproach in the midst of a ᵇcrooked and perverse generation, among whom you appear as lights in the world, ªLuke 1:6 ᵇDeut 32:5

16 holding fast the word of life, so that in the day of Christ I will have reason to glory because I did not ªrun in vain nor ᵇtoil in vain. ªGal 2:2 ᵇIs 49:4

17 But even if I am being ªpoured out as a drink offering upon ᵇthe sacrifice and service of your faith, I rejoice and share my joy with you all. ª2 Tim 4:6 ᵇNum 28:6, 7

18 You too, *I urge you,* rejoice in the same way and share your joy with me.

Timothy and Epaphroditus

19 But I hope in the Lord Jesus to ªsend Timothy to you shortly, so that I also may be encouraged when I learn of your condition. ª*Phil 2:23*

20 For I have no one *else* ªof kindred spirit who will genuinely be concerned for your welfare. ª*1 Cor 16:10; 2 Tim 3:10*

21 For they all ªseek after their own interests, not those of Christ Jesus. ª*1 Cor 10:24; 13:5*

22 But you know ªof his proven worth, that he served with me in the furtherance of the gospel like a child *serving* his father. ª*Rom 5:4; Acts 16:2*

23 ªTherefore I hope to send him immediately, as soon as I see how things *go* with me; ª*Phil 2:19*

24 and ªI trust in the Lord that I myself also will be coming shortly. ª*Phil 1:25*

25 But I thought it necessary to send to you Epaphroditus, my brother and ªfellow worker and fellow soldier, who is also your messenger and minister to my need; ª*Rom 16:3, 9, 21; Phil 4:3*

26 because he was longing for you all and was distressed because you had heard that he was sick.

27 For indeed he was sick to the point of death, but God had mercy on him, and not on him only but also on me, so that I would not have sorrow upon sorrow.

28 Therefore I have sent him all the more eagerly so that when you see him again you may rejoice and I may be less concerned *about you.*

29 Receive him then in the Lord with all joy, and ªhold men like him in high regard; ª*1 Cor 16:18*

30 because he came close to death for the work of Christ, risking his life to ªcomplete what was deficient in your service to me. ª*1 Cor 16:17; Phil 4:10*

The Goal of Life

3 Finally, my brethren, ªrejoice in the Lord. To write the same things *again* is no trouble to me, and it is a safeguard for you. ª*Phil 2:18; 4:4*

2 Beware of the ªdogs, beware of the ᵇevil workers, beware of the false circumcision; ª*Ps 22:16, 20* ᵇ*2 Cor 11:13*

3 for ªwe are the *true* circumcision, who ᵇworship in the Spirit of God and glory in Christ Jesus and put no confidence in the flesh, ª*Rom 2:29* ᵇ*John 4:23f*

4 although ªI myself might have confidence even in the flesh. If anyone else has a mind to put confidence in the flesh, I far more: ª*2 Cor 5:16; 11:18*

5 ªcircumcised the eighth day, of the ᵇnation of Israel, of the tribe of Benjamin, a ᵇHebrew of Hebrews; as to the Law, a Pharisee; ª*Luke 1:59* ᵇ*Rom 11:1*

6 as to zeal, ªa persecutor of the church; as to the righteousness which is in the Law, found blameless. ª*Acts 8:3; 22:4, 5*

7 But ªwhatever things were gain to me, those things I have counted as loss for the sake of Christ. ª*Luke 14:33*

8 More than that, I count all things to be loss in view of the surpassing value of ªknowing Christ Jesus my Lord, for whom I have suffered the loss of all things, and count them but rubbish so that I may gain Christ, ª*Jer 9:23f; John 17:3*

9 and may be found in Him, not having ªa righteousness of my own derived from *the* Law, but that which is through faith in Christ, ᵇthe righteousness which *comes* from God on the basis of faith, ª*Rom 10:5* ᵇ*Rom 9:30*

10 that I may know Him and ªthe power of His resurrection and ᵇthe fellowship of His sufferings, being conformed to His death; ª*Rom 6:5* ᵇ*Rom 8:17*

11 in order that I may ªattain to the resurrection from the dead. ª*1 Cor 15:23*

12 Not that I have already ªobtained *it* or have already become perfect, but I press on so that I may lay hold of that for which also I was laid hold of by Christ Jesus. ª*1 Cor 9:24f; 1 Tim 6:12, 19*

13 Brethren, I do not regard myself as having laid hold of *it* yet; but one thing *I do:* ªforgetting what *lies* behind and reaching forward to what *lies* ahead, ª*Luke 9:62*

14 I press on toward the goal for the prize of the ªupward call of God in Christ Jesus. ª*Rom 8:28; 11:29*

15 Let us therefore, as many as are perfect, have this attitude; and if in anything you have a different attitude, ªGod will reveal that also to you; ª*John 6:45; Eph 1:17*

16 however, let us keep ªliving by that same *standard* to which we have attained. ª*Gal 6:16*

17 Brethren, ªjoin in following my example, and observe those who walk according to the ᵇpattern you have in us. ª*1 Cor 4:16* ᵇ*1 Pet 5:3*

18 For ªmany walk, of whom I often told you, and now tell you even weeping, *that they are* enemies of ᵇthe cross of Christ, ª*2 Cor 11:13* ᵇ*Gal 6:14*

19 whose end is destruction, whose god is *their* ªappetite, and *whose* ᵇglory is in their shame, who set their minds on earthly things. ª*Rom 16:18* ᵇ*Rom 6:21*

20 For ªour citizenship is in heaven, from which also we eagerly wait for a Savior, the Lord Jesus Christ; ª*Eph 2:19; Phil 1:27*

21 who will ªtransform the body of our humble state into conformity with the body of His glory, by the exertion of the power that He has

even to subject all things to Himself. ^a*1 Cor 15:43-53*

Think of Excellence

4 Therefore, my beloved brethren whom I long *to see,* my joy and crown, in this way ^astand firm in the Lord, my beloved. ^a*1 Cor 16:13; Phil 1:27*

2 I urge Euodia and I urge Syntyche to ^alive in harmony in the Lord. ^a*Phil 2:2*

3 Indeed, true companion, I ask you also to help these women who have shared my struggle in *the cause of* the gospel, together with Clement also and the rest of my fellow workers, whose ^anames are in the book of life. ^a*Luke 10:20*

4 ^aRejoice in the Lord always; again I will say, rejoice! ^a*Phil 3:1*

5 Let your gentle *spirit* be known to all men. ^aThe Lord is near. ^a*1 Cor 16:22.mg; Heb 10:37*

6 ^aBe anxious for nothing, but in everything by ^bprayer and supplication with thanksgiving let your requests be made known to God. ^a*Matt 6:25* ^b*Eph 6:18*

7 And ^athe peace of God, which surpasses all comprehension, will guard your hearts and your minds in Christ Jesus. ^a*Is 26:3; John 14:27*

8 Finally, brethren, ^awhatever is true, whatever is honorable, whatever is right, whatever is pure, whatever is lovely, whatever is of good repute, if there is any excellence and if anything worthy of praise, dwell on these things. ^a*Rom 14:18; 1 Pet 2:12*

9 The things you have learned and received and heard and seen ^ain me, practice these things, and the God of peace will be with you. ^a*Phil 3:17*

God's Provisions

10 But I rejoiced in the Lord greatly, that now at last ^ayou have revived your concern for me; indeed, you were concerned *before,* but you lacked opportunity. ^a*2 Cor 11:9; Phil 2:30*

11 Not that I speak from want, for I have learned to be ^acontent in whatever circumstances I am. ^a*2 Cor 9:8; 1 Tim 6:6, 8*

12 I know how to get along with humble means, and I also know how to live in prosperity; in any and every circumstance I have learned the secret of being filled and going ^ahungry, both of having abundance and suffering need. ^a*1 Cor 4:11*

13 I can do all things through Him who ^astrengthens me. ^a*2 Cor 12:9; Eph 3:16*

14 Nevertheless, you have done well to ^ashare *with me* in my affliction. ^a*Heb 10:33; Rev 1:9*

15 You yourselves also know, Philippians, that at the first preaching of the gospel, after I left Macedonia, no church ^ashared with me in the matter of giving and receiving but you alone; ^a*2 Cor 11:9*

16 for even in ^aThessalonica you sent *a gift* more than once for my needs. ^a*Acts 17:1; 1 Thess 2:9*

17 ^aNot that I seek the gift itself, but I seek for the profit which increases to your account. ^a*1 Cor 9:11f; 2 Cor 9:5*

18 But I have received everything in full and have an abundance; I am amply supplied, having received from ^aEpaphroditus what you have sent, a fragrant aroma, an acceptable sacrifice, well-pleasing to God. ^a*Phil 2:25*

19 And ^amy God will supply all your needs according to His riches in glory in Christ Jesus. ^a*2 Cor 9:8*

20 Now to ^aour God and Father ^b*be* the glory forever and ever. Amen. ^a*Gal 1:4* ^b*Rom 11:36*

21 Greet every saint in Christ Jesus. ^aThe brethren who are with me greet you. ^a*Gal 1:2*

22 ^aAll the saints greet you, especially those of Caesar's household. ^a*2 Cor 13:13*

23 ^aThe grace of the Lord Jesus Christ ^b*be* with your spirit. ^a*Rom 16:20* ^b*2 Tim 4:22*

The Letter of Paul to the
COLOSSIANS

Thankfulness for Spiritual Attainments

1 Paul, an apostle of Jesus Christ ^aby the will of God, and Timothy our brother, ^a*1 Cor 1:1*

2 To the saints and faithful brethren in Christ *who are* at Colossae: ^aGrace to you and peace from God our Father. ^a*Rom 1:7*

3 ^aWe give thanks to God, ^bthe Father of our Lord Jesus Christ, praying always for you, ^a*Rom 1:8* ^b*Rom 15:6*

4 ^asince we heard of your faith in Christ Jesus and the love which you have for all the saints; ^a*Eph 1:15; Phil 5*

5 because of the hope ^alaid up for you in heaven, of which you previously ^bheard in the word of truth, the gospel ^a*2 Tim 4:8* ^b*Eph 1:13*

6 which has come to you, just as in all the world also it is constantly bearing ^afruit and increasing, even as *it has been doing* in you also since the day you ^bheard *of it* and understood the grace of God in truth; ^a*Rom 1:13* ^b*Eph 4:21*

7 just as you learned *it* from ^aEpaphras, our beloved fellow bond-servant, who is a faithful servant of Christ on our behalf, ^a*Col 4:12*

8 and he also informed us of your ^alove in the Spirit. ^a*Rom 15:30*

9 For this reason also, since the day we heard *of it,* ^awe have not ceased to pray for you and to

ask that you may be filled with the knowledge of His will in all spiritual ᵇwisdom and understanding, ᵃEph 1:16 ᵇEph 1:17

10 so that you will ᵃwalk in a manner worthy of the Lord, to please *Him* in all respects, bearing fruit in every good work and increasing in the knowledge of God; ᵃEph 4:1

11 strengthened with all power, according to His glorious might, for the attaining of all steadfastness and patience; joyously

12 giving thanks to the Father, who has qualified us to share in ᵃthe inheritance of the saints in ᵇLight. ᵃActs 20:32 ᵇActs 26:18

The Incomparable Christ

13 For He rescued us from the ᵃdomain of darkness, and transferred us to the kingdom of His beloved Son, ᵃEph 6:12

14 ᵃin whom we have redemption, the forgiveness of sins. ᵃRom 3:24

15 He is the image of the invisible God, the ᵃfirstborn of all creation. ᵃRom 8:29; Rev 3:14

16 For by Him all things were created, *both* in the heavens and on earth, visible and invisible, whether thrones or dominions or rulers or authorities—ᵃall things have been created through Him and for Him. ᵃJohn 1:3; Rom 11:36

17 He ᵃis before all things, and in Him all things hold together. ᵃJohn 1:1; 8:58

18 He is also head of ᵃthe body, the church; and He is the beginning, the firstborn from the dead, so that He Himself will come to have first place in everything. ᵃEph 1:23; Col 1:24

19 For it was ᵃthe *Father's* good pleasure for all the fullness to dwell in Him, ᵃEph 1:5

20 and through Him to ᵃreconcile all things to Himself, having made peace through ᵇthe blood of His cross; through Him, *I say,* whether things on earth or things in heaven. ᵃ2 Cor 5:18 ᵇEph 2:13

21 And although you were ᵃformerly alienated and hostile in mind, *engaged* in evil deeds, ᵃRom 5:10; Eph 2:3, 12

22 yet He has now reconciled you in His fleshly ᵃbody through death, in order to present you before Him ᵇholy and blameless and beyond reproach— ᵃRom 7:4 ᵇEph 1:4

23 if indeed you continue in the faith firmly ᵃestablished and steadfast, and not moved away from the hope of the gospel that you have heard, which was proclaimed ᵇin all creation under heaven, and of which I, Paul, was made a minister. ᵃEph 3:17 ᵇActs 2:5

24 Now I rejoice in my sufferings for your sake, and in my flesh ᵃI do my share on behalf of His body, which is the church, in filling up what is lacking in Christ's afflictions. ᵃ2 Tim 1:8; 2:10

25 Of *this church* I was made a minister according to the ᵃstewardship from God

bestowed on me for your benefit, so that I might fully carry out the *preaching of* the word of God, ᵃEph 3:2

26 *that is,* ᵃthe mystery which has been hidden from the *past* ages and generations, but has now been manifested to His saints, ᵃRom 16:25f; Eph 3:3f

27 to whom ᵃGod willed to make known what is the riches of the glory of this mystery among the Gentiles, which is ᵇChrist in you, the hope of glory. ᵃMatt 13:11 ᵇRom 8:10

28 We proclaim Him, ᵃadmonishing every man and teaching every man with all wisdom, so that we may present every man complete in Christ. ᵃCol 3:16

29 For this purpose also I ᵃlabor, striving according to His power, which mightily works within me. ᵃ1 Cor 15:10

You Are Built Up in Christ

2 For I want you to know how great a ᵃstruggle I have on your behalf and for those who are at Laodicea, and for all those who have not personally seen my face, ᵃCol 1:29; 4:12

2 that their ᵃhearts may be encouraged, having been knit together in love, and *attaining* to all the wealth that comes from the full assurance of understanding, *resulting* in a true knowledge of God's mystery, *that is,* Christ *Himself,* ᵃEph 6:22; Col 4:8

3 in whom are hidden all ᵃthe treasures of wisdom and knowledge. ᵃIs 11:2; Rom 11:33

4 I say this so that no one will delude you with ᵃpersuasive argument. ᵃRom 16:18

5 For even though I am ᵃabsent in body, nevertheless I am with you in spirit, rejoicing to see your good discipline and the stability of your faith in Christ. ᵃ1 Cor 5:3

6 Therefore as you have received Christ Jesus the Lord, *so* ᵃwalk in Him, ᵃCol 1:10

7 having been firmly ᵃrooted *and now* being built up in Him and established in your faith, just as you were instructed, *and* overflowing with gratitude. ᵃEph 3:17

8 See to it that no one takes you captive through ᵃphilosophy and empty deception, according to the tradition of men, according to the elementary principles of the world, rather than according to Christ. ᵃEph 5:6; Col 2:23

9 For in Him all the ᵃfullness of Deity dwells in bodily form, ᵃ2 Cor 5:19; Col 1:19

10 and in Him you have been ᵃmade complete, and He is the head over all ᵇrule and authority; ᵃEph 3:19 ᵇ1 Cor 15:24

11 and in Him ᵃyou were also circumcised with a circumcision made without hands, in the removal of the body of the flesh by the circumcision of Christ; ᵃRom 2:29

12 having been ᵃburied with Him in baptism, in which you were also ᵇraised up with Him

through faith in the working of God, who raised Him from the dead. ᵃRom 6:4f ᵇEph 2:6

13 When you were ᵃdead in your transgressions and the uncircumcision of your flesh, He made you alive together with Him, having forgiven us all our transgressions, ᵃEph 2:1

14 having canceled out ᵃthe certificate of debt consisting of decrees against us, which was hostile to us; and He has taken it out of the way, having nailed it to the cross. ᵃEph 2:15; Col 2:20

15 When He had ᵃdisarmed the rulers and authorities, He ᵃmade a public display of them, having triumphed over them through Him. ᵃEph 4:8

16 Therefore no one is to ᵃact as your judge in regard to ᵇfood or drink or in respect to a festival or a new moon or a Sabbath day— ᵃRom 14:3 ᵇMark 7:19

17 things which are ᵃa mere shadow of what is to come; but the substance belongs to Christ. ᵃHeb 8:5; 10:1

18 Let no one keep ᵃdefrauding you of your prize by delighting in self-abasement and the worship of the angels, taking his stand on visions he has seen, inflated without cause by his fleshly mind, ᵃ1 Cor 9:24; Phil 3:14

19 and not holding fast to the head, from whom ᵃthe entire body, being supplied and held together by the joints and ligaments, grows with a growth which is from God. ᵃEph 1:23; 4:16

20 ᵃIf you have died with Christ to the elementary principles of the world, why, as if you were living in the world, do you submit yourself to decrees, such as, ᵃRom 6:2

21 "Do not handle, do not taste, do not touch!"

22 (which all refer ᵃto things destined to perish with use)—in accordance with the ᵇcommandments and teachings of men? ᵃ1 Cor 6:13 ᵇIs 29:13

23 These are matters which have, to be sure, the appearance of wisdom in ᵃself-made religion and self-abasement and severe treatment of the body, but are of no value against fleshly indulgence. ᵃCol 2:18

Put On the New Self

3 Therefore if you have been ᵃraised up with Christ, keep seeking the things above, where Christ is, ᵇseated at the right hand of God. ᵃCol 2:12 ᵇPs 110:1

2 ᵃSet your mind on the things above, not on the things that are on earth. ᵃMatt 16:23; Phil 3:19, 20

3 For you have ᵃdied and your life is hidden with Christ in God. ᵃRom 6:2; 2 Cor 5:14

4 When Christ, who is our life, is revealed, ᵃthen you also will be revealed with Him in glory. ᵃ1 Cor 1:7; Phil 3:21

5 ᵃTherefore consider the members of your earthly body as dead to immorality, impurity, passion, evil desire, and greed, which amounts to idolatry. ᵃRom 8:13

6 For it is because of these things that ᵃthe wrath of God will come upon the sons of disobedience, ᵃRom 1:18; Eph 5:6

7 and ᵃin them you also once walked, when you were living in them. ᵃEph 2:2

8 But now you also, ᵃput them all aside: ᵇanger, wrath, malice, slander, and abusive speech from your mouth. ᵃEph 4:22 ᵇEph 4:31

9 ᵃDo not lie to one another, since you laid aside the old self with its evil practices, ᵃEph 4:25

10 and have ᵃput on the new self who is being renewed to a true knowledge according to the image of the One who created him— ᵃEph 4:24

11 a renewal in which ᵃthere is no distinction between Greek and Jew, circumcised and uncircumcised, barbarian, Scythian, slave and freeman, but Christ is all, and in all. ᵃRom 10:12; 1 Cor 12:13

12 So, as those who have been chosen of God, holy and beloved, put on a ᵃheart of compassion, kindness, ᵇhumility, gentleness and patience; ᵃGal 5:22f ᵇEph 4:2

13 bearing with one another, and ᵃforgiving each other, whoever has a complaint against anyone; ᵃjust as the Lord forgave you, so also should you. ᵃEph 4:32

14 Beyond all these things put on love, which is the perfect bond of ᵃunity. ᵃJohn 17:23

15 Let ᵃthe peace of Christ rule in your hearts, to which indeed you were called in ᵇone body; and be thankful. ᵃJohn 14:27 ᵇEph 2:16

16 Let ᵃthe word of Christ richly dwell within you, with all wisdom ᵇteaching and admonishing one another with psalms and hymns and spiritual songs, singing with thankfulness in your hearts to God. ᵃRom 10:17 ᵇCol 1:28

17 ᵃWhatever you do in word or deed, do all in the name of the Lord Jesus, giving thanks through Him to God the Father. ᵃ1 Cor 10:31

Family Relations

18 ᵃWives, be subject to your husbands, as is fitting in the Lord. ᵃCol 3:18-4:1; Eph 5:22-6:9

19 ᵃHusbands, love your wives and do not be embittered against them. ᵃEph 5:25; 1 Pet 3:7

20 ᵃChildren, be obedient to your parents in all things, for this is well-pleasing to the Lord. ᵃEph 6:1

21 ᵃFathers, do not exasperate your children, so that they will not lose heart. ᵃEph 6:4

22 ᵃSlaves, in all things obey those who are your masters on earth, not with external service, as those who merely please men, but with sincerity of heart, fearing the Lord. ᵃEph 6:5

23 Whatever you do, do your work heartily, ᵃas for the Lord rather than for men, ᵃEph 6:7

24 ᵃknowing that from the Lord you will receive the reward of the inheritance. It is the Lord Christ whom you serve. ᵃ*Eph 6:8*

25 For he who does wrong will receive the consequences of the wrong which he has done, and ᵃthat without partiality. ᵃ*Deut 10:17; Acts 10:34*

Fellow Workers

4 Masters, grant to your slaves justice and fairness, ᵃknowing that you too have a Master in heaven. ᵃ*Eph 6:9*

2 ᵃDevote yourselves to prayer, keeping alert in it with *an attitude of* thanksgiving; ᵃ*Acts 1:14; Eph 6:18*

3 praying at the same time for us as well, that God will open up to us a ᵃdoor for the word, so that we may speak forth ᵇthe mystery of Christ, for which I have also been imprisoned; ᵃ*Acts 14:27* ᵇ*Eph 3:3, 4*

4 that I may make it clear ᵃin the way I ought to speak. ᵃ*Eph 6:20*

5 ᵃConduct yourselves with wisdom toward outsiders, ᵇmaking the most of the opportunity. ᵃ*Eph 5:15* ᵇ*Eph 5:16*

6 ᵃLet your speech always be with grace, *as though* seasoned with salt, so that you will know how you should respond to each person. ᵃ*Eph 4:29*

7 ᵃAs to all my affairs, Tychicus, *our* beloved brother and faithful servant and fellow bondservant in the Lord, will bring you information. ᵃ*Col 4:7-9; Eph 6:21, 22*

8 ᵃ*For* I have sent him to you for this very purpose, that you may know about our circumstances and that he may ᵇencourage your hearts; ᵃ*Eph 6:22* ᵇ*Col 2:2*

9 and with him ᵃOnesimus, *our* faithful and beloved brother, who is one of your *number*. They will inform you about the whole situation here. ᵃ*Philem 10*

10 Aristarchus, my fellow prisoner, sends you his greetings; and *also* ᵃBarnabas's cousin Mark (about whom you received instructions; if he comes to you, welcome him); ᵃ*Acts 4:36; 12:12, 25*

11 and *also* Jesus who is called Justus; these are the only fellow workers for the kingdom of God ᵃwho are from the circumcision, and they have proved to be an encouragement to me. ᵃ*Acts 11:2*

12 ᵃEpaphras, who is one of your number, a bondslave of Jesus Christ, sends you his greetings, always laboring earnestly for you in his prayers, that you may stand perfect and fully assured in all the will of God. ᵃ*Col 1:7; Philem 23*

13 For I testify for him that he has a deep concern for you and for those who are in ᵃLaodicea and Hierapolis. ᵃ*Col 2:1; 4:15f*

14 ᵃLuke, the beloved physician, sends you his greetings, and *also* Demas. ᵃ*2 Tim 4:11; Philem 24*

15 Greet the brethren who are in Laodicea and also Nympha and ᵃthe church that is in her house. ᵃ*Rom 16:5*

16 ᵃWhen this letter is read among you, have it also read in the church of the Laodiceans; and you, for your part ᵃread my letter *that is coming* from Laodicea. ᵃ*1 Thess 5:27; 2 Thess 3:14*

17 Say to ᵃArchippus, "Take heed to the ᵇministry which you have received in the Lord, that you may fulfill it." ᵃ*Philem 2* ᵇ*2 Tim 4:5*

18 I, Paul, ᵃwrite this greeting with my own hand. Remember my ᵇimprisonment. Grace be with you. ᵃ*1 Cor 16:21* ᵇ*Phil 1:7*

The First Letter of Paul to the
THESSALONIANS

Thanksgiving for These Believers

1 ᵃPaul and ᵇSilvanus and Timothy,

To the church of the Thessalonians in God the Father and the Lord Jesus Christ: Grace to you and peace. ᵃ*2 Thess 1:1* ᵇ*2 Cor 1:19*

2 ᵃWe give thanks to God always for all of you, making mention *of you* in our prayers; ᵃ*Rom 1:8; 2 Thess 1:3*

3 constantly bearing in mind your work of faith and labor of ᵃlove and ᵇsteadfastness of hope in our Lord Jesus Christ in the presence of our God and Father, ᵃ*1 Cor 13:13* ᵇ*Rom 8:25*

4 knowing, brethren beloved by God, ᵃHis choice of you; ᵃ*2 Pet 1:10*

5 for our gospel did not come to you in word only, but also ᵃin power and in the Holy Spirit and with full conviction; just as you know what kind of men we proved to be among you for your sake. ᵃ*Rom 15:19*

6 You also became ᵃimitators of us and of the Lord, having received the word in much tribulation with the ᵇjoy of the Holy Spirit, ᵃ*1 Cor 4:16* ᵇ*Acts 13:52*

7 so that you became an example to all the believers in ᵃMacedonia and in Achaia. ᵃ*Rom 15:26*

8 For ᵃthe word of the Lord has sounded forth from you, not only in Macedonia and Achaia, but also in every place your faith toward God has gone forth, so that we have no need to say anything. ᵃ*Col 3:16; 2 Thess 3:1*

9 For they themselves report about us what kind of a reception we had with you, and how you ᵃturned to God from idols to serve a living and true God, ᵃ*Acts 14:15*

10 and to ᵃwait for His Son from heaven, whom He raised from the dead, *that is* Jesus,

who ᵇrescues us from the wrath to come.
ᵃ*1 Cor 1:7* ᵇ*Rom 5:9*

Paul's Ministry

2 For you yourselves know, brethren, that
our coming to you ᵃwas not in vain,
ᵃ*2 Thess 1:10*

2 but after we had already suffered and been
ᵃmistreated in Philippi, as you know, we had
the boldness in our God ᵇto speak to you the
gospel of God amid much opposition. ᵃ*Acts 14:5*
ᵇ*Acts 17:1-9*

3 For our exhortation does not *come* from
error or ᵃimpurity or by way of ᵇdeceit;
ᵃ*1 Thess 4:7* ᵇ*2 Cor 4:2*

4 but just as we have been approved by God
to be ᵃentrusted with the gospel, so we speak,
not as pleasing men, but God who examines
our hearts. ᵃ*Gal 2:7*

5 For we never came with flattering speech,
as you know, nor with ᵃa pretext for
greed—God is witness— ᵃ*Acts 20:33; 2 Pet 2:3*

6 nor did we ᵃseek glory from men, either
from you or from others, even though as apostles of Christ we might have asserted our
authority. ᵃ*John 5:41, 44; 2 Cor 4:5*

7 But we proved to be ᵃgentle among you, as
a nursing *mother* tenderly cares for her own
children. ᵃ*2 Tim 2:24*

8 Having so fond an affection for you, we
were well-pleased to ᵃimpart to you not only
the gospel of God but also our own lives,
because you had become very dear to us.
ᵃ*2 Cor 12:15; 1 John 3:16*

9 For you recall, brethren, our ᵃlabor and
hardship, *how* working night and day so as not
to be a ᵇburden to any of you, we proclaimed to
you the gospel of God. ᵃ*2 Thess 3:8* ᵇ*2 Cor 11:9*

10 You are witnesses, and *so is* God, ᵃhow
devoutly and uprightly and blamelessly we
behaved toward you believers; ᵃ*2 Cor 1:12;
1 Thess 1:5*

11 just as you know how we *were* ᵃexhorting
and encouraging and imploring each one of
you as ᵇa father *would* his own children,
ᵃ*1 Thess 5:14* ᵇ*1 Cor 4:14*

12 so that you would ᵃwalk in a manner worthy of the God who calls you into His own
kingdom and ᵇglory. ᵃ*Eph 4:1* ᵇ*2 Cor 4:6*

13 For this reason we also constantly thank
God that when you received the ᵃword of God
which you heard from us, you accepted *it* ᵇnot
as the word of men, but *for* what it really is,
the word of God, which also performs its work
in you who believe. ᵃ*Rom 10:17* ᵇ*Matt 10:20*

14 For you, brethren, became imitators of the
churches of God in Christ Jesus that are ᵃin
Judea, for ᵇyou also endured the same sufferings at the hands of your own countrymen,

even as they *did* from the Jews, ᵃ*Gal 1:22*
ᵇ*Acts 17:5*

15 ᵃwho both killed the Lord Jesus and the
prophets, and drove us out. They are not pleasing to God, but hostile to all men, ᵃ*Luke 24:20;
Acts 2:23*

16 hindering us from speaking to the Gentiles
so that they may be saved; with the result that
they always ᵃfill up the measure of their sins.
But wrath has come upon them to the utmost.
ᵃ*Gen 15:16; Dan 8:23*

17 But we, brethren, having been taken away
from you for a short while—ᵃin person, not in
spirit—were all the more eager with great
desire to see your face. ᵃ*1 Cor 5:3*

18 For we wanted to come to you—I, Paul,
more than once—and *yet* Satan ᵃhindered us.
ᵃ*Rom 1:13; 15:22*

19 For who is our hope or ᵃjoy or crown of
exultation? Is it not even you, in the presence
of our Lord Jesus at His ᵇcoming? ᵃ*Phil 4:1*
ᵇ*Matt 16:27*

20 For you are ᵃour glory and joy. ᵃ*2 Cor 1:14*

Encouragement of Timothy's Visit

3 Therefore when we could endure *it* no longer, we thought it best to be left behind at
ᵃAthens alone, ᵃ*Acts 17:15f*

2 and we sent ᵃTimothy, our brother and
God's fellow worker in the gospel of Christ, to
strengthen and encourage you as to your faith,
ᵃ*2 Cor 1:1; Col 1:1*

3 so that no one would be disturbed by these
afflictions; for you yourselves know that ᵃwe
have been destined for this. ᵃ*Acts 9:16; 14:22*

4 For indeed when we were with you, we
kept telling you in advance that we were going
to suffer affliction; ᵃand so it came to pass, as
you know. ᵃ*1 Thess 2:14*

5 For this reason, when I could endure *it* no
longer, I also sent to find out about your faith,
for fear that ᵃthe tempter might have tempted
you, and ᵇour labor would be in vain. ᵃ*Matt 4:3*
ᵇ*2 Cor 6:1*

6 But now that ᵃTimothy has come to us
from you, and has brought us good news of
ᵇyour faith and love, and that you always think
kindly of us, longing to see us just as we also
long to see you, ᵃ*Acts 18:5* ᵇ*1 Thess 1:3*

7 for this reason, brethren, in all our distress
and affliction we were comforted about you
through your faith;

8 for now we *really* live, if you ᵃstand firm in
the Lord. ᵃ*1 Cor 16:13*

9 For ᵃwhat thanks can we render to God for
you in return for all the joy with which we
rejoice before our God on your account,
ᵃ*1 Thess 1:2*

10 as we ᵃnight and day keep praying most
earnestly that we may see your face, and may

ᵇcomplete what is lacking in your faith?
ᵃ2 Tim 1:3 ᵇ2 Cor 13:9

11 Now may our God and Father ᵃHimself and Jesus our Lord direct our way to you;
ᵃ1 Thess 5:23; Rev 21:3

12 and may the Lord cause you to increase and ᵃabound in love for one another, and for all people, just as we also *do* for you; ᵃPhil 1:9; 1 Thess 4:1, 10

13 so that He may ᵃestablish your hearts without blame in holiness before our God and Father at the ᵇcoming of our Lord Jesus with all His saints. ᵃ1 Cor 1:8 ᵇ1 Thess 2:19

Sanctification and Love

4 Finally then, brethren, we request and exhort you in the Lord Jesus, that as you received from us *instruction* as to how you ought to ᵃwalk and ᵇplease God (just as you actually do walk), that you excel still more. ᵃEph 4:1 ᵇ2 Cor 5:9

2 For you know what commandments we gave you by *the authority of* the Lord Jesus.

3 For this is the will of God, your sanctification; *that is,* that you ᵃabstain from sexual immorality; ᵃ1 Cor 6:18

4 that ᵃeach of you know how to possess his own vessel in sanctification and honor, ᵃ1 Cor 7:2, 9

5 not in ᵃlustful passion, like the Gentiles who ᵇdo not know God; ᵃRom 1:26 ᵇGal 4:8

6 *and* that no man transgress and ᵃdefraud his brother in the matter because ᵇthe Lord is *the* avenger in all these things, just as we also told you before and solemnly warned *you.* ᵃ1 Cor 6:8 ᵇRom 12:19

7 For God has not called us for ᵃthe purpose of impurity, but in sanctification. ᵃ1 Thess 2:3

8 So, he who rejects *this* is not rejecting man but the God who ᵃgives His Holy Spirit to you. ᵃRom 5:5; 2 Cor 1:22

9 Now as to the ᵃlove of the brethren, you have no need for *anyone* to write to you, for you yourselves are ᵇtaught by God to love one another; ᵃJohn 13:34 ᵇ1 John 2:27

10 for indeed ᵃyou do practice it toward all the brethren who are in all Macedonia. But we urge you, brethren, to excel still more, ᵃ1 Thess 1:7

11 and to make it your ambition to lead a quiet life and attend to your own business and ᵃwork with your hands, just as we commanded you, ᵃActs 18:3; Eph 4:28

12 so that you will ᵃbehave properly toward outsiders and ᵇnot be in any need. ᵃRom 13:13 ᵇEph 4:28

Those Who Died in Christ

13 But we do not want you to be uninformed, brethren, about those who are asleep, so that

you will not grieve as do the rest who have ᵃno hope. ᵃEph 2:12

14 For if we believe that Jesus died and rose again, ᵃeven so God will bring with Him those who have fallen asleep in Jesus. ᵃRom 14:9; 2 Cor 4:14

15 For this we say to you by the word of the Lord, that ᵃwe who are alive and remain until ᵇthe coming of the Lord, will not precede those who have fallen asleep. ᵃ1 Cor 15:52 ᵇ1 Thess 2:19

16 For the Lord Himself will descend from heaven with a shout, with the voice of *the* archangel and with the ᵃtrumpet of God, and the dead in Christ will rise first. ᵃMatt 24:31

17 Then ᵃwe who are alive and remain will be caught up together with them in the clouds to meet the Lord in the air, and so we shall always be with the Lord. ᵃ1 Cor 15:52; 1 Thess 5:10

18 Therefore comfort one another with these words.

The Day of the Lord

5 Now as to the ᵃtimes and the epochs, brethren, you have no need of anything to be written to you. ᵃActs 1:7

2 For you yourselves know full well that ᵃthe day of the Lord will come just like a thief in the night. ᵃ1 Cor 1:8

3 While they are saying, "Peace and safety!" then ᵃdestruction will come upon them suddenly like ᵇlabor pains upon a woman with child, and they will not escape. ᵃ2 Thess 1:9 ᵇJohn 16:21

4 But you, brethren, are not in ᵃdarkness, that the day would overtake you like a thief; ᵃActs 26:18; 1 John 2:8

5 for you are all ᵃsons of light and sons of day. We are not of night nor of darkness; ᵃLuke 16:8

6 so then let us not ᵃsleep as ᵇothers do, but let us be alert and sober. ᵃRom 13:11 ᵇEph 2:3

7 For those who sleep do their sleeping at night, and those who get drunk get ᵃdrunk at night. ᵃActs 2:15; 2 Pet 2:13

8 But since we are of *the* day, let us be sober, having put on the ᵃbreastplate of faith and love, and as a ᵇhelmet, the hope of salvation. ᵃIs 59:17 ᵇEph 6:17

9 For God has not destined us for ᵃwrath, but for ᵇobtaining salvation through our Lord Jesus Christ, ᵃ1 Thess 1:10 ᵇ2 Thess 2:13f

10 ᵃwho died for us, so that whether we are awake or asleep, we will live together with Him. ᵃRom 14:9

11 Therefore encourage one another and ᵃbuild up one another, just as you also are doing. ᵃEph 4:29

Christian Conduct

12 But we request of you, brethren, that you appreciate those ᵃwho diligently labor among you, and ᵇhave charge over you in the Lord and give you instruction, ᵃRom 16:6, 12 ᵇHeb 13:17.

13 and that you esteem them very highly in love because of their work. ᵃLive in peace with one another. ᵃMark 9:50

14 We urge you, brethren, admonish ᵃthe unruly, encourage ᵇthe fainthearted, help the weak, be patient with everyone. ᵃ2 Thess 3:6, 7, 11 ᵇIs 35:4

15 See that ᵃno one repays another with evil for evil, but always seek after that which is good for one another and for all people. ᵃRom 12:17; 1 Pet 3:9

16 ᵃRejoice always; ᵃPhil 4:4

17 ᵃpray without ceasing; ᵃEph 6:18

18 in everything ᵃgive thanks; for this is God's will for you in Christ Jesus. ᵃEph 5:20

19 ᵃDo not quench the Spirit; ᵃEph 4:30

20 do not despise prophetic utterances.

21 But ᵃexamine everything *carefully;* hold fast to that which is good; ᵃ1 Cor 14:29; 1 John 4:1

22 abstain from every form of evil.

23 Now may the God of peace Himself sanctify you entirely; and may your ᵃspirit and soul and body be preserved complete, ᵇwithout blame at the coming of our Lord Jesus Christ. ᵃLuke 1:46f ᵇ2 Pet 3:14

24 ᵃFaithful is He who calls you, and He also will bring it to pass. ᵃ1 Cor 1:9; 2 Thess 3:3

25 Brethren, ᵃpray for us. ᵃEph 6:19; 2 Thess 3:1

26 ᵃGreet all the brethren with a holy kiss. ᵃRom 16:16

27 I adjure you by the Lord to ᵃhave this letter read to all the brethren. ᵃCol 4:16

28 ᵃThe grace of our Lord Jesus Christ be with you. ᵃRom 16:20; 2 Thess 3:18

The Second Letter of Paul to the
THESSALONIANS

Thanksgiving for Faith and Perseverance

1 Paul and Silvanus and Timothy,
To the ᵃchurch of the Thessalonians in God our Father and the Lord Jesus Christ: ᵃActs 17:1; 1 Thess 1:1

2 ᵃGrace to you and peace from God the Father and the Lord Jesus Christ. ᵃRom 1:7

3 We ought always ᵃto give thanks to God for you, brethren, as is *only* fitting, because your faith is greatly enlarged, and the ᵇlove of each one of you toward one another grows *ever* greater; ᵃRom 1:8 ᵇ1 Thess 3:12

4 therefore, we ourselves ᵃspeak proudly of you among ᵇthe churches of God for your perseverance and faith in the midst of all your persecutions and afflictions which you endure. ᵃ2 Cor 7:4 ᵇ1 Thess 2:14

5 *This is* a plain indication of God's righteous judgment so that you will be ᵃconsidered worthy of the kingdom of God, for which indeed you are suffering. ᵃLuke 20:35; 2 Thess 1:11

6 For after all ᵃit is *only* just for God to repay with affliction those who afflict you, ᵃEx 23:22; Col 3:25

7 and *to give* relief to you who are afflicted and to us as well ᵃwhen the Lord Jesus will be revealed from heaven with His mighty angels in flaming fire, ᵃLuke 17:30

8 dealing out retribution to those who ᵃdo not know God and to those who ᵇdo not obey the gospel of our Lord Jesus. ᵃGal 4:8 ᵇRom 2:8

9 These will pay the penalty of ᵃeternal destruction, away from the presence of the Lord and from the glory of His power, ᵃPhil 3:19; 1 Thess 5:3

10 when He comes to be ᵃglorified in His saints on that ᵇday, and to be marveled at

among all who have believed—for our testimony to you was believed. ᵃIs 49:3 ᵇIs 2:11ff

11 To this end also we ᵃpray for you always, that our God will count you worthy of your calling, and fulfill every desire for goodness and the work of faith with power, ᵃCol 1:9

12 so that the ᵃname of our Lord Jesus will be glorified in you, and you in Him, according to the grace of our God and *the* Lord Jesus Christ. ᵃIs 24:15; 66:5

Man of Lawlessness

2 Now we request you, brethren, with regard to the ᵃcoming of our Lord Jesus Christ and our ᵇgathering together to Him, ᵃ1 Thess 2:19 ᵇMark 13:27

2 that you not be quickly shaken from your composure or be disturbed either by a ᵃspirit or a ᵇmessage or a letter as if from us, to the effect that the day of the Lord has come. ᵃ1 John 4:1 ᵇ2 Thess 2:15

3 Let no one in any way deceive you, for *it will not come* unless the apostasy comes first, and the ᵃman of lawlessness is revealed, the ᵇson of destruction, ᵃDan 7:25 ᵇJohn 17:12

4 who opposes and exalts himself above every so-called god or object of worship, so that he takes his seat in the temple of God, ᵃdisplaying himself as being God. ᵃIs 14:14; Ezek 28:2

5 Do you not remember that ᵃwhile I was still with you, I was telling you these things? ᵃ1 Thess 3:4

6 And you know ᵃwhat restrains him now, so that in his time he will be revealed. ᵃ2 Thess 2:7

7 For ᵃthe mystery of lawlessness is already at work; only he who now restrains *will do so* until he is taken out of the way. ᵃRev 17:5, 7

8 Then that lawless one will be revealed whom the Lord will slay [a]with the breath of His mouth and bring to an end by the appearance of His coming; [a]Is 11:4

9 *that is,* the one whose coming is in accord with the activity of Satan, with all power and [a]signs and false wonders, [a]Matt 24:24; John 4:48

10 and with all the deception of wickedness for [a]those who perish, because they did not receive the love of [b]the truth so as to be saved. [a]1 Cor 1:18 [b]2 Thess 2:12, 13

11 For this reason [a]God will send upon them a deluding influence so that they will believe what is false, [a]1 Kin 22:22; Rom 1:28

12 in order that they all may be judged who [a]did not believe the truth, but [b]took pleasure in wickedness. [a]Rom 2:8 [b]Rom 1:32

13 But we should always give thanks to God for you, brethren beloved by the Lord, because [a]God has chosen you from the beginning for salvation [b]through sanctification by the Spirit and faith in the truth. [a]Eph 1:4ff [b]1 Thess 4:7

14 It was for this He [a]called you through our gospel, that you may gain the glory of our Lord Jesus Christ. [a]1 Thess 2:12

15 So then, brethren, stand firm and [a]hold to the traditions which you were taught, whether by word *of mouth* or by letter from us. [a]1 Cor 11:2; 2 Thess 3:6

16 [a]Now may our Lord Jesus Christ Himself and God our Father, who has loved us and given us eternal comfort and good hope by grace, [a]1 Thess 3:11

17 [a]comfort and [b]strengthen your hearts in every good work and word. [a]1 Thess 3:2 [b]2 Thess 3:3

Exhortation

3 Finally, brethren, [a]pray for us that the word of the Lord will spread rapidly and be glorified, just as *it did* also with you; [a]1 Thess 5:25

2 and that we will be [a]rescued from perverse and evil men; for not all have faith. [a]Rom 15:31

3 But [a]the Lord is faithful, and He will strengthen and protect you from the evil *one.* [a]1 Cor 1:9; 1 Thess 5:24

4 We have confidence in the Lord concerning you, that you [a]are doing and will *continue* to do what we command. [a]1 Thess 4:10

5 May the Lord [a]direct your hearts into the love of God and into the steadfastness of Christ. [a]1 Thess 3:11

6 Now we command you, brethren, in the name of our Lord Jesus Christ, that you [a]keep away from every brother who leads an unruly life and not according to the tradition which you received from us. [a]Rom 16:17; 1 Cor 5:11

7 For you yourselves know how you ought to [a]follow our example, because we did not act in an undisciplined manner among you, [a]1 Thess 1:6; 2 Thess 3:9

8 nor did we eat anyone's bread without paying for it, but with [a]labor and hardship we *kept* working night and day so that we would not be a burden to any of you; [a]1 Thess 2:9

9 not because we do not have [a]the right *to this,* but in order to offer ourselves as a model for you, so that you would follow our example. [a]1 Cor 9:4-18

10 For even when we were with you, we used to give you this order: [a]if anyone is not willing to work, then he is not to eat, either. [a]1 Thess 4:11

11 For we hear that some among you are leading an undisciplined life, doing no work at all, but acting like [a]busybodies. [a]1 Tim 5:13; 1 Pet 4:15

12 Now such persons we command and exhort in the Lord Jesus Christ to [a]work in quiet fashion and eat their own bread. [a]1 Thess 4:11

13 But as for you, brethren, [a]do not grow weary of doing good. [a]Gal 6:9

14 If anyone does not obey our instruction in this letter, take special note of that person [a]and do not associate with him, so that he will be [b]put to shame. [a]2 Thess 3:6 [b]Titus 2:8

15 *Yet* do not regard him as an enemy, but [a]admonish him as a brother. [a]1 Thess 5:14

16 Now may the Lord of peace Himself continually grant you peace in every circumstance. [a]The Lord be with you all! [a]Ruth 2:4

17 I, Paul, write this greeting [a]with my own hand, and this is a distinguishing mark in every letter; this is the way I write. [a]1 Cor 16:21

18 [a]The grace of our Lord Jesus Christ be with you all. [a]Rom 16:20; 1 Thess 5:28

The First Letter of Paul to
TIMOTHY

Misleadings in Doctrine and Living

1 Paul, an apostle of Christ Jesus [a]according to the commandment of God our Savior, and of Christ Jesus, *who is* our hope, [a]*Titus 1:3*

2 To Timothy, *my* true child in *the* faith: [a]Grace, mercy *and* peace from God the Father and Christ Jesus our Lord. [a]*Rom 1:7; 2 Tim 1:2*

3 As I urged you upon my departure for Macedonia, remain on at Ephesus so that you may instruct certain men not to [a]teach strange doctrines, [a]*Rom 16:17; 2 Cor 11:4*

4 nor to pay attention to [a]myths and endless genealogies, which give rise to mere speculation rather than *furthering* the administration of God which is by faith. [a]*1 Tim 4:7; 2 Tim 4:4*

5 But the goal of our instruction is love [a]from a pure heart and a good conscience and a sincere faith. [a]*2 Tim 2:22*

6 For some men, straying from these things, have turned aside to [a]fruitless discussion, [a]*Titus 1:10*

7 [a]wanting to be teachers of the Law, even though they do not understand either what they are saying or the matters about which they make confident assertions. [a]*James 3:1*

8 But we know that [a]the Law is good, if one uses it lawfully, [a]*Rom 7:12, 16*

9 realizing the fact that law is not made for a righteous person, but for those who are lawless and [a]rebellious, for the [b]ungodly and sinners, for the unholy and profane, for those who kill their fathers or mothers, for murderers [a]*Titus 1:6, 10* [b]*1 Pet 4:18*

10 and [a]immoral men and homosexuals and kidnappers and liars and perjurers, and whatever else is contrary to sound teaching, [a]*1 Cor 6:9*

11 according to the glorious gospel of the blessed God, with which I have been [a]entrusted. [a]*Gal 2:7*

12 I thank Christ Jesus our Lord, who has [a]strengthened me, because He considered me faithful, putting me into service, [a]*Acts 9:22; Phil 4:13*

13 even though I was formerly a blasphemer and a [a]persecutor and a violent aggressor. Yet I was shown mercy because I acted ignorantly in unbelief; [a]*Acts 8:3*

14 and the [a]grace of our Lord was more than abundant, with the faith and love which are *found* in Christ Jesus. [a]*Rom 5:20; 2 Cor 4:15*

15 [a]It is a trustworthy statement, deserving full acceptance, that Christ Jesus came into the world to save sinners, among whom I am foremost *of all.* [a]*1 Tim 3:1; 4:9*

16 Yet for this reason I found mercy, so that in me as the foremost, Jesus Christ might [a]demonstrate His perfect patience as an example for those who would believe in Him for eternal life. [a]*Eph 2:7*

17 Now to the King eternal, immortal, invisible, the [a]only God, *be* honor and glory forever and ever. Amen. [a]*John 5:44; 1 Tim 6:15*

18 This command I entrust to you, Timothy, *my* son, in accordance with the [a]prophecies previously made concerning you, that by them you [b]fight the good fight, [a]*1 Tim 4:14* [b]*2 Cor 10:4*

19 keeping [a]faith and a good conscience, which some have rejected and suffered shipwreck in regard to their faith. [a]*1 Tim 1:5*

20 Among these are Hymenaeus and [a]Alexander, whom I have [b]handed over to Satan, so that they will be taught not to blaspheme. [a]*2 Tim 4:14* [b]*1 Cor 5:5*

A Call to Prayer

2 First of all, then, I urge that [a]entreaties *and* prayers, petitions *and* thanksgivings, be made on behalf of all men, [a]*Eph 6:18*

2 [a]for kings and all who are in authority, so that we may lead a tranquil and quiet life in all godliness and dignity. [a]*Ezra 6:10; Rom 13:1*

3 This is good and acceptable in the sight of [a]God our Savior, [a]*Luke 1:47; 1 Tim 1:1*

4 [a]who desires all men to be saved and to come to the knowledge of the truth. [a]*1 Tim 4:10; Titus 2:11*

5 For there is [a]one God, *and* [b]one mediator also between God and men, *the* man Christ Jesus, [a]*Rom 3:30* [b]*Gal 3:20*

6 who gave Himself as a ransom for all, the testimony *given* at [a]the proper time. [a]*1 Tim 6:15; Titus 1:3*

7 [a]For this I was appointed a preacher and an apostle (I am telling the truth, I am not lying) as a teacher of the Gentiles in faith and truth. [a]*Eph 3:8; 1 Tim 1:11*

8 Therefore I want the men in every place to pray, [a]lifting up holy hands, without wrath and dissension. [a]*Ps 63:4; Luke 24:50*

Women Instructed

9 Likewise, *I* want [a]women to adorn themselves with proper clothing, modestly and discreetly, not with braided hair and gold or pearls or costly garments, [a]*1 Pet 3:3*

10 but rather by means of good works, as is proper for women making a claim to godliness.

11 [a]A woman must quietly receive instruction with entire submissiveness. [a]*1 Cor 14:34; Titus 2:5*

12 [a]But I do not allow a woman to teach or exercise authority over a man, but to remain quiet. [a]*1 Cor 14:34; Titus 2:5*

13 ᵃFor it was Adam who was first created, *and* then Eve. ᵃ*Gen 2:7, 22; 3:16*

14 And *it was* not Adam *who* was deceived, but ᵃthe woman being deceived, fell into transgression. ᵃ*Gen 3:6, 13; 2 Cor 11:3*

15 But *women* will be preserved through the bearing of children if they continue in ᵃfaith and love and sanctity with self-restraint. ᵃ*1 Tim 1:14*

Overseers and Deacons

3 It is a trustworthy statement: if any man aspires to the ᵃoffice of overseer, it is a fine work he desires *to do.* ᵃ*Acts 20:28; Phil 1:1*

2 ᵃAn overseer, then, must be above reproach, the husband of one wife, temperate, prudent, respectable, hospitable, able to teach, ᵃ*1 Tim 3:2-4; Titus 1:6-8*

3 not addicted to wine or pugnacious, but gentle, peaceable, ᵃfree from the love of money. ᵃ*1 Tim 3:8; 6:10*

4 *He must be* one who ᵃmanages his own household well, keeping his children under control with all dignity ᵃ*1 Tim 3:12*

5 (but if a man does not know how to manage his own household, how will he take care of ᵃthe church of God?), ᵃ*1 Cor 10:32; 1 Tim 3:15*

6 *and* not a new convert, so that he will not become ᵃconceited and fall into the condemnation incurred by the devil. ᵃ*1 Tim 6:4; 2 Tim 3:4*

7 And he must ᵃhave a good reputation with those outside *the church,* so that he will not fall into reproach and ᵇthe snare of the devil. ᵃ*2 Cor 8:21* ᵇ*2 Tim 2:26*

8 Deacons likewise *must be* men of dignity, not double-tongued, ᵃor addicted to much wine or fond of sordid gain, ᵃ*1 Tim 5:23; Titus 2:3*

9 ᵃ*but* holding to the mystery of the faith with a clear conscience. ᵃ*1 Tim 1:5, 19*

10 ᵃThese men must also first be tested; then let them serve as deacons if they are beyond reproach. ᵃ*1 Tim 5:22*

11 Women *must* likewise *be* dignified, ᵃnot malicious gossips, but temperate, faithful in all things. ᵃ*2 Tim 3:3; Titus 2:3*

12 Deacons must be ᵃhusbands of *only* one wife, *and* ᵇgood managers of *their* children and their own households. ᵃ*1 Tim 3:2* ᵇ*1 Tim 3:4*

13 For those who have served well as deacons ᵃobtain for themselves a high standing and great confidence in the faith that is in Christ Jesus. ᵃ*Matt 25:21*

14 I am writing these things to you, hoping to come to you before long;

15 but in case I am delayed, *I write* so that you will know how one ought to conduct himself in ᵃthe household of God, which is the church of the living God, the pillar and support of the truth. ᵃ*Eph 2:21f; 1 Pet 2:5*

16 By common confession, great is the mystery of godliness:

He who was ᵃrevealed in the flesh,
Was vindicated in the Spirit,
Seen by angels,
ᵇProclaimed among the nations,
Believed on in the world,
Taken up in glory. ᵃ*John 1:14* ᵇ*Rom 16:26*

Apostasy

4 But ᵃthe Spirit explicitly says that in later times some will fall away from the faith, paying attention to deceitful spirits and doctrines of demons, ᵃ*John 16:13; Acts 20:23*

2 by means of the hypocrisy of liars ᵃseared in their own conscience as with a branding iron, ᵃ*Eph 4:19*

3 *men* who forbid marriage *and advocate* abstaining from foods which ᵃGod has created to be gratefully shared in by those who believe and know the truth. ᵃ*Gen 9:3*

4 For everything created by God is good, and nothing is to be rejected if it is ᵃreceived with gratitude; ᵃ*Rom 14:6; 1 Cor 10:30f*

5 for it is sanctified by means of ᵃthe word of God and prayer. ᵃ*Gen 1:25, 31; Heb 11:3*

A Good Minister's Discipline

6 In pointing out these things to the brethren, you will be a good servant of Christ Jesus, *constantly* nourished on the words of the faith and of the sound doctrine which you ᵃhave been following. ᵃ*2 Tim 3:10*

7 But have nothing to do with worldly fables fit only for old women. On the other hand, discipline yourself for the purpose of ᵃgodliness; ᵃ*1 Tim 4:8; 6:3, 5f*

8 for ᵃbodily discipline is only of little profit, but godliness is profitable for all things, since it holds promise for the ᵇpresent life and *also* for the *life* to come. ᵃ*Col 2:23* ᵇ*Matt 6:33*

9 ᵃIt is a trustworthy statement deserving full acceptance. ᵃ*1 Tim 1:15*

10 For it is for this we labor and strive, because we have fixed ᵃour hope on the living God, who is ᵇthe Savior of all men, especially of believers. ᵃ*2 Cor 1:10* ᵇ*1 Tim 2:4*

11 ᵃPrescribe and teach these things. ᵃ*1 Tim 5:7; 6:2*

12 Let no one look down on your youthfulness, but *rather* in speech, conduct, ᵃlove, faith *and* purity, show yourself ᵇan example of those who believe. ᵃ*Titus 2:7* ᵇ*1 Tim 1:14*

13 Until I come, give attention to the *public* ᵃreading *of Scripture,* to exhortation and teaching. ᵃ*2 Tim 3:15ff*

14 Do not neglect the spiritual gift within you, which was bestowed on you through prophetic utterance with ᵃthe laying on of hands by the ᵇpresbytery. ᵃ*Acts 6:6* ᵇ*Acts 11:30*

15 Take pains with these things; be *absorbed*

in them, so that your progress will be evident to all.

16 ªPay close attention to yourself and to your teaching; persevere in these things, for as you do this you will ensure salvation both for yourself and for those who hear you. ªActs 20:28

Honor Widows

5 ªDo not sharply rebuke an older man, but *rather* appeal to *him* as a father, *to* the younger men as brothers, ªLev 19:32

2 the older women as mothers, *and* the younger women as sisters, in all purity.

3 Honor widows who are ªwidows indeed; ªActs 6:1; 9:39, 41

4 but if any widow has children or grandchildren, ªthey must first learn to practice piety in regard to their own family and to make some return to their parents; for this is ᵇacceptable in the sight of God. ªEph 6:2 ᵇ1 Tim 2:3

5 Now she who is a ªwidow indeed and who has been left alone, has fixed her hope on God and continues in entreaties and prayers night and day. ª1 Tim 5:3, 16

6 But she who ªgives herself to wanton pleasure is dead even while she lives. ªJames 5:5

7 ªPrescribe these things as well, so that they may be above reproach. ª1 Tim 4:11

8 But if anyone does not provide for his own, and especially for those of his household, he has ªdenied the faith and is worse than an unbeliever. ª2 Tim 2:12; Titus 1:16

9 A widow is to be ªput on the list only if she is not less than sixty years old, *having been* the wife of one man, ª1 Tim 5:16

10 having a reputation for ªgood works; *and* if she has brought up children, if she has ᵇshown hospitality to strangers, if she has washed the saints' feet, if she has assisted those in distress, *and* if she has devoted herself to every good work. ªActs 9:36 ᵇ1 Tim 3:2

11 But refuse *to put* younger widows *on the list,* for when they feel ªsensual desires in disregard of Christ, they want to get married, ªRev 18:7

12 *thus* incurring condemnation, because they have set aside their previous pledge.

13 At the same time they also learn *to be* idle, as they go around from house to house; and not merely idle, but also gossips and ªbusybodies, talking about ᵇthings not proper *to mention.* ª2 Thess 3:11 ᵇTitus 1:11

14 Therefore, I want younger *widows* to get ªmarried, bear children, keep house, *and* give the enemy no occasion for reproach; ª1 Cor 7:9

15 for some ªhave already turned aside to follow Satan. ª1 Tim 1:20

16 If any woman who is a believer ªhas *dependent* widows, she must assist them and

the church must not be burdened, so that it may assist those who are widows indeed. ª1 Tim 5:4

Concerning Elders

17 ªThe elders who rule well are to be considered worthy of double honor, especially those who ᵇwork hard at preaching and teaching. ªActs 11:30 ᵇ1 Thess 5:12

18 For the Scripture says, "ªYOU SHALL NOT MUZZLE THE OX WHILE HE IS THRESHING," and "The laborer is worthy of his wages." ªDeut 25:4; 1 Cor 9:9

19 Do not receive an accusation against an elder except on the basis of ªtwo or three witnesses. ªDeut 17:6; 19:15

20 Those who continue in sin, ªrebuke in the presence of all, so that the rest also will be fearful *of sinning.* ªGal 2:14; Eph 5:11

21 ªI solemnly charge you in the presence of God and of Christ Jesus and of *His* chosen angels, to maintain these *principles* without bias, doing nothing in a *spirit of* partiality. ªLuke 9:26; 1 Tim 6:13

22 ªDo not lay hands upon anyone *too* hastily and thereby share *responsibility for* the sins of others; keep yourself free from sin. ª1 Tim 3:10; 4:14

23 No longer drink water *exclusively,* but ªuse a little wine for the sake of your stomach and your frequent ailments. ª1 Tim 3:8

24 The sins of some men are quite evident, going before them to judgment; for others, their *sins* ªfollow after. ªRev 14:13

25 Likewise also, deeds that are good are quite evident, and ªthose which are otherwise cannot be concealed. ªProv 10:9

Instructions to Those Who Minister

6 ªAll who are under the yoke as slaves are to regard their own masters as worthy of all honor so that the name of God and *our* doctrine will not be spoken against. ªEph 6:5; Titus 2:9

2 Those who have believers as their masters must not be disrespectful to them because they are ªbrethren, but must serve them all the more, because those who partake of the benefit are believers and beloved. Teach and preach these *principles.* ªGal 3:28; Philem 16

3 If anyone ªadvocates a different doctrine and does not agree with sound words, those of our Lord Jesus Christ, and with the doctrine conforming to godliness, ª1 Tim 1:3

4 he is conceited *and* understands nothing; but he has a morbid interest in controversial questions and ªdisputes about words, out of which arise envy, strife, abusive language, evil suspicions, ªActs 18:15; 2 Tim 2:14

5 and constant friction between ªmen of depraved mind and deprived of the truth, who

bsuppose that godliness is a means of gain.
a2 Tim 3:8 b2 Pet 2:3

6 aBut godliness *actually* is a means of great gain when accompanied by contentment. *aLuke 12:15-21; 1 Tim 6:6-10*

7 For awe have brought nothing into the world, so we cannot take anything out of it either. *aJob 1:21; Eccl 5:15*

8 If we ahave food and covering, with these we shall be content. *aProv 30:8*

9 aBut those who want to get rich fall into temptation and a snare and many foolish and harmful desires which plunge men into ruin and destruction. *aProv 15:27; 23:4*

10 For athe love of money is a root of all sorts of evil, and some by longing for it have bwandered away from the faith and pierced themselves with many griefs. *aCol 3:5 bJames 5:19*

11 But aflee from these things, you man of God, and pursue righteousness, godliness, faith, love, perseverance *and* gentleness. *a2 Tim 2:22*

12 aFight the good fight of faith; take hold of the eternal life to which you were called, and you made the good confession in the presence of many witnesses. *a1 Tim 1:18*

13 aI charge you in the presence of God, who gives life to all things, and of Christ Jesus, who testified the bgood confession before Pontius Pilate, *a1 Tim 5:21 b2 Cor 9:13*

14 that you keep the commandment without stain or reproach until the aappearing of our Lord Jesus Christ, *a2 Thess 2:8*

15 which He will bring about at athe proper time—He who is the blessed and only Sovereign, the King of kings and Lord of lords, *a1 Tim 2:6*

16 awho alone possesses immortality and dwells in unapproachable light, whom no man has seen or can see. aTo Him *be* honor and eternal dominion! Amen. *a1 Tim 1:17*

17 Instruct those who are rich in athis present world not to be conceited or to fix their hope on the uncertainty of riches, but on God, bwho richly supplies us with all things to enjoy. *aMatt 12:32 bActs 14:17*

18 *Instruct them* to do good, to be rich in agood works, bto be generous and ready to share, *a1 Tim 5:10 bRom 12:8*

19 astoring up for themselves the treasure of a good foundation for the future, so that they may btake hold of that which is life indeed. *aMatt 6:20 b1 Tim 6:12*

20 O Timothy, guard awhat has been entrusted to you, avoiding bworldly *and* empty chatter *and* the opposing arguments of what is falsely called "knowledge"— *a2 Tim 1:12, 14 b2 Tim 2:16*

21 which some have professed and thus agone astray from the faith.

    Grace be with you.   *a2 Tim 2:18*

The Second Letter of Paul to
TIMOTHY

Timothy Charged to Guard His Trust

1 Paul, aan apostle of Christ Jesus by the will of God, according to the promise of life in Christ Jesus, *a2 Cor 1:1*

2 To Timothy, my beloved ason: Grace, mercy *and* peace from God the Father and Christ Jesus our Lord. *a1 Tim 1:2; 2 Tim 2:1*

3 aI thank God, whom I serve with a clear conscience the way my forefathers did, as I constantly remember you in my prayers night and day, *aRom 1:8*

4 alonging to see you, beven as I recall your tears, so that I may be filled with joy. *a2 Tim 4:9, 21 bActs 20:37*

5 For I am mindful of the asincere faith within you, which first dwelt in your grandmother Lois and byour mother Eunice, and I am sure that *it is* in you as well. *a1 Tim 1:5 bActs 16:1*

6 For this reason I remind you to kindle afresh athe gift of God which is in you through athe laying on of my hands. *a1 Tim 4:14*

7 For God has not given us a aspirit of timidity, but of power and love and discipline. *aJohn 14:27; Rom 8:15*

8 Therefore ado not be ashamed of the testimony of our Lord or of me His prisoner, but join with *me* in bsuffering for the gospel according to the power of God, *aMark 8:38 b2 Tim 2:3, 9*

9 who has saved us and acalled us with a holy calling, bnot according to our works, but according to His own apurpose and grace which was granted us in Christ Jesus from all eternity, *aRom 8:28ff bEph 2:9*

10 but now has been revealed by the appearing of our Savior Christ Jesus, who aabolished death and brought life and immortality to light through the gospel, *a1 Cor 15:26; Heb 2:14f*

11 afor which I was appointed a preacher and an apostle and a teacher. *a1 Tim 2:7*

12 For this reason I also suffer these things, but aI am not ashamed; for I know whom I have believed and I am convinced that He is able to guard what I have entrusted to Him until that day. *a2 Tim 1:8, 16*

13 aRetain the standard of sound words which you have heard from me, in the bfaith and love which are in Christ Jesus. *aTitus 1:9 b1 Tim 1:14*

14 Guard, through the Holy Spirit who adwells

in us, the treasure which has been entrusted to you. ªRom 8:9

15 You are aware of the fact that all who are in Asia ªturned away from me, among whom are Phygelus and Hermogenes. ªᵇ2 Tim 4:10, 16

16 The Lord grant mercy to ªthe house of Onesiphorus, for he often refreshed me and was not ashamed of my chains; ªᵇ2 Tim 4:19

17 but when he was in Rome, he eagerly searched for me and found me—

18 the Lord grant to him to find mercy from the Lord on ªthat day—and you know very well what services he rendered at Ephesus. ª1 Cor 1:8; 2 Tim 1:12

Be Strong

2 You therefore, my son, ªbe strong in the grace that is in Christ Jesus. ªEph 6:10

2 The things ªwhich you have heard from me in the presence of many witnesses, entrust these to faithful men who will be able to teach others also. ªᵇ2 Tim 1:13

3 ªSuffer hardship with *me*, as a good soldier of Christ Jesus. ªᵇ2 Tim 1:8

4 No soldier in active service ªentangles himself in the affairs of everyday life, so that he may please the one who enlisted him as a soldier. ªᵇ2 Pet 2:20

5 Also if anyone ªcompetes as an athlete, he does not win the prize unless he competes according to the rules. ª1 Cor 9:25

6 ªThe hard-working farmer ought to be the first to receive his share of the crops. ª1 Cor 9:10

7 Consider what I say, for the Lord will give you understanding in everything.

8 Remember Jesus Christ, ªrisen from the dead, descendant of David, according to my gospel, ªActs 2:24

9 for which I ªsuffer hardship even to imprisonment as a criminal; but the word of God is not imprisoned. ªᵇ2 Tim 1:8; 2:3

10 For this reason I endure all things for ªthe sake of those who are chosen, so that they also may obtain the salvation which is in Christ Jesus *and* with *it* eternal glory. ªLuke 18:7; Titus 1:1

11 It is a trustworthy statement:
For ªif we died with Him, we will also live with Him; ªRom 6:8; 1 Thess 5:10

12 If we endure, we will also reign with Him;
If we ªdeny Him, He also will deny us; ªMatt 10:33; Luke 12:9

13 If we are faithless, ªHe remains faithful, for He cannot deny Himself. ªRom 3:3; 1 Cor 1:9

An Unashamed Workman

14 Remind *them* of these things, and solemnly ªcharge *them* in the presence of God not to ᵇwrangle about words, which is useless *and*

leads to the ruin of the hearers. ª1 Tim 5:21 ᵇ1 Tim 6:4

15 Be diligent to ªpresent yourself approved to God as a workman who does not need to be ashamed, accurately handling the word of truth. ªRom 6:13

16 But avoid ªworldly *and* empty chatter, for it will lead to further ungodliness, ª1 Tim 6:20

17 and their talk will spread like gangrene. Among them are ªHymenaeus and Philetus, ª1 Tim 1:20

18 *men* who have gone astray from the truth saying that ªthe resurrection has already taken place, and they upset the faith of some. ª1 Cor 15:12

19 Nevertheless, the ªfirm foundation of God stands, having this seal, "The Lord knows those who are His," and, "Everyone who names the name of the Lord is to abstain from wickedness." ªᵇIs 28:16f; 1 Tim 3:15

20 Now in a large house there are not only gold and silver vessels, but also vessels of wood and of earthenware, and ªsome to honor and some to dishonor. ªRom 9:21

21 Therefore, if anyone cleanses himself from ªthese *things*, he will be a vessel for honor, sanctified, useful to the Master, prepared for every good work. ªᵇ2 Tim 2:16-18

22 Now flee from youthful lusts and pursue righteousness, faith, love *and* peace, with those who call on the Lord ªfrom a pure heart. ª1 Tim 1:5

23 But refuse foolish and ignorant speculations, knowing that they ªproduce quarrels. ªTitus 3:9; James 4:1

24 The Lord's bond-servant must not be quarrelsome, but be kind to all, ªable to teach, patient when wronged, ª1 Tim 3:2

25 with gentleness correcting those who are in opposition, ªif perhaps God may grant them repentance leading to ᵇthe knowledge of the truth, ªActs 8:22 ᵇ1 Tim 2:4

26 and they may come to their senses *and escape* from ªthe snare of the devil, having been held captive by him to do his will. ª1 Tim 3:7

"Difficult Times Will Come"

3 But realize this, that ªin the last days difficult times will come. ª1 Tim 4:1

2 For men will be lovers of self, ªlovers of money, ᵇboastful, arrogant, revilers, disobedient to parents, ungrateful, unholy, ªLuke 16:14 ᵇRom 1:30

3 ªunloving, irreconcilable, ᵇmalicious gossips, without self-control, brutal, haters of good, ªRom 1:31 ᵇ1 Tim 3:11

4 treacherous, reckless, ªconceited, lovers of pleasure rather than lovers of God, ª1 Tim 3:6

5 holding to a form of ªgodliness, although

they have denied its power; Avoid such men as these. ᵃ*1 Tim 4:7*

6 For among them are those who ᵃenter into households and captivate weak women weighed down with sins, led on by ᵇvarious impulses, ᵃ*Jude 4* ᵇ*Titus 3:3*

7 always learning and never able to ᵃcome to the knowledge of the truth. ᵃ*2 Tim 2:25*

8 Just as Jannes and Jambres opposed Moses, so these *men* also oppose the truth, ᵃmen of depraved mind, rejected in regard to the faith. ᵃ*1 Tim 6:5*

9 But they will not make further progress; for their ᵃfolly will be obvious to all, just as Jannes's and Jambres's folly was also. ᵃ*Luke 6:11*

10 Now you ᵃfollowed my teaching, conduct, purpose, faith, patience, ᵇlove, perseverance, ᵃ*1 Tim 4:6* ᵇ*1 Tim 6:11*

11 persecutions, *and* sufferings, such as happened to me at Antioch, at Iconium *and* at Lystra; what ᵃpersecutions I endured, and out of them all ᵇthe Lord rescued me! ᵃ*2 Cor 11:23-27* ᵇ*Rom 15:31*

12 Indeed, all who desire to live godly in Christ Jesus ᵃwill be persecuted. ᵃ*John 15:20; Acts 14:22*

13 But evil men and impostors will proceed *from bad* to worse, ᵃdeceiving and being deceived. ᵃ*Titus 3:3*

14 You, however, ᵃcontinue in the things you have learned and become convinced of, knowing from whom you have learned *them,* ᵃ*2 Tim 1:13; Titus 1:9*

15 and that from childhood you have known ᵃthe sacred writings which are able to ᵇgive you the wisdom that leads to salvation through faith which is in Christ Jesus. ᵃ*John 5:47* ᵇ*Ps 119:98f*

16 ᵃAll Scripture is inspired by God and profitable for teaching, for reproof, for correction, for training in righteousness; ᵃ*Rom 4:23f; 15:4*

17 so that the man of God may be adequate, ᵃequipped for every good work. ᵃ*2 Tim 2:21; Heb 13:21*

"Preach the Word"

4 I solemnly charge *you* in the presence of God and of Christ Jesus, who is to ᵃjudge the living and the dead, and by His appearing and His kingdom: ᵃ*Acts 10:42*

2 preach ᵃthe word; be ready in season *and* out of season; ᵇreprove, rebuke, exhort, with great patience and instruction. ᵃ*Col 4:3* ᵇ*1 Tim 5:20*

3 For ᵃthe time will come when they will not endure sound doctrine; but *wanting* to have their ears tickled, they will accumulate for themselves teachers in accordance with their own desires, ᵃ*2 Tim 3:1*

4 and ᵃwill turn away their ears from the truth

and will turn aside to myths. ᵃ*2 Thess 2:11; Titus 1:14*

5 But you, be sober in all things, endure hardship, do the work of an evangelist, fulfill your ᵃministry. ᵃ*Eph 4:12; Col 4:17*

6 For I am already being ᵃpoured out as a drink offering, and the time of ᵇmy departure has come. ᵃ*Phil 2:17* ᵇ*Phil 1:23*

7 ᵃI have fought the good fight, I have finished the course, I have kept the faith; ᵃ*1 Cor 9:25f; 1 Tim 1:18*

8 in the future there ᵃis laid up for me the crown of righteousness, which the Lord, the righteous Judge, will award to me on ᵇthat day; and not only to me, but also to all who have loved His appearing. ᵃ*Col 1:5* ᵇ*2 Tim 1:12*

Personal Concerns

9 ᵃMake every effort to come to me soon; ᵃ*2 Tim 1:4; 4:21*

10 for ᵃDemas, having loved ᵇthis present world, has deserted me and gone to Thessalonica; Crescens *has gone* to Galatia, Titus to Dalmatia. ᵃ*Col 4:14* ᵇ*1 Tim 6:17*

11 Only ᵃLuke is with me. Pick up Mark and bring him with you, for he is useful to me for service. ᵃ*Col 4:14; Philem 24*

12 But ᵃTychicus I have sent to Ephesus. ᵃ*Acts 20:4; Eph 6:21, 22*

13 When you come bring the cloak which I left at ᵃTroas with Carpus, and the books, especially the parchments. ᵃ*Acts 16:8*

14 ᵃAlexander the coppersmith did me much harm; the Lord will repay him according to his deeds. ᵃ*1 Tim 1:20*

15 Be on guard against him yourself, for he vigorously opposed our teaching.

16 At my first defense no one supported me, but all deserted me; ᵃmay it not be counted against them. ᵃ*Acts 7:60; 1 Cor 13:5*

17 But the Lord stood with me and ᵃstrengthened me, so that through me the proclamation might be ᵇfully accomplished, and that all the Gentiles might hear; and I was rescued out of the lion's mouth. ᵃ*1 Tim 1:12* ᵇ*2 Tim 4:5*

18 The Lord will rescue me from every evil deed, and will bring me safely to His ᵃheavenly kingdom; to Him *be* the glory forever and ever. Amen. ᵃ*1 Cor 15:50; 2 Tim 4:1*

19 Greet Prisca and ᵃAquila, and ᵇthe household of Onesiphorus. ᵃ*Acts 18:2* ᵇ*2 Tim 1:16*

20 ᵃErastus remained at Corinth, but ᵇTrophimus I left sick at Miletus. ᵃ*Acts 19:22* ᵇ*Acts 20:4*

21 ᵃMake every effort to come before winter. Eubulus greets you, also Pudens and Linus and Claudia and all the brethren. ᵃ*2 Tim 4:9*

22 ᵃThe Lord be with your spirit. Grace be with you. ᵃ*Phil 4:23; Philem 25*

Salutation

1 Paul, a bond-servant of God and an apostle of Jesus Christ, for the faith of those chosen of God and ªthe knowledge of the truth which is ᵇaccording to godliness, ª*1 Tim 2:4* ᵇ*1 Tim 6:3*

2 in ªthe hope of eternal life, which God, ᵇwho cannot lie, promised long ages ago, ª*2 Tim 1:1* ᵇ*Heb 6:18*

3 but ªat the proper time manifested, *even* His word, in the proclamation with which I was entrusted according to the commandment of ᵇGod our Savior, ª*1 Tim 2:6* ᵇ*Luke 1:47*

4 To Titus, ªmy true child in a ᵇcommon faith: Grace and peace from God the Father and Christ Jesus our Savior. ª*2 Tim 1:2* ᵇ*2 Pet 1:1*

Qualifications of Elders

5 For this reason I left you in Crete, that you would set in order what remains and ªappoint elders in every city as I directed you, ª*Acts 14:23*

6 *namely,* ªif any man is above reproach, the husband of one wife, having children who believe, not accused of dissipation or rebellion. ª*1 Tim 3:2-4; Titus 1:6-8*

7 For the overseer must be above reproach as ªGod's steward, not ᵇself-willed, not quick-tempered, not addicted to wine, not pugnacious, not fond of sordid gain, ª*1 Cor 4:1* ᵇ*2 Pet 2:10*

8 but ªhospitable, loving what is good, sensible, just, devout, self-controlled, ª*1 Tim 3:2*

9 ªholding fast the faithful word which is in accordance with the teaching, so that he will be able both to exhort in sound doctrine and to refute those who contradict. ª*2 Thess 2:15; 2 Tim 1:13*

10 For there are many ªrebellious men, ᵇempty talkers and deceivers, especially those of the circumcision, ª*Titus 1:6* ᵇ*1 Tim 1:6*

11 who must be silenced because they are upsetting ªwhole families, teaching ᵇthings they should not *teach* for the sake of sordid gain. ª*1 Tim 5:4* ᵇ*1 Tim 5:13*

12 One of themselves, a prophet of their own, said, "ªCretans are always liars, evil beasts, lazy gluttons." ª*Acts 2:11; 27:7*

13 This testimony is true. For this reason ªreprove them severely so that they may be sound in the faith, ª*1 Tim 5:20; 2 Tim 4:2*

14 not paying attention to Jewish ªmyths and commandments of men who turn away from the truth. ª*1 Tim 1:4*

15 To the pure, all things are pure; but ªto those who are defiled and unbelieving, nothing is pure, but both their mind and their conscience are defiled. ª*Rom 14:14, 23*

16 ªThey profess to know God, but by *their* deeds they deny *Him,* being detestable and disobedient and worthless for any good deed. ª*1 John 2:4*

Duties of the Older and Younger

2 But as for you, speak the things which are fitting for ªsound doctrine. ª*Titus 1:9*

2 Older men are to be ªtemperate, dignified, sensible, ᵇsound in faith, in love, in perseverance. ª*1 Tim 3:2* ᵇ*Titus 1:13*

3 Older women likewise are to be reverent in their behavior, ªnot malicious gossips nor ᵇenslaved to much wine, teaching what is good, ª*1 Tim 3:11* ᵇ*1 Tim 3:8*

4 so that they may encourage the young women to love their husbands, to love their children,

5 *to be* sensible, pure, ªworkers at home, kind, being ᵇsubject to their own husbands, so that the word of God will not be dishonored. ª*1 Tim 5:14* ᵇ*Eph 5:22*

6 Likewise urge ªthe young men to be sensible; ª*1 Tim 5:1*

7 in all things show yourself to be ªan example of good deeds, *with* purity in doctrine, dignified, ª*1 Tim 4:12*

8 sound *in* speech which is beyond reproach, so ªthat the opponent will be put to shame, having nothing bad to say about us. ª*2 Thess 3:14; 1 Pet 2:12*

9 *Urge* ªbondslaves to be subject to their own masters in everything, to be well-pleasing, not argumentative, ª*Eph 6:5; 1 Tim 6:1*

10 not pilfering, but showing all good faith so that they will adorn the doctrine of ªGod our Savior in every respect. ª*Titus 1:3*

11 For the grace of God has ªappeared, ᵇbringing salvation to all men, ª*2 Tim 1:10* ᵇ*1 Tim 2:4*

12 instructing us to deny ungodliness and ªworldly desires and ᵇto live sensibly, righteously and godly in the present age, ª*1 Tim 6:9* ᵇ*2 Tim 3:12*

13 looking for the blessed hope and the appearing of the glory of ªour great God and Savior, Christ Jesus, ª*Titus 1:4; 2 Pet 1:1*

14 who ªgave Himself for us ᵇto redeem us from every lawless deed, and to purify for Himself a people for His own possession, zealous for good deeds. ª*1 Tim 2:6* ᵇ*Ps 130:8*

15 These things speak and ªexhort and reprove with all authority. Let no one disregard you. ª*1 Tim 4:13; 5:20*

Godly Living

3 Remind them ªto be subject to rulers, to authorities, to be obedient, to be ᵇready for every good deed, ª*Rom 13:1* ᵇ*2 Tim 2:21*

2 to malign no one, [a]to be peaceable, gentle, showing every consideration for all men. [a]*1 Tim 3:3; 1 Pet 2:18*

3 [a]For we also once were foolish ourselves, disobedient, [b]deceived, enslaved to various lusts and pleasures, spending our life in malice and envy, hateful, hating one another. [a]*Rom 11:30* [b]*2 Tim 3:13*

4 But when the [a]kindness of God our Savior and *His* love for mankind appeared, [a]*Rom 2:4; Eph 2:7*

5 He saved us, [a]not on the basis of deeds which we have done in righteousness, but according to His mercy, by the washing of regeneration and renewing by the Holy Spirit, [a]*Eph 2:9*

6 [a]whom He poured out upon us richly through Jesus Christ our Savior, [a]*Rom 5:5*

7 so that being justified by His grace we would be made [a]heirs according to *the* hope of eternal life. [a]*Matt 25:34; Mark 10:17*

8 This is a trustworthy statement; and concerning these things I want you to speak confidently, so that those who have believed God will be careful to [a]engage in good deeds. These

things are good and profitable for men. [a]*Titus 2:7, 14; 3:14*

9 But [a]avoid [b]foolish controversies and genealogies and strife and disputes about the Law, for they are unprofitable and worthless. [a]*2 Tim 2:16* [b]*1 Tim 1:4*

10 [a]Reject a [b]factious man after a first and second warning, [a]*2 John 10* [b]*Rom 16:17*

11 knowing that such a man is [a]perverted and is sinning, being self-condemned. [a]*Titus 1:14*

Personal Concerns

12 When I send Artemas or Tychicus to you, [a]make every effort to come to me at Nicopolis, for I have decided to spend the winter there. [a]*2 Tim 4:9*

13 Diligently help Zenas the lawyer and [a]Apollos on their way so that nothing is lacking for them. [a]*Acts 18:24; 1 Cor 16:12*

14 Our people must also learn to [a]engage in good deeds to meet pressing needs, so that they will not be [b]unfruitful. [a]*Titus 3:8* [b]*Matt 7:19*

15 All who are with me greet you. Greet those who love us [a]in *the* faith.

[b]Grace be with you all. [a]*1 Tim 1:2* [b]*Col 4:18*

The Letter of Paul to
PHILEMON

Salutation

1 Paul, [a]a prisoner of Christ Jesus, and Timothy our brother,

To Philemon our beloved *brother* and fellow worker, [a]*Eph 3:1*

2 and to Apphia our sister, and to [a]Archippus our [b]fellow soldier, and to the church in your house: [a]*Col 4:17* [b]*Phil 2:25*

3 [a]Grace to you and peace from God our Father and the Lord Jesus Christ. [a]*Rom 1:7*

Philemon's Love and Faith

4 [a]I thank my God always, making mention of you in my prayers, [a]*Rom 1:8f*

5 because I [a]hear of your love and of the faith which you have toward the Lord Jesus and toward all the saints; [a]*Eph 1:15; Col 1:4*

6 *and I pray* that the fellowship of your faith may become effective through the [a]knowledge of every good thing which is in you for Christ's sake. [a]*Phil 1:9; Col 1:9*

7 For I have come to have much [a]joy and comfort in your love, because the hearts of the saints have been [b]refreshed through you, brother. [a]*2 Cor 7:4, 13* [b]*1 Cor 16:18*

8 Therefore, [a]though I have enough confidence in Christ to order you *to do* what is proper, [a]*2 Cor 3:12; 1 Thess 2:6*

9 yet for love's sake I rather appeal *to you*—since I am such a person as Paul, the

aged, and now also [b]a prisoner of Christ Jesus— [a]*Titus 2:2* [b]*Philem 1*

Plea for Onesimus, a Free Man

10 I appeal to you for my [a]child [b]Onesimus, whom I have begotten in my imprisonment, [a]*1 Cor 4:14f* [b]*Col 4:9*

11 who formerly was useless to you, but now is useful both to you and to me.

12 I have sent him back to you in person, that is, *sending* my very heart,

13 whom I wished to keep with me, so that on your behalf he might minister to me in my [a]imprisonment for the gospel; [a]*Phil 1:7; Philem 10*

14 but without your consent I did not want to do anything, so that your goodness would [a]not be, in effect, by compulsion but of your own free will. [a]*2 Cor 9:7; 1 Pet 5:2*

15 For perhaps [a]he was for this reason separated *from you* for a while, that you would have him back forever, [a]*Gen 45:5, 8*

16 no longer as a slave, but more than a slave, [a]a beloved brother, especially to me, but how much more to you, both in the flesh and in the Lord. [a]*Matt 23:8; 1 Tim 6:2*

17 If then you regard me a [a]partner, accept him as *you would* me. [a]*2 Cor 8:23*

18 But if he has wronged you in any way or owes you anything, charge that to my account;

19 [a]I, Paul, am writing this with my own hand, I will repay it (not to mention to you that you

owe to me even your own self as well).
[a]*1 Cor 16:21*
20 Yes, brother, let me benefit from you in the Lord; [a]refresh my heart in Christ.   [a]*Philem 7*
21 [a]Having confidence in your obedience, I write to you, since I know that you will do even more than what I say.   [a]*2 Cor 2:3*
22 At the same time also prepare me a lodg-

ing, for I hope that through [a]your prayers I will be given to you.   [a]*2 Cor 1:11*
23 [a]Epaphras, my fellow prisoner in Christ Jesus, greets you,   [a]*Col 1:7; 4:12*
24 *as do* [a]Mark, Aristarchus, [b]Demas, [b]Luke, my fellow workers.   [a]*Col 4:10* [b]*Col 4:14*
25 [a]The grace of the Lord Jesus Christ be with your spirit.   [a]*Gal 6:18*

The Letter to the
HEBREWS

God's Final Word in His Son

1 God, after He spoke long ago to the fathers in the prophets in many portions and [a]in many ways,   [a]*Num 12:6, 8; Joel 2:28*
2 in these last days has spoken to us in His Son, whom He appointed [a]heir of all things, through whom also He made the world.   [a]*Ps 2:8; Matt 28:18*
3 And He is the radiance of His glory and the exact [a]representation of His nature, and [b]upholds all things by the word of His power. When He had made purification of sins, He sat down at the right hand of the Majesty on high,
[a]*2 Cor 4:4* [b]*Col 1:17*
4 having become as much better than the angels, as He has inherited a more excellent [a]name than they.   [a]*Eph 1:21*
5 For to which of the angels did He ever say,
"[a]YOU ARE MY SON,
 TODAY I HAVE BEGOTTEN YOU"?
And again,
"[b]I WILL BE A FATHER TO HIM
 AND HE SHALL BE A SON TO ME"?   [a]*Ps 2:7*
 [b]*2 Sam 7:14*
6 And when He again brings the firstborn into the world, He says,
"[a]AND LET ALL THE ANGELS OF GOD WORSHIP
 HIM."   [a]*Ps 97:7*
7 And of the angels He says,
"WHO MAKES HIS ANGELS WINDS,
 AND HIS MINISTERS A FLAME OF FIRE."
8 But of the Son *He says,*
"[a]YOUR THRONE, O GOD, IS FOREVER AND
 EVER,
 AND THE RIGHTEOUS SCEPTER IS THE SCEPTER
 OF HIS KINGDOM."   [a]*Ps 45:6*
9 "[a]YOU HAVE LOVED RIGHTEOUSNESS AND HATED
 LAWLESSNESS;
 THEREFORE GOD, YOUR GOD, HAS [b]ANOINTED
 YOU
 WITH THE OIL OF GLADNESS ABOVE YOUR
 COMPANIONS."   [a]*Ps 45:7* [b]*Is 61:1, 3*
10 And,
"[a]YOU, LORD, IN THE BEGINNING LAID THE
 FOUNDATION OF THE EARTH,
 AND THE HEAVENS ARE THE WORKS OF YOUR
 HANDS;   [a]*Ps 102:25*

11 [a]THEY WILL PERISH, BUT YOU REMAIN;
 AND THEY ALL WILL BECOME OLD LIKE A GAR-
 MENT,   [a]*Ps 102:26*
12 [a]AND LIKE A MANTLE YOU WILL ROLL THEM
 UP;
 LIKE A GARMENT THEY WILL ALSO BE
 CHANGED.
 BUT YOU ARE THE SAME,
 AND YOUR YEARS WILL NOT COME TO AN
 END."   [a]*Ps 102:26, 27*
13 But to which of the angels has He ever said,
"[a]SIT AT MY RIGHT HAND,
 UNTIL I MAKE YOUR ENEMIES
 A FOOTSTOOL FOR YOUR FEET"?   [a]*Ps 110:1;
 Matt 22:44*
14 Are they not all [a]ministering spirits, sent out to render service for the sake of those who will inherit salvation?   [a]*Ps 103:20f; Dan 7:10*

Give Heed

2 For this reason we must pay much closer attention to what we have heard, so that [a]we do not drift away *from it.*   [a]*Prov 3:21*
2 For if the word spoken through [a]angels proved unalterable, and every transgression and disobedience received a just penalty,
[a]*Acts 7:53*
3 [a]how will we escape if we neglect so great a salvation? After it was at the first spoken through the Lord, it was confirmed to us by those who heard,   [a]*Heb 10:29; 12:25*
4 God also testifying with them, both by signs and wonders and by various miracles and by [a]gifts of the Holy Spirit according to His own will.   [a]*1 Cor 12:4, 11; Eph 4:7*

Earth Subject to Man

5 For He did not subject to angels [a]the world to come, concerning which we are speaking.
[a]*Matt 24:14; Heb 6:5*
6 But one has testified somewhere, saying,
"[a]WHAT IS MAN, THAT YOU REMEMBER HIM?
 OR THE SON OF MAN, THAT YOU ARE CON-
 CERNED ABOUT HIM?   [a]*Ps 8:4*
7 "[a]YOU HAVE MADE HIM FOR A LITTLE WHILE
 LOWER THAN THE ANGELS;

YOU HAVE CROWNED HIM WITH GLORY AND
HONOR,
AND HAVE APPOINTED HIM OVER THE WORKS
OF YOUR HANDS; [a]*Ps 8:5, 6*
8 YOU HAVE PUT ALL THINGS IN SUBJECTION
UNDER HIS FEET."

For in subjecting all things to him, He left
nothing that is not subject to him. But now [a]we
do not yet see all things subjected to him.
[a]*1 Cor 15:25*

Jesus Briefly Humbled

9 But we do see Him who was made for a little while lower than the angels, *namely,* Jesus,
[a]because of the suffering of death crowned
with glory and honor, so that by the grace of
God He might taste death for everyone.
[a]*Acts 3:13; 1 Pet 1:21*

10 For it was fitting for Him, [a]for whom are
all things, and through whom are all things, in
bringing many sons to glory, to [b]perfect the
author of their salvation through sufferings.
[a]*Rom 11:36* [b]*Heb 5:9*

11 For both He who [a]sanctifies and those who
are sanctified are all from one *Father;* for
which reason He is not ashamed to call them
brethren, [a]*Heb 13:12*

12 saying,
"[a]I WILL PROCLAIM YOUR NAME TO MY
BRETHREN,
IN THE MIDST OF THE CONGREGATION I WILL
SING YOUR PRAISE." [a]*Ps 22:22*

13 And again,
"[a]I WILL PUT MY TRUST IN HIM."
And again,
"[b]BEHOLD, I AND THE CHILDREN WHOM GOD
HAS GIVEN ME." [a]*Is 8:17* [b]*Is 8:18*

14 Therefore, since the children share in [a]flesh
and blood, He Himself likewise also partook of
the same, that through death He might render
powerless him who had the power of death,
that is, the devil, [a]*Matt 16:17*

15 and might free those who through [a]fear of
death were subject to slavery all their lives.
[a]*Rom 8:15*

16 For assuredly He does not give help to
angels, but He gives help to the descendant of
Abraham.

17 Therefore, He had [a]to be made like His
brethren in all things, so that He might become
a merciful and faithful high priest in things
pertaining to God, to [b]make propitiation for the
sins of the people. [a]*Phil 2:7* [b]*Dan 9:24*

18 For since He Himself was [a]tempted in that
which He has suffered, He is able to come to
the aid of those who are tempted. [a]*Heb 4:15*

Jesus Our High Priest

3 Therefore, holy brethren, partakers of a
[a]heavenly calling, consider Jesus, the

Apostle and High Priest of our confession;
[a]*Phil 3:14*

2 He was faithful to Him who appointed
Him, as [a]Moses also was in all His house.
[a]*Ex 40:16; Num 12:7*

3 [a]For He has been counted worthy of more
glory than Moses, by just so much as the
builder of the house has more honor than the
house. [a]*2 Cor 3:7-11*

4 For every house is built by someone, but
the builder of all things is God.

5 Now Moses was faithful in all His house as
[a]a servant, [b]for a testimony of those things
which were to be spoken later; [a]*Num 12:7*
[b]*Deut 18:18f*

6 but Christ *was faithful* as a Son over His
house—[a]whose house we are, if we hold fast
our confidence and the boast of our hope firm
until the end. [a]*1 Cor 3:16; 1 Tim 3:15*

7 Therefore, just as the Holy Spirit says,
"[a]TODAY IF YOU HEAR HIS VOICE, [a]*Ps 95:7;*
Heb 3:15

8 [a]DO NOT HARDEN YOUR HEARTS AS WHEN THEY
PROVOKED ME,
AS IN THE DAY OF TRIAL IN THE WILDERNESS,
[a]*Ps 95:8*

9 [a]WHERE YOUR FATHERS TRIED *Me* BY TESTING
Me,
AND SAW MY WORKS FOR [b]FORTY YEARS.
[a]*Ps 95:9-11* [b]*Acts 7:36*

10 "[a]THEREFORE I WAS ANGRY WITH THIS GENERA-
TION,
AND SAID, 'THEY ALWAYS GO ASTRAY IN
THEIR HEART,
AND THEY DID NOT KNOW MY WAYS';
[a]*Ps 95:10*

11 [a]AS I SWORE IN MY WRATH,
'THEY SHALL NOT ENTER MY REST.' "
[a]*Ps 95:11; Heb 4:3, 5*

The Peril of Unbelief

12 [a]Take care, brethren, that there not be in
any one of you an evil, unbelieving heart that
falls away from the living God. [a]*Col 2:8;*
Heb 12:25

13 But [a]encourage one another day after day,
as long as it is *still* called "Today," so that
none of you will be hardened by the [b]deceitful-
ness of sin. [a]*Heb 10:24f* [b]*Eph 4:22*

14 For we have become partakers of Christ, [a]if
we hold fast the beginning of our [b]assurance
firm until the end, [a]*Heb 3:6* [b]*Heb 11:1*

15 while it is said,
"[a]TODAY IF YOU HEAR HIS VOICE,
DO NOT HARDEN YOUR HEARTS, AS WHEN THEY
PROVOKED ME." [a]*Ps 95:7f; Heb 3:7*

16 For who [a]provoked *Him* when they had
heard? Indeed, did not all those who came out
of Egypt *led* by Moses? [a]*Jer 32:29; 44:3, 8*

17 And with whom was He angry for forty

years? Was it not with those who sinned, ªwhose bodies fell in the wilderness?
ªNum 14:29; 1 Cor 10:5

18 And to whom did He swear ªthat they would not enter His rest, but to those who were disobedient? ªNum 14:23; Deut 1:34f

19 So we see that they were not able to enter because of ªunbelief. ªJohn 3:18, 36; Rom 11:23

The Believer's Rest

4 Therefore, let us fear if, while a promise remains of entering His rest, any one of you may seem to have ªcome short of it. ª2 Cor 6:1; Gal 5:4

2 For indeed we have had good news preached to us, just as they also; but ªthe word they heard did not profit them, because it was not united by faith in those who heard. ªRom 10:17; Gal 3:2

3 For we who have believed enter that rest, just as He has said,

"ªAs I SWORE IN MY WRATH,
    THEY SHALL NOT ENTER MY REST,"

although His works were finished from the foundation of the world. ªPs 95:11; Heb 3:11

4 For He has said somewhere concerning the seventh day: "ªAND GOD RESTED ON THE SEVENTH DAY FROM ALL HIS WORKS"; ªGen 2:2

5 and again in this passage, "ªTHEY SHALL NOT ENTER MY REST." ªPs 95:11; Heb 3:11

6 Therefore, since it remains for some to enter it, and those who formerly had good news preached to them failed to enter because of ªdisobedience, ªHeb 3:18; 4:11

7 He again fixes a certain day, "Today," saying through David after so long a time just ªas has been said before,

"ᵇTODAY IF YOU HEAR HIS VOICE,
    DO NOT HARDEN YOUR HEARTS."

        ªHeb 3:7fᵇPs 95:7f

8 For ªif Joshua had given them rest, He would not have spoken of another day after that. ªJosh 22:4

9 So there remains a Sabbath rest for the people of God.

10 For the one who has entered His rest has himself also rested from his works, as ªGod did from His. ªGen 2:2; Heb 4:4

11 Therefore let us be diligent to enter that rest, so that no one will fall, through following the same ªexample of disobedience. ª2 Pet 2:6

12 For ªthe word of God is living and active and sharper than any two-edged sword, and piercing as far as the division of soul and spirit, of both joints and marrow, and able to judge the thoughts and intentions of the heart. ªJer 23:29; Eph 5:26

13 And ªthere is no creature hidden from His sight, but all things are open and laid bare to

the eyes of Him with whom we have to do. ª2 Chr 16:9; Ps 33:13-15

14 Therefore, since we have a great ªhigh priest who has ᵇpassed through the heavens, Jesus the Son of God, let us hold fast our confession. ªHeb 2:17 ᵇEph 4:10

15 For we do not have a high priest who cannot sympathize with our weaknesses, but One who has been ªtempted in all things as we are, yet ᵇwithout sin. ªHeb 2:18 ᵇ2 Cor 5:21

16 Therefore let us ªdraw near with confidence to the throne of grace, so that we may receive mercy and find grace to help in time of need. ªHeb 7:19

The Perfect High Priest

5 For every high priest ªtaken from among men is appointed on behalf of men in things pertaining to God, in order to offer both gifts and sacrifices for sins; ªEx 28:1

2 ªhe can deal gently with the ignorant and misguided, since he himself also is beset with weakness; ªHeb 2:18; 4:15

3 and because of it he is obligated to offer sacrifices for sins, ªas for the people, so also for himself. ªLev 9:7; 16:6

4 And ªno one takes the honor to himself, but receives it when he is called by God, even as Aaron was. ªNum 16:40; 18:7

5 So also Christ did not glorify Himself so as to become a high priest, but He who said to Him,

"ªYOU ARE MY SON,
    TODAY I HAVE BEGOTTEN YOU"; ªPs 2:7

6 just as He says also in another passage,
"ªYOU ARE A PRIEST FOREVER
    ACCORDING TO THE ORDER OF MELCHIZEDEK."

        ªPs 110:4; Heb 7:17

7 In the days of His flesh, ªHe offered up both prayers and supplications with loud crying and tears to the One able to save Him from death, and He was heard because of His piety. ªMatt 26:39, 42, 44; Mark 14:36, 39

8 Although He was ªa Son, He learned ᵇobedience from the things which He suffered. ªHeb 1:2 ᵇPhil 2:8

9 And having been made ªperfect, He became to all those who obey Him the source of eternal salvation, ªHeb 2:10

10 being designated by God as ªa high priest according to the order of Melchizedek. ªHeb 2:17; 5:5

11 Concerning him we have much to say, and it is hard to explain, since you have become dull of hearing.

12 For though by this time you ought to be teachers, you have need again for someone to teach you the ªelementary principles of the oracles of God, and you have come to need milk and not solid food. ªHeb 6:1

13 For everyone who partakes *only* of milk is not accustomed to the word of righteousness, for he is an [a]infant. [a]*1 Cor 3:1; 14:20*

14 But solid food is for [a]the mature, who because of practice have their senses trained to discern good and evil. [a]*1 Cor 2:6; Eph 4:13*

The Peril of Falling Away

6 Therefore [a]leaving the elementary teaching about the Christ, let us press on to maturity, not laying again a foundation of repentance from [b]dead works and of faith toward God, [a]*Phil 3:13f* [b]*Heb 9:14*

2 of [a]instruction about washings and laying on of hands, and the [b]resurrection of the dead and eternal judgment. [a]*John 3:25* [b]*Acts 17:31f*

3 And this we will do, [a]if God permits. [a]*Acts 18:21*

4 For in the case of those who have once been [a]enlightened and have tasted of the heavenly gift and have been made partakers of the Holy Spirit, [a]*2 Cor 4:4, 6; Heb 10:32*

5 and [a]have tasted the good word of God and the powers of the age to come, [a]*1 Pet 2:3*

6 and *then* have fallen away, it is [a]impossible to renew them again to repentance, since they again crucify to themselves the Son of God and put Him to open shame. [a]*Heb 10:26f; 2 Pet 2:21*

7 For ground that drinks the rain which often falls on it and brings forth vegetation useful to those [a]for whose sake it is also tilled, receives a blessing from God; [a]*2 Tim 2:6*

8 but if it yields thorns and thistles, it is worthless and [a]close to being cursed, and it ends up being burned. [a]*Gen 3:17f; Deut 29:22ff*

Better Things for You

9 But, [a]beloved, we are convinced of better things concerning you, and things that accompany salvation, though we are speaking in this way. [a]*1 Cor 10:14; 2 Cor 7:1*

10 For [a]God is not unjust so as to forget your work and the love which you have shown toward His name, in having ministered and in still ministering to the saints. [a]*Prov 19:17; Matt 10:42*

11 And we desire that each one of you show the same diligence so as to realize the [a]full assurance of [b]hope until the end, [a]*Heb 10:22* [b]*Heb 3:6*

12 so that you will not be sluggish, but [a]imitators of those who through faith and patience inherit the promises. [a]*Heb 13:7*

13 For when God made the promise to Abraham, since He could swear by no one greater, He [a]swore by Himself, [a]*Gen 22:16; Luke 1:73*

14 saying, "[a]I WILL SURELY BLESS YOU AND I WILL SURELY MULTIPLY YOU." [a]*Gen 22:17*

15 And so, [a]having patiently waited, he obtained the promise. [a]*Gen 12:4; 21:5*

16 For men swear by one greater *than themselves,* and with them [a]an oath *given* as confirmation is an end of every dispute. [a]*Ex 22:11*

17 In the same way God, desiring even more to show to [a]the heirs of the promise the unchangeableness of His purpose, interposed with an oath, [a]*Heb 11:9*

18 so that by two unchangeable things in which [a]it is impossible for God to lie, we who have taken refuge would have strong encouragement to take hold of the hope set before us. [a]*Num 23:19; Titus 1:2*

19 This hope we have as an anchor of the soul, a *hope* both sure and steadfast and one which [a]enters within the veil, [a]*Lev 16:2, 15; Heb 9:3, 7*

20 [a]where Jesus has entered as a forerunner for us, having become a high priest forever according to the order of Melchizedek. [a]*John 14:2; Heb 4:14*

Melchizedek's Priesthood Like Christ's

7 For this [a]Melchizedek, king of Salem, priest of the Most High God, who met Abraham as he was returning from the slaughter of the kings and blessed him, [a]*Gen 14:18-20; Heb 7:6*

2 to whom also Abraham apportioned a tenth part of all *the spoils,* was first of all, by the translation *of his name,* king of righteousness, and then also king of Salem, which is king of peace.

3 Without father, without mother, without genealogy, having neither beginning of days nor end of life, but made like [a]the Son of God, he remains a priest perpetually. [a]*Heb 7:28*

4 Now observe how great this man was to whom Abraham, the [a]patriarch, gave a tenth of the choicest spoils. [a]*Acts 2:29; 7:8f*

5 And those indeed of [a]the sons of Levi who receive the priest's office have commandment in the Law to collect a tenth from the people, that is, from their brethren, although these are descended from Abraham. [a]*Num 18:21, 26; 2 Chr 31:4f*

6 But the one whose genealogy is not traced from them collected a tenth from Abraham and blessed the one who [a]had the promises. [a]*Rom 4:13*

7 But without any dispute the lesser is blessed by the greater.

8 In this case mortal men receive tithes, but in that case one *receives them,* [a]of whom it is witnessed that he lives on. [a]*Heb 5:6; 6:20*

9 And, so to speak, through Abraham even Levi, who received tithes, paid tithes,

10 for he was still in the loins of his father when Melchizedek met him.

11 [a]Now if perfection was through the Levitical priesthood (for on the basis of it [b]the people received the Law), what further need

was there for another priest to arise according to the order of Melchizedek, and not be designated according to the order of Aaron? [a]*Heb 7:18f* [b]*Heb 10:1*

12 For when the priesthood is changed, of necessity there takes place a change of law also.

13 For [a]the one concerning whom these things are spoken belongs to another tribe, from which no one has officiated at the altar. [a]*Heb 7:14*

14 For it is evident that our Lord was [a]descended from Judah, a tribe with reference to which Moses spoke nothing concerning priests. [a]*Num 24:17; Is 11:1*

15 And this is clearer still, if another priest arises according to the likeness of Melchizedek,

16 who has become *such* not on the basis of a law of [a]physical requirement, but according to the power of an indestructible life. [a]*Heb 9:10*

17 For it is attested *of Him,*

"[a]YOU ARE A PRIEST FOREVER
ACCORDING TO THE ORDER OF MELCHIZEDEK."
[a]*Ps 110:4; Heb 5:6*

18 For, on the one hand, there is a setting aside of a former commandment [a]because of its weakness and uselessness [a]*Rom 8:3; Gal 3:21*

19 (for [a]the Law made nothing perfect), and on the other hand there is a bringing in of a better hope, through which we draw near to God. [a]*Acts 13:39; Rom 3:20*

20 And inasmuch as *it was* not without an oath

21 (for they indeed became priests without an oath, but He with an oath through the One who said to Him,

"[a]THE LORD HAS SWORN
AND WILL NOT CHANGE HIS MIND,
'YOU ARE A PRIEST FOREVER' "); [a]*Ps 110:4*

22 so much the more also Jesus has become the [a]guarantee of a better covenant. [a]*Ps 119:122; Is 38:14*

23 The *former* priests, on the one hand, existed in greater numbers because they were prevented by death from continuing,

24 but Jesus, on the other hand, because He continues [a]forever, holds His priesthood permanently. [a]*Is 9:7; John 12:34*

25 Therefore He is able also to save forever those who draw near to God through Him, since He always lives to [a]make intercession for them. [a]*Rom 8:34; Heb 9:24*

26 For it was fitting for us to have such a high priest, holy, [a]innocent, undefiled, separated from sinners and [b]exalted above the heavens; [a]*1 Pet 2:22* [b]*Heb 4:14*

27 who does not need daily, like those high priests, to offer up sacrifices, first for His own sins and then for the *sins* of the people, because this He did [a]once for all when He offered up Himself. [a]*Heb 9:12, 28; 10:10*

28 For the Law appoints men as high priests [a]who are weak, but the word of the oath, which came after the Law, *appoints* a Son, [b]made perfect forever. [a]*Heb 5:2* [b]*Heb 2:10*

A Better Ministry

8 Now the main point in what has been said *is this:* we have such a high priest, who has taken His seat at [a]the right hand of the throne of the Majesty in the heavens, [a]*Ps 110:1; Heb 1:3*

2 a minister in the sanctuary and in the [a]true tabernacle, which the Lord pitched, not man. [a]*Heb 9:11, 24*

3 For every [a]high priest is appointed to offer both gifts and sacrifices; so it is necessary that this *high priest* also have something to offer. [a]*Heb 2:17*

4 Now if He were on earth, He would not be a priest at all, since there are those who [a]offer the gifts according to the Law; [a]*Heb 5:1; 7:27*

5 who serve a copy and shadow of the heavenly things, just as Moses was warned *by God* when he was about to erect the tabernacle; for, "[a]SEE," He says, "THAT YOU MAKE all things ACCORDING TO THE PATTERN WHICH WAS SHOWN YOU ON THE MOUNTAIN." [a]*Ex 25:40*

6 But now He has obtained a more excellent ministry, by as much as He is also the [a]mediator of a better covenant, which has been enacted on better promises. [a]*1 Tim 2:5*

A New Covenant

7 For [a]if that first *covenant* had been faultless, there would have been no occasion sought for a second. [a]*Heb 7:11*

8 For finding fault with them, He says,

"[a]BEHOLD, DAYS ARE COMING, SAYS THE LORD,
WHEN I WILL EFFECT A NEW COVENANT
WITH THE HOUSE OF ISRAEL AND WITH THE
HOUSE OF JUDAH; [a]*Jer 31:31*
9 [a]NOT LIKE THE COVENANT WHICH I MADE WITH
THEIR FATHERS
ON THE DAY WHEN I TOOK THEM BY THE HAND
TO LEAD THEM OUT OF THE LAND OF EGYPT;
FOR THEY DID NOT CONTINUE IN MY COVE-
NANT,
AND I DID NOT CARE FOR THEM, SAYS THE
LORD. [a]*Ex 19:5; Jer 31:32*
10 "[a]FOR THIS IS THE COVENANT THAT I WILL MAKE
WITH THE HOUSE OF ISRAEL
AFTER THOSE DAYS, SAYS THE LORD:
I WILL PUT MY LAWS INTO THEIR MINDS,
AND I WILL WRITE THEM ON THEIR HEARTS.
AND I WILL BE THEIR GOD,
AND THEY SHALL BE MY PEOPLE. [a]*Jer 31:33;
Rom 11:27*
11 "[a]AND THEY SHALL NOT TEACH EVERYONE HIS
FELLOW CITIZEN,

AND EVERYONE HIS BROTHER, SAYING, 'KNOW
THE LORD,'
FOR ALL WILL KNOW ME,
FROM THE LEAST TO THE GREATEST OF THEM.
[a]*Jer 31:34*

12 "*[a]*FOR I WILL BE MERCIFUL TO THEIR INIQUITIES,
AND I WILL REMEMBER THEIR SINS NO MORE."

[a]*Is 43:25; Jer 31:34*

13 When He said, "*A new covenant,*" He has
made the first obsolete. But whatever is
becoming obsolete and growing old is ready to
disappear. [a]*Luke 22:20; 2 Cor 3:6*

The Old and the New

9 Now even the first *covenant* had [a]regula-
tions of divine worship and the earthly
sanctuary. [a]*Heb 9:10*

2 For there was [a]a tabernacle prepared, the
outer one, in which *were* the lampstand and the
table and the sacred bread; this is called the
holy place. [a]*Ex 25:8, 9; 26:1-30*

3 Behind [a]the second veil there was a tabernacle which is called the Holy of Holies,
[a]*Ex 26:31-33; 40:3*

4 having a golden [a]altar of incense and the
ark of the covenant covered on all sides with
gold, in which was a golden jar holding the
manna, and Aaron's rod which budded, and
the tables of the covenant; [a]*Ex 30:1-5; 37:25f*

5 and above it *were* the cherubim of glory
[a]overshadowing the mercy seat; but of these
things we cannot now speak in detail. [a]*Ex 25:17,
20; Lev 16:2*

6 Now when these things have been so prepared, the priests [a]are continually entering the
outer tabernacle performing the divine worship, [a]*Num 18:2-6; 28:3*

7 but into the second, only the high priest
enters once a year, [a]not without *taking* blood,
which he offers for himself and for the [b]sins of
the people committed in ignorance. [a]*Lev 16:11,
14* [b]*Num 15:25*

8 The Holy Spirit *is* signifying this, [a]that the
way into the holy place has not yet been disclosed while the outer tabernacle is still standing, [a]*John 14:6; Heb 10:20*

9 which *is* a symbol for the present time.
Accordingly [a]both gifts and sacrifices are
offered which cannot make the worshiper perfect in conscience, [a]*Heb 5:1*

10 since they *relate* only to [a]food and drink
and various washings, regulations for the body
imposed until [b]a time of reformation.
[a]*Lev 11:2ff* [b]*Heb 7:12*

11 But when Christ appeared *as* a [a]high priest
of the good things to come, *He entered* through
the greater and more perfect tabernacle, not
made with hands, that is to say, not of this creation; [a]*Heb 2:17*

12 and not through the blood of goats and

calves, but [a]through His own blood, He entered
the holy place once for all, having obtained
eternal redemption. [a]*Heb 9:14; 13:12*

13 For if [a]the blood of goats and bulls and the
ashes of a heifer sprinkling those who have
been defiled sanctify for the cleansing of the
flesh, [a]*Lev 16:15; Heb 9:19*

14 how much more will [a]the blood of Christ,
who through the eternal Spirit offered Himself
without blemish to God, cleanse your conscience from dead works to serve the living
God? [a]*Heb 9:12; 13:12*

15 For this reason He is the [a]mediator of a new
covenant, so that, since a death has taken place
for the redemption of the transgressions that
were *committed* under the first covenant, those
who have been called may receive the promise
of the eternal inheritance. [a]*1 Tim 2:5; Heb 8:6*

16 For where a covenant is, there must of
necessity be the death of the one who made it.

17 For a covenant is valid *only* when men are
dead, for it is never in force while the one who
made it lives.

18 Therefore even the first *covenant* was not
inaugurated without blood.

19 For when every commandment had been
spoken by Moses to all the people according to
the Law, [a]he took the blood of the calves and
the goats, with [b]water and scarlet wool and
hyssop, and sprinkled both the book itself and
all the people, [a]*Ex 24:6ff* [b]*Lev 14:4, 7*

20 saying, "[a]THIS IS THE BLOOD OF THE COVENANT
WHICH GOD COMMANDED YOU." [a]*Ex 24:8; Matt 26:28*

21 And in the same way he [a]sprinkled both the
tabernacle and all the vessels of the ministry
with the blood. [a]*Ex 24:6; 40:9*

22 And according to the Law, *one may*
[a]almost *say,* all things are cleansed with blood,
and without shedding of blood there is no forgiveness. [a]*Lev 5:11f*

23 Therefore it was necessary for the [a]copies
of the things in the heavens to be cleansed with
these, but [a]the heavenly things themselves with
better sacrifices than these. [a]*Heb 8:5*

24 For Christ [a]did not enter a holy place made
with hands, a *mere* copy of the true one, but
into heaven itself, now to appear in the presence of God for us; [a]*Heb 4:14; 9:12*

25 nor was it that He would offer Himself
often, as [a]the high priest enters the holy place
[a]year by year with blood that is not his own.
[a]*Heb 9:7*

26 Otherwise, He would have needed to suffer
often since the foundation of the world; but
now [a]once at the consummation of the ages He
has been manifested to put away sin by the
sacrifice of Himself. [a]*Heb 7:27; 9:12*

27 And inasmuch as [a]it is appointed for men to
die once and after this [b]*comes* judgment,
[a]*Gen 3:19* [b]*2 Cor 5:10*

28 so Christ also, having been offered once to [a]bear the sins of many, will appear a second time for salvation without *reference to* sin, to those who eagerly await Him. [a]*Is 53:12; 1 Pet 2:24*

One Sacrifice of Christ Is Sufficient

10 For the Law, since it has *only* a shadow of the good things to come *and* not the very form of things, can [a]never, by the same sacrifices which they offer continually year by year, [b]make perfect those who draw near. [a]*Rom 8:3* [b]*Heb 7:19*

2 Otherwise, would they not have ceased to be offered, because the worshipers, having once been cleansed, would no longer have had [a]consciousness of sins? [a]*1 Pet 2:19*

3 But [a]in those *sacrifices* there is a reminder of sins year by year. [a]*Heb 9:7*

4 For it is impossible for the [a]blood of bulls and goats to take away sins. [a]*Heb 9:12f*

5 Therefore, when He comes into the world, He says,

"[a]SACRIFICE AND OFFERING YOU HAVE NOT
　　DESIRED,
BUT A BODY YOU HAVE PREPARED FOR ME;
　　[a]*Ps 40:6*

6 [a]IN WHOLE BURNT OFFERINGS AND *sacrifices*
　　FOR SIN YOU HAVE TAKEN NO PLEASURE.
　　[a]*Ps 40:6*

7 "[a]THEN I SAID, 'BEHOLD, I HAVE COME
　　(IN THE SCROLL OF THE BOOK IT IS WRITTEN OF
　　　ME)
　　TO DO YOUR WILL, O GOD.' ". [a]*Ps 40:7, 8*

8 After saying above, "[a]SACRIFICES AND OFFERINGS AND WHOLE BURNT OFFERINGS AND *sacrifices* FOR SIN YOU HAVE NOT DESIRED, NOR HAVE YOU TAKEN PLEASURE *in them*" (which are offered according to the Law), [a]*Ps 40:6; Heb 10:5f*

9 then He said, "[a]BEHOLD, I HAVE COME TO DO YOUR WILL." He takes away the first in order to establish the second. [a]*Ps 40:7, 8; Heb 10:7*

10 By this will we have been [a]sanctified through [b]the offering of the body of Jesus Christ once for all. [a]*John 17:19* [b]*Eph 5:2*

11 Every priest stands daily ministering and [a]offering time after time the same sacrifices, which [b]can never take away sins; [a]*Heb 5:1* [b]*Mic 6:6-8*

12 but He, having offered one sacrifice for sins for all time, [a]SAT DOWN AT THE RIGHT HAND OF GOD, [a]*Ps 110:1; Heb 1:3*

13 waiting from that time onward [a]UNTIL HIS ENEMIES BE MADE A FOOTSTOOL FOR HIS FEET. [a]*Ps 110:1; Heb 1:13*

14 For by one offering He has [a]perfected for all time those who are sanctified. [a]*Heb 10:1*

15 And [a]the Holy Spirit also testifies to us; for after saying, [a]*Heb 3:7*

16 "[a]THIS IS THE COVENANT THAT I WILL MAKE
　　WITH THEM

AFTER THOSE DAYS, SAYS THE LORD:
I WILL PUT MY LAWS UPON THEIR HEART,
AND ON THEIR MIND I WILL WRITE THEM,"
He then says, [a]*Jer 31:33; Heb 8:10*

17 "[a]AND THEIR SINS AND THEIR LAWLESS DEEDS
I WILL REMEMBER NO MORE." [a]*Jer 31:34;*
　　Heb 8:12

18 Now where there is forgiveness of these things, there is no longer *any* offering for sin.

A New and
Living Way

19 Therefore, brethren, since we have confidence to [a]enter the holy place by the blood of Jesus, [a]*Heb 9:25*

20 by a new and living way which He inaugurated for us through [a]the veil, that is, His flesh, [a]*Heb 6:19; 9:3*

21 and since *we have* a great priest [a]over the house of God, [a]*1 Tim 3:15; Heb 3:6*

22 let us [a]draw near with a sincere heart in full assurance of faith, having our hearts sprinkled *clean* from an evil conscience and our bodies washed with pure water. [a]*Heb 7:19; 10:1*

23 Let us hold fast the [a]confession of our hope without wavering, for He who promised is faithful; [a]*Heb 3:1*

24 and let us consider how [a]to stimulate one another to love and good deeds, [a]*Heb 13:1*

25 not forsaking our own assembling together, as is the habit of some, but [a]encouraging *one another;* and all the more as you see the day drawing near. [a]*Heb 3:13*

Christ or Judgment

26 For if we go on [a]sinning willfully after receiving [b]the knowledge of the truth, there no longer remains a sacrifice for sins, [a]*Num 15:30* [b]*1 Tim 2:4*

27 but a terrifying expectation of judgment and [a]THE FURY OF A FIRE WHICH WILL CONSUME THE ADVERSARIES. [a]*Is 26:11; 2 Thess 1:7*

28 [a]Anyone who has set aside the Law of Moses dies without mercy on *the testimony of* two or three witnesses. [a]*Deut 17:2-6; 19:15*

29 How much severer punishment do you think he will deserve who has trampled under foot the Son of God, and has regarded as unclean the blood of the covenant by which he was sanctified, and has insulted the Spirit of grace? [a]*Ex 24:8; Matt 26:28*

30 For we know Him who said, "[a]VENGEANCE IS MINE, I WILL REPAY." And again, "[b]THE LORD WILL JUDGE HIS PEOPLE." [a]*Rom 12:19* [b]*Deut 32:36*

31 It is a terrifying thing to fall into the hands of the [a]living God. [a]*Matt 16:16; Heb 3:12*

32 But remember the former days, when, after being [a]enlightened, you endured a great [b]conflict of sufferings, [a]*Heb 6:4* [b]*Phil 1:30*

33 partly by being [a]made a public spectacle through reproaches and tribulations, and partly

by becoming [b]sharers with those who were so treated. [a]*1 Cor 4:9* [b]*Phil 4:14*

34 For you showed sympathy to the prisoners and accepted [a]joyfully the seizure of your property, knowing that you have for yourselves a better possession and a lasting one. [a]*Matt 5:12*

35 Therefore, do not throw away your [a]confidence, which has a great reward. [a]*Heb 10:19*

36 For you have need of [a]endurance, so that when you have done the will of God, you may [b]receive what was promised. [a]*Luke 21:19* [b]*Heb 9:15*

37 [a]FOR YET IN A VERY LITTLE WHILE,
HE WHO IS COMING WILL COME, AND WILL NOT DELAY. [a]*Hab 2:3; Heb 10:25*

38 [a]BUT MY RIGHTEOUS ONE SHALL LIVE BY FAITH;
AND IF HE SHRINKS BACK, MY SOUL HAS NO PLEASURE IN HIM. [a]*Hab 2:4; Rom 1:17*

39 But we are not of those who shrink back to destruction, but of those who have faith to the preserving of the soul.

The Triumphs of Faith

11 Now faith is the [a]assurance of *things* hoped for, the conviction of things not seen. [a]*Heb 3:14*

2 For by it the men of old [a]gained approval. [a]*Heb 11:4, 39*

3 By faith we understand that the [a]worlds were prepared by the word of God, so that what is seen was not made out of things which are visible. [a]*John 1:3; Heb 1:2*

4 By faith [a]Abel offered to God a better sacrifice than Cain, through which he obtained the testimony that he was righteous, God testifying about his gifts, and through faith, though he is dead, he still speaks. [a]*Gen 4:4; Matt 23:35*

5 By faith [a]Enoch was taken up so that he would not see death; AND HE WAS NOT FOUND BECAUSE GOD TOOK HIM UP; for he obtained the witness that before his being taken up he was pleasing to God. [a]*Gen 5:21-24*

6 And without faith it is impossible to please *Him,* for he who [a]comes to God must believe that He is and *that* He is a rewarder of those who seek Him. [a]*Heb 7:19*

7 By faith [a]Noah, being warned *by God* about things not yet seen, in reverence prepared an ark for the salvation of his household, by which he condemned the world, and became an heir of the righteousness which is according to faith. [a]*Gen 6:13-22*

8 By faith [a]Abraham, when he was called, obeyed by going out to a place which he was to receive for an inheritance; and he went out, not knowing where he was going. [a]*Gen 12:1-4; Acts 7:2-4*

9 By faith he lived as an alien in [a]the land of promise, as in a foreign *land,* dwelling in tents with Isaac and Jacob, fellow heirs of the same promise; [a]*Acts 7:5*

10 for he was looking for [a]the city which has foundations, whose architect and builder is God. [a]*Heb 12:22; 13:14*

11 By faith even [a]Sarah herself received ability to conceive, even beyond the proper time of life, since she considered Him faithful who had promised. [a]*Gen 17:19; 18:11-14*

12 Therefore there was born even of one man, and [a]him as good as dead at that, *as many descendants* [b]AS THE STARS OF HEAVEN IN NUMBER, AND INNUMERABLE AS THE SAND WHICH IS BY THE SEASHORE. [a]*Rom 4:19* [b]*Gen 22:17*

13 All these died in faith, [a]without receiving the promises, but having seen them and having welcomed them from a distance, and [b]having confessed that they were strangers and exiles on the earth. [a]*Heb 11:39* [b]*Gen 23:4*

14 For those who say such things make it clear that they are seeking a country of their own.

15 And indeed if they had been thinking of that *country* from which they went out, [a]they would have had opportunity to return. [a]*Gen 24:6-8*

16 But as it is, they desire a better *country,* that is, a [a]heavenly one. Therefore God is not ashamed to be called their God; for [b]He has prepared a city for them. [a]*2 Tim 4:18* [b]*Heb 11:10*

17 By faith [a]Abraham, when he was tested, offered up Isaac, and he who had [b]received the promises was offering up his only begotten *son;* [a]*Gen 22:1-10* [b]*Heb 11:13*

18 *it was he* to whom it was said, "[a]IN ISAAC YOUR DESCENDANTS SHALL BE CALLED." [a]*Gen 21:12; Rom 9:7*

19 He considered that [a]God is able to raise *people* even from the dead, from which he also received him back as a type. [a]*Rom 4:21*

20 By faith [a]Isaac blessed Jacob and Esau, even regarding things to come. [a]*Gen 27:27-29, 39f*

21 By faith [a]Jacob, as he was dying, blessed each of the sons of Joseph, and worshiped, *leaning* on the top of his staff. [a]*Gen 48:1, 5, 16, 20*

22 By faith [a]Joseph, when he was dying, made mention of the exodus of the sons of Israel, and gave orders concerning his bones. [a]*Gen 50:24f; Ex 13:19*

23 By faith [a]Moses, when he was born, was hidden for three months by his parents, because they saw he was a beautiful child; and they were not afraid of the [b]king's edict. [a]*Ex 2:2* [b]*Ex 1:16, 22*

24 By faith Moses, [a]when he had grown up, refused to be called the son of Pharaoh's daughter, [a]*Ex 2:10, 11ff*

25 choosing rather to [a]endure ill-treatment with the people of God than to enjoy the passing pleasures of sin, [a]*Heb 11:37*

26 ªconsidering the reproach of Christ greater riches than the treasures of Egypt; for he was looking to the reward. ª*Luke 14:33; Phil 3:7f*

27 By faith he ªleft Egypt, not ᵇfearing the wrath of the king; for he endured, as seeing Him who is unseen. ª*Ex 2:15* ᵇ*Ex 2:14*

28 By faith he ªkept the Passover and the sprinkling of the blood, so that he who destroyed the firstborn would not touch them. ª*Ex 12:21ff*

29 By faith they ªpassed through the Red Sea as though *they were passing* through dry land; and the Egyptians, when they attempted it, were drowned. ª*Ex 14:22-29*

30 By faith ªthe walls of Jericho fell down ᵇafter they had been encircled for seven days. ª*Josh 6:20* ᵇ*Josh 6:15f*

31 By faith ªRahab the harlot did not perish along with those who were disobedient, after she had welcomed the spies in peace. ª*Josh 2:9ff; 6:23*

32 And what more shall I say? For time will fail me if I tell of Gideon, ªBarak, Samson, Jephthah, of David and Samuel and the prophets, ª*Judg ch 4, 5*

33 who by faith conquered kingdoms, performed *acts of* righteousness, ªobtained promises, shut the mouths of lions, ª*2 Sam 7:11f*

34 ªquenched the power of fire, escaped the edge of the sword, from weakness were made strong, became mighty in war, put foreign armies to flight. ª*Dan 3:23ff*

35 ªWomen received *back* their dead by resurrection; and others were tortured, not accepting their release, so that they might obtain a better resurrection; ª*1 Kin 17:23; 2 Kin 4:36f*

36 and others experienced mockings and scourgings, yes, also ªchains and imprisonment. ª*Gen 39:20; 1 Kin 22:27*

37 They were ªstoned, they were sawn in two, they were tempted, they were put to death with the sword; they went about in sheepskins, in goatskins, being destitute, afflicted, ill-treated ª*1 Kin 21:13; 2 Chr 24:21*

38 (*men* of whom the world was not worthy), ªwandering in deserts and mountains and caves and holes in the ground. ª*1 Kin 18:4, 13; 19:9*

39 And all these, having gained approval through their faith, ªdid not receive what was promised, ª*Heb 10:36; 11:13*

40 because God had provided ªsomething better for us, so that ᵇapart from us they would not be made perfect. ª*Heb 11:16* ᵇ*Rev 6:11*

Jesus, the Example

12 Therefore, since we have so great a cloud of witnesses surrounding us, let us also ªlay aside every encumbrance and the sin which so easily entangles us, and let us run with endurance the race that is set before us, ª*Rom 13:12; Eph 4:22*

2 fixing our eyes on Jesus, the ªauthor and perfecter of faith, who for the joy set before Him ᵇendured the cross, despising the shame, and has sat down at the right hand of the throne of God. ª*Heb 2:10* ᵇ*Phil 2:8f*

3 For ªconsider Him who has endured such hostility by sinners against Himself, so that you will not grow weary and lose heart. ª*Rev 2:3*

A Father's Discipline

4 ªYou have not yet resisted ᵇto the point of shedding blood in your striving against sin; ª*Heb 10:32f* ᵇ*Phil 2:8*

5 and you have forgotten the exhortation which is addressed to you as sons,

"ªMY SON, DO NOT REGARD LIGHTLY THE DISCI-
    PLINE OF THE LORD,
    NOR FAINT WHEN YOU ARE REPROVED BY HIM;
      ª*Job 5:17; Prov 3:11*

6 ªFOR THOSE WHOM THE LORD LOVES HE DISCI-
    PLINES,
    AND HE SCOURGES EVERY SON WHOM HE
    RECEIVES." ª*Prov 3:12*

7 It is for discipline that you endure; ªGod deals with you as with sons; for what son is there whom *his* father does not discipline? ª*Deut 8:5; 2 Sam 7:14*

8 But if you are without discipline, ªof which all have become partakers, then you are illegitimate children and not sons. ª*1 Pet 5:9*

9 Furthermore, we had earthly fathers to discipline us, and we respected them; shall we not much rather be subject to ªthe Father of spirits, and ᵇlive? ª*Num 16:22* ᵇ*Is 38:16*

10 For they disciplined us for a short time as seemed best to them, but He *disciplines us* for *our* good, ªso that we may share His holiness. ª*2 Pet 1:4*

11 All discipline for the moment seems not to be joyful, but sorrowful; yet to those who have been trained by it, afterwards it yields the ªpeaceful fruit of righteousness. ª*Is 32:17; James 3:17f*

12 Therefore, ªstrengthen the hands that are weak and the knees that are feeble, ª*Is 35:3*

13 and ªmake straight paths for your feet, so that *the limb* which is lame may not be put out of joint, but rather be healed. ª*Prov 4:26; Gal 2:14*

14 ªPursue peace with all men, and the sanctification without which no one will see the Lord. ª*Rom 14:19*

15 See to it that no one comes short of the grace of God; that no ªroot of bitterness springing up causes trouble, and by it many be ᵇdefiled; ª*Deut 29:18* ᵇ*Titus 1:15*

16 that *there be* no immoral or ªgodless person

like Esau, ^bwho sold his own birthright for a *single* meal. ^a*1 Tim 1:9* ^b*Gen 25:33f*

17 For you know that even afterwards, ^awhen he desired to inherit the blessing, he was rejected, for he found no place for repentance, though he sought for it with tears. ^a*Gen 27:30-40*

Contrast of Sinai and Zion

18 For you have not come to ^a*a mountain* that can be touched and to a blazing fire, and to darkness and gloom and whirlwind, ^a*Ex 19:12, 16ff; Deut 4:11*

19 and to the ^ablast of a trumpet and the sound of words which *sound was such that* those who heard ^bbegged that no further word be spoken to them. ^a*Matt 24:31* ^b*Ex 20:19*

20 For they could not bear the command, "^aIF EVEN A BEAST TOUCHES THE MOUNTAIN, IT WILL BE STONED." ^a*Ex 19:12f*

21 And so terrible was the sight, *that* Moses said, "^aI AM FULL OF FEAR and trembling." ^a*Deut 9:19*

22 But ^ayou have come to Mount Zion and to ^bthe city of the living God, the heavenly Jerusalem, and to myriads of angels, ^a*Rev 14:1* ^b*Heb 11:10*

23 to the general assembly and church of the firstborn who ^aare enrolled in heaven, and to God, the Judge of all, and to the spirits of *the* righteous made perfect, ^a*Luke 10:20*

24 and to Jesus, the ^amediator of a new covenant, and to the ^bsprinkled blood, which speaks better than *the blood* of Abel. ^a*1 Tim 2:5* ^b*Heb 9:19*

The Unshaken Kingdom

25 See to it that you do not refuse Him who is speaking. For if those did not escape when they refused him who ^awarned *them* on earth, much less *will* we *escape* who turn away from Him who ^a*warns* from heaven, ^a*Ex 20:22; Heb 8:5*

26 And His voice shook the earth then, but now He has promised, saying, "^aYET ONCE MORE I WILL SHAKE NOT ONLY THE EARTH, BUT ALSO THE HEAVEN." ^a*Hag 2:6*

27 This *expression,* "Yet once more," denotes ^athe removing of those things which can be shaken, as of created things, so that those things which cannot be shaken may remain. ^a*Is 34:4*

28 Therefore, since we receive a ^akingdom which cannot be shaken, let us show gratitude, by which we may offer to God an acceptable service with reverence and awe; ^a*Dan 2:44*

29 for ^aour God is a consuming fire. ^a*Deut 4:24; Heb 10:27, 31*

The Changeless Christ

13 Let ^alove of the brethren continue. ^a*Rom 12:10; 1 Thess 4:9*

2 Do not neglect to show hospitality to strangers, for by this some have ^aentertained angels without knowing it. ^a*Gen 18:1ff; 19:1f*

3 ^aRemember the prisoners, as though in prison with them, *and* those who are ill-treated, since you yourselves also are in the body. ^a*Col 4:18*

4 Marriage *is to be held* in honor among all, and the *marriage bed is to be* undefiled; ^afor fornicators and adulterers God will judge. ^a*1 Cor 6:9; Gal 5:19, 21*

5 *Make sure that* your character is free from the love of money, being content with what you have; for He Himself has said, "^aI WILL NEVER DESERT YOU, NOR WILL I EVER FORSAKE YOU," ^a*Deut 31:6, 8; Josh 1:5*

6 so that we confidently say,

"^aTHE LORD IS MY HELPER, I WILL NOT BE AFRAID.

WHAT WILL MAN DO TO ME?" ^a*Ps 118:6*

7 Remember ^athose who led you, who spoke the word of God to you; and considering the result of their conduct, imitate their faith. ^a*Heb 13:17, 24*

8 ^aJesus Christ *is* the same yesterday and today and forever. ^a*Heb 1:12*

9 ^aDo not be carried away by varied and strange teachings; for it is good for the heart to be strengthened by grace, not by foods, ^bthrough which those who were so occupied were not benefited. ^a*Eph 4:14* ^b*Heb 9:10*

10 We have an altar ^afrom which those who serve the tabernacle have no right to eat. ^a*1 Cor 10:18*

11 For ^athe bodies of those animals whose blood is brought into the holy place by the high priest *as an offering* for sin, are burned outside the camp. ^a*Ex 29:14; Lev 4:12, 21*

12 Therefore Jesus also, that He might sanctify the people ^athrough His own blood, suffered outside the gate. ^a*Heb 9:12*

13 So, let us go out to Him outside the camp, ^abearing His reproach. ^a*Luke 9:23; Heb 11:26*

14 For here we do not have a lasting city, but we are seeking ^a*the city* which is to come. ^a*Heb 11:10, 16; 12:22*

God-pleasing Sacrifices

15 Through Him then, let us continually offer up a sacrifice of praise to God, that is, ^athe fruit of lips that give thanks to His name. ^a*Is 57:19; Hos 14:2*

16 And do not neglect doing good and ^asharing, for ^bwith such sacrifices God is pleased. ^a*Rom 12:13* ^b*Phil 4:18*

17 Obey your leaders and submit *to them,* for ^athey keep watch over your souls as those who will give an account. Let them do this with joy and not with grief, for this would be unprofitable for you. ^a*Ezek 3:17; Acts 20:28*

18 Pray for us, for we are sure that we have a ^agood conscience, desiring to conduct our-

selves honorably in all things. [a]*Acts 24:16; 1 Tim 1:5*

19 And I urge *you* all the more to do this, [a]so that I may be restored to you the sooner. [a]*Philem 22*

Benediction

20 Now [a]the God of peace, who brought up from the dead the [b]great Shepherd of the sheep through the blood of the eternal covenant, *even* Jesus our Lord, [a]*Rom 15:33* [b]*John 10:11*

21 [a]equip you in every good thing to do His will, [b]working in us that which is pleasing in His sight, through Jesus Christ, to whom *be* the glory forever and ever. Amen. [a]*1 Pet 5:10* [b]*Phil 2:13*

22 But I urge you, [a]brethren, bear with this [a]word of exhortation, for [b]I have written to you briefly. [a]*Heb 3:1* [b]*1 Pet 5:12*

23 Take notice that [a]our brother Timothy has been released, with whom, if he comes soon, I will see you. [a]*Acts 16:1; Col 1:1*

24 Greet [a]all of your leaders and all the saints. Those from Italy greet you. [a]*1 Cor 16:16; Heb 13:7, 17*

25 [a]Grace be with you all. [a]*Col 4:18*

The Letter of
JAMES

Testing Your Faith

1 [a]James, a bond-servant of God and of the Lord Jesus Christ,

To the twelve tribes who are dispersed abroad: Greetings. [a]*Acts 12:17; Jude 1*

2 [a]Consider it all joy, my brethren, when you encounter [b]various trials, [a]*Matt 5:12* [b]*1 Pet 1:6*

3 knowing that the testing of your faith produces [a]endurance. [a]*Luke 21:19*

4 And let endurance have *its* perfect result, so that you may be [a]perfect and complete, lacking in nothing. [a]*Matt 5:48; Col 4:12*

5 But if any of you [a]lacks wisdom, let him ask of God, who gives to all generously and without reproach, and [b]it will be given to him. [a]*1 Kin 3:9ff* [b]*Matt 7:7*

6 But he must [a]ask in faith without any doubting, for the one who doubts is like the surf of the sea, driven and tossed by the wind. [a]*Matt 21:21*

7 For that man ought not to expect that he will receive anything from the Lord,

8 *being* a [a]double-minded man, unstable in all his ways. [a]*James 4:8*

9 [a]But the brother of humble circumstances is to glory in his high position; [a]*Luke 14:11*

10 and the rich man *is to glory* in his humiliation, because [a]like flowering grass he will pass away. [a]*1 Cor 7:31; 1 Pet 1:24*

11 For the sun rises with [a]a scorching wind and [b]withers the grass; and its flower falls off and the beauty of its appearance is destroyed; so too the rich man in the midst of his pursuits will fade away. [a]*Matt 20:12* [b]*Is 40:7f*

12 [a]Blessed is a man who perseveres under trial; for once he has been approved, he will receive the crown of life which *the Lord* [b]has promised to those who love Him. [a]*Luke 6:22* [b]*James 2:5*

13 Let no one say when he is tempted, "[a]I am being tempted by God"; for God cannot be tempted by evil, and He Himself does not tempt anyone. [a]*Gen 22:1*

14 But each one is tempted when he is carried away and enticed by his own lust.

15 Then when lust has conceived, it gives birth to sin; and when [a]sin is accomplished, it brings forth death. [a]*Rom 5:12; 6:23*

16 [a]Do not be deceived, my beloved brethren. [a]*1 Cor 6:9*

17 Every good thing given and every perfect gift is [a]from above, coming down from the Father of lights, with whom there is no variation or shifting shadow. [a]*James 3:15, 17*

18 In the exercise of His will He [a]brought us forth by the word of truth, so that we would be a kind of [b]first fruits among His creatures. [a]*1 Pet 1:3, 23* [b]*Rev 14:4*

19 *This* you know, my beloved brethren. But everyone must be quick to hear, [a]slow to speak *and* slow to anger; [a]*Prov 10:19; 17:27*

20 for [a]the anger of man does not achieve the righteousness of God. [a]*Matt 5:22; Eph 4:26*

21 Therefore, [a]putting aside all filthiness and *all* that remains of wickedness, in humility receive the word implanted, which is able to save your souls. [a]*Eph 4:22; 1 Pet 2:1*

22 [a]But prove yourselves doers of the word, and not merely hearers who delude themselves. [a]*Matt 7:24-27; Luke 6:46-49*

23 For if anyone is a hearer of the word and not a doer, he is like a man who looks at his natural face [a]in a mirror; [a]*1 Cor 13:12*

24 for *once* he has looked at himself and gone away, he has immediately forgotten what kind of person he was.

25 But one who looks intently at the perfect law, the *law* of liberty, and abides by it, not having become a forgetful hearer but an effectual doer, this man will be [a]blessed in what he does. [a]*John 13:17*

26 If anyone thinks himself to be religious, and yet does not [a]bridle his tongue but deceives

his *own* heart, this man's religion is worthless. [a]Ps 39:1; 141:3

27 Pure and undefiled religion in the sight of *our* God and Father is this: to visit orphans and widows in their distress, *and* to keep oneself unstained by [a]the world. [a]2 Pet 1:4; 1 John 2:15-17

The Sin of Partiality

2 My brethren, do not hold your faith in our glorious Lord Jesus Christ with *an attitude of* [a]personal favoritism. [a]Acts 10:34; James 2:9

2 For if a man comes into your assembly with a gold ring and dressed in fine clothes, and there also comes in a poor man in [a]dirty clothes, [a]Zech 3:3f

3 and you pay special attention to the one who is wearing the [a]fine clothes, and say, "You sit here in a good place," and you say to the poor man, "You stand over there, or sit down by my footstool," [a]Luke 23:11

4 have you not made distinctions among yourselves, and become judges [a]with evil motives? [a]Luke 18:6; John 7:24

5 Listen, my beloved brethren: did not [a]God choose the poor of this world *to be* rich in faith and [b]heirs of the kingdom which He promised to those who love Him? [a]Job 34:19 [b]Matt 5:3

6 But you have dishonored the poor man. Is it not the rich who oppress you and personally [a]drag you into court? [a]Acts 8:3; 16:19

7 [a]Do they not blaspheme the fair name by which you have been called? [a]Acts 11:26; 1 Pet 4:16

8 If, however, you are fulfilling the royal law according to the Scripture, "[a]YOU SHALL LOVE YOUR NEIGHBOR AS YOURSELF," you are doing well. [a]Lev 19:18

9 But if you [a]show partiality, you are committing sin *and* are convicted by the law as transgressors. [a]Acts 10:34; James 2:1

10 For whoever keeps the whole law and yet [a]stumbles in one *point*, he has become guilty of all. [a]James 3:2; 2 Pet 1:10

11 For He who said, "[a]DO NOT COMMIT ADULTERY," also said, "[b]DO NOT COMMIT MURDER." Now if you do not commit adultery, but do commit murder, you have become a transgressor of the law. [a]Ex 20:14 [b]Deut 5:17

12 So speak and so act as those who are to be judged by [a]*the* law of liberty. [a]James 1:25

13 For [a]judgment *will be* merciless to one who has shown no mercy; mercy triumphs over judgment. [a]Prov 21:13; Matt 5:7

Faith and Works

14 [a]What use is it, my brethren, if someone says he has faith but he has no works? Can that faith save him? [a]James 1:22ff

15 [a]If a brother or sister is without clothing and in need of daily food, [a]Matt 25:35f; Luke 3:11

16 and one of you says to them, "[a]Go in peace, be warmed and be filled," and yet you do not give them what is necessary for *their* body, what use is that? [a]1 John 3:17f

17 Even so [a]faith, if it has no works, is dead, *being* by itself. [a]Gal 5:6; James 2:20, 26

18 But someone may *well* say, "You have faith and I have works; show me your [a]faith without the works, and I will show you my faith by my works." [a]Rom 3:28; Heb 11:33

19 You believe that God is one. You do well; [a]the demons also believe, and shudder. [a]Matt 8:29; Mark 1:24

20 But are you willing to recognize, you foolish fellow, that [a]faith without works is useless? [a]Gal 5:6; James 2:17, 26

21 [a]Was not Abraham our father justified by works when he offered up Isaac his son on the altar? [a]Gen 22:9, 10, 12, 16-18

22 You see that [a]faith was working with his works, and as a result of the [b]works, faith was perfected; [a]Heb 11:17 [b]1 Thess 1:3

23 and the Scripture was fulfilled which says, "[a]AND ABRAHAM BELIEVED GOD, AND IT WAS RECKONED TO HIM AS RIGHTEOUSNESS," and he was called the friend of God. [a]Gen 15:6; Rom 4:3

24 You see that a man is justified by works and not by faith alone.

25 In the same way, was not [a]Rahab the harlot also justified by works [b]when she received the messengers and sent them out by another way? [a]Heb 11:31 [b]Josh 2:4, 6, 15

26 For just as the body without *the* spirit is dead, so also [a]faith without works is dead. [a]Gal 5:6; James 2:17, 20

The Tongue Is a Fire

3 [a]Let not many *of you* become teachers, my brethren, knowing that as such we will incur a stricter judgment. [a]Rom 2:20f; 1 Tim 1:7

2 For we all stumble in many *ways*. [a]If anyone does not stumble in what he says, he is a perfect man, able to bridle the whole body as well. [a]Matt 12:34-37; James 3:2-12

3 Now [a]if we put the bits into the horses' mouths so that they will obey us, we direct their entire body as well. [a]Ps 32:9

4 Look at the ships also, though they are so great and are driven by strong winds, are still directed by a very small rudder wherever the inclination of the pilot desires.

5 So also the tongue is a small part of the body, and *yet* it [a]boasts of great things. [b]See how great a forest is set aflame by such a small fire! [a]Ps 12:3f [b]Prov 26:20f

6 And [a]the tongue is a fire, the *very* world of iniquity; the tongue is set among our members as that which defiles the entire body, and sets on fire the course of *our* life, and is set on fire by hell. [a]Ps 120:2, 3; Prov 16:27

7 For every species of beasts and birds, of

reptiles and creatures of the sea, is tamed and has been tamed by the human race.

8 But no one can tame the tongue; *it is* a restless evil *and* full of ᵃdeadly poison. ᵃ*Ps 140:3; Eccl 10:11*

9 With it we bless *our* Lord and Father, and with it we curse men, ᵃwho have been made in the likeness of God; ᵃ*Gen 1:26; 1 Cor 11:7*

10 from the same mouth come *both* blessing and cursing. My brethren, these things ought not to be this way.

11 Does a fountain send out from the same opening *both* fresh and bitter *water?*

12 ᵃCan a fig tree, my brethren, produce olives, or a vine produce figs? Nor *can* salt water produce fresh. ᵃ*Matt 7:16*

Wisdom from Above

13 Who among you is wise and understanding? Let him show by his ᵃgood behavior his deeds in the gentleness of wisdom. ᵃ*1 Pet 2:12*

14 But if you have bitter ᵃjealousy and selfish ambition in your heart, do not be arrogant and *so* lie against the truth. ᵃ*Rom 2:8; 2 Cor 12:20*

15 This wisdom is not that which comes down ᵃfrom above, but is earthly, natural, demonic. ᵃ*James 1:17*

16 For where ᵃjealousy and selfish ambition exist, there is disorder and every evil thing. ᵃ*Rom 2:8; 2 Cor 12:20*

17 But the wisdom from above is first pure, then peaceable, gentle, reasonable, full of mercy and good fruits, unwavering, without ᵃhypocrisy. ᵃ*Rom 12:9; 2 Cor 6:6*

18 And the ᵃseed whose fruit is righteousness is sown in peace by those who make peace. ᵃ*Prov 11:18; Is 32:17*

Things to Avoid

4 What is the source of quarrels and ᵃconflicts among you? Is not the source your pleasures that wage ᵇwar in your members? ᵃ*Titus 3:9* ᵇ*Rom 7:23*

2 You lust and do not have; *so* you ᵃcommit murder. You are envious and cannot obtain; *so* you fight and quarrel. You do not have because you do not ask. ᵃ*James 5:6; 1 John 3:15*

3 You ask and ᵃdo not receive, because you ask with wrong motives, so that you may spend *it* on your pleasures. ᵃ*1 John 3:22; 5:14*

4 You adulteresses, do you not know that friendship with the world is ᵃhostility toward God? ᵇTherefore whoever wishes to be a friend of the world makes himself an enemy of God. ᵃ*Rom 8:7* ᵇ*Matt 6:24*

5 Or do you think that the Scripture speaks to no purpose: "He jealously desires ᵃthe Spirit which He has made to dwell in us"? ᵃ*1 Cor 6:19; 2 Cor 6:16*

6 But He gives a greater grace. Therefore *it* says, "ᵃGOD IS OPPOSED TO THE PROUD, BUT GIVES GRACE TO THE HUMBLE." ᵃ*Prov 3:34; 1 Pet 5:5*

7 ᵃSubmit therefore to God. Resist the devil and he will flee from you. ᵃ*1 Pet 5:6*

8 ᵃDraw near to God and He will draw near to you. ᵇCleanse your hands, you sinners; and purify your hearts, you double-minded. ᵃ*2 Chr 15:2* ᵇ*Job 17:9*

9 ᵃBe miserable and mourn and weep; let your laughter be turned into mourning and your joy to gloom. ᵃ*Prov 14:13; Luke 6:25*

10 ᵃHumble yourselves in the presence of the Lord, and He will exalt you. ᵃ*Job 5:11; Luke 1:52*

11 ᵃDo not speak against one another, brethren. He who speaks against a brother or judges his brother, speaks against the law and judges the law; but if you judge the law, you are not a doer of the law but a judge *of it.* ᵃ*2 Cor 12:20; James 5:9*

12 There is *only* one ᵃLawgiver and Judge, the One who is able to save and to destroy; but who are you who judge your neighbor? ᵃ*Is 33:22; James 5:9*

13 Come now, you who say, "ᵃToday or tomorrow we will go to such and such a city, and spend a year there and engage in business and make a profit." ᵃ*Prov 27:1; Luke 12:18-20*

14 Yet you do not know what your life will be like tomorrow. ᵃYou are *just* a vapor that appears for a little while and then vanishes away. ᵃ*Job 7:7; Ps 39:5*

15 Instead, *you* ought to say, "ᵃIf the Lord wills, we will live and also do this or that." ᵃ*Acts 18:21*

16 But as it is, you boast in your arrogance; ᵃall such boasting is evil. ᵃ*1 Cor 5:6*

17 Therefore, ᵃto one who knows *the* right thing to do and does not do it, to him it is sin. ᵃ*Luke 12:47; John 9:41*

Misuse of Riches

5 Come now, ᵃyou rich, weep and howl for your miseries which are coming upon you. ᵃ*Luke 6:24; 1 Tim 6:9*

2 ᵃYour riches have rotted and your garments have become moth-eaten. ᵃ*Is 50:9; Matt 6:19f*

3 Your gold and your silver have rusted; and their rust will be a witness against you and will consume your flesh like fire. It is ᵃin the last days that you have stored up your treasure! ᵃ*James 5:7, 8*

4 Behold, ᵃthe pay of the laborers who mowed your fields, *and* which has been withheld by you, cries out *against you;* and ᵇthe outcry of those who did the harvesting has reached the ears of the Lord of Sabaoth. ᵃ*Lev 19:13* ᵇ*Ex 2:23*

5 You have ᵃlived luxuriously on the earth and led a life of wanton pleasure; you have fattened your hearts in a day of slaughter. ᵃ*Ezek 16:49; Luke 16:19*

6 You have condemned and ªput to death the righteous *man;* he does not resist you. ªJames 4:2

Exhortation

7 Therefore be patient, brethren, ªuntil the coming of the Lord. ᵇThe farmer waits for the precious produce of the soil, being patient about it, until it gets the early and late rains. ªJohn 21:22 ᵇGal 6:9

8 ªYou too be patient; ᵇstrengthen your hearts, for the coming of the Lord is near. ªLuke 21:19 ᵇ1 Thess 3:13

9 Do not complain, brethren, against one another, so that you yourselves may not be judged; behold, ªthe Judge is standing ᵇright at the door. ª1 Cor 4:5 ᵇMatt 24:33

10 As an example, brethren, of suffering and patience, take ªthe prophets who spoke in the name of the Lord. ªMatt 5:12

11 We count those ªblessed who endured. You have heard of the endurance of Job and have seen the outcome of the Lord's dealings, that ᵇthe Lord is full of compassion and *is* merciful. ªMatt 5:10 ᵇEx 34:6

12 But above all, my brethren, ªdo not swear, either by heaven or by earth or with any other oath; but your yes is to be yes, and your no, no, so that you may not fall under judgment. ªMatt 5:34-37

13 Is anyone among you suffering? ªThen he must pray. Is anyone cheerful? He is to sing praises. ªPs 50:15

14 Is anyone among you sick? *Then* he must call for the elders of the church and they are to pray over him, ªanointing him with oil in the name of the Lord; ªMark 6:13

15 and the ªprayer offered in faith will restore the one who is sick, and the Lord will ᵇraise him up, and if he has committed sins, they will be forgiven him. ªJames 1:6 ᵇJohn 6:39

16 Therefore, ªconfess your sins to one another, and pray for one another so that you may be ᵇhealed. The effective prayer of a righteous man can accomplish much. ªMatt 3:6 ᵇHeb 12:13

17 Elijah was ªa man with a nature like ours, and ᵇhe prayed earnestly that it would not rain, and it did not rain on the earth for three years and six months. ªActs 14:15 ᵇ1 Kin 17:1

18 Then he ªprayed again, and ᵇthe sky poured rain and the earth produced its fruit. ª1 Kin 18:42 ᵇ1 Kin 18:45

19 My brethren, ªif any among you strays from the truth and one turns him back, ªMatt 18:15; Gal 6:1

20 let him know that he who turns a sinner from the error of his way will ªsave his soul from death and will cover a multitude of sins. ªRom 11:14; 1 Cor 1:21

The First Letter of
PETER

A Living Hope, and a
Sure Salvation

1 Peter, an apostle of Jesus Christ,
To those who reside as ªaliens, scattered throughout Pontus, Galatia, Cappadocia, Asia, and Bithynia, ᵇwho are chosen ª1 Pet 2:11 ᵇMatt 24:22

2 according to the ªforeknowledge of God the Father, ᵇby the sanctifying work of the Spirit, to obey Jesus Christ and be sprinkled with His blood: May grace and peace be yours in the fullest measure. ªRom 8:29 ᵇ2 Thess 2:13

3 Blessed be the God and Father of our Lord Jesus Christ, who ªaccording to His great mercy has caused us to be born again to a living hope through the ᵇresurrection of Jesus Christ from the dead, ªTitus 3:5 ᵇ1 Cor 15:20

4 to *obtain* an ªinheritance *which is* imperishable and undefiled and will not fade away, reserved in heaven for you, ªActs 20:32; Rom 8:17

5 who are ªprotected by the power of God ᵇthrough faith for a salvation ready to be revealed in the last time. ªJohn 10:28 ᵇEph 2:8

6 ªIn this you greatly rejoice, even though now ᵇfor a little while, if necessary, you have been distressed by various trials, ªRom 5:2 ᵇ1 Pet 5:10

7 so that the proof of your faith, *being* more precious than gold which is perishable, even though tested by fire, ªmay be found to result in praise and glory and honor at the revelation of Jesus Christ; ªRom 2:7

8 and ªthough you have not seen Him, you ᵇlove Him, and though you do not see Him now, but believe in Him, you greatly rejoice with joy inexpressible and full of glory, ªJohn 20:29 ᵇEph 3:19

9 obtaining as ªthe outcome of your faith the salvation of your souls. ªRom 6:22

10 ªAs to this salvation, the prophets who prophesied of the grace that *would come* to you made careful searches and inquiries, ªMatt 13:17; Luke 10:24

11 seeking to know what person or time ªthe Spirit of Christ within them was indicating as He predicted the sufferings of Christ and the glories to follow. ª2 Pet 1:21

12 It was revealed to them that they were not serving themselves, but you, in these things which now have been announced to you

through those who preached the gospel to you by ªthe Holy Spirit sent from heaven—things into which angels long to look. ªActs 2:2-4

13 Therefore, ªprepare your minds for action, ᵇkeep sober *in spirit,* fix your hope completely on the grace to be brought to you at the revelation of Jesus Christ. ªEph 6:14 ᵇ1 Thess 5:6, 8

14 As obedient children, do not ªbe conformed to the former lusts *which were yours* in your ignorance, ªRom 12:2; 1 Pet 4:2f

15 but like the Holy One who called you, ªbe holy yourselves also ᵇin all *your* behavior; ª2 Cor 7:1 ᵇJames 3:13

16 because it is written, "ªYOU SHALL BE HOLY, FOR I AM HOLY." ªLev 11:44f; 19:2

17 If you ªaddress as Father the One who impartially judges according to each one's work, conduct yourselves in fear during the time of your stay *on earth;* ªPs 89:26; Jer 3:19

18 knowing that you were not ªredeemed with perishable things like silver or gold from your ᵇfutile way of life inherited from your forefathers, ªIs 52:3 ᵇEph 4:17

19 but with precious ªblood, as of a lamb unblemished and spotless, *the blood* of Christ. ªActs 20:28; 1 Pet 1:2

20 For He was ªforeknown before the foundation of the world, but has appeared in these last times for the sake of you ªActs 2:23; Eph 1:4

21 who through Him are ªbelievers in God, who raised Him from the dead and gave Him glory, so that your faith and hope are in God. ªRom 4:24; 10:9

22 Since you have in obedience to the truth ªpurified your souls for a sincere love of the brethren, fervently love one another from the heart, ªJames 4:8

23 for you have been ªborn again not of seed which is perishable but imperishable, *that is,* through the living and enduring ᵇword of God. ªJohn 3:3 ᵇHeb 4:12

24 For,

"ªALL FLESH IS LIKE GRASS,
    AND ALL ITS GLORY LIKE THE FLOWER OF
        GRASS.
    THE GRASS WITHERS,
    AND THE FLOWER FALLS OFF,
        ªIs 40:6ff; James 1:10f

25 ªBUT THE WORD OF THE LORD ENDURES FOREVER."

And this is the word which was preached to you. ªIs 40:8

As Newborn Babes

2 Therefore, ªputting aside all malice and all deceit and hypocrisy and envy and all slander, ªEph 4:22, 25, 31; James 1:21

2 ªlike newborn babies, long for the pure milk of the word, so that by it you may grow in respect to salvation, ªMatt 18:3; 19:14

3 if you have ªtasted ᵇthe kindness of the Lord. ªHeb 6:5 ᵇPs 34:8

As Living Stones

4 And coming to Him as to a living stone which has been ªrejected by men, but is choice and precious in the sight of God, ª1 Pet 2:7

5 you also, as living stones, are being built up as a spiritual house for a holy ªpriesthood, to ᵇoffer up spiritual sacrifices acceptable to God through Jesus Christ. ªIs 61:6 ᵇRom 15:16

6 For *this* is contained in Scripture:

"ªBEHOLD, I LAY IN ZION A CHOICE STONE, A
    PRECIOUS CORNER *stone,*
    AND HE WHO BELIEVES IN HIM WILL NOT BE
        DISAPPOINTED." ªIs 28:16; Rom 9:32, 33

7 This precious value, then, is for you who believe; but for those who disbelieve,

"ªTHE STONE WHICH THE BUILDERS REJECTED,
    THIS BECAME THE VERY CORNER *stone,*"
        ªPs 118:22; Matt 21:42

8 and,

"ªA STONE OF STUMBLING AND A ROCK OF
    OFFENSE";

for they stumble because they are disobedient to the word, and to this *doom* they were also appointed. ªIs 8:14

9 But you are A CHOSEN RACE, A royal PRIESTHOOD, A ªHOLY NATION, A PEOPLE FOR *God's* OWN POSSESSION, so that you may proclaim the excellencies of Him who has called you out of darkness into His marvelous light; ªEx 19:6; Deut 7:6

10 ªfor you once were NOT A PEOPLE, but now you are THE PEOPLE OF GOD; you had NOT RECEIVED MERCY, but now you have RECEIVED MERCY. ªHos 1:10; Rom 9:25

11 Beloved, I urge you as ªaliens and strangers to abstain from fleshly lusts which wage ᵇwar against the soul. ªLev 25:23 ᵇJames 4:1

12 Keep your behavior excellent among the Gentiles, so that in the thing in which they slander you as evildoers, they may because of your good deeds, as they observe *them,* glorify God ªin the day of visitation. ªIs 10:3; Luke 19:44

Honor Authority

13 ªSubmit yourselves for the Lord's sake to every human institution, whether to a king as the one in authority, ªRom 13:1

14 or to governors as sent by him ªfor the punishment of evildoers and the ᵇpraise of those who do right. ªRom 13:4 ᵇRom 13:3

15 For ªsuch is the will of God that by doing right you may silence the ignorance of foolish men. ª1 Pet 3:17

16 ªAct as ªfree men, and do not use your freedom as a covering for evil, but *use it* as ᵇbondslaves of God. ªJohn 8:32 ᵇRom 6:22

17 ªHonor all people, love the brotherhood, ᵇfear God, honor the king. ªRom 12:10 ᵇProv 24:21

18 ᵃServants, be submissive to your masters with all respect, not only to those who are good and gentle, but also to those who are unreasonable. ᵃEph 6:5

19 For this *finds* favor, if for the sake of ᵃconscience toward God a person bears up under sorrows when suffering unjustly. ᵃRom 13:5; 1 Pet 3:14, 16f

20 For what credit is there if, when you sin and are harshly treated, you endure it with patience? But if ᵃwhen you do what is right and suffer *for it* you patiently endure it, this *finds* favor with God. ᵃ1 Pet 3:17

Christ Is Our Example

21 For you have been called for this purpose, ᵃsince Christ also suffered for you, leaving you an example for you to follow in His steps, ᵃ1 Pet 3:18; 4:1, 13

22 WHO ᵃCOMMITTED NO SIN, NOR WAS ANY DECEIT FOUND IN HIS MOUTH; ᵃIs 53:9; 2 Cor 5:21

23 and while being ᵃreviled, He did not revile in return; while suffering, He uttered no threats, but kept entrusting *Himself* to Him who judges righteously; ᵃIs 53:7; Heb 12:3

24 and He Himself ᵃbore our sins in His body on the cross, so that we might die to sin and live to righteousness; for ᵇby His wounds you were healed. ᵃIs 53:4, 11 ᵇIs 53:5

25 For you were ᵃcontinually straying like sheep, but now you have returned to the ᵇShepherd and Guardian of your souls. ᵃIs 53:6 ᵇJohn 10:11

Godly Living

3 In the same way, you wives, ᵃbe submissive to your own husbands so that even if any *of them* are disobedient to the word, they may be won without a word by the behavior of their wives. ᵃEph 5:22; Col 3:18

2 as they observe your chaste and respectful behavior.

3 ᵃYour adornment must not be *merely* external—braiding the hair, and wearing gold jewelry, or putting on dresses; ᵃIs 3:18ff; 1 Tim 2:9

4 but *let it be* ᵃthe hidden person of the heart, with the imperishable quality of a gentle and quiet spirit, which is precious in the sight of God. ᵃRom 7:22

5 For in this way in former times the holy women also, ᵃwho hoped in God, used to adorn themselves, being submissive to their own husbands; ᵃ1 Tim 5:5; 1 Pet 1:3

6 just as Sarah obeyed Abraham, ᵃcalling him lord, and you have become her children if you do what is right ᵇwithout being frightened by any fear. ᵃGen 18:12 ᵇ1 Pet 3:14

7 ᵃYou husbands in the same way, live with *your wives* in an understanding way, as with someone weaker, since she is a woman; and show her honor as a fellow heir of the grace of life, so that your prayers will not be hindered. ᵃEph 5:25; Col 3:19

8 To sum up, ᵃall of you be harmonious, sympathetic, brotherly, ᵇkindhearted, and humble in spirit; ᵃRom 12:16 ᵇEph 4:32

9 not returning evil for evil or insult for insult, but giving a ᵃblessing instead; for you were called for the very purpose that you might inherit a blessing. ᵃLuke 6:28; Rom 12:14

10 For,

"ᵃTHE ONE WHO DESIRES LIFE, TO LOVE AND SEE GOOD DAYS,
MUST KEEP HIS TONGUE FROM EVIL AND HIS LIPS FROM SPEAKING DECEIT. ᵃPs 34:12, 13

11 "ᵃHE MUST TURN AWAY FROM EVIL AND DO GOOD;
HE MUST SEEK PEACE AND PURSUE IT. ᵃPs 34:14

12 "ᵃFOR THE EYES OF THE LORD ARE TOWARD THE RIGHTEOUS,
AND HIS EARS ATTEND TO THEIR PRAYER,
BUT THE FACE OF THE LORD IS AGAINST THOSE WHO DO EVIL." ᵃPs 34:15, 16

13 ᵃWho is there to harm you if you prove zealous for what is good? ᵃProv 16:7

14 But even if you should suffer for the sake of righteousness, you are blessed. ᵃAND DO NOT FEAR THEIR INTIMIDATION, AND DO NOT BE TROUBLED, ᵃIs 8:12f

15 but sanctify Christ as Lord in your hearts, always *being* ready ᵃto make a defense to everyone who asks you to give an account for the hope that is in you, yet ᵇwith gentleness and reverence; ᵃCol 4:6 ᵇ2 Tim 2:25

16 and keep a ᵃgood conscience so that in the thing in which you are slandered, those who revile your good behavior in Christ will be put to shame. ᵃ1 Tim 1:5; Heb 13:18

17 For ᵃit is better, ᵇif God should will it so, that you suffer for doing what is right rather than for doing what is wrong. ᵃ1 Pet 2:20 ᵇActs 18:21

18 For Christ also died for sins ᵃonce for all, *the* just for *the* unjust, so that He might bring us to God, having been put to death in the flesh, but made alive in the spirit; ᵃHeb 9:26, 28; 10:10

19 in which also He went and made proclamation to the spirits *now* in prison,

20 who once were disobedient, when the patience of God ᵃkept waiting in the days of Noah, during the construction of ᵇthe ark, in which a few, that is, eight persons, were brought safely through *the* water. ᵃGen 6:3, 13f ᵇHeb 11:7

21 Corresponding to that, baptism now saves you—ᵃnot the removal of dirt from the flesh, but an appeal to God for a good conscience—through the resurrection of Jesus Christ, ᵃHeb 9:14; 10:22

22 ᵃwho is at the right hand of God, having

gone into heaven, after angels and authorities and powers had been subjected to Him. [a]Heb 1:3f; Eph 1:20f

Keep Fervent in Your Love

4 Therefore, since [a]Christ has suffered in the flesh, arm yourselves also with the same purpose, because he who has suffered in the flesh has ceased from sin, [a]1 Pet 2:21

2 [a]so as to live the rest of the time in the flesh no longer for the lusts of men, but for the will of God. [a]Rom 6:2; Col 3:3

3 For [a]the time already past is sufficient for you to have carried out the desire of the Gentiles, having pursued a course of sensuality, lusts, drunkenness, carousing, drinking parties and abominable idolatries. [a]1 Cor 12:2

4 In all this, they are surprised that you do not run with them into the same excesses of [a]dissipation, and they [b]malign you; [a]Eph 5:18 [b]1 Pet 3:16

5 but they will give account to Him who is ready to judge [a]the living and the dead. [a]Acts 10:42; Rom 14:9

6 For [a]the gospel has for this purpose been preached even to those who are dead, that though they are judged in the flesh as men, they may live in the spirit according to the will of God. [a]1 Pet 3:18

7 [a]The end of all things is near; therefore, be of sound judgment and sober spirit for the purpose of prayer. [a]Rom 13:11; James 5:8

8 Above all, [a]keep fervent in your love for one another, because [b]love covers a multitude of sins. [a]1 Pet 1:22 [b]Prov 10:12

9 [a]Be hospitable to one another without complaint. [a]1 Tim 3:2; Heb 13:2

10 [a]As each one has received a special gift, employ it in serving one another as good [b]stewards of the manifold grace of God. [a]Rom 12:6f [b]1 Cor 4:1

11 [a]Whoever speaks, is to do so as one who is speaking the utterances of God; whoever serves is to do so as one who is serving [b]by the strength which God supplies; so that in all things God may be glorified through Jesus Christ, to whom belongs the glory and dominion forever and ever. Amen. [a]Titus 2:1 [b]Eph 6:10

Share the Sufferings of Christ

12 Beloved, do not be surprised at the [a]fiery ordeal among you, which comes upon you for your testing, as though some strange thing were happening to you; [a]1 Pet 1:6f

13 but to the degree that you [a]share the sufferings of Christ, keep on rejoicing, so that also at the revelation of His glory you may rejoice with exultation. [a]Rom 8:17; 2 Cor 1:5

14 If you are reviled [a]for the name of Christ, [b]you are blessed, because the Spirit of glory and of God rests on you. [a]John 15:21 [b]Matt 5:11

15 Make sure that none of you suffers as a murderer, or thief, or evildoer, or a [a]troublesome meddler; [a]2 Thess 3:11; 1 Tim 5:13

16 but if anyone suffers as a Christian, he is not to be ashamed, but is to [a]glorify God in this name. [a]1 Pet 4:11

17 For it is time for judgment [a]to begin with [b]the household of God; and if it begins with us first, what will be the outcome for those who do not obey the gospel of God? [a]Amos 3:2 [b]Heb 3:6

18 [a]AND IF IT IS WITH DIFFICULTY THAT THE RIGHTEOUS IS SAVED, WHAT WILL BECOME OF THE [b]GODLESS MAN AND THE SINNER? [a]Prov 11:31 [b]1 Tim 1:9

19 Therefore, those also who suffer according to [a]the will of God shall entrust their souls to a faithful Creator in doing what is right. [a]1 Pet 3:17

Serve God Willingly

5 Therefore, I exhort the elders among you, as your fellow elder and [a]witness of the sufferings of Christ, and a [b]partaker also of the glory that is to be revealed, [a]Luke 24:48 [b]1 Pet 1:5

2 shepherd [a]the flock of God among you, exercising oversight [b]not under compulsion, but voluntarily, according to the will of God; and not for sordid gain, but with eagerness; [a]John 21:16 [b]Philem 14

3 nor yet as [a]lording it over those allotted to your charge, but proving to be examples to the flock. [a]Ezek 34:4; Matt 20:25f

4 And when the Chief [a]Shepherd appears, you will receive the unfading crown of glory. [a]1 Pet 2:25

5 You younger men, likewise, be subject to your elders; and all of you, clothe yourselves with [a]humility toward one another, for [b]GOD IS OPPOSED TO THE PROUD, BUT GIVES GRACE TO THE HUMBLE. [a]1 Pet 3:8 [b]Prov 3:34

6 Therefore [a]humble yourselves under the mighty hand of God, that He may exalt you at the proper time, [a]Matt 23:12; Luke 14:11

7 casting all your [a]anxiety on Him, because He cares for you. [a]Ps 55:22; Matt 6:25

8 [a]Be of sober spirit, [b]be on the alert. Your adversary, the devil, prowls around like a roaring lion, seeking someone to devour. [a]1 Pet 1:13 [b]Matt 24:42

9 [a]But resist him, firm in your faith, knowing that the same experiences of suffering are being accomplished by your brethren who are in the world. [a]James 4:7

10 After you have suffered [a]for a little while, the God of all grace, who [b]called you to His eternal glory in Christ, will Himself perfect, confirm, strengthen and establish you. [a]1 Pet 1:6 [b]1 Cor 1:9

11 [a]To Him be dominion forever and ever. Amen. [a]Rom 11:36; 1 Pet 4:11

12 Through ªSilvanus, our faithful brother (for so I regard *him),* I have written to you briefly, exhorting and testifying that this is the true grace of God. Stand firm in it! ª*2 Cor 1:19*

13 She who is in Babylon, chosen together with you, sends you greetings, and *so does* my son, ªMark. ª*Acts 12:12, 25; 15:37, 39*

14 ªGreet one another with a kiss of love.

Peace be to you all who are in Christ. ª*Rom 16:16*

The Second Letter of
PETER

Growth in Christian Virtue

1 Simon Peter, a bond-servant and apostle of Jesus Christ,

To those who have received ªa faith of the same kind as ours, by ᵇthe righteousness of our God and Savior, Jesus Christ: ª*Rom 1:12* ᵇ*Rom 3:21-26*

2 Grace and peace be multiplied to you in ªthe knowledge of God and of Jesus our Lord; ª*John 17:3; Phil 3:8*

3 seeing that His divine power has granted to us everything pertaining to life and godliness, through the true knowledge of Him who ªcalled us by His own glory and excellence. ª*1 Thess 2:12; 2 Thess 2:14*

4 For by these He has granted to us His precious and magnificent ªpromises, so that by them you may become ᵇpartakers of *the* divine nature, having escaped the corruption that is in the world by lust. ª*2 Pet 3:9, 13* ᵇ*1 John 3:2*

5 Now for this very reason also, applying all diligence, in your faith supply moral excellence, and in *your* moral excellence, ªknowledge, ª*Col 2:3; 2 Pet 1:2*

6 and in *your* knowledge, ªself-control, and in *your* self-control, ᵇperseverance, and in *your* perseverance, godliness, ª*Acts 24:25* ᵇ*Luke 21:19*

7 and in *your* godliness, ªbrotherly kindness, and in *your* brotherly kindness, love. ª*Rom 12:10; 1 Pet 1:22*

8 For if these *qualities* are yours and are increasing, they render you neither useless nor ªunfruitful in the true knowledge of our Lord Jesus Christ. ª*Col 1:10*

9 For he who lacks these *qualities* is ªblind *or* short-sighted, having forgotten *his* purification from his former sins. ª*1 John 2:11*

10 Therefore, brethren, be all the more diligent to make certain about His ªcalling and ᵇchoosing you; for as long as you practice these things, you will never stumble; ª*Rom 11:29* ᵇ*1 Thess 1:4*

11 for in this way the entrance into the eternal kingdom of our Lord and Savior Jesus Christ will be ªabundantly supplied to you. ª*Rom 2:4; 1 Tim 6:17*

12 Therefore, I will always be ready to remind you of these things, even though you *already* know *them,* and have been established in ªthe truth which is present with *you.* ª*Col 1:5f; 2 John 2*

13 I consider it right, as long as I am in ªthis *earthly* dwelling, to ᵇstir you up by way of reminder. ª*2 Cor 5:1, 4* ᵇ*2 Pet 3:1*

14 knowing that ªthe laying aside of my *earthly* dwelling is imminent, ᵇas also our Lord Jesus Christ has made clear to me. ª*2 Tim 4:6* ᵇ*John 21:19*

15 And I will also be diligent that at any time after my ªdeparture you will be able to call these things to mind. ª*Luke 9:31*

Eyewitnesses

16 For we did not follow cleverly devised ªtales when we made known to you the ᵇpower and coming of our Lord Jesus Christ, but we were eyewitnesses of His majesty. ª*1 Tim 1:4* ᵇ*Mark 13:26*

17 For when He received honor and glory from God the Father, such an ªutterance as this was made to Him by the Majestic Glory, "This is My beloved Son with whom I am well-pleased"— ª*Matt 17:5; Mark 9:7*

18 and we ourselves heard this utterance made from heaven when we were with Him on the ªholy mountain. ª*Ex 3:5; Josh 5:15*

19 *So* we have the prophetic word *made* more sure, to which you do well to pay attention as to ªa lamp shining in a dark place, until the day dawns and the ᵇmorning star arises in your hearts. ª*Ps 119:105* ᵇ*Rev 22:16*

20 But know this first of all, that ªno prophecy of Scripture is *a matter* of one's own interpretation, ª*Rom 12:6*

21 for ªno prophecy was ever made by an act of human will, but men moved by the Holy Spirit spoke from God. ª*Jer 23:26; 2 Tim 3:16*

The Rise of False Prophets

2 But ªfalse prophets also arose among the people, just as there will also be false teachers among you, who will secretly introduce destructive heresies, even denying the Master who bought them, bringing swift destruction upon themselves. ª*Deut 13:1ff; Jer 6:13*

2 Many will follow their ªsensuality, and because of them the way of the truth will be ᵇmaligned; ª*Gen 19:5ff* ᵇ*Rom 2:24*

3 and in *their* greed they will exploit you with false words; ᵇtheir judgment from long ago is not idle, and their destruction is not asleep. ª*1 Tim 6:5* ᵇ*Deut 32:35*

4 For ªif God did not spare angels when they sinned, but cast them into hell and committed them to pits of darkness, reserved for judgment; ªJude 6

5 and did not spare ªthe ancient world, but preserved Noah, a preacher of righteousness, with seven others, when He brought a flood upon the world of the ungodly; ªEzek 26:20; 2 Pet 3:6

6 and *if* He ªcondemned the cities of Sodom and Gomorrah to destruction by reducing *them* to ashes, having made them an example to those who would live ungodly *lives* thereafter; ªGen 19:24; Jude 7

7 and *if* He ªrescued righteous Lot, oppressed by the sensual conduct of unprincipled men ªGen 19:16, 29

8 (for by what he saw and heard *that* ªrighteous man, while living among them, felt *his* righteous soul tormented day after day by *their* lawless deeds), ªHeb 11:4

9 ªthen the Lord knows how to rescue the godly from temptation, and to keep the unrighteous under punishment for the day of judgment, ª1 Cor 10:13; Rev 3:10

10 and especially those who indulge the flesh in *its* corrupt desires and ªdespise authority.

Daring, self-willed, they do not tremble when they ªrevile angelic majesties, ªEx 22:28; Jude 8

11 ªwhereas angels who are greater in might and power do not bring a reviling judgment against them before the Lord. ªJude 9

12 But ªthese, like unreasoning animals, born as creatures of instinct to be captured and killed, reviling where they have no knowledge, will in the destruction of those creatures also be destroyed, ªJude 10

13 suffering wrong as the wages of doing wrong. They count it a pleasure to ªrevel in the daytime. They are stains and blemishes, ªreveling in their deceptions, as they carouse with you, ªRom 13:13

14 having eyes full of adultery that never cease from sin, enticing ªunstable souls, having a heart trained in greed, accursed children; ªJames 1:8; 2 Pet 3:16

15 forsaking ªthe right way, they have gone astray, having followed ᵇthe way of Balaam, the *son* of Beor, who loved the wages of unrighteousness; ªActs 13:10 ᵇNum 22:5, 7

16 but he received a rebuke for his own transgression, ªfor a mute donkey, speaking with a voice of a man, restrained the madness of the prophet. ªNum 22:21, 23, 28, 30ff

17 These are ªsprings without water and mists driven by a storm, ᵇfor whom the black darkness has been reserved. ªJude 12 ᵇJude 13

18 For speaking out ªarrogant *words* of vanity they entice by fleshly desires, by sensuality, those who barely escape from the ones who live in error, ªJude 16

19 promising them freedom while they themselves are slaves of corruption; for ªby what a man is overcome, by this he is enslaved. ªJohn 8:34; Rom 6:16

20 For if, after they have escaped the defilements of the world by the knowledge of the Lord and Savior Jesus Christ, they are again entangled in them and are overcome, ªthe last state has become worse for them than the first. ªMatt 12:45; Luke 11:26

21 ªFor it would be better for them not to have known the way of righteousness, than having known it, to turn away from the holy commandment ᵇhanded on to them. ªEzek 18:24 ᵇJude 3

22 It has happened to them according to the true proverb, "ªA DOG RETURNS TO ITS OWN VOMIT," and, "A sow, after washing, *returns* to wallowing in the mire." ªProv 26:11

Purpose of This Letter

3 This is now, beloved, the second letter I am writing to you in which I am ªstirring up your sincere mind by way of reminder, ª2 Pet 1:13

2 that you should ªremember the words spoken beforehand by ᵇthe holy prophets and the commandment of the Lord and Savior *spoken* by your apostles. ªJude 17 ᵇLuke 1:70

The Coming Day of the Lord

3 Know this first of all, that ªin the last days ᵇmockers will come with *their* mocking, following after their own lusts, ª1 Tim 4:1 ᵇJude 18

4 and saying, "ªWhere is the promise of His coming? For *ever* since the fathers ᵇfell asleep, all continues just as it was from the beginning of creation." ªMal 2:17 ᵇActs 7:60

5 For when they maintain this, it escapes their notice that by the word of God *the* heavens existed long ago and *the* earth was ªformed out of water and by water, ªPs 24:2; 136:6

6 through which ªthe world at that time was ᵇdestroyed, being flooded with water. ª2 Pet 2:5 ᵇGen 7:11, 12, 21f

7 But by His word ªthe present heavens and earth are being reserved for ᵇfire, kept for the day of judgment and destruction of ungodly men. ª2 Pet 3:10, 12 ᵇIs 66:15

8 But do not let this one *fact* escape your notice, beloved, that with the Lord one day is like a thousand years, and ªa thousand years like one day. ªPs 90:4

9 ªThe Lord is not slow about His promise, as some count slowness, but is patient toward you, ᵇnot wishing for any to perish but for all to come to repentance. ªHab 2:3 ᵇ1 Tim 2:4

A New Heaven and Earth

10 But ªthe day of the Lord ᵇwill come like a

thief, in which the heavens will pass away with a roar and the elements will be destroyed with intense heat, and the earth and its works will be burned up. ^a*1 Cor 1:8* ^b*1 Thess 5:2*

11 Since all these things are to be destroyed in this way, what sort of people ought you to be in holy conduct and godliness,

12 looking for and hastening the coming of the day of God, because of which ^athe heavens will be destroyed by burning, and the elements will melt with intense heat! ^a*2 Pet 3:7, 10*

13 But according to His ^apromise we are looking for ^bnew heavens and a new earth, in which righteousness dwells. ^a*Is 65:17* ^b*Rom 8:21*

14 Therefore, beloved, since you look for these things, be diligent to be found by Him in peace, ^aspotless and blameless, ^a*Phil 2:15; 1 Thess 5:23*

15 and regard the ^apatience of our Lord *as* sal-

vation; just as also ^bour beloved brother Paul, according to the wisdom given him, wrote to you, ^a*2 Pet 3:9* ^b*Acts 15:25*

16 as also in all *his* letters, speaking in them of these things, ^ain which are some things hard to understand, which the untaught and unstable distort, as *they do* also the rest of the Scriptures, to their own destruction.   ^a*Heb 5:11*

17 You therefore, beloved, knowing this beforehand, be on your guard so that you are not carried away by ^athe error of ^bunprincipled men and fall from your own steadfastness, ^a*2 Pet 2:18* ^b*2 Pet 2:7*

18 but grow in the grace and knowledge of our ^aLord and Savior Jesus Christ. To Him *be* the glory, both now and to the day of eternity. Amen. ^a*2 Pet 2:20*

The First Letter of
JOHN

Introduction, The Incarnate Word

1 What was ^afrom the beginning, what we have heard, what we have ^bseen with our eyes, what we have looked at and touched with our hands, concerning the Word of Life— ^a*John 1:1f* ^b*2 Pet 1:16*

2 and ^athe life was manifested, and we have seen and testify and proclaim to you ^bthe eternal life, which was with the Father and was ^amanifested to us— ^a*John 1:4* ^b*John 10:28*

3 what we have seen and ^aheard we proclaim to you also, so that you too may have fellowship with us; and indeed our ^bfellowship is with the Father, and with His Son Jesus Christ. ^a*Acts 4:20* ^b*John 17:3, 21*

4 ^aThese things we write, so that our ^bjoy may be made complete. ^a*1 John 2:1* ^b*John 3:29*

God Is Light

5 This is the message we have heard from Him and announce to you, that ^aGod is Light, and in Him there is no darkness at all. ^a*1 Tim 6:16; James 1:17*

6 ^aIf we say that we have fellowship with Him and *yet* walk in the darkness, we ^blie and do not practice the truth; ^a*John 8:12* ^b*1 John 2:4f*

7 but if we ^awalk in the Light as ^bHe Himself is in the Light, we have fellowship with one another, and the blood of Jesus His Son cleanses us from all sin. ^a*Is 2:5* ^b*1 Tim 6:16*

8 ^aIf we say that we have no sin, we are deceiving ourselves and the ^btruth is not in us. ^a*Job 15:14* ^b*John 8:44*

9 ^aIf we confess our sins, He is faithful and righteous to forgive us our sins and to cleanse us from all unrighteousness. ^a*Ps 32:5; Prov 28:13*

10 ^aIf we say that we have not sinned, we

^bmake Him a liar and His word is not in us. ^a*Job 15:14* ^b*1 John 5:10*

Christ Is Our Advocate

2 My little children, I am writing these things to you so that you may not sin. And if anyone sins, ^awe have an ^bAdvocate with the Father, Jesus Christ the righteous; ^a*Rom 8:34* ^b*John 14:16*

2 and He Himself is the propitiation for our sins; and not for ours only, but also ^afor *those of* the whole world. ^a*John 4:42; 11:51f*

3 By this we know that we have come to know Him, if we ^akeep His commandments. ^a*John 14:15; 15:10*

4 The one who says, "I have come to know Him," and does not keep His commandments, is a ^aliar, and ^bthe truth is not in him; ^a*1 John 1:6* ^b*1 John 1:8*

5 but whoever ^akeeps His word, in him the ^blove of God has truly been perfected. By this we know that we are in Him: ^a*John 14:23* ^b*1 John 4:12*

6 the one who says he ^aabides in Him ought himself to walk in the same manner as He walked. ^a*John 15:4*

7 Beloved, I am not writing a new commandment to you, but an old commandment which you have had ^afrom the beginning; the old commandment is the word which you have heard. ^a*1 John 2:24; 3:11*

8 On the other hand, I am writing a new commandment to you, which is true in Him and in you, because ^athe darkness is passing away and ^bthe true Light is already shining. ^a*Rom 13:12* ^b*John 1:9*

9 The one who says he is in the Light and *yet*

[a]hates his brother is in the darkness until now. [a]*1 John 2:11; 3:15*

10 [a]The one who loves his brother abides in the Light and there is no cause for stumbling in him. [a]*John 11:9; 1 John 2:10, 11*

11 But the one who hates his brother is in the darkness and walks in the darkness, and does not know where he is going because the darkness has [a]blinded his eyes. [a]*2 Cor 4:4; 2 Pet 1:9*

12 I am writing to you, little children, because [a]your sins have been forgiven you for His name's sake. [a]*Acts 13:38; 1 Cor 6:11*

13 I am writing to you, fathers, because you know Him who has been from the beginning. I am writing to you, young men, because [a]you have overcome the evil one. I have written to you, children, because you know the Father. [a]*John 16:33; 1 John 5:4f*

14 I have written to you, fathers, because you know Him [a]who has been from the beginning. I have written to you, young men, because you are [b]strong, and the word of God abides in you, and you have overcome the evil one. [a]*1 John 1:1* [b]*Eph 6:10*

Do Not Love the World

15 Do not love the world nor the things in the world. [a]If anyone loves the world, the love of the Father is not in him. [a]*James 4:4*

16 For all that is in the world, [a]the lust of the flesh and the lust of the eyes and the boastful pride of life, is not from the Father, but is from the world. [a]*Rom 13:14; Eph 2:3*

17 [a]The world is passing away, and *also* its lusts; but the one who does the will of God lives forever. [a]*1 Cor 7:31*

18 Children, it is the last hour; and just as you heard that [a]antichrist is coming, [b]even now many antichrists have appeared; from this we know that it is the last hour. [a]*Matt 24:5, 24* [b]*Mark 13:22*

19 [a]They went out from us, but they were not *really* of us; for if they had been of us, they would have remained with us; but *they went out*, so that it would be shown that they all are not of us. [a]*Acts 20:30*

20 But you have an [a]anointing from [b]the Holy One, and you all know. [a]*2 Cor 1:21* [b]*Mark 1:24*

21 I have not written to you because you do not know the truth, but [a]because you do know it, and because no lie is [b]of the truth. [a]*James 1:19* [b]*John 8:44*

22 Who is the liar but [a]the one who denies that Jesus is the Christ? This is the antichrist, the one who denies the Father and the Son. [a]*1 John 4:3; 2 John 7*

23 [a]Whoever denies the Son does not have the Father; the one who confesses the Son has the Father also. [a]*John 8:19; 16:3*

24 As for you, let that abide in you which you heard from the beginning. If what you heard from the beginning abides in you, you also [a]will abide in the Son and in the Father. [a]*John 14:23; 1 John 1:3*

The Promise Is Eternal Life

25 [a]This is the promise which He Himself made to us: eternal life. [a]*John 3:15; 6:40*

26 These things I have written to you concerning those who are trying to [a]deceive you. [a]*1 John 3:7; 2 John 7*

27 As for you, the anointing which you received from Him abides in you, and you have no need for anyone to teach you; but as His anointing [a]teaches you about all things, and is [b]true and is not a lie, and just as it has taught you, you abide in Him. [a]*John 14:26* [b]*John 14:17*

28 Now, little children, abide in Him, so that when He [a]appears, we may have confidence and [b]not shrink away from Him in shame at His coming. [a]*1 John 3:2* [b]*Mark 8:38*

29 If you know that [a]He is righteous, you know that everyone also who practices righteousness is born of Him. [a]*John 7:18; 1 John 3:7*

Children of God Love One Another

3 See [a]how great a love the Father has bestowed on us, that we would be called [b]children of God; and *such* we are. For this reason the world does not know us, because it did not know Him. [a]*John 3:16* [b]*John 1:12*

2 Beloved, now we are children of God, and it has not appeared as yet what we will be. We know that when He appears, we will be [a]like Him, because we will [b]see Him just as He is. [a]*Rom 8:29* [b]*John 17:24*

3 And everyone who has this [a]hope *fixed* on Him purifies himself, just as He is pure. [a]*Rom 15:12; 1 Pet 1:3*

4 Everyone who practices sin also practices lawlessness; and [a]sin is lawlessness. [a]*Rom 4:15; 1 John 5:17*

5 You know that He appeared in order to [a]take away sins; and [b]in Him there is no sin. [a]*John 1:29* [b]*2 Cor 5:21*

6 No one who abides in Him [a]sins; no one who sins has seen Him or knows Him. [a]*1 John 3:9*

7 Little children, make sure no one [a]deceives you; [b]the one who practices righteousness is righteous, just as He is righteous; [a]*1 John 2:26* [b]*1 John 2:29*

8 the one who practices sin is [a]of the devil; for the devil has sinned from the beginning. The Son of God appeared for this purpose, to destroy the works of the devil. [a]*John 8:44; 1 John 3:10*

9 No one who is [a]born of God practices sin, because His seed abides in him; and he cannot sin, because he is born of God. [a]*John 1:13; 3:3*

10 By this the [a]children of God and the chil-

dren of the devil are obvious: anyone who does not practice righteousness is not of God, nor the one who does not love his [b]brother. [a]*John 1:12* [b]*1 John 2:9*

11 For this is the message which you have heard from the beginning, [a]that we should love one another; [a]*John 15:12; 1 John 4:7, 11f, 21*

12 not as [a]Cain, *who* was of [b]the evil one and slew his brother. And for what reason did he slay him? Because his deeds were evil, and his brother's were righteous. [a]*Gen 4:8* [b]*1 John 2:13f*

13 Do not be surprised, brethren, if [a]the world hates you. [a]*John 15:18; 17:14*

14 We know that we have [a]passed out of death into life, because we love the brethren. He who does not love abides in death. [a]*John 5:24*

15 Everyone who [a]hates his brother is a murderer; and you know that no murderer has eternal life abiding in him. [a]*Matt 5:21f; John 8:44*

16 We know love by this, that [a]He laid down His life for us; and we ought to lay down our lives for the brethren. [a]*John 10:11; 15:13*

17 But [a]whoever has the world's goods, and sees his brother in need and [b]closes his heart against him, how does the love of God abide in him? [a]*James 2:15f* [b]*Deut 15:7*

18 Little children, let us not love with word or with tongue, but in deed and [a]truth. [a]*2 John 1; 3 John 1*

19 We will know by this that we are [a]of the truth, and will assure our heart before Him [a]*1 John 2:21*

20 in whatever our heart condemns us; for God is greater than our heart and knows all things.

21 Beloved, if our heart does not condemn us, we have [a]confidence before God; [a]*1 John 2:28; 5:14*

22 and whatever we ask we receive from Him, because we [a]keep His commandments and do [b]the things that are pleasing in His sight. [a]*1 John 2:3* [b]*John 8:29*

23 This is His commandment, that we [a]believe in [b]the name of His Son Jesus Christ, and love one another, just as He commanded us. [a]*John 6:29* [b]*John 1:12*

24 The one who [a]keeps His commandments abides in Him, and He in him. We know by this that [b]He abides in us, by the Spirit whom He has given us. [a]*1 John 2:3* [b]*1 John 2:5*

Testing the Spirits

4 Beloved, do not believe every [a]spirit, but test the spirits to see whether they are from God, because many false prophets have gone out into the world. [a]*Jer 29:8; 1 Thess 5:20f*

2 By this you know the Spirit of God: [a]every spirit that [b]confesses that Jesus Christ has come in the flesh is from God; [a]*1 Cor 12:3* [b]*1 John 2:23*

3 and every spirit that [a]does not confess Jesus

is not from God; this is the *spirit* of the antichrist, of which you have heard that it is coming, and [b]now it is already in the world. [a]*1 John 2:22* [b]*2 Thess 2:3-7*

4 You are from God, little children, and [a]have overcome them; because greater is He who is in you than [b]he who is in the world. [a]*1 John 2:13* [b]*John 12:31*

5 [a]They are from the world; therefore they speak *as* from the world, and the world listens to them. [a]*John 15:19; 17:14, 16*

6 We are from God; he who knows God listens to us; he who is not from God does not listen to us. By this we know [a]the spirit of truth and [b]the spirit of error. [a]*John 14:17* [b]*1 Tim 4:1*

God Is Love

7 Beloved, let us [a]love one another, for love is from God; and everyone who loves is born of God and knows God. [a]*1 John 3:11*

8 The one who does not love does not know God, for [a]God is love. [a]*1 John 4:7, 16*

9 By this the love of God was manifested in us, that [a]God has sent His only begotten Son into the world so that we might live through Him. [a]*John 3:16f; 1 John 4:10*

10 In this is love, [a]not that we loved God, but that He loved us and sent His Son *to be* [b]the propitiation for our sins. [a]*Rom 5:8, 10* [b]*1 John 2:2*

11 Beloved, if God so loved us, [a]we also ought to love one another. [a]*1 John 4:7*

12 [a]No one has seen God at any time; if we love one another, God abides in us, and His love is perfected in us. [a]*John 1:18; 1 Tim 6:16*

13 [a]By this we know that we abide in Him and He in us, because He has given us of His Spirit. [a]*Rom 8:9; 1 John 3:24*

14 We have seen and testify that the Father has [a]sent the Son *to be* the Savior of the world. [a]*John 3:17; 1 John 2:2*

15 [a]Whoever confesses that Jesus is the Son of God, God abides in him, and he in God. [a]*1 John 2:23*

16 [a]We have come to know and have believed the love which God has for us. [b]God is love, and the one who abides in love abides in God, and God abides in him. [a]*John 6:69* [b]*1 John 4:7, 8*

17 By this, love is perfected with us, so that we may have [a]confidence in [b]the day of judgment; because as He is, so also are we in this world. [a]*1 John 2:28* [b]*Matt 10:15*

18 There is no fear in love; but [a]perfect love casts out fear, because fear involves punishment, and the one who fears is not perfected in love. [a]*Rom 8:15*

19 [a]We love, because He first loved us. [a]*1 John 4:10*

20 If someone says, "I love God," and [a]hates his brother, he is a liar; for the one who does not love his brother whom he has seen, cannot love God whom he has not seen. ᵃ*1 John 2:9, 11*

21 And ᵃthis commandment we have from Him, that the one who loves God should love his brother also. ᵃ*Lev 19:18; Matt 5:43f*

Overcoming the World

5 ᵃWhoever believes that Jesus is the Christ is born of God, and whoever loves the Father loves the *child* born of Him. ᵃ*1 John 2:22f; 4:2, 15*

2 By this we know that ᵃwe love the children of God, when we love God and observe His commandments. ᵃ*1 John 3:14*

3 For ᵃthis is the love of God, that we keep His commandments; and ᵇHis commandments are not burdensome. ᵃ*John 14:15* ᵇ*Matt 11:30*

4 For whatever is born of God ᵃovercomes the world; and this is the victory that has overcome the world—our faith. ᵃ*1 John 2:13; 4:4*

5 Who is the one who overcomes the world, but he who ᵃbelieves that Jesus is the Son of God? ᵃ*1 John 4:15; 5:1*

6 This is the One who came by water and blood, Jesus Christ; not with the water only, but with the water and with the blood. It is ᵃthe Spirit who testifies, because the Spirit is the truth. ᵃ*Matt 3:16f; John 15:26*

7 For there are ᵃthree that testify: ᵃ*Matt 18:16*

8 the Spirit and the water and the blood; and the three are in agreement.

9 ᵃIf we receive the testimony of men, the testimony of God is greater; for the testimony of God is this, that He has testified concerning His Son. ᵃ*John 5:34, 37; 8:18*

10 The one who believes in the Son of God ᵃhas the testimony in himself; the one who does not believe God has made Him a liar, because he has not believed in the testimony that God has given concerning His Son. ᵃ*Rom 8:16; Gal 4:6*

11 And the testimony is this, that God has given us ᵃeternal life, and ᵇthis life is in His Son. ᵃ*1 John 1:2* ᵇ*John 1:4*

12 ᵃHe who has the Son has the life; he who does not have the Son of God does not have the life. ᵃ*John 3:15f, 36*

This Is Written That You May Know

13 ᵃThese things I have written to you who ᵇbelieve in the name of the Son of God, so that you may know that you have eternal life. ᵃ*John 20:31* ᵇ*1 John 3:23*

14 This is ᵃthe confidence which we have before Him, that, if we ask anything according to His will, He hears us. ᵃ*1 John 2:28; 3:21f*

15 And if we know that He hears us *in* whatever we ask, ᵃwe know that we have the requests which we have asked from Him. ᵃ*1 John 5:18-20*

16 If anyone sees his brother committing a sin not *leading* to death, ᵃhe shall ask and *God* will for him give life to those who commit sin not *leading* to death. There is a sin *leading* to death; ᵇI do not say that he should make request for this. ᵃ*James 5:15* ᵇ*Jer 7:16*

17 ᵃAll unrighteousness is sin, and there is a sin not *leading* to death. ᵃ*1 John 3:4*

18 We know that ᵃno one who is born of God sins; but He who was born of God keeps him, and ᵇthe evil one does not touch him. ᵃ*1 John 3:9* ᵇ*1 John 2:13*

19 We know that ᵃwe are of God, and that the whole world lies in *the power of* the evil one. ᵃ*1 John 4:6*

20 And we know that the Son of God has come, and has ᵃgiven us understanding so that we may know ᵇHim who is true; and we are in Him who is true, in His Son Jesus Christ. This is the true God and eternal life. ᵃ*Luke 24:45* ᵇ*John 17:3*

21 Little children, guard yourselves from ᵃidols. ᵃ*1 Cor 10:7, 14; 1 Thess 1:9*

The Second Letter of
JOHN

Walk According to His Commandments

1 The elder to the chosen lady and her children, whom I love in truth; and not only I, but also all who ᵃknow the truth, ᵃ*John 8:32; 1 Tim 2:4*

2 for the sake of the truth which abides in us and will be ᵃwith us forever: ᵃ*John 14:16*

3 ᵃGrace, mercy *and* peace will be with us, from God the Father and from Jesus Christ, the Son of the Father, in truth and love. ᵃ*Rom 1:7; 1 Tim 1:2*

4 ᵃI was very glad to find *some* of your children walking in truth, just as we have received commandment *to do* from the Father. ᵃ*3 John 3f*

5 Now I ask you, lady, ᵃnot as though *I were* writing to you a new commandment, but the one which we have had ᵃfrom the beginning, that we love one another. ᵃ*1 John 2:7*

6 And ᵃthis is love, that we walk according to His commandments. This is the commandment, just as you have heard ᵇfrom the beginning, that you should walk in it. ᵃ*1 John 5:3* ᵇ*1 John 2:7*

7 For ᵃmany deceivers have ᵇgone out into the world, those who do not acknowledge Jesus Christ *as* coming in the flesh. This is ᵃthe deceiver and the antichrist. ᵃ*1 John 2:26* ᵇ*1 John 2:19*

8 Watch yourselves, ᵃthat you do not lose

what we have accomplished, but that you may receive a full reward. ª*1 Cor 3:8; Heb 10:35*

9 Anyone who goes too far and ªdoes not abide in the teaching of Christ, does not have God; the one who abides in the teaching, he has both the Father and the Son. ª*John 7:16; 8:31*

10 If anyone comes to you and does not bring this teaching, do not receive him into *your* house, and do not give him a greeting;

11 for the one who gives him a greeting ªparticipates in his evil deeds. ª*Eph 5:11; 1 Tim 5:22*

12 ªThough I have many things to write to you, I do not want to *do so* with paper and ink; but I hope to come to you and speak face to face, so that your joy may be made full. ª*3 John 13, 14*

13 The children of your ªchosen sister greet you. ª*2 John 1*

The Third Letter of
JOHN

You Walk in the Truth

1 The elder to the beloved Gaius, whom I ªlove in truth. ª*1 John 3:18; 2 John 1*

2 Beloved, I pray that in all respects you may prosper and be in good health, just as your soul prospers.

3 For I ªwas very glad when brethren came and testified to your truth, *that is,* how you ªare walking in truth. ª*2 John 4*

4 I have no greater joy than this, to hear of my children ªwalking in the truth. ª*2 John 4*

5 Beloved, you are acting faithfully in whatever you accomplish for the brethren, and especially *when they are* ªstrangers; ª*Rom 12:13; Heb 13:2*

6 and they have testified to your love before the church. You will do well to send them on their way in a manner ªworthy of God. ª*Col 1:10; 1 Thess 2:12*

7 For they went out for the sake of ªthe Name, accepting nothing from the Gentiles. ª*John 15:21; Acts 5:41*

8 Therefore we ought to support such men, so that we may be fellow workers with the truth.

9 I wrote something to the church; but Diotrephes, who loves to ªbe first among them, does not accept what we say. ª*2 John 9*

10 For this reason, if I come, I will call attention to his deeds which he does, unjustly accusing us with wicked words; and not satisfied with this, he himself does not ªreceive the brethren, either, and he forbids those who desire *to do so* and ᵇputs *them* out of the church. ª*2 John 10* ᵇ*John 9:34*

11 Beloved, ªdo not imitate what is evil, but what is good. The one who does good is of God; the one who does evil has not seen God. ª*Ps 34:14; 37:27*

12 Demetrius has received a *good* testimony from everyone, and from the truth itself; and we add our testimony, and ªyou know that our testimony is true. ª*John 19:35; 21:24*

13 ªI had many things to write to you, but I am not willing to write *them* to you with pen and ink; ª*2 John 12*

14 but I hope to see you shortly, and we will speak face to face. ª*John 10:3*

15 Peace *be* to you. The friends greet you. Greet the friends by name.

The Letter of
JUDE

The Warnings of History to the Ungodly

1 Jude, a bond-servant of Jesus Christ, and brother of James,

To ªthose who are the called, beloved in God the Father, and ᵇkept for Jesus Christ: ª*Rom 1:6* ᵇ*John 17:11f*

2 May mercy and peace and love ªbe multiplied to you. ª*1 Pet 1:2; 2 Pet 1:2*

3 Beloved, while I was making every effort to write you about our common salvation, I felt the necessity to write to you appealing that you ªcontend earnestly for ᵇthe faith which was once for all handed down to the saints. ª*1 Tim 6:12* ᵇ*Acts 6:7*

4 For certain persons have crept in unnoticed, those who were long beforehand

ªmarked out for this condemnation, ungodly persons who turn the grace of our God into licentiousness and ᵇdeny our only Master and Lord, Jesus Christ. ª*1 Pet 2:8* ᵇ*2 Tim 2:12*

5 Now I desire to remind you, though you know all things once for all, that the Lord, ªafter saving a people out of the land of Egypt, subsequently destroyed those who did not believe. ª*Ex 12:51; 1 Cor 10:5-10*

6 And ªangels who did not keep their own domain, but abandoned their proper abode, He has ᵇkept in eternal bonds under darkness for the judgment of the great day, ª*2 Pet 2:4* ᵇ*2 Pet 2:9*

7 just as Sodom and Gomorrah and the cities around them, since they in the same way as these indulged in gross immorality and went

after strange flesh, are exhibited as an example in undergoing the ªpunishment of eternal fire. *Matt 25:41; 2 Thess 1:8f*

8 Yet in the same way these men, also by dreaming, ªdefile the flesh, and reject authority, and revile angelic majesties. ª2 Pet 2:10

9 But Michael ªthe archangel, when he disputed with the devil and argued about the body of Moses, did not dare pronounce against him a railing judgment, but said, "ᵇThe Lord rebuke you!" ª2 Pet 2:11 ᵇZech 3:2

10 But ªthese men revile the things which they do not understand; and the things which they know by instinct, ªlike unreasoning animals, by these things they are destroyed. ª2 Pet 2:12

11 Woe to them! For they have gone ªthe way of Cain, and for pay they have rushed headlong into the error of Balaam, and ᵇperished in the rebellion of Korah. ªGen 4:3-8 ᵇNum 16:1-3, 31-35

12 These are the men who are hidden reefs ªin your love feasts when they feast with you without fear, caring for themselves; ᵇclouds without water, carried along by winds; autumn trees without fruit, doubly dead, uprooted; ª1 Cor 11:20ff ᵇProv 25:14

13 ªwild waves of the sea, casting up their own shame like foam; wandering stars, ᵇfor whom the black darkness has been reserved forever. ªIs 57:20 ᵇ2 Pet 2:17

14 *It was* also about these men *that* ªEnoch, *in* the seventh *generation* from Adam, prophesied, saying, "Behold, the Lord came with many thousands of His holy ones, ªGen 5:18, 21ff

15 to execute judgment upon all, and to convict all the ungodly of all their ungodly deeds which they have done in an ungodly way, and of all the harsh things which ªungodly sinners have spoken against Him." ª1 Tim 1:9

16 These are ªgrumblers, finding fault, following after their *own* lusts; they speak ᵇarrogantly, flattering people for the sake of *gaining an* advantage. ªNum 16:11, 41 ᵇ2 Pet 2:18

Keep Yourselves in the Love of God

17 But you, beloved, ªought to remember the words that were spoken beforehand by the apostles of our Lord Jesus Christ, ª2 Pet 3:2

18 that they were saying to you, "ªIn the last time there will be mockers, following after their own ungodly lusts." ªActs 20:29; 1 Tim 4:1

19 These are the ones who cause divisions, ªworldly-minded, devoid of the Spirit. ª1 Cor 2:14f; James 3:15

20 But you, beloved, ªbuilding yourselves up on your most holy faith, praying in the Holy Spirit, ªCol 2:7; 1 Thess 5:11

21 keep yourselves in the love of God, ªwaiting anxiously for the mercy of our Lord Jesus Christ to eternal life. ªTitus 2:13; Heb 9:28

22 And have mercy on some, who are doubting;

23 save others, ªsnatching them out of the fire; and on some have mercy with fear, ᵇhating even the garment polluted by the flesh. ªAmos 4:11 ᵇZech 3:3f

24 Now to Him who is able to keep you from stumbling, and to ªmake you stand in the presence of His glory blameless with great joy, ª2 Cor 4:14

25 to the ªonly ᵇGod our Savior, through Jesus Christ our Lord, *be* glory, majesty, dominion and authority, before all time and now and forever. Amen. ªJohn 5:44 ᵇ

THE REVELATION
to John

The Revelation of
Jesus Christ

1 The Revelation of Jesus Christ, which ªGod gave Him to ᵇshow to His bond-servants, the things which must soon take place; and He sent and communicated *it* by His angel to His bond-servant John, ªJohn 17:8 ᵇRev 22:6

2 who testified to ªthe word of God and to the testimony of Jesus Christ, *even* to all that he saw. ªRev 1:9; 6:9

3 ªBlessed is he who reads and those who hear the words of the prophecy, and heed the things which are written in it; ᵇfor the time is near. ªLuke 11:28 ᵇRev 22:10

Message to the
Seven Churches

4 John to the seven churches that are in ªAsia: Grace to you and peace, from ᵇHim who is and who was and who is to come, and from the seven Spirits who are before His throne, ªActs 2:9 ᵇRev 1:8; 17

5 and from Jesus Christ, ªthe faithful witness, the ᵇfirstborn of the dead, and the ruler of the kings of the earth. To Him who loves us and released us from our sins by His blood— ªRev 3:14 ᵇ1 Cor 15:20

6 and He has made us *to be* a ªkingdom, priests to ᵇHis God and Father—to Him *be* the glory and the dominion forever and ever. Amen. ªRev 5:10 ᵇRom 15:6

7 ªBEHOLD, HE IS COMING WITH THE CLOUDS, and every eye will see Him, even those who pierced Him; and all the tribes of the earth will mourn over Him. So it is to be. Amen. ªDan 7:13; 1 Thess 4:17

8 "I am ªthe Alpha and the Omega," says the

Lord God, "who is and who was and who is to come, the Almighty." ªRev 21:6; 22:13

The Patmos Vision

9 I, John, your brother and ªfellow partaker in the tribulation and kingdom and ᵇperseverance *which are* in Jesus, was on the island called Patmos because of the word of God and the testimony of Jesus. ªActs 14:22 ᵇ2 Thess 3:5

10 I was ªin the Spirit on the Lord's day, and I heard behind me a loud voice ᵇlike *the sound* of a trumpet, ªMatt 22:43 ᵇRev 4:1

11 saying, "ªWrite in a book what you see, and send *it* to the seven churches: to Ephesus and to Smyrna and to Pergamum and to Thyatira and to Sardis and to Philadelphia and to Laodicea." ªRev 1:19

12 Then I turned to see the voice that was speaking with me. And having turned I saw ªseven golden lampstands; ªEx 25:37; 37:23

13 and in the middle of the lampstands *I saw* one ªlike a son of man, clothed in a robe reaching to the feet, and girded across His chest with a golden sash. ªDan 7:13; Rev 14:14

14 His head and His hair were white like white wool, like snow; and ªHis eyes were like a flame of fire. ªDan 7:9; 10:6

15 His ªfeet *were* like burnished bronze, when it has been made to glow in a furnace, and His ᵇvoice *was* like the sound of many waters. ªEzek 1:7 ᵇEzek 1:24

16 In His right hand He held seven stars, and out of His mouth came a ªsharp two-edged sword; and His ᵇface was like the sun shining in its strength. ªIs 49:2 ᵇMatt 17:2

17 When I saw Him, I ªfell at His feet like a dead man. And He placed His right hand on me, saying, "Do not be afraid; ᵇI am the first and the last, ªDan 8:17 ᵇIs 44:6

18 and the ªliving One; and I ᵇwas dead, and behold, I am alive forevermore, and I have the keys of death and of Hades. ªLuke 24:5 ᵇRev 2:8

19 "Therefore ªwrite ᵇthe things which you have seen, and the things which are, and the things which will take place after these things. ªRev 1:11 ᵇRev 1:12-16

20 "As for the mystery of the seven stars which you saw in My right hand, and the seven golden lampstands: the seven stars are the angels of ªthe seven churches, and the seven lampstands are the seven churches. ªRev 1:4, 11

Message to Ephesus

2 "To the angel of the church in ªEphesus write:

The One who holds the seven stars in His right hand, the One who walks among the seven golden lampstands, says this: ªRev 1:11

2 'I know your deeds and your toil and perseverance, and that you cannot tolerate evil men, and you ªput to the test those who call them-

selves apostles, and they are not, and you found them *to be* false; ª1 John 4:1

3 and you have perseverance and have endured ªfor My name's sake, and have not grown weary. ªJohn 15:21

4 'But I have *this* against you, that you have ªleft your first love. ªJer 2:2; Matt 24:12

5 'Therefore remember from where you have fallen, and ªrepent and ᵇdo the deeds you did at first; or else I am coming to you and will remove your lampstand out of its place—unless you repent. ªRev 2:16, 22 ᵇHeb 10:32

6 'Yet this you do have, that you hate the deeds of the ªNicolaitans, which I also hate. ªRev 2:15

7 'He who has an ear, let him hear what the Spirit says to the churches. To him who overcomes, I will grant to eat of ªthe tree of life which is in the ᵇParadise of God.' ªGen 2:9 ᵇEzek 28:13

Message to Smyrna

8 "And to the angel of the church in Smyrna write:

ªThe first and the last, who ᵇwas dead, and has come to life, says this: ªIs 44:6 ᵇRev 1:18

9 'I know your ªtribulation and your ᵇpoverty (but you are ᵇrich), and the blasphemy by those who say they are Jews and are not, but are a synagogue of Satan. ªRev 1:9 ᵇ2 Cor 6:10

10 'Do not fear what you are about to suffer. Behold, the devil is about to cast some of you into prison, so that you will be tested, and you will have tribulation for ten days. Be ªfaithful until death, and I will give you the crown of life. ªRev 2:13; 12:11

11 'He who has an ear, let him hear what the Spirit says to the churches. He who overcomes will not be hurt by the ªsecond death.' ªRev 20:6, 14; 21:8

Message to Pergamum

12 "And to the angel of the church in Pergamum write:

The One who has ªthe sharp two-edged sword says this: ªRev 1:16; 2:16

13 'I know where you dwell, where Satan's throne is; and you hold fast My name, and did not deny My faith even in the days of Antipas, My ªwitness, My faithful one, who was killed among you, where Satan dwells. ªActs 22:20; Rev 1:5

14 'But I have a few things against you, because you have there some who hold the teaching of Balaam, who kept teaching Balak to put a stumbling block before the sons of Israel, ªto eat things sacrificed to idols and to commit *acts of* immorality. ªNum 25:1f; Acts 15:29

15 'So you also have some who in the same way hold the teaching of the ªNicolaitans. ªRev 2:6

16 'Therefore ^arepent; or else I am coming to
you quickly, and I will make war against them
with ^bthe sword of My mouth. ^a*Rev 2:5* ^b*Rev 1:16*
17 'He who has an ear, let him hear what the
Spirit says to the churches. To him who overcomes, to him I will give *some* of the hidden
manna, and I will give him a white stone, and a
^anew name written on the stone ^bwhich no one
knows but he who receives it.' ^a*Is 62:2* ^b*Rev 19:12*

Message to Thyatira

18 "And to the angel of the church in Thyatira
write:

The Son of God, ^awho has eyes like a flame
of fire, and His feet are like burnished bronze,
says this: ^a*Rev 1:14f*
19 '^aI know your deeds, and your love and
faith and service and perseverance, and that
your deeds of late are greater than at first.
^a*Rev 2:2*
20 'But I have *this* against you, that you tolerate the woman ^aJezebel, who calls herself a
prophetess, and she teaches and leads My
bond-servants astray so that they commit *acts
of* immorality and eat things sacrificed to idols.
^a*1 Kin 16:31; 21:25*
21 '^aI gave her time to repent, and she ^bdoes
not want to repent of her immorality. ^a*2 Pet 3:9*
^b*Rom 2:5*
22 'Behold, I will throw her on a bed *of sickness,* and those who ^acommit adultery with her
into great tribulation, unless they repent of her
deeds. ^a*Rev 17:2; 18:9*
23 'And I will kill her children with pestilence, and all the churches will know that I am
He who ^asearches the minds and hearts; and I
will give to each one of you according to your
deeds. ^a*Ps 7:9; Jer 11:20*
24 'But I say to you, the rest who are in
Thyatira, who do not hold this teaching, who
have not known the ^adeep things of Satan, as
they call them—I ^bplace no other burden on
you. ^a*1 Cor 2:10* ^b*Acts 15:28*
25 'Nevertheless ^awhat you have, hold fast
until I come. ^a*Rev 3:11*
26 'He who overcomes, and he who keeps My
deeds until the end, ^aTO HIM I WILL GIVE AUTHOR-
ITY OVER THE NATIONS; ^a*Ps 2:8*
27 AND HE SHALL ^aRULE THEM WITH A ROD OF IRON,
^bAS THE VESSELS OF THE POTTER ARE BROKEN TO
PIECES, as I also have received *authority* from
My Father; ^a*Ps 2:9* ^b*Is 30:14*
28 and I will give him ^athe morning star.
^a*1 John 3:2; Rev 22:16*
29 '^aHe who has an ear, let him hear what the
Spirit says to the churches.' ^a*Rev 2:7*

Message to Sardis

3 "To the angel of the church in Sardis write:
He who has the seven Spirits of God and
^athe seven stars, says this: 'I know your deeds,

that you have a name that you are alive, but
you are ^bdead. ^a*Rev 1:16* ^b*1 Tim 5:6*
2 'Wake up, and strengthen the things that
remain, which were about to die; for I have not
found your deeds completed in the sight of My
God.
3 'So ^aremember what you have received and
heard; and keep *it,* and ^arepent. Therefore if
you do not wake up, ^aI will come like a thief,
and you will not know at what hour I will
come to you. ^a*Rev 2:5*
4 'But you have a few people in Sardis who
have not ^asoiled their garments; and they will
walk with Me ^bin white, for they are worthy.
^a*Jude 23* ^b*Eccl 9:8*
5 'He who overcomes will thus be clothed in
white garments; and I will not erase his name
from the book of life, and ^aI will confess his
name before My Father and before His angels.
^a*Matt 10:32*
6 '^aHe who has an ear, let him hear what the
Spirit says to the churches.' ^a*Rev 2:7*

Message to Philadelphia

7 "And to the angel of the church in Philadelphia write:

He who is holy, who is true, who has ^athe
key of David, who opens and no one will shut,
and who shuts and no one opens, says this:
^a*Is 22:22; Matt 16:19*
8 'I know your deeds. Behold, I have put
before you ^aan open door which no one can
shut, because you have a little power, and have
kept My word, and ^bhave not denied My name.
^a*Acts 14:27* ^b*Rev 2:13*
9 'Behold, I will cause *those* of ^athe synagogue of Satan, who say that they are Jews and
are not, but lie—I will make them ^bcome and
bow down at your feet, and *make them* know
that I have loved you. ^a*Rev 2:9* ^b*Is 45:14*
10 'Because you have kept the word of My
perseverance, I also will keep you from the
hour of testing, that *hour* which is about to
come upon the whole ^aworld, to test those who
dwell on the earth. ^a*Rev 16:14*
11 'I am coming quickly; ^ahold fast what you
have, so that no one will take your ^bcrown.
^a*Rev 2:25* ^b*Rev 2:10*
12 'He who overcomes, I will make him a
^apillar in the temple of My God, and he will not
go out from it anymore; and I will write on him
the ^bname of My God, and the name of the city
of My God, the new Jerusalem, which comes
down out of heaven from My God, and My
new name. ^a*Gal 2:9* ^b*Rev 14:1*
13 '^aHe who has an ear, let him hear what the
Spirit says to the churches.' ^a*Rev 3:6*

Message to Laodicea

14 "To the angel of the church in Laodicea
write:

[a]The Amen, [b]the faithful and true Witness, the Beginning of the creation of God, says this: [a]*2 Cor 1:20* [b]*Rev 3:7*

15 '[a]I know your deeds, that you are neither cold nor hot; I wish that you were cold or hot. [a]*Rev 3:1*

16 'So because you are lukewarm, and neither hot nor cold, I will spit you out of My mouth.

17 'Because you say, "[a]I am rich, and have become wealthy, and have need of nothing," and you do not know that you are wretched and miserable and poor and blind and naked, [a]*Hos 12:8; Zech 11:5*

18 I advise you to [a]buy from Me gold refined by fire so that you may become rich, and white garments so that you may clothe yourself, and *that* the shame of your nakedness will not be revealed; and eye salve to anoint your eyes so that you may see. [a]*Matt 13:44*

19 '[a]Those whom I love, I reprove and discipline; therefore be zealous and repent. [a]*Prov 3:12; 1 Cor 11:32*

20 'Behold, I stand at the door and knock; if anyone hears My voice and opens the door, [a]I will come in to him and will dine with him, and he with Me. [a]*John 14:23*

21 'He who overcomes, I will grant to him to sit down with Me on My throne, as [a]I also overcame and sat down with My Father on His throne. [a]*John 16:33; Rev 5:5*

22 '[a]He who has an ear, let him hear what the Spirit says to the churches.' " [a]*Rev 2:7*

Scene in Heaven

4 After these things I looked, and behold, a door *standing* open in heaven, and the first voice which I had heard, [a]like *the sound* of a trumpet speaking with me, said, "[b]Come up here, and I will show you what must take place after these things." [a]*Rev 1:10* [b]*Rev 11:12*

2 Immediately I was [a]in the Spirit; and behold, [b]a throne was standing in heaven, and One sitting on the throne. [a]*Rev 1:10* [b]*1 Kin 22:19*

3 And He who was sitting *was* like a jasper stone and a sardius in appearance; and *there was* a [a]rainbow around the throne, like an emerald in appearance. [a]*Ezek 1:28*

4 Around the throne *were* [a]twenty-four thrones; and upon the thrones *I saw* [b]twenty-four elders sitting, clothed in white garments, and golden crowns on their heads. [a]*Rev 11:16* [b]*Rev 4:10*

The Throne and Worship of the Creator

5 Out from the throne come flashes of lightning and sounds and peals of thunder. And *there were* [a]seven lamps of fire burning before the throne, which are the seven Spirits of God; [a]*Ex 25:37; Zech 4:2*

6 and before the throne *there was something* like a sea of glass, like crystal; and in the center and around the throne, four living creatures [a]full of eyes in front and behind. [a]*Ezek 1:18; 10:12*

7 [a]The first creature *was* like a lion, and the second creature like a calf, and the third creature had a face like that of a man, and the fourth creature *was* like a flying eagle. [a]*Ezek 1:10; 10:14*

8 And the four living creatures, each one of them having six wings, are full of eyes around and within; and day and night they do not cease to say,

   "[a]HOLY, HOLY, HOLY *is* THE LORD GOD, THE ALMIGHTY, WHO WAS AND WHO IS AND WHO IS TO COME." [a]*Is 6:3*

9 And when the living creatures give glory and honor and thanks to Him who [a]sits on the throne, to Him who lives forever and ever, [a]*Ps 47:8; Is 6:1*

10 the twenty-four elders will [a]fall down before Him who sits on the throne, and will worship Him who lives forever and ever, and will cast their crowns before the throne, saying, [a]*Rev 5:8, 14; 7:11*

11 "Worthy are You, our Lord and our God, to receive glory and honor and power; for You [a]created all things, and because of Your will they existed, and were created." [a]*Acts 14:15; Rev 10:6*

The Book with Seven Seals

5 I saw in the right hand of Him who sat on the throne a [a]book written inside and on the back, [b]sealed up with seven seals. [a]*Ezek 2:9, 10* [b]*Is 29:11*

2 And I saw a [a]strong angel proclaiming with a loud voice, "Who is worthy to open the book and to break its seals?" [a]*Rev 10:1; 18:21*

3 And no one [a]in heaven or on the earth or under the earth was able to open the book or to look into it. [a]*Phil 2:10; Rev 5:13*

4 Then I *began* to weep greatly because no one was found worthy to open the book or to look into it;

5 and one of the elders *said to me, "Stop weeping; behold, the Lion that is [a]from the tribe of Judah, the [b]Root of David, has overcome so as to open the book and its seven seals." [a]*Heb 7:14* [b]*Rev 22:16*

6 And I saw between the throne (with the four living creatures) and the elders a Lamb standing, as if slain, having seven horns and [a]seven eyes, which are the seven Spirits of God, sent out into all the earth. [a]*Zech 3:9; 4:10*

7 And He came and took [a]the book out of the right hand of Him who [a]sat on the throne. [a]*Rev 5:1*

8 When He had taken the book, the four living creatures and the twenty-four elders fell down before the Lamb, each one holding a

harp and golden bowls full of incense, which are the [a]prayers of the saints. [a]*Ps 141:2; Rev 8:3f*

9 And they *sang a new song, saying,

"Worthy are You to take the book and to break its seals; for You were slain, and [a]purchased for God with Your blood *men* from [b]every tribe and tongue and people and nation.   [a]*1 Cor 6:20* [b]*Dan 3:4*

10 "You have made them *to be* a [a]kingdom and priests to our God; and they will [b]reign upon the earth."   [a]*Rev 1:6* [b]*Rev 20:4*

Angels Exalt the Lamb

11 Then I looked, and I heard the voice of many angels around the throne and the [a]living creatures and the elders; and the number of them was [b]myriads of myriads, and thousands of thousands. [a]*Rev 4:6* [b]*Dan 7:10*

12 saying with a loud voice,

"Worthy is the [a]Lamb that was slain to receive power and riches and wisdom and might and honor and glory and blessing."
[a]*John 1:29; Rev 5:6, 13*

13 And every created thing which is in heaven and on the earth and under the earth and on the sea, and all things in them, I heard saying,

"To Him who sits on the throne, and to the Lamb, [a]*be* blessing and honor and glory and dominion forever and ever."
[a]*Rev 1:6*

14 And the four living creatures kept saying, "[a]Amen." And the elders fell down and worshiped.   [a]*1 Cor 14:16; Rev 7:12*

The Book Opened; The First Seal—The False Christ

6 Then I saw when the Lamb broke one of the [a]seven seals, and I heard one of the four living creatures saying as with a voice of thunder, "Come." [a]*Rev 5:1*

2 I looked, and behold, a white horse, and he who sat on it had a bow; and [a]a crown was given to him, and he went out conquering and to conquer. [a]*Zech 6:11; Rev 14:14*

The Second Seal—War

3 When He broke the second seal, I heard the [a]second living creature saying, "Come."
[a]*Rev 4:7*

4 And another, [a]a red horse, went out; and to him who sat on it, it was granted to [b]take peace from the earth, and that *men* would slay one another; and a great sword was given to him.
[a]*Zech 1:8* [b]*Matt 10:34*

The Third Seal—Famine

5 When He broke the third seal, I heard the [a]third living creature saying, "Come." I looked, and behold, a black horse; and he who sat on it had a pair of scales in his hand. [a]*Rev 4:7*

6 And I heard *something* like a voice in the center of the [a]four living creatures saying, "A

quart of wheat for a denarius, and three quarts of barley for a denarius; and do not damage the oil and the wine." [a]*Rev 4:6f*

The Fourth Seal—Death

7 When the Lamb broke the fourth seal, I heard the voice of the [a]fourth living creature saying, "Come." [a]*Rev 4:7*

8 I looked, and behold, an ashen horse; and he who sat on it had the name [a]Death; and Hades was following with him. Authority was given to them over a fourth of the earth, to kill with sword and with famine and with pestilence and by the wild beasts of the earth.
[a]*Prov 5:5; Hos 13:14*

The Fifth Seal—Martyrs

9 When the Lamb broke the fifth seal, I saw underneath the altar the [a]souls of those who had been slain [b]because of the word of God, and because of the testimony which they had maintained; [a]*Rev 20:4* [b]*Rev 1:2, 9*

10 and they cried out with a loud voice, saying, "How long, O Lord, [a]holy and true, will You refrain from [b]judging and avenging our blood on those who dwell on the earth?"
[a]*Rev 3:7* [b]*Deut 32:43*

11 And [a]there was given to each of them a white robe; and they were told that they should rest for a little while longer, until *the number of* their fellow servants and their brethren who were to be killed even as they had been, would be [b]completed also. [a]*Rev 3:4, 5* [b]*Acts 20:24*

The Sixth Seal—Terror

12 I looked when He broke the sixth seal, and there was a great earthquake; and the [a]sun became black as sackcloth *made* of hair, and the whole moon became like blood; [a]*Is 13:10; Joel 2:10, 31*

13 and [a]the stars of the sky fell to the earth, as a fig tree casts its unripe figs when shaken by a great wind. [a]*Matt 24:29*

14 The sky was split apart like a scroll when it is rolled up, and [a]every mountain and island were moved out of their places. [a]*Is 54:10; Jer 4:24*

15 Then [a]the kings of the earth and the great men and the commanders and the rich and the strong and every slave and free man hid themselves in the caves and among the rocks of the mountains; [a]*Is 2:10f, 19, 21*

16 and they *said to the mountains and to the rocks, "Fall on us and hide us from the presence of Him [b]who sits on the throne, and from the wrath of the Lamb; [a]*Hos 10:8* [b]*Rev 4:9*

17 for [a]the great day of their wrath has come, and [b]who is able to stand?" [a]*Joel 2:11* [b]*Mal 3:2*

An Interlude

7 After this I saw four angels standing at the four corners of the earth, holding back [a]the four winds of the earth, so that no wind would

blow on the earth or on the sea or on any tree. ªJer 49:36; Dan 7:2

2 And I saw another angel ascending from the rising of the sun, having the ªseal of ᵇthe living God; and he cried out with a loud voice to the four angels to whom it was granted to harm the earth and the sea, ªRev 7:3 ᵇMatt 16:16

3 saying, "Do not harm the earth or the sea or the trees until we have ªsealed the bond-servants of our God on their ᵇforeheads." ªRev 7:3-8 ᵇEzek 9:4, 6

A Remnant of Israel—144,000

4 And I heard the number of those who were sealed, ªone hundred and forty-four thousand sealed from every tribe of the sons of Israel: ªRev 14:1, 3

5 from the tribe of Judah, twelve thousand *were* sealed, from the tribe of Reuben twelve thousand, from the tribe of Gad twelve thousand,

6 from the tribe of Asher twelve thousand, from the tribe of Naphtali twelve thousand, from the tribe of Manasseh twelve thousand,

7 from the tribe of Simeon twelve thousand, from the tribe of Levi twelve thousand, from the tribe of Issachar twelve thousand,

8 from the tribe of Zebulun twelve thousand, from the tribe of Joseph twelve thousand, from the tribe of Benjamin, twelve thousand *were* sealed.

A Multitude from the Tribulation

9 After these things I looked, and behold, a great multitude which no one could count, from ªevery nation and *all* tribes and peoples and tongues, standing before the throne and ᵇbefore the Lamb, clothed in white robes, and palm branches *were* in their hands; ªRev 5:9 ᵇRev 22:3

10 and they cry out with a loud voice, saying, "ªSalvation to our God who sits on the throne, and to the Lamb." ªPs 3:8; Rev 12:10

11 And all the angels were standing ªaround the throne and *around* ªthe elders and the four living creatures; and they fell on their faces before the throne and worshiped God, ªRev 4:4

12 saying,
"Amen, ªblessing and glory and wisdom and thanksgiving and honor and power and might, *be* to our God forever and ever. Amen." ªRev 5:12

13 Then one of the elders answered, saying to me, "These who are clothed in the ªwhite robes, who are they, and where have they come from?" ªRev 7:9

14 I said to him, "My lord, you know." And he said to me, "These are the ones who come out of the great tribulation, and they have washed their robes and made them white in the ªblood of the Lamb. ªHeb 9:14; 1 John 1:7

15 "For this reason, they are ªbefore the throne of God; and they serve Him day and night in His temple; and ᵇHe who sits on the throne will spread His tabernacle over them. ªRev 7:9 ᵇRev 4:9

16 "ªThey will hunger no longer, nor thirst anymore; nor will the sun beat down on them, nor any heat; ªPs 121:5f; Is 49:10

17 for the Lamb in the center of the throne will be their ªshepherd, and will guide them to springs of the water of life; and ᵇGod will wipe every tear from their eyes." ªPs 23:1f ᵇIs 25:8

The Seventh Seal— the Trumpets

8 When the Lamb broke the ªseventh seal, there was silence in heaven for about half an hour. ªRev 5:1; 6:1, 3, 5, 7, 9, 12

2 And I saw ªthe seven angels who stand before God, and seven trumpets were given to them. ªRev 8:6-13; 9:1, 13

3 Another angel came and stood at the ªaltar, holding a golden censer; and much ᵇincense was given to him, so that he might add it to the ᵇprayers of all the saints on the golden altar which was before the throne. ªRev 6:9 ᵇRev 5:8

4 And ªthe smoke of the incense, with the prayers of the saints, went up before God out of the angel's hand. ªPs 141:2

5 Then the angel took the censer and ªfilled it with the fire of the altar, and threw it to the earth; and there followed ᵇpeals of thunder and sounds and flashes of lightning and an earth-quake. ªLev 16:12 ᵇEx 19:16

6 ªAnd the seven angels who had the seven trumpets prepared themselves to sound them. ªRev 8:2

7 The first sounded, and there came ªhail and fire, mixed with blood, and they were thrown to the earth; and a third of the earth was burned up, and a third of the trees were burned up, and all the green grass was burned up. ªEx 9:23ff; Ezek 38:22

8 The second angel sounded, and *something* like a great mountain burning with fire was thrown into the sea; and a third of the ªsea became blood, ªEx 7:17ff; Rev 11:6

9 and a third of the creatures which were in the sea and had life, died; and a third of the ªships were destroyed. ªIs 2:16

10 The third angel sounded, and a great star ªfell from heaven, burning like a torch, and it fell on a third of the rivers and on the ᵇsprings of waters. ªIs 14:12 ᵇRev 14:7

11 The name of the star is called Wormwood; and a third of the waters became ªwormwood,

and many men died from the waters, because they were made bitter. [a]Jer 9:15; 23:15

12 The fourth angel sounded, and a third of the [a]sun and a third of the [a]moon and a third of the stars were struck, so that a third of them would be darkened and the day would not shine for a third of it, and the night in the same way. [a]Ex 10:21ff; Is 13:10

13 Then I looked, and I heard an eagle flying in [a]midheaven, saying with a loud voice, "Woe, woe, woe to [b]those who dwell on the earth, because of the remaining blasts of the trumpet of the three angels who are about to sound!" [a]Rev 14:6 [b]Rev 3:10

The Fifth Trumpet— the Bottomless Pit

9 Then the fifth angel sounded, and I saw a star from heaven which had fallen to the earth; and the key of the [a]bottomless pit was given to him. [a]Luke 8:31; Rev 9:2, 11

2 He opened the bottomless pit, and [a]smoke went up out of the pit, like the smoke of a great furnace; and the sun and the air were darkened by the smoke of the pit. [a]Gen 19:28; Ex 19:18

3 Then out of the smoke came [a]locusts upon the earth, and power was given them, as the scorpions of the earth have power. [a]Ex 10:12-15; Rev 9:7

4 They were told not to hurt the grass of the earth, nor any green thing, nor any tree, but only the men who do not have the [a]seal of God on their foreheads. [a]Ezek 9:4; Rev 7:2, 3

5 And they were not permitted to kill anyone, but to torment for five months; and their torment was like the torment of a [a]scorpion when it stings a man. [a]2 Chr 10:11, 14; Ezek 2:6

6 And in those days [a]men will seek death and will not find it; they will long to die, and death flees from them. [a]Job 3:21; 7:15

7 The [a]appearance of the locusts was like horses prepared for battle; and on their heads appeared to be crowns like gold, and their faces were like the faces of men. [a]Joel 2:4

8 They had hair like the hair of women, and their [a]teeth were like the teeth of lions. [a]Joel 1:6

9 They had breastplates like breastplates of iron; and the [a]sound of their wings was like the sound of chariots, of many horses rushing to battle. [a]Jer 47:3; Joel 2:5

10 They have tails like scorpions, and stings; and in their [a]tails is their power to hurt men for [b]five months. [a]Rev 9:19 [b]Rev 9:5

11 They have as king over them, the angel of the [a]abyss; his name in Hebrew is Abaddon, and in the Greek he has the name Apollyon. [a]Luke 8:31; Rev 9:1, 2

12 [a]The first woe is past; behold, two woes are still coming after these things. [a]Rev 8:13; 11:14

The Sixth Trumpet— Army from the East

13 Then the sixth angel sounded, and I heard a voice from the four horns of the [a]golden altar which is before God, [a]Rev 8:3

14 one saying to the sixth angel who had the trumpet, "Release the four angels who are bound at the [a]great river Euphrates." [a]Gen 15:18; Deut 1:7

15 And the four angels, who had been prepared for the hour and day and month and year, were [a]released, so that they would kill a third of mankind. [a]Rev 20:7

16 The number of the armies of the horsemen was [a]two hundred million; I heard the number of them. [a]Rev 5:11

17 And this is how I saw in the vision the horses and those who sat on them: *the riders* had breastplates *the color* of fire and of hyacinth and of [a]brimstone; and the heads of the horses are like the heads of lions; and [b]out of their mouths proceed fire and smoke and [a]brimstone. [a]Rev 9:18 [b]Rev 11:5

18 A [a]third of mankind was killed by these three plagues, by the fire and the smoke and the brimstone which proceeded out of their mouths. [a]Rev 8:7; 9:15

19 For the power of the horses is in their mouths and in their tails; for their tails are like serpents and have heads, and with them they do harm.

20 The rest of mankind, who were not killed by these plagues, [a]did not repent of the works of their hands, so as not to worship demons, and the idols of gold and of silver and of brass and of stone and of wood, which can neither see nor hear nor walk; [a]Rev 2:21

21 and they did not repent of their murders nor of their [a]sorceries nor of their immorality nor of their thefts. [a]Is 47:9, 12; Rev 18:23

The Angel and the Little Book

10 I saw another strong angel coming down out of heaven, clothed with a cloud; and the [a]rainbow was upon his head, and [b]his face was like the sun, and his feet like pillars of fire; [a]Rev 4:3 [b]Matt 17:2

2 and he had in his hand a [a]little book which was open. He placed his right foot on the sea and his left on the land; [a]Rev 5:1; 10:8-10

3 and he cried out with a loud voice, [a]as when a lion roars; and when he had cried out, the seven peals of thunder uttered their voices. [a]Is 31:4; Hos 11:10

4 When the seven peals of thunder had spoken, [a]I was about to write; and I heard a voice from heaven saying, "Seal up the things which the seven peals of thunder have spoken and do not write them." [a]Rev 1:11, 19

5 Then the angel whom I saw standing on the sea and on the land [a]lifted up his right hand to heaven, [a]*Deut 32:40; Dan 12:7*

6 and swore by Him who lives forever and ever, [a]WHO CREATED HEAVEN AND THE THINGS IN IT, AND THE EARTH AND THE THINGS IN IT, AND THE SEA AND THE THINGS IN IT, that there will be delay no longer, [a]*Ex 20:11; Rev 4:11*

7 but in the days of the voice of the [a]seventh angel, when he is about to sound, then [b]the mystery of God is finished, as He preached to His servants the prophets. [a]*Rev 11:15* [b]*Amos 3:7*

8 Then [a]the voice which I heard from heaven, *I heard* again speaking with me, and saying, "Go, take [b]the book which is open in the hand of the angel who [b]stands on the sea and on the land." [a]*Rev 10:4* [b]*Rev 10:2*

9 So I went to the angel, telling him to give me the little book. And he *said to me, "[a]Take it and eat it; it will make your stomach bitter, but in your mouth it will be sweet as honey." [a]*Jer 15:16; Ezek 2:8*

10 I took the little book out of the angel's hand and ate it, and in my mouth it was sweet as honey; and when I had eaten it, my stomach was made bitter.

11 And they *said to me, "You must prophesy again concerning [a]many peoples and nations and tongues and [b]kings." [a]*Rev 5:9* [b]*Rev 17:10, 12*

The Two Witnesses

11 Then there was given me a [a]measuring rod like a staff; and someone said, "Get up and measure the temple of God and the altar, and those who worship in it. [a]*Ezek 40:3-42:20*

2 "Leave out the court which is outside the temple and do not measure it, for [a]it has been given to the nations; and they will [a]tread under foot the holy city for [b]forty-two months. [a]*Luke 21:24* [b]*Dan 7:25*

3 "And I will grant *authority* to my two witnesses, and they will prophesy for twelve hundred and sixty days, clothed in [a]sackcloth." [a]*Gen 37:34; 2 Sam 3:31*

4 These are the [a]two olive trees and the two lampstands that stand before the Lord of the earth. [a]*Zech 4:3, 11, 14*

5 And if anyone wants to harm them, [a]fire flows out of their mouth and devours their enemies; so if anyone wants to harm them, he must be killed in this way. [a]*2 Kin 1:10-12; Jer 5:14*

6 These have the power to [a]shut up the sky, so that rain will not fall during the days of their prophesying; and they have power over the waters to turn them into blood, and to strike the earth with every plague, as often as they desire. [a]*1 Kin 17:1; Luke 4:25*

7 When they have finished their testimony, [a]the beast that comes up out of the abyss will make war with them, and overcome them and kill them. [a]*Rev 13:1ff; 17:8*

8 And their dead bodies *will lie* in the street of the great city which mystically is called [a]Sodom and Egypt, where also their Lord was crucified. [a]*Is 1:9, 10; Jer 23:14*

9 Those from [a]the peoples and tribes and tongues and nations *will* look at their dead bodies for three and a half days, and will not permit their dead bodies to be laid in a tomb. [a]*Rev 5:9; 10:11*

10 And [a]those who dwell on the earth *will* rejoice over them and celebrate; and they will send gifts to one another, because these two prophets tormented [a]those who dwell on the earth. [a]*Rev 3:10*

11 But after the three and a half days, [a]the breath of life from God came into them, and they stood on their feet; and great fear fell upon those who were watching them. [a]*Ezek 37:5, 9, 10, 14*

12 And they heard a loud voice from heaven saying to them, "[a]Come up here." Then they [b]went up into heaven in the cloud, and their enemies watched them. [a]*Rev 4:1* [b]*2 Kin 2:11*

13 And in that hour there was a great [a]earthquake, and a tenth of the city fell; seven thousand people were killed in the earthquake, and the rest were terrified and gave glory to the God of heaven. [a]*Rev 6:12; 16:18*

14 The second [a]woe is past; behold, the third woe is coming quickly. [a]*Rev 8:13; 9:12*

The Seventh Trumpet—
Christ's Reign Foreseen

15 Then the seventh angel sounded; and there were loud voices in heaven, saying,
"The kingdom of the world has become *the kingdom* of our Lord and of His Christ; and [a]He will reign forever and ever." [a]*Ex 15:18; Dan 2:44*

16 And the twenty-four elders, who [a]sit on their thrones before God, [b]fell on their faces and worshiped God, [a]*Matt 19:28* [b]*Rev 4:10*

17 saying,
"We give You thanks, [a]O Lord God, the Almighty, who are and who were, because You have taken Your great power and have begun to [b]reign. [a]*Rev 1:8* [b]*Rev 19:6*

18 "And [a]the nations were enraged, and Your wrath came, and the time *came* for the dead to be judged, and *the time* to reward Your bondservants the prophets and the saints and those who fear Your name, the small and the great, and to destroy those who destroy the earth." [a]*Ps 2:1*

19 And [a]the temple of God which is in heaven was opened; and [b]the ark of His covenant appeared in His temple, and there were flashes of lightning and sounds and peals of thunder

and an earthquake and a great hailstorm.
[a]*Rev 15:5* [b]*Heb 9:4*

The Woman, Israel

12 A great [a]sign appeared in heaven: a woman clothed with the sun, and the moon under her feet, and on her head a crown of twelve stars; [a]*Matt 24:30; Rev 12:3*

2 and she was with child; and she *[a]cried out, being in labor and in pain to give birth. [a]*Is 26:17; 66:6-9*

The Red Dragon, Satan

3 Then another sign appeared in heaven: and behold, a great red [a]dragon having seven heads and [b]ten horns, and on his heads *were* seven diadems. [a]*Is 27:1* [b]*Dan 7:7, 20, 24*

4 And his tail *swept away a [a]third of the stars of heaven and [b]threw them to the earth. And the dragon stood before the woman who was about to give birth, so that when she gave birth he might devour her child. [a]*Rev 8:7, 12* [b]*Dan 8:10*

The Male Child, Christ

5 And [a]she gave birth to a son, a male *child,* who is to [b]rule all the nations with a rod of iron; and her child was caught up to God and to His throne. [a]*Is 66:7* [b]*Ps 2:9*

6 Then the woman fled into the wilderness where she *had a place prepared by God, so that there she would be nourished for [a]one thousand two hundred and sixty days. [a]*Rev 11:3; 13:5*

The Angel, Michael

7 And there was war in heaven, [a]Michael and his angels waging war with the dragon. The dragon and [b]his angels waged war, [a]*Dan 10:13, 21* [b]*Matt 25:41*

8 and they were not strong enough, and there was no longer a place found for them in heaven.

9 And the great dragon was thrown down, the [a]serpent of old who is called the devil and Satan, who deceives the whole world; he was thrown down to the earth, and his angels were thrown down with him. [a]*Gen 3:1; 2 Cor 11:3*

10 Then I heard a loud voice in heaven, saying,

"Now the salvation, and the power, and the kingdom of our God and the authority of His Christ have come, for the [a]accuser of our brethren has been thrown down, who accuses them before our God day and night. [a]*Job 1:11; 2:5*

11 "And they overcame him because of [a]the blood of the Lamb and because of the word of their testimony, and they did not love their life even when faced with death. [a]*Rev 7:14*

12 "For this reason, [a]rejoice, O heavens and you who dwell in them. Woe to the earth and

the sea, because the devil has come down to you, having great wrath, knowing that he has *only* a short time." [a]*Ps 96:11; Is 44:23*

13 And when the [a]dragon saw that he was thrown down to the earth, he persecuted the woman who gave birth to the male *child.* [a]*Rev 12:3*

14 But the [a]two wings of the great eagle were given to the woman, so that she could fly into the wilderness to her place, where she *was nourished for a time and times and half a time, from the presence of the serpent. [a]*Ex 19:4; Deut 32:11*

15 And the [a]serpent poured water like a river out of his mouth after the woman, so that he might cause her to be swept away with the flood. [a]*Gen 3:1; 2 Cor 11:3*

16 But the earth helped the woman, and the earth opened its mouth and drank up the river which the dragon poured out of his mouth.

17 So the dragon was enraged with the woman, and went off to [a]make war with the rest of her children, who keep the commandments of God and hold to the testimony of Jesus. [a]*Rev 11:7; 13:7*

The Beast from the Sea

13 And the dragon stood on the sand of the seashore.

Then I saw a beast coming up out of the sea, having [a]ten horns and seven heads, and on his horns *were* ten diadems, and on his heads *were* [b]blasphemous names. [a]*Rev 12:3* [b]*Dan 7:8*

2 And the beast which I saw was [a]like a leopard, and his feet were like *those* of a bear, and his mouth like the mouth of a lion. And the dragon gave him his power and his [b]throne and great authority. [a]*Dan 7:6* [b]*Rev 2:13*

3 *I saw* one of his heads as if it had been slain, and his [a]fatal wound was healed. And the whole earth was amazed *and followed* after the beast; [a]*Rev 13:12, 14*

4 they worshiped the [a]dragon because he gave his authority to the beast; and they worshiped the beast, saying, "Who is like the beast, and who is able to wage war with him?" [a]*Rev 12:3; 13:2, 12*

5 There was given to him a mouth [a]speaking arrogant words and blasphemies, and authority to act for forty-two months was given to him. [a]*Dan 7:25; 2 Thess 2:3f*

6 And he opened his mouth in blasphemies against God, to blaspheme His name and His tabernacle, *that is,* [a]those who dwell in heaven. [a]*Rev 7:15; 12:12*

7 It was also given to him to [a]make war with the saints and to overcome them, and authority over every tribe and people and tongue and nation was given to him. [a]*Dan 7:21; Rev 11:7*

8 All who dwell on the earth will worship

him, *everyone* whose name has not been written [a]from the foundation of the world in the book of life of the Lamb who has been slain. [a]*Rev 17:8*

9 [a]If anyone has an ear, let him hear. [a]*Rev 2:7*

10 [a]If anyone *is destined* for captivity, to captivity he goes; if anyone kills with the sword, with the sword he must be killed. Here is the perseverance and the faith of the saints. [a]*Jer 15:2; 43:11*

The Beast from the Earth

11 Then [a]I saw another beast coming up out of the earth; and he had two horns like a lamb and he spoke as a dragon. [a]*Rev 13:1; 16:13*

12 He exercises all the authority of the first beast [a]in his presence. And he makes the earth and those who dwell in it to worship the first beast, whose fatal wound was healed. [a]*Rev 13:14; 19:20*

13 He [a]performs great signs, so that he even makes [b]fire come down out of heaven to the earth in the presence of men. [a]*Matt 24:24* [b]*1 Kin 18:38*

14 And he deceives those who dwell on the earth because of [a]the signs which it was given him to perform in the presence of the beast, telling those who dwell on the earth to make an image to the beast who *had the [b]wound of the sword and has come to life. [a]*2 Thess 2:9f* [b]*Rev 13:3*

15 And it was given to him to give breath to the image of the beast, so that the image of the beast would even speak and cause [a]as many as do not worship the image of the beast to be killed. [a]*Dan 3:3ff*

16 And he causes all, [a]the small and the great, and the rich and the poor, and the free men and the slaves, to be given a mark on their right hand or on their forehead, [a]*Rev 11:18*

17 and *he provides* that no one will be able to buy or to sell, except the one who has the mark, *either* [a]the name of the beast or [b]the number of his name. [a]*Rev 14:11* [b]*Rev 15:2*

18 [a]Here is wisdom. Let him who has understanding calculate the number of the beast, for the number is that of a man; and his number is six hundred and sixty-six. [a]*Rev 17:9*

The Lamb and the 144,000 on Mount Zion

14 Then I looked, and behold, the Lamb *was* standing on Mount Zion, and with Him one hundred and forty-four thousand, having [a]His name and the name of His Father written on their foreheads. [a]*Rev 3:12*

2 And I heard a voice from heaven, like [a]the sound of many waters and like the sound of loud thunder, and the voice which I heard *was* like *the sound* of harpists playing on their harps. [a]*Rev 1:15*

3 And they *sang [a]a new song before the throne and before the four living creatures and the elders; and no one could learn the song except the [b]one hundred and forty-four thousand who had been [a]purchased from the earth. [a]*Rev 5:9* [b]*Rev 7:4*

4 [a]These are the ones who have not been defiled with women, for they have kept themselves chaste. These *are* the ones who [b]follow the Lamb wherever He goes. These have been purchased from among men as first fruits to God and to the Lamb. [a]*2 Cor 11:2* [b]*Rev 3:4*

5 And [a]no lie was found in their mouth; they are blameless. [a]*Ps 32:2; Zeph 3:13*

Vision of the Angel with the Gospel

6 And I saw another angel flying in midheaven, having [a]an eternal gospel to preach to those who live on the earth, and to every nation and tribe and tongue and people; [a]*1 Pet 1:25*

7 and he said with a loud voice, "[a]Fear God, and give Him glory, because the hour of His judgment has come; worship Him who made the heaven and the earth and sea and springs of waters." [a]*Rev 15:4*

8 And another angel, a second one, followed, saying, "[a]Fallen, fallen is Babylon the great, she who has [b]made all the nations drink of the wine of the passion of her immorality." [a]*Is 21:9* [b]*Jer 51:7*

Doom for Worshipers of the Beast

9 Then another angel, a third one, followed them, saying with a loud voice, "If anyone [a]worships the beast and his image, and receives a mark on his forehead or on his hand, [a]*Rev 13:12; 14:11*

10 he also will drink of the [a]wine of the wrath of God, which is mixed in full strength [b]in the cup of His anger; and he will be tormented with fire and brimstone in the presence of the holy angels and in the presence of the Lamb. [a]*Is 51:17* [b]*Ps 75:8*

11 "And the [a]smoke of their torment goes up forever and ever; they have no rest day and night, those who worship the beast and his image, and whoever receives the [b]mark of his name." [a]*Is 34:8-10* [b]*Rev 13:17*

12 Here is [a]the perseverance of the saints who [b]keep the commandments of God and their faith in Jesus. [a]*Rev 13:10* [b]*Rev 12:17*

13 And I heard a voice from heaven, saying, "Write, 'Blessed are the dead who [a]die in the Lord from now on!' " "Yes," says the Spirit, "so that they may [b]rest from their labors, for their deeds follow with them." [a]*1 Thess 4:16* [b]*Heb 4:9ff*

The Reapers

14 Then I looked, and behold, a white cloud,

and sitting on the cloud *was* one [a]like a son of man, having a golden crown on His head and a sharp sickle in His hand. [a]*Dan 7:13; Rev 1:13*

15 And another angel came out of the temple, crying out with a loud voice to Him who sat on the cloud, "[a]Put in your sickle and reap, for the hour to reap has come, because the [b]harvest of the earth is ripe." [a]*Joel 3:13* [b]*Matt 13:39-41*

16 Then He who sat on the cloud swung His sickle over the earth, and the earth was reaped.

17 And another angel [a]came out of the temple which is in heaven, and he also had a sharp sickle. [a]*Rev 11:19; 14:15*

18 Then another angel, the one who has power over fire, came out from [a]the altar; and he called with a loud voice to him who had the sharp sickle, saying, "Put in your sharp sickle and gather the clusters from the vine of the earth, because her grapes are ripe." [a]*Rev 6:9; 8:3*

19 So the angel swung his sickle to the earth and gathered *the clusters from* the vine of the earth, and threw them into [a]the great wine press of the wrath of God. [a]*Is 63:2f; Rev 19:15*

20 And [a]the wine press was trodden outside the city, and blood came out from the wine press, up to the horses' bridles, for a distance of two hundred miles. [a]*Is 63:3; Lam 1:15*

A Scene of Heaven

15 Then I saw another sign in heaven, great and marvelous, seven angels who had [a]seven plagues, *which are* the last, because in them the wrath of God is finished. [a]*Lev 26:21*

2 And I saw something like a [a]sea of glass mixed with fire, and those who had [b]been victorious over the beast and his image and the number of his name, standing on the [a]sea of glass, holding harps of God. [a]*Rev 4:6* [b]*Rev 12:11*

3 And they *sang the [a]song of Moses, the bond-servant of God, and the song of the Lamb, saying,

"[b]Great and marvelous are Your works,
O Lord God, the Almighty;
Righteous and true are Your ways,
King of the nations! [a]*Ex 15:1ff* [b]*Deut 32:3f*

4 "Who will not fear, O Lord, and glorify Your name?
For You alone are holy;
For [a]ALL THE NATIONS WILL COME AND WORSHIP BEFORE YOU,
FOR YOUR RIGHTEOUS ACTS HAVE BEEN REVEALED." [a]*Ps 86:9; Is 66:23*

5 After these things I looked, and [a]the temple of the tabernacle of testimony in heaven was opened, [a]*Rev 11:19*

6 and the [a]seven angels who had the seven plagues came out of the temple, clothed in linen, clean *and* bright, and girded around their chests with golden sashes. [a]*Rev 15:1*

7 Then one of the [a]four living creatures gave to the seven angels seven golden bowls full of the wrath of God, who lives forever and ever. [a]*Rev 4:6*

8 And the temple was filled with [a]smoke from the glory of God and from His power; and no one was able to enter the temple until the seven plagues of the seven angels were finished. [a]*Ex 19:18; 40:34f*

Six Bowls of Wrath

16 Then I heard a loud voice from [a]the temple, saying to the seven angels, "Go and pour out on the earth the seven bowls of the wrath of God." [a]*Rev 11:19*

2 So the first *angel* went and poured out his bowl on the earth; and it became a loathsome and malignant [a]sore on the people who had the mark of the beast and who worshiped his image. [a]*Ex 9:9-11; Deut 28:35*

3 The second *angel* poured out his bowl [a]into the sea, and it became blood like *that* of a dead man; and every living thing in the sea died. [a]*Ex 7:17-21; Rev 8:8f*

4 Then the third *angel* poured out his bowl into the [a]rivers and the springs of waters; and they became blood. [a]*Rev 8:10*

5 And I heard the angel of the waters saying, "[a]Righteous are You, [b]who are and who were, O Holy One, because You judged these things; [a]*John 17:25* [b]*Rev 11:17*

6 for they poured out [a]the blood of saints and prophets, and You have given them blood to drink. They deserve it." [a]*Rev 17:6; 18:24*

7 And I heard the altar saying, "Yes, O Lord God, the Almighty, [a]true and righteous are Your judgments." [a]*Rev 15:3; 19:2*

8 The fourth *angel* poured out his bowl upon [a]the sun, and it was given to it to scorch men with fire. [a]*Rev 6:12*

9 Men were scorched with fierce heat; and they [a]blasphemed the name of God who has the power over these plagues, and they did not repent so as to give Him glory. [a]*Rev 16:11, 21*

10 Then the fifth *angel* poured out his bowl on the [a]throne of the beast, and his kingdom became darkened; and they gnawed their tongues because of pain, [a]*Rev 13:2*

11 and they blasphemed the God of heaven because of their pains and their [a]sores; and they did not repent of their deeds. [a]*Rev 16:2*

12 The sixth *angel* poured out his bowl on the [a]great river, the Euphrates; and its water was dried up, so that the way would be prepared for the kings [b]from the east. [a]*Rev 9:14* [b]*Rev 7:2*

Armageddon

13 And I saw *coming* out of the mouth of the dragon and out of the mouth of the beast and out of the mouth of the false prophet, three [a]unclean spirits like [b]frogs; [a]*Rev 18:2* [b]*Ex 8:6*

14 for they are [a]spirits of demons, [b]performing

signs, which go out to the kings of the whole world, to gather them together for the war of the great day of God, the Almighty. [a]*1 Tim 4:1* [b]*Rev 13:13*

15 ("Behold, [a]I am coming like a thief. Blessed is the one who stays awake and keeps his clothes, so that he will not walk about naked and men will not see his shame.") [a]*Matt 24:43f; Luke 12:39f*

16 And they [a]gathered them together to the place which in Hebrew is called [b]Har-Magedon. [a]*Rev 19:19* [b]*Zech 12:11*

Seventh Bowl of Wrath

17 Then the seventh *angel* poured out his bowl upon the air, and a loud voice came out of the temple from the throne, saying, "[a]It is done." [a]*Rev 10:6; 21:6*

18 And there were flashes of [a]lightning and sounds and peals of thunder; and there was a great earthquake, such as there had not been since man came to be upon the earth, so great an earthquake *was it, and* so mighty. [a]*Rev 4:5*

19 The great city was split into three parts, and the cities of the nations fell. [a]Babylon the great was [b]remembered before God, to give her the cup of the wine of His fierce wrath. [a]*Rev 14:8* [b]*Rev 18:5*

20 And [a]every island fled away, and the mountains were not found. [a]*Rev 6:14; 20:11*

21 And huge hailstones, about one hundred pounds each, *came down from heaven upon men; and men blasphemed God because of the [a]plague of the hail, because its plague *was extremely severe. [a]*Ex 9:18-25*

The Doom of Babylon

17 Then one of the seven angels who had the seven bowls came and spoke with me, saying, "Come here, I will show you the judgment of the [a]great harlot who [b]sits on many waters, [a]*Rev 19:2* [b]*Jer 51:13*

2 with whom [a]the kings of the earth committed *acts of* immorality, and those who dwell on the earth were made drunk with the wine of her immorality." [a]*Rev 2:22; 18:3, 9*

3 And [a]he carried me away in the Spirit into a wilderness; and I saw a woman sitting on a scarlet beast, full of blasphemous names, having seven heads and ten horns. [a]*Rev 21:10*

4 The woman [a]was clothed in purple and scarlet, and adorned with gold and precious stones and pearls, having in her hand [b]a gold cup full of abominations and of the unclean things of her immorality, [a]*Ezek 28:13* [b]*Jer 51:7*

5 and on her forehead a name *was* written, a mystery, "BABYLON THE GREAT, THE MOTHER OF HARLOTS AND OF THE ABOMINATIONS OF THE EARTH." [a]*2 Thess 2:7; 17:7*

6 And I saw the woman drunk with [a]the blood of the saints, and with the blood of the witnesses of Jesus. When I saw her, I wondered greatly. [a]*Rev 16:6*

7 And the angel said to me, "Why do you wonder? I will tell you the mystery of the woman and of the beast that carries her, which has the [a]seven heads and the ten horns. [a]*Rev 17:3*

8 "The beast that you saw [a]was, and is not, and is about to [b]come up out of the abyss and go to destruction. And those who dwell on the earth, whose name has not been written in the book of life from the foundation of the world, will wonder when they see the beast, that he was and is not and will come. [a]*Rev 13:3, 12, 14* [b]*Rev 11:7*

9 "Here is the mind which has wisdom. The [a]seven heads are seven mountains on which the woman sits, [a]*Rev 17:3*

10 and they are seven [a]kings; five have fallen, one is, the other has not yet come; and when he comes, he must remain a little while. [a]*Rev 10:11*

11 "The beast which [a]was and is not, is himself also an eighth and is *one* of the seven, and he goes to destruction. [a]*Rev 13:3, 12, 14; 17:8*

12 "The [a]ten horns which you saw are ten kings who have not yet received a kingdom, but they receive authority as kings with the beast for one hour. [a]*Dan 7:24; Rev 12:3*

13 "These have [a]one purpose, and they give their power and authority to the beast. [a]*Rev 17:17*

Victory for the Lamb

14 "These will wage [a]war against the Lamb, and the Lamb will overcome them, because He is [b]Lord of lords and King of kings, and those who are with Him *are the* called and chosen and faithful." [a]*Rev 16:14* [b]*1 Tim 6:15*

15 And he *said to me, "The [a]waters which you saw where the harlot sits, are peoples and multitudes and nations and tongues. [a]*Is 8:7; Jer 47:2*

16 "And the [a]ten horns which you saw, and the beast, these will hate the harlot and will make her desolate and naked, and will eat her flesh and will burn her up with fire. [a]*Rev 17:12*

17 "For [a]God has put it in their hearts to execute His purpose by having a common purpose, and by giving their kingdom to the beast, until the words of God will be fulfilled. [a]*2 Cor 8:16*

18 "The woman whom you saw is [a]the great city, which reigns over the kings of the earth." [a]*Rev 11:8; 16:19*

Babylon Is Fallen

18 After these things I saw another [a]angel coming down from heaven, having

great authority, and the earth was illumined with his glory. [a]Rev 17:1, 7

2 And he cried out with a mighty voice, saying, "[a]Fallen, fallen is Babylon the great! She has become a dwelling place of demons and a prison of every [b]unclean spirit, and a prison of every unclean and hateful bird." [a]Is 21:9 [b]Rev 16:13

3 "For all the nations have drunk of the [a]wine of the passion of her immorality, and the kings of the earth have committed *acts of* immorality with her, and the merchants of the earth have become rich by the wealth of her sensuality." [a]Jer 51:7; Rev 14:8

4 I heard another voice from heaven, saying, "[a]Come out of her, my people, so that you will not participate in her sins and receive of her plagues; [a]Is 52:11; Jer 50:8

5 for her sins have [a]piled up as high as heaven, and God has [b]remembered her iniquities. [a]Jer 51:9 [b]Rev 16:19

6 "[a]Pay her back even as she has paid, and give back *to her* double according to her deeds; in the cup which she has mixed, mix twice as much for her. [a]Ps 137:8; Jer 50:15, 29

7 "[a]To the degree that she glorified herself and lived sensuously, to the same degree give her torment and mourning; for she says in her heart, "[b]I SIT *AS* A QUEEN AND I AM NOT A WIDOW, and will never see mourning.' [a]Ezek 28:2-8 [b]Is 47:7f

8 "For this reason in one day her plagues will come, pestilence and mourning and famine, and she will be [a]burned up with fire; for the Lord God who judges her [b]is strong. [a]Rev 17:16 [b]Rev 11:17f

Lament for Babylon

9 "And [a]the kings of the earth, who committed *acts of* immorality and lived sensuously with her, will weep and lament over her when they see the smoke of her burning, [a]Rev 17:2; 18:3

10 [a]standing at a distance because of the fear of her torment, saying, '[b]Woe, woe, the great city, Babylon, the strong city! For in one hour your judgment has come.' [a]Rev 18:15, 17 [b]Rev 18:16, 19

11 "And the merchants of the earth [a]weep and mourn over her, because no one buys their cargoes any more— [a]Ezek 27:27-34

12 cargoes of [a]gold and silver and precious stones and pearls and fine linen and purple and silk and scarlet, and every *kind of* citron wood and every article of ivory and every article *made* from very costly wood and bronze and iron and marble, [a]Ezek 27:12-22; Rev 17:4

13 and cinnamon and spice and incense and perfume and frankincense and wine and olive oil and fine flour and wheat and cattle and sheep, and *cargoes* of horses and chariots and slaves and [a]human lives. [a]1 Chr 5:21; Ezek 27:13

14 "The fruit you long for has gone from you, and all things that were luxurious and splendid have passed away from you and *men* will no longer find them.

15 "The [a]merchants of [b]these things, who became rich from her, will stand at a distance because of the fear of her torment, weeping and mourning, [a]Rev 18:3 [b]Rev 18:12, 13

16 saying, '[a]Woe, woe, the great city, she who was clothed in fine linen and purple and scarlet, and adorned with gold and precious stones and pearls; [a]Rev 18:10, 19

17 for in one hour such great wealth has been laid [a]waste!' And [b]every shipmaster and every passenger and sailor, and as many as make their living by the sea, stood at a distance, [a]Rev 17:16 [b]Ezek 27:28f

18 and were [a]crying out as they [b]saw the smoke of her burning, saying, 'What *city* is like the great city?' [a]Ezek 27:30 [b]Rev 18:9

19 "And they threw [a]dust on their heads and were crying out, weeping and mourning, saying, '[b]Woe, woe, the great city, in which all who had ships at sea became rich by her wealth, for in [b]one hour she has been laid waste!' [a]Josh 7:6 [b]Rev 18:10

20 "Rejoice over her, O heaven, and you saints and apostles and prophets, because God has pronounced judgment for you against her."

21 Then a strong angel [a]took up a stone like a great millstone and threw it into the sea, saying, "So will Babylon, the great city, be thrown down with violence, and [b]will not be found any longer. [a]Jer 51:63f [b]Ezek 26:21

22 "And [a]the sound of harpists and musicians and flute-players and trumpeters will not be heard in you any longer; and no craftsman of any craft will be found in you any longer; and the sound of a mill will not be heard in you any longer; [a]Is 24:8; Ezek 26:13

23 and the light of a lamp will not shine in you any longer; and the [a]voice of the bridegroom and bride will not be heard in you any longer; for your [b]merchants were the great men of the earth, because all the nations were deceived by your sorcery. [a]Jer 7:34 [b]Is 23:8

24 "And in her was found the [a]blood of prophets and of saints and of [b]all who have been slain on the earth." [a]Rev 16:6 [b]Matt 23:35

The Fourfold Hallelujah

19 After these things I heard something like a [a]loud voice of a great multitude in heaven, saying,

"Hallelujah! Salvation and glory and power belong to our God; [a]Jer 51:48; Rev 11:15

2 [a]BECAUSE HIS JUDGMENTS ARE TRUE AND RIGHTEOUS; for He has judged the great harlot who

was corrupting the earth with her immorality, and HE HAS ᵇAVENGED THE BLOOD OF HIS BOND-SERVANTS ON HER." ᵃPs 19:9 ᵇDeut 32:43

3 And a second time they said, "Hallelujah! ᵃHER SMOKE RISES UP FOREVER AND EVER." ᵃIs 34:10; Rev 14:11

4 And the ᵃtwenty-four elders and the ᵇfour living creatures fell down and worshiped God who sits on the throne saying, "Amen. Hallelujah!" ᵃRev 4:4, 10 ᵇRev 4:6

5 And a voice came from the throne, saying,

"Give praise to our God, all you His bond-servants, ᵃyou who fear Him, the small and the great." ᵃRev 11:18

6 Then I heard *something* like ᵃthe voice of a great multitude and like the sound of many waters and like the sound of mighty peals of thunder, saying,

"ᵃHallelujah! For the Lord our God, the Almighty, reigns. ᵃJer 51:48; Rev 11:15

Marriage of the Lamb

7 "Let us rejoice and be glad and give the glory to Him, for ᵃthe marriage of the Lamb has come and His bride has made herself ready." ᵃEph 5:23, 32; Rev 19:9

8 It was given to her to clothe herself in ᵃfine linen, bright *and* clean; for the fine linen is the ᵇrighteous acts of the saints. ᵃRev 19:14 ᵇRev 15:4

9 Then ᵃhe *said to me, "ᵇWrite, 'Blessed are those who are invited to the marriage supper of the Lamb.' " And he *said to me, "These are true words of God." ᵃRev 17:1 ᵇRev 1:19

10 Then ᵃI fell at his feet to worship him. ᵇBut he *said to me, "Do not do that; I am a fellow servant of yours and your brethren who hold the testimony of Jesus; worship God. For the testimony of Jesus is the spirit of prophecy." ᵃRev 22:8 ᵇActs 10:26

The Coming of Christ

11 And I saw heaven opened, and behold, a white horse, and He who sat on it *is* called ᵃFaithful and True, and in ᵇrighteousness He judges and wages war. ᵃRev 3:14 ᵇPs 96:13

12 His ᵃeyes *are* a flame of fire, and on His head *are* many diadems; and He has a name written *on Him* which no one knows except Himself. ᵃDan 10:6; Rev 1:14

13 *He is* clothed with a robe dipped in blood, and His name is called ᵃThe Word of God. ᵃJohn 1:1

14 And the armies which are in heaven, clothed in fine linen, ᵃwhite *and* clean, were following Him on white horses.   ᵃRev 3:4; 19:8

15 From His mouth comes a sharp sword, so that with it He may strike down the nations, and He will ᵃrule them with a rod of iron; and

He treads the wine press of the fierce wrath of God, the Almighty. ᵃPs 2:9; Rev 2:27

16 And on His robe and on His thigh He has a name written, "ᵃKING OF KINGS, AND LORD OF LORDS." ᵃRev 17:14

17 Then I saw an angel standing in the sun, and he cried out with a loud voice, saying to all the birds which fly in midheaven, "ᵃCome, assemble for the great supper of God, ᵃ1 Sam 17:44; Ezek 39:17

18 so that you may ᵃeat the flesh of kings and the flesh of commanders and the flesh of mighty men and the flesh of horses and of those who sit on them and the flesh of all men, both free men and slaves, and ᵇsmall and great." ᵃEzek 39:18-20 ᵇRev 13:16

19 And I saw ᵃthe beast and ᵇthe kings of the earth and their armies assembled to make war against Him who sat on the horse and against His army. ᵃRev 11:7 ᵇRev 16:14, 16

Doom of the Beast and False Prophet

20 And the beast was seized, and with him the false prophet who performed the signs ᵃin his presence, by which he deceived those who had received the ᵇmark of the beast and those who worshiped his image; these two were thrown alive into the lake of fire which burns with brimstone. ᵃRev 13:12 ᵇRev 13:16f

21 And the rest were killed with the sword which came from the mouth of Him who sat on the horse, and ᵃall the birds were filled with their flesh. ᵃRev 19:17

Satan Bound

20 Then I saw an angel coming down from heaven, holding the ᵃkey of the abyss and a great chain in his hand. ᵃRev 1:18; 9:1

2 And he laid hold of the ᵃdragon, the serpent of old, who is the devil and Satan, and bound him for a thousand years; ᵃGen 3:1; Rev 12:9

3 and he threw him into the abyss, and shut *it* and ᵃsealed *it* over him, so that he would not deceive the nations any longer, until the thousand years were completed; after these things he must be released for a short time. ᵃDan 6:17; Matt 27:66

4 Then I saw ᵃthrones, and ᵇthey sat on them, and judgment was given to them. And I *saw* the souls of those who had been beheaded because of their testimony of Jesus and because of the word of God, and those who had not worshiped the beast or his image, and had not received the mark on their forehead and on their hand; and they came to life and reigned with Christ for a thousand years. ᵃDan 7:9 ᵇMatt 19:28

5 The rest of the dead did not come to life until the thousand years were completed. ᵃThis is the first resurrection. ᵃLuke 14:14; Phil 3:11

6 ᵃBlessed and holy is the one who has a part in the first resurrection; over these the second death has no power, but they will be priests of God and of Christ and will reign with Him for a thousand years. ᵃ*Rev 14:13*

Satan Freed, Doomed

7 When the thousand years are completed, Satan will be ᵃreleased from his prison, ᵃ*Rev 20:2f*

8 and will come out to deceive the nations which are in the four corners of the earth, ᵃGog and Magog, to gather them together for the war; the number of them is like the sand of the seashore. ᵃ*Ezek 38:2; 39:1, 6*

9 And they ᵃcame up on the broad plain of the earth and surrounded the camp of the saints and the beloved city, and ᵇfire came down from heaven and devoured them. ᵃ*Ezek 38:9, 16* ᵇ*Ezek 38:22*

10 And the devil who deceived them was thrown into the ᵃlake of fire and brimstone, where the ᵇbeast and the ᵇfalse prophet are also; and they will be tormented day and night forever and ever. ᵃ*Rev 19:20* ᵇ*Rev 16:13*

Judgment at the Throne of God

11 Then I saw a great white throne and Him who sat upon it, from whose presence earth and heaven fled away, and ᵃno place was found for them. ᵃ*Dan 2:35; Rev 12:8*

12 And I saw the dead, the ᵃgreat and the small, standing before the throne, and books were opened; and another book was opened, which is *the book* of life; and the dead ᵃwere judged from the things which were written in the books, according to their deeds. ᵃ*Rev 11:18*

13 And the sea gave up the dead which were in it, and ᵃdeath and Hades ᵇgave up the dead which were in them; and they were judged, every one *of them* according to their deeds. ᵃ*1 Cor 15:26* ᵇ*Is 26:19*

14 Then death and Hades were thrown into the lake of fire. This is the ᵃsecond death, the lake of fire. ᵃ*Rev 20:6*

15 And if anyone's name was not found written in ᵃthe book of life, he was thrown into the lake of fire. ᵃ*Rev 3:5; 20:12*

The New Heaven and Earth

21 ᾽Then I saw ᵃa new heaven and a new earth; for the first heaven and the first earth passed away, and there is no longer *any* sea. ᵃ*Is 65:17; 66:22*

2 And I saw the holy city, ᵃnew Jerusalem, ᵇcoming down out of heaven from God, made ready as a bride adorned for her husband. ᵃ*Rev 3:12* ᵇ*Heb 11:10, 16*

3 And I heard a loud voice from the throne, saying, "Behold, ᵃthe tabernacle of God is among men, and He will ᵇdwell among them, and they shall be His people, and God Himself will be among them, ᵃ*Lev 26:11f* ᵇ*2 Cor 6:16*

4 and He will ᵃwipe away every tear from their eyes; and there will no longer be *any* death; there will no longer be *any* mourning, or crying, or pain; the first things have passed away." ᵃ*Is 25:8; Rev 7:17*

5 And ᵃHe who sits on the throne said, "Behold, I am making all things new." And He *said, "Write, for these words are faithful and true." ᵃ*Rev 4:9; 20:11*

6 Then He said to me, "It is done. I am the Alpha and the Omega, the beginning and the end. ᵃI will give to the one who thirsts from the spring of the water of life without cost. ᵃ*Is 55:1; John 4:10*

7 "ᵃHe who overcomes will inherit these things, and ᵇI will be his God and he will be My son. ᵃ*Rev 2:7* ᵇ*2 Sam 7:14*

8 "ᵃBut for the cowardly and unbelieving and abominable and murderers and immoral persons and sorcerers and idolaters and all liars, their part *will be* in the lake that burns with fire and brimstone, which is the second death." ᵃ*1 Cor 6:9*

9 ᵃThen one of the seven angels who had the seven bowls full of the seven last plagues came and spoke with me, saying, "ᵃCome here, I will show you the ᵇbride, the wife of the Lamb." ᵃ*Rev 17:1* ᵇ*Rev 19:7*

The New Jerusalem

10 And ᵃhe carried me away in the Spirit to a great and high mountain, and showed me ᵇthe holy city, Jerusalem, coming down out of heaven from God, ᵃ*Ezek 40:2* ᵇ*Rev 21:2*

11 having the glory of God. Her brilliance was like a very costly stone, as a ᵃstone of crystal-clear jasper. ᵃ*Rev 4:3; 21:18, 19*

12 It had a great and high wall, ᵃwith twelve gates, and at the gates twelve angels; and names *were* written on them, which are *the names* of the twelve tribes of the sons of Israel. ᵃ*Ezek 48:31-34*

13 *There were* three gates on the east and three gates on the north and three gates on the south and three gates on the west.

14 And the wall of the city had ᵃtwelve foundation stones, and on them *were* the twelve names of the ᵇtwelve apostles of the Lamb. ᵃ*Heb 11:10* ᵇ*Acts 1:26*

15 The one who spoke with me had a gold measuring rod to measure the city, and its ᵃgates and its wall. ᵃ*Rev 21:12, 21, 25*

16 The city is laid out as a square, and its length is as great as the width; and he measured the city with the rod, fifteen hundred

miles; its length and width and height are equal.

17 And he measured its wall, seventy-two yards, *according to* [a]human measurements, which are *also* angelic *measurements*. [a]*Deut 3:11; Rev 13:18*

18 The material of the wall was [a]jasper; and the city was [b]pure gold, like clear glass. [a]*Rev 21:11* [b]*Rev 21:21*

19 [a]The foundation stones of the city wall were adorned with every kind of precious stone. The first foundation stone was jasper; the second, sapphire; the third, chalcedony; the fourth, emerald; [a]*Ex 28:17-20; Is 54:11f*

20 the fifth, sardonyx; the sixth, [a]sardius; the seventh, chrysolite; the eighth, beryl; the ninth, topaz; the tenth, chrysoprase; the eleventh, jacinth; the twelfth, amethyst. [a]*Rev 4:3*

21 And the twelve [a]gates were twelve pearls; each one of the gates was a single pearl. And the street of the city was pure gold, like transparent glass. [a]*Rev 21:12, 15, 25*

22 I saw no temple in it, for the [a]Lord God the Almighty and the [b]Lamb are its temple. [a]*Rev 1:8* [b]*Rev 5:6*

23 And the city [a]has no need of the sun or of the moon to shine on it, for the glory of God has illumined it, and its lamp *is* the Lamb. [a]*Is 60:19, 20; Rev 22:5*

24 [a]The nations will walk by its light, and the kings of the earth will bring their glory into it. [a]*Is 60:3, 5*

25 In the daytime (for there will be no night there) its gates [a]will never be closed; [a]*Is 60:11*

26 and [a]they will bring the glory and the honor of the nations into it; [a]*Ps 72:10f; Is 49:23*

27 and [a]nothing unclean, and no one who practices abomination and lying, shall ever come into it, but only those whose names are [b]written in the Lamb's book of life. [a]*Is 52:1* [b]*Rev 3:5*

The River and the Tree of Life

22 Then he showed me a [a]river of the water of life, clear as crystal, coming from the throne of God and of the Lamb, [a]*Ps 46:4; Ezek 47:1*

2 in the middle of its street. On either side of the river was [a]the tree of life, bearing twelve *kinds of* fruit, yielding its fruit every month; and the leaves of the tree were for the healing of the nations. [a]*Gen 2:9; Rev 2:7*

3 [a]There will no longer be any curse; and the throne of God and of the Lamb will be in it, and His bond-servants will serve Him; [a]*Zech 14:11*

4 they will [a]see His face, and His name *will be* on their foreheads. [a]*Ps 42:2; Matt 5:8*

5 And there will no longer be *any* night; and

they will not have need [a]of the light of a lamp nor the light of the sun, because the Lord God will illumine them; and they will reign forever and ever. [a]*Is 60:19; Rev 21:23*

6 And he said to me, "[a]These words are faithful and true"; and the Lord, the God of the spirits of the prophets, sent His angel to show to His bond-servants the things which must soon take place. [a]*Rev 19:9; 21:5*

7 "And behold, I am coming quickly. [a]Blessed is he who heeds the words of the prophecy of this book." [a]*Rev 1:3; 16:15*

8 [a]I, John, am the one who heard and saw these things. And when I heard and saw, [b]I fell down to worship at the feet of the angel who showed me these things. [a]*Rev 1:1* [b]*Rev 19:10*

9 But he *said to me, "Do not do that. I am a fellow servant of yours and of your brethren the prophets and of those who heed the words of [a]this book. Worship God." [a]*Rev 1:11; 22:10, 18f*

The Final Message

10 And he *said to me, "[a]Do not seal up the words of the prophecy of this book, for the time is near. [a]*Dan 8:26; Rev 10:4*

11 "[a]Let the one who does wrong, still do wrong; and the one who is filthy, still be filthy; and let the one who is righteous, still practice righteousness; and the one who is holy, still keep himself holy." [a]*Ezek 3:27; Dan 12:10*

12 "Behold, I am coming quickly, and My [a]reward *is* with Me, to render to every man according to what he has done. [a]*Is 40:10; 62:11*

13 "I am the Alpha and the Omega, [a]the first and the last, the beginning and the end." [a]*Is 44:6; 48:12*

14 Blessed are those who [a]wash their robes, so that they may have the right to the tree of life, and may [b]enter by the gates into the city. [a]*Rev 7:14* [b]*Rev 21:27*

15 [a]Outside are the dogs and the sorcerers and the immoral persons and the murderers and the idolaters, and everyone who loves and practices lying. [a]*Matt 8:12; 1 Cor 6:9f*

16 "I, Jesus, have sent [a]My angel to testify to you these things for the churches. I am the root and the descendant of David, the bright morning star." [a]*Rev 1:1; 22:6*

17 The [a]Spirit and the bride say, "Come." And let the one who hears say, "Come." And let the one who is thirsty come; let the one who wishes take the water of life without cost. [a]*Rev 2:7; 14:13*

18 I testify to everyone who hears the words of the prophecy of this book: if anyone [a]adds to them, God will add to him the plagues which are written in this book; [a]*Deut 4:2; 12:32*

19 and if anyone takes away from the words of the book of this prophecy, God will take

away his part from the tree of life and from the holy city, ᵃwhich are written in this book. ᵃRev 21:10-22:5

20 He who testifies to these things says, "Yes,

ᵃI am coming quickly." Amen. ᵇCome, Lord Jesus. ᵃRev 22:7 ᵇ1 Cor 16:22

21 ᵃThe grace of the Lord Jesus be with all. Amen. ᵃRom 16:20

WHERE TO FIND HELP WHEN:

AFRAID	Mark 4:35-41	INSULTED OR INTIMIDATED	1 Peter 2:20-23
ATTACKED	Luke 23:34	JUST RETIRED	Matthew 6:33, 34
BEREAVED	1 Thessalonians 4:13-18		Philippians 4:12, 13
	Revelation 21:3-5	TEMPTED TO LIE	John 8:44
BITTER OR CRITICAL	Matthew 7:1-5		Ephesians 4:25
	Romans 14:10-13		Revelation 21:8
	1 Corinthians 4:5	LONELY	Revelation 3:20
CHOOSING A CAREER	Romans 12:1,2	LOOKING FOR A JOB /	Colossians 3:17, 23
	James 1:5-8	MADE REDUNDANT	
CONSCIOUS OF SIN	Luke 15:11-24	NEEDING GUIDANCE	Romans 12:1, 2
	1 John 1:5-10	NEEDING PEACE	John 14:27
CONSIDERING MARRIAGE	Matthew 19:4-6		Romans 5:1-2
	Ephesians 5:22-33		Philippians 4:4-7
	Hebrews 13:4	PRAYING	Luke 11:1-13
CONTEMPLATING REVENGE	Romans 12:17-19		John 14:12-14
	1 Thessalonians 5:15		James 5:13, 16
	1 Peter 2:21-23		1 John 5:14, 15
DISTRESSED OR TROUBLED	Romans 8:28-39	TEMPTED TO COMMIT	1 Corinthians 6:9, 10, 13-20
	2 Corinthians 4:8, 9, 16-18	SEXUAL IMMORALITY	Galatians 5:19-24
CONSIDERING DIVORCE	Mark 10:1-12		1Thessalonians 4:3-7
	Romans 7:2-3	SLEEPLESS	Matthew 11:28
DOUBTING	Mark 9:23, 24	STEAL	Romans 13:9, 10
	John 20:24-29		Ephesians 4:28
TEMPTED BY DRINK ABUSE	Ephesians 5:18		Hebrews 13:5
	1 Thessalonians 5:6-8	TEMPTED TO COMMIT	1 Corinthians 3:16, 17
TEMPTED BY DRUG ABUSE	John 8:34-36	SUICIDE	
	Psalm 139:1-5, 13, 14	THANKFUL	2 Corinthians 2:14
	1 Corinthians 6:12, 19-20		Ephesians 5:18-20
TEMPTED TO ENVY	Galatians 5:26	UNEMPLOYED	Philippians 4:11-13
	Philippians 4:11	UNFAIRLY TREATED OR	Luke 6:27, 28
	James 3:14-18	WRONGLY ACCUSED	Hebrews 12:1-3
FACING DEATH	John 3:16		1 Peter 2:19-24
	John 14:1-3	VICTIMISED	Hebrews 13:6
	Revelation 21:4	WANTING TO BE A CHRISTIAN	John 1:12
FAILURE COMES	Hebrews 4:14-16		John 3:14-18
FAITH IS WEAK	Matthew 8:5-13		Acts 16:30-31
	Mark 9:23,24	WEARY	Matthew 11:28-30
	Luke 12:22-31		2 Corinthians 4:16-18
	Hebrews 11		Galatians 6:9
FAR FROM GOD	James 4:8	WITNESSING	Acts 1:8
	Luke 19:10		Acts 22:15
FEELING INADEQUATE	1 Corinthians 1:25-31		1 Peter 3:15, 16
	2 Corinthians 12:9, 10	WORRIED	Matthew 6:25-34
	Philippians 4:12, 13		Phillipians 4:6, 7
FRIENDS FAIL	Luke 17:3, 4	YOU HAVE LEFT HOME	Mark 10:28-30
	2 Timothy 4:16-18		Luke 15:11-32
ILL OR IN PAIN	2 Corinthians 12:9, 10		
	James 5:14-16		
IN DANGER OR THREATENED	Mark 4:37-41		
	1 Peter 3:13,14		
	Psalm 27:1-3		
	Psalm 118:6-9		